social
psychology

social

psychology

STAN L. ALBRECHT
DARWIN L. THOMAS
BRUCE A. CHADWICK

Brigham Young University

PRENTICE-HALL, INC. Englewood Cliffs, New Jersey 07632

Library of Congress Cataloging in Publication Data

Albrecht, Stan. L.
  Social psychology.

  Bibliography: p. 412
  Includes index.
  1. Social psychology. I. Chadwick, Bruce A.,
joint author. II. Thomas, Darwin L., joint
author. III. Title.
HM251.A517   301.1   79-21533
ISBN 0-13-817882-8

Prentice-Hall Series in Sociology,
Neil J. Smelser, Editor

Printed in the United States of America

10 9 8 7 6 5 4 3 2 1

Editorial/production supervision
and interior design by
Barbara Kelly
Cover design by
Mario Piazza
Manufacturing buyer: Ray Keating

Prentice-Hall International, Inc., *London*
Prentice-Hall of Australia Pty. Limited, *Sydney*
Prentice-Hall of Canada, Ltd., *Toronto*
Prentice-Hall of India Private Limited, *New Delhi*
Prentice-Hall of Japan, Inc., *Tokyo*
Prentice-Hall of Southeast Asia Pte. Ltd., *Singapore*
Whitehall Books Limited, *Wellington, New Zealand*

contents

preface

This book has grown out of our shared conviction that in the study of social psychology the student can find the unique combination of (1) an exciting intellectual challenge that comes from the development of increased knowledge and understanding of human social behavior, and (2) a ready application of learned principles and ideas to everyday experiences and reality.

The discipline of social psychology is itself somewhat unique in that it stands between social-structure-oriented disciplines such as sociology and cultural anthropology and individually-oriented disciplines such as psychology. Thus, social psychologists can draw from the important theoretical and research traditions in each of these as well as other fields in order to increase our overall understanding of human behavior.

While social psychology has important historical roots in both sociology and psychology, the tendency of most textbook writers in the field has been to draw primarily from one of these traditions at the expense of the other. The emphasis given has been dependent largely upon whether the author came out of a sociology or a psychology department. If the former, the book was likely to have a strong symbolic interactionist flavor; if the latter, the emphasis was more likely to be placed upon research findings that have come out of an experimental social psychology tradition. In a very real sense, we have attempted to be integrative and to draw from the breadth of the literature of social psychology, whatever the background or orientation of an individual author or researcher. Some of our chapters will appear more social-structure-oriented while others will be more individually-oriented; however, we feel that this is a clear reflection of the current state of the discipline.

Throughout the book, we have sought to be professionally rigorous and accurate in the treatment of social psychological topics. At the same time, we have also tried to maintain a high level of student interest. To achieve the former, a broad range of empirical literature is integrated into each of the individual chapters. Where applicable, this literature is treated critically and yet-to-be-answered questions are noted. To achieve the latter, numerous examples are developed in each chapter that draw from current events and experiences, and applications are made to the everyday life of the individual reader. For example, social psychological theory and insight are used to amplify understanding of events such as the mass murder/suicide in Guyana, looting behavior in recent big-city blackouts, changing sex role orientations that are emerging out of an important contemporary social movement, and so on.

While there are a number of different ways to organize the material that should be presented in a social psychology textbook, we have chosen to begin at the individual level by discussing such issues as the development of the self, the learning of language and the ability to communicate, and the basic socialization processes which transmit social values, beliefs, and behavior patterns from one individual or group to another. Areas of critical interaction between individual-level variables and group-level variables are then covered in chapters dealing with social influence, social roles, attitudes, attitude change, and person perception and attribution. Specific social behaviors such as altruism and aggression that have been discovered to be important to group survival and to the personal satisfaction of group members are then covered. We conclude by examining group behavior where large numbers of people act together in what has been referred to as collective behavior. The final chapter of the book deals with research methods. In this chapter we attempt to help the reader understand how one does social psychology as well as to present the basis for much of the literature that is presented in earlier chapters. We have placed this chapter at the end of the book for several reasons. Some instructors may choose not to include the chapter at all in their assigned readings, and the book has been written so that the remaining chapters are not dependent upon this one. However, the chapter is also written in such a way that the individual instructor can choose to assign it at the beginning of the course to aid the student in understanding the materials in the remainder of the book. This is left entirely to the preference of the individual instructor.

As is always the case in an effort such as this, appreciation must be expressed to a number of people without whose influence and assistance the book may never have come about. We were each taught by gifted social psychologists who instilled in us a sense of excitement with the field. Important among these were Melvin DeFleur of the University of New Mexico and Robert Hamblin of the University of Arizona. Through their influence, we each became most familiar with some rather different traditions in social psychology that we have attempted to blend in this book. For Albrecht, this included a strong emphasis on cognitive social psychology with particular application to the study of attitudes and attitude-behavior relationships; for Thomas, the graduate school experience was directed more toward symbolic interactionism and the research traditions that have grown out of this orientation; for Chadwick, the emphasis was on experimental social psychology and research traditions growing out of social learning theory.

We are grateful to the many professional colleagues who read and commented on either the complete manuscript or various chapters. Among these are David Alcorn, Angelo State University; Neil Smelser, editor, Prentice-Hall Series in Sociology; H. W. Smith, University of Missouri; Howard Robboy, Rutgers University; Andrew Gordon, Northwestern University; Clark McPhail, University of Illinois; Jerold Starr, West Virginia University; H. Andrew Michener, University of Wisconsin; Bernard C. Rosen, Cornell University; Charlotte Weissberg, Brandeis University; Frank Miyamoto, University of Washington; James A. Wiggins, University of North Carolina; Sharon Guten, Case Western Reserve University; and Sheldon Stryker, Indiana University. We appreciate the patience and willing assistance of LeAnn Edvalson, Leslie Gaynes, Trina Redford, and Karen Denney in typing endless pages of manuscript, finding lost references in the library, obtaining permissions, and numerous other critical but usually thankless tasks.

Finally, the book surely would not have come about without the continuous encouragement and support from Ed Stanford, Sociology Editor for Prentice-Hall; Barbara Kelly, our able production editor; Patrice Goor, who handled most of the copy-editing on the manuscript; and Irene Springer for her help with the numerous photos used in the text.

social
psychology

introduction

An Invitation to Social Psychology

On November 15, 1978, U.S. Representative Leo Ryan of California and four others were shot to death in the hot, humid jungles of Guyana, South America. This event and what followed during the next few hours shocked millions of Americans.

Congressman Ryan was investigating reports that some members of the People's Temple, an American religious cult that had recently moved from California to Guyana, were being held against their will and were being denied the opportunity to return to the United States. Several requests to visit the cult's headquarters in Jonestown—named after the cult's leader, the Rev. Jim Jones—were required before Congressman Ryan and his party were granted permission. For two days, the Ryan party observed life in the jungle commune and interviewed Jones and some of his followers. However, the initial picture of happy communards baking bread and doing laundry was broken by quiet whisperings of discontent and secret notes indicating that some cult members wanted to leave but were afraid. The image of a jungle paradise that Jones and his followers had created for investigators started to crack.

Rumors of discord and defections quickly changed the social atmosphere in Jonestown. When Ryan and his group prepared to leave Jonestown, the Congressman was attacked by a knife-wielding cult member. Ryan was unharmed, but he and his group, accompanied by several defectors, quickly boarded the truck to be transported to the airstrip for a flight back to Georgetown, the capital of Guyana. However, before the two small planes were able to get off the ground, gunmen from the commune opened fire. Five members of the Ryan party, including the Congressman, were killed. Several other

Reverend Jim Jones, charismatic leader of the Peoples Temple *Source:* Wide World Photos, Inc.

members were seriously wounded and had to spend a terrifying night in the jungle before help arrived the following day.

Following this attack, an event occurred back in Jonestown that has few parallels in recent history. Jones assembled his followers into the main courtyard and announced that Ryan and several others had been killed. He commanded that commune members all join together in committing suicide. Exhorted by their leader and intimidated by armed guards, parents and nurses squirted a mixture of Kool Aid and potassium cyanide down the throats of the babies and young children. Adults and other children then drank cups filled with the deadly poison sweetened by strawberry-flavored Kool Aid. The steamy jungle air was filled with screams and agonizing cries as hundreds of cult members followed their leader in death. For some unexplained reason, Jones and several of his closest followers shot themselves to death rather than take the poison. More than nine hundred members of the People's Temple died, the bodies later found heaped upon each other in the compound.

The five cold-blooded murders, followed by the mass murder-suicide, stunned the world. The questions were asked over and over again: "How could parents squirt syringes filled with poison down the throats of their children?" "How could so many people be convinced to terminate their lives?" "Why did so few even try to resist or escape into the jungle during the final moments of confusion?" The mass suicides at Jonestown were not entirely voluntary; nevertheless, the orderliness of the rows of dead and the linked arms of family members offered mute testimony that Jones' disciples, if they did not die because they wanted to, lacked the ability to resist his demand.

Vat of Kool-Aid laced with potassium cyanide and some of the 900 victims of Jamestown. *Source:* Wide World Photos, Inc.

Although the field of social psychology does not promise definitive answers to these questions, it does provide tentative ones that should prove useful to the student in increasing his or her understanding of this as well as a wide array of other, less spectacular events of everyday life.

Identifying with and acquiescing to Jones can be understood when we apply social-psychological theories about the development of the self, the process of socialization, and the formation of individual personality. Most members of any cult have some emotional need or problem before they join. Many of them lack a sense of personal value and join out of a desire to become a part of something meaningful. Personal judgment then becomes subjected to the group and its leader.

In addition, explanations of Jones' ability to sway and persuade his followers to give up their families, their belongings, and eventually their lives are available in the literature on mass communication. Similarly, theories of collective behavior contribute to understanding the importance of the group setting of the Guyana tragedy. Obviously, the sanctioning power of the leaders of the group, inherent in the totally isolated location, was an important factor in the settlement of Jonestown. The mass suicide can be understood through applying theories of conformity, compliance, and obedience as they explain the process through which individuals commit themselves to a charismatic and authoritarian leader, such as Jim Jones, Adolph Hitler, or Charles Manson.

We have reviewed the tragic events at Jonestown as a means of introducing the field of social psychology. As illustrated by this example, a broad range of individual and group behaviors, including both normal and deviant behavior, constitute the subject matter of the field. We recognize that many different interests and activities, including academics, social activities, athletics, and service projects, compete for the attention of the college student and that the study of social psychology will demand only a relatively small part of the student's time. It should be recognized that the serious student can obtain information about social behavior that is directly relevant to the other events and activities in which he or she participates. For example, a great deal of scientific information has been collected concerning interpersonal attraction, dating, communication, educational achievement, attitude formation, value formation, violence, and helping others in times of need —all of which relate to the student's everyday activities. In other words, as the student studies this discipline, he or she is not confined to a world of theory and research divorced from real experiences. Instead, the social world surrounding the student is a laboratory.

The Field of Social Psychology

Social psychology focuses primarily on the *processes of social influence.* For example, a widely accepted definition of *social psychology,* presented in the *Handbook of Social Psychology,* is "an attempt to understand and explain how the thoughts, feelings, and behavior of individuals are influenced by the actual, imagined, or implied presence of others" (Allport, 1968, p. 3). In other words, social psychology studies the relationship between social institutions, social groups, and individual behavior. In order to do this, it inte-

Contact between traditional African tribal culture and modern industrial culture illustrates the importance of anthropology's contribution to understanding social behavior. *Source:* United Nations.

grates the fields of cultural anthropology, sociology, psychology, and, to a lesser degree, political science and economics. Anthropology's primary focus is on the unique set of beliefs, values, and behavior patterns that constitute a given culture. Sociology studies social institutions, such as the family and the large variety of social groups varying from informal peer groups to nation-states. Psychology examines individual characteristics, including patterns of thought, feelings, and perception and their relationship to individual behavior. Social psychology synthesizes the information from these different disciplines to account for individual behavior within a social context.

Social psychology explores the relationship between the culture in which the individual has been socialized, the social institutions in which he or she participates, the groups to which he or she belongs, his or her personal characteristics, and his or her behavior toward others. Only occasionally is attention directed to how a single individual's behavior affects the emergence of cultural elements or social groups.

This synthesis of information from several disciplines to explain a particular behavior can be illustrated by attempting to understand why nine hundred individuals committed suicide in Jonestown. Cultural beliefs and values of the commune created hope for a socialistic paradise, which had not materialized and suddenly did not seem likely to appear in this life. The logical alternative was for the group to seek it in the next. The norms of the

A friendship group, an example of the social groups that most people belong to, illustrates the importance of sociology's contribution to social behavior.

group called for total loyalty to the cult and absolute obedience to Jones. The command to commit suicide was enforced to a large degree by the collective involvement in the emotional arousal and contagion of example arising in the social situation, as well as by the social pressures to conform to the group's demands. Finally, a typical psychological characteristic of cult joiners is a need to be associated with something meaningful, and this trait probably contributed to the obedience apparent in the mass suicide-murder. Social psychology, by synthesizing the limited explanations of different disciplines, produces a more complete, albeit a more complex, explanation of this behavior.

History of Social Psychology

Philosophers have long mused over the social nature of people, and the "roots" of social psychology can be found in their writings. The development of social psychology as an independent discipline occurred in the United States in this century. Allport (1968) suggests that the tradition of free inquiry, the ethics of a democracy, and strong interest in natural and biological sciences in twentieth-century America precipitated the emergence of social psychology. In addition, the American pragmatic tradition of seeking rational answers to problems has resulted in political, civic, and business leaders looking to social psychology for scientific answers to pressing social problems. Conflict between labor unions and employers, racial conflict, war, crime, economic depression, cold war, urban rioting, student protest, civil disobedience, and atomic threat have all stimulated theory and research into the causes of such behaviors and how to cope with them.

The first social-psychology textbook was published in 1908 by a sociolo-

Understanding social behavior involves examining the psychological aspects of the individual, including the processes of thought and perception.

gist, Edward A. Ross. Ross had a Ph.D. in history, politics, and economics and combined these disciplines with psychology and sociology to write the first text, *Social Psychology*. The major emphasis was how imitation and suggestability account for the transfer of ideas, habits, and attitudes between members of social groups. The same year, William McDougall (1908), a psychologist, published a text entitled, *Introduction to Social Psychology*. He also explored the role of imitation in explaining the similarity of behaviors of members of a given social group.

Since the discipline's humble beginning in the form of these two textbooks, it has flourished in the succeeding seventy years. In 1954, there were 52 social-psychology texts available, and Allport estimated that by 1968 the number had risen to nearly 100 (1968, p. 68). The growth of social psychology has continued, until today we estimate that there are approximately 150 textbooks, half a dozen journals, and numerous collections of readings available to the student.

Traditionally, social psychology has emphasized psychology to the neglect of the other disciplines. It is estimated that two-thirds of the social-psychology textbooks have been written by psychologists and tend to emphasize psychological principles and processes (Allport, 1968, p. 68). In this text, we have included a strong foundation of psychology but, in addition, have added considerably more material from sociology and cultural anthropology. Those topics normally covered in psychological social-psychology texts are included, but where possible the relevant social theories and research findings have been included. For example, the chapter on aggression has sections on television violence and urban riots, which would not be part of the typical psychologically oriented text. Also, topics normally neglected in psychologically slanted texts, such as social roles and collective behavior, have been added.

Social psychology, as a science, endeavors to understand the social behavior of individuals by discovering principles of behavior. To understand a behavior implies that information about the circumstances surrounding its occurrence or that information about why it occurs has been discovered and that this knowledge can be used to predict or control the behavior in question. Theories or theoretical orientations are expressions of this type of information. They are sets of propositions stating the relationship between phenomena or variables (Shaw and Costanzo, 1970). For example, we may develop a theory that a group norm prescribing obedience to the leader of the group is related to group members' conformity to the leader's commands. This theory asserts that, as in the case of the People's Temple, if a group norm of obedience to the leader has emerged, members of the group will obey their leader to a greater degree than members of groups not having such a norm.

If the relationship between the variables is causal, control of the behavior may be possible. If a norm of obedience and conformity are causally related, then obedience by members of a group with such a norm will be high. Accepting a causal relationship, group organizers, public officials, and leaders of social groups may create a norm of obedience and sanctions to support conformity and to punish disobedience, thus ensuring a high rate of compliance to their requests. However, causal relationships do not always allow control of behavior as at times it is not possible to manipulate the relevant variables. It may be that certain social groups have such a strong democratic ideology and tradition that members will not accept a norm of obedience as legitimate, and therefore the level of conformity will not be changed even though the relationship is causal.

If the relationship is not causal but only predictive, then the existence of an obedience norm will predict the likelihood of conformity but not allow the control of such behavior. Such prediction is valuable as it allows leaders, politicians, and other interested persons to anticipate a given level of obedience to the group's leader. However, it must be stressed that because the relationship is only predictive, introducing such a norm will not influence the conformity, and thus other means of control must be sought. (See chapter 13 for a more extensive discussion of this topic.)

At times, social-psychological theories are not specific about the relationship between the relevant variables, but rather provide a general approach to the analysis and interpretation of behavior (Shaw and Costanzo, 1970). General approaches are usually called theoretical orientations, general frameworks from which to derive a specific theory. Although we recognize this difference, we have treated both as theories to simplify the presentation of material.

The utility of theories to science is that they summarize observations and research findings and suggest new relationships to research. For example, thousands of observations of parent/child interaction that fill volumes could be reduced to a single equation that could be written on a single three-by-five card if an adequate theory of such behavior were derived. In addition, theories direct or guide research in the discovery of specific relationships between variables. The circular relationship between theory and research should be noted because theories are tested by empirical research and research findings suggest new or modified theories.

Given the high financial costs of conducting social research, society seems to be placing greater emphasis on practical or relevant research than on "basic research." There is pressure for social psychologists to develop and test theories about behavior that is important to large numbers of individuals, to powerful groups, or to society as a whole. The problems of war, violence, poverty, discrimination, crime, mental illness, alcoholism, drug abuse, and child abuse are examples of areas in which considerable amounts of public money have been expended on research. The hope has been that theories expressing causal relationships would be forthcoming, permitting the amelioration of these social problems. Unfortunately, the social sciences in general, and social psychology in particular, have been only partially successful in this endeavor. Some social-psychological theories have been and are being applied by individuals, groups, and society as a whole to alter specific behavior with remarkable success.

Given the importance of theory in the study of social psychology, we will now review three major theoretical orientations and several specific theories derived from them. These theories will be used throughout the book to organize and interpret the material presented in the various chapters.

None of the theories are complete explanations of all human behavior, and thus certain behaviors or subjects will be discussed in terms of one theory and others will be analyzed using another. At times, behaviors such as socialization, conformity, altruism, or aggression will be discussed from competing theoretical orientations and the research evaluated as to which theory is the best explanation. Wherever possible, the competing theories will be synthesized into a single, more comprehensive explanation of the behavior.

PSYCHOANALYTIC THEORY

Psychoanalytic theory emerged out of the work of Sigmund Freud (1856–1939). A remarkable individual, Freud entered medical school at age seventeen, became a noted physician and scientist, authored over twenty volumes of scientific reports, and at the age of seventy developed his theory of personality. Throughout his distinguished career, Freud tested and revised his concepts and theory, and since his death others have continued this revision. Because of the vast literature on psychoanalytic theory, a comprehensive review of it as first developed by Freud and then modified by him and his followers is beyond the scope of this book. Rather, a brief review of the basic psychoanalytic principles of human behavior will be presented. The interested reader is referred to two excellent summaries of Freud's psychoanalytic theory: Hall (1954), and Rapaport (1959).

Psychoanalytic theory assumes that every person has a given amount of vital psychic or mental energy called *libido energy*. The libido, the source of this psychic energy and the various channels through which it is expressed, are of utmost importance to personality development.

Freud perceived the mind as divided into two parts, the conscious and the unconscious. The mind, according to psychoanalytic theory, is like an iceberg, with the conscious part represented by the portion of the iceberg above the water. That part of the mind of which the individual is aware includes all the information that can be recalled from memory, but even so is much smaller than the unconscious. The unconscious part of the mind consists of emotions, desires, instincts, and knowledge of which the person is not aware, yet it has an influence on his or her behavior. The researcher or therapist obtains information about the material in the unconscious or subconscious using the techniques of free association, dream analysis, recall of information under the influence of hypnosis or drugs, and subjective tests. All these techniques are supposed to measure covert or indirect expressions of the force contained in the unconscious.

Structure of the Personality The personality, according to psychoanalytic theory, is the interaction between three components: the *id;* the *ego;* and the *superego.* The *id,* present at birth, is the original component of the personality and is the source of all psychic energy, including libido energy, instincts, and drives. The id cannot tolerate increases in energy and operates according to the *pleasure principle* to immediately reduce such tension. It does not distinguish reality and thus cannot differentiate between an imagined image of a steak dinner and actual food, or between an imagined sexual partner and an actual person. Obviously, the image of food or a sexual partner will not reduce the psychic energy the id has derived from hunger or from the sex drive. Therefore, the *ego* comes into existence to deal with reality on behalf of the id.

The ego differentiates between subjective objects or experiences and real ones. In doing this, it operates according to the *reality principle.* The id supplies images of objects or experiences that will produce the desired reduction in tension or energy, and the ego engages in reality testing to determine if the images are real or imagined. The ego has the psychological apparatus, the sensory system, the perceptual system, the motor system, and the memory to assist in the processes of reality testing.

In order to locate appropriate opportunities for tension reduction, the ego requires the id to delay gratification for a while. The id objects to these delays and will tolerate only a limited amount before overruling the ego and forcing the individual to engage in what appears to be irrational behavior.

The ego is also responsible to the third component of the personality, the *superego.* The superego is the internal representation of society or of the traditional values of society as the person has learned them. It is the moral component of the personality and operates according to the *perfection principle.* This principle pushes the individual to behave in morally prescribed ways rather than to seek pleasure. The superego includes a conscience, which has developed from punishment the person has received and defines what the person should not do. The ego ideal, a second subsystem of the super ego, emerges from behaviors that have been rewarded and spells out praiseworthy behavior. The superego is as nonrational as the id and is opposed to both the id and ego as it seeks a permanent blocking of physical gratification. The superego has the ability to enforce its wishes by either punishing or rewarding the person. On one hand, it may reward the individual by temporarily relaxing inhibitions against physical gratification by stating "you have been good for a long time, you may now indulge in a gourmet meal, a sexual encounter, or a similar gratification." On the other hand, the superego may punish the individual who has violated an internalized rule by influencing the body to have an upset stomach, to misplace a valued object, or to have an accident causing a physical injury. An example frequently cited is that of the young man who wrecked his automobile shortly after having premarital sex with his girlfriend. The inference is that his superego punished him for violating this sexual standard by influencing him to have an accident.

The ego has the responsibility to balance the demands of the id and the superego. The need for water and food must be satisfied if the person is to survive, and sexual behavior must occur for the survival of the species, but the superego demands that the gratification of these basic drives be met via socially or morally acceptable means.

Defense Mechanisms As the executive branch of the personality, the ego is frequently placed in the impossible position of reconciling irreconcilable demands. To accomplish this task, the ego has a set of defense mechanisms that it can use to deceive the id and superego into believing that their demands have been met and thus reduce the tension or conflict between them. These defense mechanisms also deceive the ego, which uses them as they occur at the unconscious level. Because of this, their use frequently interferes with the ego's adjustment to reality. *Repression* involves the shift of painful or dangerous ideas, memories, perceptions, or wishes from the conscious mind to the unconscious. Following repression, the individual is not aware of them, and thus they are not threatening. *Projection* is the attribution of a person's unacceptable traits or behaviors to another person or group. Again, the threatening event or impulse is moved away from the individual, and it ceases to be frightening. *Reaction formation* occurs when the ego blocks an unacceptable impulse from the id or superego with the impulse's acceptable opposite. Thus, the person who is experiencing a desire to hate someone may respond with love, fear may be replaced by courage, and immorality by extreme morality. *Denial* is the process of simply denying that a threatening impulse, object, or event exists. This is a dangerous defense mechanism because reality may eventually force the person to recognize the threatening object or event. *Sublimation* involves the ego channeling unacceptable impulses, drives, and so on into acceptable alternatives. For example, an aggressive drive can legitimately be expressed in hard-hitting football play, competitive performance in business, and so forth.

Stages of Personality Development Freud contended that the personality progresses through stages related to psychosexual development. This psychosexual development focuses on various zones or regions of the body at different ages. The *oral stage* occurs during the first year of life, and the primary region of pleasure is the mouth. Although this stage is brief, Freud felt that it is very important to the development of trust in other people and has a lasting influence on social relationships the person enters into during his or her entire life. People may experience *fixation* at any given stage and carry some of the characteristics of that stage into subsequent ones. Examples of oral fixation are thumb sucking, excessive gum chewing, smoking, or overeating, as all focus on sensations associated with the mouth.

The *anal stage* occupies the time between the first and fourth years of life. During this stage, attention concerning pleasurable sensations moves from the mouth to the anus, especially during toilet training. Although attention is directed to the anus during this stage, it also involves other important motor-skill development, including walking and speech.

The *phallic stage* usually lasts only a year and occurs during the fourth or fifth year. During this stage, the genitals become the primary erogenous area. The child becomes interested in sexual matters, including masturbation and exhibitionism, and this interest culminates in a conflict with the same-sex parent for the sexual favors of the opposite-sex parent. For the male child, this is known as an Oedipal conflict, so named for the tragic hero of Greek drama. Freud felt that during the phallic stage all male children desire their mother as a sexual partner and want to remove or kill their competitor, their father. The eventual resolution of the Oedipal conflict is for the boy to identify with his father and to surrender his mother to him. The similar experience for the female child is called an Electra conflict, a name also referring to a Greek tragedy. Freud maintained that it was essential that the child resolve the Oedipal or Electra conflict in order for normal adult sexual development to occur.

After the phallic stage, the individual enters a *latency stage* during which he or she is free from the intense conflict and anxiety of the three previous stages. This latency period lasts until about age twelve or thirteen, when the child enters puberty. The final stage is the *genital stage* and involves the significant emotional and physical changes associated with puberty. The end product of the genital stage is a well-socialized adult who follows the prescribed sexual values and customs of society.

The characteristics of many of the critical components of psychoanalytic theory have made it very difficult to empirically test its validity. Many researchers refuse to even attempt to test the relationships suggested by the theory because of this difficulty of measuring unobservable concepts or variables. Others have attempted to infer the occurrence of psychoanalytical processes from observable events, with rather limited success. The unobservability of psychoanalytic processes is also responsible for the criticism that psychoanalytic theory is incapable of predicting future behavior. For example, in the case of Guyana, psychoanalytic theory could not have been utilized to predict whether or not a given person would have followed Jones's command to commit suicide. If the person had complied, then the psychoanalytic theorist would have interpreted the suicide as being the consequences of unobservable psychoanalytic processes. On the other hand, if the person had refused Jones and survived, then a logical explanation for this response would have been developed using the same concepts and processes.

Although not strongly supported by research, and limited in the prediction of behavior, psychoanalytic theory has been applied to many aspects of American life in such areas as child-training practices, the treatment of the mentally ill, and the rehabilitation of criminals.

SOCIAL-LEARNING THEORY

There are a large number of theories based on the principles of social-learning theory, such as operant conditioning (Skinner, 1959, 1969), behavior modification (Bandura, 1969; Staats, 1975), and social-exchange theory

(Thibaut and Kelley, 1959; Homans, 1961; Blau, 1964). It is not possible to review each of these theories; rather, we will present the basic principles of social-learning theory from which the more specific theories have been derived. (Social learning, in the context of this section, is used interchangeably with the traditional term behaviorism.)

Social-learning theory argues that theories of human behavior must be built on observable events and processes, thus omitting unobservable mentalistic concepts or processes such as the id, ego, repression, and so on. Social-learning theory does not deny the existence of such processes but argues that, because they are unobservable, they are useless in explaining human behavior. Rather, relationships between observable conditions in the individual's environment and observable behaviors are the subject matter of social-learning theory.

Respondent Behavior and Classical Conditioning Learning theory divides human behavior into two categories, respondent and operant behavior. *Respondent behaviors* are those actions that are controlled by stimuli that preceed them and are referred to as $S \rightarrow R$ behavior (where S is the eliciting stimulus and R is the respondent response). Examples of respondent behaviors are the contraction of the pupil of the eye elicited by a bright light, the salivation in the mouth and the release of gastric juices in the stomach elicited by the smell of food, and the acceleration in heartbeat elicited by a sudden loud noise. As indicated by the examples, respondent behavior involves the smooth muscles and glands of the body. These responses are involuntary in that stimuli that follow them have no effect on them. A person generally cannot make them occur in the absence of the eliciting stimulus nor prevent them from happening when the appropriate stimulus is present.

Pavlov, the Russian physiologist (1927), discovered the process of *classical conditioning*, which later became known as *respondent conditioning*. Pavlov was studying the digestive system of dogs, including salivation. He noted that although originally only the smell or taste of food (an unconditioned stimulus) elicited salivation, later the sound of the footsteps of the animal keeper

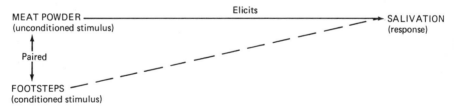

After pairing unconditioned stimulus and conditioned stimulus, the conditioned stimulus elicits the response.

Figure 1–1 Classical or Respondent Conditioning in Pavlov's Pioneering Experiment

(conditioned stimulus) elicited the response. This observation led to a series of experiments demonstrating that other stimuli, such as the ringing of a bell or the sound of a buzzer, could elicit the salivation response (see figure 1–1).

The physiological nature of respondent behavior may suggest that it is of limited interest to social psychology, but it should be noted that emotional behavior is respondent behavior that is extremely important to the study of social behavior. The conditioning of emotional behavior was powerfully demonstrated by Watson and Raynor (1920) in a famous experiment with a nine-month-old baby boy. It was discovered that little Albert had no fear reaction to white rats, rabbits, or dogs, but that a loud sudden noise behind his head elicited a strong fear reaction as evidenced by crying and crawling away. The loud noise (unconditioned stimulus) and a white rat (conditioned stimulus) were paired seven times over a four-day period, at which point the rat alone elicited the same strong emotional reaction.

Higher-order conditioning, where a conditioned stimulus such as the white rat conditions the eliciting function to another conditioned stimulus, has been demonstrated in the laboratory. It is probable that chains or

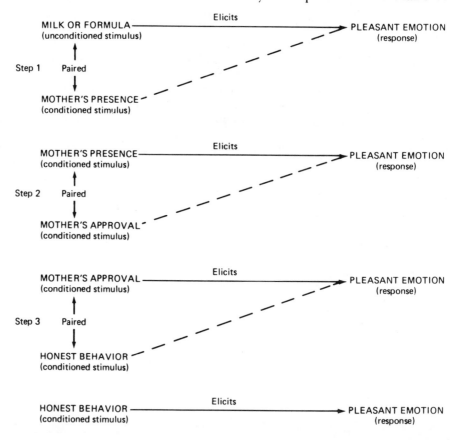

Figure 1–2 Example of Higher-Order Classical or Respondent Conditioning. Honest Behavior to Elicit a Pleasant Emotional Reaction

sequences of higher order conditioning, as illustrated in figure 1–2 explain the ability of various stimuli to affect people's emotional behavior. The process of higher-order conditioning is used by some to account for why some people feel proud when a flag with red and white stripes and white stars on a blue background passes by, or why some people feel fear at the sight of a failing grade in school, or why some feel guilty when they take something that is not theirs. A short hypothetical chain of higher-order conditioning moving from food to pride for honesty is presented in figure 1–2. In this example, the food mother provides is an unconditioned stimulus with the ability to elicit pleasurable feelings, and because it is paired with her, mother's presence is conditioned to also elicit the pleasant emotional state. Mother's presence is then paired with mother's approval, which gains the eliciting ability, and in turn mother's approval is associated with honest behavior so that honesty elicits pleasant feelings. Once honest behavior, by the individual or by others he or she observes, comes to elicit a pleasant emotional state, honesty has become part of the person's value system. The person will now engage in honest behavior because of the pleasurable feelings he or she experiences from so doing. By the same process, it is possible to use an unconditioned stimulus that elicits pain so that dishonest behavior elicits fear, anxiety, or guilt.

Classical conditioning is used in aversion therapy, with which a very negative emotional reaction is elicited when an inappropriate behavior occurs, and in desensitization, with which irrational fears (phobias) are reduced or eliminated via conditioning of pleasant emotions. Aversion therapy has been used to condition a strong negative reaction to the use of alcohol, the use of specific drugs, or homosexual behavior. Treatment usually involves the pairing of a drug (unconditioned stimulus) that elicits a very powerful vomiting response with alcohol, marijuana, or viewing a film of a homosexual act. After a sufficient number of pairings, the smell or taste of alcohol or marijuana or the sight of the initiation of a homosexual act will elicit violent vomiting. The person being conditioned may be aware of the process and may even oppose it, but, because respondent behavior is involuntary, the effect will be the same as for someone who is not aware or who desires help with changing a behavior.

Operant Behavior and Conditioning Operant behavior refers to voluntary behavior that the individual uses to operate on the environment and is controlled by stimuli that follow it. Operant behavior is generally referred to as R→S behavior (where R is the response that is followed by the stimulus S). The strength of an operant response is determined by the stimulus that follows it. If the consequence of the behavior is a highly valued experience, object, or event, then the behavior will occur more often with greater intensity. If the stimulus is painful, then the response will occur much less often, if at all. The stimulus or set of stimuli that follow the response is called *reinforcement* or *punishment*. *Positive reinforcement* refers to a response obtaining a valued stimulus; *negative reinforcement* refers to the removal of a painful stimulus. *Punishment* occurs when the response has a painful or aversive consequence. *Extinction* happens when a behavior that initially obtained reinforcement is no longer reinforced and gradually decreases in frequency of occurrence.

The principles of *operant conditioning* or *behavior modification,* as it has come to be known, were originally developed by B. F. Skinner (1959, 1969). Behavior modification is accomplished by manipulating reinforcement or punishment to strengthen desired behavior and to extinguish or inhibit undesirable behavior.

Not only is the reinforcer important to the rate of behavior but so is the schedule with which it is dispensed. There are five basic schedules of reinforcement that have been discovered in extensive experimental research to have somewhat different effects on behavior. *Continuous reinforcement* is the reinforcing of every appropriate response and produces a steady rate of responding; however, such behavior extinguishes easily. A *fixed ratio* is the reinforcement of every nth response, which produces a high rate of behavior and is fairly resistant to extinction. Piece work in factories or production incentives are examples of a fixed ratio of reinforcement. A *variable ratio* affords reinforcement following a varying number of responses, and thus the person cannot predict which response will be reinforced. This schedule creates a very high rate of response and is very resistant to extinction. Gambling is an example of variable-ratio reinforcement, and those individuals who are unable to quit gambling illustrate the resistance to extinction. The feeling is that reinforcement will occur on the next response, the next response, the next response, and so on. Raises, promotions, and awards are generally scheduled on a variable ratio.

A *fixed interval* is reinforcement for the first response after a set time period. Most workers in American society are paid on a fixed interval. It produces a moderate rate of response but is easy to extinguish. A *variable interval* is reinforcement for the first response after varying intervals of time, which produces a slow but steady rate of behavior, resistant to extinction. Generally, the reinforcement people receive in their social contacts and relationships occurs as a combination of the various schedules.

Operant conditioning or behavior modification is achieved by the parent, therapist, teacher, researcher, or whoever, deciding the desired level of the behavior being modified. For example, a leader of a cult may decide that cult members should give 100 percent of their wealth to the group. The second step is to observe the baseline or operant level at which the behavior is presently occurring. The cult leader may observe that followers give an average of only 25 percent of their money and other assets. The third step is the selection of a reinforcer that is appropriate for the individuals whose behavior is being modified. For commune members, praise from a charismatic leader or promise of involvement in creating a unique society may be quite reinforcing. The next step is to determine the schedule of reinforcement, and this decision is made in light of the type of change in behavior desired. The commune members could be given praise or opportunities to hold responsible positions in the group for every 10 percent of wealth contributed (fixed ratio) or for every month of turning over all their income (fixed interval). At this point, the leader can either explain to the members the reinforcement contingencies or let them learn them from experience. In the first case, the leader would explain how to be worthy of praise or of a position in the group; in the second, praise and positions would be handed out as they were earned and the members would learn that the praise and involvement are contingent on contributions. Based on a large number of experiments, it is anticipated that these procedures would successfully increase the level of financial contribution to the desired 100 percent.

Behavior modification has been and is currently being used in a large variety of institutional settings, including homes, schools, mental hospitals, and prisons, to alter an even larger variety of behaviors with remarkable success. Token economies have been created in institutional settings where food, recreational opportunities, visitation rights, and similar privileges can be purchased with tokens earned. Token economies have been very efficient in changing many different patterns simultaneously and in assisting participants in institutions to become more self-sufficient and self-governing.

Modeling, Imitation, and Vicarious Learning Modeling or imitation is an extension of learning theory important to the understanding of social behavior. It has been demonstrated that both respondent conditioning and behavior modification can be accomplished by vicariously observing models (Bandura and Walters, 1963; Bandura, 1969). Emotional responses (respondents) have been conditioned by having subjects watch the pairing of the eliciting stimulus and the model's emotional behavior. Fear and avoidance behavior elicited by a given stimulus can be reduced and the positive emotional reaction elicited by a stimulus can be increased by vicarious classical conditioning.

Operant conditioning or behavior modification can also be achieved through modeling because the way to perform a behavior as well as the behavior's consequences can be learned from watching models. Modeling is a very efficient means of teaching people how to perform a novel or new response. Everyday life is full of examples of individuals learning vicariously from the experiences of others. For example, drivers who see a highway patrol officer writing a ticket for a motorist generally slow down. The observation of a person putting money in a candy machine and receiving nothing in return reduces the tendency of those who witnessed the event to invest their money in the machine. The list is long because modeling, imitation, and vicarious learning are important processes of social learning.

Social-Exchange Theory Building on the foundation of learning theory, and, to a lesser degree, economics, exchange theory explains social behavior in terms of the mutual reinforcement people exchange with each other. Learning theory has generally focused on only the experimental subject or animal and has neglected the exchange that takes place between the researcher and his or her subjects. For example, the rat in the typical conditioning experiment is seen as pushing a lever in return for food pellets, but it is also true that the experimenter is exchanging pellets for lever pushes.

Exchange theory explains how individuals seek to initiate exchanges with others by weighing the "profit" they would anticipate from potential exchanges with alternative partners (Thibaut and Kelley, 1959). Profit is determined in light of the investment a person must have to be eligible to enter the exchange, the costs he or she has to pay, and the reward obtained. If investments, say education; and costs, say time expended; are high, then rewards must be high for the exchange to be profitable. The basic principle of exchange theory is that behavior performed in exchanges that have been profitable in the past will increase in frequency, and those from unprofitable exchanges will decrease.

If the exchange partners' profits are out of balance, the "law of distributive justice" (Homans, 1961) or the "law of equity" (Blau, 1964) has been violated. When this happens, the offended partner will experience anger and will seek redress or terminate the exchange.

Exchange theory assumes that people are rational to the extent that each person will enter into and continue in exchanges that maximize that which is reinforcing to them (Homans, 1961). Related to this theory is recognition of the importance of social reinforcers, such as approval, acceptance, status, esteem, recognition, and love, and the identification of social punishment, such as rejection and ridicule. As discussed earlier, these are secondary reinforcers that are learned, and thus there is considerable variation in what social behavior is reinforcing to different people. There is a great deal of similarity in learned secondary reinforcers in a given society, but there also is sufficient diversity to make exchanging interesting and profitable. Also, people do not satiate on secondary reinforcers as readily as with primary reinforcers—another reason they play such an important role in explaining social behavior.

Social-exchange theory attempts to explain social behavior and thus at times utilizes mental processes to explain the behavior in question. The existence of a memory and the ability to recall it is inherent in the notion of a history of past reinforcement. Also, the individual's calculation of the profit level of potential exchanges implies mental processes because possible outcomes are predicted. The heavy reliance on the established principles of learning theory, modified by the inclusion of limited mental processes, has made social-exchange theory very popular as an explanation of social behavior.

Traditional social learning theory's rejection of unobservable mental processes remains a source of criticism. Although many reject the psychoanalytic conception of these mental processes, everyone personally experiences internal mental experiences of thought, contemplation, and self conversation; and most realize that such processes greatly influence their behavior. Therefore, social learning theory is frequently accused of ignoring that behavior which is the essence of the human experience.

The success of social learning theory in changing the behavior of school children, mental patients, delinquents, criminals, and so on, has led to a very real concern about personal freedom. Behavior modification, operant conditioning, and respondent conditioning have been criticized for violating the freedom and the opportunity to exercise self control of those whose behavior is being modified or conditioned. Skinner (1971) in *Beyond Freedom and Dignity* eloquently describes how the principles of social learning theory could be used to design a society which maximizes freedom and dignity.

COGNITIVE THEORY

Cognitive theories of human behavior stress mental processes, such as perception, knowledge, ideas, and expectations, as the major determinants of behavior. The processes of gathering information, giving it meaning, organizing it into knowledge, and similar mental activities are seen as the most important components of human behavior. The unobservable nature of these mental events has hindered the empirical testing of cognitive theories.

Their existence has to be inferred from behaviors that can be measured, and such inferences are frequently difficult to defend.

In addition, cognitive theories contend that in order to understand a person's behavior the unit of analysis must be the individual's entire behavior system. This holistic approach argues that a particular behavior must be studied as part of the individual's total behavior with special emphasis on cognitive activities. A number of cognitive theories of behavior have been developed, but we will limit our review to the two most widely discussed theories: symbolic-interaction theory and cognitive-consistency theory.

Symbolic-Interaction Theory Symbolic-interaction theory emerged in the early 1900s, having roots in philosophy, psychology, and sociology. George Herbert Mead (1934) was the most influential spokesperson during the early formative period, largely through his social-psychology courses taught at the University of Chicago. Although Mead himself published very little, his students integrated his written material along with their class notes into four books, all published after his death.

The major focus of the theory is upon human social interaction. Social interaction, the theory assumes, can best be understood by studying humans because people evidently possess the ability to perform the process of thinking, reasoning, and planning, which is not possessed by other animals. Thus, the theory calls attention to cognitive processes and therefore has a psychological base.

The approach is likewise very sociological in that one of its major concerns is to understand the cooperative dimension of human social behavior, which was the essence of society in Mead's view. Human cooperative behavior is different from cooperative behavior in animals, which is controlled by instincts. Society (cooperative behavior) is made possible precisely because humans possess the higher mental process and therefore live in a symbolic world as well as a physical world. Unlike animals, which respond to stimuli directly, people respond to stimuli mediated by their symbolic world. The stimuli impinging upon people are given meaning through cognitive processes and then are responded to according to the attached meaning.

The basic processes underlying social interaction are graphically depicted in figure 1–3. The cognitive processes are depicted as dotted lines with directional arrows (– – →); an individual's initiation of action toward another, and the other person's behavioral responses are depicted as solid lines with arrows (→). Social interaction is thought to begin with action of one person directed toward another. Because the theory assumes a person is an actor as well as a reactor, it emphasizes the initiation of behavior as well as reactions to the behavior of others.

Symbolic-interaction theory, as indicated in step 1 of figure 1–3, suggests that people mentally explore the possible reactions of others to specific behaviors and use this information to decide how to act toward other people. People, unlike other animals, possess the ability to experience themselves in their imaginations. Through *role taking,* a person places himself or herself in another person's social role and imagines the other's reaction to the planned course of action. For example, a person can mentally role play how a teacher, spouse, or friend would feel about a particular behavior or act in order to decide if the behavior will likely achieve the desired effect.

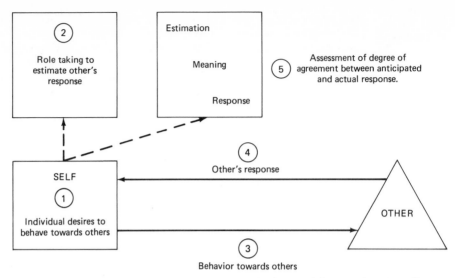

Figure 1–3 Illustration of Individual Initiating Behavior Involving Another According to Symbolic-Interaction Theory

If the response of the other is similar to what was anticipated, then the other's behavior is said to have *social meaning* (see step 5 in figure 1–3). Out of this role-taking process, cooperative behavior emerges, and society is created. The degree of consensus between anticipated and actual behavior is usually quite high but generally is not perfect. Social interaction that always achieves total agreement between anticipated and actual responses would probably be boring. However, little or no overlap would produce anarchy or chaos, and cooperation could not occur.

As seen in the foregoing discussion and in figure 1–3, the *self* is a central concept in symbolic-interaction theory. People can interact with themselves, just as they do with others. By taking another person's role, they can generate new information about themselves and their behavior that may motivate change. The reactions of some individuals—*significant others*— have a greater impact on self-conceptions. Significant others usually are people who have power to give rewards or to administer punishment. A person's significant others generally change as he or she moves through the life cycle. Parents may be replaced by peers as significant others during the teenage years; a spouse appears as one in later life.

The *generalized other* is a set of roles that a person uses for comparative self-evaluation. This involves simultaneously taking the roles of a group of others, such as all the members of a family, all the members of a friendship group, or all the citizens of a country. This allows the individual to view himself or herself from the collective perspective of the group or society. In short, the self is a reflection of the group or society.

The self is composed of two elements: the *I,* and the *Me.* The *I* is the impulsive tendency of the person; the *Me* is the generalized others and gives direction to the propulsion. Every behavior begins with the *I* and then is directed by the *Me.* In other words, the *I* suggests an action, and the *Me* inhibits it by saying "let's examine the alternatives." The anticipated reactions of the significant and generalized others to the original act and the alternatives are imagined, and agreement is reached regarding which behavior should be performed.

Social interaction is seen by symbolic-interaction theory as occurring within a common *definition of the situation.* The role taking occurs within the context of a perceived social setting (such as within a basketball game, a marriage, or a delinquent gang) and the surrounding environment (a gymnasium, home, or street). Symbolic-interaction theory assumes that even if the definition of the situation does *not* reflect social reality, the consequences are real for the people involved. Thus, if the members of a group *believe* that another group hates them, then the first group will probably attack the other even though in reality there is no hatred.

A symbolic-interaction theorist trying to explain the Guyana episode would observe that Jim Jones was able to accurately anticipate his followers' response to his order to commit suicide by symbolically placing himself in the social category of follower and identifying their potential reactions to his behavior. He obviously concluded from his role taking that his followers would obey his order; what followed substantiated his role taking, as the anticipated and the actual responses seemed to be very similar. In addition, he and his followers shared a common definition of the situation, which gave meaning to the command to die. With the five murders, the cult had created a situation that was defined as probable arrest and prison for some members and disbanding for the others. Given this definition of the situation, mass suicide became for many the most meaningful response because continued existence without the cult was unacceptable to them, and those who resisted were engaging in irrational or nonsensical behavior. Lieutenants executed the resistors in order to make everyone's behavior meaningful according to the shared definition. Although their definition may not have corresponded to social reality, the death that followed as a consequence was starkly real.

The advantage of symbolic-interaction theory is its emphasis upon cognitive processes and on the processes of social interaction. The use in this theory of mentalistic constructs, such as the self, which have a subjective reality to both the social psychologist and the layperson, contributes to the understanding of human behavior. One weakness of the theory is the emphasis on people as rational and problem-solving beings, which neglects the contribution of emotions in understanding behavior, particularly irrational behavior. The child and adult are not perceived as ever being influenced by temper tantrums, depression, exhilaration, or humorous feelings.

Another weakness of the theory is the difficulty of testing propositions derived from it because mentalistic phenomena are impossible to observe. Thus, the theory can only be supported, rejected, or modified on the basis of inferences from observable behavior, which has limited support for symbolic-interaction theory.

Role theory is a loose set of concepts and hypotheses that developed out of symbolic-interaction theory but that has been adapted by a number of other theoretical orientations, including learning theory. Role theory, while acknowledging the mental connections between the self and significant and generalized others, focuses on the actual interaction between people. For example, the interaction between a doctor and a patient is explained in terms of the roles of doctor and patient. Each role includes *role obligations,* such as giving competent medical advice, arriving for an appointment on time, or promptly paying the bill. As is evident from this example, the obligations of one role partner generally are the *role rights* or *privileges* of the other partner. This exchange of obligations and rights has resulted in the merger of role theory and exchange theory by some theorists and researchers.

Role theory contends that *role performances* are evaluated by *role partners* and, to a degree, by society or groups in it. Good performances are rewarded, and inadequate ones punished. Frequently, people enter into role relationships with conflicting role expectations. An example of *role conflict* may be the doctor who defines part of the doctor role as saving lives, and whose role as a hospital staff surgeon requires the performance of abortions. If he or she happens to believe that abortion is in conflict with saving life, then the doctor is caught in conflicting demands of the roles of doctor and hospital staff surgeon.

Role strain occurs when the individual occupies too many roles and cannot adequately perform each one because he or she does not have sufficient time, energy, or resources. The doctor who does not have time to treat all his or her patients, to spend the expected time with his or her family, or to attend the meetings of the Chamber of Commerce is a victim of role strain. When either role conflict or role strain occurs, the person engages in behavior that appears to certain others as inappropriate, irrational, or deviant. This discussion of role theory is very superficial, and the interested reader is referred to an excellent detailed discussion by Biddle and Thomas (1966), and to Chapter 4 in this book.

Cognitive-Consistency Theory Cognitions are those things that each of us uses to make sense out of our everyday worlds. Robert Zajonc (1968, p. 320) has argued that no social psychologist honestly questions the general assumption that cognitions are organized wholes made up of interdependent parts. Cognitions include our perceptions—how we perceive and code events and experiences that occur around us—as well as the knowledge, opinions, and beliefs that we hold about ourselves, about our behavior, and about the environment (Festinger, 1957). The question of how these interdependent cognitive elements are, in fact, organized together into larger wholes has been one of the primary concerns of consistency theory.

The underlying assumption that has influenced the majority of the work in this area is that each individual attempts to establish and maintain some degree of consistency or balance among those cognitions that are related to each other. For example, if I am strongly convinced that there is a direct link between cigarette smoking and lung cancer, it would be inconsistent for me to smoke cigarettes. Similarly, if I were to observe a close friend—to whom I have previously attributed characteristics of honesty and morality —shoplifting, I would experience inconsistency among related cognitive elements.

Cognitive-consistency theory grows directly out of important gestalt traditions in psychology. For example, Fritz Heider (1946, 1958) is generally credited with developing much of the original work on which consistency theories are based, and for originating the concept of cognitive balance. Heider's work in this regard is closely related to his work on perception. His belief that people seek to develop an orderly and coherent view of their environment clearly influenced both areas.

Cognitive-consistency theories have been proposed under a variety of names (balance, symmetry, dissonance, congruity, and so forth), but all have in common the belief that individuals will tend to behave in ways that minimize the internal inconsistency among their interpersonal relations, their intrapersonal cognitions, and their beliefs, feelings, and actions. Although resembling each other in their adoption of this fundamental postulate, the various theories differ in many other respects, such as the ways they define consistency, the assumptions they make about the relationship between cognitions, and the realms in which their predictions can be used to explain behavior (McGuire, 1966).

The consistency principle holds that the individual not only attempts to behave in ways that would be consistent to an observer, but that he or she also tries to appear consistent to his or her own observation. In other words, it is assumed that a person has a need to establish and maintain consistent orientations toward self, other persons, and the elements of the nonperson environment. These orientations emerge out of the person's everyday experiences. Effective goal attainment requires a degree of stability in a given situation and the person's orientation toward it. Difficulty is encountered when operating in unorderly situations because the person is unable to determine or predict the consequences of his or her behavior.

In addition to maintaining that individuals strive to attain cognitive balance, cognitive-consistency theories also assume that when inconsistency occurs it is a noxious or uncomfortable state. Consequently, it creates pressures within the individual to eliminate or reduce it. Inconsistency or imbalance thus has a motivational quality and may be a major force for attitudinal or behavioral change in the individual.

As all this implies, there are numerous areas in which cognitive inconsistency can occur. For example, Aronson (1969) argues that it may arise in any of four situations:

1. When a logical inconsistency exists. For example, I believe that all men are mortal but that I, a man, will live forever. In this example, the second cognitive element is clearly inconsistent with the first. However, it should be pointed out that the inconsistency must be recognized by the person in order for the motivational properties inherent in inconsistency to become operative.

2. When there is a conflict between actions and self-definitions or cultural mores. For example, I may consider myself a relatively intelligent, mild-mannered, self-controlled college professor. Therefore, if I lost my temper in class and hit a student, I would probably feel some psychological imbalance growing out of the conflict between my action and my definition of self. My action would also be inconsistent with my definitions of what constitutes appropriate behavior for college professors.

3. When there is an inconsistency between a cognition and a more encompassing cognition. For example, suppose I am a lifelong, committed, true-believing member of the Democratic party but have just voted for a

Republican Presidential candidate. The behavior would be inconsistent with the more encompassing definition of self as a Democrat.

4. When inconsistency is created by conflict between present and past experiences. Aronson's example in this case involves an individual who has just stepped on a thumbtack with his bare foot but felt no pain. The two cognitive elements of stepping on a tack but feeling nothing simply do not follow.

Research findings reveal that people do tend to seek consistency and balance among related cognitions. The most positive support for this contention comes from data revealing that when an obvious inconsistency exists, people will tend to make changes in their attitudes or behavior that move them back toward a more consistent state. For example, when a person engages in attitude-discrepant behavior, the attitude often changes toward greater consistency with the act. Similarly, when a triadic relationship is unbalanced—I like you, you smoke cigarettes, I despise cigarette smoking—there is a tendency to change the unbalanced situation toward a more balanced state. Much more will be said about consistency theory in later chapters on attitudes and attitude change.

At this point, it is clear that cognitive theory differs in important ways from psychoanalytic theory and social-learning theory. Although psychoanalytic theory and cognitive theory both involve mental processes, there are several important differences. For example, in contrast to psychoanalytic theory, cognitive theory is not as strongly influenced by physiological characteristics such as instincts, drives, and energy. Before such motivations are acted upon, according to cognitive theory, the person generally engages in conscious thought about alternative behaviors and anticipated reactions from others. Also, psychoanalytic theory's emphasis on the unconscious or subconscious is absent in cognitive theory.

In contrast to social-learning theory, cognitive theory conceives of action as instigated not by some external source of stimulation but by the receipt and transformation of information within the individual. External *or* internal events are encoded, categorized, and transformed into a belief or course of action (Weiner, 1972). Thus, people are assumed to be capable of self-induced motion and to have the ability to think abstractly and to communicate their thinking to others. According to this perspective, thoughts intervene between incoming information and the final behavioral response. Individuals attach meanings, define situations, and then respond, and the focus of the cognitive theory is largely directed toward the analysis of these cognitive processes. Whether one adopts the perspective of the symbolic interactionist or the cognitive-consistency theorist, the emphasis remains upon the interpretive processes that occur within the individual.

Organization of the Book

Although there are a number of different ways to organize the material that should be included in a social-psychology textbook, we have opted to begin at the individual level and then to discuss the processes of communication that facilitate the formation of social groups. The socialization processes that transmit social values, beliefs, and behavior patterns from one individual or group to another are then covered. Specific social behavior, such as aggression or helping behavior, that have been discovered to be important to the survival of social groups and to the personal satisfaction members derive from their membership are discussed. We conclude our specific study by examining group behavior—large numbers of people acting together. It is hoped that moving from the individual to interpersonal behavior to group behavior will facilitate an orderly presentation of social-psychological theories and principles and a reasonably adequate summary of social-psychological research, which is the basis for this book and future studies, and the subject of our final chapter.

2

the self

In the 1950s, psychiatrist Cornelia Wilbur unraveled one of psychiatry's most amazing cases of multiple personality (Schreiber, 1973). A young woman, Sybil Dorsett (a pseudonym), was discovered to be not a unified personality but rather sixteen different persons sharing the same body. Sybil, the person who consciously directed the body the majority of the time, was not even aware of the other fifteen people and because of this would frequently discover that she could not account for significant periods of time. She would have no memory of what had occurred when one of the fifteen other selves had emerged and expressed itself. Sybil's childhood and early adulthood were filled with occurrences of being one place and suddenly discovering that she was now somewhere else and that minutes, hours, and even days had passed. For example, one day in 1953 she left a chemistry laboratory at Columbia University in New York City and found herself walking the streets in Philadelphia five days later. Occasionally, the other selves would engage in behavior that would place them in a difficult situation and then would retreat from consciousness, leaving Sybil, who did not know what "she" had done, to resolve the difficulty. For example, "Peggy" once broke the window of a locked car that she thought was her father's and, when apprehended, faded from consciousness, leaving Sybil to placate the irate owner.

What is especially relevant to the study of the self is that each of the sixteen individuals had different conceptions of themselves and what they could accomplish with the same body. They varied from Sybil Ann, who was pale, timid, and listless, to Victoria Antoinette Schorleau, an attractive, sophisticated and self-assured young woman. Even though the body was definitely that of a female, two of the persons conceived of themselves as males and kept insisting that besides being skilled carpenters they could also "give a girl a baby." Several considered themselves artists, and their paintings exhibited unique styles.

It seems that because of certain childhood experiences, Sybil had not developed a unified self but rather sixteen different selves, each with unique strengths and weaknesses. The link between self and behavior is readily apparent as each of the sixteen behaved in quite different ways, vividly illustrating the importance of the self in defining who an individual is and how he or she behaves.

Definitions of the *Self*

Each individual is very much aware that he or she exists; that he or she has had and is currently having certain experiences; and that he or she has specific physical, psychological, and social characteristics. People frequently seek to discover the "true" nature of their self as they search for an "identity" or "sense of being." Given the subjective nature of the self, it is not surprising that many different definitions and conceptions of it have emerged. The *self* has been defined as the combination of one's physical appearance, personal memories, and sensory images (Ausubel, 1952, p. 13). Yinger (1971, p. 158) characterizes the self as the mental images of "who I am" or "what I want to be." Sullivan conceptualized the self as "an organization of educative experiences called into being by the necessity to avoid or to minimize incidents of anxiety" (1953, p. 165). The "good me" avoids unpleasant social disapproval—the main function of the self.

Social scientists generally refer to perceptions of the self as an individual's *self-concept* or feelings of *self-esteem.* The self-concept is the more general of the two and includes an identification of the characteristics of the individual as well as an evaluation of them. For example, a person's self-concept may be built around the perception that he or she is a good basketball player. Self-esteem is sometimes used as a synonym for self-concept, but usually it emphasizes the evaluation of the person's characteristics. An individual with high self-esteem feels that he or she is a person of worth who possesses valuable characteristics, experiences, or traits; a person with low self-esteem feels incompetent or of little value.

The self has been the subject of literally thousands of studies, and, although the results have not been completely consistent, certain overall patterns in the development of the self have been observed. For example, some theorists and researchers have differentiated different components of the self. The components most frequently identified are the *material self* and the *social self.* The material self includes the perceptions the individual has of his or her own body, usually determined from the physical sensations provided by the various limbs, organs, and parts of the body. A steady stream of sensations indicating the body's state of being, including feelings of touch, pain, and pleasure; the image of its various parts; and sounds made by it; is sent to the brain. Frequently, the material self is extended beyond the person's own body and includes other people and objects. A spouse, children, brothers, sisters, work, club, school, house, community, or car can become part of an individual's material self. In this case, an attack on any of these persons or objects is experienced as an attack on the self, and achievement by them is a source of pride to the self.

The social self is defined by the perceptions a person has of the social roles he or she occupies and how they are performed. Students probably conceive of themselves as students, which provides meaning to the interaction with their fellow students, instructors, and administrators and how they think that others feel about them as students. It is possible that a person may have several social selves, one for each of the major social roles occupied in society. Occupational, marital, parental, family, and recreational roles are examples of a few of the major roles around which most people develop a social self.

Self-conceptions generally are stable over time, but different aspects of the self may be more salient as the individual shifts from one social role to another. Shibutani (1961) suggests that conceptions of the self may vary on five dimensions as the person performs in different social roles: the degree of integration; extent of conscious awareness; degree of stability; nature of evaluation; and social consensus.

Integration refers to the consistency of the elements of the self and its manifestation in behavior. People with an integrated self will not feel and act hostile one minute and placid the next, unless social conditions have changed drastically. Although integration of self varies individually, it is the consistency of self that makes each person a recognizable individual whose behavior can be predicted with some degree of accuracy. Even in the case of Sybil, each of the sixteen selves had a reasonably high level of integration as they each tended to behave in a consistent way.

In addition, people seem to vary in the degree to which they are *consciously aware* of their selves. Some people have highly integrated selves but lack a strong sense of identity. In other words, they are not very aware of what they think they are and how this affects their behavior.

Although the self appears to be reasonably *stable* over time, it does change as people shift social roles and reference groups. It has been observed that youngsters have somewhat more flexible self-concepts, which solidify as they become older. However, even adults usually experience some change in self as they take on new roles, such as entering college, getting married, becoming a parent, starting a new job, or retiring from work. People vary greatly in how they *evaluate* their self. The large literature dealing with self-concept and self-esteem documents variations in perceptions of self held by different social groups including age, racial, ethnic, and class groups. *Consensus* between individuals' perceptions of their selves and how other people perceive them may also vary. It is difficult to feel that you are an outstanding student when you frequently are ridiculed by classmates for stupid comments in class and when you usually receive low grades. But it appears that people do rationalize or explain away both success and failure that is inconsistent with their concepts of self. We are all aware of people who seem to feel that they are really something special when we and most other people see them as rather ordinary, and we have all met people who are very competent and who are "good" or "nice" people but have a negative concept of themselves. Although such exceptions do occur, generally the reaction of others towards us results in a fairly high degree of consensus.

THE SYMBOLIC-INTERACTIONIST VIEW OF THE SELF

The early founders of the symbolic-interactionist view of the self (James; Mead; Cooley) were influenced by philosophy and by the relatively new discipline of psychology, which was breaking away from its philosophical traditions at the turn of the century. Both disciplines were concerned with distinctly human characteristics and concluded that people were qualitatively different from animals because of their greater ability to use and interpret symbols. Symbolic interactionists treat language as a set of symbols with shared meaning. Language enables communication between individuals; it also allows people to talk to themselves (thought).

One very important consequence of language and thought is that people have the ability to possess knowledge about themselves as objects. A person is simultaneously the *knower* and the *known*. William James in particular emphasized this aspect of human nature: "Whatever I may be thinking of, I am always at the same time more or less aware of myself, or my personal existence. At the same time it is I who am aware; so that the total self of me . . . must have two aspects discriminated in it, of which for shortness we may call one the 'Me' and the other 'I' " (reprinted in Gorden and Gergen, 1968, p. 41). For James, the undeniable subjective reality of being aware of both dimensions simultaneously, the *I* (knower) and the *Me* (known), was the self. However, he stressed the *Me* more than the I. To him, the *Me* was a social object that was identified by how others respond to the person.

Charles Horton Cooley, a sociologist, built upon the work of James. Cooley defined the social self as "a system of ideas, drawn from the communicative life, that the mind cherishes as its own" (1902, p. 179). According to Cooley, the self develops via the reactions of others to the person. The resulting self-conception was labeled the *looking-glass self.* The self is thus shaped by the responses (or, more accurately, the interpretations of the responses) one receives from other people. Just as we see our faces and figures reflected in a looking glass, we also see ourselves in the social mirror of others as they react to our presence, words, and deeds.

Development of the Self According to Cooley (1902, pp. 102–103), there are three steps in the development of the looking-glass self: (1) imagination of one's appearance to others (did they see me as bright, as fat, as bumbling, or as old?); (2) the imagination of others' judgment of that appearance (did they evaluate my appearance in a positive or negative way?); and (3) some resulting *self*-feeling—pride and personal satisfaction if one imagines that the judgment of others was positive, and embarrassment, fear, or humiliation if one imagines that the appearance was judged negatively. It is important to note that the looking-glass self develops from our *imagination* of the response of others. To paraphrase W. I. Thomas (1928, p. 572), this imagination will be real in its consequences for the individual, whatever its accuracy. Thus, if we feel that others are responding to us negatively, this could seriously affect our self-concept, even though those others may have intended to communicate approval and acceptance.

The hypothesized relationship between perceived feedback from others

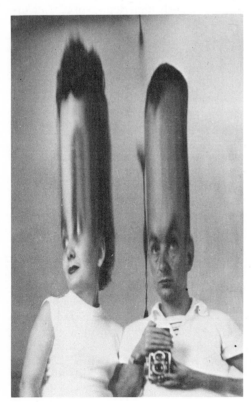

Just as mirrors in amusement parks give distorted images, people frequently receive distorted views of themselves from others. *Source:* Strickler, Monkmeyer Press Photo Service.

and the development of individual self-concepts implied in the work of the symbolic interactionists is clearly reflected in the following letter, which was written to one of the nationally syndicated columnists who specializes in solving personal problems:

> Dear Ann: I saw myself in your column the other day—the homely child whose mother was so ashamed she covered the little girl's face with a heavy veiling when she took her out in the baby carriage. I hope your message got through to that mother because nobody got through to mine. I grew up believing I was the ugliest person in the world. I didn't make friends because I felt I was too homely to be seen with. My posture was bad because I kept my shoulders hunched so no one would have to look at my face.
>
> One day a kind teacher asked me to stay after school. I swear I thought she was going to tell me I was too ugly to be in her class, and I was being transferred. Instead, she told me I had very pretty hair and nice eyes and I shouldn't worry about my nose and chin—that my face would develop nicely in time and I might even be considered a beauty. She showed me magazine pictures of models who had weak chins and prominent noses and explained that irregular features could be "interesting".
>
> That wonderful teacher changed my life. After our visit, I stood a little straighter and started to believe that one day I might be considered attractive. I began to open up to others and accept friendship—something I couldn't do before. Today I am happily married and we have two beautiful children. Please print this letter for other Ugly Ducklings and their mothers. It might help someone—somewhere (Ann Landers, *The Salt Lake Tribune*, 22 July, 1971. p. C-1. Permission of Field Newspaper Syndicate).

The process of the development of the self that is implied here is illustrated in figure 2–1. As can be seen, the reactions of others need not always be consistent with each other. In most instances, we would anticipate that they would not be. Father may evaluate the risk-taking behavior of his son, such as swimming in a swift river, much differently than does mother. The self-concept that emerges is a summary of the reactions of various others interacted with. The illustration also indicates that the individual is not influenced equally by all others because the feedback from some is more important in shaping the self-concept. These *significant others* tend to be those who have the *power* to give or withhold rewards and punishments. During childhood, when parents are the major source of emotional as well as material support, they are generally significant others. As the child moves through adolescence, friends take on greater importance, and when he or she obtains employment and becomes economically independent, parental influence declines further. At this point, friends, employers, or marriage partners become more significant.

George Herbert Mead (1968) provided an even more detailed account of the development of the self. He strongly stressed, as did Cooley, that the self arises out of and is maintained through social interaction. For Mead, symbols permit the individual to receive information about herself or himself from others and, even more importantly, to anticipate through role taking (see chapter 1) how others will react to her or his behavior.

It is important to realize that the role taker may not have previously interacted with the other but still can successfully role take. If the other can

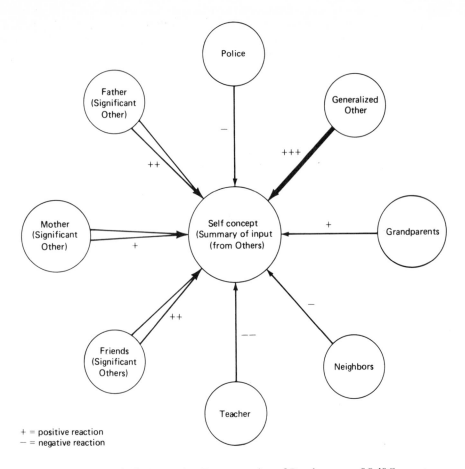

+ = positive reaction
− = negative reaction

Figure 2–1 Symbolic-Interaction Representation of Development of Self-Concept

be identified as a father, teacher, police officer, and so on, the social norms of how someone should behave in any of these positions permit fairly accurate predictions of how they will behave. Obviously, not all teachers behave exactly the same, but the norms and sanctions associated with the social position of a teacher produce a great deal of similarity so that we can predict how a teacher will react to a given situation. A college student who refuses to attend class or to hand in assignments can quite accurately predict the grade he or she will receive. In addition to assisting role taking, learning the behavior appropriate to a given role internalizes "society" within the individual. The individual can then move outside himself or herself and evaluate his or her characteristics and behavior. A man can say to himself, "I am a father, a good father, a lousy policeman."

According to Mead, the child progresses through two stages in developing self-awareness through role taking. The first is the *play* stage, in which the child plays doctor, mother, teacher, fireman, cowboy, and so forth. Usually, this involves other children, and the one who plays the role of teacher, for example, has an opportunity to view another child's behavior from the perspective of a teacher. Often, the performance is distorted, but gradually additional role-playing information is gleaned from other children, movies, books, and experiences with adults so that acceptable role behavior is learned. During this stage, the child will often move freely and easily from one role to another. Children playing school, for example, may alternatively play the role of teacher or student.

The second stage is the *game* stage. The name should not be misinterpreted to mean playing games; *game* implies that the individual can now simultaneously take a number of roles relevant to a particular behavior. Mead utilizes a baseball team as an example. As the novice player, say a first baseman, learns what the pitcher, catcher, second baseman, and outfielders expect of a first baseman, he combines the expectations of the other eight baseball players in a *generalized other.* The role of student has a generalized other that involves the mutual role expectations of instructor, classmates, dean, and society in general. Once the generalized other is learned, the person can self-evaluate from this position. The first baseman can evaluate his own performance from the combined perspective of his teammates. The individual has thus become a "society in miniature."

Mead, like James, conceptualized a self divided into an "I" and a "Me." He argued that the *I* includes the impulsive tendencies of the individual— what psychologists call drives, needs, and instincts. These impulses are spontaneous and unorganized, and the *Me* gives them direction. The *Me* is the social dimension of the self, the generalized other, and directs the impulses of the *I* into socially acceptable behavior. Every act starts with the *I* and ends with the *Me.* The *I* and *Me* cooperate to satisfy the initial impulse in the most efficient and socially acceptable way. Mead labeled this internal conversation the *Mind.*

One can develop a perception of self by imitating the role behavior of significant others. *Source:* S. M. Wakefield.

Multiple Selves Symbolic-interaction theory implies that somewhere within the individual there is a "core" self that provides meaning and identity as well as direction for action. Some symbolic interactionists contend, however, that we have multiple selves to deal with social contexts. Our behavior changes to the extent that we have developed a different self for each of the different roles that are occupied. For example, the teenage boy behaves quite differently before a group of his peers than he does in front of his parents. If the friends and parents were asked to describe the boy, quite different pictures might emerge because each has known him in a different setting.

The idea of multiple selves is implied in the work of Cooley when he maintains that we are what we think others think we are. In other words, our self-attitudes are at least in part situationally determined. The college instructor who receives strong positive feedback from a class of students and boredom and avoidance from his girlfriend may develop two rather different self-images for those two different audiences. The strong, assertive classroom lecturer may react quite differently when speaking to his girlfriend.

However, the recognition that behavior changes from audience to audience does not demand that the notion of a core self be eliminated. This core self may account for the stability and consistency that is evident in the behavior of most people. At the same time, it does not deny changes from situation to situation. The core self may provide the boundaries outside of which change will not occur or will occur only infrequently. The teenage boy may behave differently with his peers than with his parents, but there are certain things he will not do in the presence of either because his core self finds them too contrary to his self-definition.

THE BEHAVIORAL VIEW OF THE SELF

The internal self discussed by symbolic-interaction theory is replaced in behavioral theory by a conception of the self in terms of how it is measured. A behavioral definition of the *self* is the corpus of verbal statements a person makes about himself or herself (Staats and Staats, 1963; Staats, 1975). In other words, the measures themselves are the self. Thus, a favorable self-concept or high self-esteem is stating positive evaluations about oneself or receiving a high score on a self-concept scale. The contrast between these observable measures and symbolic interaction is obvious. The behaviorist treats the verbal statement or the response to the scale as the self; the symbolic interactionist maintains that the various measures are only "indicators" of the inner self. The behavioral concept of the self does not deny that inner processes exist but contends that only as scientists are able to observe and measure such processes can they be used as scientific concepts explaining behavior. Because verbal or written self-descriptive statements are the only *observations* we have of the internal state labeled the self, these statements become the behavioral definition of the self.

A somewhat more elaborate behavioral definition of the *self* has emerged out of social-learning theory. The development of self-reinforcing and self-punishing behavior has been viewed as a significant aspect of the self-concept (Bandura, 1969a, 1969b). Through the process of learning, including social learning and modeling, the individual sets standards of behavior and self-administers rewarding or punishing consequences depending on whether his or her performances fall short of, match, or exceed self-prescribed standards (Bandura, 1969a, p. 32). Thus, according to social-learning theory, self-concept, self-esteem, or any other self-construct is defined as the frequency of self-reinforcement or self-punishment. A favorable self-concept or high self-esteem is conceived of as a high rate of self-reinforcement; a negative self-concept or low self-esteem is a high rate of self-punishment.

Self-reinforcement and self-punishment may involve observable behavior, such as treating oneself to a hot fudge sundae after completing some task or noteworthy accomplishment, or denying oneself a customary Saturday night steak dinner because of failing to complete an assignment. In addition, self-reinforcement and punishment may involve internal states, such as feelings of pride or guilt. However, this makes this theory vulnerable to the same criticism as symbolic-interaction theory. Behavioral theorists have recognized the dangers and have attempted to develop more observable means of identifying nonobservable mental events or processes. For example, Staats and Staats argue that mental processes can be inferred by carefully establishing the link between an observable antecedent event and the nonobservable mental event and then between the mental event and an observable consequence (Staats and Staats, 1964, p. 95). This social-learning conceptualization of the self is an initial merging of the symbolic-interaction emphasis on mental processes and the behavioral empirical emphasis.

The development of the self can be considered a specific case of the processes of attitude change, which will be treated in chapter 8. In the behaviorist perception, two basic processes, respondent conditioning and operant conditioning are used to explain the development and change in attitudes, including self-attitudes.

Classical Conditioning According to the classical conditioning paradigm, the self is paired with an event or object that elicits a pleasurable emotional reaction and by this pairing the self is conditioned to elicit the same reaction. Two examples of this process are presented in figure 2–2. In the first case, a famous athlete's presence elicits a strong emotional reaction (respect or pride) in the person. Through association with the athlete, the person gains the ability to elicit the same reaction in him or herself. Thus, when the individual focuses attention on him or herself, he or she feels the same respect or pride that is felt in the presence of the athlete. The second example illustrates the classical conditioning of a negative self-concept. In this case, the person associates with a convicted felon, whose presence elicits a painful emotional reaction (fear, disgust, or anxiety). After sufficient association, the person will elicit in him or herself the same reaction, which in behavioral terms is a negative self-concept or evaluation.

In both these cases, the reaction elicited by the self is completely involuntary and is not contingent on any behavior performed by the person. Whenever introspection or focusing of attention on the self occurs, a positive emotional reaction (pride and so on) is elicited in the first case; in the second, a painful emotional reaction (such as shame or guilt) occurs. A number of studies have demonstrated the classical conditioning of feelings about the self (Lazarus, 1971). For example, Ryan, Krall, and Hodges (1976)

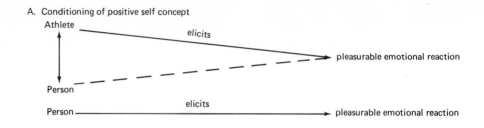

A. Conditioning of positive self concept

Athlete — elicits → pleasurable emotional reaction

Person

Person — elicits → pleasurable emotional reaction

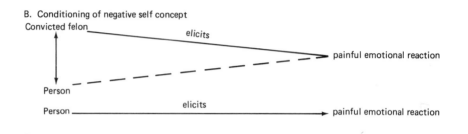

B. Conditioning of negative self concept

Convicted felon — elicits → painful emotional reaction

Person

Person — elicits → painful emotional reaction

Figure 2–2   Classical Conditioning of a Positive and a Negative Self-Concept

describe how desensitization of test anxiety not only reduced anxiety to test situations but also resulted in increased feelings of self-esteem.

Operant Conditioning   The operant paradigm of attitude change maintains that positive or negative reinforcement of statements about the self will increase or decrease the frequency of their occurrence. In other words, an individual's reinforcement history conditions the frequency with which the person makes negative or positive statements about him or herself. The nature and frequency of such responses constitute the person's self-concept. The process of operant conditioning of these statements is illustrated in figure 2–3.

As illustrated, self-praise is reinforced by obtaining salary increases, which strengthened the likelihood of self-praise. In this case, the person developed a positive self-concept or high self-esteem. In the second example, self-derogatory statements are strengthened by social approval from those with whom the individual associates. The person is reinforced to develop a negative self-concept or low self-esteem. The history of race relations in America provides numerous examples of reinforcing minorities to accept their consigned inferiority in society. A poignant example is given by a four and one-half year old black girl who wrote the following limerick: "The people that are white, they can go up. The people that are brown, they have to go down" (Goodman, 1964, p. 45).

Generally, the operant model does not emphasize internal processes or "internalization." Rather, the emphasis is upon observable behavior that is under the control of external reinforcement contingencies. Although the subtleties of this basic model cannot be developed here, figure 2–3 illustrates how behavioral theory explains the development of the self.

The social-learning model adds an additional element to the operant

A. Conditioning of positive self statements

acquires

Self praise ─────────────────────────────────────→ money

increase in response strength

B. Conditioning of negative self statements

acquires

Self derogation ─────────────────────────────────────→ social approval

increase in response strength

Figure 2–3 Operant Conditioning of Positive and Negative Self-Statements

conditioning model by focusing on self-reinforcement, self-punishment, and vicarious learning (modeling). Through the process of classical conditioning, certain behaviors, such as academic achievement, sharing, helping, honesty, and so on, gain the ability to elicit a positive emotional reaction. Conversely, other behaviors, such as cheating, aggression, or vulgarity, are conditioned to elicit painful emotional reactions. This classical conditioning may occur directly, by pairing the person's own behavior with valued reinforcers, or vicariously, by witnessing the behavior performed and its consequences realized by someone else. The emotional reaction occurs whenever the person engages in the behavior or sees the behavior performed by another. A person may engage in a patriotic act or view one in a motion picture and in both instances may feel proud, or he or she may either participate with or watch a favorite football team beaten and feel angry or ashamed. The important point is that the behavior is now self-reinforcing, and the person engages in it in order to experience the pleasant or painful emotional feelings. For example, an individual returns a wallet not because of an anticipated financial reward but because it creates a good feeling.

Reinforcers, both internal and external, are of differing strengths, and in any given situation the strongest anticipated reinforcement will control the behavior. Thus, if the person for whom honesty is modestly self-reinforcing is faced with a situation in which dishonesty will produce substantial financial reinforcement, the individual will probably engage in the dishonest act. On the other hand, the conditioning of self-reinforcing behaviors may be so strong that even death will not persuade the person to forgo the desired behavior or to commit the inappropriate act.

Evidently, the social-learning view of the self, although purportedly emphasizing behavior rather than internal processes, nevertheless incorporates a number of concepts that are internal to the individual. Once the behaviorist accepts vicarious learning, he or she has moved well beyond either the classical or operant conditioning model. Although these mental processes are not named, they are implicitly assumed.

The greatest departure from the behavioral position occurs, however, with the concepts of self-reinforcing and self-punishing behavior. Here, mental and emotional processes make it possible for the individual to engage in a particular behavior in order to create an emotionally enjoyable state. Once the individual instrumentally controls his or her behavior in order to create these conditions, the behavioral theory is very near the position of symbolic interaction in advocating future-oriented behavior, self-control, and self-direction.

Measurement of the Self

As indicated in the discussion of theories about the development of the self, how perceptions of the self are obtained are very important. Whether the measures of self are indicators of a nonobservable internal entity or are actually the self, the same basic measurement strategies are utilized. The first strategy is to ask the individual to objectively describe him or herself. The Twenty Statement Test (TST), a frequently used technique, involves asking a person to complete the following task: "There are twenty numbered blanks on the page below. Please write in the blanks twenty answers to the simple question 'Who am I?'" (Kuhn and McPartland, 1954). An example of a completed TST is presented in table 2–1.

The strength of the TST is found in the freedom given the respondent to describe him or herself. This strength is also a major weakness in that the results from the TST are difficult to analyze and interpret. In response to this problem, a number of different coding schemes have been devised, but

Table 2–1   Answers to the TST Given by a Mother and a Son

In the space below, please give twenty answers to the question, "Who am I?" Answer as if you were giving the answers to yourself, not to somebody else. Write rapidly for time is limited.

FORTY-YEAR-OLD MARRIED FEMALE	FIFTEEN-YEAR-OLD BOY
1. I am a wife. (F) (G)*	1. I am a boy. (G)
2. I am a mother. (F)	2. I am an athlete.
3. I am a sister. (F)	3. I am a music lover.
4. I am a daughter. (F)	4. I am the oldest. (F)
5. I am a granddaughter. (F)	5. I am 15 years old.
6. I am a child of God. (R)	6. I am a Christian. (R)
7. I am a Christian. (R)	7. I am a guitarist, sort of.
8. I am a teacher.	8. I am a good eater.
9. I am a seamstress. (F)	9. I am a horse rider.
10. I am a homemaker. (F)	10. I am an animal lover.
11. I am a chauffeur. (F)	11. I am a first counselor. (R)
12. I am a friend. (P)	12. I am a big brother. (F)
13. I am a laundress. (F)	13. I am an example (for good or bad).
14. I am a singer.	14. _____
15. I am a pianist.	15. _____
16. I am someone who enjoys reading.	16. _____
17. I am someone who needs people.	17. _____
18. _____	18. _____
19. _____	19. _____
20. _____	20. _____

*These refer to typical identity-coding procedures, where F = family identity; P = peer identity; R = religious identity; G = gender identity.

unfortunately none completely resolve it (Kuhn and McPartland, 1954; Gorden and Gergen, 1968).

A large number of self-concept or self-esteem scales have been developed that ask respondents to check descriptive adjectives or to indicate the degree to which certain statements are true about them (Robinson and Shaver, 1969). Sample items from the Butler-Haigh Q-Sort List (Rogers and Dymond, 1954) are: "I doubt my sexual powers"; "It is difficult to control my aggression"; "I am a responsible person"; "I am sexually attractive to the opposite sex"; and "I feel emotionally mature."

The advantages of such scales are that the results are easy to quantify and most have been standardized with a sample population so that the researcher can evaluate the nature of the self-concept or the strength of the self-esteem in comparison to the population with which the scale was developed. The disadvantage is that the test imposes restrictions upon the respondent and forces a self-description in the researcher's terms. Given the ease of analysis and the level of reliability of self-scales, they will undoubtedly continue to be used extensively in the study of the self.

Measurement strategies have also been developed to assess the unconscious self. The problems of identifying the dimensions of the unconscious self are much more formidable than those of assessing the conscious self. If the person does not recognize or understand these dimensions of self, how can the researcher be told about them? The psychoanalytic orientation asserts that the person will give sufficient information in the proper setting so that the the investigator can infer the nature of the self. Thus, the strategy of projective techniques is to ask the person to define and interpret ambiguous stimuli that reveal the nature of the unconscious self. The Thematic Apperception Test (TAT), Rorschach, Sentence Completion Test, and Draw a Person Test are examples of projective techniques that supposedly measure unconscious attitudes, including attitudes about the self.

The TAT is a series of pictures that are presented to the respondent, who tells a story about each. The investigator then looks for meaning hidden in the stories. For example, the following story was given in response to a picture of three young men with a gun and a knife in the background.

> These two boys have gone out hunting. They shot a lot of boys—I mean, animals, and decided to split up to get more pheasants. They agreed to meet at 8:30 at night to count the game and to go home. This boy was standing in the bushes. Twenty feet from him he heard something move. He goes to look at what he caught and finds his friend and rushes him to the doctor. The doctor says the boy will be all right, and in the end the boy gets OK and forgives him for what he did (Bellak, 1971, p. 122).

At first glance, the story seems confusing, with minimal information. The background of the person who wrote the story makes interpretation somewhat easier and illustrates how a researcher may use the TAT to assess the unconscious self.

> . . . I was asked to help determine whether or not a young boy should be released from an institution. He had killed a small child, apparently in some sexual excitement. Institutionalized, he was a model inmate on a behavioral

level—bland, noncommital, and inaccessible to psychotherapy. At the time of commitment and again when he came for disposition at the end of the year, he was given the TAT and other tests by the staff for help in understanding his problems. When none of the tests threw any light on the psychodynamics of the crime, he was referred to me for the administration of the TAT under the influence of intravenous Amytal Socium. After the intravenous administration of 7-½ gr. of Amytal Sodium and 1-½ gr. of Nembutal orally, a marked psychomotor effect of the drugs was noted: general relaxation, drowsiness, slurring of speech, and occasionally such lack of motor control and sleepiness that the TAT cards dropped out of his hands. Despite the action of the drugs, the boy gave 15 stories which in no single instance revealed any primary pathological evidence in the theme itself that would have permitted one to pick out his TAT as belonging to a noticeably disturbed person.

However, although it was impossible from his TAT stories to predict his actual behavior, small breakthroughs of original impulses came to light. For instance, he made one slip of the tongue in the story to picture 8BM.

The slip betrays the apparently original aggressive impulse which becomes absorbed in a perfectly acceptable hunting story, then breaks through again with the boy's injury. An inquiry into the small detail of 8:30 at night revealed that was the time for lights out at the institution and strongly suggested that it was at this time that his fantasies were permitted to emerge (Bellak, 1971, p. 122).

The weakness of projective techniques is obvious. The stimuli and the responses are so ambiguous that it is extremely difficult to extract information with any degree of validity or reliability. However, the importance of the effect of unconscious or subconscious processes on human behavior justifies the effort to develop better means of measuring this component of the self. It was only through such techniques, using hypnosis, that the therapist working with Sybil was able to make contact with all the sixteen different selves.

SOCIAL CLASS AND SELF-CONCEPT

It has been assumed by many scientists, and by the general public to a degree, that children raised in poor homes are socialized to see themselves in the same negative terms that are often used by the larger society to describe them. The general stereotype of the poor as being hedonistic, lazy, and intellectually inferior was assumed to be internalized by those living in poverty. A large number of studies, primarily with school children, have confirmed this hypothesis (Long and Henderson, 1968; Wylie, 1963). However, to the surprise of many, more recent studies have discovered that the self-concepts of students from different social classes are basically the same (Coleman et al., 1966; McDaniel, 1967; Scott, 1969). Even more surprising, several studies have reported that lower-class children have stronger self-concepts than do middle- and upper-class children (Clark and Trowbridge, 1971; Green and Rohwer, 1971; Trowbridge, 1972). For example, in a study of over three thousand elementary-school children in Iowa (Trowbridge, 1972), the children from families with lower socio-economic status had stronger self-concepts than did children from middle-class families. Trowbridge speculates that this difference may be due to the lower-class children's attitude that school is relatively unimportant to them, and therefore their self-concepts and self-esteem are not affected by their school performance.

The relationship between social class and self-concept originally hypothesized that upper-class people would have stronger self-concepts as compared to those living in poverty. The research indicates that because perceptions of the self are more sensitive to one's immediate social environment, lower-class individuals develop their self-concepts by comparing themselves with other lower-class individuals in the context of lower-class culture. Thus, lower-class people on the average have self-concepts or self-esteem just as positive as that of upper-class individuals.

RACE AND SELF-CONCEPT

Researchers have long postulated a low level of self-esteem or negative self-concepts for members of ethnic and/or racial groups. The examples used to illustrate the negative self-concepts of minority-group members are those of "Uncle Tom," "Sambo," "Step and Fetch It," or "Uncle Tomohawk." Each of these stereotypic characters has accepted the majority's definition of them as being inferior. A series of early studies with black children provided support for this idea (Horowitz, 1939; Clark and Clark, 1952; Radke and Trager, 1950). Children were given black and white dolls to play with, were asked to make up stories about black and white children, or were asked to interpret photographs of blacks and whites interacting. These studies clearly demonstrated that at a very early age children perceived differences in skin color. More importantly, it was found that black children sought to play with the white doll and defined it as good, labeled the black doll as bad, and gave black characters in the stories or photographs the roles of servants, maids, or gardeners. The doll play, stories, and self-portraits all gave frightening evidence of the negative self-concepts of black children.

The civil-rights movement of the late 1960s and early 1970s has facilitated the emergence of "Black is beautiful," "Red is beautiful," "Yellow is beautiful," and "Brown is beautiful" attitudes. The ethnic pride generated in minority individuals, especially the young, suggests that the earlier studies are now outdated. More recent studies have found little or no difference between the self-concepts of members of different racial groups. Zirkel (1971) reviewed over a dozen studies of black and white students attending elementary and secondary schools, and similar self-concepts or levels of self-esteem were determined. Robert Havighurst and his associates conducted a national study of Indian education between 1967 and 1971. They reported that the self-concepts and self-esteem of Indian students were about the same as that of white students (Fuchs and Havighurst, 1972). The famous Coleman Report concerning equality of educational opportunity in American society found mixed results, as black and white students had similar self-concepts, but Mexican-American students evidenced more negative self-conceptions (Coleman et al., 1966).

A number of studies have also discovered that minority students have stronger self-concepts than do majority students (Simmons et al., 1978). Zirkel and Moses (1971) assessed the self-concepts of fifth- and sixth-grade students in the same classes, and the black students evidenced the strongest self-concepts. Several studies found stronger black self-concepts among high-school students (Trowbridge, 1972; Wilson, 1967; Hodgkins and Stakenas, 1969).

One attempt to reconcile the inconsistent findings concerning differences between black and white self-concepts is provided by Rosenberg and Simmons (1971). They speculate that black students who attend white-majority schools experience greater discrimination and compare themselves with the higher-achieving, middle-class white students. The result is a lower self-concept. On the other hand, black students who attend segregated, all-black schools compare themselves to their black peers, receive evaluations about themselves from these same peers, and develop reasonably positive self-concepts and feelings of self-esteem. This suggests that minority students placed in integrated schools may experience strain on their self-concepts.

An alternative explanation, mentioned above, is that the civil-rights movement has greatly increased racial pride. The change in attitudes and behavior associated with the civil-rights movement has occurred at different rates in different sections of the country. The large metropolitan areas on the east and west coasts have experienced such social change to a greater degree than have other areas of the country. Studies conducted in communities where racial pride has increased discover minority students with strong self-concepts; inferior self-attitudes still persist in other communities.

SEX AND SELF-CONCEPT

Anthropologists have long noted that the division of labor and assignment of status on the basis of sex can be found in virtually all societies (Linton, 1936). Although the effort to deemphasize longstanding sex-role definitions is having some obvious impact on our society, the traditional subordinate status granted women is assumed to have some important consequences on the self-concepts of both males and females. According to Freeman (1970), the inferior social status of women is generally reflected in more negative self-concepts or lower self-esteem as compared to men. Support for this hypothesis has also been provided by Simmons, Rosenberg, and Rosenberg (1973) in their research on 2,000 adolescents in the public schools of Baltimore. These authors concluded that youngsters twelve- and thirteen-years old exhibit a greater awareness of self than did students of other ages. This greater awareness was accompanied by less-stable and somewhat weaker self-concept. More importantly, Simmons and her associates (1973, 1975, and 1978) reported significant differences in self-concepts exhibited by male and female students at this age. The girls revealed somewhat weaker or more negative self-concepts or feelings of self-esteem.

On the other hand, other researchers have reported that in certain situations women have equal or stronger levels of self-esteem than do men. It appears that differences in self-concepts between large social groups, such as social classes, racial groups, or sex groups, are fairly small and that the variation within each group results in great overlap between the members of the different groups. The overlap is so large that it is difficult to predict a person's self-concept or self-esteem on the basis of their social class, race, or sex.

Self as Determinant of Behavior

In the past, personality theorists argued that internal states, including the self, largely control human behavior. Today, most scientists accept the position that the self is a determinant of behavior that interacts with biological factors and external situational constraints in guiding behavior, as illustrated in figure 2–4. The degree of contribution of each of the three factors has long been a source of discussion and debate within the scientific community. We are not implying that the self is the major determinant of behavior but rather that it is one of many factors influencing the actions of the individual. Much of the research linking self and behavior appears in the areas of education and deviant behavior. Numerous studies have attempted to document the effects of self on learning by both children and adults. In addition, "labeling" theorists have attempted to account for various types of deviant behavior, such as juvenile delinquency, crime, and mental illness, using the theory that self-concept develops in response to the labels others place on the individual and that this self-concept in turn influences the delinquent or criminal behavior. Labeling theory is a specific application of the symbolic-interaction theory of the looking-glass self described earlier.

THE SELF AND EDUCATIONAL ACHIEVEMENT

An education study that frequently is interpreted as supporting the self-concept/behavior link is *Pygmalion in the Classroom* (Rosenthal and Jacobson, 1968). As the title indicates, *Pygmalion* has to do with the effect that one person's *belief* in the goodness of another person has on what that other person becomes. (The title is derived from the Greek myth and the 1912 comedy, *Pygmalion*, by George Bernard Shaw, that was later the basis for "My Fair Lady;" which has generated folk-wisdom variants on the theme that to be a lady is not so much determined by what you are, but by how you are treated.)

Rosenthal and Jacobson (1968) selected a random sample of elementary-school children, told their teachers these students were going to bloom academically during the coming year, and then compared their achievement

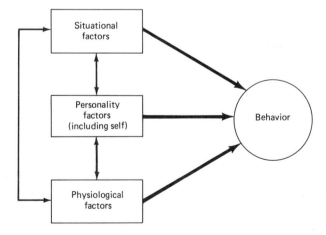

Figure 2–4 Interaction of Situational, Personality, and Physiological Factors in Influencing Behavior

to that of the control-group children. The researchers' hypothesis was that the teacher's belief in the potential of these children would increase the children's self-concept, which in turn would enhance their performance. The involvement of the self-concept in the learning process is explained by Rosenthal and Jacobson:

> To summarize our speculations, we may say that by what she said, by how and when she said it, by her facial expressions, postures, and perhaps by touch, the teacher may have communicated to the children of the experimental group that she expected improved intellectual performance. Such communications together with possible changes in teaching techniques may have helped the child learn by changing his self-concept, his expectations of his own behavior, and his motivation, as well as his cognitive style and skills (1968, p. 180).

The study was conducted in a public elementary school serving a lower-class community in a medium-sized city in Northern California. Students of Mexican-American origin accounted for one-sixth of the student population. In May 1964, all the students were tested with a standard nonverbal test of intelligence. Twenty percent of the students were randomly selected as experimental subjects; the other 80 percent served as the control group.

In September 1964, during the first staff meeting, teachers were told, "By the way, in case you're interested in who did what in those tests we did for Harvard. . . ." The teachers were then shown the list of randomly selected students labeled as bloomers. The only difference between the students whose names appeared on the list and those whose names did not was in the minds of the teachers. Nothing else was said, nothing else was done. The children were retested in January and May 1965. The differences in increases in IQ scores for bloomers and control students were impressive. The IQ gains of the "bloomers" were extraordinary! The Pygmalion effect was significantly more pronounced for the younger students. For the children in the first and second grades, 21 percent increased by thirty or more points, 48 percent increased twenty or more points, and 78 percent increased by at least ten IQ points. Perhaps the self-concepts of first and second graders are more malleable, and thus they responded more strongly to teacher expectations. Additional support for this idea was obtained when the students were tested one year after the Pygmalion experiment, as the effect on the younger students had faded much more than that on the older students. This suggests that the older children's self-concepts were more resistant to change but once altered the change persisted. The implications of this study for education are enormous. While costing the taxpayer nothing, student IQs were substantially improved without any crash program of tutoring, field trips, special curricula, or teacher aids.

This study has generated considerable controversy, and some serious methodological criticisms have been raised. Pertaining to self theory, it is pointed out that no observations of the students' self-concepts were ever made, and thus there is no evidence that changes in self-concept affected IQ scores.

Rosenthal (1973) reviewed 242 studies that had attempted to replicate the Pygmalion effect using a variety of subjects in different social settings. Only

84 studies (35 percent) had obtained the predicted Pygmalion effect. Rosenthal argues that because this success rate is higher than chance, the Pygmalion effect is real. He suggests that future research should seek to identify the conditions under which the effect is produced.

A more rigorous test of the social interaction/self-concept/behavior hypothesis was conducted utilizing junior-high school students in a midwest community (Brookover et al., 1965). The study assessed the impact of three significant others—parents, learning expert, and school counselor—on student self-concepts and subsequently on academic achievement. The first experiment involved coaching *parents* to give their children positive input about their academic abilities. The researchers met regularly with the parents during the school year, both in a group and as couples, to train them how to encourage their children. The theory was supported in that by the end of the school year both self-concepts and grade-point averages of the experimental group had significantly improved as compared to the control group.

The second experiment conducted in a different junior-high school had a *learning expert*—a university professor—give encouragement to students to alter their self-concepts about their ability to succeed. The expert met with the students seven times during the year, presenting pep talks about their academic ability. The self-concept of these students remained unchanged. Given that self-concepts did not improve, it was predicted that grades would also stay constant. This prediction held true.

The third experiment utilized a *school counselor* as the significant other. The counselor met with students in a group six times and with each student individually every ten days during the school year. Despite this intense interaction, there were no significant changes in self-concept or grade-point averages.

This study indicates that the self-concepts of junior-high school students are difficult to alter. The only significant other to accomplish this was the parent. However, the results support the theory that self-concept influences academic achievement. In the school where self-concepts were strengthened, better schoolwork also appeared. In the other two cases where self-concepts were not affected, grades remained the same.

An example of research that failed to replicate the Pygmalion effect is a study of the relationship between self-concept and academic achievement of first-grade students in Colorado (Williams, 1973). It was discovered that self-concepts of these young students were not related to their reading achievement. In other words, students with weak self-concepts were as likely to excel in reading as were students with strong self-concepts. These findings suggest that changes in the students' self-concepts would not affect their reading achievement. Also, the findings indicate that children who succeed in school tasks were not more likely to develop strong self-concepts than were students who did poorly in their schoolwork.

Alpert (1975) attempted to trace the link between teacher expectations, teacher behavior, and student performance in order to unravel the inconsistencies in the findings concerning the Pygmalion effect. Although not explicitly including measures of self-concept in the research, the implicit assumption was that student self-image was being altered by the teachers' behavior. It was discovered that for a sample of seventeen second-grade teachers and 138 students with reading difficulties, changes in teacher be-havior, specifically "good" teaching behavior, did not alter the students' reading performance. The author concluded that one reason the Pygmalion effect has not been replicated with any degree of consistency is that re-searchers have focused on teacher behaviors, which were assumed to im-prove student performance, when such behaviors in reality have no effect.

Finally, Rogers, Smith, and Coleman (1978) tested the notion that the relationship between self-concept and academic achievement is contingent upon the student's perceptions of how his or her achievement compares to those of classmates, rather than to some absolute level of achievement. They found that classroom achievement and self-concept were related when achievement was compared to that of classmates.

Although the relationship between self-concept and academic achieve-ment is not clearly understood, research is slowly unraveling the conditions that influence the relationship. The dramatic promise of studies such as *Pygmalion in the Classroom* tantalizes researchers to continue attempts to understand the relationship between self and school performance.

THE SELF AND DEVIANT BEHAVIOR

A large literature has developed concerning the relationship between self-conceptions and deviant behavior, such as juvenile delinquency, crime, drug abuse, alcoholism, suicide, and mental illness. The relationship between the self and deviant behavior is hypothesized to be reciprocal: a negative self-concept increases the probability of deviant behavior, and the commitment of deviant acts shapes a negative self-concept of being deviant.

A number of theorists have proposed that the development of deviant identities follows pretty much the symbolic-interactionist orientation of the development of the self-concept. Biesanz and Biesanz (1969) draw from the work of Lemert (1951), Becker (1963), Goffman (1963), and other "interac-tionist" theorists in discussing the sequential process involved. They sug-gest that engaging in deviant acts does not *ipso facto* make one a deviant. Rather, one must come to be defined as deviant by others and then incorpo-rate this definition into his or her self-concept.

When a person commits a deviant act, it may be perceived by others—perhaps a teacher, a police officer, a parent, or some other agent of social control—and the act can be ignored or handled privately, thereby limiting the probability of the act coming to the attention of others. However, if the act is publicized, then a stigma is attached to the actor—he or she is defined as a problem child, a cheat, a delinquent, a drug addict, and so forth. The stigma may lead to further commission of the negative act, if only because it closes off opportunities to return to a more conforming lifestyle. For example, the youth who is labeled a troublemaker may be unable to obtain a job, the student who is labeled a cheat may not be allowed to finish a course, and consequently, to graduate with his or her class. As the stigma continues to affect the opportunities of the person to whom it is applied, the looking-glass self process comes into operation. If the feedback a person gets from everyone else says he or she is no good, then this definition is likely to be incorporated into his or her self-concept. Once this has oc-curred, we reach the stage Lemert refers to as "secondary deviance." The person defines him or herself as a deviant, accepts the role, and behaves accordingly. Deviance, in other words, has become a way of life because this is the identity that is most central to the individual's concept of self.

Why this occurs is made more clear by a recent attempt to develop a general theory of deviance utilizing the self-attitude/behavior link. Kaplan (1975) has hypothesized a universal self-esteem motive. He contends that every person has a need to maximize the experience of positive feedback about the self and to minimize negative self-information experiences. Kaplan's theory of deviance is built on this basic self-esteem need as the person with a history of negative self-attitude experiences is predicted to change significant others and to change behavior patterns in order to maximize positive and minimize negative self-attitude experiences. Because positive experiences cannot be maximized in general society, law-abiding significant others are replaced by deviant significant others, and conformity to societal norms is abandoned to deviant behavior. The expectation is that the deviant significant others will approve of the deviant activities, and the person will receive the positive self-attitude experiences that he or she craves but is denied by traditional society.

It is considerably more difficult to test the link between self-attitudes and deviant behavior than it is to test the relationship between the self and academic achievement. Ethical values prohibit the purposeful creation of negative self-attitudes in order to assess their effect on engagement or nonengagement in deviance. The best alternative would be to take deviants and utilize positive self-attitude experiences in order to shape them into nondeviants. The difficulty of controlling the choice of significant others of delinquents, criminals, alcoholics, and other deviants has limited this type of research. Some support has been obtained in experiments involving very minor acts of deviance. For example, Aronson and Mattee (1968) manipulated self-attitude experiences and then observed the degree of cheating behavior. The subjects, female psychology students, were told the experiment was testing the association between personality traits and extrasensory perception (ESP) and were given a battery of personality-trait tests. Regardless of test results, one-third of the subjects (fifteen) were given rather negative self-concept feedback, another third neutral results, and the other one-third positive test scores. Cheating was determined by having the subjects participate in a modified blackjack game in which it was relatively easy to cheat. In order to provide additional motivation to cheat, the game was structured so that cheating was the only means by which the subjects could win. The results revealed that 87 percent of those given negative self-attitude feedback cheated, as compared to 60 percent of the neutral and only 40 percent of the positive self-attitude subjects. These large differences are interpreted as support for the relationship between one's view of self and deviant behavior.

Another strategy for testing the influence of self-attitudes on deviant behavior has been to compare the self-concepts of deviants to those of nondeviants. For example, Kaplan and Meyerowitz (1970) obtained several different measures of self-attitude from 300 recent drug addicts as well as from a control group of similar age and education in the state of Texas. The drug addicts evidenced significantly more negative self-attitudes on all the different measures. It is not possible to assert that the self-attitudes caused the drug addiction any more than it is possible to assert that the addiction caused the negative evaluations of the self. It is suspected that the relationship was reciprocal, producing a vicious cycle of increasing self-derogation and drug abuse. Similar findings were reported by Steffenhagen (1978), who found that self-esteem was related to drug abuse. Those persons with stronger self-esteem used drugs significantly less frequently than those with lower self-esteem and were more able to resist social pressures to use drugs.

Similar results have been obtained concerning mental illness as Harrow et al. (1968) discovered that psychiatric patients had lower self-ratings than did nonpatients. They compared thirty-four adolescent and young-adult psychotics to twenty normal people matched for age and education. The results strongly support the hypothesis that self-attitudes and mental illness are related. A review of studies testing labeling theory as an explanation of mental illness (Scheff, 1975) concluded that the research evidence supports the theory. Eighteen studies ranging from controlled experiments to surveys were examined, and in thirteen cases the results supported the theory.

Summary

Although several definitions of the self have been offered, most focus on the individual's mental image of who or what the individual perceives him or herself to be. Attitudes about the self usually describe the characteristics of the person and include an evaluation of these characteristics. A person's *self-concept* usually includes both an identification of characteristics as well as an evaluation of them; the level of *self-esteem* generally emphasizes the evaluation. The various elements of information contained in a self-concept tend to be integrated, thus contributing to a unified personality. The self also is reasonably stable over time, although it appears to change some as people shift social roles. Finally, an individual's self-perceptions tend to be consistent with those held of him or her by other people. There are exceptions, but generally the feedback a person receives from others results in a fairly high degree of consensus.

Symbolic-interaction theories conceptualize the self as an internal mental process that develops out of and continually influences social interaction. The various theories show society's influence in the self-development process, explaining it in terms of role taking or feedback. Some think this results in multiple selves that are alternately present for different audiences. There does not have to be a conflict between the notions of a core versus multiple selves, however. The core self may provide the boundaries as we change roles and audiences.

Behavioral psychology defines the self in terms of how it is measured, and shows self-development as the result of two conditioning or learning processes: classical conditioning and operant conditioning. Conditioning can result in positive or negative self-concept, as measured by such observable behavior as the statements made about oneself.

Social-learning theory somewhat bridges the gap between symbolic-interaction theory and behavioral psychology as it focuses on self-reinforcement, self-punishment, and vicarious learning. Once behavior has become self-reinforcing or self-punishing, it is influenced by internal processes and is not solely under the control of external reinforcement contingencies.

Numerous techniques have been developed to measure the self. Standardized scales and checklists involve asking the respondent to objectively describe him or herself using a list of adjectives or characteristics. These scales are fairly easy to analyze, but there is concern that the respondent has been forced to describe him or herself in terms he or she normally would not use. On the other hand, strategies such as the Twenty Statement Test permit the person to use his or her own terms, but such tests are much more difficult to interpret. In addition to these methods, projective techniques such as the TAT, Rorschach, Sentence Completion, and Draw a Person tests are used to measure the unconscious self. Recent studies using measurement techniques refute older findings in that they find little or no difference in self-concepts across social groups; some have even found lower-class people, minority-group members, and women with stronger self-concepts than their counterparts. This change can be explained by changes in society or by viewing the differences between these large social groups as being so small with so much overlap that any observed differences are unreliable and meaningless.

Much of the literature is concerned with the relationship between self-concept and behavior. The "Pygmalion" and Brookover research studies found that changes in the self-concepts can be tied to better school performance. Finally, it has been argued that there is a strong relationship between self-concept and engagement in deviant behavior. Presumably, if the individual is labeled negatively by others (as a delinquent, drug addict, alcoholic), that individual will eventually come to internalize the label and will behave accordingly. Research findings have been generally supportive of this supposition.

In conclusion, although much controversy still exists regarding the usefulness of self-concept in understanding human behavior, it continues to be widely used. In addition, although we recognize the important measurement and definitional problems associated with the term, the research on the relationship between self and behavior seems to justify this continued use.

3

language and communication

Each one of us is involved daily in efforts to communicate meanings and intentions to others. People are social animals largely because language allows them to be. However, the inherent hazards that are built into the communication process are well illustrated by the following incident:

> I learned something of the intricacies of plain English at an early stage in my career. A woman of thirty-five came in one day to tell me that she wanted a baby but that she had been told that she had a certain type of heart-disease which might not interfere with a normal life but would be dangerous if she ever had a baby. From her description I thought at once of mitral stenosis. This condition is characterized by a rather distinctive rumbling murmur near the apex of the heart, and especially by a peculiar vibration felt by the examining finger on the patient's chest. The vibration is known as the "thrill" of mitral stenosis.
>
> When this woman had been undressed and was lying on my table in her white kimono, my stethoscope quickly found the heart-sounds I had expected. Dictating to my nurse, I described them carefully. I put my stethoscope aside and felt intently for the typical vibration which may be found in a small but variable area of the left chest.
>
> I closed my eyes for better concentration, and felt long and carefully for the tremor. I did not find it and with my hand still on the woman's bare breast, lifting it upward and out of the way, I finally turned to the nurse and said: "No thrill."
>
> The patient's black eyes snapped open, and with venom in her voice she said: "Well, isn't that just too bad? Perhaps it's just as well you don't get one. That isn't what I came for."
>
> My nurse almost choked, and my explanation still seems a nightmare of futile words (F. Loomis, 1939. Cited in Krech, Crutchfield, and Ballachey, 1962, p. 305).

Introduction

People live in a symbolic world. Through the use of symbols, they can call out in others the same meaning as the symbols call out in themselves. Thus, a mother and father can talk of and weep over their daughter's death in Guyana long after the event. Not only can they weep again about their daughter's death, they can make plans to prevent a similar fate for their other daughter. All this is made possible because symbols free them from the constraints of the here and now. In this sense, people never just respond to objects in the real world, but rather to objects and events in the real world that are given meaning by placing them in the categories inherent in their symbolic worlds. Thus, it is not just a young woman who dies, but "daughter." Once the event is placed in its appropriate category, then meaningful lines of action are identified toward the event or object. The past can be symbolically relived, even redefined, and the future can be anticipated, even anxiously awaited.

The complexities of the process of human communication are easily recognized by the professional and the layperson alike. This is demonstrated in the example at the beginning of this chapter. Unless the "sender" and the "receiver" attach similar meaning to a symbol, communication breaks down. The importance people attach to sending the message they actually intend to send can be seen in the amount of time they sometimes take in seeking just the right word or phrase or in selecting the proper nonverbal symbol to communicate their feelings and intents to others.

Although we have created numerous symbolic systems, such as mathematics, music, and painting to communicate our feelings and intentions to others, the most universal system is language itself. In this chapter, we seek to understand something about the nature of language, including language acquisition, the relationship of language to thought, and the importance of communication patterns as they relate to social order.

The Nature of Language

ORIGIN OF LANGUAGE

Because language is such a universal, human possession, some have attempted to illuminate this dimension of human behavior by inquiring how humans came to use language. One such explanation is the onomatopoeic or the "bow-wow" theory of the origin of language. It assumes that language arose because of people's efforts to create words that were similar to the sounds of the thing being described. Thus, people heard the bark of a dog and said "bow-wow." The "bow-wow" theory of the origin of language has a certain plausible ring to the average person. We can all identify words that do in fact sound like their referent, such as the "toot" of a train, the "buzz" of a bee, or the "bong" of a drum. However, this explanation has not faired well under even minimal examination. Comparative linguists (those who study languages in different cultures) find that the same sound is often "heard" differently in different languages. To the English speaker, "snip, snip" refers without question to the sound of scissors; to the Greek, the snipping of scissors sounds like "krits-krits." To us, "ting-a-ling" sounds like a bell, whereas to the Finnish ear a bell clearly sounds like "kili" (Pei, 1968).

An alternative theory of language development is that it is the product of an evolutionary process. Ancient people living in caves intended their first vocalizations to communicate feelings of fear, hunger, anger, or contentment. Gradually, the spoken sounds evolved into a complicated language. Although this explanation may fit well with our views of human evolution, there is an absence of concrete evidence supporting this view. In fact, the evidence compiled by the comparative linguists shows that the order of development may be the direct opposite. Jesperson, as early as 1921, presented considerable evidence that the further back in time one goes in the study of language, the more complex the languages were.

More contemporary linguists (Kiparski, 1976) note that although there is no generally agreed upon measure of linguistic complexity, the evidence tends to support Jesperson's conclusion that linguistic change is toward greater simplification. Kiparski also notes that the complexity of the language is not positively correlated with the complexity of the society. In fact, he argues that what evidence is available may indicate an inverse relationship; namely, that the more complex the society, the more simplified the language form. He notes that language groups that have a relatively small number of speakers tend to have very complex language structure, whereas, "the spread of a single language over great areas . . . usually brings with it a drift toward structural simplification" (Kiparski, 1976, p. 98).

Studies of the origin of the written word as a derivative of the spoken word have also assumed an evolutionary explanation. It is assumed that written language developed gradually and slowly from the spoken language and may have begun with the drawing of pictures to represent things. This pictograph writing was gradually refined into a more complex symbolic system. Again, this explanation for slow, gradual change may seem reasonable, but it lacks convincing evidence. The earliest written records reveal a complex written language (Nibley, 1978). This, of course, does not mean that language did not develop slowly; it merely means we have no evidence.

The great complexity of both written and spoken languages has apparently existed from the earliest historical times. Because of this, the invention of language must be seen as one of the greatest human inventions. As Tanner and Zihlman note, "We still do not know how the first language was invented" (1976, p. 476). It may well have been the invention of one person or a relatively few people. In very recent historical times, there are at least two remarkable instances of writing systems, each having been developed by a single person. These cases are described in the box below.

Inventions of Reading and Writing by American Indians

CASE 1

Some early Americans desired to "civilize" the American Indians by developing a written language for them. A number of them attempted to develop a phonetic system that could be used by the Indian in his native language. In the midst of one of these earliest attempts, a most remarkable invention was made by George Guess, an Indian known as Sequoyah. Jeffrey Wollock describes what happened.

While scholars were pondering the best way to represent the simple sounds of English, Sequoyah, an Indian of the civilized Cherokee tribe, applied himself to the same task in respect of his native language (the only language he ever knew). In the year 1809, in Northern Alabama, during the course of a discussion with some other Indians regarding the white man's "talking leaves," Sequoyah expressed the belief that it was neither a divine gift, nor magic, nor imposture, but that the marks on paper stood for words, and that *he could invent a way to do the same thing.* It took him twelve years, but by 1821, he had a *nearly phonetic syllabary of 86 characters.* His method had been the same as the elocutionists'. He went to all public gatherings, listening carefully to speeches and conversations. Eventually an English book came his way, and *although he could not read it,* he set about adapting the letters to his own use, *modifying* some and *inventing* new forms. *What happened next has no parallel in history.* Not a schoolhouse was built and not a teacher was hired, but within a few months the syllabary had spread spontaneously to every corner of the Cherokee country. It generally took a native speaker *three* or *four* days to *learn to read,* seldom more than a week. A short time later the tribe had obtained a *printing press* and type, and *started a newspaper* (Davis, 1930, italics added).

In the beginning of 1825 John Pickering was at work on a Cherokee grammar. . . . As soon as he heard of Sequoyah's syllabary, he gave up the project, despite the fact that 48 pages had already been printed (Pickering, 1887). Yet the American Missionary Board doggedly continued to insist on the Pickering orthography for years to come, despite the opposition of the Indians and even some of the missionaries. As Sheehan puts it: "An apparently workable system of Indian writing encroached on the exclusivity of English as the necessary precondition for civilized life. Many philanthropists, consequently, kept a distinct reserve in their reaction to Sequoyah's invention" (Sheehan, 1973, p. 139).

(Source: Jeffrey Wollock, "William Thornton, An Eighteenth Century American Psycholinguist: Background and Influence," *Annals of New York Academy of Sciences* 284, 291 (1977): 264–76 © 1977 NY Academy of Sciences).

CASE 2

The cover story of *Science,* June 8, 1973, describes the invention of an unusual writing system. In 1904, in a quiet corner of the Fort Apache Indian Reservation in Arizona, this most remarkable invention occurred. Basso and Anderson, an anthropology professor and an Apache third-year law student, respectively, rank this among the most "significant intellectual achievements of an American Indian during the 20th Century" (1973, p. 1013).

Silas John, a twenty-one year old Apache, received in a vision one night a complicated set of sixty-two prayers that were to form the corpus of his teachings. At the same time he received the prayers, he was given a writing system in order to record and preserve them for succeeding generations. Silas John described what took place:

There were 62 prayers. They came to me in rays from above. At the same time I was instructed. He [God] was advising me and telling me what to do, at the same time teaching me the chants. They were presented to me—one by one. All of these and the writing were given to me at one time in one dream . . . (Basso and Anderson, 1973, p. 1014).

Silas John recorded the sixty-two prayers on separate pieces of buckskin. By 1920, his teachings were widely accepted, and he chose twelve *assistants.* He taught them the writing system and the prayers. Silas John's system spread throughout the Fort Apache and San Carlos reservations in East-Central Arizona, where it is still in use today. When one assistant died, another was chosen to take his place. Each new assistant was carefully taught the writing system and the prayers. In 1973, Silas John was ninety-one years old and very active. The remarkable invention of the writing system was undoubtedly responsible for the fact that the system of prayers and writing have "continued unmodified up to the present" (Basso and Anderson, 1973, p. 1015).

A detailed linguistic analysis revealed the underlying rules that gave order and meaning to the writing system. The underlying logic and rules formed a coherent and very useful system that was unlike any with which the psycholinguists were familiar. Even though Silas John could read and write English, this could in no way "account for the . . . form of his script, of its underlying structural principles. . . . The writing system of Silas John represents . . . the creation of a totally unique cultural form" (Basso and Anderson, 1973, p. 1013).

(Source: Keith H. Basso and Neal Anderson, "A Western Apache Writing System: The Symbols of Silas John," *Science* 180, no. 4090 (June 1973): 1013–22.)

Linguists have succeeded in identifying basic components of language. Their research has demonstrated that language can be understood by focusing on its components, and in so doing its universal characteristics are highlighted.

When language is thought of as a spoken system of communication, it can then be broken into its component parts. Consider the following simple dialogue between a mother and a three-year-old child:

Mother: Where have you and dad been?
Child: Outside feeding the dog.

The written form of what both mother and child said and heard breaks the string of sound into words. Look at the mother's question written with no word structure identified:

Mother: wherehaveyouanddadbeen

What the child hears is a string of sounds more like the last phrase than the first phrase. In order to understand what the mother has said, the child must have a working knowledge of the phonetic structure of the language. Thus, the child must have the ability to recognize distinct sounds *(phonology)* as well as combine sounds together to form words *(morphology)*. This simple conversation also illustrates that in addition to phonology and morphology, the child must also have attached to those words their common meaning *(semantics)*.

Although the child may not consciously know that he has learned something about phonology and morphology and semantics, he has in fact developed the ability to make all the differentiations that are required in each of those components of language. This is not all the three-year-old child has accomplished, however; he must also know that the words must be ordered in a particular way *(syntax)*.

Phonology, morphology, semantics, and syntax are the four basic components of language. It is the purpose of the linguist to study languages along these dimensions in order to understand the underlying rules governing language use. Psycholinguistics and sociolinguistics are areas of study that seek to ask questions of how this ordered and structured system of language relates to and influences the social-psychological world of each individual.

Unspoken Languages

It is not necessary that all these four components be present for a system of communication to be classified as a language. Unspoken languages do not have the phonetic component, but they possess all the other characteristics of language, namely, morphology, in the sense of combining signs and symbols into words with meaning (semantics), and then combining words into sentences (syntax). The most prominent and well-known unspoken language is that of Ameslan, the name given to American Sign Language for the deaf. Other such examples are Morse Code and computer languages. Analysis of Ameslan reveals that it contains all the elements with the exception of phonetics, qualifying it as a language (Katz, 1976; Brown, 1973).

Language as a communication system can take a number of different forms—spoken, written, or gestural. The communication system of the bee would not be classified as a language because it does not possess morphology or syntax (see box). However, there are other communication systems in animals that may help illuminate the psycholinguistic dimensions of human language.

Communication in Bees

A striking example of the potential for complex communication behavior in infrahuman species is the "body language" of the honeybee. The studies of the German naturalist Von Frisch (1954) have shown that bees are able to convey the location and direction of food discoveries to others in the swarm by means of a series of maneuvers as stylized, in some respects, as the figures in classical ballet.

Von Frisch constructed a hive with glass walls that permitted him to observe the behavior of the bee tenants when they returned from a food-seeking flight. When the source of the nectar was close, say within 100 feet or less, the finder bee would perform a "dance" consisting of a circular movement. To indicate longer distances, the bee would run in a straight line while moving its abdomen rapidly from side to side, then make a turn and repeat the maneuver. For distances in excess of 200 yards, the number of turns made by the bee decreased. A run followed by only two turns, for example, might indicate that the food source was several miles away.

After observing this behavior, the other bees were able to fly directly to the food. It was apparent that they received cues to the location of the food from the direction of the "run" made by the finder bee. An upward vertical run in the hive indicated that the food source would be found by flying into the sun, whereas a downward vertical run indicated that the food source was away from the sun. Von Frisch found that bees that were restricted to a horizontal surface and deprived of sunlight were unable to communicate the direction of their finds (Vetter, 1969, p. 14, reprinted by permission).

CHIMPS AND LANGUAGE?

The remarkable research conducted with chimpanzees in the last two decades is causing careful reevaluation of earlier assumptions that only humans possess the ability to develop language. Students of language are divided, with some insisting that the research evidence leads to the conclusion that chimpanzees utilize a language very similar to that of children, arguing that whatever differences there may be are probably "ones of degree, not kind" (Miles, 1976, p. 596). Other linguists assert that "language is a uniquely human attribute," and the recent research has strengthened that conclusion (Katz, 1976, p. 33).

If linguists are divided on the issue, it is not surprising to find that social psychologists likewise express differing opinions. Some assert that "humans are the only animals capable of language" (Lindesmith, Strauss, and Denzin, 1977, p. 74). Others conclude that "chimpanzees are capable of learning to use the functional properties of language in embarrassingly human ways" (Gallup, et al., 1977, p. 308).

Gua and Vicki The early attempts at teaching chimps language were designed to discover whether chimps could learn to vocalize anything that appeared to be similar to words. Kellogg and Kellogg (1933) reported on their efforts of teaching Gua language by having the chimp live in their home. Gua made sounds, but these appeared to be species-specific sounds of the chimp rather than anything that sounded like human words. In the book, *The Ape In Our House* (1951), Hayes reported that Vicki acquired sounds that were approximations of the words mama, papa, and cup. Brown (1973, p. 33) concludes that these words "seem to mark the upper limits of her productive linguistic capacity."

What this research clearly shows is that chimps lack the necessary vocal apparatuses to produce spoken language in a human sense. These early efforts led Lenneberg to conclude: "There is no evidence that any non-human form has the capacity to acquire even the most primitive stages of language development" (1964, p. 67, quoted in Brown, 1973, p. 33). Anatomical research clearly shows that the chimps' vocal organs cannot produce the sounds of human speech (Lieberman, Crelin, and Klatt, 1972). However, research designed to measure the chimps' linguistic abilities in communication not requiring the vocal medium is providing an exciting array of findings.

Project Sarah David Premack (1970a, 1970b, 1971) succeeded in teaching a full-grown, adult chimpanzee named Sarah to use a complicated symbol system. Plastic chips stood for various aspects of language, such as questions, sentences, and words, as well as a series of qualifiers, such as one, all, several, or none.

Through standard conditioning procedures based on Sarah's food needs, Premack taught Sarah discrimination learning to the point that she could differentially respond to the various chips. Sarah's accomplishments are impressive. It seems clear that not only did Sarah learn the symbol system, she was able to respond to the symbol as a symbol. She learned that objects in the real world had names. Her use of the symbol system seemed to indicate that Sarah had a cognitive structure capable of using the symbol system to solve problems about the symbolic system itself. For example, "Sarah could respond correctly to questions concerning the shape or the color of an apple when all she was shown was the symbol for an apple—a blue triangle. She could also answer questions about the plastic symbol itself" (Terrace and Bever, 1976, p. 583).

The debate is unsettled as to whether Sarah has learned something about the rules governing the ordering of words (syntax). Premack has presented evidence that he feels supports the conclusion that this learning has occurred. He shows that Sarah is able to respond correctly to the sentence, "Sarah insert banana pail apple dish." This sentence is taken to mean that Sarah is supposed to place the banana in the pail and an apple in a dish when she is given a choice of both fruit and containers. Premack argues that the fact that Sarah can do this shows that she has mastered two relationships:

banana and pail and apple and dish going together linguistically in the sentence and also going together in the real nonsymbolic world. This allows her to place those objects in the respective containers. Others, however, are not sure that this shows linguistic knowledge of word order but rather believe that it may have just been a result of training on successive trials. As Terrace and Bever note: "If the pail and dish were empty before the problem was given, then she need only pay attention to the extra linguistic cue provided by the condition of the container in front of her" (1976, p. 583). Although the research with Sarah has not settled the question of language ability in chimps, it certainly has generated considerable research.

Project Washoe Unlike Sarah, who was a full-grown adult caged chimpanzee, Washoe was a young chimp that was raised in a normal family environment, very similar to that of the human child. The medium of communication was Ameslan. Whereas Sarah was taught the highly unnatural plastic-disc symbolic system, Washoe was taught what has come to be recognized as natural language. The chimp has the necessary equipment to be able to engage in that activity freely; the biological base does not restrict what she can do. Thus, the abilities the chimp develops ought to more correctly mirror cognitive or linguistic learning.

The trainers began exposing Washoe to signs early in her life. Their purpose was to make the social environment rich and to communicate to the chimp in sign language in a number of different social settings. In many ways, Washoe's accomplishments parallel and support Sarah's accomplishments. Washoe learned the symbolic system relatively easily; she learned signs early, and began chaining them together. The chaining of the signs is important because it can imply the possibility of semantic and syntactic development.

Initially, the chaining together of the signs in sequence occurred apparently at random. As Brown notes, this random combination of signs appears to be quite different from what occurs with children (1973, p. 41). The production of key word structure by children apparently is done because they wish to communicate different meaning; this apparently does not hold for chimps, at least in the early stages.

As the chaining of signs developed, it became clear that the combinations of the signs were no longer random but were used by the chimp to convey meaning. Not only did Washoe use the chaining of signs to convey meaning, but there was clear evidence that novel semantic formulations were produced. Washoe and her trainer were walking past a pond, and a duck landed on the water. Washoe saw the duck, became excited, and combined the signs for "water" and "bird" together, signaling "water bird." This is significant because it not only demonstrates cognitive processes occurring but also the use of linguistic formulations to communicate about those cognitive processes. Washoe rejected the sign of "duck" for the bird but instead preferred her newly created signs "water-bird" to communicate what was observed (Rumbaugh and Gill, 1976, p. 565).

One of the chief differences coming from the research is that Washoe appeared to initiate a greater number of conversations than did Sarah. This may be a function of different types of symbolic systems that each of the chimps had learned. Sign language may be more conducive to conversation than is the rigidity of the plastic-disc system. It also underscores the social dimension of language because the Gardners raised Washoe in the socially enriched signing environment.

Project Lana Project Lana began at the Yerkes Primate Laboratories in Georgia. The basic purpose was to create a computer-controlled language training situation that would not only take the trainer out of the system but would put the chimpanzee much more in control. It was also set up so that the language system would be available to the chimp twenty-four hours a day, and the computer technology would allow for almost total recording of behavior initiated by the chimp as well as by the trainers. It was assumed that this would not only allow for greater understanding of language itself but might perfect training methods that might be applied to language deficient children (Rumbaugh and Gill, 1976, p. 568).

The language that was developed is called Yerkish. The technological setup consisted of two boards—one for the trainer, and one for the chimp. The keyboards were equivalent in function, although the keyboard used by the chimp had the keys coded by the use of geometric configurations or "lexograms" on the surface of each key. Linguistic expressions were created by selecting and pressing the various keys, which functioned as words representing basic parts of the grammar of the artificial language. The location of the keys on the keyboard were scrambled so that Lana had to learn what keys to depress on the basis of the geometric figure on the key rather than the location of the key on the keyboard. When each key was pressed, a light would flash and the lexogram of the particular key that was pressed would appear on the projector right above the keyboard. As it turned out, this was a serendipitous aspect of the keyboard construction. Lana would look at the picture of the lexogram that flashed above by the keyboard. She did this over and over.

Initially, the project developers thought it might be difficult to teach Lana the "meaning" behind each of the keys. To their surprise, she learned it all on her own; she equated the image presented above the computer with the image on the key itself. Basic stock sentences were taught through conditioning procedures.

The results clearly indicate that not only did Lana learn the symbolic system, but she learned to use the system for communication. She quickly learned to respond to questions in yes-no form as well as to ask questions. She also learned names of objects and events distant in time and space. Lana was able to respond with better than 90 percent accuracy to the questions asking for the name of the objects. Lana would respond, "banana name of this," or "M&M candy name of this." It was also clear that Lana used the stock sentences she had learned in novel situations.

The project also demonstrated rather convincingly Lana's conversational ability. Conversation in the Lana project was defined as, "(1) There must be a linguistic type of exchange between the ape subject and [trainer]; (2) There must be novelty in at least one of the messages transmitted by either party; (3) The topic of the exchange must be relatively coherent and stable across the time of its duration" (Rumbaugh and Gill, 1976, p. 571).

One of the most frequently quoted examples of Lana's novel construction in conversation deals with a box of candy. Lana had not been given a name for the box, and, although she did not understand what the box was called, she knew that it was filled with candy. She evidently wanted the candy. There were also bowls and cans present, and Lana knew the names for these objects. In her first requests, Lana repeatedly asked for a "can" or a "bowl." Each time she asked for these, the trainer, Tim, gave her a can or bowl, all of which were empty. After this had occurred a number of times and Lana still did not have what she evidently wanted, she initiated the following request: " 'Tim, give Lana name of this.' To which Tim responded, 'Box, name of this.' Lana then asked, 'Tim, give Lana this box.' Tim complied, Lana got her box and candy and the conversation stopped" (Rumbaugh and Gill, 1976, p. 573).

NATURAL LANGUAGE IN CHIMPS

The more recent research with artificial languages and Ameslan has generated some evidence of the existence of natural languages in chimps. Although the evidence for or against the question is still too incomplete for a conclusive decision, some of the preliminary research is demonstrating some unusual findings.

Menzel's research (1971a, 1971b, 1973, 1974) shows that when one chimpanzee is taken from the group and given information about the location of food, he is able to go back to the group and communicate this basic information to the other chimps. How this communication takes place in natural language is not yet known. Further research will undoubtedly better identify how the communication takes place. What is known, however, is that if the chimp receives information about an object that is fearful to the chimps, he can clearly communicate this fear-inducing aspect to the other chimps, and the other chimps follow far behind the "leader" as they explore for the location of this object of fear. When they finally encounter it, they will poke at it with sticks rather than get close to it. However, if the object that the chimp has information about is desired, such as food, the chimps run far in advance of the "leader" in an apparent effort to try and locate the food before the leader gets there.

Penny Talking to Her Friend, Koko

During the past decade researchers have successfully taught several chimpanzees to converse with signs. In a project partly funded by the National Geographic Society, Koko is the first gorilla to achieve proficiency.

After six years of study, author Francine "Penny" Patterson, a Stanford University doctoral candidate, evaluates Koko's working vocabulary at about 375 signs, including airplane, belly button, lollipop, friend, and stethoscope.

Koko responds to and asks questions, tells Penny when she feels "happy" or "sad," refers to past and future events, and has begun to give definitions for objects. She also shows an impish sense of humor, insults human companions—usually with good reason—and lies on occasion to avoid blame (Patterson and Cohn, 1978, p. 438).

As Penny tells the story of the three little kittens who lost their mittens, Koko comments that their mother is angry and that the kittens are crying. Then she dramatically signs, "Bad."

What does this abstract word mean to a gorilla? "When she breaks or steals something," Penny says, "I tell her that is 'bad.' Sometimes when I scold her she signs, 'Bad.' I've seen her rip up a toy and sign, 'Bad,' while destroying it" (Patterson and Cohn, 1978, p. 448).

KOKO LEARNS TO LIE

Perhaps the most telling, yet elusive, evidence that a creature can displace events is lying. When someone tells a lie, he is using language to distort the listener's perception of reality. He is using symbols to describe something that never happened, or won't happen. Evidence I have been accumulating strongly suggests that Koko expresses a make-believe capacity similar to humans'.

At about the age of 5 Koko discovered the value of the lie to get herself out of a jam. After numerous repeat performances I'm convinced that Koko really is lying in these circumstances and not merely making mistakes. One of her first lies also involved the reconstruction of an earlier happening. My assistant Kate Mann was with Koko, then tipping the scales at 90 pounds, when the gorilla plumped down on the kitchen sink in the trailer and it separated from its frame and dropped out of alignment. Later, when I asked Koko if she broke the sink, she signed, "Kate there bad," pointing to the sink. Koko couldn't know, of course, that I would never accept the idea that Kate would go around breaking sinks.

Some of Koko's lies are startlingly ingenious. Once, while I was busy writing, she snatched up a red crayon and began chewing on it. A moment later I noticed and said, "You're not eating that crayon are you?" Koko signed, "Lip," and began moving the crayon first across her upper, then her lower lip as if applying lipstick." (Patterson and Cohn, 1978, p. 459–61).

(Source: Francine Patterson and R. H. Cohn. "Conversations with a Gorilla," *National Geographic,* October 1978, pp. 438–65. Reprinted by permission.)

The research also shows that if a chimp is carried over a field and shown the location of various types of food, some desired and some undesired, when turned loose he will use this information to get to the food selectively. He will go first to the more desirable, and then to the less desirable.

Another study, in which a gorilla, Koko, was taught approximately 375 signs, showed further evidence of "human" thought processes and communication. Koko not only showed the ability to react to stories and to recall earlier events, but the researchers became convinced that she lied to avoid disapproval, thereby showing recall, communication ability, and ingenuity (Patterson and Cohn, 1978).

SUMMARY

Taken together, this research with chimps and the research it has generated with other primates, such as the gorilla, shows ability on the part of these primates to possess higher cortical processes and to use a linguistic system to convey informational content to others about themselves and their environment.

Chimps and apparently gorillas can create words, learn symbolic systems, combine words into novel semantic utterances, and utilize that symbolic system in commenting upon the system itself, upon the environment, as well as upon their own needs. Thus, morphology and semantics are clearly present along with novelty as parts of the linguistic system of these primates.

What is yet to be determined is the extent to which they develop syntactic abilities—to understand the rules underlying language. Research currently underway with groups of chimps being taught sign languages may well begin to answer the questions of not only human-chimpanzee communication but chimpanzee-chimpanzee communication and the degree to which natural languages of the chimpanzee differ from natural human languages. Future research will undoubtedly be better able to compare language development in chimps with language development in children. We now turn to a consideration of human language development.

Language Development

There are few accomplishments made by the average child that compare with the learning of his or her own native tongue. The average child begins using the first words at the beginning of the second year of life, and finishes learning the bulk of the language during the last half of the fourth year of life. Thus, in shortly over twenty-four months the young child acquires the basic vocabulary of his or her native language, as well as the rules underlying combining these words into sentences to convey the desired meaning.

BEHAVIORAL PRECURSORS OF LANGUAGE DEVELOPMENT

The research of the last decade that has videotaped mother and infant interaction patterns has revealed a striking reciprocity in their behavior (Brazeltan, 1976; Schaffer, 1977). This research demonstrates that both the mother and infant gauge their own behavior according to behavior of the other. When gazing and smiling behavior is analyzed, it becomes apparent that the mother and infant engage in a conversation, in the sense that the mother gazes at the infant and then waits appropriately for the infant's response. The infant in turn gazes or smiles at the mother and then waits for the mother's response. A variety of behaviors of the mother and the infant are characterized by this rhythmic interactional pattern. Thus, long before the infant begins to speak, he or she has acquired a whole repertoire of conversational abilities (Schaffer, 1977).

At some point between the ages of six and twelve months, the infant engages in a sustained production of varied sounds. These sounds appear to be very much like words, in the sense that two or three sounds are combined together. The intonation, the frequency, and the pitch are all varied. These words are not words in the sense of conveying meaning to either the hearer or producer (we assume), but are described as babbling on the part of the infant. The frequency and intensity of the babbling increases to a high point, and then begin to drop off toward the latter part of the first year.

Consensus among social psychologists and linguists is that this babbling is undoubtedly related to the maturation of the child. Also, studies of children in a number of different settings seem to indicate that the sounds made by the babbling child are universal. During the babbling stage, a child, no matter what the native language, will produce all the sounds of his own

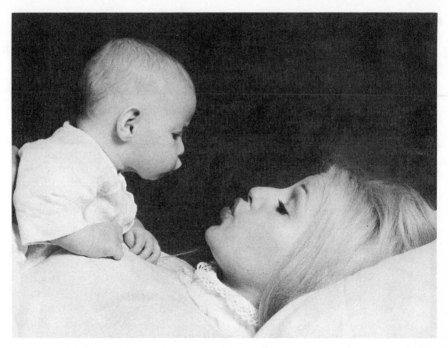

Mother and infant in intimate interpersonal interaction using nonverbal communication. *Source:* H. Armstrong Roberts.

native tongue as well as sounds heard in other languages. The child produces sounds that he has never heard before. Children everywhere seem to be biologically equipped to speak any language in the world (Jakobson, 1968; McNeill, 1970a; Nakazima, 1962). As the babbling begins to decrease in frequency, toward the end of the first year and the beginning of the second year, the child's first words will be heard.

SINGLE-WORD UTTERANCES

By the middle of the second year, the average child will produce—singly—dozens of different words. The first words spoken will very likely be sounds approximating "papa" or "mama." Common, single-word utterances in addition to "mama" and "papa" are "byby," "dada," "bebe," and so forth. The child evidently uses one-word utterances, each with a variety of meanings. The word "dada," for example, may mean "there's my daddy" or "come here and take me" or "I am hungry" or "read me a story." These one-word sentences have been referred to as *holophrases.*

Different interpretations have been given to the meaning of these single-word utterances. Some researchers favor a "rich" interpretation (Greenfield and Smith, 1976), believing that the meaning of the single-word utterance represents different stages of development through which the child is going during the first part of the second year. They theorize that initially the single-word utterances represent a combination of both action and language. For example, the child will say "by by" whenever either the child or someone else comes or goes. The child then moves to the second stage, where a specific word is attached to a specific object: saying "mama" in the presence of mama, or "ball" when a ball is at hand. The child then moves to the third stage, where the single word is used for requests. He or she may say "milk" when hungry.

Psycholinguists favoring a "poor" explanation are cautious about inferring an undue array of meaning attached to the single word. Bloom (1973), a proponent of the "poor" theory, notes that during the time the child is using the single word, the child can in fact utter a number of different words and can in fact say these single words one right after another. Even when a string of such words is created, they are still single-word utterances. This leads Bloom to conclude that the reason the child does not produce the two-word utterance is because he or she lacks the requisite cognitive development to put two words together meaningfully.

TWO-WORD UTTERANCES

The average child moves into the two-word stage of language development at the beginning of the third year of life. Interpretation of the meaning of two-word utterances is much easier than of single words. With two words, the child has learned that words can be combined to communicate a meaning behind the utterance. Some common two-word utterances are, "there book," "my ball," "more milk," "baby fall," "where mama?" Psycholinguists and psychologists have analyzed the dual phrase in depth, noting that there are a number of repeated meanings captured in these two-word phrases. Roger Brown (1973) sees a variety of different classes of meaning. For example: *agent location,* there book"; *agent action,* "baby fall"; and *nonexistence,* "where mama."

The striking thing with the analysis of the two-word phrases is that most of the words used are either nouns or verbs. This has led Brown to describe the language of children as *telegraphic.* As is true for adults when they have a constraint upon the number of words that can be used (as in writing a telegram), those words retained are the most dominant information giving words, namely, verbs and nouns.

An alternative explanation is that the child simply learns those words that are emphasized more by the adults in his or her environment. In speaking to the child, the adult will emphasize those words the child knows and likely can remember, which are usually references to objects. Research, however, does not support this interpretation as well as the telegraphic formulation. McNeill (1966b) has shown that in foreign languages where the stress is on other parts of speech, children show the same telegraphic tendency. Indeed, children constructing two-word phrases in a variety of languages tend to talk about the same things the world over.

BROADENING THE MEANING

In the third year, the child moves beyond the single-word and dual-word utterances, and begins to create three-word, four-word, and longer sentences. The most frequently used sentences will be simple declarative sentences, such as "Mama, come here." "Susie fall down." The child may begin to create compound sentences, but these will be very rare. The child would say, "The ball is round. The ball is green." rather than making a compound sentence by saying, "The ball is round and green." The child will begin asking simple "wh" questions: the whys, the whats, and the wheres. At first, these questions may be used incorrectly gramatically, such as "Why you go away?" It will be some time into the next year before the child can rearrange the word orders to make these grammatically correct.

Brown's research (1973) shows this to be the time that the child begins adding "ed" and "ing" endings to the nouns and the verbs to produce variation of meaning. Thus, the child acquires the added linguistic structure that allows him or her to communicate the added meaning that his or her cognitive structure has developed.

It is during this time that the syntactic development becomes apparent in the child's use of language. Not only has he or she learned the underlying grammatical rules for constructing phrases and sentences, but he or she uses these rules in creating novel utterances. Researchers have devised intriguing strategies to investigate the child's comprehension of underlying grammatical rules. One such research device is presented in figure 3–1. The child's speech during this stage of development exhibits many examples of use of the underlying rules in constructing utterances that are not "gramatically" correct in English because the language has words that are exceptions to the rules. The child will say "goed" instead of "went," or when he or she learns the meaning of "raining outside" he may describe the blowing wind as "winding outside."

This is a wug.

Now there is another one.
There are two of them.
There are two _____ .

Figure 3–1 Procedure for Measuring a Child's Knowledge and Use of Linguistic Rules. (*Source:* Berko, 1958, p. 154.)

Table 3–2   General Linguistic Accomplishments of the Average Child

AGE	
0–6 months	The infant produces the normal sounds of laughing, crying, and cooing. Sounds approaching babbling begin to appear in the latter months as the infant further explores production of sounds.
7–12 months Babbling	The infant's babbling increases in intensity and duration reaching a high just before the end of the first year. Babbling then drops off dramatically. During this stage, the infant masters the sounds of his or her own language as well as having produced many sounds foreign to his or her own tongue. At the end of the year, he or she will usually have said his or her first word—very likely *mama* or *papa*.
13–18 months Single-word utterances	By a year and a half, the infant's production vocabulary consists of a dozen or more words spoken singly; comprehension vocabulary far exceeds that. He or she is able to understand simple commands: "Bring me the ball"; "Drink your milk", and so on.
19–24 months Dual-Word Utterances	The child's production vocabulary continues to develop with single words. Toward the latter months of this period, he or she begins producing two-word phrases of essentially nouns and verbs.
25–36 months Further Development of Meaning	The first half of the third year shows a further development of dual-word construction. In the last half, the child moves to three- and four-word declarative sentences. Not until the child is three or over will he or she be able to change word order to create negatives that are correct grammatically. The first signs of the child overgeneralizing linguistic rules may be seen. Plurals, possessives, and past tenses are the most common ones. He or she may say "taked" for took, "mices" for mice, "goed" for went, and so on.

Note: The average child is used to describe general patterns while at the same time recognizing tremendous differences among children. Some children may begin their first utterances well before their first birthday, while others may utter few words until well after their second birthday.

Children's talk shows great flexibility by the end of the third year. The overall development of the child to this point makes possible considerable creativity, as is described in table 3–2.

Theories of Language Acquisition

Our description of the child's acquisition of language underscores the rapidity with which the whole process occurs. Although we may be able to describe some of the major stages of the acquisition process, and roughly when they occur, we still cannot truly understand, explain, or accurately predict language acquisition itself. Some psycholinguists and social psychologists have attempted to develop theories that may help give us this explanation. In this section, we consider two very different and in many ways opposing views as to how the child acquires language: social-learning theory and cognitive theory.

If asked why a child learns language, most people would likely respond that parents and other family members teach the child the language. Researchers, studying language acquisition from the conditioning framework, have proposed that language acquisition can be explained by the same principles of learning that hold for any other area in social psychology (Miller and Dollard, 1941; Mowrer, 1960a, 1960b; Skinner, 1957). They argue that the principles of classical and operant conditioning ought to hold for language acquisition. A minimal explanation of language acquisition from conditioning theory asserts that at first the child will emit a variety of sounds, none of which have any meaning to either the child or to the adults in that child's environment. Eventually, the child emits sounds that are similar to sounds in the adult language, and the adults respond positively to those sounds. Thus, through systematic recognition and rewarding by the parents, the child begins to learn the meanings that are attached to each of those sounds (phonological development). In essence, the sounds become conditioned responses to the rewarding stimuli emitted by the parents through their reactions. The theory assumes a general tendency on the part of the child to imitate or model adult speech patterns, and this along with the rewarding behavior of the parents gradually shapes the child's language behavior to conform more closely to the adult pattern. The child first learns to put sounds together to form words (morphological development) and then, on the basis of the adult reactions to those words, begins to put words together to form larger meaning systems (semantic development). The child is able to make all the necessary discriminations between the multitude of possible sounds and begin to produce only those relevant to his or her linguistic group.

One of the most consistent advocates of social-learning theory has been Arthur Staats. In a series of publications (Staats, 1961, 1968; Staats and Staats, 1963), he has extended social-learning approaches to language development and has shown how the child progresses step by step through language acquisition. He focuses upon the concept of discrimination learning and also on stimulus generalizations to allow for the acquisition of words as well as for the combining of words into novel formulations.

Staats assumes, following Mowrer (1960a), that the vocalizations of the parents in association with positive reinforcers (such as food) quickly lead to the development of secondary reinforcing qualities for the parents' voices. Additional stimulus generalization moving from the parents' vocalizations to the child's own vocalizations quickly leads to the child's own productions acquiring secondary reinforcing quality. Thus, the child's own verbalizations become reinforcing in and of themselves. In short, then, direct reinforcement by the parents for the production of sounds of their own tongue is replaced by the self-reward of the child's own vocalizations.

Staats addresses himself to the question of novel behavior in language, noting that "any conception of human behavior that cannot deal with original behaviors . . . is inadequate" (1968, p. 168). He attempts to build the links between basic stimulus-response connections and novel combinations of words in generating a sentence.

Let us say that the child has been reinforced for saying MAN in the presence of different "man stimulus objects" and such a stimulus has come [as a discriminative stimulus] to control the vocal response MAN. Let us also say that the child has also had the same experience with respect to the vocal response RUNNING. That is, in the presence of a running dog, a running boy, a running girl and so on, the child has been reinforced for saying RUNNING. This response, however, has never been reinforced in the presence of a man running. Let us also say, however, that the child sees a man who is running. Under these circumstances the child would be likely to say MAN RUNNING or RUNNING MAN. The total response would be entirely novel, since the child would never before have emitted the sequence (Staats, 1968, p. 169).

Thus, for Staats the conditioning theory allows for original behavior but such behavior is learned behavior, and it is learned as any other behavior is learned—through basic conditioning principles.

Critical evaluation of social-learning theory is difficult because in such research it is impossible to control all the reinforcements that a child receives. Aside from the intuitive evidence that children do grow up learning the language spoken by their parents, there is not a great deal of evidence that seems to suggest that children do imitate very closely adult speech patterns. Some of the earliest dual phrases the children construct, as was indicated earlier, are telegraphic in nature. They differ markedly from the parents' speech. A child who has been eating candy and has sticky hands, after having those hands washed, will very likely say "all gone sticky." This construction by the child is most likely not an imitation of the adult phrases.

Not only does the research seem to indicate that social-learning theory has trouble demonstrating that children imitate adult speech patterns, but some evidence seems to indicate that children do not hear exceptions to their own regularity in speech patterns, even when those exceptions are grammatically correct. McNeill (1970b, p. 1103) quotes the following exchange between a mother and a child:

Child: Nobody don't like me.
Mother: No, say nobody likes me.
Child: Nobody don't like me.

(The mother and the child then repeat this same dialogue over eight times.)

Mother: No, now listen carefully; say, "Nobody likes me."
Child: Oh! Nobody don't likes me.

This seems to imply that children hear the adult's speech in their own terms of understanding and comprehension rather than the particular grammatical form used by the parent.

Social-learning theory also has trouble providing evidence that parents do in fact reward or punish a child's grammatical constructions. Roger Brown and his associates have conducted some of the best research isolating the role of the parents in shaping the child's linguistic behavior. He and his associates have carefully followed the language development of three children since they began to speak and analyzed the incidences when the child's utterances were either approved or disapproved by the parents. They conclude that direct teaching by the parents in terms of reinforcement or punishment cannot be an important factor. Summarizing, they state:

> What circumstances did govern approval and disapproval directed at child utterances by parents? Gross errors of word choice were sometimes corrected, as when Eve said *What the guy idea*. Once in awhile an error of pronunciation was noticed and corrected. Most commonly, however, the grounds on which an utterance was approved or disapproved . . . were not strictly linguistic at all. When Eve expressed the opinion that her mother was a girl by saying *He a girl*, her mother answered *That's right*. The child's utterance was ungrammatical, but her mother did not respond to that fact; instead, she responded to the truth of the proposition the child intended to express. In general, the parents fitted the propositions to the child's utterances, however incomplete or distorted the utterances, and then approved or not according to the correspondence between proposition and reality. Thus, *Her curl my hair* was approved because the mother was, in fact, curling Eve's hair. However, Sara's grammatically impeccable *There's the animal farmhouse* was disapproved because the building was a lighthouse, and Adam's *Walt Disney comes on Tuesday* was disapproved because Walt Disney came on some other day. It seems, then, to be truth value rather than syntactic well-formedness that chiefly governs explicit verbal reinforcement by parents (Brown, Cazden, and Bellugi-Klima, 1969, pp. 70–71).

In additional research reported by Brown and Hanlon (1970), parents' approval or disapproval of errors in verb forms, plurals, and so on, were analyzed. They also did not find that parents corrected such errors. They did find that parents corrected a child's insults or foolishness, but in essence paid little or no attention to grammatical errors. Later, Brown (1973) studied the child's acquisition of morpheme words and related this to the frequence with which the parents used these words. There was a very low correlation. He concluded that the order of word acquisition apparently is influenced by factors other than modeling the language of the parents.

Cazden (1965) reported similar findings. In one group of children, the experimenter took care not to repeat the child's words or phrases. In another group, the experimenter carefully repeated the child's utterances and in addition placed them into proper grammatical form. The research was designed to see if, in fact, children would learn the grammatical structure more quickly when they heard their own words repeated back to them in grammatically correct form. A variety of linguistic measures were used to assess the linguistic development of the child. The group that was corrected did not score higher on these linguistic measures. In fact, the opposite was true. Namely, the children that were allowed to converse with each other without having their words repeated seemed to develop faster than the others on a number of the measures.

Although studies have not been impressive in documenting the conditioning theory of language acquisition, common sense still leads us to assume that adult spoken language does in fact influence what the child acquires. We, in our own common-sense world, know that children do acquire the dialects spoken by their parents, which must involve some type of modeling.

Also, there is some research (Sailor, 1971) that demonstrates reinforcement does have controlling influence over some linguistic behaviors. What is yet to be demonstrated from research, however, is under what conditions the child seems to imitate the linguistic behavior of the parents and under what conditions reinforcement seems to affect the child's acquisition of language.

COGNITIVE THEORY

The theoretical orientation that we label cognitive owes most of its intellectual heritage to the work of Chomsky, a linguist, and Piaget, a child psychologist. In the mid-fifties, Chomsky's formulation not only revolutionized the study of languages but also influenced psychologists and, more particularly, psycholinguists. In addition, developmental psychologists were influenced by his ideas and combined some of them with Piagetian formulations to address themselves to the question of language acquisition. In 1959, Chomsky published a powerful critique of Skinner's book, *Verbal Behavior*, which had appeared two years earlier. He criticized Skinner by asserting that the conditioning theories, more specifically operant conditioning, were inadequate in explaining the acquisition of languages.

Chomsky's work, along with later work by McNeill (1966a, 1966b), called attention to the biological capabilities of the child, asserting that the child has innate predispositions for language acquisition. Given these biological predispositions and interaction with the adults in the environment, the child constructs his own language. McNeill has argued that any attempt to explain language from this point of view must focus on the innate capacities of the child and then identify how these interact with experience to bring about the almost automatic, effortless, and extremely rapid acquisition of the native language of the very young child.

This particular approach has developed the concepts of "transformational grammars." Chomsky identifies two levels of language that must be kept separate in an analysis of language acquisition. One is referred to as "deep structure," and is the underlying level involved with meaning. The other is the surface structure, which is produced and heard in ordinary conversation. The purpose of this approach is to develop the rules of correspondence between the surface structure and the deep structure that allow each to be understood. These rules thus formulated have become known as "rules of transformation of grammar."

The two utterances, "You need to wash," and "You need to wash," clearly have the same surface structure, that is, the same sounds, words, and ordering among words (phonetics, morphology, and syntax). However, the deep structure—the meaning—can be vastly different. The first sentence is spoken by a teenage daughter to her mother. The daughter has just unsuccessfully searched through her clothes for a clean pair of jeans to wear. The second is spoken by the same daughter to her mother. The daughter has just come home from school and sees her mother as she is finishing painting the bedroom.

Those concerned with transformational grammar have focused on defining how the child constructs the grammar of the underlying structure that is appropriate to the language she or he hears. Transformational grammar is seen as a universal grammar that, once learned, can be employed with any particular language. The child searches for these universal characteristics of the language and constructs a personal grammar out of them, which then allows him or her to acquire the language of his or her given group. This gives the child the ability to convert the universal aspects of language to a specific aspect of the language that is spoken locally.

This approach has underscored the native capacity of the child and has emphasized the biological base for language. Lieberman (1974) has analyzed the vocal apparatus and shown how it is intricately prepared for the production of sound. Likewise, Lenneberg (1967) has called attention to the fact that the left cerebral hemisphere appears to be specifically developed for processing language stimuli. Because of the structure of the nerve system in the brain, some have argued (Chomsky, 1975a, 1975b; Fodor, 1975) that knowledge of language is, in a sense, prewired into the brain.

Developmental psycholinguists working on language universals have noted that children in various parts of the world seem to construct very similar first words and dual phrases, no matter which language they speak, and that these first words seem to be part of the sensory motor intelligence that Piaget has described. Intelligence comes to the child by manipulating objects in the real world and then creating cognitive structures that portray the nature of the relationships between those objects in the real world. From this point of view, then, the child constructs the language appropriate to describe these discovered relationships. Thus, the reason the child acquires language is because of biological preprogramming and the subsequent unfolding of this ability as the child interacts with his or her environment.

Although both the conditioning and cognitive theories help us understand the child's acquisition of language, there are still many unresolved issues. The two approaches seem to be alternative rather than complementary statements about language acquisition. There have been some attempts at synthesis or construction of alternative paradigms, but as yet these have not been adequately formulated. One such attempt is that by Denzin (1977), who sees problems with the transformation-of-grammar approach of Chomsky. He asks, "If the child does not learn how to make proper utterances based on the usual variables of reinforcement, imitation, and indifference, then how does he learn the rules necessary to make such utterances?" (1977, p. 79). Denzin rejects the notion that the underlying cognitive structure in the human brain determines how the child acquires that language. He proposes a three-phase model of language acquisition. In the beginning phase, stimulus reinforcement operates with the child making the first crude sounds approximating words and being reinforced by the parents. In phase two, Denzin postulates the existence of inner thought, but the child is still unable to produce a symbol that conveys the intended meaning to the listener. The third phase is characterized by face-to-face interaction in which the child produces the verbal stimuli that are understood and responded to by significant others.

Denzin's three-phase model does not appear to be promising. The first phase suffers from the same problems as does the conditioning theory. Research evidence has failed to support the notion that reinforcement plays an important part in which sounds the child produces or drops from his or her repertoire. The internal thought of phase two remains problematic in that it is only vaguely formulated, and few predictions could be made from it about language acquisition. Phase three seems to be little more than a general kind of sociological statement that does not lend itself to critical analysis.

Denzin's criticism that the cognitive theories do not explain how the child learns the rules of grammar seems valid. This seems to be one of the questions left unanswered by the conditioning theorists and the transformation grammarians, unless one accepts the assumptions of the latter that the rules are innate and therefore do not have to be learned. Although the cognitive approach unambiguously confirms that language is an intricate and rule-governed symbolic system, it does not shed much light on how those rules are acquired by the child; neither does conditioning theory adequately explain it. The child acquires this intricate, symbolic system that is above all rule governed in an incredibly short period of time. This acquisition of rules appears to occur almost independently of the reward/punishment behavior of people around the child.

Rule-governed language is obviously a social construction, and the child learns a language within the context of a specific social setting. Children raised in Israel do not grow up learning German unless all those around them speak German. Thus, the social dimension of language acquisition must be of prime importance even though it is little understood. As Grimshaw and Holden have argued, learning the rules underlying grammar (linguistic rules) may be "far more compacted into the very earliest years than is true of that of social and sociolinguistic skills" (1976, p. 34). The research of the past three decades has clearly demonstrated the importance of the *biological, cognitive,* and *social* dimensions. Perhaps research in language acquisition is ready for a concerted interdisciplinary effort of sociologists, psychologists, and biologists in an effort to further understand the intriguing processes of language development.

Language and Thought

Social psychologists for some time have been intrigued by the nature of the relationship between language and thought. Nearly all agree that the two are intricately related; but the specific nature of that relationship becomes the focal point of discussion. Is language best seen as a molder of thought or a vehicle used to express one's thought? Or, is it some combination?

The position that language molds thought has been most forcefully presented through the works of Benjamin Lee Whorf and Edward Sapir. These linguists and anthropologists studied language in a variety of different settings. Their work led them to conclude that the particular language an individual grew up learning does indeed influence not only the way in which he or she perceives the world but the way that he or she acts towards objects within that world. Sapir writes:

> Human beings do not live in the objective world alone; nor alone in the world of social activity as ordinarily understood, but are very much at the mercy of the particular language which has become the medium of expression for their society. It is quite an illusion to imagine that one adjusts to reality essentially without the use of language and that language is merely an incidental means of solving specific problems of communication or reflection. The fact of the matter is that the 'real world' is to a large extent unconsciously built on the language habits of the group. . . . We see and hear and otherwise experience very largely as we do because the language habits of our community predispose certain choices of interpretation (cited in Whorf, 1956, p. 134).

The work of Whorf, Sapir, and others has documented the fact that languages differ greatly on the number and type of category systems used to describe objects in the real world. A boy growing up in the Philippines whose language has ninety-two names for different varieties of rice obviously learns a category system quite different from the American boy who has one word to refer to all those varieties of rice (Brown, 1965, p. 317). The linguists are quick to point out that it is rare to find a word in one language that can be translated directly into another language, unless those languages both derive from a common source. Whorf and others have pointed to this widespread occurrence of nonequivalence across languages. If, indeed, reality can be so differentially cut up according to the category system of a particular language, then Whorf holds that linguistic structure underlies thought. He states that the greatest understanding of thought will come by studying language that:

> . . . shows that forms of a person's thoughts are controlled by inexorable laws of pattern of which he is unconscious. These patterns are the unperceived intricate systematizations of his own language. His thinking itself is in a language—in English, in Sanskrit, in Chinese (Whorf, 1956, p. 252).

The basic causal relationship underlying the Sapir-Whorf hypothesis as contrasted to Piaget's cognitive theory is shown in figure 3–2.

The Sapir-Whorf position has sometimes been described as the language-relativity hypothesis, asserting that one's view of reality will be relative to the language that is spoken. Whorf states, "We are thus introduced to a new principle of relativity, which holds that all observers are not led by the same physical evidence to the same picture of the universe, unless their linguistic backgrounds are similar, or can in some way be calibrated" (Whorf, 1956, p. v).

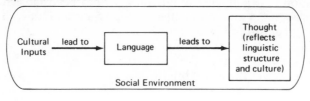

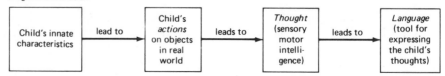

Cognitive–development
explanation
Piaget's formulation

Figure 3–2 Alternative Views of the Relationship Between Thought and Language

A strong version of the language-relativity hypothesis implies that the language one learns, because of the nature of the category systems and the structure of the language, determines one's perception and thought. This strong version of the hypothesis has not been widely accepted. A weaker version, which is more readily accepted, asserts that the language one speaks, because of its basic structure, will facilitate some perceptions as opposed to others and therefore will lead to some type of thought as opposed to other types of thought. This weaker version has been tested in considerable research.

Brown and Lenneberg (1954) first devised an ingenious study to determine whether the category systems of a language used to differentiate colors would, in fact, influence the ability of the perceiver to identify shades of color. Languages vary greatly in the number of words used to identify categories of colors. In some languages, only one word is used for what we in English call blue or green. In addition, for the English-speaking person green is not only one color but describes a variety of shades and hues. Twenty-four colors were selected from a large array of 124 colors on the basis of their degree of codability. If a color is highly codable, it will have one or two words used to describe it. Dark brown would be highly codable, whereas blue-green combinations might have to be described in combinations of words or phrases; thus, its codability would be low. The subjects were shown colors selected from the 24 and then were asked to find that same color in the larger collection of 124 different colors. The data clearly indicated that codability of the color was strongly related to the ability of the subject to find it in the larger collection. The research seemed to indicate that the linguistic codes facilitated memory. Additional research has tended to support the relationship that language may in fact facilitate memory. However, research conducted by Lantz and Stefflre (1964) indicates that the choice of colors may inadvertently influence the results of the research. They selected a different color array in the blue-green regions than that used in the Brown and Lenneberg research and did not find that codability predicted memory. They interpreted their findings to mean that because the colors were very similar the subjects had to invent their own terms to distinguish between these colors. Because they had to do this inventing, codability did not facilitate memory.

Research conducted by Lenneberg and Roberts (1956) hypothesized that Pueblo Indians of the American Southwest would have greater difficulty than would an English-speaking person in recognizing orange from an array of colors that contained both oranges and yellows. They predicted this because the Pueblo language uses one word to categorize both yellow and orange, whereas English uses two words. Their research supported their hypothesis. This research has been used by proponents of the Sapir-Whorf hypothesis as evidence of its validity.

However, the bulk of the research studying perception across cultures provides very little support of the Sapir-Whorf hypothesis. Brown (1976) says that the evidence supporting the hypothesis is so meager that the research tradition is quickly dying out in social psychology. Rosch (1973) reviewed the research evidence of perception cross-culturally and concluded that perception appears to be very similar around the world and is largely independent of language. This appears to hold despite vastly different experiences. The only evidence at all supporting the Sapir-Whorf hypothesis is related to memory. There is evidence (McNeil, 1965) that if the language categories are so constructed that one word can stand for a number of different items within its class, it will facilitate the person's ability to recall that class of items, more than would a language that has separate words for each item.

Although this research can be construed to be supportive of the hypothesis, it is very limited (Stam, 1977; Wertheimer, 1977). Indeed, some recent research with four-month infants demonstrated that the infants categorized stimuli into basic hue categories of red, green, blue, and yellow. This obviously occurs before the child has learned the category system of his or her own language and before the culture could have sufficiently trained the child to make these discriminations (Bornstein, 1975). Thus, from birth the child appears capable of perceiving different colors. All that remains, then, is to attach the respective cultural labels to these different stimuli.

LANGUAGE AS AN EXPRESSION OF THOUGHT

Piaget (1923, 1963) argued that language is a tool that is used to express thought. The child, during the sensory-motor stage of development, is seen as developing thought patterns by initiating action upon objects in the real world. This action leads to thought in that the child learns relationships between objects in the real world and begins to develop categories for manipulating, sorting, pushing, and reaching for objects of various types.

Researchers working with deaf children have tended to corroborate Piaget's formulation (Youniss, Firth, and Ross, 1971). In these studies, deaf children, who are said to lack language in the ordinary sense, appeared to be able to solve problems and play games involving logic on a level comparable to the ability of children who can hear. Research in which investigators have not been able to enhance children's cognitive capacities by improving their language skills (Sinclair-de-Zwart, 1967) also supports the Piagetian interpretation. This research attempted to teach children concepts more or less through a language-therapy program. The language therapy failed to improve their scores on cognitive tests.

Although research with young children seems to support the Piagetian formulation that thought clearly develops before the child acquires language, many laypeople feel uncomfortable with the statement that language is used to merely express thought; and common sense seems to argue persuasively that language does facilitate thought. Even the ability to think about and discuss some topics requires that the requisite vocabulary be learned. Once the vocabulary of mathematics is learned, for example, a person can think and solve problems utilizing the mathematical vocabulary. The same thing is true of philosophical issues. Is there something basic in the relationship between thought and language aside from what has been hypothesized in either the Sapir-Whorf or Piagetian formulations? At least one researcher/theorist has proposed a synthesis.

PARALLEL DEVELOPMENT OF THOUGHT AND LANGUAGE

The single most important attempt at compromise between the cultural-relativity formulations and the Piagetian formulation is that presented by Vygotsky (1962). The early stages of development in Vygotsky's formulation are not markedly different from those in the Piagetian formulation (see figure 3–3 for a diagrammatic presentation, and compare that with figure 3–2). Vygotsky assumes that the innate characteristics of the infant/child lead to two simultaneous but parallel developments: thought and language. These separate streams emerge over time. On the language side, the very young infant is producing and mastering the sounds, the tones, and many words of the language of the local culture. At the same time, through the sensory-motor phase of development, the child is initiating action upon the objects in the real world and developing his or her own sensory-motor thought patterns. He or she is able to categorize and understand the consequences of actions that he or she exerts upon objects in the environment.

Vygotsky argues that these two streams of development are virtually independent, having little influence upon each other during these early stages. However, at about the age of two, the child becomes intently interested in naming objects in the real world. This is an important occurrence in Vy-

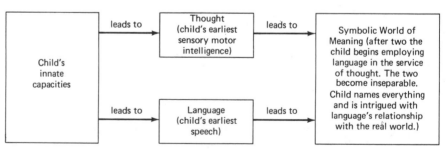

Figure 3–3 Vygotsky's Formulation of the Parallel Development of Thought and Language

gotsky's formulation because it signals a basic change in the child's thought and language systems. The two streams of development begin to merge. At this point, the child has an intense need to learn the names of all the objects that he or she has encountered in the action-object world and endlessly asks adults what things are called. The child, at this point, begins to move into a symbolic world, realizing that objects in the real world are also referred to linguistically. The experience of Helen Keller is a poignant example of this (see Keller, 1917, pp. 22–24).

A number of students of cognitive development note that about this time the child often appears to be thinking out loud. For Vygotsky, this is when thought becomes verbal and speech becomes rational. Speech rapidly begins to take on the forms inherent in the larger language community.

Macnamara (1972) feels that the argument that thought emerges in the early sensory-motor stages is well supported by research. Linguistic development in these early stages may be just a matter of learning how what you already know can be expressed in your own native language. Twelve to twenty-month-old infants can intelligently group and categorize objects on the basis of functional and physical relationships that hold among those objects even though they are not able, we suppose, to understand linguistically or name any of those categories or relationships (Ricciuti, 1965). The months and months of development during the sensory-motor stage has led to a considerable intellectual growth on the part of the child.

> I have continually insisted on the child possessing nonlinguistic cognitive processes before he learns their linguistic signal. By this I do not intend to endow the infant at birth with a complete ready-made set of cognitive structures. I accept Piaget's thesis that children gradually develop many of their cognitive structures, which they employ in association with language. Neither do I suggest that the child has a complete set of cognitive structures at the moment when he begins to learn language. All that is needed for my position is that the development of those basic cognitive structures to which I referred should precede the development of the corresponding linguistic structures. Since the acquisition of linguistic structures is spread over a long period, there is no reason that the acquisition of the corresponding nonlinguistic one should not also extend well into the period of language learning (Macnamara, 1972, p. 11).

From the available evidence, it appears that in the early stages thought and language are relatively independent. This independence seems to end as further stages of development occur and language and thought become part of an inextricably mingled amalgam.

Social Structure and Communication

Our emphasis to this point has been on the development of language and its relationship to thought. Another aspect of communication is *how* something is said, rather than *what* is said. The *what* focuses on the content, that is, language; the *how* relates to the social setting. Obviously, the two are not mutually exclusive because how something is said will often influence what is said. In this section, we examine the communicants themselves as well as the social surroundings within which the communication occurs. Obviously, different groups and cultures develop norms about how communications are to be sent! We consider two of these normative dimensions, proximics and body language.

PROXIMICS

Until the 1960s, proximics was an area that was little studied by social psychologists, but, with the publication of work by anthropologist Edward Hall (1959), it began receiving long-overdue interest. Hall was impressed by the cultural variation that occurred in what was considered to be the proper distance between two people conversing. For the Arabs, the proper distance was a few inches between each person's nose; for Americans, a distance of between two and three feet was preferred. Research has indicated that the distance between people is an indication of the perceived attitudes created through previous interpersonal relations, which then exist between the people. People tend to increase the distance between themselves and others who they dislike or do not know. People trying to be friendly will try to sit closer than will people who are attempting to convey negative feelings (Heshka and Nelson, 1972). People who stand close together also perceive that the other person likes them more than does someone standing further away (Mehrabian, 1968a, 1968b). When people are strangers, the physical distance between them is increased as much as possible (Becker, 1973).

Not only are there norms about appropriate distances between two people communicating, there are also norms about appropriate and inappropriate touching during communication. Because touch is clearly as close as two people can come, the norms do not refer to distance but rather who can touch whom and where. Jourard (1968) has conducted research exploring these normative patterns. Not surprisingly, different parts of the body are touched by different people. Most often, the top of the head is touched by the mother and friends of the opposite sex. Women are touched more often by other women than are men by other men except for shaking hands. Shaking hands itself is a more predominantly male custom.

BODY LANGUAGE AND NONVERBAL COMMUNICATION

A great deal of human interaction involves nonverbal communication. For example, things such as posture, facial expressions, and gestures can communicate attitudes and feelings toward others even more effectively than can the spoken word in many instances. Although the communicator will often spend more time dealing with the explicit (or spoken) aspects of his or her message, the implicit information transmitted to the audience nonverbally may have a far greater effect on their response. Drawing upon some earlier work by Goffman (1959), Cuzzort (1969) identifies two different classes of symbolic interaction; content (the actual message the communicator is trying to put across) and symptomatic behavior (those actions and characteristics that validate or lend reality to what is being said). Cuzzort (1969, p. 177) summarizes the relationship between content and symptomatic behavior as follows:

CONTENT	SYMPTOMATIC BEHAVIOR	AUDIENCE REACTION
1. Positive	Positive	A person possessing control over both levels of expression will be highly effective.
2. Positive	Negative	Despite content mastery, such a person may lose his audience because of incongruities in his performance.
3. Negative	Positive	This person may prove acceptable so long as he can conceal the existing incongruity.
4. Negative	Negative	This person will be highly ineffective.

This suggests that our response to someone is more influenced by *how* they present themselves than by *what* they say.

It has now become almost a social-psychological maxim that "first we define, then we respond." This means simply that our response to others will often be based on how we define those others. That definition is frequently developed on the basis of nonverbal cues before the other person even has a chance to present his or her arguments. We define persons on the basis of such external cues as skin color, hair length, name, or physical attractiveness and are influenced by what they have to say only to the extent that these prior cues have told us that they are someone who deserves our attention.

A wide variety of nonverbal cues are used in the communication process. For example, research by Mehrabian (1972) shows that the positioning of the limbs during conversation conveys something about the status differential between people. When an individual is talking to someone from a lower social status or with less power, the arms and legs will be more relaxed. While speaking with someone from a higher status, the body posture tends to be more erect in general and the limbs more rigid. The erect position with the head thrown back may communicate aloofness; the more relaxed position inclining toward the other person would communicate interest and friendliness (Mehrabian, 1968a, 1968b, 1972).

Research investigating courting behavior (Scheflen, 1965) corroborates much folk wisdom about the place of nonverbal communication in expressing interest and affection. Interest in courting the other person is associated with increased muscle tone, with a decrease in body sagging, and changes in facial expressions. The skin tends to become flushed and the eyes may brighten. The woman interested in courting may even exhibit what is called "preening" behavior by straightening her clothes or hair, by moving her hair back from her face or making sure her makeup is appropriate. In addition, the courting couples exchange long involved glances.

Eye contact has been studied considerably lately by social psychologists. It is an interesting phenomenon in that normative dimensions apparently exist that define some types of intense eye contact as threatening. Although people who are courting will not define long, intense eye contact as staring, staring behavior in other situations appears to be very threatening. Even monkeys appear to react aggressively to stares by a human (Exline, 1972). Automobiles drivers who were stopped at an intersection found the stares of a research confederate, who posed either as a pedestrian or as a man on

Consciously or unconsciously, the position of our limbs, face, and eyes communicates our feelings to others.

a motorcycle pulled up alongside of them, to be threatening or at least uncomfortable. The subjects of stares in this research drove across the intersection at the change of the light much more rapidly than did drivers who were stopped and not stared at. In general, the research on eye contact seems to show that a limited amount of eye contact communicates liking or need for affiliation (Exline, 1963; Exline and Winters, 1965), whereas excessive eye contact communicates threat. Couples who are in love exhibit more than normal eye contact (Rubin, 1970). Success and failure experiences seem to be related to the amount of eye contact; contact drops after a failure experience and increases after a success experience (Modigliani, 1971).

If the posture of the body, movement of the limbs, eyes, and other facial expressions do in fact convey a wide range of information, it might well be hypothesized that one would find some universals in body languages across cultures. Charles Darwin, in *Expression of the Emotions in Man and Animals,* proposed that the universal gestures might well be the last evidence of behavioral responses that in their earlier forms were adaptive for the survival of the organism. Crying, with its downturned mouth, might be a vestige of a universal cry for help. When answered, such a cry increased survival chances. Research (Ekman, Friesen, and Ellsworth, 1972; Ekman, Sorenson, and Friesen, 1969; Eibl-Eibesfeldt, 1970) gives some support for the universal interpretations for nonverbal behavior. The nonverbal expressions of sadness, fear, happiness, or surprise, for example, appear common to all societies studied. The research seems to show that so long as the response patterns are in fairly broad, general categories, such as sadness, there is

A nonverbal expression of feelings is often the most effective and most universal means of communication. *Source:* Wide World Photos, Inc.

evidence of the existence of universals. However, finer distinctions do not appear to be universal in their modes of expression. For example, it does not appear to be universal what gestures accompany fear as opposed to distress in general. The research leads to the conclusion that there is no universal language of gestures, but that some broad, general expressions such as sadness, fear, or happiness appear to carry the same gestural components across many cultures.

To this point, we have focused on language and nonverbal communication occurring between two people. The social psychologist's interest, however, does not stop with dyadic analysis, but includes attempts to understand communication flow in groups of varying sizes.

GROUP-COMMUNICATION PATTERNS

One of the characteristics of social structure is that communication patterns are normatively defined and reflect the inherent status pattern that exists. As was indicated previously, status differences between members of a dyad influence the type of body position as well as other nonverbal cues. Likewise, within groups, the flow of communication is evidently related to status.

One universal group characteristic is that the amount of talking engaged in by various members of the group is not randomly distributed. In fact, some of the first research on communication within groups (Stephan and Mishler, 1952) showed that the patterns of communication in different-sized groups (of four, six, and eight) are very similar. Essentially, in all groups, two people end up contributing more than half the total communication. For example, in a group of eight, the two most talkative members contributed 60 percent of the total communication. The third member contributed 14 percent, and the other five members of the group contributed only 26 percent. These characteristics of group-communication patterns appear to hold for structured or unstructured groups; groups with members varying in age, from children to adults; and groups that include strangers or long-time friends.

From this and similar research, one might well conclude that by varying communication patterns within a group one might influence who emerges as group leaders. Some research seems to support this contention (Bavelas, et al., 1965). Subjects who did not know each other were recruited and asked to be members of a four-person problem-solving group. In the first observation, subjects were charted as to the amount of communication that they contributed to the group. From this first observation, the subjects who were ranked near the bottom of the verbal-output rankings were selected to be positively reinforced in each group. Whenever the chosen subject spoke, he or she was positively reinforced, and the rest of the group were negatively reinforced when they spoke. The control groups for this research were not reinforced either negatively or positively. At the completion of the discussion in the problem-solving session, all members of the group filled out their rating forms on each group member. The results clearly showed that not only did the absolute amount of talking increase considerably by the reinforced group member, but, importantly, other members of the group were much more inclined to rate him or her higher on leadership qualities. This research seems to indicate that, at least for these types of groups, verbal behavior is an important pattern that emerges within groups and is related to the leadership structure.

Types of Communication Not only do groups show patterns of communication in terms of amount of speaking and who speaks to whom, but additional research shows that different types of leaders emerge, and the type of communication in which they engage is related to their specific leadership role. One of the earliest to identify the nature of these leaders and communication patterns within groups was Robert F. Bales (1950). He constructed a detailed category system for analyzing the interaction that emerged in groups. He initially became interested in studying group structure as he visited Alcoholics Anonymous organizations in an attempt to better understand the success of those groups. He developed his category system and then applied it in the study of emerging leadership. Not only did he observe the behavior and the communication patterns within the groups behind one-way mirrors, he also had group members rate and rank each other on a number of different dimensions. From both the observational data and the group members' ratings, it became clear that communication patterns could be described on three different dimensions. One was the *activity,* or the total amount of communication. The other two were called *task-oriented activity* and *social-emotional activity.*

From Bales' research and subsequent studies, it was discovered that the common group structure that emerged had a task leader and a social-emotional leader. These two leaders consistently engaged in different types of communication. The task leader asked questions, gave instructions, and clarified points related to problem-solving activity. The social-emotional leader encouraged others with praise, reduced tension with humor, and performed other functions designed to maintain social solidarity among group members.

Although it is common for one person to engage in most of the task-oriented behavior and another person to engage in most of the social-emotional behavior within a group, sometimes one individual will be unusually high on both these dimensions. This has been referred to as the "great man" theory of leadership and communication patterns within groups. Borgatta, Couch, and Bales (1954) initiated research designed to test and to better understand this "great man" theory of communication patterns in groups. They selected eleven men who were high on these two dimensions of communication and then placed these individuals in new groups to observe the leadership patterns that emerged. Their research clearly shows that even in these new groups these individuals quickly emerged as leaders. Seven out of the eleven were ranked as tops in all the groups in which they participated.

Communication Networks The social-psychological research of the last decades has demonstrated that communication within any group is a vital part of that group's functioning. This insight has been utilized by revolutionaries and reactionaries alike for centuries. One of the most common things for revolutionary groups to do in their efforts at seizing power is to seize control of the major communication networks of the society, such as newspapers, radio, or television. Those who are struggling to preserve the status quo realize they must retain control of those communication channels. Controlling the communication networks and their content within any social order will influence the outcome of the group's functioning.

Leavitt (1951) conducted early research that sought to identify different types of communication networks and then to study the efficiency of those groups and the satisfaction level of group members. Four communication networks were created—wheel, chain, circle, and "Y"—by having the subjects seated around the table with partitions in between each subject (see Figure 3–4). The openings in the partitions allowed notes with information on them to be passed from one to the other. By controlling the openings that were allowed between each partition, Leavitt could, in effect, create four different types of communication networks. In the wheel formation, there is obviously one member of the five-member group who has a very centralized position in the communication network. In the chain, communication information can flow up and down the chain but, of course, cannot complete the entire circle. In the circle, no one is central, and communication is allowed to flow in all directions. The "Y" communication system has one person who becomes more central in that communication than in any other.

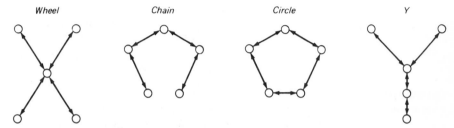

Figure 3–4 Communication Networks in Five-Person Groups. (Adapted from Leavitt, 1951, p. 42). Note: The double-headed arrows indicate directions of communication patterns allowed in the research.

Thus, Leavitt was, in essence, able to create two relatively centralized communication systems (the wheel and the "Y") and two relatively decentralized communication networks (the chain and the circle).

Group performance, both in terms of achieving its goals and its ability to satisfy its group members, appears to be related to its communication network. Communication patterns such as the circle are characterized by slow flow of the communication and inefficiency in terms of problem solving, but results in greater satisfaction for group members, who participate almost equally in the communication flow. The more highly centralized patterns, such as the wheel and the "Y," are characterized by greater efficiency, but less satisfaction for the outlying members. One additional finding from the Leavitt research was that the highly centralized patterns, while they tended to be efficient in terms of task-oriented behavior, tended to perpetuate errors made by people in those highly centralized positions. The circle communication pattern, for example, allowed for greater correction of errors by other members of the group than did the wheel or "Y."

In later experiments designed to compare the efficiency and satisfaction associated with wheel and circle networks, Burgess (1968) found that if errors were punished and reinforcements were introduced, differences in outcome virtually disappeared. Similarly, when the two groups were allowed to reach a steady state, no differences between them remained.

Subsequent research has shown that communication patterns are related to other dimensions of the group. Shaw (1954a, 1954b) shows that when information is distributed unequally among members of the group, the highly centralized groups emerged as less efficient in problem solving than were the circle or the chain. This is evident on intuitive grounds in that the more open communication networks allow information possessed by members who are not in the centralized position to get into the decision-making process. Shaw's research also shows that if the problem requires thinking and innovation rather than merely a collection of available information, it is better solved by the less centralized networks. Shaw (1964) has also shown that when the problem-solving dimension is unusually high with respect to the task confronting the group, the person occupying the centralized position in the highly centralized network may become frustrated and overloaded with the unmanageable amount of communication.

Similar research in large-scale organizations (Janis, 1972) shows that equal communication in government is very directly related to good and bad decision making. Janis argued that the "Bay of Pigs" fiasco occurred because the people within the government who had important information were not consulted. They were, in effect, outside the communication net. The decision of the highly centralized communication structure did not produce the best decisions.

Summary

As our major symbolic system, language has universal characteristics. Any one language is very much like any other language, existing or dead. The evidence seems to indicate that languages are evolving into more simple linguistic structures. The invention of written language was very likely the work of one person or a limited few and has probably occurred at different times and places in history.

Languages are studied as communicative systems consisting of phonetic, morphologic, semantic, and syntactic components. Some languages, such as unspoken ones, may not have all four components but are still clearly languages. Some animals, such as chimps, have the ability to learn and use some unspoken languages. Such language-possessing chimps can learn a symbolic system and can come to understand that objects have names; they can use the symbolic system to comment on objects in the real world as well as the symbolic system itself; and they can create novel word orders to communicate newly discovered information.

Language development in humans appears to originate basically out of characteristics of mother/infant interaction. The child moves successively through several stages in language acquisition: babbling, one- and two-word utterances, and expanded meaning. By the middle of the fourth year, the child has acquired the basic vocabulary and syntactic structure of its native tongue.

The cognitive and conditioning theories of language acquisition illuminate much about the processes of learning language. What neither theory addresses adequately is how the social, rule-governing aspect of language is internalized by the child. When the average child is two and one-half to three, he or she has internalized the underlying linguistic rules and uses them in creating new words and phrases. This social dimension is yet to be adequately understood.

Alternative explanations of the relationship between thought and language have been proposed. One approach (Sapir-Whorf) asserts that language, as part of the cultural milieu, molds thought. Piaget's alternative explanation asserts that language is merely a tool of thought. Vygotsky has attempted a synthesis by proposing that thought and language begin as two separate systems but quickly merge together when the child is about two years old. Language then begins to be employed in the service of developing new thought patterns, and new thought patterns in turn influence language development. At this stage, language and thought are really inseparable, each influencing the other.

Communication in the larger social setting has to be understood not only in terms of *what* is communicated but also *how* things are communicated. Research on proximics indicates prescribed norms, with great variations occurring between cultures. Although there are some gross body postures and gestures that convey similar meanings in virtually all cultures, there is no universal language of gestures. Nonverbal communication is receiving more and more attention, particularly because there is some evidence that nonverbal cues carry the major part of the communication load, at least in terms of how we define and respond to others.

Communication patterns in groups demonstrate regularities across groups. Groups of differing size seem to have similar patterns, with two people in each group contributing over half of all conversation. The flow of information within groups is related to how efficient the group is in reaching decisions and how satisfying the group is to each member. Groups typically have both a task and social-emotional leader, each specializing in appropriate types of communication, namely, the task or social-emotional needs of the group.

socialization

4

For hundreds of years, observers of human behavior have been intrigued with how infants become functioning members of society and with other basic social-psychological questions about the relationship of the social order to individual characteristics. In Aldous Huxley's *Brave New World,* the controllers of society determine the adult characteristics of each social class by giving the people in each identical genetic endowments and experiences. We join the Director of Hatcheries and Conditioning as he enters the infant nursery with a group of students:

The nurses stiffened to attention as the D.H.C. (and students) came in.

"Set out the books," he said curtly.

In silence the nurses obeyed his command. Between the rose bowls the books were duly set out—a row of nursery quartos opened invitingly, each at some gaily coloured image of beast or fish or bird.

"Now bring in the children."

They hurried out of the room and returned in a minute or two, each pushing a kind of tall dumb-waiter laden, on all its four wire-netted shelves, with eight-month-old babies. . . .

"Put them down on the floor."

The infants were unloaded.

"Now turn them so that they can see the flowers and books."

Turned, the babies at once fell silent, then began to crawl toward those clusters of sleek colours, those shapes so gay and brilliant on the white pages . . . small hands reached out uncertainly, touched, grasped, unpetaling the transfigured roses, crumpling the illuminated pages of the books. The Director waited until all were happily busy. Then, "Watch carefully," he said. And, lifting his hand, he gave the signal.

The Head Nurse . . . pressed down a little lever.

There was a violent explosion. Shriller and ever shriller, a siren shrieked. Alarm bells maddeningly sounded.

The children started, screamed; their faces were distorted with terror.

"And now," the Director shouted (for the noise was deafening), "Now we proceed to rub in the lesson with a mild electric shock.". . .

The Head Nurse pressed a second lever. The screaming of the babies suddenly changed its tone. There was something desperate, almost insane, about the sharp spasmodic yelps to which they now gave utterance. Their little bodies twitched and stiffened; their limbs moved jerkily as if to the tug of unseen wires.

"We can electrify that whole strip of floor," bawled the Director in explanation. "But that's enough," he signalled to the nurse.

The explosions ceased, the bells stopped ringing, the shriek of the siren died down from tone to tone into silence. The stiffly twitching bodies relaxed, and what had become the sob and yelp of infant maniacs broadened out once more into a normal howl of ordinary terror.

"Offer them the flowers and books again."

The nurses obeyed; but at the approach of the roses, at the mere sight of those gaily-coloured images of pussy and cock-a-doodle-doo and baa-baa black sheep, the infants shrank away in horror; the volume of their howling suddenly increased.

"Observe," said the Director triumphantly, "observe."

Books and loud noises, flowers and electric shocks—already in the infant mind these couples were compromisingly linked; and after two hundred repetitions of the same or a similar lesson would be wedded indissolubly. What man has joined, nature is powerless to put asunder.

"They'll grow up with what the psychologists used to call an 'instinctive' hatred of books and flowers. Reflexes unalterably conditioned. They'll be safe from books and botany all their lives" (Huxley, 1932, pp. 21–23).

Introduction

In this chapter, we address the general question of how the human infant becomes social and, more particularly, consider the basic relationships between things social and things individual. Social psychology by definition concerns itself with the study of the interplay between social structure and the individual. As a subset of social psychology, *socialization* focuses directly upon this interplay. How does the child come to believe that he or she should go to school, should learn to read, and should get good grades? How does the young adult come to believe that he or she should become a registered nurse? Socialization has traditionally been the study of the processes by which a human organism becomes a social being concerned with the rights and duties of self and others, with ethical and unethical behavior, and so on.

After considering some basic terms and theoretical approaches to the study of socialization and some recurring questions about the nature of the human organism and of social order, we attempt to study basic socialization processes and products occurring in the social institution of the family, and in other social groups across time and social space.

Basic Concepts

The traditional approach to socialization begins from the point of view that the social order precedes the existence of the individual. The starting point for socialization inquiry is the already functioning social group; the purpose is to understand how any one individual acquires the requisite knowledge, skills, and attitudes for membership in that group. Although students of socialization are quick to point out that they recognize that the individual can also change the nature and functioning of the social order, they usually focus first on that learning which allows the individual to engage in meaningful and sustained social interaction in an already existing social order.

DEFINITION OF SOCIALIZATION

Although a variety of definitions of *socialization* exist in the literature, they generally share a number of common elements. For example, consider the following:

Socialization [is] the process by which we learn the ways of a given society or social group so that we can function within it (Elkin and Handel 1978, p. 4).

Socialization deals essentially with the practical problem of how to rear children so that they will become adequate adult members of the society to which they belong (Zigler and Child, 1973, p. 4).

The term socialization designates the processes whereby the infant and child is led to take on the way of life of his family and of the larger social groups in which he must relate and perform adequately in order to qualify for full adult status (Clausen, 1966, p. 4).

Socialization refers to the process whereby individuals acquire the personal system properties—the knowledge, skills, attitudes, values, needs and motivations, cognitive, affective and connotative patterns—which shape their adaptation to the physical and social cultural setting in which they live (Inkeles, 1969, p. 616).

These definitions essentially all refer to the learning required by the individual to become a part of the existent social order. For our purposes, we can define *socialization* as those learning processes and resultant products that allow the individual to become an adequately functioning member of a social order. The definition is relatively broad and allows us to consider socialization as it deals with young children and as it occurs in the latter stages of the life cycle. Thus, if a person joins a union, for example, he or she will be socialized in the sense that he or she will take on those attitudes, values, and behaviors required by union membership.

Our definition obviously does not imply that socialization is nothing more than a synonym for learning. Socialization is a subset of learning in the sense that in order for socialization to occur, learning must take place; however, not all learning is necessarily socialization. Socialization entails learning those things that are necessary for sustained social interaction. As Zigler and Child emphasized in their definition, successful socialization implies the full (adult) acceptance into the social order, be it family or larger society.

This definition requires another clarification because, along with most of the others, it either explicitly or implicitly refers to process and product.

Source: © 1960 United Feature Syndicate.

The distinction between *process* and *product* is very useful. Socialization includes those social processes in which the individual engages that bring about his or her acquisition of socialization's products—the attitudes, values, and behavior appropriate to that particular social system. Thus, a child will engage in repeated interactions with father and mother involving talking, instructing, holding, caressing, toilet training, and so on. Over time, the child develops the necessary behavior to become an adult member not only of that family, but also of the larger society within which the family is imbedded.

Finally, it should be pointed out that the definition emphasizes the fact that the individual is seen as "conforming" to the normative expectations found in the existent social order. It does not call attention to deviant or other nonnormative behavior.

INTERNALIZATION

Social order exists precisely because out of sustained social interaction people develop and maintain shared expectations about appropriate and inappropriate behavior. These shared expectations are referred to as the *normative values* that characterize a given group or society. As a new member of a social order begins to interact with others, she or he gradually adopts the commonly shared standards as her or his own. This process of adopting as one's own the values, attitudes, and behavior of significant others is generally referred to as *internalization.* The concept obviously points toward processes of one type or another occurring internally to the organism. Most theories of socialization, be they psychoanalytic, social-learning, or cognitive, accept the assumption that internalization occurs.

Thus, if the child learns in the home that part of the appropriate behavior at meal time is to eat with a fork, and this becomes the child's standard of behavior, the child will also eat with a fork wherever he may be. The child will engage in the socially appropriate behavior even though the socializing agents (parents) are not present. Although different approaches to socialization give varying emphasis to this concept, all acknowledge that something akin to internalization occurs.

Human Nature

Our discussion of socialization so far has assumed that the social order already exists. A second assumption is also needed: namely, the new unsocialized member must possess the necessary biological endowments. A child born with severe mental deficiencies will not become an adequately functioning adult in society. Other deficiencies, such as missing limbs, deafness, blindness, or sexual abnormalities, require specialized socialization processes in order to maximize human development. Because socialization basically addresses normal interpersonal interaction and also assumes adequate genetic potential, the study has centered on questions concerning the innate qualities of the human organism. In short, it addresses the question, what is the basic nature of the human animal?

TABULA RASA VIEW

Traditionally, students of social relations have tended to view the human infant in a *tabula rasa* framework. This is to say the infant is considered to be born *asocial* rather than *antisocial* or *prosocial*. The individual in this traditional view is seen much like a lump of unmolded clay, possessing whatever biological equipment is necessary to engage in social interaction, having no predispositions that would lead him or her into one type of behavior as opposed to another. In its extreme form, this view of the child tends to see the products of socialization as being largely a result of the social pressures encountered in growing up in a given social system. In short, the organism is molded by society rather than having a hand in his or her own social creation.

The tabula rasa view tends to paint the individual as being basically passive, only responding to stimuli impinging upon him or her from the environment. Thus, differences in socialization outcomes are attributed not so much to differences in individual characteristics but rather to differences in the nature of the social order. This passive view has come under attack. For example, Dennis Wrong (1961) criticizes this perspective as contributing to an oversocialized view of people. More recently, others have continued with this criticism, arguing for a view of humans as actively engaging in their own socialization processes (Franks and Marolla, 1976; Brazelton, 1976; Schaffer, 1977; Zigler and Seitz, 1978).

ACTIVE-PARTICIPANT VIEW

Those who argue for a conception of people as active participants in their own socialization processes are much more likely to emphasize factors possessed by the infant at birth that influence the initial social behavior. In the child-psychology and child-development circles, proponents of the active view tend to emphasize the importance of cognitive development in the socialization process. For them, the child never just responds to the stimuli "out there" but selectively perceives and places the perceptions into a cognitively structured meaning system; the child acts toward stimuli on the basis of ascribed meanings. Socialization from this point of view is never seen as merely stamping in of cultural prescriptions but as a very complex interactional process between characteristics of the environment and the individual's characteristics. Socialization is not just the transmission of culture; it is really the study of the process of "becoming human."

A question logically follows from the active versus passive, or the nature-nurture, controversies, namely: "Who or what is responsible for socialization outcomes?" If one adopts the *tabula rasa* stance, then one is led to conclude that whatever differences occur are largely the result of environmental influences. The social order is ultimately responsible for the outcomes.

In practice, however, most societies reject this point of view. Nearly all judicial systems are based upon the view that the individual is at least partly responsible for his or her own behavior; otherwise, justice, judgment, rewards, and punishment would all be irrational. The issue of responsibility is frequently debated in the court cases involving punishment for flagrant violation of some of society's most strictly enforced norms, such as murder.

Another issue that comes to center stage as one wrestles with questions of responsibility is whether people are basically good or bad. In nonscientific literature, this discussion generally focuses around the question of whether people are "inherently evil or inherently good" (Zigler and Child, 1973, p. 31).

The person in the street is forced to consider explanations based upon the good/bad dimension of human nature when confronted with seemingly inexplicable behavior, such as the mass suicide-murder in Guyana (see chapter 1). As the investigations into that bizarre tragedy turned up evidence of how Jim Jones led or coerced his followers to accept punishment, deprivation, and finally death, people repeatedly asked, "Why?" Answers offered by some newscasters, journalists, and editorial writers showed the reasons lying in the various socialization experiences of Jim Jones's life. Those who opted for a people-are-basically-good interpretation saw the motivation for the suicide-murder as coming from some combination of the religious and political experiences and beliefs of Jim Jones and his followers; the chief source of the causes lay with the political and religious institutions in society (*Newsweek* 1978). Others argued that the underlying causes of such blatant evil were nothing more than the basic nature of people. Such events could not be explained away by pointing to political or religious institutions as culprits. These writers warned that the real lesson to be learned from Guyana was that this darker side of human nature was frighteningly close for everyone; that the jungle for all of us "is only a few yards away" (Greenfield, 1978). The box below exemplifies this view.

Heart of Darkness

I thought of one of those automatic ceiling sprinkler systems that go on of their own accord at the first sign of fire. The strange and terrifying news had hardly begun to come in from Guyana when I and the people I know . . . started trying to douse the flames in familiar and reassuring explanations. First would come the requisite cosmic sigh about how incomprehensible were the ways of man. And then would come the sly suggestion that the events weren't really so incomprehensible after all. Whereupon the speaker would proceed to interpret the Jonestown horror in a way that could best by summed up: I told you so.

Accordingly, it was a great week for the anti-left right, the anti-system left, and the anti-clerical of every political persuasion. The anti-clerical interpretation vaguely, but lovingly, put forward by skeptics and committed nonbelievers holds that this—carnage, hysteria and insanity—is what you get when you start down that leap-of-faith, suspension-of-reason road to religion. Crazy Reverend Jonesism is argued to be but a priest's step or two away from much, if not most or all, of religious experience. Under this construction, the irrational acquiescence of Jones's followers in their own mortification and doom is viewed as evidence of the dangers inherent in any form of spiritualism.

The anti-left interpretation has been made almost too easy to be sporting. Beans and rice and interracial harmony and blather about socialism and communal living and endorsements from liberal-left politicians and involvement of people like Huey Newton and Angela Davis and Mark Lane . . . The wages of interracial living [are] not mass suicide and mass murder.

RATIONALIZING THE BIZARRE

In fact, I would turn the thing around and say that the left politics, from what I have read, seem to have been less a source of the bizarre behavior than a rationalization of it. People who were submitting to terror and indulging some masochistic fantasy with their suicide drills and beatings and the rest, somehow justified it with a wash of sentimental, cockeyed class politics. Only ponder the intellectual confusion of those who could say in extenuation of a system characterized by physical privation, violence and abuse that, on the other hand, the medical care was good.

The anti-system implications have been indirectly drawn from the beginning. Practically the first voice I heard from Guyana was that of lawyer Mark Lane, just out of the jungle, expounding his theory to a radio interviewer that it was a *bleak comment* on life in the United States that these people would have chosen to go to Jonestown in the first place. In Jonestown, at least, they were free from drugs and crime in the streets . . . and so on. A variety of other observers, including newspapers abroad and, of course, the ever-ready Tass, have pitched in to help explain along these lines, citing sexual promiscuity, religious battiness and the general decadence of the American way of life as the true nub of the matter.

The confounding, inconvenient fact is that none of these interpretations will stand, any more than the related single-premise theories concerning mesmerization, brainwashing and similar mechanical processes will. The Guyana horror was not imposed on its victims by an external force or process. It was also not the inevitable or even probable outcome of dalliance with religion or left-wing politics. It's not where you necessarily come out if you go in those other doors. . . . Why then do we insist on trying to construe the various shocks and terrors that light up the sky as the predictable result of somebody or other's politics or faith? Well, at the simplest, most obvious level, it makes the night less frightening for the rest of us if we can attribute grotesque behavior to ordinary, manageable causes. And it justifies our own behavior and beliefs as well, sparing us along the way from having to face up to a world out there that is not conforming to the model with which we have become comfortable.

PROMPTINGS TO VIOLENCE

So we tame and domesticate the horror by making it fit our prejudices and predilections and we justify our own way of thinking about things, and we impose a certain consoling, if deceptive, order on the unsettling chaos of events outside us. But I think there is something more at play. I think we don't want to acknowledge that the aberrational behavior we have witnessed is at least dimly familiar to us in an individual, human way, that in some respects it represents not an antithesis of our own behavior, but rather a parody or caricature of it.

The desire to follow the mystique of a charismatic leader; the blindness and self-deception and unyielding resistance to evidence that our heroes may be weak and our commitments misguided and crazy; the fantasy of escape into another place or into the toil-free world of total obedience and repression of self; the reversion to infantilism ("Motherl Motherl" Jones is said to have cried out at the end); the contained, yet real, promptings to violence we have all felt—there are the things the Guyana nightmare put in stark relief.

They are not the vices of some cult or the end product of some political position. They are the dark impulses that lurk in every private psyche, the impulses whose control and channeling into constructive humane acts is the very definition of civilization. What made the Jonestown affair such a disturbing metaphor and called forth so many diversionary "explanations" was its reminder that the jungle is only a few yards away. (Italics added.)

(Greenfield 1978.)

The sharpest distinction in the social-psychological literature between the good and bad views of human nature can be seen in the works of Freud and

Maslow. The Freudian formulation with its emphasis upon energy being a motivator toward immediate gratification often views the individual as basically antisocial. Freud argued that the purpose of the social order is to control the diffused energy of the id into appropriately defined channels. Thus, the ego and the superego interrelate to channel the individual into socially constructive behavior. The social order must protect itself from the innate destructive tendencies of the human organism.

In Maslow's (1943) formulation of the self-actualized individual, a different view of human nature emerges. It is basically a positive view in which the individual is seen as progressively moving from one stage to another in social development. This progression is not a result of society's imposition of normative structure upon the individual but rather emerges because of innate human characteristics. The good person is seen as one who allows this natural development to take place and in the end becomes a fully functioning adult member of society—the actualized person. From this perspective, society is not so much the "good guy" keeping generally destructive tendencies from emerging but rather can become the "bad guy" if it inhibits the natural development from taking place. That which is "good" is so because of our basic nature. One of the weaknesses of this emphasis, however, is in explaining antisocial behavior, unless one is willing to assume that antisocial behavior is also caused by the organism. As a number of people have remarked, Maslow's ethics are reduced to a biological base. In fact, as Smith (1974) indicates, Maslow's biology is forced to carry his ethics.

HUMAN DEVELOPMENT UNDER MINIMAL SOCIAL CONTACT

Few accounts in the literature cause more discussion about basic socialization questions than do reports of children raised with wild animals or in extreme isolation. Such accounts serve as valuable sources of information about basic socialization processes and products. To what extent would a child raised in a den of wolves behave like a wolf? What type of behavior would be found in a child reared with almost no contact with adults or other socializing agents? A few cases have been adequately documented and verified and afford considerable insight.

Although stories and myths about humans reared with animals have been repeated since the dawn of history, the story of Kamala and Amala is well documented and reliable. The two "wolf children" were captured in a wolves' lair on October 17, 1920, in an isolated rural area of India. Kamala was judged to be about eight years of age, and Amala, about one and one-half. They had evidently been adopted by the wolves when they were infants—probably placed out in the fields to die as the local practice sometimes dictated for unwanted female children. Amala died shortly after being captured, but Kamala lived for years, supplying a rich source of information about the power of socialization processes and the resilience of human beings. When Kamala was captured, she ran on all fours; lapped milk with her tongue; devoured raw meat; carried dead chickens into the underbrush, where she ate them, entrails and all; howled mournfully and regularly at night; was relatively inactive during the day, sleeping for long periods, but became very active at night; and preferred the company of dogs to children.

Kamala spent nine years at the orphanage before she died from an illness. During this time, extensive efforts were made to resocialize her. At the time of death, she preferred to wear clothes rather than go naked; picked up her own clothes; preferred cooked meat to raw; became frightened at the barking of dogs; came to morning religious services and joined the singing; did not go outside at night; called doctors by their names; and understood many commands and instructions. The attitude and behavioral change over the nine-year period are really remarkable (see Singh and Zingg, 1966, for a published diary of Kamala's life at the orphanage).

Although there is always some question as to the validity of stories about children raised by wild animals, instances in which children have been raised in virtual isolation from other human contact have been more thoroughly documented. One of the first and most important accounts of a child being reared in extreme isolation is the case of Isabelle (Davis, 1940, 1947). She was an illigitimate child reared by her deaf-mute mother, alone in one room until she was about six years old. Because Isabelle had been conceived out of wedlock, her grandfather forced her mother to keep the child's birth a secret and to keep her from contact with people. When she was found, she could not speak and showed signs of fear and hostility toward people. It was difficult to determine at first whether she could hear. Upon careful examination, the child appeared to have normal hearing faculties, and an extensive training program was begun. By the time Isabelle was fourteen, she appeared to be normal and had acquired the learning equivalent of a sixth-grade education.

A more recent example of extreme isolation is the case of Genie, who was discovered when her nearly blind mother inadvertently went to a family-aids building. Her pitiful story and an account of the attempts to socialize her are set forth in the box below.

The Case of Genie

GENIE'S HISTORY

Genie was first encountered when she was thirteen years, nine months. At the time of her discovery and hospitalization, she was an unsocialized, primitive human being; emotionally disturbed, unlearned, and without language. She had been taken into protective custody by the police and, on November 4, 1970, was admitted into the Childrens Hospital of Los Angeles for evaluation with a tentative diagnosis of severe malnutrition. She remained in the Rehabilitation Center of the hospital until August 13, 1971. At that time, she entered a foster home where she has been living ever since as a member of the family.

When admitted to the hospital, Genie was painfully thin, had the distended abdomen commonly seen in cases of malnutrition, and appeared to be six or seven years younger than her age. She was 54.5 inches tall and weighed 62.25 pounds. She was unable to stand erect, could not chew solid or even semisolid foods, had great difficulty in swallowing, was incontinent of feces and urine, and was mute.

The tragic and bizarre story that was uncovered revealed that for most of her life Genie suffered physical and social restriction, nutritional neglect, and extreme experience deprivation. There is evidence that, from about the age of twenty months until shortly before admission to the hospital, Genie had been isolated in a small closed room where she was tied into a potty chair most or all hours of the day, sometimes overnight. A cloth harness, constructed to keep her from handling her feces, was the only thing she wore. When not strapped into the chair, she was kept in a covered infant crib, also confined from the waist down. The door to the room was kept closed, and the windows were curtained. She was hurriedly fed (only cereal and baby food) and minimally cared for by her mother, who was almost blind during most of the years of Genie's isolation. There was no radio or television in the house, and her father's intolerance of noise of any kind kept any accoustic stimuli that she received behind the closed door to a minimum. Genie was physically punished by the father if she made any sounds. According to her mother, the father and older brother never spoke to Genie; they did bark at her like dogs. The mother was forbidden to spend more than a few minutes with Genie during feeding.

It is reported that Genie's father regarded her as a hopelessly retarded child who was destined to die at a young age and convinced the mother of this. His prediction was based at least in part on Genie's failure to walk at a normal age. Genie was born with a congenital dislocation of the hips, which was treated in the first year by the application of a Frejka pillow splint to hold both legs in abduction, and the father placed the blame for her "retardation" on this device.

On the basis of what is known about the early history, and what has been observed so far, it appears that Genie was normal at the time of birth and that the retardation observed at the time of discovery was due principally to the extreme isolation to which she was subjected, with its accompanying social, perceptual, and sensory deprivation.

Genie's birth was relatively normal. She was born in April 1957, delivered by Caesarian section. Her birth problems included an Rh negative incompatibility, for which she received an exchange transfusion and the hip dislocation spoken of above. Genie's development was otherwise initially normal. At birth, she weighed 7 pounds, 7.5 ounces. By three months, she had gained 4.5 pounds. According to the pediatrician's report, at six months she was doing well and taking food well. At eleven months, she was still within normal limits. At fourteen months, Genie developed an acute illness and was seen by another pediatrician. The only other medical visit until she admitted to the hospital was when Genie was just over three and one half years of age. From these meager medical records, there was no indication of early retardation (Fromkin, et al. 1974).

GENIE'S DEVELOPMENT

When Genie was discovered, she did not speak. On the day after admission to the hospital, she was seen by Dr. James Kent.

Throughout this period she retained saliva and frequently spit it out into a paper towel or into her pajama top. She made no other sounds except for a kind of throaty whimper. . . . [Later in the session] . . . she imitated "back" several times, as well as "fall" when I said "The puppet will fall." . . . She could communicate [her] needs non-verbally, at least to a limited extent. . . . Apart from a peculiar laugh, frustration was the only other clear affective behavior we could discern. . . . When very angry she would scratch at her own face, blow her nose violently into her clothes and often void urine. During these tantrums there was no vocalization. . . . We felt that the eerie silence that accompanied these reactions was probably due to the fact that she had been whipped by her father when she made noise (Kent, 1972).

Within a few days, she began to respond to the speech of others and also to imitate single words.

There has been dramatic improvement in Genie's speech production. Among the grammatical structures that Genie comprehends are singular-plural contrasts of nouns, negative-affirmative sentence distinctions, possessive constructions, modifications, a number of prepositions (including *under, next to, beside, over,* and probably *on* and *in*), conjunction with *and,* and the comparative superlative forms of adjectives.

A number of relatively successful efforts have been directed at teaching her written language. She recognizes names, can print the letters of the alphabet, can read a large number of printed words, can assemble printed words into grammatically correct sentences, and can understand sentences (and questions) constructed of these printed words. On this level of performance, she seems to exceed normal children at a similar stage of language development.

Her cognitive growth seemed to be quite rapid. In a seven-month span, her score on the Leiter International Performance Scale had increased from fifteen to forty-two months; six months after admission, she passed all the items at the four-year level, two at the five-year level, and two out of four at the seven-year level. In May 1973, her score on this test was on the six-to-eight year level. At the same time, the Stanford Binet Intelligence Scale elicited a mental age of five-to-eight years old.

(Adapted from Fromkin, et. al. 1974, and Curtiss, 1977.)

Taken together, these and other examples of socialization under unusual and extreme conditions underscore the resilient and remarkable capabilities of the human organism. Kamala, for example, lived through two successive crises, each requiring fantastic changes in her behavior: (1) from the human culture to the wolf den as an infant; and (2) from the wolf culture to the orphanage. Kamala's experiences, along with the remarkable progress of Isabelle and Genie after being taken from their extremely deprived social environments, demonstrates the tremendous adaptability of the human animal. These examples also underscore the pervasive influence the ongoing social order has on human behavior, as Davis (1966) convincingly argued. Although the human organism sets the parameters within which culture can leave its imprint, the myriad forms of adult human behavior cannot be derived from innate individual characteristics. It can only be explained as an emergent phenomenon created out of the interplay between individual characteristics and society's normative order.

Theories of Socialization

PSYCHOANALYTIC APPROACH

Largely the contribution of five decades of work by Sigmund Freud, the psychoanalytic approach to socialization presents the view that the quality of the parent/child relationship is the central element in personality development. Not only does the psychoanalytic approach underscore the parent/child relationship, but it makes fundamental assumptions about the nature of the organism and postulates a developmental view of the emerging socialized being. The concept of development was one of the most revolutionary contributions of the psychoanalytic approach (Zigler and Child, 1973, p. 7).

The Freudian approach delineates several psychosexual stages of development, and the processes of interaction during these stages occurring in the family are seen as basic to the child's becoming socialized. These familiar interaction patterns are analyzed according to the quality of the emotional relationship. Thus, the ways the mother interacts with the child while toilet training, feeding, and so on, are seen as the social foundation out of which grow different personality characteristics. As Zigler and Child note, "Differences between one family and another then came to be viewed as a major cause of variation from person to person in socialization and the resulting personality of individuals" (1973, p. 7).

The formulations of the initial nature of the human organism as it moves through the stages of development places considerable emphasis upon the source of energy, namely, the id. The ever-present energies from the id result in tension in the organism, which seeks to reduce these tensions by filling its needs. The specific type of behavior selected for fulfillment will depend upon the stage of development. In the earlier psychosexual stages, the need for immediate gratification is strongest; the infant is hungry and demands to eat. As the child develops, other dimensions of the intellectual processes, namely the ego and superego functions, begin to appear.

The primary purpose of the ego is reality formation and a channeling of the energies of the id into ways that will reduce tension, built upon the nature of reality (both social and physical). The child learns that it is more realistic to postpone immediate gratification (wait until the dinner is ready) because the organism will be better off in the long run (the full meal will be prepared and hence the reward much better than a hastily prepared piece of bread demanded immediately). As Freud explains, this emphasis upon reality is not a triumph over the pleasure principle but merely a "safeguarding of it. A momentary pleasure, uncertain in its results, is given up, but only in order to gain . . . an assumed pleasure coming later" (1963, p. 26).

Identification is a central concept in Freud's formulation that is used to explain the development of and relationships among the three parts of the personality (id, ego, and superego). At the basic level of integration of the three parts, the identification mechanism makes possible the emergence of both the ego and superego. In the id, no distinction is made between image and object. However, an image cannot fill basic physiological needs; thus, ego functions emerge that link mental images with objects in the real world, taking energy away from the id. "At this point, logical thinking takes the place of wish-fulfillment" (Hall, 1954, p. 42) which is characteristic of the id. Once superego functions emerge, then energy is invested in objects or things as they "should" be. This basic process of investing energy in a mental representation of some object in the real world is spoken of as identification.

In Freudian formulations, the first important social objects in the child's world are parents. As the child moves through the psychosexual stages of development, he or she is said to be identifying with the parents. In this sense, *identification* is defined as "the incorporation of the qualities of an external object, usually those of another person, into one's personality" (Hall, 1954, p. 74). By *anaclitic identification,* the child incorporates characteristics of the person who is very warm and loving to him or her. By *identification with the aggressor,* the child adopts as his or her own characteristics of the powerful or aggressive person. The Mother and Father, respectively, are seen as central figures in these processes. Thus, children come to resemble their parents by assimilating "the characteristics of their parents" (Hall, 1954, p. 74).

The final phase in the identification process is reached when the child has internalized as his or her own the parents' moral dimensions of right and wrong contained in their superego structure, which strives for "perfection rather than for reality or pleasure" (Hall, 1954, p. 31). Once the superego is said to have been developed, the child can be considered to be fully socialized.

The Freudian formulation sees tension in the organism as inherently unpleasant, and shows that the child engages in activity until a state of balance is again created. This basically negative view of stimulation is rejected in much of the later work in ego psychology, and pleasure gotten from the initiation of activity is as desirable as that derived from the restoration of a homeostatic condition. Thus, much of contemporary work in ego psychology tends to reject the passive view of the organism (White, 1963) and investigates "intrinsic pleasure . . . attributed to an activity entailing initiative . . . such as play, manipulation, exploration and the expression of curiosity" (Miller, 1969, p. 483).

SOCIAL-LEARNING APPROACH

The social-learning approach tends to deemphasize internalization processes because these refer to states of the organism that cannot be measured and hence do not make important contributions to the scientific study of socialization. Although behaviorists recognize that internalization occurs, they refer to it as only response acquisition or learning by the organism. Thus, learning is seen as taking place in more narrowly defined limits than those (such as tending to imitate one's parent) set forth by Freud. In its simplest form, social learning sees the child as learning what is appropriate and inappropriate behavior in any social setting because she or he is rewarded for some behavior and not rewarded for others. Because of the child's basic nature, she or he tends to repeat rewarded behaviors and does not repeat nonrewarded behaviors. Thus, rather than "learning" general traits, the child learns which response is tied to a given stimulus.

Given the above, it follows that this theoretical approach would pay considerable attention to a *discriminative stimulus,* which is a stimulus that "precedes a reinforced response. . . . a child may become conditioned to respond (e.g., reaching out and smiling) to the appearance of his mother's face if these responses, when she appears, are systematically followed by functional reinforcers" (Gewirtz, 1969, p. 64). The learned tendency of an individual to perform in a given manner in the presence of discriminative stimuli is spoken of as *habit strength* (Hull, 1943). Learning, then, is seen basically as establishing links between stimuli and reinforcers. Rewards and punishment are central in the stamping in or stamping out processes of connecting specific stimuli with specific reinforcers.

Students working out of the social-learning orientation have made important contributions, especially the neo-Hullians (such as Dollard and Miller, 1950; Whiting and Child, 1953; and Sears, Maccoby, and Levin, 1957), by their willingness to include motives and drives in their work (Zigler and Child, 1973, p. 25). Although the neo-Hullians depart somewhat from strict behaviorism by talking of motives and needs, they refer to them as secondary drives or secondary needs, think of them as social in nature, and see them as emerging out of social interaction that is directed at reducing tension in the organism caused by primary needs. Thus, when the infant is hungry (primary need), the mother approaches the crying infant to feed it. The baby stops crying when the bottle is put in its mouth. Gradually, over time, the bottle being put in the mouth acquires other cue-arousing properties, such as the mother's picking up the baby. This becomes a secondary reward and will stop the crying. In short, the child develops a "need" for being picked up. As mother/child interaction continues, the mother approaching the bed will also stop the crying or, in effect, becomes rewarding in and of itself. Through these processes, the child develops elaborate stimulus/response connections that are social in nature.

Although social learning explains with facility the acquisition of behavior and demonstrates the external or stimulus control over that behavior, it has more difficulty explaining the maintenance of acquired behavior patterns over time. Why should a child repeat a given behavior for which he or she is not rewarded? This problem is usually discussed in terms of intermittent reinforcement schedules. If the observer sees behavior engaged in for which there is no reward, the explanation is offered that if the observer could be present long enough, he or she would observe a reward. After all, an intermittent reward schedule is the most effective in establishing learning that is resistent to extinction.

Perhaps the most apparent weakness of social learning is its difficulty in handling incidental or observational learning. If a child merely observes other people being rewarded or punished for their behavior, why should she or he learn appropriate or inappropriate behavior from that? The tendency to avoid any constructs that point to internal cognitive processes does not lead to easy answers.

The social-learning theorist and researcher who has contributed most to the study of observational learning is Albert Bandura. Initially, Bandura referred to this area of learning as *vicarious learning* with no attempt at explaining what was going on within the organism. In his later formulation, however, he has chosen to use concepts that refer to symbolic or cognitive processes in describing socialization. In one of his later works, he states that his purpose is to "provide a unified theoretical framework for analyzing human thought and behavior" (1977, p. vi). It is significant that Bandura equates thought and behavior in relative importance.

For Bandura, the same principles of learning hold in that connections are made between stimulus and response (reward), but he attempts to show how the development of cognitive formulations partly determines what will be connected in the stimulus/response chains. He rejects the "mechanistic models of an earlier period" and emphasizes the "vicarious, symbolic and self-regulatory processes" in human learning (1977, pp. vi–vii). Bandura urges that social-learning approaches reject the traditional passive view of the human and replace it with a cognitively operative and action-initiating organism. He argues that "people are not simply reactors to external influences. They select, organize, and transform the stimuli that impinge upon them. Through self-generated inducements and consequences they can exercise some influence over their own behavior. . . . Recognition of people's self-directing capacities provided the impetus for self-regulatory paradigms of research in which individuals themselves serve as the principal agents of their own change . . ." (1977, p. vii).

Whereas behaviorism initially rejected the internalization processes postulated by psychoanalytic and cognitive approaches, Bandura's recent emphasis would make social learning much more similar to other approaches in postulating various internalization processes. To date, the central construct that Bandura has developed pointing toward the cognitive and social side of human behavior is *self-regulation.* By this, he refers to a process in which individuals enhance and maintain their own behavior by rewarding themselves (positive reinforcers) and withdrawing rewards (negative reinforcers), whenever they attain or fail to attain self-prescribed standards. Bandura also assumes another internalization process that he does not fully describe. He asserts that people tend to adopt as their own those standards of behavior that they have observed in others. Thus, the presence of an internalized standard of conduct is largely created in the social milieu, and the presence of this internalized standard makes possible control of one's own behavior. "Actions that measure up to internal standards give rise to positive appraisals, while those that fall short are judged negatively" (Bandura, 1977, p. 131). As was stated in chapter 2, Bandura defines "negative self-concepts in terms of proneness to devalue oneself and positive self-concepts as a tendency to judge oneself favorably" (1977, p. 139).

Some will hail Bandura's formulations as the needed antedote to problems in the social-learning approach; others will see it as an unfortunate regression to inadequate approaches that give undue emphasis to processes that cannot be measured but have to be inferred from the very behavior that they intend to explain. Thus, negative self-concept is inferred from the self-devaluing behavior it is supposed to help us understand. Whether one accepts or rejects these formulations will likely depend upon her or his basic view of the nature of the human organism. Bandura's work clearly points toward possible points of reconciliation between behaviorist and cognitive approaches.

SYMBOLIC—COGNITIVE APPROACH

The last theoretical approach we consider is created by joining two different but related bodies of literature. The first comes from the more sociological sources of symbolic interaction, and the second from child psychology. The symbolic-interaction approach underscores a number of processes that are seen as basic to socialization. It emphasizes that self and society (individual and the social order) cannot be understood as distinct entities. Indeed, as was seen in chapter 2, the self arises and is maintained in social interaction.

Society is taken to exist in the sense of interrelated social institutions, each consisting of interrelated sets of roles. These roles define for the individual society's expected behavior for any person moving into a given role. The person who adopts as his or her own a given role internalizes the expected behavior and acts accordingly.

> That which creates the duties, rights, customs, laws, and the various institutions in the human society . . . is the capacity of the human individual to assume the organized attitude of the community toward himself as well as toward each other (Mead, 1938, p. 625).

Once the individual has moved into a role and adopted as personally appropriate those behaviors ascribed by society, then it can be said that she or he has become socialized. She or he can evaluate her or his own behavior from society's perspective and initiate behavior toward others consonant with her or his view of self (Mead, 1934).

The self is said to exist when the individual can initiate action toward himself or herself as a social object as well as being the subject or initiator of the action. Thus, the symbolic-interaction approach emphasizes that the individual is an actor as well as reactor (Dager, 1964; Stryker, 1964). This body of writing has much in common with the literature coming from the cognitive framework. Indeed, some of the cognitive-development theorists, such as Kohlberg (1973), make explicit their reliance upon the writings from both traditions.

Kohlberg lists a number of assumptions descriptive of the cognitive-development approach, among which are the following:

> Development of cognitive structure is the result of processes of interaction between the structure of the organism and the structure of the environment, rather than being the direct result of maturation or the direct result of learning. . . .
>
> Cognitive structures are always structures . . . of action. . . .
>
> There is a fundamental unity of personality organization and development termed the ego, or the self; . . . Social development is, in essence, the restructuring of the (1) concept of self, (2) in its relationship to concepts of other people, (3) conceived as being in a common social world with social standards. . . .
>
> . . . Social cognition always involves role-taking, i.e., awareness that the other is in some way like the self, and that the other knows or is responsive to the self in a system of complementary expectations. Accordingly developmental changes in the social self reflect parallel changes in conceptions of the social world (1973, pp. 348–49).

From these bodies of literature comes a conceptualization of socialization that emphasizes the interactional nature of the organism and the social order. The child or emerging self is seen as progressing through related steps of development. The rate of progress through the stages is determined by the maturational potential of the child as well as the characteristics of the social order. The child is seen as selectively and actively processing information according to his own stage of cognitive development.

As can be seen, this view of socialization places emphasis upon the outcome of action initiated by the organism in selecting and giving meaning to stimuli, which is always dependent upon the organism's cognitive-development stage. This approach leads researchers to ask about universal characteristics of the developing social being and discounts cultural or societal differences. Individual differences are minimized because all children are seen as going through the same sequence of stages—merely at different rates.

Kohlberg (1973) developed a model for this approach consisting of three levels of moral development; each level has two stages. The first level is called the *premoral level.* At stage 1, the child's behavior is primarily controlled by punishment, and behavior centers around avoiding punishment. As the child matures, he or she becomes aware of rewards and moves into stage 2, where his or her behavior shifts to obtaining rewards. Kohlberg reviews studies that suggest that about 100 percent of ten-year old children are at the first level.

The second level is called *conventional morality* and involves internalization of expectations that others have of the child. During stage 3, the child conforms to societal rules and norms in order to meet the expectations of individual others. For example, the child will return a pocket knife he or she has found to its owner because he or she feels that the owner expects him or her to. Stage 4 occurs when the child internalizes general standards of behavior, regardless of the role partner. In this stage, the child would return the pocket knife because it is a duty to return objects that belong to someone else. According to Kohlberg, most children go through this second level between the ages of thirteen and sixteen.

The third level, called *principled morality,* involves the internalization of abstract principles. Stage 5 occurs when the individual behaves according to rational, agreed-upon standards. The emphasis is on obeying the letter of the law. Stage 6 involves the acceptance of abstract moral principles, such as justice, freedom, honesty, and so on. A person in stage 5, while arguing that it should be changed, would obey an unjust law; a person in stage 6 would disobey for the sake of justice or freedom. Kohlberg's study of the levels of moral development included children only up to age sixteen; by this age, only 20 percent had entered stage 5, and less than 10 percent had entered stage 6. Additional research is needed to determine at what age the individual moves into these higher stages.

In testing his model, Kohlberg and his associates (Rest, Turiel, and Kohlberg, 1969) presented subjects with a situation that created a moral dilemma and then provided several alternative actions that could be taken. Each alternative action was supported by arguments developed according to the principles associated with the different developmental stages. Each situation included an argument one stage below where the subject should have been, a second argument one stage above, and a third, two stages above. The prediction of the model was that children would accept the argument a little more sophisticated or abstract than their current level and thus would agree with the argument one stage above theirs. The evidence was generally supportive of the model.

Most of the research conducted on moral development from this perspective has focused on what is most accurately described as moral *reasoning,* or what type of thinking or reasoning the child tends to engage in at various stages of development. It has not focused on the actual moral *behavior* of the child. Just because a child would resolve a hypothetical dilemma in a particular way does not mean that the child would actually behave that way in a real-life social situation. Research on moral behavior as opposed to moral reasoning may generate findings that can clarify the relationship between the reasoning and behavior dimensions.

Additional insight into this approach comes from research reported by Kohlberg on children and their dreams, which are universal experiences that normal children have. Kohlberg studied dreams in American and Atayal (a Malaysian Aboriginal group on Formosa) children. The meaning given dreams in these societies differ dramatically; American adults believe that dreams are subjective experiences and not real, whereas Atayal adults believe in the reality of dreams. It is considered that, in the first cognitive-development stages, American children accept dreams as real. At about five, they begin to learn that dreams are not real. Shortly thereafter, they understand that other people cannot see their dreams and that they come from within themselves. At about six and one-half, American children learn that dreams are not a material substance, but are thoughts; and at seven and one-half, they learn that dreams are not caused by God or another agency, but are caused by themselves (thoughts). What would the progression of stages look like in a culture in which dreams are believed to be real by the adult world?

If cognitive development follows universal patterns and if thinking is related to the underlying cognitive structure, then the Atayal children should show a sequence of stages similar to that of American children, even though the cultural input is different. If, however, the belief structure of the child is dependent upon what is rewarded and punished in his or her society, the Atayal children should never develop a belief that dreams are not real. The Atayal society would not reward them for believing something "false," and the adult world believes dreams are real.

The research shows that the sequence of stages is similar as it begins because the Atayal children, like the Americans, begin by believing that dreams are real. Next, they believe that the objects and experiences in dreams are not really in the room with them and that therefore dreams are not really real. The data indicate that through the age of eleven Atayal children go through a stage sequence similar to that of American children, but at a slower rate. At this age, the cultural input about the reality of dreams apparently begins to be effective, and the Atayal children who up until then believe dreams are not real gradually "regress" to their earliest formulations that the dream is real. Eventually, they accept the complete adult view that the soul departs the body during dreams and actually experiences things in far places (Kohlberg, 1973).

The social-learning view would have a difficult time explaining the sequence of beliefs of the Atayal children. The Atayal society would not have differentially rewarded or punished the children in those sequences to engender the observed change in belief structure from dream as real to unreal at about age eight and then back to real at about eleven.

The cognitive-developmental view sees the individual as selector of available stimuli in an effort to give them meaning and that much of the attached meaning is related to the underlying cognitive structure. Perhaps the most important potential contribution of the developmental view of socialization would be its focus on the question of which types of learning are related to the reward/punishment structure in the environment and which aspects are best seen as resulting from the child's own efforts at selecting, organizing, and giving meaning to the stimuli. Perhaps when these questions are further researched, social psychology will be better able to give meaningful answers to the controversies centering around nature versus nurture, active versus passive, and individual versus environment as responsible for socialization outcomes.

The three theoretical approaches to socialization discussed have generated many valuable socialization studies. The Freudian view has shown that emotional attachments between parents and offspring are central in socialization. The social-learning thrust has demonstrated the importance of focusing on reward/punishment patterns in social interaction. The symbolic-cognitive approach has shown the necessity for understanding the human organism as actor forming his or her own cognitive and symbolic view of the world as he or she becomes a functioning member of society.

Socialization in the Family

Regardless of the theoretical approach being used, researchers have virtually all recognized the family as the first important social group into which the typical child is socialized (Zigler and Seitz, 1978). Although the form of the family organization as well as the specific functions it performs may vary from culture to culture, families in virtually all parts of the world have one thing in common: adult caretakers interact with the child, out of which the first learning of appropriate and inappropriate behavior emerges. Several socialization practices have been shown to be related to specific behavioral patterns in the child; the more important of these are discussed below.

PARENTAL SUPPORT

There is rather remarkable agreement that the emotional or supportive relationship that develops between parent and offspring is very important in predicting certain socialization products in the form of attitudes and behavior. There exists general agreement that children reared in supportive interpersonal relationships generally tend to develop those characteristics that are valued in that society. In the Western world, they tend to develop high self-esteem, to be sufficiently creative, to see themselves as agents of cause rather than the results of environmental causes, to develop sufficient cognitive abilities, to exhibit moral attitudes and behavior, and to adopt the dominant values of their society. The ubiquitous influence of supportive interpersonal relationships has led many researchers to comment on the essential nature of love, support, and warmth in the adequate development of the human infant (Bronfenbrenner, 1977; Thomas et al., 1974; Rohner, 1975; Straus, 1964; Schaefer, 1965a, 1965b; Becker, 1964).

Deprivation of this life-sustaining, emotionally supportive relationship has been repeatedly associated with the emergence of severe problems. The classic research conducted and reported by René Spitz decades ago demonstrated the devastating effects of the lack of love. Spitz compared infants

Children often use tangible articles when they practice adult behavior. *Source*: © Marjorie Pickens.

reared in emotionally supportive (nursery) and nonsupportive (foundling home) environments. The startling findings are summarized by Munroe:

> Considered as a group, the nursery babies made normal progress as determined by (1) the general impression of activity and emotional responsiveness, (2) maintenance of the developmental quotient on regularly administered psychological tests, and (3) physical examination and health records. There were no deaths or serious epidemics, even though only common-sense precautions were taken against infection.
>
> The fate of the foundling home babies was tragic on all these counts: (a) The general impression was one of apathy and deathly silence. (b) The mean developmental quotient dropped progressively with age to a group mean of 45 (low-grade moron). This statistical finding is made more vivid by the statement that among 21 children ages 2½ to 4½ years (there were 91 in the total group), only five could walk unassisted, eight could not even stand alone, only one had a vocabulary of a dozen words, six could not talk at all, and 11 had only two words. (c) The health record shows that, despite elaborate medical precautions (no person whose clothes and hands were not sterilized could approach the babies), 34 of these 91 babies died. All but one of the older group was seriously underweight, despite a carefully supervised and varied diet (1955; pp. 185–86).

In reviewing the research literature, Rollins and Thomas (1979) found considerable evidence that parental support was related to a number of attitudinal and behavior characteristics of children. It was found that emotional support from parents was associated with high self-esteem, advanced cognitive development, creativity, instrumental competence, acceptance of societal moral values, and conformity to societal norms. On the other hand, absence of parental support was related to socially disapproved behaviors, including aggression, learning disabilities, mental illness, and delinquency.

PARENTAL CONTROL

Although there has been general agreement upon the importance of the support dimension in parent/child relations, such agreement has not characterized studies on the consequences of parental discipline or control techniques used in the socialization processes. Hypothesized relationships have often not been observed. In many cases, investigators have reported results contrary to what they predicted. There has been a great number of inconsistent findings reported across different studies in any given area of investigation. A number of researchers have identified the parental-control area as especially problematic (Rollins and Thomas, 1975; Thomas et al., 1974; Maccoby, 1968; Coopersmith, 1967; Schaefer, 1965a, 1965b). In addition, these researchers have called for new conceptualization and research in an effort to help resolve the ambiguity and attempt to bring some semblance of order to the findings.

It seems obvious that different styles of parental discipline might have very different consequences for child behavior and attitude. Following the earlier work of Hoffman (1960) and others (Baumrind, 1971; Aaronfreed, 1969; Hoffman and Saltzstein, 1967), Rollins and Thomas (1975, 1979) suggest that there are two main types of discipline used by parents. The first, *induction,* refers to control attempts of the parents embedded in an informational matrix. Parents reason with the child, giving information about possible consequences of behavior either for the child or others in the social encounters. Inductive-control attempts seek to avoid direct contest of wills between parent and child and rely upon reason to *induce* in the child voluntary behavior. The second, *coercion,* refers to the parents' use of their greater status, control of resources, and/or physical strength in attempting to elicit the appropriate behavior.

In reviewing the research on discipline techniques, Rollins and Thomas (1979) classified the parental behavior studied as either inductive or coercive. They discovered consistent relationships between the type of discipline exercised and the child's behavioral characteristics. In general, inductive control by parents was found to enhance the child's competence in dealing with his environment. The socially approved attributes of social competence, moral development, self-esteem, conformity, and belief in being able to control the environment rather than being a victim of fate, were all found to be more prevalent in children raised in homes characterized by parental use of inductive discipline techniques. Coercive discipline, on the other hand, tends to decrease those same characteristics in children. In addition, children from homes characterized by coercive parental discipline were more likely to be aggressive and to have other behavioral problems, such as drug abuse, learning disabilities, and schizophrenia. When the effects of both parental support and parental control are combined, the results are impressive. Children reared in emotionally supportive homes where parents use inductive disciplinary techniques are more likely to emerge with distinct advantages within the larger social setting. In short, children from these types of homes tend to be creative, to demonstrate sufficient conformity to the expectations of others in the social milieu to carry on sustained social interaction, to see themselves as capable and therefore responsible for what they do, to exhibit moral behavior, and to have relatively high self-esteem.

The relationship between inductive-discipline techniques and socially disapproved behavior is not clear because of the lack of research. The studies that have been done suggest that induction may tend to lower inappropriate behavior. We anticipate that future research will further substantiate and clarify this relationship.

The effects of coercive disciplinary practices appear to be multiplied when combined with a cold, nonsupportive parental relationship. The child raised in a nonsupportive home with coercive discipline tends to manifest inappropriate behavior significantly more frequently than those raised in supportive homes with inductive discipline. Table 4–1 presents a summary of the research evidence showing the influence of parents' supportive, inductive, and coercive control attempts upon various child characteristics.

EFFECTS OF GENDER ON SOCIALIZATION OUTCOMES

Up to this point, we have not made any distinctions between mother or father because the available evidence suggests that the parental behavior of support and control, whether it is from mother or father, has similar effects upon both boys and girls. Thus, the relationships between support, induction, and coercion are generalizable across mothers, fathers, sons, and

Table 4–1   Summary of the Relationship Between Parents' Behavior and Various Characteristics of the Child

CHILD'S CHARACTERISTICS	NUMBER OF STUDIES	NUMBER OF SUBJECTS	SUPPORT	COERCION	INDUCTION
Socially Valued					
1. Cognitive development	12	1,176	+ (S)	− (M)	
2. Conformity	7	11,833	+ (M)	− (M)	+ (M)
3. Creativity	8	2,143	+/−(M)	− (S)	
4. Instrumental competence	5	212	+ (S)	− (S)	+ (S)
5. Internal locus of control	11	2,020	+ (S)	− (W)	+ (W)
6. Moral behavior	18	1,402	+ (S)	− (M)	+ (S)
7. Self-esteem	8	2,800	+ (S)	− (W)	+ (W)
Socially Devalued					
1. Aggression	5	2,815	− (S)	+ (S)	
2. Behavior problems	11	2,128	− (S)	+ (W)	
3. Drug abuse	5	1,109	− (W)	+ (W)	
4. Learning disabilities	5	271	− (S)	+ (S)	
5. Schizophrenia	11	954	− (M)	+ (S)	

Adapted from Rollins and Thomas, 1979.

Key: + =Positive relationship between the parental behavior and the child characteristic.
*   − =Negative relationship between the parental behavior and the child characteristic.*
*   (S) (M) (W)=On the basis of the empirical evidence (chiefly the consistency of the relationships across the studies), the authors gave an overall rating to the strength of the research evidence: (S)=strong; (M)=moderate; (W)=weak.*

daughters. However, gender-related differences occur in academic achievement and sex-role identification.

Academic Achievement Over the decades, academic achievement has received a great deal of attention in social psychology. The influence of parent/child interaction patterns has been repeatedly studied. From the evidence in twenty-one studies, Rollins and Thomas conclude (1979, p. 342), "For sons, academic achievement seems to be facilitated by the same patterns of parental behaviors as other aspects of social competence," namely an emotionally supportive environment with reasoning-based discipline. However, a striking difference occurs for girls. Here, academic achievement appears to be fostered by a socialization environment that is conducive to socially devalued behavior in other areas. For the girl, a social environment with not too much support and a relatively high amount of control appears to facilitate academic achievement.

Any reasons for this unexpected finding given at this time will, at best, be guesses. One explanation offered is that in contemporary American society, academic achievement is differentially valued for boys and for girls. In essence, this explanation asserts that support and induction predict academic achievement for boys because it is valued for them, as are the other characteristics that are enhanced by these same parental behaviors. For girls, academic achievement is not valued as highly as self-esteem, moral development, competence, cognitive development, and so on. Thus, girls who achieve academically tend to come from home environments that are somewhat cold and controlling. Girls from these homes are seen as turning to academic achievement as an alternative to an environment that is not all that satisfying.

Traditionally, college graduation has been more highly valued for males than for females. The contemporary emphasis upon women's liberation, however, has tended to equalize these values. It may be that once this fundamental value change is reflected in different home environments, we will see a difference in those parental behaviors associated with academic achievement. We would expect that, if this equalization of values occurs, similar results in the area of academic achievement for boys and girls would be forthcoming.

A second possible explanation is more biological than sociological. If females are by nature less disposed to exhibiting aggressive behavior in the form of striving for accomplishment, then the findings become understandable. Because the male by nature is more prone to aggressiveness, then a home environment that mitigates against this tendency, namely, highly supportive and induction-controlled, will assist the boy in achieving academically. The male's most frequent school-related problem is one of too much aggressiveness rather than too little, whereas the female tends toward passivity. Hence, a home environment that is cold with high demands for performance encourages achievement for the female child.

Although this biologically based explanation has some support in published research (Maccoby and Jacklin, 1974), it is not currently in vogue and will likely be slow in being accepted. Even though biological differences between male and female are not popular explanations, social psychologists ought not to close their eyes to such possibilities.

Sex-Role Identification Following the initial clarification developed by Lynn (1966), we define *sex-role identification* as the degree of internalization of the typical role defined in a given culture as belonging to the male or female. Studies of sex-role identification in children have generally emphasized the importance of the differential effects of same-sex and opposite-sex parents on sex-role identification in children (Walters and Stinnett, 1971). The dominance of parents relative to each other has also emerged as an important influence. The results of research published through 1974 are congruent with these ideas (Rollins and Thomas, 1979). Twenty tests of the relationship between parental support and sex-role identification in children, in general, suggest that for both boys and girls the behavior of the same-sex parent is more important in engendering an acceptance of the child's own sex role.

Parental coercion appears to have a different effect depending on whether it is the father or the mother doing the coercing and whether the child is a son or daughter. Coercion from father appears to increase the male child's tendency to accept his own sex role, but it decreases the tendency of the daughter to accept her role. Coercion from mother in the two studies reporting this analysis showed that it did not seem to make any difference for the daughter. However, coercion from mother toward the son tends to decrease the son's acceptance of his own sex role. No studies were located that measured induction, so its relationship to sex-role identification remains unknown.

If the father is dominant over the mother in the husband-wife relationship, it tends to enhance the male child's acceptance of his own sex role. Likewise, greater feminine sex-role identification appears to occur in families in which the mother is more powerful.

A major difficulty with the material covered in the review of research up to the mid-seventies (Rollins and Thomas, 1979) is that sex-role identification is conceptualized as the person having either masculine or feminine characteristics, but not possessing both. This traditional view has undergone considerable modification since the early and mid-seventies. Research since that time has contributed to a better understanding of how traditionally defined masculine and feminine characteristics do not exist in isolation in any one individual, but rather are found in any one person in a blend of both (Bem, 1975; Hetherington, Cox, and Cox, 1978; Kelly and Worell, 1976).

Research that has focused on socialization for androgyny reveals slightly different findings than that focused on masculinity or femininity. Kelly and Worell (1976) found that masculine-typed males reported a cool, nonsupportive relationship with both parents. Feminine-typed males reported a warm, supportive relationship with their mother, and androgynous males reported high emotional support from both their father and mother. Hetherington, Cox, and Cox (1978) also found that support from mother was related to androgyny in boys.

Although warm, supportive relationships with both parents appeared to facilitate androgyny in males, a somewhat different pattern emerged for females. The support dimension from father appears to be important in encouraging androgyny in daughters when it comes from a father who also encourages early independence and achievement. Encouragement of independence and achievement by mothers was the one maternal behavior that appeared to foster androgyny in daughters (Hetherington, Cox, and Cox, 1978). In summary, it appears that androgyny in sons will be enhanced by warm, supportive relationships with both parents, and that support from father combined with encouragement for independence and achievement from both parents will lead to androgyny for daughters.

These findings, when combined with those for academic achievement of sons and daughters, point toward a possible synthesis. With both academic achievement and androgyny, the female must incorporate attitudes and behaviors that have traditionally been defined as masculine but that are valued by society. These qualities of assertiveness, intellectual achievement, independence, and accomplishment appear to be fostered in the female by a family environment that is high on demands and controlling parental behaviors combined with relatively high supportive behavior from the father.

RECIPROCAL CAUSATION

To this point, the research evidence has emphasized the environmental influence upon the individual who is being socialized, and this is the traditional conception of socialization. Although the research in the early socialization literature is usually conducted from a parent to child causal framework, some alternative viewpoints are also emerging in literature. In literally all the theoretical orientations used to focus on socialization, the human organism is seen as an *active* participant in his or her own socialization process. The emphasis upon the passive view of the human organism is partly a result of inadequate methodologies for the study of the human organism as cause. Many have observed that the time is ripe for the development of additional methodologies allowing research to focus on the human being as at least part of the cause of the socialized outcome (Rheingold, 1969; Rollins and Thomas, 1979; Bandura, 1977; Gewirtz, 1969; Cottrell, 1969; Klaus and Kennell, 1976; Brazelton, 1976; and Zigler and Seitz, 1978).

If social interaction is the stuff out of which socialization emerges and if social interaction by definition consists of reciprocal causation (each person being a cause), then socialization by definition will be a process with outcomes that are partly caused by the behavior *initiated* by the person being socialized. Gewirtz (1969) has argued that even from the most behavioristic formulations of stimulus/response theory, what is really postulated are S-R-S chains, not merely *a* stimulus that elicits *a* response. Even the most basic stimulus/response formulations require a dyadic analysis, not just a monadic or one-way casual relationship. Bandura (1977) has argued that social psychologists adopt a reciprocal causation model and begin to study the individual as initiator of action. When this is done, it will help to fill a current void in social-psychological research.

Environmental control is minutely analyzed, whereas personal control has been relatively neglected. To cite one example, there exist countless demonstrations of how behavior varies under different schedules of reinforcement, but one looks in vain for studies of how people succeed, either individually or by collective action, in negotiating the reinforcement schedules to their own liking (Bandura, 1977, p. 204).

Changing View of the Child There is a growing body of research evidence that calls into question the traditional view of the young infant as a passive organism unable to discriminate between stimuli. Descriptions of the infant as being unable to see objects distinctly at birth and having only the gross emotional responses of either pleasant or unpleasant (Hurlock, 1968, pp. 116 and 119) are rapidly changing in the face of new research evidence.

Those studies dealing specifically with the infant reveal a very active organism even within the first minutes of life. Infants from two minutes to nine minutes old will fixate on a representation of a human face and turn the head "to attempt to maintain fixation from a neutral position as far as 90°" (Vaughan, 1976, p. 126). When given a choice, infants prefer to look at a figure resembling a human face rather than scrambled arrangements of facial components. As the infant gets older, he or she will prefer to interact visually with a patterned stimulus over a nonpatterned one, and with more complex stimuli than with simple ones (Appleton, Clifton, and Goldberg, 1975).

Although the visual response pattern is the easiest to study in focusing on intentional behavior of the infant, it is reasonable to assume that similar choices between alternative stimuli occur with other sensory input, such as auditory and tactile. The infant is equipped to make rather complicated differentiations in sound. It is clear that very young infants engage in "selective attention, discrimination of voices, and early phoneme perception" such that they are able to "process speech sounds in their appropriate mode." Research now indicates that "infants of one to five months . . . make some of the same discriminations as adults" (Appleton, Clifton, and Goldberg, 1975, pp. 115–16). As Schaffer notes, "the notion that a baby is functionally deaf can certainly be discounted" (1977, p. 38). In addition, research findings coming out of Russia (Fradkina, 1971, cited in Appleton, Clifton, and Goldberg, 1975, pp. 115–16) indicate that once the child has begun to create his own meaning systems (for example, begins to comprehend simple commands), the child can be conditioned four times faster to words than to other sounds. Intentional cognitive processes of the child are undoubtedly related to the differential learning because before the child is seven or eight months old the conditioning time for words compared to other sounds is the same.

Thus, the newer view of the infant is one of great capability at birth to engage in the initial social interaction with parents. In Brazelton's words, after studying mother-child interaction intently for years, "I no longer see him as a passive lump of clay, but as a powerful force for stabilizing and influencing those around him" (1976, p. 135). Given the characteristics now known to be possessed by the infant at birth, the former *asocial* perspective is giving way to a prosocial view. Out of the uterus comes a socially preadapted infant (Schaffer, 1977, p. 38).

Changing View of the Environment Not only does the infancy research reveal a very active, prosocial, and competent human organism, but it reveals a very important and complicated set of interrelated mother/infant behavior. The repeated finding from much of this research underscores the importance of early reciprocal interaction. Each person—mother and child —initiates action toward the other and then modifies her or his own behavior on the basis of how the other responds. If parents are not responsive to the behavior of the infant, the "infant turns off his attention" and spends most of his time just checking back on the parent from time to time. A smooth, rhythmical interaction pattern is not established but rather a jagged attentional system having some similarities to the infant/object system (Brazelton, 1976, p. 137).

Interactional systems are established early with the infant moving in rhythm with the voice and movements of the mother. The mother takes her cues predominantly from the eye movements of the infant, and the infant takes cues from the mother's facial and voice changes. Studies show that infants in the first day of life move in rhythm with the spoken word "whether English or Chinese, but not with discontinuous symbols" (Klaus and Kennell, 1976, p. 117). The researchers assert that the quality of these early reciprocal systems of interaction is related to subsequent behavior of both the parent and the child. Studies have shown that parents who develop these early synchronous interaction patterns with their child, when compared to a control group having jagged interactional styles, have a significantly different style of interaction with their new infant as well as two years later. Parents tend to be less anxious, more supportive, and the child shows a freer and easier repertoire of behavior when interacting with others (Vaughan, 1976; Klaus and Kennell, 1976; Brazelton, 1976).

The infancy research focusing on reciprocal interaction fits well with the earlier research on the child's characteristics associated with parents who use induction and support. These parents and children would undoubtedly move in rhythm with each other. As will be remembered from the empirical review, the child behavior characteristics that are taken as consequences of supportive behavior of parents were both numerous and consistent. The presence of supportive behavior from one person to another appears to have a facilitative effect upon the recipient. Humans appear to grow physically, emotionally, and socially in the presence of a supportive relationship, and they encounter considerable problems in its absence.

When action is initiated by an individual, the responsiveness to that action by the other individual is very important. The mother who loves her child becomes very responsive to the first signs of intentional behavior of the child. The first smiles, intentional or not, are responded to as if they are intentional. The first sounds, be they intentional or not, are repeated by the mother to the child. There are even now some research results in language development that indicate that the mother changes her manner of speaking to the child once the child begins to speak and she makes the change on the basis of verbal feedback from the child (Phillips, 1973).

From the reciprocal-causation model, it follows that the nonsupportive environment is not responsive to the individual's initial and continuing efforts at producing an effect upon the environment. In such environments, a sense of competency will develop with greater difficulty.

Significant others who try to influence the behavior of the individual in an information-giving context by pointing out possible consequences of different types of behavior facilitate the sense of competency. In effect, this additional information (reason-based control) about causes and consequences to the individual and others should help the individual more fully understand the nature of the world and thus be able to cope more successfully with it.

Coercive-control attempts have essentially the opposite effect of both support and induction. As the coercive-control attempts increase by significant others in the individual's environment, the responsiveness of that environment to that individual's intentional behavior decreases. In such an unresponsive environment, the individual develops a view of self as being unable to deal effectively with the environment. This becomes the mirror image of the self-fulfilling prophecy of the positive relationships. The unresponsive environment generates fewer attempts at intentional behavior, which further reinforces the individual's view of self as socially incompetent.

With a view of the child as part of the cause of her or his own socialization outcomes (Zigler and Seitz, 1978), future research focusing upon a responsive environment will help us better understand both the socialization processes and products occurring in the family as well as in larger social environments.

Socialization in the Larger Social Setting

At the close of childhood or adolescence, socialization does not end. Indeed, it is virtually a lifelong process. All that an individual needs to know to be an adequately functioning member of society cannot be learned during the first eighteen years of life, nor the first fifty. Life itself is characterized by taking on, changing, and finally discarding social roles, all of which require the individual to learn new behavior in new social settings. The adolescent decides to become an electrician, then to get married, to become a parent, to live in Los Angeles, to retire, and so on. Adults socialize themselves and are socialized by others into a variety of social roles during their lives. Adult socialization, in many ways similar to childhood socialization, differs in some important dimensions.

SELF-SOCIALIZATION

One of the chief characteristics of adult socialization is the role of *choice* (Elkin and Handel, 1978, p. 235). The adult decides to become an electrician instead of a lawyer. The executive decides to become a mother as well as being vice president in charge of advertising in a national agency. Adults choose to change employment and place of residence, to marry or not to marry, to have none, one, or many children, to live in a commune or a suburban home. With each choice, adults not only determine the type and content of future social relations but also future social contexts in which they will be socialized. Thus, the adult is seen as being largely responsible for these socialization outcomes.

With greater emphasis being given to adult-socialization research (Rosow, 1965; Brim, 1966; Zigler and Seitz, 1978), it can be expected that more frequent analysis will be given to the central role of the individual in his or her own socialization. If childhood socialization has now begun to emphasize the child's role in his or her own socialization more than ever before (Zigler and Seitz, 1978, p. 740), then adult-socialization research will continue to expand social psychology's knowledge about choice and responsibility in socialization processes and products.

A second characteristic of self-socialization is the process of *anticipatory socialization.* This is defined as "the acquisition of values and orientations found in statuses and groups in which one is not yet engaged but which one is likely to enter" (Merton, 1957a, p. 384).

Before an individual makes the decision to enter a new role, he or she will often be attracted to the group by the attitudes and values that group members are perceived as possessing. The individual may even rehearse or practice the behavior in which he or she will engage once the new role is taken on. The anticipation of future behavior and adoption of accompanying attitudes and values facilitates socialization into the new role. Research shows that new army recruits who, through anticipatory socialization, have already "accepted the official values of the army hierarchy were more likely than others to be promoted." They are more readily received by the new group and make easier adjustments (Merton, 1957a, p. 265).

SOCIALIZATION INTO ROLES

A second distinguishing characteristic of adult socialization is the emphasis upon the acquisition of role-specific attitudes and behavior. Whereas childhood socialization tends to be of a general nature, equipping the child for general social competence across a number of different social settings, such as at home, at school, or with peers, adult socialization focuses more directly upon role-specific information. As Elkin and Handel (1978, p. 233) note, this arises because much of what an adult needs to know about the role can only be learned by actually being "in the new situation."

In a modern, industrialized society, such as the United States, a variety of roles exist that require vast amounts of specialized knowledge. The average person who reaches adulthood will have only a limited knowledge of even the existence of many of these roles, much less an awareness of the specific rights and duties that identify appropriate and inappropriate behavior. In no way could families, schools, or other institutions in society prepare individuals to move into a multiplicity of these specialized roles. Thus, most socialization into the roles, aside from what occurs through anticipatory socialization and preparatory training, takes place after the decision is made to assume a given role. Much of the behavior appropriate in any one of a large number of adult roles, such as politician, police officer, or parent, can be learned only in the social setting in which the individual is called upon to enact the role.

Social psychologists have sensed the importance and complexity of this dimension of socialization for some time:

> In role learning, the importance of persons enacting complementary roles, the importance of teachers, models and coaches, and the importance of relevant audiences cannot be overemphasized. . . . Research on role learning must deal with the particular kind of learning that occurs in interactional settings and must recognize the complexity of the content of the learning, the persuasiveness of the influence of other persons, and

the crucial importance of the role relationship itself (Sarbin and Allen, 1968, p. 545).

Research focusing on child abuse in the United States illustrates the importance of studying the role relationship itself in understanding how a person is socialized into a role. The actual occurrence of child abuse is probably as old as society itself. In Greece and Rome, child abuse was known to exist (Radbull, 1968), and infanticide has been practiced in many societies. Others have practiced the maiming or otherwise deforming of young children to enhance their effectiveness as beggars. Widespread professional and lay concern for this as a social problem needing attention is of relatively recent origin.

Professional concern in the United States began in 1946 with the publication of an article by a young medical doctor (Caffey, 1946), in which he detailed the presence of severe bruises, broken bones, and so forth, as an indication of possible abuse by caretakers. Other medical doctors (Wooley and Evans, 1955) further defined the problem and alerted the medical profession. In 1961, the United States adopted a law requiring that all child-abuse cases had to be reported to legal authorities, and in 1974 the Child Abuse Prevention and Treatment Act was passed. A national center for gathering information on child abuse was set up in Denver, Colorado. In addition, the federal government allocated millions of dollars for research and experimental treatment programs during the late 1960s and the 1970s. These and other efforts have succeeded in alerting virtually all segments of the population to the child-abuse problem.

What was not understood, however, was the *causes* of such inexplicable behavior. Why would a parent fracture the child's skull, break ribs, dislocate a hip, fracture an arm, or seriously damage internal organs? Could parents with the potential for abusing their children be identified beforehand and could programs be developed to reduce the incidence of child abuse?

Social-psychological research is in the process of supplying possible answers to some of these questions. Some of this research emphasizes the understanding of role relationships and how parents are or are not socialized into their roles. Some of the best research has been conducted at the national center in Denver, Colorado (Helfer and Kempe, 1976; Kempe and Kempe, 1978).

Data have been gathered from parents at four different points in time to attempt to identify those likely to abuse their children. The first step involved an in-depth clinical interview of the parents before the birth of the baby that probed problems of depression, anxiety over the prospects of birth, feelings of aloneness, and desires to deny the pregnancy. Second, the parents filled out an extensive questionnaire on similar areas of concern. Third, members of the delivery staff took detailed notes on the parent-to-parent and parent-to-infant interaction in the labor and delivery rooms. Fourth, observations were made of the parents in the postpartum wards and during the first six weeks of the child's life at home (Kempe and Kempe, 1978, pp. 60–61).

Of the four, observation of the beginning of the parent-child role relationship during labor, delivery, and immediately following birth was by far the best predictor of future propensity for abuse. Seventy-seven percent of the time, correct predictions could be made from these observational data. Combining all four sources of data increased accurate predictions only to 79 percent, "which is not significantly different from the labor and delivery observations alone." The researchers conclude:

> Doctors and nurses working with expectant parents are ideally placed to make sensitive significant observations of the way parents react to their new babies. . . . We suggest that such observations should, therefore, become a routine part of *all* obstetrical and neonatal care. . . . This information gathering will significantly improve every child's chance of escaping physical injury (Kempe and Kempe, 1978, pp. 62–63).

By observing the initial parent-infant role behavior, the researchers were able to accurately identify abnormal parental role behavior. Some of the role behavior that best discriminated between high- and low-risk parents was a failure of the mother to make and maintain eye contact with the newborn, failure to speak affectionately to the infant or to touch or handle the baby, disappointment over the baby's sex, failure to respond to movement of the baby, making hostile or disparaging remarks about the baby, and failure to show affection toward her husband or him toward the mother (Kempe and Kempe, 1978, p. 61).

The second encouraging aspect of this research, in addition to the predictive dimension, is the intervention program. Parents were randomly separated into three groups of twenty-five families each: (1) low-risk nonintervention; (2) high-risk intervention; and (3) high-risk nonintervention. The intervention consisted of a doctor working with each family during labor and delivery with repeated later contact by telephone and office visits with the parents and infant. He or she would check on problems, explain characteristics of infant behavior, answer questions about the infant's behavior, or in other ways instruct parents about their roles as well as offering his or her support. Sometimes, if they had problems, he or she would recommend specialists to assist them.

When the children in the study were between seventeen and thirty-five months of age, assessment was made of the effect of the intervention program. None of the children

> . . . in either the low-risk group or the high-risk *intervention* group was hospitalized for abuse or neglect. But five high-risk, nonintervention children did need hospital treatment for serious injury. These included a fractured femur, a fractured skull, barbituate poisoning, a subdural hematoma (hemorrhage on the surface of the brain), and third-degree burns. . . . Furthermore, the short-term and long-term cost of the five injuries to the State of Colorado has been calculated at $1 million. By comparison the extra cost of our intervention with the treated group was only $12,000 (Kempe and Kempe, 1978, p. 65).

If these preliminary findings are supported by additional research, perhaps social psychologists will be able to offer hope to otherwise confused and discouraged parents. Parents might have the hope of becoming better prepared for their role by creating confidence in themselves and a more realistic expectation about what to expect from the infant in the parent/

child relationship. Many skills can only be learned in the role, but the research seems to indicate parents can be helped in this essential learning. Given needed information, the parents in this research at least successfully carried out their role to the extent of not abusing their children.

SOCIAL CLASS AND SOCIALIZATION

Great differences exist between people in any society in terms of power, prestige, ease of access to the decision-making and law-enforcing segments of the society, and material possessions. These differences are often referred to as social-class differences. The influence of social class upon individual behavior is pervasive. The single most important decision that an adult makes with respect to determining so far as he or she can determine, the social class that he or she will occupy is the decision about what occupation to pursue. This decision will largely affect the values developed as well as the types of socialization practices that will likely be used in the individual's own family. One researcher who has done considerable work to clarify the relationship between social class values and socialization is Melvin Kohn (Kohn and Schooler, 1963).

One of the key concepts in Kohn's formulation is values. He takes values to mean "conceptions of the desirable," which are seen as products of the social conditions that surround people.

> Members of different social classes, by virtue of enjoying or suffering different conditions of life, come to see the world differently—to develop different conceptions of social reality, different aspirations and hopes and fears, different conceptions of the desirable (Kohn and Schooler, 1963, p. 471).

Kohn's purpose, however, is not to study values in general but more particularly values held by parents because he sees these values as directly related to how parents socialize their children. For Kohn, the single most important source of values held by parents comes from their occupational world.

If these basic value differences emerge in different socio-economic strata, it is easy to see how socialization practiced by parents would be expected to vary by social class. Gecas (1979) outlines the basic relationship identified

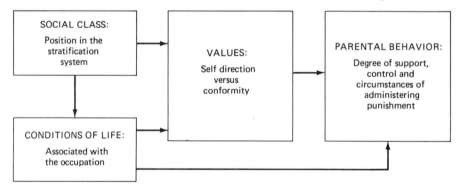

Figure 4–1 Basic Relationship Identified in Kohn's View of Variations in Socialization by Social Class (Adapted from Gecas 1979 p. 380).

in Kohn's model (see figure 4–1) and then assesses the degree of empirical evidence for the postulated relationships. He concludes that there is strong evidence that social class is directly related to parental values, even when researchers control for the influence of "race, region, community size, religion, and national background" (Gecas, 1979, p. 380). Wright and Wright (1976) tend to corroborate these findings. One important finding in the Wright and Wright research is that there has been a change in values in that people give more importance to values of self-direction, regardless of social class.

Although the evidence is impressive that occupational strata are related to parental values, what the relationship is between social class and parental behavior is not as well documented. The empirical evidence tends to support the conclusion that the "lower-class parents are more likely to use physical punishment, whereas middle-class parents rely more on psychological techniques, such as threat of love withdrawal, appeals to guilt, and reason with the child" (Gecas, 1979, p. 382).

SOCIALIZATION INTO AN OCCUPATION

Because the choice of occupation influences so much of what adults are socialized into as well as how they will socialize their children, it is important to look more closely at how the socialization occurs. Occupational socialization is one of the most universal socialization processes and requires learning over generally long time frames. Our discussion follows Moore's analysis in general outline (1969). For our purposes, we divide the occupational socialization process into three different stages: background experiences; deciding on an occupation; and developing requisite commitment.

Background Experiences Obviously, early-childhood experiences are crucial in determining what career patterns will be followed. Here, the influence of the family is central. An individual receives from her or his family two basic types of attributes that differentially equip her or him for one occupational pursuit instead of another. The two, genetic endowments and the opportunities that result from the family's position in the social structure, mesh to produce the chosen occupational outcome. One can easily see how Mohammud Ali, for example, with the gift of a superb physique combined with his family's position in the social structure, achieves his remarkable excellence in the world of boxing. Boxing has traditionally been one of the occupational avenues to achievement open to the lower socio-economic strata. As upwardly mobile ethnic and racial groups, the Germans, Irish, blacks, and Mexican Americans have had or are having their respective days in the boxing world. Individuals from higher social strata, who have the genetic endowment allowing them to excel in sports, often move into other careers, such as playing golf, basketball, or tennis.

Not surprisingly, the educational world and the family provide the bulk of those early background experiences that coalesce to prepare one to choose an occupation. As Moore notes (1969, p. 871), what one receives from the family and school works to delimit the range of alternatives in a negative sense, in that required qualifications are not met. If the individual does not possess the necessary training to be able to select a given career path, then this occupational career remains closed. Likewise, if an individual

A drill instructor attempts to socialize a raw recruit into a soldier. *Source*: U.S. Army.

is not endowed genetically with requisite qualifications, he or she will not be able to pursue given careers. A 150-pound sixteen-year old can hardly aspire to be a jockey.

Deciding on an Occupation Not a great deal is known about the occupational-choice phase of the socialization process. Moore assumes, without the supporting evidence, that a few teachers in the lives of most occupationally successful people have great influence upon the person's occupational choice. Parents' preferences will likewise have an influence. In some cases, the child may decide that he or she wants the same career as his or her father or mother, and in other cases he or she may explicitly decide that this is not desirable. In addition to teachers and parents, other significant people, such as friends, relatives, and neighbors, influence the decision-making process. This array of significant others becomes an important source of information about possible occupational careers.

In some areas of life, the person choosing an occupation may receive on-the-job training before a total commitment to that occupation is required. Thus, during high school one may have a part-time job in a gas station and learn rudimentary auto mechanics. The college student may do some teaching before committing to an educational career.

Although apprenticeship training is available to some, by and large the socialization that takes place in this early decision-making phase overwhelmingly occurs symbolically. The individual gathers information and imagines what life would be like in that occupation. This process of *anticipatory socialization* not only aids the individual in deciding upon an occupation but undoubtedly facilitates the development and acceptance of values needed in a given occupation. Many of those values typical of an occupation become internalized during the process of occupational identity formation, for example, the process of saying to oneself and believing that "I am a flight attendant, a doctor, a jockey."

Occupational Commitment After the person has decided on an occupation, the next phase is the development of the necessary commitment. This sustained intrapsychic commitment comes largely from the development of the occupational identity, which forms over time as one performs the ascribed work role. Each occupation requires the worker to meet expectations. As the person repeatedly meets those expectations, he or she comes to accept the newly acquired occupational status as truly descriptive of him or her as an individual. Once this cognitive connection is made between social-status characteristics and individually possessed characteristics, the identity formation is complete.

Most occupations require a trial period in which individuals train and are tried to see if they can adequately perform the new work. University professors receive tenure after years in a "temporary" position. Doctors spend years as interns. Jockeys, during the beginning years, are given special advantages in races, after which they must compete on a par with fully accepted jockeys. During these trial periods, either the individual or those representing the occupational world (social structure) can choose to end the association. If not severed, it is expected that the individual develops the requisite occupational identity and meets the minimal commitment requirements.

SOCIALIZATION INTO DEVIANT GROUPS

The various phases of socialization described to this point have all been "mainstream" socialization. The influences involved in the socialization process (family, occupation, education, and so on) thus far are all accepted parts of the larger social fabric and tend to reflect the basic value structure found in the larger social setting. Generally, the goals and means of socialization practiced by the different social institutions or groups are consistent with each other. However, occasionally a group emerges with goals and purposes contrary to those of most of the other social institutions. Because such groups are trying to socialize attitudes and behavior counter to other institutions, they must be very explicit about the socialization of new members and therefore often utilize extreme techniques. The conflict in socialization between such deviant groups and the rest of society provides valuable information about the effectiveness of different socialization techniques.

The Unification Church, whose members are commonly known as "Moonies" after its leader, Rev. Sun Myung Moon, is an example of a force for deviant socialization that received widespread attention in the mass media during the 1970s. The attention centered around the issue of whether people are simply products of their environments or whether they can direct their own courses. Parents of young converts of the Unification Church

Socialization concerning appropriate dress is apparent in the appearance of these members of a deviant social group. *Source*: Nancy Kaye, Leo de Wys, Inc.

claim that their adult children have been unwillingly brainwashed and are not responsible for what they have become. Many parents have gone to the extreme of having professional deprogrammers "kidnap" their children and resocialize them into the mainstream of American society. The courts have become the battleground. The Unification Church claims that forced deprogramming violates the civil rights of the young adults; parents contend that their children are powerless against the Moonies' socialization techniques.

The Unification Church has had considerable success in winning converts, claiming to have seven thousand "core" members in the United States in 1976. The typical convert is a middle-class young adult with some college education (*Newsweek* 1976, p. 61). The conversion process starts by inviting potential converts to spend a weekend at a "Creative Community Project." The activity is designed to interest young adults and to make them feel a part of something worthwhile or meaningful. Those participants who react favorably are invited to return for longer periods of time, and those that do are exposed to a very rigorous socialization process. Letters, phone calls, and visitors are all turned away. Long sessions of interrogation and indoctrination alternate with work to deprive the recruit of sleep. Diet is restricted as well. The individual is subjected to very strong group pressures from members to accept the doctrines being taught. The content of the indoctrination involves a rejection of American society, including the family, as they are defined as "satanic" ways of the world (*Newsweek* 1976, pp. 61–62). This initial stage of the socialization process is to convince the recruit to become a permanent member of the group.

Once the individual makes this commitment, he or she then participates in months of mental, moral, social, and physical reform. As the member accepts the doctrine, she or he is permitted greater exposure to the outside world and may be involved in recruiting others. Eventually, the new member develops an identity as a member of the Unification Church and accepts Dr. and Mrs. Moon as his true parents. She or he renounces ties with the traditional world, gives all her or his wealth to the church, and works for her or his new parents.

Parents, educators, religious leaders, and others in society have become somewhat alarmed by these activities. However, the professional deprogrammers use resocialization techniques that in some ways are similar to those used by the Moonies themselves. The captured Moonie is taken to a motel or a hotel and kept in relative isolation under constant guard. The stay is usually for only a few days and involves intensive interrogation and indoctrination by the deprogrammer and former family and friends. The intent is to raise enough doubts in the person's mind so that he or she will cooperate and not attempt to run away. After two or three days, the person is taken to a rehabilitation center where the "true nature of the Moonies" is taught while his or her ties with the traditional world are reestablished.

Whether one considers the socialization practices of the "Moonies" and other cults extreme and bordering on mind control, or whether one considers the capturing of "Moonies" as illegally violating human rights, both the cults and deprogrammers practice some basic socialization processes. In both instances, the youth are given normative information, asked to make their behavior conform to these expectations, and asked to fashion an identity as a cult member or as a member of their "real" family and "real" society. Once internalization of the group's normative standards has occurred, the individual is then accepted as a functioning member of that group.

Summary

Socialization is the process by which an individual becomes an adequately functioning member of a group. The individual internalizes the normative dimensions of the social group, and these internalized social norms govern behavior.

The study of socialization raises some very basic questions about the nature of humans and the nature of the social order. Traditional socialization research has begun with the existing social group and has asked how a new member comes to acquire the appropriate values and behavior required for group membership. This approach tends to see the existent social order as responsible for the socialization outcome; thus, the individual is seen as a passive rather than an active agent in the socialization process. Self-actualization theorists tend to ascribe to the individual basic characteristics that facilitate socialization. The psychoanalytic approach tends to see society as necessary in order to restrain basic antisocial tendencies inherent in the human being.

Socialization under extreme conditions allows some insight into these basic questions. Children raised with little or no human contact fail to acquire human characteristics, but, when given normal training, some of them show remarkable ability to acquire many of the attitudes, values, and speech behavior characteristic of normal social adults.

The psychoanalytic approach to socialization calls attention to the importance of the basic parent/child relationship and the identification process that channels the id's energy sources into adult use of the ego and superego. The social-learning approach has traditionally focused on behavior and analyzed reward and punishment schedules associated with the acquisition and extinction of various behaviors. Social learning uses few concepts referring to mental processes, such as internalization. However, more recent social-learning researchers and theorists have begun to develop concepts that point to internal cognitive processes in an effort to better understand thought and behavior in socialization.

The symbolic-cognitive approach highlights the individual as an actor who continually constructs his or her own meaning system. Any socialization outcome, to be adequately understood, must be seen as part of the person's cognitive development. Each theoretical approach gives differential emphasis to feelings, behavior, and thought, respectively.

In the family, the first and most important socialization institution in contemporary societies, research shows that parental behavior characterized by a relatively high amount of emotional support and a reason-based discipline is positively associated with socially valued outcomes in the child, and environments characterized by low parental support and coercive discipline appear to be associated with outcomes that are not valued.

Socialization does not end with childhood or adolescence but continues throughout a person's life. Adult socialization is distinguished from childhood socialization by the importance of choice and anticipatory socialization. The adult chooses which social roles he or she will move into and as a result is seen as more responsible for the socialized outcomes. Whereas early socialization tends to equip the individual in a general nature for adequate membership in the group, socialization into roles prepares the individual to function in role-specific situations. Thus, much adult socialization occurs only after the individual has moved into a specific role.

Socialization varies in its processes and products by social class. The blue-collar classes tend to use more direct and physical methods of control and have a set of values emphasizing conformity to external standards. The white-collar classes emphasize symbolic modes of discipline with a set of values giving primacy to self-direction and creativity. Socialization into an occupation appears to be completed when the individual has accepted as descriptive of himself or herself the social occupational label. He or she then has the requisite commitment to perform the necessary behavior and regulate his or her occupational life according to the normative structure.

Generally, socialization proceeds rather smoothly because most social groups are mutually supportive. However, deviant groups with purposes counter to the more basic institutions in the society create considerable strain on the individual as these institutions struggle to assert their own right to carry out the socialization of members, thereby vying for the individual's commitment.

5

social influence:
norms,
conformity,
obedience,
and independence

SAN DIEGO (UPI)—The Marines who gave Pvt. Lynn McClure the beating that killed him say he was on his knees screaming "God make them stop," as relays of bigger recruits bashed him with pugil sticks for about 45 minutes to prove to their drill sergeants they were "motivated."

The Marine Corps Wednesday ordered three sergeants and a captain to face courts martial on charges ranging up to negligent homicide and manslaughter in the death of McClure, 20, of Lufkin, Texas.

The colonel commanding McClure's regiment was disciplined by unspecified punishment announced Maj. Gen. Kenneth Houghton, commander of the Marine Corps Recruit Depot.

McClure, described as mentally retarded, died March 13, three months after he suffered massive brain damage in a beating during training at the depot. He never regained consciousness.

In interviews published today by the Los Angeles Times, four former recruits said drill sergeants ordered them to beat McClure, one after another, in bouts with pugil sticks, padding-tipped poles used in bayonet training.

According to the article, they said McClure repeatedly complained that he was injured and refused to fight, threw down his stick and helmet and ran screaming from the ring. But they said the sergeants dragged him back, ordering the others to beat him as he lay on the ground.

"We were like animals," said Robert Evans, now discharged, who said he struck the final blow and has been troubled by nightmares ever since.

Recruits could get out of the undesirable platoon by showing motivation, he said, and with the sergeants egging them on they took turns beating McClure "to prove to the drill instructor that we could make good Marines."

"Just to beat on this guy gave us the feeling that the drill instructor liked this and that we were really showing motivation."[1]

Few issues have attracted as much attention in the popular press in the past decade as have the closely related issues of *conformity* to group expectations and *obedience* to the commands and dictates of others. This was the period in which 104 unarmed men, women, and children were massacred in the now infamous My Lai "incident." The court martial and trial of Lieutenant William Calley wrestled at length with the question of the extent to which an individual can be held personally responsible for his or her behavior when under orders from someone else. Like the Nazi war criminals of over two decades earlier, many of the My Lai participants attempted to justify their behavior by asserting that they were only doing what they were commanded to do. Similarly, participants in the beating of the marine recruit found justification in noting that they were only doing what the drill instructor wanted them to do. The criminal convictions following the Watergate scandal of many Presidential allies and advisors also raised this question. Again, the common excuse for participation in these illegal activities by several men who were themselves highly trained in the law was that they felt a need to "go along" and to not question the directives of those placed over them.

My Lai, Watergate, the Nazi war crimes, and the beating death of Pvt. Lynn McClure all have a common element: they all involve individuals

---

[1]Source: "Courts Ordered in Beating Death." *The Daily Herald,* Provo, Utah. April 29, 1976, p. 20. Reprinted by permission of United Press International.

engaging in actions having serious negative consequences, including death, for other individuals, at the instruction of a third individual or set of individuals. How can we account for what happens when the individual almost totally turns over to someone else the right and ability to make the decisions that govern his or her action, even when the required action has such potentially horrible consequences? Wrightsman has proposed that "... conscience operates when each individual is working on his or her own, but when the person functions in the 'organizational mode', ... one's individual conscience is no longer relevant. Such persons are operating in an *agentic state*, or a condition in which the person sees himself as an agent for carrying out another person's wishes, in contrast to a state of *autonomy*, or acting on one's own. Hence, we get the obedient subject, the Eichmann, the Lt. Calley, the Watergate conspirators" (1974, p. 804).

However, does being in an *agentic state* fully explain the actions described? Do we live in a society in which "going along to get along" is the accepted mode of response? What conditions are likely to promote independence and greater individual willingness to assume and accept personal responsibility for behavior with its attendant consequences? These are some of the questions we will strive to answer in this chapter.

Norms and Social Influence

As noted in chapter 1, the influence of the social group on individual behavior has been one of the primary concerns of social psychology since its beginning. Social-psychological research has consistently noted that the presence of others, "whether in the immediate sense or in the actor's psychological definition of the situation" (Warner and DeFleur, 1969, p. 155), exerts influence on the individual to act in a manner that is consistent with what those others are perceived to feel is appropriate and desirable conduct.

In some of the earliest experimental work done in social psychology (Allport, 1920), it was noted that behavior in groups tends to differ from behavior that occurs in private settings. Allport found that the presence of a coworking group, as compared to subjects working alone, was distinctly favorable to the speed of progress subjects attained in a free word-association problem.

In a similar study designed to test whether the presence of others facilitated the speed with which subjects performed various tasks, Dashiell (1930) found that persons working in group settings did indeed work faster than when working alone. Of perhaps even more interest was the observation that it was not necessary for the others to be present in the immediate situation. Subjects who performed the task knowing that others were working simultaneously with them on identical tasks worked much faster, even though the others were not immediately present.

The idea of social influence or of conforming to the expectations of the group implies the existence of some *standard* around which our attitudes and behavior cluster. That standard is most often socially defined and so can be referred to as a *social norm*. Social norms constitute "ought to" definitions; they define for us the behaviors and attitudes that are appropriate for given situations; they tell us what we ought to do and, conversely, what we ought not to do.

From a sociological perspective, norms constitute one of the essential ingredients that hold the fabric of society together. Along with attending sanctions, they account largely for the existence of social order. Without some degree of adherence to normative prescriptions, social life would be characterized by general disorganization and chaos. This can be readily demonstrated from the observation of what happens in countries during the initial stages of great crises, such as depression and war: the normative structure of society that has guided the behavior of individual citizens often breaks down, and social life is characterized by disarray and anarchy until new norms emerge to help provide meaning and direction to individual behavior.

From a social-psychological perspective, adherence to social norms helps to account for the regularities in individual behavior. As we grow to maturity, we are taught through the socialization process that certain types of behavior are appropriate and acceptable and others are inappropriate and unacceptable. Sanctions, in the form of approval, praise, scorn, or punishment, are used to enforce the norms. Behavior that is consistent with social norms brings approval from others, and this increases the probability of such behavior occurring again. Behavior contrary to norms, on the other hand, usually elicits disapproval or some other form of negative sanction, decreasing the probability that similar behavior will be repeated.

THE ORIGIN OF SOCIAL NORMS

The early American sociologist William Graham Sumner (1904) proposed that much of our daily action is governed by *folkways,* or relatively informal traditions and customs that are passed from one generation to the next. Sumner argued that the ability to rely on such norms in reaching decisions about the action we should take or the attitude we should express is a great advantage in most instances because otherwise the burden of rationally considering all possible choices in each action or situation would be unendurable.

Perhaps the best explanation of how norms originate lies in the observation that norms emerge to provide meaning and structure in what would otherwise be an ambiguous situation. Sumner's folkways are rules of behavior that have developed in the past to define appropriate and inappropriate responses as individuals confront new situations and new decisions. The particular sets of rules or responses that are adopted over a period of time are probably those that have contributed most to group survival and adaptation to group environment. We continue to follow many of these folkways because we face similar situations today. This point can be further illustrated when we note how uncomfortable we feel in situations for which we feel inadequately prepared, such as when we are first introduced into a new group of people or begin our first day on a job. In such situations, the norms or standards of behavior may not be clearly defined and provided. Therefore, new groups will often spend their first hours together "establishing the ground rules."

As shown in *Lord of the Flies* (Golding, 1954), the need for norms to govern behavior was quickly felt by the English schoolboys whose airplane crashed on an uninhabited island. There were no adults; however, they realized they needed rules, and they structured a society that relied heavily on their English schoolboy rules and traditions. Because the situation created needs not covered by their norms (such as food gathering) and because they could not agree on a new set of rules, their society broke down, and murder ensued. New norms emerge, then, to fill gaps left by the ambiguity or the inapplicability of existing norms. Some degree of consensus on the new norms is necessary, or the outcome is likely to be anarchy and destruction.

The emergence of norms in response to ambiguity is vividly illustrated by early research conducted by Muzafer Sherif (1936), who employed what is called the *autokinetic effect* in studying the process of norm formation. The autokinetic effect is the phenomenon that occurs when a pinpoint of light is viewed in what is otherwise a totally dark room: a totally stationary light will appear to move. In one of his experiments, Sherif brought a group of subjects into a dark room to observe a pinpoint of light and then asked them to estimate how far the light moved. Sherif was very successful in creating a situation totally ambiguous in a physical sense because there were no criteria available for the subjects to use in estimating movement of the light.

After a series of trials, Sherif began to observe a most interesting social-psychological phenomenon: the range of estimates by his respondents began to converge toward the mean. For example, after the first trial, the range of estimated movement varied from two or three inches to several times that amount. After additional trials, the more extreme estimates tended to become less extreme, therefore moving toward the mean. Eventually, the group came to establish a *norm* or a generally agreed-upon estimate of light movement. Respondents who helped develop this group norm then tended to continue to use it in responding in later trials when they were by themselves. In other words, a social norm developed to provide meaning to an ambiguous situation.

Other social psychologists (see Secord and Backman, 1974) have noted that we rely on at least two sources of information to determine the validity of our opinions and actions—*physical reality* and *social reality.* Our senses obtain a good deal of information from the physical environment around us and, to some extent, our opinions and behaviors are evaluated and determined on the basis of this physical reality. However, social reality, or the evaluation and judgment of other persons, often acts as an even more important source of information. In this sense, other people define and interpret our world for us, which is why we often look to the response of others before taking action ourselves. The key seems to be that the more ambiguous the physical stimuli, the more likely we are to rely on social definitions of reality. There are many situations in which we find ourselves (for example, we have just taken a new job) where the physical cues are insufficient to provide us with adequate direction concerning the most appropriate response. In such situations, we must rely heavily on group direction—what is the generally accepted social definition of the situation?

Numerous examples are available in the social-psychological literature that support this contention. One of the most interesting is the study (Cantril, 1940) of the widespread panic brought on by Orson Welles' reading of H. G. Welles's "War of the Worlds," a science fiction tale of the invasion of the Eastern United States by aliens from outer space. The radio drama was presented in the format of on-the-scene descriptions and vivid accounts of destruction and chaos. Thousands of listeners, many of whom apparently tuned in after the program had begun, defined the events as real, and panicked. Police switchboards were clogged with incoming calls, and intersections were jammed by people fleeing their homes.

With our current knowledge of science and entertainment, it is difficult for us to understand why so many listeners failed to realize that it was simply a dramatization and, instead, feared that their lives were endangered by the alien invaders. However, social definitions of the situation, which would be based on state-of-the-art radio drama compared to Welles' innovative reading, apparently filled the gap provided by physical ambiguity. Listeners could not rush to the window and see the invaders, but they could interpret their inability to get a call through to the local police as a result of alien destruction of communication lines. In the heat of panic, the same definition could apparently be applied to very different conditions. For example, some people rushed to the window and saw a great deal of traffic, which they defined as a result of large numbers of people fleeing before their attackers. Some others looked out and saw no traffic, but they defined this as the result of everyone having already been killed. Both interpretations led to panic.

CHANGING NORMS IN CHANGING CONDITIONS

Although social norms usually arise in response to ambiguous situations to provide guidelines for future behavior, society is not static, and in some instances normative definitions change rather quickly and dramatically. A vivid illustration of changing norms is set forth in the box below.

New Norms for New Conditions

One of the most poignant illustrations of how norms change in response to immediate pressures of the situation is found in the actions taken by a group of young Uruguayan rugby players in their effort to survive.

On October 12, 1972, at Carrasco Airport near Montevideo, forty-five passengers boarded a Uruguayan Air Force plane en route to Santiago, Chile. Fourteen of the passengers were members of a rugby club composed primarily of socially prominent young men from Montevideo. Most of the remaining passengers were friends and family of the club members. While crossing the Andes, the plane was caught in a late winter storm and crashed. The fuselage of the airliner slid back from the point of impact into a bowl-like valley where shadows helped hide it from the search planes that flew overhead. The plane crashed above the vegetation level; temperatures hovered around five to fifteen degrees, and winds reached up to eighty miles per hour. Sixteen people were killed in the crash or died in the first few days. The only things on the plane for the others to eat were some chocolates, some bottles of wine, and toothpaste. These were soon gone, and the group of survivors faced a critical decision: they could either starve to death, or they could choose to eat the only food source that was available to them—their dead companions.

By about the eighth day, several of the hungry survivors had begun seriously discussing eating the dead. These were very religious young men, and one can hardly imagine the difficulty of the decision they faced. On the tenth day, after the air search had been called off and after they had been declared lost, the first members of the group turned to cannibalism.

Sixteen of the young Uruguayans survived the horror of seventy-two days on the mountain before the weather warmed and two of them were able to walk down for help. During this time they had been forced to make a decision that most individuals hope they will never have to make. The decision was clearly contrary to what most would recognize as an important social norm. However, it was made because of a commitment to another—that of survival and self-preservation.

> The moment came when we had no food, and we thought: if Jesus shared His body and blood with the apostles at the Last Supper, up there He was letting us know that we must do the same. We took His body and blood that had been reincarnated
> (Alfredo Delgado, in explanation).

> It was then that we made the dramatic decision: in order to survive, we would leap any obstacle, break any biological or religious barrier. Thanks to that decision we are alive
> (Fernando Parrado, in Santiago).

(Source: Richard Cunningham, *The Place Where the World Ends* New York: Sheed and Ward, 1973.)

Even in familiar situations (as opposed to the "new world" in *Lord of the Flies* or that faced by the Uruguayan survivors), new norms are developing, and old ones are changing. Normative changes being institutionalized in American society in response to the contemporary feminist movement pro-

Two bodies lie in the snow in the Andes Mountains beside the wreckage of their plane. 16 of 45 passengers survived 69 days in the freezing mountains, some of whom acknowledged eating human flesh to stay alive. *Source:* Wide World Photos, Inc.

vide a good example. The lives of very few Americans remain untouched by these changes, which include an ever-increasing percentage of women in the labor force, the opening to women of careers and professions that have, in the past, been largely the domain of men, efforts to eliminate sexism in our language, and so on. Public attitudes toward the proper and acceptable roles of women in society reflect these important changes. For example, between 1935 and 1971, the percentage of Americans who expressed a willingness to vote for a woman for President increased from 34 percent to 66 percent (Gallup, 1972).

Similar normative shifts have occurred in other areas of behavior. Clothing and hair styles, consumption patterns, and political behavior are examples. Continual changes in each of these areas suggest that although we must certainly agree that much of our behavior is determined by social definitions of appropriate and inappropriate conduct, those definitions continue to change.

Conformity

We noted above that the more ambiguous the physical stimuli, the more likely we are to rely on social definitions of the situation. Interest in the study of conformity by social psychologists increased dramatically when they began to accumulate systematic data indicating that many individuals go along with group definitions even when doing so means behaving contrary to the evidence provided by available physical stimuli. In effect, *conformity* in social-psychological research has come to be defined as yielding to group expectations or definitions of the situation. It implies some degree of conflict between what the group demands of the individual and what the individual would otherwise do.

Conformity has become a much-maligned concept in America in recent years, perhaps in part because of the popularity of such works as *The Lonely Crowd* (Riesman, Glazer, and Denney, 1950). These authors argued that societies are characterized by different types and degrees of conformity. Individuals living in *tradition-directed* societies rely primarily on norms and standards handed down from the past. Acceptable behaviors are those behaviors approved by the elders. *Inner-directed* societies are characterized by individuals who rely primarily on a set of internalized norms to govern their behavior. Through the socialization process, they have learned and accepted a particular behavioral code, and this internalized code provides a guide in decision-making situations. Whereas the tradition-directed society relies on sanctions imposed by the elders or other persons occupying traditionally defined positions of social control, the inner-directed society relies on self-imposed sanctions. The inner-directed person who behaves contrary to an internalized norm feels guilty for having broken the rules.

More characteristic of American society of the middle twentieth century is what the authors call the *other-directed* person, who continually looks to others for directives concerning appropriate and inappropriate behavior. This is the person who goes along with the crowd in order to be popular and feel accepted, even when going along with the crowd means engaging in behavior that is contrary to personal norms and values. The other-directed person is governed by expediency; behavior fluctuates as the situation and the audience change. To predict behavior, we really need to know very little about the attitudes of the actor. Rather, we should try to determine the orientation of the group in which the actor happens to find himself. Sanctions are imposed by the group on the individual when nonconformity occurs, and the other-directed person wants to avoid these sanctions. The other-directed person is a conformist in a negative sense of the word because he or she goes along even when to do so is contrary to personal values. Although we all conform, and conformity to a degree is necessary in order to avoid societal chaos, the other-directed person carries it too far.

Overconformity can often have consequences that are as dysfunctional to society as are those associated with nonconformity. Robert Merton (1957a) defined the overconformer as a *ritualist* and suggested that such a person loses sight of important goals or ends because of a ritual overemphasis of the means that have been specified to attain those goals. More recently, Janis (1972) has suggested that the *groupthink* syndrome grows out of overconformity and group efforts to maintain consensus. Groupthink is most likely to occur in highly cohesive groups and involves the process whereby the group becomes so involved in maintaining unanimity of thought that its ability to evaluate issues critically is seriously impaired. According to Janis, groupthink seriously impairs decision making, reality testing, and moral judgment, and has contributed to such seriously faulty decisions as the Bay

Problems of overconformity led to events such as Watergate. *Source:* Wide World Photos, Inc.

of Pigs invasion of Cuba. Janis summarizes the groupthink syndrome as having the following properties (1972, pp. 197–98):

1. An illusion of invulnerability, shared by most or all the members, that creates excessive optimism and encourages taking extreme risks.
2. Collective efforts to rationalize in order to discount warnings that might lead the members to reconsider their assumptions before they recommit themselves to their past policy decisions.
3. An unquestioned belief in the group's inherent morality, inclining the members to ignore the ethical or moral consequences of their decisions.
4. Stereotyped views of enemy leaders as too evil to warrant genuine attempts to negotiate, or as too weak and stupid to counter whatever risky attempts are made to defeat their purposes.
5. Direct pressure on any member who expresses strong arguments against any of the group's stereotypes, illusions, or commitments, making clear that this type of dissent is contrary to what is expected of all loyal members.
6. Self-censorship of deviations from the apparent group consensus, reflecting each member's inclination to minimize to himself the importance of his doubts and counter-arguments.
7. A shared illusion of unanimity concerning judgments conforming to the majority view (partly resulting from self-censorship of deviations, augmented by the false assumption that silence means consent).
8. The emergence of self-appointed mindguards—members who protect the group from adverse information that might shatter their shared complacency about the effectiveness and morality of their decisions.

Although "types" of personality orientations are factors affecting conformity, personal values and attributes do not develop independently of

Group conformity: worshippers praying inside a Mosque in Lahore, Pakistan. *Source:* United Nations.

group orientations. That is, inner-directed people are products of societies that approve and encourage inner direction, and other-directed individuals are products of groups that stress other direction. It is recognition of the importance of different historical emphases that adds significance to *The Lonely Crowd,* in which the authors contend that different historical periods have "produced" different personality types because of their different emphases.

GROUP CONFORMITY VERSUS INDIVIDUAL JUDGMENT

As noted above, conformity as a social psychological phenomenon takes on more interest in those instances in which going along with group definitions entails behavior that is either contrary to individual values and preferences or to input from physical stimuli. The central question becomes that of what happens when the individual's privately held attitudes, perceptions, and definitions of the situation conflict with the position taken by the group. A series of classic studies by Solomon Asch (1951, 1952, 1956) demonstrate one example of what happens when the individual's privately held attitudes, perceptions, and definitions of the situation conflict with the position taken by the group.

Asch's basic experimental procedure involved using a number of student assistants who acted as confederates in order to assess the conforming behavior of a naive subject. Several individuals were brought together in the experimental laboratory. If there were eight subjects in the study, for example, seven of these were actually working for the experimenter, though this was not known to the eighth. The group was told that they were going to participate in a study of perception. Each member of the group was requested to draw a number from a hat that would designate the seating arrangement. All the slips of paper in the hat were marked with the number seven to guarantee that the experimental subject would be in the next to final seat; the confederates sat themselves in a prearranged order in the row of desks provided. The experimenter came into the room with two stacks of 6 x 18 inch cards. The cards were shown to the subjects in pairs; one card of each pair had a single line, and the second had three lines, one of which was equal in length to the single line on the first card (see figure 5–1). The subjects were to indicate which line on the second card was equal in length to the line on the first card.

CARD 1　　　　　　　CARD 2

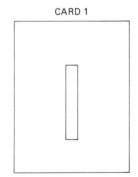
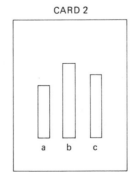

Figure 5–1 The Asch Conformity Experiment. The Asch experiment involved a procedure somewhat like that depicted here. The subjects were simultaneously shown the two cards and were asked to indicate which of the lines of Card 2 was equal in length to the single line on Card 1. The correct answer was usually quite obvious, as demonstrated by the fact that when alone the subjects were able to make the right choice almost without exception.

The situation developed by Asch was hardly ambiguous in that it was relatively easy to make the correct selection. This was demonstrated by having subjects in a control group respond to the two cards by themselves, without the intervening effect of the group. In such cases, almost perfect scores were recorded by the subjects. During the first two trials of the group experiments, each of the confederates were instructed to give the correct response. Following this, they began systematically to give a preselected incorrect response. Suddenly, what had been an easy and somewhat monotonous task for the experimental subject became a source of great concern and attention. Were his eyes deceiving him? Had all the rest of the group gone crazy? Did they have a different angle? Perhaps little concern was registered as the first one or two subjects gave an obviously incorrect answer, but after hearing six prior respondents agree on a choice that appeared very obviously incorrect, the naive subject was faced with a dilemma.

In this basic experimental condition, Asch found that the subject would conform with the group and give an obviously incorrect answer in approximately 37 percent of the trials. Although this is not an overwhelmingly high figure, it is interesting that, on the average, a respondent would give an answer contrary to what all of his senses indicated as correct in order to go along with the group over one-third of the time.

Several other experimental conditions were tried by Asch and later by other colleagues (Crutchfield, 1955; Deutsch and Gerard, 1955; Levy, 1960). In general, these studies have demonstrated that the size of the majority is not critical after it reaches about three. The naive subject was as likely to conform if three or five other respondents gave a unanimous incorrect response as he or she would be if seven other respondents gave the incorrect response. One finding of particular interest was the observation that if the naive subject was given one confederate, the probability of conforming to the group decreased dramatically. In other words, assuming the eight-person experimental situation, if someone else gave the correct response, then the probability of the naive subject giving the correct answer was greatly increased (conformity to the erroneous group judgment declined from an average of over 30 percent to approximately 5 percent). This finding has been confirmed by Allen and Levine (1971), who observed that even when this social support comes from someone who is wearing thick glasses (thus throwing some doubt on his or her ability to correctly evaluate line lengths) conformity to majority-group opinion is reduced. Overall, the Allen and Levine research found that the more valid and credible the information provided by the ally, the more likely the subject was to concur with him or her in opposition to majority-group opinion. In addition, certain personality factors along with things such as self-confidence, a previous history of success, and the public versus private nature of response were all found to be important.

Building upon the observation of the importance of having an ally, Kimball and Hollander (1974) observed that this effect is compounded when the stimuli are more ambiguous and when the ally is believed to be experienced. In fact, research by Kimball and Holland has shown that the presence of a group member who was defined as being experienced in such tasks and who exhibited a high level of independence from the group led to significantly increased independence by the naive subject from *all* the others, including the independent role model.

Some recent critics interpret the findings of all these experiments as a result of the demand characteristics of the experimental procedures. That is, subjects are not conforming to the behavior of the experimental confederates but to what they define as the expectations of the experimenter. It is important to recognize, however, that the value of this research for understanding conformity remains, no matter which interpretation of results holds.

NORMATIVE AND INFORMATIONAL INFLUENCE

Deutsch and Gerard (1955), in commenting upon some of the early conformity experiments, have pointed out that we need to distinguish between *normative influence* and *informational influence.* The individual under normative influence goes along with the group largely out of a desire to be accepted by the group, even when to do so may involve behavior that is potentially contrary to the individual's own values and perceptions. Informational influence emerges out of the desire to increase certainty about the correctness of the response; the individual sometimes conforms to the group simply because he or she is personally unsure about the appropriate course of action. This is not rejecting individuality in favor of the group but is relying on the group for assistance in making the proper decision. In more ambiguous situations, such as in Sherif's autokinetic-effect studies, informational influence is probably operating. However, in the Asch studies and in research on obedience (see next section), normative influence becomes more critical.

What about historical trends in conforming behavior? Riesman, Glazer, and Denney (1950) argued that we are becoming more conformity-oriented in the "normative influence" meaning of the word. They felt that the socialization experience of young people in American society was coming to emphasize more and more the importance of popularity and group acceptance. Being popular, in other words, was becoming more important than being right. On the other hand, James Davis (1975) presented evidence that indicates that we are becoming more tolerant of nonconformity in others. In 1955, Samuel Stouffer published an important study of American attitudes toward Communists, atheists, and socialists using data from a large national sample. During 1972–1973, the National Opinion Research Center reused the Stouffer items in another national survey, and Davis has analyzed these data in light of the earlier study. Table 5–1 summarizes responses from both national surveys on two items.

Overall, Davis found that during the two decades there had been an average increase of about 23 percent in tolerant responses. In other words, in the 1970s Americans were much more willing to allow free expression of ideas by someone who was different from them. These results suggest that perhaps the trend toward overconformity set forth in *The Lonely Crowd* has reversed itself in more recent years.

BEYOND CONFORMITY: OBEDIENCE

Although the Asch experiments suggested the degree to which group definitions can affect individual responses, critics observed that there may be few significant applications of the findings; going along with the group in specifying the length of lines does not mean that such behaviors would be gener-

Table 5–1 Public Tolerance Toward Communists and Atheists in 1954 and 1972–73

	PROPORTION GIVING TOLERANT RESPONSE	
Questions	*1954*	*1972–1973*
There are always some people whose ideas are considered bad or dangerous by other people, for instance, somebody who is against all churches and religion.		
A. If such a person wanted to make a speech in your city (town, community) against churches and religion, should he be allowed to speak, or not?	38	66
B. Should such a person be allowed to teach in a college or university, or not?	12	42
C. If some people in your community suggested that a book he wrote against churches and religion should be taken out of your public library, would you favor removing this book, or not?	37	71
Now, I should like to ask you some questions about a man who admits he is a Communist.		
A. Suppose this admitted Communist wanted to make a speech in your community. Should he be allowed to speak, or not?	28	57
B. Suppose he is teaching in a college. Should he be fired, or not?	06	38
C. Suppose he wrote a book which is in your public library. Somebody in your community suggests that the book should be removed from the library. Would you favor removing it, or not?	29	58

Adapted from Davis, 1975, p. 495, 506.

alized to other types of social situations. For example, could these findings be generalized to situations wherein going along with the group could cause physical or psychological pain to someone else? In a series of studies that paralleled and went well beyond the Asch research, Stanley Milgram (1963, 1964, 1965, 1974) provided interesting experimental evidence on this question.

The Milgram Experiments Under the guise of doing research on social learning, Milgram conducted a series of studies that are both exciting and frightening in their implications. The research has generated extensive debate on the ethical issues involved in doing such studies. (These ethical questions are discussed in chapter 13.) In addition, many of Milgram's conclusions have come under attack by professional colleagues (Wrightsman, 1974).

The basic design of the Milgram experiments involved inviting volunteers to participate in what was billed as a study of the effects of punishment on memory and learning. Volunteers were recruited from the local community through a newspaper advertisement, which simply stated that five hundred men were needed to participate in a study of memory and learning to be conducted at Yale University. Volunteers were to be paid $4 plus car fare for approximately one hour of their time. No further obligations were entailed. The ad emphasized that no special training, education, or experience was needed. The only requirements were that participants be between twenty and fifty years old and that they not be high school or college students. Individuals who responded to the ad were contacted and appointments were set up.

Upon their arrival, volunteers were met by one of Milgram's research associates who conducted them into the research lab. At this point, they found themselves in one of several different experimental conditions that were really designed to assess their conformity to group pressure or their obedience to commands issued by the experimenter rather than to assess the effect of punishment on learning.

In one of the experimental conditions (Milgram, 1964), the volunteer was part of a four-person group. Unknown to him, the other three people were working for the experimenter. The four people were told that each would be assigned a different role and, to make the role assignments fair, each would draw a slip of paper with the designated role from a hat. In all cases, the drawing was rigged so that the naive subject was assigned the role of Teacher 3. The different role assignments that subjects drew from the hat were as follows (Milgram, 1964, p. 138, reprinted by permission):

ROLE TITLE	PARTICIPANT	TASK
Teacher 1	Confederate C	First, you will read word pairs to the learner. Then you will read a stimulus word along with four possible answers.
Teacher 2	Confederate A	When the learner gives his answer, your task is to indicate whether he is correct or incorrect. When he has erred, you will provide him with the correct answer.
Teacher 3	Naive Subject	Whenever the learner gives an incorrect answer, you will administer punishment by activating a shock generator.
Learner	Confederate B	Your task will be to learn a list of word pairs read to you by Teacher 1.

When the roles were assigned, the learner was taken to an adjoining room where he was strapped into an apparatus that looked like an electric chair. The other three participants sat before "an imposing shock generator" that had thirty lever switches labeled from 15 to 450 volts in 15-volt increments. The switches also had written designations ranging from "Slight Shock" to "Danger: Severe Shock."

Instructions given the participants indicated that the learner was to be tested on a "paired-associate" learning test that involved Teacher 1 reading through a list of paired words and then going back and reading the first word of the pair again along with four alternatives from which the learner was to select the correct second word of the pair. The teachers were instructed that the learner had to be shocked each time he gave an incorrect answer. However, the level of punishment was to be decided upon by the teachers themselves. Each had to suggest a shock level, beginning with Teacher 1. However, the shock administered was to be the lowest level suggested by any of the three. Thus, the naive subject (Teacher 3) actually had control at all times over the shock he administered *if* he resisted going along with the two confederates.

Once the study began, the confederates called for a one-step (15 volt) increase in shock level each time the learner made a mistake. The naive subject had the option of submitting to group pressure, continuing to increase the shock level along with the assumed suffering and pain for the learner, or maintaining his independence and administering low-level, less-painful shocks. The decision was made more difficult by the fact that the learner did more than just provide correct or incorrect answers; as the shock level increased, he began to protest, and the protests became more vociferous at each increase in voltage. At 75 volts, he grunted; at 120 volts, he shouted that the shocks were becoming painful; at 150 volts, the learner demanded to be released from the experiment, citing a heart condition. "Cries of this type continue with generally rising intensity, so that at 180 volts, the learner cries out 'I can't stand the pain,' and by 285 volts his response to the shock is clearly an agonized scream. At 300 volts the victim shouts in desperation that he will no longer provide answers to the memory test, and so forth through 450 volts. In other words, increases in shock level are met by increasingly severe reactions from the person being punished" (Milgram, 1964, p. 139).

To demonstrate the effect of group pressure in this particular experiment, Milgram randomly assigned half his subjects to a control condition wherein the roles of the three teachers were collapsed into one role that was performed by the naive subject so that the condition included only the naive subject (teacher) and the learner. The naive subject could always make the decision as to which shock level would be administered for incorrect responses without pressure or input from anyone else.

Figure 5–2 shows the shock level administered by subjects in the group condition (where the other two teachers always suggested 15-volt increases in shock levels) compared to the nongroup condition. The effect of group influence is demonstrated by the gap between lines *A* and *B*. The resistance to group pressure is demonstrated by the gap between line A and the line representing the shock level suggested by the two stooges. The mean shock level rises systematically for the experimental group but remains rather stable in the control-group situation. In the experimental group, "subjects are induced by the group to inflict pain on another person at a level that goes well beyond levels chosen in the absence of social pressure" (Milgram, 1964, p. 141). Though the learner continued to express displeasure and pain, a significant percentage of subjects were willing to continue to both administer that pain *and* increase its intensity simply because other persons in the social situation suggested that was what should be done.

In comparing his findings with those of Asch, Milgram observed: "Here

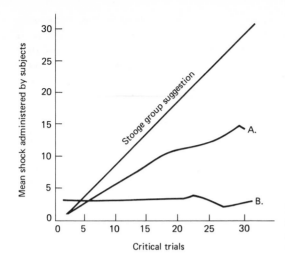

Figure 5–2 Mean Shock Levels in Experimental and Control Conditions Over 30 Critical Trials. Adapted from Milgram, (1964) p. 140. *A* = experimental group, *B* = control group.

the subject does not merely feign agreement with a group on a perceptual task of undefined importance; and he is unable to dismiss his action by relegating it to the status of a trivial gesture, for a person's suffering and discomfort are at stake" (1964, p. 142).

The provocative nature of Milgram's findings is further reinforced by a second experimental condition he employed in his research. In this condition, the roles of the teacher-confederates were eliminated and the subject responded to the commands of the experimenter. In this case, the instructions were that if the learner gave an incorrect response, the shock administered was to start at the lowest level but was to increase by one level each time there was a miss. Responses of the learner were the same as before: grunting and moaning began at 75 volts and increased in intensity up to 300 volts. After that, only an ominous silence came from the room where the learner was strapped in the electric chair. If the subject hesitated or expressed some concern about the pain inflicted on the learner or the possible serious harm, the experimenter simply stated that "the experiment requires that you must go on," or something like, "please continue." For stronger protestations, the experimenter said something like, "whether the learner likes it or not, you must go on until he has learned all the pairs correctly. So please go on" (Elms, 1972, p. 115). Milgram found that under this condition, over 60 percent of the subjects continued to administer shocks to the maximum level of 450 volts. Thus, a surprising majority were willing to engage in actions that they believed were causing serious pain and discomfort to another in simple obedience to the commands of the experimenter.

The reader who is surprised by these findings is certainly not alone. Milgram asked a group of psychiatrists at a leading medical school to predict at which shock level his subjects would refuse to continue. They predicted that less than one percent would administer the full 450 volts.

In evaluating these experiments, it is important to consider the possibility that many of the obedient subjects, though experiencing very real personal stress, were willing to continue administering shocks because they did not believe that an experiment conducted in a university lab (and, particularly, at a place so prestigious as Yale) would really allow them to hurt others. In an important variation of his basic study, Milgram (1965) conducted his research in an office in a commercial building in the downtown shopping area of Bridgeport, Connecticut. The elimination of the scientific trappings and prestige of Yale resulted in a drop in the percentage of obedient subjects from over 60 to 48. Although this is an important shift, it must be emphasized that the 48 percent who were still willing to administer the highest voltage remains a surprisingly high figure.

Proximity and Obedience One of the more interesting findings from the Milgram research came from an analysis of the effect of teacher/learner *proximity* on willingness to obey the instructions of the experimenter. Four conditions of proximity were analyzed. In the first (remote-feedback condition), the teacher and learner were in separate rooms, and the learner could not be heard or seen except for pounding on the wall that occurred at the 300-volt level. In the second condition (voice feedback), vocal protests could be heard through the wall and through a partially open doorway that separated the two rooms. (This was the condition described in the previous section.) In the third (proximity condition), the teacher and learner were placed in the same room approximately 1.5 feet apart. Thus, the subject could readily receive both audible and visible cues to the learner's pain. In the final condition (touch proximity), the shock plate was placed under the learner's hand and the teacher (after 150 volts) actually had to force the learner's hand down upon the plate to administer the shock.

The percentage of obedient subjects administering the highest shock level for each of the four conditions was as follows: remote feedback, 65.0 percent; voice feedback, 62.5 percent; proximity, 40.0 percent; touch proximity, 30.0 percent. Thus, although touch proximity reduced the totally obedient responses by more than half, almost one-third of the subjects were still willing to actually *force* the victim's hand into contact with the shock plate so that the called-for punishment could be given.

Of course, in none of the conditions were shocks actually being administered to the learner. The responses from the learner were all recorded and played back to the naive subject via tape so that all the experimental subjects would hear the same responses. However, they *believed* that they were administering electrical shocks to the learner and that he was feeling pain of increasing intensity as the shock level was increased. Under such conditions, subjects were still willing to administer harm to others either at the suggestion of persons like themselves or the person conducting the experiment.

COMPLIANCE, IDENTIFICATION, AND INTERNALIZATION

The action of Milgram's subjects probably was motivated by factors both similar to and different from those that motivate the teenager who refuses to cut his hair or wear outmoded styles of clothing because none of his peers would do these things. Kelman (1961) has made a rather critical distinction between three different types of conformity. *Compliance* involves acquiescence to group demands *not* because one really identifies with and accepts these demands but because noncompliance could result in punishment or loss of reward. Compliance, then, depends on the observability of one's behavior. We go along so long as others can observe our action and administer sanctions. When that external constraint is removed, behavior is likely to change significantly.

The second type of conformity also involves external factors, but rather than being a response to the threat of punishment or the promise of reward, it involves responding to one's *identification* with another person. The individual goes along with another or adopts an idea or behavior pattern not because it is intrinsically satisfying but because he or she desires to be like the influencer. Conformity contributes to a highly valued, satisfying relationship with another person, such as that between a child and his or her parents. Television commercials rely heavily on identification when they hire famous athletes to endorse their products.

The third mode of conformity noted by Kelman is *internalization*. At this level, the individual has accepted the action and made it a part of her or his own value system. The individual chooses a particular behavior not because of the threat of punishment for not doing so and not because another with whom she or he identifies urges that particular course of action, but because she or he really believes that it is the correct and appropriate way things should be done. The reward in this case is largely internal—the individual feels good when she or he behaves as she or he believes is right.

Several important differences can be noted in these different modes of conformity. Compliance depends on the existence of external constraints, and it is effective only so long as these exist. Identification is effective as a mechanism of conformity only so long as the particular rewarding relationship exists with someone else. If the relationship shifts for some reason, identification is no longer an effective means of social control. Internalization relies on internal rather than external sources of motivation and therefore is likely to be a more permanent means of control than are the other two types, as well as more dependable and less costly. For example, if citizens of a country all have internalized the laws and norms that have been

The imposition of sanctions against one who fails to comply with group norms is a very real part of "club house justice" among some members of various gangs. *Source:* Wide World Photos, Inc.

established to govern their behavior, there is little need for strong external enforcing powers, such as police or military forces. However, if few have internalized the dictates of the state, control can usually be maintained only through force. Thus, so-called police states are just that—stability depends on a strong and effective system of policing the behavior of the citizenry and instituting swift and forceful sanctions to curb deviant behavior. Because of this difference, internalization is likely to be more resistant to change. Certainly, an individual can change attitudes and values as a result of new experiences, but this is usually a gradual, long-term process.

Kelman's three processes can be used to account for the common action of different individuals in the same behavioral context. For example, many Americans conform to the 55 mph maximum speed limits that were instituted for most of the nation's highways, but the reasons for different persons doing so may vary. One person may drive 55 mph because he or she suspects that there is a radar trap just ahead or because he or she has noted that a highway patrolman is following. Another may stick to the limit not because he or she personally feels it is justifiable but because a significant other (such as a religious leader) has just emphasized the importance of obeying the laws of the land, including traffic laws that may or may not be justifiable. A third person may stick to the limit because he or she feels that the law is an excellent law because it saves gasoline and has greatly reduced the number of traffic fatalities. Remove the radar trap or have the patrolman turn off at the next exit, and the first driver is likely to speed up immediately. The second will drive slowly only so long as the instructions of the valued and trusted leader remain salient; these will probably fade soon, and his or her speed will also increase. Only the third driver will continue to travel along at a speed dictated by the law. A few hours experience on practically any freeway in the country is convincing evidence of how few people limit their driving speed because of internalized values and how many are influenced by the existence of external constraints.

FACTORS INFLUENCING CONFORMITY AND OBEDIENCE

Any careful observation of human behavior soon reveals significant variation in the extent and nature of conformity and obedience. Some of Lieutenant Calley's troops refused to participate in the slaughter of civilians at My Lai, and a significant majority of the subjects in Asch's conformity study continued to give the correct answer when matching lines, even in the face of unanimous opposition by the group. Several factors have been identified in social-psychological research as being important determinants of these variations in degree of conformity and obedience.

Disclosure as a Determinant of Conformity Disclosure is a key to Kelman's concept of compliance. Unless others can monitor our behavior, they will have an extremely difficult time of forcing us to comply with their expectations.

The term *disclosure* is generally used to refer to the degree to which other persons may know of the behavior performed by an individual. When one's behavior is open to surveillance by others, he or she is subject to possible negative sanctions if his or her behavior deviates from the others' expectations, norms, or values. We have already noted the effect of group influence as observed in laboratory experiments conducted by Asch, Sherif, and Milgram. One of Milgram's most interesting findings, however, also reveals the critical importance of observability of behavior in obedience to dictates from an authority figure. Under one of the experimental conditions, the naive subject in the teacher role was given his instructions via telephone from the experimenter who was not in sight. In these cases, a number of subjects "cheated" by reporting to the experimenter via telephone that they were administering a higher shock level than was actually the case.

The importance of the distinction between public and private behavior has also been noted in research conducted outside the laboratory. For example, Menzel (1957) found important discrepancies in a study of the private and public behavior of a group of physicians. One-half of the doctors studied stated that they had first used a new drug at a date earlier—often many months earlier—than that established from the prescriptions they had written. Menzel found that the preponderant direction of the discrepancies between the prescription record and the interview statements was such that the interview statements made the doctor appear more "up-to-date". When the physician's standing in his or her medical community was considered, the discrepancies in this direction occurred most frequently among low-status physicians, who tried to make themselves appear more "modern" than they had in fact been. In other words, physicians behaved one way in private but tried to express a rather different public image—one that would show them to be more in the vanguard of their profession.

Gordon (1952) has also noted that individuals often alter their private opinion when stating that opinion in public, particularly if the audience is perceived as holding views contrary to the private opinion. Specifically, Gordon was interested in the extent to which the opinions of the members of a group of individuals who shared a common residence house would be influenced by their conception of how others in the group felt toward the issue of concern when such opinions were expressed in a group setting. His results showed that typically the individual tried to reach a compromise between his private opinion and conception of the group opinion when expressing his public opinion. Gordon concluded that the following factors were important in affecting conformity: (1) the degree to which the individual identified with the group (the more the individual identified with the group, the more likely he was to express public opinions that were consistent with the perceived group position); (2) his conception of the group's attitude toward nonconformity (if the group was seen as likely to negatively sanction nonconformity, the individual was more likely to go along with group expectations); (3) personal conception of his own role in relationship to the group (this can involve both acceptance by the group and particular function within the group—if acceptance is more important or if the individual occupies a role that by its very nature requires going along with group norms, conformity is likely to be higher); (4) individual personality traits (those more confident in their own opinion are more willing to state a position in opposition to the group standard).

Robert Merton has long been interested in the influence that visibility of behavior has upon individual response. He has suggested that one of the important defining variables of a group is the degree of observability of behavior within that group—the extent to which the role performance of an individual member of the group is open to monitoring by other group members. Observability allows feedback, which, in turn, contributes to group stability.

> The structural conditions which make for ready observability or visibility of role performance will . . . provide appropriate feedback when the role performance departs from the patterned expectations of the group. For under such conditions, the responses of other members of the group, tending to bring the deviant back into line with the norms, will begin to operate soon after the deviant behavior has occurred. Collaterally, when there are structural impediments to such direct and immediate observability, deviant behavior can cumulate, depart ever more widely from the prevailing norms before coming to the notice of others in the group, and then often elicit an "over-reaction" which serves only to alienate the deviants, rather than to "correct" their deviations (Merton, 1957a, p. 320).

Although Merton's primary concern is with group properties, he is clearly suggesting that the extent to which an individual's behavior is public will, in part, determine the extent to which that behavior will remain consistent with group norms and standards.

The effect of disclosure on conformity can be illustrated further by a study of attitudes toward marijuana among college students (Albrecht, DeFleur, and Warner, 1972). In this study, students whose attitudes toward marijuana had been measured earlier in the semester in the context of another project were brought into the small-groups laboratory to ascertain the effects of different levels of "social participation" on attitude/behavior consistency. Three different conditions were employed. In the *individualistic* condition, three subjects were placed in private booths, and they were not allowed to see or speak with each other. The subjects were instructed to simply think about "the pros and cons of legalizing marijuana" for a few minutes. The experimenter then returned to the room and asked each respondent to indicate whether he or she favored marijuana legalization by registering an opinion on a voting machine. This machine consisted of a panel with two rows of lights, one row red, the other white. There were three lights per row, one labeled for each of the three booths. The white lights represented a vote "for legalizing marijuana," and the red lights signified a vote "against legalizing marijuana." In all cases, the first two respondents to vote were working for the experimenter and were instructed to vote consistently with each other in a manner that opposed or supported the known attitude (obtained in the earlier study) of the naive subject. The naive subject could thus see the position taken by the other two participants and knew that they, in turn, would know his or her opinion when it was registered on the machine. The naive subject also knew that the others did not know him or her and that he or she would be able to leave the lab anonymously.

In the *anonymous-participation* condition, the same basic procedure was employed, but the three participants were to argue audibly the pros and cons of marijuana legalization before registering their vote. Though they could not see each other, they were to verbally express arguments in favor of their position and to have these attacked (or supported) by the other participants. Again, the confederates took the same stand on the issue (in support of or in opposition to the known attitude of the naive subject) and registered their vote prior to his.

The *public* condition involved sitting the three subjects around a small table where they could discuss the issue face to face. The vote on the marijuana issue was also registered publicly, and the naive subject again voted last.

As would be expected, greatest conformity to the position of the confederates occurred in the public condition and least conformity occurred in the individualistic condition. All this evidence suggests that, as the degree of disclosure or visibility of our position becomes known to others, we are more likely to exhibit attitudes and behavior that are like their attitudes and behavior. When our acts are known to others, they have the ability to impose sanctions that could not or would not be imposed in response to private expressions. Disclosure and visibility, then, become important keys in our understanding of conforming behavior.

GROUP CHARACTERISTICS—ATTRACTIVENESS AND COHESIVENESS

Several group characteristics have been found important in understanding conformity. The more attractive a group is to its individual members, the higher the probability of their conforming to group goals and expectations and the more likely prospective members are to be willing to adjust their attitude and behavior patterns in order to obtain membership. The highly attractive group can demand more than other groups can because the individual member will get more in return, such as higher satisfaction and status.

Similarly, highly cohesive groups are likely to exhibit a high level of conformity among group members. Attractive groups are those in which membership is highly appealing; cohesive groups are those that have a strong esprit de corps or a strong commitment to a common set of values or goals. Such groups tend to exhibit more positive and friendly interactions among group members (Deutsch, 1949), whose individual goals are likely to be represented in the goals of the larger group. The more cohesive the group, the more likely it is able to impose negative sanctions on nonconforming group members. Sanctions imposed by less cohesive groups, those to which members are less committed, are likely to lack the effectiveness that would coincide with high cohesiveness and commitment.

However, cohesive groups are not only characterized by higher levels of conformity, but they also face the very real danger of overconformity. Thus, "the more amiability and esprit de corps among the members of an in-group of policy makers, the greater is the danger that independent critical thinking will be replaced by groupthink, which is likely to result in irrational and dehumanizing actions directed at outgroups" (Janis, 1972, p. 198). "A high degree of group cohesiveness is conducive to a high frequency of symptoms of groupthink, which, in turn, are conducive to a high frequency of defects in decision-making" (Janis, 1972, p. 199). Cohesiveness, then, is an important factor affecting conformity, but its consequences can be dysfunctional as well as functional.

In addition to the group or social situational factors, a number of characteristics of the individual have been found to correlate with conformity or its absence. For example, if an individual has had a *personal history of success* in performing tasks that are similar to the one being studied, he or she is less likely to go along with the group than is someone without such a history. Mausner (1954) observed that when subjects who were asked to judge the length of lines were reinforced for their responses, they were less likely to be influenced by their partners' judgment when placed in a group context. On the other hand, if a subject was frequently pronounced incorrect when judging the line lengths while alone, he or she was much more likely to submit to group opinion in later trials. Similarly, Walters and Karal (1960) found that subjects characterized by high levels of *anxiety* were more likely to conform to the group than were low-anxiety subjects.

A number of studies have assessed the effect of personality characteristics on individual susceptibility to influence. One of the important variables identified in these studies is what Crowne and Marlowe (1964) have called *need for social approval.* Subjects who exhibit a strong need for social approval from others are much more likely to conform to what they perceive as the conduct expected and considered appropriate by others (Moeller and Applezweig, 1957; Strickland and Crowne, 1962). On the other hand, people with a low need for social approval are more likely to feel greater independence from group judgment and to emphasize their own individual values and preferences in decision making.

There appears to be a significant degree of similarity between the need for approval discussed by Crowne and Marlowe and the typology of *inner* and *other directedness* (Riesman, Glazer, and Denney, 1950). *Other directed* has been used to describe the individual who alters behavior to maintain consistency with shifting *group* expectations; *inner directed* has been applied to the person who is more independent of perceived expectations of others. Research conducted by Albrecht and Warner (1975) has shown that both the need for approval and the inner-/other-directedness concepts are useful in assessing the effect of the larger social group on individual behavior. In a study of the relationship between the attitudes and behavior of college students toward marijuana use, these researchers found that, for inner-directed subjects with low need for approval, attitude was a good predictor of behavior. However, for other-directed subjects with high need for approval, reference-group expectations surpassed the influence of individual attitudes.

George Homans (1974) has noted that *individual position* within a group's social status system has an important bearing on degree of conformity. In general, persons of middle status show the highest level of conformity. If a person of high status moves in a new direction and the correctness of this new direction is confirmed, then the legitimacy of his or her higher status is also confirmed. However, if proven wrong, the high-status person can use some of what Hollander (1964) has called "idiosyncrasy credit". In other words, the high-status person has probably attained his or her position by performing acts that reward group members, and he or she is therefore allowed by the group to act differently without losing status. Low-status individuals are already at the bottom of the heap and so have little more to lose through nonconformity. On the other hand, if they do act differently and are proven correct, this may provide a way for them to increase their status. Middle-level persons, however, are stuck: if they do not conform they could lose status; strict conformity may be a mechanism for gaining status.

Some important individual differences were found in the subjects that participated in the Milgram experiments. For example, Catholics were somewhat more obedient than were members of other religious groups, and those with better education and in professions, such as law, medicine, and teaching, were more likely to defy the experimenter and not give high-voltage shocks. Republicans and Democrats were not significantly different in their responses. However, in detailed interviews with a number of the Milgram subjects several months after the initial experiments, Elms (Elms and Milgram, 1966) was unable to note consistent and significant personality differences between the subjects who defied the experimenter and those who willingly administered the 450 volts. Elms failed to find significant differences on any of twelve standard tests included in the MMPI (Minnesota Multiphasic Personality Inventory) to measure tendencies toward paranoia, schizophrenia, psychopathic deviancy, or other such pathologies. Elms' disappointment in his results is reflected in the following statement: "Milgram had constructed a reality that divided men on an important behavior. I had constructed a questionnaire that looked as though it should yield similar divisions. But however I analyzed the answers to this questionnaire . . . the obedients and the defiants weren't much different. That wouldn't have bothered me much, except that I knew they *were* different, dammit!" (Elms, 1972, pp. 135–36).

Although other individual characteristics have been studied, those such as need for approval and others we have identified have gained the most attention. In assessing their overall effect, the best conclusion seems to be that they are important in *interaction with* social-situational factors. The evidence noted by Elms does not negate the supportive evidence found in a large number of other projects. To understand different levels of conformity, we must look both at the characteristics of the social situation in which the behavior is to occur and the characteristics of the individual actor. Simply knowing *either* social-situational factors *or* individual characteristics is inadequate because the behavior is a function of the interaction of factors at both levels. As noted several years ago by Milton Yinger: "To know how a person will behave, one must know the group within which he is behaving, the position he occupies (position implies counter-positions and roles— mutual patterns of expectations), the sanctions and rewards of the surrounding environment (which facilitate the expression of certain tendencies and inhibit the expression of others), and the stream of events around him (which activate some predispositions while others remain latent)" (1965, p. 248). We would only add that knowledge of individual tendencies and predispositions, *combined* with these activating or inhibiting social-situational factors, is critical.

Independence versus Conformity

For a number of years, social psychology has seemed to have had a much greater interest in studying conformity than its obverse—independence. At the same time, extensive lip service has been paid to the importance of nonconformity.

> The American educated middle class is firm in its admiration of nonconformity and dissent. The right to be nonconformist, the right to dissent, is part of our conception of community. Everybody says so . . . How good that is, and how right! And yet, when we examine the content of our idea of nonconformity, we must be dismayed by the smallness of the concrete actuality this very large idea contains. The rhetoric is as sincere as it is capacious, yet . . . we cannot really imagine nonconformity at all, not in art, not in moral or social theory, certainly not in the personal life—it is probably true that there never was a society which required so entire an eradication of personal differentiation, so bland a uniformity of manner. Admiring nonconformity and loving community, we have decided that we are all nonconformists together (Trilling, p. 51–52).

As the excerpt from Lionel Trilling, American moralist, humanist, and social critic, suggests, independence of judgment and behavior is supposed to be one of the important values in our highly mobile, constantly changing society.

Hollander (1975) argues that the primary reason for the overemphasis on conformity in social psychology is historical. Such classic research projects as those by Munsterberg (1914), Moede (1920), Allport (1924), Jenness (1932), Sherif (1935), Asch (1951), and Crutchfield (1955), have all been devoted to the study, in one form or another, of the effect that knowing the judgments of others has on an individual's own judgments. As Hollander notes, the major dependent variable in this range of studies is conformity of the individual to the judgment of a group (the latter often being erroneous).

It cannot be assumed that the reason for limited research on independence is that it is always the direct opposite of conformity; that is, it cannot be said that once we have determined the factors that contribute to conformity we can conclude that the opposite of these leads to nonconformity. Instead, much more is probably involved.

Hollander has defined *independence* as, "action which reflects critical judgment by the individual in responding to social demands" (1975, p. 57). The key is *critical judgment.* According to Hollander, "It means sometimes accepting and going along with the majority view and sometimes rejecting that view, deviating from it, and trying to get others to do so as well." Thus, independence does not mean that one automatically rejects the views of the majority. In fact, one may accept them most of the time. One can even be a good "team player" and yet often strike out in a new direction. Independence simply implies the real potential of selecting an alternative course of action if such a course is consistent with one's own definition of the situation.

As we have noted, traditional forces operating in society appear directed more toward conformity than toward independence. The educational system in this country has been criticized for fostering the pat answer and the simple regurgitation of memorized notes rather than critical independent thought. Though few teachers would admit it, many of them feel more comfortable with rote memorization and recital than with critical analysis, which may mean challenging even the ideas of the teacher.

Peer pressure also acts as an important influence. During the teen years especially, acceptance by peers is vital for most young people. It is not uncommon for the bright student to purposely miss a question or to score lower than he or she is capable of scoring in order to avoid criticism by peers.

Hollander (1975) has identified six primary impediments to independence. It should be noted that although we have suggested that independence and conformity are not necessarily the two end points on a continuum, these six factors could just as well be viewed as contributors to conformity as impediments to independence.

RISK OF DISAPPROVAL

Probably the most important single factor that limits independence and causes the individual to go along with the group is fear of rejection and disapproval. For example, a teenage youth participates in a deviant act because to not do so would cause significant others to label him "chicken," "square," or whatever. An ambitious stockbroker buys the suit with a conservative cut and drab colors not because he or she likes that particular suit best but because another choice would be viewed negatively by peers, clients, and employers.

Of course, the risks of negative sanctions can be far more critical in some instances than others. Verbal disapproval may or may not be as effective as physical punishment. A graduate student working for one of the authors discovered this while interviewing in a small, rural, very conservative community. The student wore his hair below the shoulders, but to try to "fit" better with local norms, he bought a pair of cowboy boots. Both the boots and hair went after the student was informed by a group of local men that the only thing they hated worse than a "hippie" was a "hippie wearing cowboy boots."

LACK OF PERCEIVED ALTERNATIVES

Independence from a course of action decided upon by a group is impossible if there are no alternatives. Although a case of *no alternatives* may be rare, people are often faced with the availability of less attractive alternatives only. Thibaut and Kelley (1959) have argued that whether or not we stay with a given relationship or course of action is determined in large part by the "comparison level for alternatives." Even though a given relationship may be unrewarding, we will stick with it if the perceived alternatives are even less rewarding. Similarly, we may abandon a rewarding activity if an even more rewarding one presents itself. The perceived availability of alternatives, then, is critical in determining the course of action that is chosen.

FEAR OF DISRUPTING PROCEEDING

Hollander notes that in many groups there is a prevailing reluctance to have confrontations. Apparently, some people feel that open disagreements can create wounds and hard feelings that will be difficult to heal. Consequently, subtle pressure is frequently exerted to "go along to get along." Some groups and organizations seek to establish consensus before striking out on a new course of action. Although one may not wholly agree with that course of action, he or she may decide to go along in order not to be the reason for total inaction.

ABSENCE OF SHARED COMMUNICATION

Perhaps one of the most prevalent reasons for a lack of independence is the absence of shared communication. The rebel often feels that he or she is alone in his or her opposition and so fails to speak out. However, a number of others, perhaps even a majority, may feel the same, but they also fail to verbalize their feelings publically. In such cases, failure to communicate can lead to "pluralistic ignorance," and all go along with something with which they do not totally agree. This principle was illustrated by a study by Schank (1932), who collected data from residents of a relatively small, rural, Methodist community regarding their beliefs about a series of church principles and teachings. In his conversations with residents of the community, Schank found almost total verbal support for the church prohibitions against smoking, drinking, and playing cards. Yet, before leaving the community, he played cards and drank with a substantial percentage of the town's residents, always behind closed doors and with the shades drawn. Each person with whom Schank so participated felt that he was alone in his opposition to church teachings.

INABILITY TO FEEL RESPONSIBLE

The inability to feel responsible is illustrated by the practice of "passing the buck." Maybe we do not like what we see happening, but we rationalize that it is not our responsibility or not in our department and so we effectively ignore it. Schwartz has argued that two important factors must be activated before we are willing to strike out on a course of action (particularly a course of action that involves "helping behavior"): first, a person must have some awareness that his potential acts may have consequences for the welfare of others, and second, he must *ascribe* some degree of *responsibility* for these acts and their consequences to himself. Ascription of responsibility, which is very similar to Hollander's concept, refers to the willingness on the part of the individual to personally assume responsibility for the consequences that are likely to follow from his or her actions (or conversely, from failure to take action). Schwartz argues that "it is only when there is both awareness of interpersonal consequences and acceptance of responsibility for them that norms governing these consequences are likely to be experienced as applicable and to influence behavior, except insofar as other pressures supporting them are brought to bear (e.g., they are invoked by someone else in the situation)" (1968, p. 234).

Rather than accept responsibility ourselves, we tend to "diffuse responsibility" (Latane and Darley, 1969). Therefore, we are never directly responsible for a course of action—we can always diffuse that responsibility to someone else or to some generalized other, such as society. As Flip Wilson retorts in one of his famous lines, we can always claim that "the Devil made me do it!"

SENSE OF IMPOTENCE

The final factor that Hollander feels inhibits individual independence is simply a feeling of personal impotence. In other words, the person feels that speaking out would not make any difference anyway: no one would listen, and, if they did, they surely would not do anything about it. This person could perhaps be characterized by a high degree of personal alienation. Because the individual feels independent action is futile, he or she goes through the motions of behaving in accordance with group expectations. Many people living in totalitarian societies may not personally agree with the course taken by their governments but nevertheless go along because of a sense of individual impotence in the face of the powerful monolithic state.

One of the difficulties associated with this whole topic is that of deciding how much individual independence is good. To put it another way, when do individual idiosyncrasies start to become such a disruptive force that the group can no longer function effectively? Any social group must have a certain degree of conformity to group goals and rules, or they become meaningless. A meeting will soon become chaotic unless rules of order are adopted and followed. Without such rules, communication often becomes disruptive rather than a mechanism for sharing and transmitting ideas. Independence, then, is not synonymous with total deviation. Rather, as Hollander (1975) has noted, true independence probably involves conformity to some group positions and nonconformity to others. The individual acts and reacts on the basis of his or her own best thinking and the information made available by others. Judgment becomes in a true sense critical judgment, and compromise remains an important strategy to accomplish goal achievement.

In an other-directed society, independence would probably not be a highly valued goal. However, evidence, such as that concerning tolerance garnered from Davis' research (1975), suggests that perhaps the focus of the socialization experience is now more likely to emphasize a greater degree of independence of thought. At least, we appear to be somewhat more tolerant of those who express independence and individuality than we used to be. Although it may be less efficient, a society that guarantees a healthy portion of "freedom and dignity" still seems to be important to many of us.

Summary

Many of the regularities of human thought and action can be linked directly to the operation of social norms. These norms provide definitions of appropriate and inappropriate thoughts and actions. They have developed largely to provide meaning and direction in what would otherwise be conditions of ambiguity. Once norms develop, they are reinforced by systems of formal

153

and informal sanctions. When behavior is consistent with the norms, it is generally rewarded (or, at least, is not punished). Deviation from social norms usually elicits disapproval or other, more formal, negative sanctions. We usually attempt to define situations before responding to them, and a critical aspect of that definition includes as assessment of the relevant social norms.

Behavior that is consistent with normative expectations can be defined as conforming behavior. All groups must have a certain degree of conformity if they are to avoid total chaos and disruption. Yet, we have a tendency to view conformity in a negative sense. This probably results from the fact that conformity also implies going along with group expectations and definitions of the situation even when doing so means behavior that is contrary to individual values and perceptions.

Obedience is really one type of conformity and usually involves engaging in behavior that is dictated by some authority figure, such as a parent, an employer, or a commanding officer. Again, obedience is necessary in many instances if the group is to function successfully and achieve its goals, but, like conformity, it also has its negative side, especially when the individual obeys the illegitimate wishes of a third party.

Clearly, situational constraints are critical in our understanding of conformity and obedience. One of the most important of these is the extent to which our behavior will be disclosed or made public to others. Without disclosure, others are unaware of our actions and so are unable to impose sanctions should those actions be inconsistent with their expectations. Disclosure is especially important to compliance in that compliance involves action that would not occur in the absence of external social constraints. Conformity to other norms occurs without such external constraints because we have internalized the norm.

In addition to these external constraints, individual response tendencies are also important in our understanding of rates of conformity. It has been found that we are less likely to conform if we have had a past history of success on similar tasks, if we exhibit lower anxiety levels, if we have high or low (as opposed to middle-range) status in the group, if the group is not highly attractive to us, and if we are characterized by a low need for social approval or by inner-directedness in contrast to other-directedness.

Finally, more social-psychological interest and attention has been turning to the study of independence in recent years. We are now asking questions concerning the factors that contribute to independence of thought and action rather than concentrating on just those things that contribute to conformity. Hollander (1975) has identified six impediments to independence: (1) risk of disapproval; (2) lack of perceived alternatives; (3) fear of disrupting proceeding; (4) absence of shared communication; (5) inability to feel responsible; and (6) sense of impotence.

No doubt, each of us can recognize the operation of one or more of these factors at various times in our lives. Whether or not they are becoming less important and whether or not we feel greater freedom to develop and express our individuality are matters of important debate. However, before we conclude that all of the most negative ramifications of conformity and obedience have faded, we should remember how recently the situations concerning Private McClure, Lieutenant Calley, and the Watergate conspirators took place.

social

roles

An air of excitement electrified all the animals on the Animal Farm. Each could hardly wait for the day's work to end when all would gather for a hurriedly called meeting. When Mr. Jones' bedroom light went out, all the animals met in the big red barn where Major, the wise prize-winning boar, stood upon his platform to address them.

What is the nature of this life of ours? Let us face it: our lives are miserable, laborious and short. . . . We are given just so much food as will keep the breath in our bodies, and those of us who are capable of it are forced to work to the last atom of our strength; and the very instant that our usefulness has come to an end we are slaughtered with hideous cruelty. . . .

But is this . . . the order of nature? . . . . No, . . . a thousand times no! . . . . This single farm of ours would support a dozen horses, twenty cows, hundreds of sheep—and all of them living in comfort and dignity. . . . Why then do we continue in this miserable condition? Because nearly the whole of the produce of our labour is stolen from us by human beings. There . . . is the answer to all our problems. It is summed up in a single word—Man.

Man is the only creature that consumes without producing. . . . He is lord of all the animals. He sets them to work, he gives back to them the bare minimum that will prevent them from starving and the rest he keeps for himself. . . . What then must we do? Why, work night and day, body and soul, for the overthrow of the human race! . . . .

I have little more to say. . . . Remember that in fighting against Man, we must not come to resemble him. Even when you have conquered him, do not adopt his vices. No animal must ever live in a house, or sleep in a bed, or wear clothes, or drink alcohol, or smoke tobacco, or touch money, or engage in trade. . . . Above all, no animal must ever tyrannize over his own kind. No animal must ever kill any other animal. All animals are equal.

The animals successfully drove Mr. Jones and all his men from the farm. Enthusiastically, they set about creating their new social order. It soon became apparent that some organization was needed and, without the other animals being exactly aware of why they should do so, the pigs gradually assumed this supervisory role. The pigs soon discovered that they needed to learn to read and write, and to do this more effectively they needed to live in the farm house. The pigs decided they had to get rid of all old animals, to buy and sell produce, to walk upright on two legs, and to have their social drinks. Finally, the pigs called the neighboring farmers to a special meeting with the purpose of resolving old differences. All the animals watched the historic meeting through the farmhouse windows. Six of the most prominent pigs and six farmers all sat around the table, enjoying a game of cards. The game was interrupted when Mr. Pilkington, head of the farmers, suggested they all drink a toast in honor of the remarkable prosperity achieved on Animal Farm. This was followed by a toast of continuing prosperity by Napoleon, the pig in charge of Animal Farm. Loud applause followed each toast.

As the animals outside gazed at the scene, it seemed to them that some strange thing was happening. What was it that had altered in the faces of the pigs? . . . What was it that seemed to be changing? Then, the applause having come to an end, the company took up their cards and continued the game . . . and the animals crept silently away.

But they had not gone twenty yards when they stopped short. An uproar of voices was coming from the farmhouse. They rushed back and looked through the window again. Yes, a violent quarrel was in progress. There were shoutings, bangings on the table, sharp suspicious glances, furious denials. The source of the trouble appeared to be that Napoleon and Mr. Pilkington had each played an ace of spades simultaneously.

Twelve voices were shouting in anger, and they were all alike. No question, now, what had happened to the faces of the pigs. The creatures outside looked from pig to man, and from man to pig, and from pig to man again; but already it was impossible to say which was which (Orwell 1946, pp. 117–118).

Introduction

Few concepts are as useful for the student of social psychology as is that of social role. This concept allows the student to simultaneously study the nature and function of the social order *and* the behavior of the individual actor in that social order. It also helps us to understand the extent to which our behavior is determined by the various roles that we occupy as illustrated in the excerpt from Orwell's *Animal Farm.* Shakespeare observed that the world was a stage, and men and women were merely players having their exits and their entrances. During a life time each actor plays many parts. In the theater, the script outlining the general content of the role exists independently of any one actor who may fill the role at any one time. So, too, in social-psychological analysis, social order and the individual exist independently of each other. In this chapter, we begin with a discussion of role and related concepts. Throughout the chapter, our purpose is to better understand social structure and the individual's behavior in any social role.

THE DEVELOPMENT OF THE CONCEPT "ROLE" _____

In studying societies and their members, social scientists frequently employ the term *social system.* The term *system* connotes a configuration of individual parts that are interdependent. Many of the social groups studied by social psychologists can be seen as social systems inasmuch as they are comprised of several individual members, any one of whose actions are, at least in part, interdependent with the actions of other members of the group.

Social systems are composed of a series of *positions.* For example, if we consider the family as a social system, we can readily see that it is composed of such positions as father, mother, son, daughter, husband, wife, brother, sister, and so on. The interdependence of these positions and the fact that the group shows recurrent normative patterns and structure allows us to describe the family as a social system in much the same manner that a scientist might describe the solar system.

Associated with each of the positions in a social system is a set of expected attitudinal and behavioral patterns. These expectations are normative in nature—they define what the occupant of the position ought to do and ought not to do—and constitute what we define as the *social role*. Thus, the expected set of behaviors that are associated with the position of father in the family system constitutes the social role of father.

One of the earliest discussions foreshadowing much of contemporary role theory in social psychology is found in the writing of George Simmel (1858–1912). Although in the translations of Simmel's work the word *role* is not used, it is clear that Simmel's concept of "vocation" is similar in meaning to role. The concept of vocation, for Simmel, made society possible because in it he saw the existent social order offering to the individual a "position which in content and outline differs from others, but which in principle may be filled by any man" (Martindale, 1960, p. 239). For Simmel, the existence of the vocation and the individual's choice to take up the particular vocation resulted in a social order created by the "association of independent persons" (Martindale, 1960, p. 239).

While Simmel's works were influencing some of the sociologically oriented social psychologists, the work of Linton, an anthropologist, provided further insight in linking role to other concepts utilized to describe social structure. For the cultural anthropologist, a social structure, or social system, consists of a set of interrelated statuses. *Status* is simply defined as a social position in a given social order; for example, the status of husband in the social system we call the family. In Linton's words, role is "used to designate the sum total of the cultural patterns associated with a particular status. It included the attitudes, values, and behavior ascribed by the society to any and all persons occupying the status" (Linton, 1947, p. 77).

Although Linton's work emphasized the normative dimension of role—that is, what society expects from the occupant of any social position—it did not specifically speak to the question of whether it would be best to conceive of one or many roles attached to a given social position. More recently,

When we assume a role, we must learn the behaviors as well as the attitudes and values that go with that role. *Source:* U.S. Army.

Merton (1957*b*) has influenced thinking in the direction of defining a particular position as consisting of multiple role expectations. In a similar vein, underscoring the multiplicity of expectations associated with a given role, Bates defined *role* as a "part of a social position consisting of a more or less integrated or related subset of social norms . . ." (1956, p. 314). Taken together, Merton's and Bates' formulations lead to the conceptualization that normative expectations cluster together to form a role, and roles cluster together to form a position.

Occupants of the social position of spouse/parent in the family, for example, generally accept the responsibility of meeting clusters of expectations related to specific *duties* that they must perform as well as inherent *rights* attached to the social position. There is some research evidence (Nye, 1976) that indicates that these social norms within the family cluster together to define at least eight different social roles, which in turn define the normative dimension of the spouse/parent position. These eight roles are child socialization, provider, homemaker, child care, therapeutic, recreational, sexual and kinship. Some of the expectations that define the content of the parent's socialization role are to help the child acquire appropriate tastes for given foods and accompanying eating habits, to feel good about self and significant others, to learn the value of work, and to like school. Figure 6–1 presents this conceptualization for the position of spouse/parent in the family (Nye and Gecas, 1976).

POSITION — Spouse/Parent

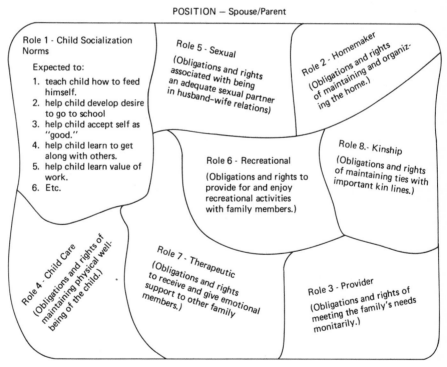

Figure 6–1 Relationship Between Norms, Roles, and Social Positions. (Adapted from Nye and Gecas in Nye 1976, pp. 1–14.)

Reciprocity In addition to this basic formulation of the concept of role, we need to look at additional concepts to more fully understand the social structural dimensions. No role exists in isolation. Roles are *reciprocal* in nature in that they point toward another person and the respective social obligations that the role performer has toward that other person, who is called the *role partner*. For example, the parents' role of socializing the child shown in figure 6–1 obviously only exists in terms of the needs and rights of the child. In role analysis, the needs and rights of one person are reciprocal to the obligations of the role partner. Thus, the need of the child to be nourished with food becomes the parents' obligation to provide food for the child and in addition to teach the child appropriate and inappropriate behaviors related to filling that need. Not only are roles reciprocal in nature, but many and varied demands or expectations are made upon the individual occupant of a role. These varied demands come from at least two sources: (1) multiple demands within one role, and (2) multiple roles. The child-socialization role has many demands, but the spouse/parent must also meet accompanying demands associated with the roles of provider, homemaker, sexual partner, and so forth.

Role Strain If an individual occupies many different positions at one time with many and varied expectations emanating from multiple roles, he or she is very likely to find that some expectations run counter to others. For example, the role of the accountant may dictate that the employee take work home at night, but the accountant who also occupies the spouse/parent role is also expected to give his or her time and attention to spouse and children. Likewise, in just one position it is possible for some role expectations to be in opposition to others. The executive assistant is expected to be efficient and on time with his or her work, but at the same time may be expected to accompany the boss to meet and socialize with given clients. *Role strain* refers to the subjectively experienced difficulty in performing one's role that results from these role conflicts.

Role Conflict Social psychologists have developed two useful distinctions within the concept of role conflict—*inter-* and *intra*role conflict. The former is conflict created by incompatible expectations from more than one role; the latter is created by conflicting demands arising within one role.

Interrole conflict results when someone who occupies multiple social positions is faced with conflicting performance demands arising out of those positions. It is very likely that the demands associated with one or more of these roles will inhibit the effectiveness with which others are performed, or that the person cannot choose between the conflicting demands and will suffer role strain. President Carter is not only father to his children but also commander in chief of all military forces, chief executive officer of the federal government, president of the wealthiest nation on earth, and husband to his wife. In his role of father, he is expected to spend time with his children and care for their safety. However, in his role of President, he is expected to spend time with foreign leaders and to protect the country, even to call for war if necessary. The conflict is obvious.

Intrarole conflict refers to contradictory role expectations emanating from one social position. A study of intrarole conflict is found in an early and detailed analysis of school superintendents. Gross, McEachern, and Mason (1966) describe the conflicting demands inherent in this social position. The superintendent's role set is naturally self-contradictory as the position calls for interaction with many very distinct groups. Each of these different groups has, not surprisingly, different expectations about what the superintendent ought to be doing. Figure 6–2 presents the superintendents' perceptions of conflicting expectations from six different groups about whether they should recommend high or low salaries for teachers. Most of the superintendents perceived that politicians, taxpayers' associations, and city council members expect the superintendent to recommend as low a salary as possible but that labor unions, P.T.A.'s, and teachers expect a high salary recommendation. In attempting to discharge his or her duties, each decision made by a superintendent will create intrarole conflict as each group evaluates the superintendent's performance in light of its expectations about appropriate role behavior. It is safe to predict that any occupant of the school superintendent position will experience role strain resulting from this high amount of role conflict.

Another level of intrarole conflict creates an additional source of role strain. In the school superintendent research, role strain emerged because various groups had differing expectations about what was appropriate behavior. Another source of role strain emerges when ego's role performance does not measure up to the expectations that both ego and the role partner

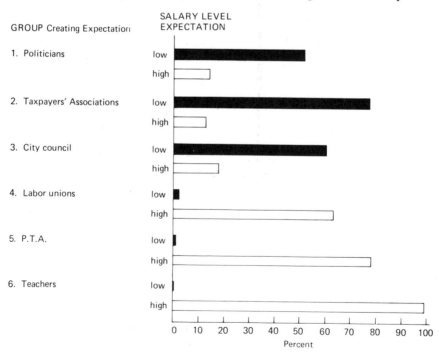

Figure 6–2   School Superintendents' Perception of Differing Expectations about Whether the Superintendent Should Recommend High or Low Salaries for Teachers. (Adapted from Gross, McEachern, and Mason, 1968, p. 290.)

have. There is no set of conflicting expectations since both ego and the role partner agree about what *should* be done but rather ego and the role partner both experience a discrepancy between the actual performance and the agreed upon role expectations.

Other Sources of Strain and Conflict Role strain and conflict can also result from other sources. For example, it is extremely difficult to perform a role adequately if the expectations that are associated with that role are not clearly defined and specified. To know that one should be doing something while not knowing exactly what should be done may cause role strain under some conditions. The first day or two on a new job can cause this strain unless someone takes the novice by the hand and teaches him or her the informal as well as the formal (job description) role expectations.

Similarly, we often find that behavior patterns we have learned for one role and for which we have been rewarded are not acceptable for another role. For example, children are expected to turn to their parents for guidance in decision making, even on simple matters. However, as they mature they are expected to make their own decisions. Anthropologists frequently talk about the strain that results from discontinuities in status passage or from the serial progression from one position in society to another. Unless one has been adequately trained and prepared for the change, it can often result in serious strain.

HANDLING ROLE STRAIN

Because of the conflicting role expectations within and across social positions, it might be anticipated that people would be hesitant to take on additional roles and the potential of increased role strain associated with such accumulation. However, people obviously do handle conflicting role expectations, and they systematically take on roles throughout the life cycle. A lawyer may become a university president and still remain a partner in the law firm. A plumber who is also father and husband, in addition becomes a scout master or a Big Brother. If the social order is characterized by anything, it is the phenomenon of role accumulation. What are some of the mechanisms that make the relatively smooth social order possible even in the face of role strain?

Role Expectation Hierarchy One obvious way of handling role strain created by role overload is to rearrange one's priorities. A conscious decision can be made to reduce the involvement and time commitment to social positions that are least important to the person's central identity hierarchy (McCall and Simmons, 1966). A businessman may consciously decide that he will work his regular eight-hour day for five days a week, but he will not take work home to do at night or on the weekend. His self-identity as husband and father is salient enough to require a rearrangement of time commitments to better fit his basic identity hierarchy. Time with his family is more important than advancement in the firm, which might come if he were to put in the extra time. A mother may decide to place her children in a day-care center and in addition insist that her husband share in household tasks so she can pursue an advertising career. Her identity as an advertising agent is more important than the homemaker identity, so she rearranges her commitments, thus reducing role strain.

Some situations do not require the individual role occupant to rearrange priorities in order to satisfy personal expectations. In some cases, society recognizes explicitly a hierarchy of role expectations that prevents role strain from arising and offers a ready-made course of action that frees the individual from one of the conflicting expectations. One's obligations as a family member are given greater priority over the expectations of the occupational world at the death of an immediate family member. At such times of socially recognized moments of grief, not only does the recognized hierarchy of role expectations reduce role strain, but one social group will marshal its resources to assist its member to more adequately meet the role expectations in the other social group. Thus, the occupational group sends flowers to the funeral, provides assistance to the bereaved in arranging the funeral, and sends money to the family. After all things connected with the funeral are over, the expectations are that the role of worker will resume its normal place in the hierarchy.

When a recognized hierarchy of role expectations exists, not only will one social group move to facilitate smooth interaction in another social setting, but formal procedures are often instituted to protect the person from experiencing harm because of the unavoidable role strain. The role expectation of a citizen called as a witness in a criminal case is to provide the court with *all* the relevant information. However, if the witness also happens to be the accused's priest or lawyer, the witness occupies another social position that carries the right of privileged communication. There are formal rules stating that the role expectations of priest or lawyer take precedence over the role expectations of witness, and the lawyer or priest cannot be prosecuted for withholding information that was spoken in confidence.

However, the effectiveness of establishing a hierarchy of role expectations as a mechanism for reducing strain and conflict is dependent upon the various partners in the relationship agreeing upon that hierarchy. If role partners do not agree on which set of expectations takes precedence, the conflict may be increased rather than diminished.

The Third Party Conflicting role expectations existing over time will often lead to the creation of a third-party role to reduce the role strain. For example, some of the school superintendents faced with the conflicting expectations about salary increases for teachers utilized committees as third parties to advise them. In the words of one such superintendent:

> I put it all in the hands of the school committee. It's a hot potato so I let the school committee handle it. . . . I'd hang myself by getting involved. But I go along with the school committee recommendation one hundred percent, whatever they decide (Gross, McEachern, and Mason, 1966, p. 291).

By removing himself or herself from the conflicting expectations, the superintendent avoids the role strain. So long as the committee represents various points of view, their recommendation will be seen as a relatively fair compromise. Social institutions move over time to formally define the arbitrator role. The arbitrator is protected from reprisals from dissatisfied groups but must simultaneously accept a set of norms outlining the responsibilities in settling disputes.

Social analysts, in their effort to clarify the role of the third party in dispute resolution, have made an important distinction between the role of arbitrator as judge and the role of arbitrator as problem solver (Fuller, 1963; Mueller, 1963). If the parties to a dispute agree that the third party is to function largely in the judicial dimension of the role, then they expect the arbitrator to hear all the relevant information and to arrive at a decision. The parties may then be ordered to comply with the decision as a way of enforcing the underlying agreement of the contract. As Fuller (1963, pp. 23–24) notes, the purpose is to reach a fair decision, and the morality of this type of arbitration lies in the correctness of the "decision according to the law of the contract." Arbitrators will likely function in this role where there are clear contractual agreements.

When the underlying norms and/or contracts are not this clear, the third-party role may be defined predominantly by its problem-solving or mediating dimension. Whereas the judicial aspect underscores the fairness and legal dimension of the decision and calls for a third party of impeccable "principles" (Fuller, 1963, p. 3), the problem-solving role may well require an adaptive and innovative role performer. As Fuller (1971, p. 308) notes, this mediator role is "commonly directed, not toward achieving conformity to norms, but toward the creation of the relevant norms themselves." The arbitrator functioning in this role is expected to adapt the procedure according to the case at hand. His or her primary purpose is to reorient the parties such that they will achieve the most mutually satisfying settlement. As Fuller argues, the "morality of mediation lies in optimum settlement in which each party gives up what he values less in return for what he values more" (1963, pp. 23–24).

ROLE ACCUMULATION

Since Goode's formal identification of role strain and his observation that "difficulty in meeting given role demands is therefore normal" (1960, p. 485), social psychologists have generally assumed that adding more roles inevitably results in increased role strain. Some have questioned this one-sided approach and asked what the positive outcomes of role accumulation might be.

Seiber (1974, p. 569) insists that the "larger social order is determined more so by the efforts of individuals to acquire and enjoy the *normal,* net *benefits* of role accumulation" rather than the development of social structures designed to reduce role strain. He notes that benefits of the acquisition of multiple roles can be classified into four types: (1) role privileges; (2) status security; (3) resources for status enhancement and role performance; and (4) personality and ego gratification.

Every role is comprised of *rights* as well as duties. Seeking any additional role that carries a net increase of rights over duties may actually make the role occupant's future social encounters easier rather than more difficult. Seiber notes that occupying a new status often carries with it many *freedoms* that are not associated with specific obligations to partners in the role set. Many positions provide these freedoms to the occupants in such forms as freedom from physical abuse, freedom from dismissal without cause, freedom to choose one's own representatives for bargaining purposes, freedom to regulate one's own work schedule; freedom to interact with friends while at work; and the freedom to make suggestions for improving the working conditions (Seiber, 1974, p. 571).

A primary positive payoff in occupying multiple social positions is the visibility and status enhancement that follows. Rewards and recognitions for role performance in one role will many times have positive influence in other social spheres. This phenomenon can be clearly seen in the likes of Henry Kissinger who, because of his outstanding role performance at Harvard, was selected for government service, which in turn opened up numerous opportunities in the political and business worlds and other university settings. The movement of top business and academic officials in and out of government circles confirms Mills' (1968) observation that this transfer of influence from one sphere to another makes possible the powerful elite groupings in any society. In Seiber's words, "it would be surprising if ego did not find that the tension engendered by [role] conflict and overload was not totally overshadowed by the rewards of role multiplicity" (1974, p. 576).

Social Roles as Process

To define the basic ideas needed to study the concept of *role*, we have thus far presented static societal dimensions. Positions, roles, and norms are seen as parts of the social order, and individuals are seen as moving in and out of social positions exhibiting the appropriate behavior according to role expectations. Society, in this view, is seen as a "structure of relations" (Blumer, 1966, p. 541). Although this emphasis upon social structure has been useful to social psychologists, a number of them have spoken of the need to view society as an "ongoing process of action" (Blumer, 1966, p. 541). They see a need to describe human interaction in process terms underscoring the dynamic nature of social relations rather than in static, structural terms. Social roles are forged in social interaction. Each actor creates his or her own particular style of role performance depending upon his or her view of self and others.

ROLE TAKING

In its most basic process form, social interaction proceeds smoothly only because each person takes into account the role expectations of the other person and uses these expectations to channel or modify his or her own behavior toward the other person. Role taking, in its "most general form is a process of looking at or anticipating another's behavior by viewing it in the context of a role imputed to that other" (Turner, 1966, p. 151). Social behavior is made possible precisely because humans do not respond directly to stimuli but to stimuli (behavior of another person) that are placed into meaning systems. One of the chief mechanisms for doing this is to place the other person in an appropriate social position, anticipate the behavior that would be associated with that position, and then align one's own action with the total definition of the situation concerning self and others.

Taking the role of the other is not only bound up with ongoing social interaction but also gives rise to the socially appropriate emotional responses to a given behavior. By accurately attributing the appropriate role to the other person, one experiences the emotion that fits in the social context of the action. Different social contexts make different responses appropriate, even though the specific behavior may not change across social settings. Thus, a slap in the face will give rise to a very different set of emotions depending upon the roles that are assigned to self and others as part of the definition of the situation. For example, a slap that occurs when two people are arguing may be defined as insult and may result in increased anger on the part of the participants. The same slap given by a parent to a child may be defined as punishment for inappropriate behavior and may result in shame or guilt. A slap initiated by a very young child against his or her father may occur during horseplay and may lead to amusement and laughter, and so forth. None of these behaviors may be completely understandable to an observer who did not know the context in which they occurred.

Thus, in virtually all social interaction, be it the first encounter or routinized action, each actor sees himself or herself as an object of the actions and perceptions of the other person. Simultaneously, the person experiences self as subject or initiator of action.

As is apparent from the foregoing, role taking relies on many social cues to generate sustained social interaction. The nature of the social positions ascribed to self and others will partly determine how accurate a person is at taking the role of the other. For example, it might be argued that in the family, parents would be more accurate role takers than children because they are older, have spent years observing and caring for their children, and have come to know them well. On the other hand, if the parent role in the family carries the privilege of power over the children, the children out of necessity might be more adept at perceiving what their parents would do. Thomas, Franks, and Calonico, (1972) tested the hypothesis that adolescent daughters would be more perceptive than adolescent sons, who would be more perceptive than mothers, who would be more perceptive than fathers. The reasoning was that the less formal power the person had in a social system the more he or she would rely on accurate role taking as an influence strategy. Because the father was the most powerful by virtue of legitimate authority in the family, he would be the least accurate role taker. In general, the data supported the hypothesis. There was no significant difference between adolescent daughters and sons, but they were both more accurate than their mothers, who in turn were more accurate than fathers.

ROLE MAKING

A second process of social interaction is role making (Turner, 1962, p. 21). Not only do people ascribe roles to self and others, but they create their own version of their role performance over time. There is considerable leeway allowed between the role expectations and any one person's performance; thus, people develop their own distinct style of role performance. In creating the role, the person does not just comply with existent role expectations but selectively chooses those expectations to which he or she conforms, those that he or she modifies extensively, and those that he or she rejects completely. This process of role making generates a considerable amount of social change over time as the role created by one occupant becomes the accepted role expectation for a later occupant of that social position.

Such social change can be readily seen in a number of common roles. For example:

> The priest of 1970 could conduct a marriage service jointly with a protestant minister, while the priest of 1950 would have viewed such behavior as intolerable. A female in the 1970s could decide to be a jockey, while females in the 1950s would have viewed such a decision as bizarre. A college professor in the 1970s might appear in class in anything from shorts to jeans, while the professor of 1950 would consider the removal of his suit coat in class as highly inappropriate. Numberless priests, women, and college professors interacting with numberless others modified their roles over time, and as the examples . . . show, over a short period of time (Lauer and Handel, 1977, p. 81).

The amount of change that occurs between the expectations and the performance appears to be related to how closely the role expectations fit with the actor's basic self-concept. So long as there is close congruence between the cultural expectations and the self, there will likely be little modification of the role. When there is great discrepancy, the actor will develop a more personalized style of performance.

ROLE DISTANCE

Goffman (1961, pp. 105–52) has carefully analyzed face-to-face social encounters by introducing the concept *role distance* to refer to the discrepancy between the actor's view of self and the "self that is implied in the role" (1961, p. 108). Goffman's extensive analysis of the merry-go-round rider shows the emergence of role distance as the child's view of his or her own capable self develops and changes over time. At two or younger, the role of a merry-go-round rider is too much for the child to handle. The role may be rejected completely because the child's view of self is that of not being capable of performing the role. At three or four, he or she embraces the role enthusiastically and performs with serious dedication. The self and role mesh and "doing is being." At five, the child's view of self is now that of being much more capable than just riding a wooden horse, and hence he or she develops a personal, mocking style of riding. The intent is to create distance between the self and the role; to clearly communicate to all observers that the real self is not to be confused with the role of rider. Role distance affords people a process by which they can apologize to observers for performing a role that they perceive to be inappropriate and by which they can rationalize the behavior.

ROLES AND THE STAGE

Another important usage of the concept of role in the social-psychology literature helps us further understand some of the relationships existing between the behavior as it is performed in a given role and the individual

Establishing role distance is often used as a means to justify engaging in what would otherwise be defined as an inappropriate behavior. *Source:* Forsyth, Monkmeyer Press Photo Service.

performing the role. This usage draws directly from another of its historical roots—the theater. It implies that when we perform in a role we are to one degree or another actively wearing a mask and that in wearing the mask we are presenting to the audience only part of the behavior we take to be representative of us as a total person.

From this perspective, role playing may be seen as a type of dishonesty if the particular behavior selected is radically different from what the person would do in a different social setting. We may engage in behavior because that is what the role calls for and not because that is the type of behavior we would prefer. Henry (1973) refers to the most blatant examples of this as "sham" and provides us with some rather vivid examples: "President Johnson tells us that war is peace, Martin Luther King pats the Illinois National Guard on the back for their politeness while Hubert Humphrey suggests the appropriateness of Negro revolt. The officers of a famous university issue engraved invitations to a 'reception opening the Conference of Poverty in America;' and those who direct antipoverty programs are the upper-middle class, who are not in want. It is clear that our civilization is a tissue of contradictions and lies; and that therefore the main problem for psychiatry is not to cure mental illness but to define sanity and account for its occurrence" (p. 120).

The major proponent of the theatrical view of role in contemporary social psychology is Erving Goffman (1959, 1961). Goffman exhibits an uncanny skill in analyzing interpersonal relationships. In our everyday encounters, according to Goffman, each of us attempts to manage the impressions that others will have of us; we strive to create a certain definition of the situation that will cause others to attach appropriate meaning to the behavior under question. To do this, we develop defensive and protective behavior to safeguard against a breakdown in this impression management, which would result in others developing a different impression of us than that which we desire them to have.

According to Goffman, most social behavior can be viewed as a "performance." It involves a stage or setting where the performance takes place, an actor who is playing a role, and an audience that reacts to the performance of the actor. In order to have some degree of control over the impression that the audience receives, the actor will attempt to manipulate the setting or stage. For example, furniture and other room decorations will be arranged and rearranged until they are "just right" for creating the desired impression. A woman who has invited to dinner at her apartment a man in whom she is particularly interested will often carefully arrange the setting in order to help create a desired impression. For example, she may light candles, select music that conveys just the right mood, ask roommates to stay away for the evening, carefully select her outfit, and so on. A role has been chosen, and the performer does what can be done to facilitate an effective and successful performance of that role.

While the individual is rehearsing the soon to be performed role, careful scrutiny is given to the smallest detail if the performance is an important one. John Dean deliberately changed from contact lenses to eye glasses before testifying at the Watergate hearings. One day while Dean was watching himself on television during one of the prehearing interviews, he noticed that his contacts made him blink repeatedly, which he felt would threaten his credibility. In his words, "That's when I said, John, get the old glasses out and get your hair cut so you don't look like the White House hippie" (*Newsweek* Sept. 12, 1977, p. 73).

In situations such as this, *each* individual will be engaging—either consciously or unconsciously—in a role performance attempting to insure that the role as performed is believable. If one of the actors is a novice, he or she has probably received some instruction and coaching from a more experienced performer. Goffman notes that if the performance is to be successful, the setting and the appearance and manner of the actors must be congruent. Roles must be played according to an unwritten, but generally accepted, script. If some unplanned for or unanticipated event occurs, the mood may be destroyed, and the effort at careful impression management may fail.

Given the fact that the individual effectively projects a definition of the situation when he enters the presence of others, we may assume that events may occur within the interaction which contradict, discredit, or otherwise throw doubt upon this projection. When these disruptive events occur, the interaction itself may come to a confused and embarrassed halt. Some of the assumptions upon which the responses of the participants had been predicated become untenable, and the participants find themselves lodged in an interaction for which the situation has been wrongly defined and is now no longer defined. At such moments the individual whose presentation has been discredited may feel ashamed while the others present may feel hostile, and all the participants may come to feel ill at ease, nonplussed, out of countenance, embarrassed, experiencing the kind of anomy that is generated when the minute social system of face-to-face interaction breaks down (Goffman, 1959, p. 12, reprinted by permission).

Embarrassment As an instance of the breakdown of the underlying social expectations in face-to-face interaction, embarrassment has been studied by social psychologists. These studies help us to understand the importance of role performance. Gross and Stone (1964) carefully analyzed approximately one thousand cases of embarrassment. Like Goffman, they see embarrassment arising out of unexpected events that unequivocally "discredit" the underlying assumptions about the identity and role performance of "at least one participant" (Gross and Stone, 1964, p. 1). Thus, embarrassment is a result of the nature of the social setting rather than a consequence of a personality trait.

Gross and Stone identify three necessary conditions that must be maintained in order to insure adequate role performance: establishment and maintenance of poise; retention of trust in each social participant; and presentation and maintenance of the appropriate identity. The loss of poise was a frequent source of embarrassment in the Gross and Stone research. Failure to maintain expected control over body, clothing, or physical objects caused the loss of poise in many cases. Stumbling, trembling, tearing clothing, or having a chair collapse as one sits are examples of events that can destroy poise.

When someone arrives at the checkout stand in a grocery store and finds that he or she has no money, both the shopper and the checkout clerk will feel embarrassed. Having no money violates an agreed upon assumption about the identity of customer, which carries with it the expectation of paying for the goods. This identity is established behaviorally when a shopper gets the cart and fills it with groceries. Having discredited this identity, the otherwise smooth social interaction is abruptly halted.

Front and Back Regions Goffman makes an interesting and important distinction between front and back regions in his analysis of role behavior. *Front regions* are those areas where the performance is actually given. The individual carefully arranges both stage props and mask for the front-region performance; lines are memorized; actions are rehearsed; potential pitfalls that would disrupt the proceedings are assessed and carefully avoided. In Goffman's analysis, a front region can be considered "on stage."

However, each of us also has *back regions*—those places relative to a given performance where we can remove the mask, let our hair down, and no longer have to worry about the performance. In Goffman's terms, a back region is a place where the impression that has been fostered by the performance in the front region may be knowingly contradicted if the actor wishes to portray behavior characteristic of a different dimension of self. "Here stage props and items of personal front can be stored in a kind of compact collapsing of whole repertoires of actions and character. . . . Here the team can run through its performance, checking for offending expressions when no audience is present to be affronted by them. . . . Here the performer can relax; he can drop his front, forgo speaking his lines, and step out of character" (1959, p. 112).

The actor keeps backstage those vital secrets that would cause the impression that is being fostered on stage to break down. For example, "if the bereaved are to be given the illusion that the dead one is really in deep and tranquil sleep, then the undertaker must be able to keep the bereaved from the workroom where the corpses are drained, stuffed, and painted in preparation for their final performance" (Goffman 1959, p. 114).

We even attempt to manage our homes and our workplaces to keep distinct front and back regions. For example, some people may keep on public display in their living rooms copies of magazines and books seldom read, and they may have hidden away in another room those items they frequently read but that they would never admit to someone else.

One of the more interesting occurrences from the perspective of the social psychologist is when back-region behavior intrudes into front-region settings. Some fascinating examples of this intrusion have occurred in the political world. For example, following a political address to a Canadian audience, former Secretary of State Henry Kissinger was publicly embarrassed when it was discovered that the supposedly "dead" mike at the table where he was chatting informally with some Canadian government officials was in fact on and was carrying his conversation into a crowded newsroom at another place in the building. The surprised reporters were more than delighted to record Secretary Kissinger's back-region remarks on his feelings toward Richard Nixon, his impressions of Jackie Kennedy Onassis' sexuality, and so on. Former Secretary of Agriculture Earl Butz was forced to resign from the Ford cabinet when he told a back-region racial joke to some friends on a plane and was overheard by reporters, who made it public. Most individuals have clearly defined front and back regions, and the difference in behavior from one to the other probably varies significantly. However, to assume that either the front region or back region describes the "real" person is to miss the power of Goffman's insights. Both front- and back-region behavior is governed by normative expectations, and both need to be analyzed to better understand interpersonal behavior.

Discrepant Roles To study social roles from the perspective developed by Goffman, one must always ask whether or not things are really what they appear to be. Does the observer attach the same meaning to the performed role as does the actor? The answer to this question is made even more difficult by the fact that some people play *discrepant roles;* that is, they consciously misrepresent themselves by causing us to assume that they are playing one particular role when in fact they are really playing another. Goffman discusses a series of discrepant roles, some of which are the informer, the shill, and the agent.

The *informer* is the individual who pretends to the performers to be a member of their team, but who is in fact there to obtain vital secrets that will be given to the audience or revealed to an opposing group. Because the informer is accepted by the actors as one of them, he or she is allowed to come backstage and to have access to information that is potentially damaging when it is revealed or made public. Political, military, and industrial spies are examples of informers.

The *shill* is someone who acts as a member of the audience, but who is in fact in league with the performers. For example, speakers or other performers may "plant" members of their team in an audience to influence the behavior of that audience. At appropriate times, the shill may laugh, applaud, cheer, stand, or engage in some other behavior to influence the role of other members of the audience. Standing ovations following what are, from an objective point of view, mediocre performances, are often triggered by the behavior of shills.

Another important discrepant role is that of the *agent*. The agent is the individual who acts as an ordinary member of an audience, but who is actually there to observe or check up on the behavior of the performer. Police decoys who are used to combat prostitution and muggings in many cities are examples of agents, as are company representatives who act as regular customers in order to judge and evaluate the performance of salespeople and clerks.

The fascinating thing about Goffman's analysis is that he helps us to realize that many of the roles that we play during the course of our daily activities are carefully selected bits of behavior that fit a particular social setting but are not a description of the entire person. We may sit quietly and listen to a professor's dull lecture because we are playing, for the moment, the role of a student, even though we are bored stiff. We may smile pleasantly at an irate customer, although we would much prefer to punch him or her in the nose because we are playing the role of representative of some reputable business. Again, the behavior in which we engage as role performers is normative behavior. The social groups to which we belong define the role, and we take this as the script and perform accordingly. Moments later, we may move into a very different role that will allow another bit of behavior to be selected and performed according to a different script.

ROLES AND SELF

Whether we are just "playing at" roles or whether we are performing in a role that requires long-term commitments, the effect of roles on our individual personalities and behavior patterns can sometimes be rather dramatic. Role theorists have long assumed that a person can be significantly affected by the roles he or she occupies in a given social system. The excerpt from Orwell's *Animal Farm* beginning the chapter is a fictional example of this process. In many cases, a person internalizes the norms of a role, so a role that is taken up reluctantly or with distance becomes an important one. The role and the person merge.

This process has been demonstrated in several important social-psychological experiments. In an early field experiment, Lieberman (1956) studied the attitudes and perceptions of a large group of factory employees who produced home-appliance equipment. Lieberman examined such things as attitudes toward work conditions, toward management, and toward the local labor union. In the year following the initial survey, several of the workers in the factory were promoted to the role of foreman and others had been selected as union stewards. Lieberman was then able to go back and again measure the attitudes of these men who had changed roles and compare them with another group of men, controlling relevant characteristics and initial attitudes, who had not changed jobs. Lieberman found that the change in roles had a significant effect upon their attitudes. Those promoted to foreman positions became more favorable toward management and less

At times, role and self almost merge and become one—both in the eyes of actors and in the eyes of observers. *Source:* Culver Pictures Inc.

favorable toward unions, and those who had assumed positions as union stewards made changes in almost the opposite direction.

In the second year following the initial study, an economic recession forced a cutback at the plant, and some men who had been serving as foremen had to be demoted and some workers who had been union stewards were placed back in regular work roles. Again, the change in roles significantly affected the attitudes of the workers. By this time, the men who had become foremen and who remained foremen exhibited attitudes that were almost diametrically opposed to those of the men who had retained the roles of worker or who had become union officials, although they were very similar two years earlier.

More recently, a study by Zimbardo (1971) demonstrated the importance of the link between role and other social-psychological characteristics of the individual. Zimbardo established a simulated prison at Stanford University as his experimental lab. A number of mature and apparently stable young men who volunteered for the experiment were then assigned, on the basis of the flip of a coin, to be either prisoners or guards at the prison. Those selected to be prisoners were stripped of their clothing, fingerprinted, photographed, assigned a number and uniform, and locked in cells. Guards wore uniforms and dark glasses and were assigned to run the prison complex. Zimbardo's initial plan had been to continue the experiment for about two weeks, but the study had to be terminated after only six days. By that point, the volunteers had so internalized their roles that the situation was becoming frightening and dangerous. According to Zimbardo, most had indeed become "guards" and "prisoners" and appeared unable to clearly differentiate between role playing and self.

These experimental examples are repeated daily in everyday encounters.

The apparently shy and retiring individual blossoms into a dynamic and forceful executive when given the responsibility. The radical becomes a strong defender of the status quo when elected as mayor of the city. In each case, role behavior learned in one setting merges with the individual's self-concept and influences behavior in other social settings.

Turner has observed that with some individuals "roles are put on and taken off like clothing without lasting personal effect. Other roles are difficult to put aside . . . and continue to color the way in which many of the individual's roles are performed" (1978, p. 1). Some of the factors that Turner believes lead to a merger of the role with the person are social or situational factors and some are personal characteristics. If the individual's social world does not contain "contradictory roles," then merger will more likely occur. Those who observe the actor perform the role and who have not observed conflicting roles will tend to see the role and person merge. Likewise, the actor will tend to converge his opinion of self with that of the other social observers and merge the role behavior with his or her view of self. The greater the role is differentiated and the greater the power ascribed to the role, the greater the merger of person with role will be (Turner, 1978, pp. 7, 8). If the social order defines any performer's role behavior as relatively temporary, this will reduce the amount of person-role merger (Turner, 1978, p. 12).

Turner's analysis leads him to conclude that some of the individual factors that influence role merger are the degree of autonomy the person develops in enacting the role and the amount of reward the person believes he or she receives from the role. An autonomous individual who believes he or she will receive considerable reward from the role performance will likely see

Table 6–1   Conditions under Which Person and Role Will Likely be Merged

1. The more intensely and consistently significant others identify a person on the basis of a certain role, the greater the tendency for the individual to merge that role with his or her person.

2. The more actor discretion incorporated in a role and the wider the range of settings in which the role behavior can be made meaningful, the greater the tendency for the individual to merge the role with his or her person.

3. Individuals tend to merge positively evaluated roles with their persons.

4. Individuals tend to locate their persons in the roles they enact most adequately.

5. The greater the investment of time and effort in gaining or maintaining the opportunity to claim a role or in learning to play *a* role, the greater the tendency to merge the role with the person.

6. The greater the sacrifices made in the course of gaining or maintaining the opportunity to claim a role, or in learning to play a role, the greater the tendency to merge the role with the person.

7. The more publicly a role is played and the more an individual has engaged in explaining and justifying a role and its standpoint, the greater the tendency to merge the role with the person.

8. The greater the unresolved role strain, the greater the tendency to merge the role with the person.

Adapted from Turner, 1978, pp. 14–15.

his or her role behavior merging with view of self (1978, p. 14). A more complete list of Turner's propositions about this merger is given in table 6–1.

Sex: A Universal Social Role?

To this point, we have viewed the person as moving into various social positions and performing the expected behavior. The role performer may create a distinctive style of role performance and may contribute to social change in creating different expectations for a particular social position. Likewise, the social processes may lead the individual performer to alter his or her views about his or her own individual characteristics. Thus, both the social order and the individual are likely to change because of social interaction.

We now turn to an examination of the most universal of all social roles —the sex role. It is the earliest and most persistent social role learned and adopted. Most sex-role performances require lifelong commitments with very few opting to change their sex-role identity. For most people, the sex role has become basically merged with the person. The beginnings of this sex-role learning occurs so early that most cannot remember when the sex role was not part of the person.

Once the concept of sex role is learned and children place people in this social category, a whole array of appropriate and inappropriate behavior can then be ascribed to boys and girls, and men and women. By considering how children acquire this universal role, we can better understand not only sex roles but other social roles as well.

THE DEVELOPMENT OF SEX-TYPED BEHAVIOR

Given that virtually all cultures place men and women in different social statuses and children quickly learn appropriate and inappropriate behavior based upon these social categories, we now ask, how does a child learn appropriate behavior for a given social position? We use the learning of sex-typed behavior to illustrate the basic processes.

One of the earlier explanations of the acquisition of sex-typed behavior comes from the work of Freud, who postulated that girls identified with their mothers (anaclytic identification) and boys identified with their fathers (the aggressor) and adopted the appropriate sex-role identity with the accompanying sex-typed behavior (see chapters 2 and 4). Although the Freudian explanation enjoyed considerable professional and lay popularity for some time, the research evidence has failed to substantiate it. We will therefore concentrate on more recent explanations.

Social-Learning Approach The social learning approach sees the acquisition of sex-typed behavior as just another type of learning that can be explained according to basic learning principles. In the words of one social learning theorist:

> Sex-typing is the process by which the individual acquires sex-typed behavior patterns: first he learns to *discriminate* between sex-typed behavior pat-

terns, then to *generalize* from these specific learning experiences to new situations, and finally to *perform* sex-typed behavior (Mischel, 1966, p. 57).

Sex-typed behavior is seen as a consequence of the rewards and punishments that a child experiences as he or she engages in various behaviors. This explanation assumes, for example, that a male child will be rewarded for engaging in behavior characteristic of male children and punished for doing what girls do. Girls likewise will be rewarded and punished for appropriate and inappropriate sex-typed behavior. Parents are seen as critical in this rewarding and punishing paradigm. Boys are given trucks to play with, and girls are given dolls. Gradually, the child learns to discriminate between appropriate and inappropriate behavior and then generalizes from these specific instances of rewarding and punishing behaviors to other children and adults in general, based upon their appropriate sex label.

The social-learning model also postulates a second process—that of observational learning. It is generally acknowledged that a child learns many things by merely observing a role model (parent or peer) engaging in behavior. The child need not be rewarded or punished personally; through observational learning he or she comes to discriminate between appropriate and inappropriate sex-typed behavior. Therefore, the same-sex parent becomes a powerful model in learning appropriate sex-typed behavior. A daughter

"In the interests of science, Miss Mellish, I'm going to make a rather strange request of you."

Source: Peter Arno; © 1937, 1965 The New Yorker Magazine, Inc.

learns the requisite feminine behavior by observing her mother in the kitchen, for example. Thus, when the child plays at making bread, she is very adept at reproducing all the intricate sequences of behavior associated with her mother's "feminine behavior" of making bread. She carefully arranges the pans, adds the ingredients, mixes, puts the pans in the oven, and times the baking.

Taken together, the rewarding-punishing and the modeling processes lead to the three major steps in the acquisition of sex-typed behavior (see figure 6–3). First, the child becomes attached to the same-sex parent as the major source of rewards and punishments. From the series of specific rewarding and punishing acts, the child generalizes or identifies with the same-sex parent. The next step in the generalization process leads to the appropriate sex-typed identity with the accompanying appropriate sex-typed behavior.

Some researchers question the validity of using the rewarding/punishing and observational processes to fully explain acquisition of sex-typed behavior. In a review of available evidence, Maccoby and Jacklin (1974) conclude that these social-learning processes are not really adequate to account for sex-typed behavior. In order for the first process to explain sex-typed behavior, it would be necessary for parents, teachers, and peers to differentially reward and punish boys and girls on the basis of culturally defined sex-typed behavior. In other words, it would have to be shown, for example, that parents and teachers rewarded aggressive behavior for boys and punished this behavior in girls. The research evidence does not support such a conclu-

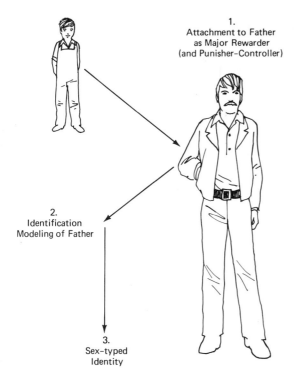

1.
Attachment to Father
as Major Rewarder
(and Punisher–Controller)

2.
Identification
Modeling of Father

3.
Sex-typed
Identity

Figure 6–3 Social-Learning Sequence of the Acquisition of Sex-Typed Behavior. (Adapted from Kohlberg, 1966, p. 128.)

sion. Even though some research finds no difference, the bulk of the available evidence indicates that parents punish boys for aggressive behavior more than girls. Likewise, there is some research that indicates that if the aggressive child is a boy, nursery-school teachers will more likely "intervene and scold" the guilty child (Maccoby and Jacklin, 1974, p. 361). The evidence seems to contradict the social-learning explanation of aggression in the larger social setting. Maccoby and Jacklin conclude that "although differential reinforcement of boys and girls may account for some sex typing as narrowly defined (e.g., the fact that boys avoid wearing dresses and playing with dolls), there are large areas of sex-differentiated behavior where parental sanctions and encouragement seem to play only a very minor role" (1974, p. 364).

The observational learning and modeling explanation of sex-typed behavior is also found wanting when carefully weighed against other available evidence. If the observational and modeling explanation could explain sex-typed behavior, it would logically follow that boys as compared to girls would model and therefore be more like their father and girls as compared to boys would be more like their mother. Maccoby and Jacklin conclude that "children have not been shown to resemble closely the same-sex parent. . . . The rather meager evidence suggests that a boy resembles other children's fathers as much as he does his own" (1974, p. 363). In addition, considerable research as well as anecdotal evidence indicates that children's sex-typed behavior does not closely resemble adult models. Maccoby and Jacklin note, "Boys choose to play with trucks and cars, even though they may have seen their mothers driving the family car more frequently than their fathers; girls play hopscotch and jacks, highly sex-typed games, although these games are totally absent from their mother's observable behavior" (1974, p. 363).

One of the weaknesses of much of the published research on modeling is that data are collected from models in only one social setting. For example, children are studied to judge the degree to which they model their parents. Social reality is not this simple. Children have a variety of models to observe, such as parents, siblings, teachers, and peers. However, because research seems to show that children do not model parents completely, one cannot conclude that children do not model. They may well have chosen other models, such as peers. Sex roles are obviously greatly influenced by peer pressure. Teenage girls spend hours in front of a mirror before going to school so they can look "right" (like their friends). Boys go to great lengths to model peers so they will be "with it" or appropriately "tough."

Cognitive-Developmental View As Maccoby and Jacklin assert, the social pressures from differential rewards and punishments and observational learning "do not by any means tell the whole story of the origins of sex differences" (1974, p. 363). We need additional explanations to help account for the observed differences. An alternative view that has been most fully developed by Kohlberg (1966) can add some additional insight. Kohlberg begins by identifying the basic casual model underlying the social-learning approach to sex typing and then compares it to the cognitive-developmental view. Using the boy as an example, in abbreviated form the basic social-learning model is:

1. I want rewards.
2. I am rewarded for doing boy things.
3. *Therefore,* I want to be a boy (Kohlberg, 1966, p. 89).

The cognitive-developmental view of sex typing argues for a very different sequence of events leading up to sex-typed behavior. This view underscores the active, knowledge-assimilating dimension of the human organism. This explanation asserts that the child develops a view of self as being male or female at about the same age that he or she is developing some other rather stable cognitive abilities, specifically that of *conservation.* At some point in the child's cognitive development, he or she learns that substances, such as water in a bottle, conserve their quantity even though they appear to change. The child concludes that the substance has conserved its original quantity even though this is not readily apparent.

Kohlberg reasons that a child will likely develop a sense of constancy about his or her own sex-role identity about the same time he or she is developing the analogous cognitive processes of conservation. He presents evidence to show that this generally occurs at about five to seven years of age in western cultures. Once the child forms his own sex-role identity by coming to know that he is a boy and that he will always be a boy, he then matches his own behavior to the internalized standard of what a boy should do. Before the child develops this permanent view of himself, he may believe that he could become a girl by dressing differently. Once he has developed his sex-role identity, he knows that he will always be a boy no matter how he might dress. The basic underlying casual chain from the developmental point of view is:

1. I am a boy.
2. I want to do boy things.
3. *Therefore,* doing boy things is rewarding (adapted from Kohlberg, 1966, p. 89).

As is readily apparent, the cognitive-developmental view reverses the basic underlying motivational sequence by beginning with sex-role identity (see figure 6–4). The motivation to engage in sex-typed behavior grows out of that, and, therefore, engaging in sex-typed behavior is rewarding. Likewise, the underlying motivational model leads to a very different sequence of events from those of the social learning sequence.

Maccoby and Jacklin (1974) call this approach to sex typing self-socialization and note that there is considerable evidence to support it as a partial explanation of what occurs. They cite research that shows that once children have formed their own gender identity and believe that they will always be a boy or girl (gender constancy) they systematically choose to observe same-sex role models, whereas children who have not achieved gender constancy do not.

However, the available evidence is not entirely supportive of Kohlberg's formulations either. What does not hold up is the assertion that sex-typed behavior follows from the formation of sex-role identity, which can only be developed after the child develops the cognitive processes built upon the

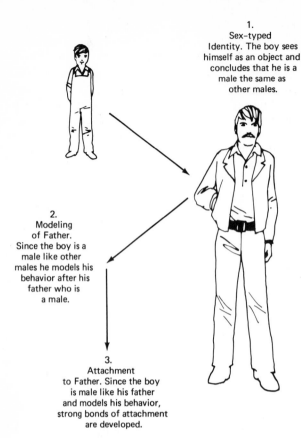

1.
Sex-typed
Identity. The boy sees
himself as an object and
concludes that he is a
male the same as
other males.

2.
Modeling
of Father.
Since the boy is a
male like other
males he models his
behavior after his
father who is
a male.

3.
Attachment
to Father. Since the boy
is male like his father
and models his behavior,
strong bonds of attachment
are developed.

Figure 6–4 Cognitive-Developmental
Sequence of the Acquisition of Sex-Typed
Behavior. (Adapted from Kohlberg, 1966,
p. 128.)

principles of conservation. There is abundant evidence that children consistently choose appropriate sex-typed behavior long before they have achieved gender constancy. As early as twenty months, children begin exhibiting sex-typed behavior even though they will not develop gender constancy until age five or six.

In carefully controlled research with twenty-month-old infants, Fein et al. (1975) observed sex-typed preferences for toys. They observed that male infants imitated the model more if the model used a male toy, such as a truck, hammer, or gun. Girls imitated more when the model had female toys. This sex-typed preference held even when the researchers controlled for how familiar the infant was with the respective toys. In addition, this and other research shows that even in twenty-month-old infants the male sex role seems to be more clearly defined with greater consistency in male behavior compared to female behavior. Cross-sex "interests are less likely to appear in boys than girls" (Fein et al., 1975, p. 527). Girls aged twenty months are more likely to play with cross-sex toys. Even though this difference emerges early, knowledge about sex roles appears to develop in similar ways for boys and girls. They both learn about the male role at an earlier age than the female role (Williams, Bennet, and Best, 1975, p. 641).

Maccoby and Jacklin show that the child, as early as three years of age, begins to formulate rudimentary cognitions of his or her own gender identity and that he or she actively attempts to match his or her own behaviors to that internalized sex-role standard. The early formulations may be incomplete and very different from adult standards, but they are a beginning, and as the child develops his or her sex-typed behavior will likewise change.

> We believe that the processes of direct reinforcement and simple imitation are clearly involved in the acquisition of sex-typed behavior, but that they are not sufficient to account for the developmental changes that occur in sex typing. . . . The third process . . . in its simplest terms . . . means that a child gradually develops concepts of "masculinity" and "femininity" and when he has understood what his own sex is, he attempts to match his behavior to his conceptions. His ideas may be drawn only minimally from observing his own parents. The generalizations he constructs do not represent acts of imitation, but are organizations of information distilled from a wide variety of sources (Maccoby and Jacklin, 1974, pp. 365–66).

The evidence seems to indicate that a number of different processes are involved. Clearly, the rewards and punishments that the society attaches to sex-typed behavior as well as the modeling process influence what the child sees as behavior that he or she wants to perform because he or she is of that sex. For example, adolescent girls show much more interest in babies than do boys. This difference does not show up before adolescence nor is it present in "single, cohabiting or married young adults" (Feldman, Nash, and Cutrona, 1977, p. 676). It is believed that the adolescent develops this interest in anticipation of adopting the role of mother as her orienting future identity. Self-socialization begins early and continues through life and clearly influences what the individual sees as behavior typical and appropriate for his or her sex. Social psychologists have identified some of the basic processes but have many unanswered questions still before them.

MYTHS AND REALITIES ABOUT SEX-ROLE DIFFERENCES

Given all the discussion about sex roles in western societies, it is not surprising to find many differing opinions about the clear differences between male and female sex roles. After carefully analyzing a large number of studies, the following differences—that at one time were taken as *real differences* between the sexes—are *not substantiated* in the social-psychological research literature (Maccoby and Jacklin, 1974, pp. 349–52).

1. Girls are more "social" than boys.
2. Girls are more "suggestible" than boys.
3. Girls have lower self-esteem.
4. Girls are better at role learning and simple repetitive tasks, and boys are better at tasks that require higher-level cognitive processing and the inhibition of previously learned responses.
5. Boys are more "analytic."
6. Girls are more affected by heredity, boys by environment.
7. Girls lack achievement motivation.
8. Girls are auditory, boys visual.

These are probably best considered as myths about sex role differences; the following differences appear to be well supported by research findings:

1. Girls have greater verbal ability than boys do.
2. Boys excel in visual-spatial ability.
3. Boys excel in mathematical ability.
4. Males are more aggressive.

Some of the available research evidence (Guttman, 1975; Maccoby and Jacklin, 1974) leads to the conclusion that some of the differences probably have a biological base. For example, there is evidence of a biological base for aggression in that: (1) the sex difference manifests itself in similar ways in man and the subhuman primates; (2) it is universal across cultures; and (3) levels of aggression are responsive to sex hormones (Maccoby and Jacklin, 1974, p. 360). Although Maccoby and Jacklin are confident that the available evidence strongly supports their conclusion that a biological base underlies some of the observed differences, they are quick to acknowledge that biology is not destiny. They do argue, however, that the biological base in the form of "genetically controlled characteristics . . . may take the form of a greater *readiness* to learn a particular kind of behavior" (1974, p. 363).

At present, it is not clear how a biological readiness to learn one kind of behavior interacts with cultural patterns to produce observed male/female differences. Anthropologists have studied enough different societies to learn that there are great differences in male and female personality characteristics across cultures. Margaret Mead's conclusion of some years ago seems particularly appropriate for our own time.

> We are forced to conclude that human nature is almost unbelievably maleable, responding accurately and contrastingly to contrasting cultural conditions. . . . Personality differences between the sexes are of this order, cultural creations to which each generation, male or female, is trained to conform (Mead, 1935, p. 191, cited in D'Andrade, 1966, p. 185).

Thus, we ought to consider the sex-typed male-female differences we have discussed as characteristic of western societies and not generalize them unthinkingly to other cultures, which might be radically different.

VARIATION IN SEX ROLES

Sex Roles in Different Societies Although biology may not be destiny, virtually all societies develop a division of labor between the sexes that is based upon perceived differences between men and women. These socially accepted differences, whether they are biologically based or not, become the basis for the institutionally sanctioned expectations about what men and women should do.

Anthropologists studying different societies have compared the ways the societies assign tasks. These basic tasks that must be done in order for its members to live are called *subsistence activities.* Some regularities appear in a number of different societies, and these regularities appear to be based upon biological differences. Table 6–2 presents the general findings. Fish-

Table 6-2   Cross-Cultural Data from 224 Societies on Subsistence Activities and Division of Labor by Sex

	NUMBER OF SOCIETIES IN WHICH ACTIVITY IS PERFORMED BY				
Activity	*Men always*	*Men usually*	*Either sex*	*Women usually*	*Women always*
Pursuing sea mammals	34	1	0	0	0
Hunting	166	13	0	0	0
Trapping small animals	128	13	4	1	2
Herding	38	8	4	0	5
Fishing	98	34	19	3	4
Clearing land for agriculture	73	22	17	5	13
Dairy operations	17	4	3	1	13
Preparing and planting soil	31	23	33	20	37
Erecting and dismantling shelter	14	2	5	6	22
Tending fowl and small animals	21	4	8	1	39
Tending and harvesting crops	10	15	35	39	44
Gathering shellfish	9	4	8	7	25
Making and tending fires	18	6	25	22	62
Bearing burdens	12	6	35	20	57
Preparing drinks and narcotics	20	1	13	8	57
Gathering fruits, berries, nuts	12	3	15	13	63
Gathering fuel	22	1	10	19	89
Preserving meat and fish	8	2	10	14	74
Gathering herbs, roots, seeds	8	1	11	7	74
Cooking	5	1	9	28	158
Carrying water	7	0	5	7	119
Grinding grain	2	4	5	13	114

Source: D'Andrade, 1966, p. 177, who adapted this from Murdock, 1937, p. 552.

ing, hunting, trapping, and herding flocks are those activities almost always performed by men in a comparison of 224 societies. Women are almost exclusively assigned such tasks as grinding grain, carrying water, cooking, gathering herbs, roots, and seeds, and preserving meat. In the words of one analyst, the "male activities appear to involve behavior which is strenuous, cooperative, and which may require long periods of travel. The female activities, on the other hand, are more likely to involve the physically easier, more solitary, and less mobile activities. These differences appear to be more or less the direct result of physical male-female differences" (D'Andrade, 1966, p. 176). The functions of bearing and rearing children are the mother's responsibilities, and they restrict her mobility. Societies therefore develop a logical division of labor based upon the need for the mother to remain in one area for longer periods of time during childbirth and child-rearing activities, which leaves to the husband-father those subsistence activities that take him into remote regions.

However, when societies are analyzed according to the types of objects that men and women make it is not apparent that this division of labor is assigned on the basis of physical differences between the sexes. The data presented in table 6–3 show quite clearly that some objects are always produced by women and others almost always produced by men. It does not hold that those activities that are solely the province of men are the most

Table 6-3   Cross-Cultural Data on the Manufacture of Objects and Division of Labor by Sex

Activity	Men always	Men usually	Either sex	Women usually	Women always
Metalworking	78	0	0	0	0
Weapon making	121	1	0	0	0
Boat building	91	4	4	0	1
Manufacture of musical instruments	45	2	0	0	1
Work in wood and bark	113	9	5	1	1
Work in stone	68	3	2	0	2
Work in bone, horn, shell	67	4	3	0	3
Manufacture of ceremonial objects	37	1	13	0	1
House building	86	32	25	3	14
Net making	44	6	4	2	11
Manufacture of ornaments	24	3	40	6	18
Manufacture of leather products	29	3	9	3	32
Hide preparation	31	2	4	4	49
Manufacture of nontextile fabrics	14	0	9	2	32
Manufacture of thread and cordage	23	2	11	10	73
Basket making	25	3	10	6	82
Mat making	16	2	6	4	61
Weaving	19	2	2	6	67
Pottery making	13	2	6	8	77
Manufacture and repair of clothing	12	3	8	9	95

The column headers fall under the overarching label: NUMBER OF SOCIETIES IN WHICH ACTIVITY IS PERFORMED BY

Source: D'Andrade, 1966, p. 178, who adapted this from Murdock, 1937, p. 552.

strenuous, nor do they require more cooperative behavior, nor do they require more mobility. Weapon making is the province of men in virtually all societies, but this is not necessarily more strenuous than making pottery or manufacturing and repairing clothing, which are clearly what women do in those societies. Likewise, one cannot make the case that the reason men almost always make the musical instruments is that this is strenuous work requiring great mobility. Clearly, although some division of labor, specifically subsistence activity, seems to be based upon physical differences between the sexes, this can account for only a small part of those activities that any society defines as falling into either the male or female domain. It is the social order itself that creates and sustains most of the observed differences between male and female activities.

As can be seen from both tables 6-2 and 6-3, there is greater consistency in the "male" activities across societies than in the "female" activities (compare the greater number of zeros in the "always" and "usually" columns for both sexes). This greater variety seen in women's activities is similar to that of the cross-sexual behavior in female infants in our society. This tendency for the male to be more fully sex typed begins as early as twenty months of age and carries into adulthood. Research shows that men tend to choose masculine activity over feminine activity even when "they would be paid more for performing feminine activity." Women's choices "are more sex-neutral" (Maccoby and Jacklin, 1974, p. 284).

This greater sex typing in very young children as well as adults may be a function of greater social pressure put on males to make appropriate sex choices. Hartup and Moore's research (1963) showed that, especially when an investigator was present, boys were less likely to choose a sex-inappropriate toy. Subsequent research shows that when a son chooses a feminine activity parents are deeply concerned but that they demonstrate little concern about a girl's choice of masculine activity. Maccoby and Jacklin conclude that "more social pressure against inappropriate sex typing is directed at boys than at girls" (1974, p. 328).

Sex-Role Changes Within a Society In addition to finding similarities and differences across societies in the assignment of sex roles, it is also apparent to social psychologists that sex roles change within any one society over time. It is generally assumed that the rate of change in our contemporary western society is much greater now than it was centuries or even decades ago, thus speeding sex-role changes. The women's liberation movement has sensitized major segments of our population to basic questions centering around those opportunities that should be made available to women that have traditionally been reserved for men. Clearly, there have been great changes in sex roles in the United States in the 1960s and 1970s. Our primary concern in this section is to ask whether sex-role changes in the society at large are best seen as cause or consequence of the women's liberation movement.

Although there has been considerable discussion about changes in sex-role orientations and women's liberation in the popular press, there is not a great deal of good research available that has focused on the question of how the changes in sex-role attitudes relate to the movement. The best of the available research evidence comes from a careful analysis of data from surveys taken between 1964 and 1974 (Mason, Czajke, and Arber, 1976). This important analysis covers a time period

Changing expectations of parents and community for their children may expose the extent to which socialization rather than biology has dictated sex roles. *Source:* S. M. Wakefield.

that allows examination of sex-role attitudes before, during, and after the rise of the movement.

The available evidence indicates that by 1970, women in the United States were likely to have become aware of the liberation movement. Mason, Czajke, and Arber, conclude, after reviewing the relevant research that "most women in the United States were not exposed to the movement's activities or ideas until very late in the 1960s or early 1970s" (1976, p. 575). Thus, any change occurring before 1970 cannot convincingly be attributed to the women's movement, but would have to be attributed to other social-psychological dynamics. Change occurring after 1970 could be influenced by the highly visible women's movement.

Figure 6–5 shows the change occurring in women's sex-role attitudes from 1964 to 1970. The one item that shows no significant change is that dealing with parents encouraging independence equally for sons and daughters. This shows a 4 percent increase, but virtually everyone agreed that daughters should be encouraged to be independent as much as sons in 1964. Because 88 percent agreed with this item, there was little possibility for upward change. In 1964, only 55 percent of the women disagreed with the opinion that a man can make long-range plans but a woman must take things as they come. By 1970, 88 percent of the women disagreed. This is

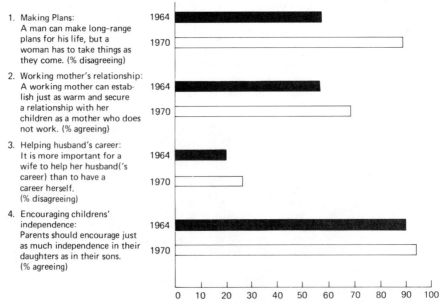

Figure 6–5 Percentage of Women Giving the Egalitarian Response in 1964 and 1970 on Sex-Role Attitude Items. Adapted from Mason, Czajke, and Arber, 1976, p. 585. The 1964 percentages reported here are from a sample from the National Opinion Research Center's College Seniors Study. These women were seniors in 1961 and were sampled again in 1964. The 1970 data comes from a national probability sample as part of the National Fertility Study. The samples were equated on a number of variables, such as women's ages, husband's education, occupational experience, etc., in order to make the samples comparable. Thus, any differences observed are most likely the result of attitude change rather than of comparing two very different samples.

a remarkable shift in attitudes over the six-year period. In 1970, 67 percent of the women agreed that a working mother could establish just as warm a relationship with her children as a nonworking mother. This was an increase of 15 percent over 1964. The research indicates that there were sizeable shifts in women's sex-role attitudes (children, work, careers, and planning for life) in the United States before the movement's "public" rise (Mason, Czajke, and Arber, 1976, p. 585).

Figure 6–6 shows the change in sex-role attitudes occurring between 1970 and 1974. As in the earlier time period, the change in attitudes is very marked across many of the items. It is significant to note that by 1974 80 percent or more of the women agree that a woman's job should be kept for her when she has a baby; that men should share in the housework; that equal prestige should be accorded women as executives, politicians, or even as President; that women should be granted equal job opportunities; and that women should receive equal pay. With the exception of the equal-pay item, with which 94 percent already agreed in 1970, all these items show marked increases from 1970 to 1974. The average increase across those four items was 23 percent. The shift in attitudes was general in nature in that the marked increase occurred across items relating to the prestige of women in both the home and the work world.

Mason, Czajke, and Arber analyzed the rate of change occurring before and after 1970 and concluded that the rate of change was more rapid from 1970 to 1974 than in the earlier six-year period. They concluded that there were forces operating in the society at large before the rise of the women's movement that were causing sex-role attitudes to change.

> The movement may have accelerated the rate at which women's attitudes changed in this period. . . . The sizeable shifts observed between 1964 and 1974 are certainly consistent with the rise of the movement and may help explain the movement's apparent popularity and rapid spread. But we find it difficult to conclude from these data that the movement per se was responsible for lowering women's support for the traditional roles of the sexes (Mason, Czajke, and Arber, 1976, p. 589).

What the women's movement has apparently accomplished is to create a more consistent set of sex-role attitudes between the woman's world at home and at work; a set that became stronger over the four-year period between the two surveys.

In addition, the researchers concluded that the marked sex-role attitude change did not only occur in the higher socio-economic statuses. "The relationship between education and attitudes has remained fairly constant over time. . . . [The] better-educated women changed their attitudes no more than have less-educated women" (Mason, Czajke, and Arber, 1976, p. 584). They observed changes in college-educated women, married Southern women, and Northern metropolitan working women. The sex-role change is obviously a widespread phenomenon that was caused by widespread social changes before 1970. The women's movement evidently further accelerated the change and in addition produced greater consistency of home and work attitudes in women centering around the concept of equality among the sexes.

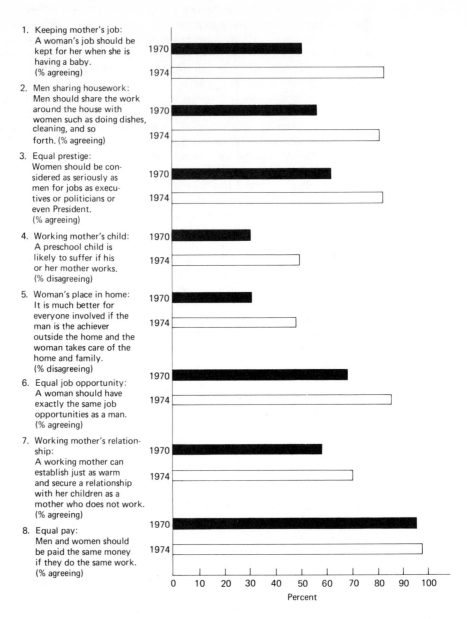

1. Keeping mother's job:
   A woman's job should be kept for her when she is having a baby.
   (% agreeing)

2. Men sharing housework:
   Men should share the work around the house with women such as doing dishes, cleaning, and so forth. (% agreeing)

3. Equal prestige:
   Women should be considered as seriously as men for jobs as executives or politicians or even President.
   (% agreeing)

4. Working mother's child:
   A preschool child is likely to suffer if his or her mother works.
   (% disagreeing)

5. Woman's place in home:
   It is much better for everyone involved if the man is the achiever outside the home and the woman takes care of the home and family.
   (% disagreeing)

6. Equal job opportunity:
   A woman should have exactly the same job opportunities as a man.
   (% agreeing)

7. Working mother's relationship:
   A working mother can establish just as warm and secure a relationship with her children as a mother who does not work.
   (% agreeing)

8. Equal pay:
   Men and women should be paid the same money if they do the same work.
   (% agreeing)

Percent

Figure 6–6 Percentage of Women Giving the Egalitarian Response in 1970 and 1974 on Sex-Role Attitude Items. Adapted from Mason, Czajke, and Arber, 1976, p. 586. The 1970 sample is the National Fertility Survey, and the 1974 sample is the Detroit Area Survey. The two samples are equated on a number of criteria such that observed differences are likely the result of attitude change rather than an artifact of comparing very different samples. The number of women surveyed for the 1970 and 1974 samples were 384 and 164, respectively.

Summary

Role is one of the social-psychological concepts that points simultaneously toward the social order and the individual. It is extremely useful to the student who wishes to better understand both individual behavior and normative expectations. *Social systems* are comprised of interrelated positions that are in turn comprised of clusters of roles. *Roles* are defined as clusters of normative expectations affixed to a social position. Roles do not exist in isolation, but are reciprocal in nature. The role of one person exists in conjunction with another, the role partner. The rights of one role become the role obligations of another.

At any one point in time a person is simultaneously a member of multiple social systems; the multiplicity of roles with their differing role expectations will often cause role strain. For example, the social actor finds that some role expectations will make more difficult role performance in other roles. In the face of the possibility of universal and abundant role strain, human beings in social interaction have created a number of mechanisms, that tend to reduce role strain, thus insuring continuing, satisfying social relations. Recognized and agreed upon hierarchies of formal role expectations exist to reduce role strain in certain cases. In other cases, social actors can decide to engage or not engage in the expected behavior on the basis of which is most important.

When social systems exist that repeatedly have conflicting expectations about role performance, they often move to create a recognized third-party role, such as the arbitrator, with the express purpose of resolving basic recurring differences. In some cases, the arbitrator is expected to be impartial and is protected legally from reprisals from either side. In other situations, the arbitrator role may be defined more in terms of creating shared normative expectations rather than making a decision according to contractual agreement. This distinction between arbitration and mediation has served to further clarify the role expectations of third parties in dispute resolution.

An additional characteristic of the social order that reduces role strain is the positive benefits accrued by the social actor from acquiring more privileges and benefits as roles are accumulated. In many instances, accumulating additional roles will make other role performances easier because increased esteem in one role transfers to others.

A number of social psychologists have objected to the traditional role analysis that underscores the social structural dimensions to the virtual exclusion of the individual and the dynamic nature of the social process. Most cultural expectations are for classes of behavior and leave a wide array of choices up to the individual. Therefore, each individual often helps create his or her own role as he or she develops his or her role performance. Thus, because of role making, normative expectations change dramatically over time as the role made by one individual becomes the role expectations of a later occupant of that same social position. It appears that processes of role taking, role making, and the generating of role distance are all part of social change that is characteristic of every society.

Another important use of the role concept in social psychology employs the analogy of the stage and analyzes front-stage and back-stage behavior to improve our understanding of those things the individual does that are designed to insure that the role enactment generates a believable performance both for the actor and the audience. However, in some social roles, the performance is meant to be very discrepant from the real self, as in the case of the informer, the shill, and the agent. There are conditions under which the role and the person merge and when a person will put on and take off roles with relatively little influence on self-perceptions. Generally, those roles that are perceived by a host of significant others as descriptive of the person will be merged with the self. Likewise, roles of lasting duration are seen as descriptive of the real self.

One of the first and most central roles that a person learns about is sex role. Sex-typed behavior is typical of virtually all societies, but societies demonstrate also the tremendous variability in what is defined as appropriate and inappropriate sex-role behavior. Both social-learning and cognitive-developmental theories appear to be able to explain some of the phenomena associated with the acquisition of sex-typed behavior. The rewards and punishments that are attached to sex-typed behavior in any society obviously assist the individual in learning appropriate and inappropriate behavior. It is also clear that through self-socialization the individual creates his or her own gender identity and then matches the behavior to the internalized standard. Much of the contemporary western world is in the middle of rapid change in sex roles. In the United States, the women's liberation movement has focused on sex-role change. However, the movement itself appears to be a result of dynamics in the larger society itself rather than a major cause of sex-role changes. The movement appears to have accelerated the rate of sex-role changes as well as having resulted in greater consistency in women's attitudes after 1970, especially in the home and work world.

With continued research by social psychologists centering around the concept of role, we may better understand both the nature of the individual and the nature of the social order.

attitudes: definition, measurement, and relationship with behavior

During the middle and late 1960s, American involvement in Southeast Asia had gotten increasingly costly both in terms of the loss of American lives and in financial expenditures. Still, two U.S. Presidents and their advisors refused to significantly alter the policy of escalating that involvement, claiming that the *attitudes* of the vast majority were supportive of the policies that were being followed. The administrations contended that the vocal critics constituted only a small minority of the American population.

During this same period, a number of American cities erupted in racial violence. A national commission concluded that the riots resulted from Blacks' frustration engendered by their inability to "melt" into the melting pot and become real participants in the "American Dream" (U.S. Riot Commission Report, 1968). One solution suggested by the Commission was to bring about significant changes in the *attitudes* of majority-group members so that prejudice and discrimination could be eliminated.

In the 1970s, we have witnessed important changes in numerous state and federal policies. Abortion was legalized by the Supreme Court. Several states removed the harsh criminal penalties associated with the use of marijuana, and the rights of women have been extended. All these actions have been justified, in part, because they were assumed to be consistent with the *attitudes* of the majority of the American population.

Each of these brief statements highlights the importance of attitudes in our study of human behavior. The concept of *attitude* occupies a central position in the field of social psychology. For at least half a century, it has been a primary focus of both sociologists and psychologists. Sociologist W. I. Thomas (1918) referred to it as the subject matter "par excellence" of the discipline, and psychologist Gordon Allport (1935) referred to attitude as

Large numbers of people can express their individual attitudes in a united front through rallies and demonstrations. *Source:* Wide World Photos, Inc.

the "keystone in the edifice" of the growing field of social psychology. In fact, several early social psychologists defined their field as the *scientific study of attitudes* (Allport, 1935).

Attitudes are measured, studied, and manipulated by a variety of groups other than social scientists in American society. Politicians want reassurance that they are on the popular side of the issues. Manufacturers want to know the public's preference in breakfast cereal, perfume, and headache remedies. National and regional opinion-polling companies have appeared with sophisticated research methodologies to provide the information about attitudes desired by these interest groups. In fact, many readers of this book may have participated in an attitude survey about inflation, legalization of marijuana, capital punishment, preference for consumer goods, or some such issue. Many of the groups who are interested in the public's current attitudes use the information they gather to attempt to change public opinion. The politician is eager to convince the electorate that his position is reasonable, manufacturers want to convince the public that they need their product, and service companies such as travel agencies want to influence a positive attitude towards their service.

After a brief historical overview, this chapter will cover the major issues associated with defining and measuring attitudes. We will then turn to the question of attitude organization and the problem of cognitive consistency. Finally, the controversy regarding the influence attitudes have in directing behavior will be explored. The topic of attitude change, which has attracted a large and rather independent body of literature, will be treated in the next chapter.

Historical Overview

The use of the concept of attitude in the social-science literature dates back at least to the writings of Herbert Spencer (1862) and Alexander Bain (1868), who suggested that an individual's mind would fall into a set pattern or attitude that would influence and color his or her perception of a situation. Important experimental advances were made a few years later by several German scientists who treated attitude as a mental preparedness that could significantly affect physical reaction time.

The introduction of the attitude concept into the sociological literature is usually attributed to Thomas and Znaniecki (1918) in their monumental work, *The Polish Peasant.* Allport has noted that prior to the publication of this book, the term *attitude* had made only sporadic appearances in sociological literature. However, after this work was published, the concept was adopted with enthusiasm by an ever-growing number of writers.

The rise in popularity of the concept of *attitude* must be seen in conjunction with the demise of the concept of *instinct.* Although *instinct* had received a great deal of attention from both psychologists and sociologists during the first two decades of the twentieth century, it was shortly to come under devastating attacks from several directions.

The primary impetus in the popularity of the attitude concept, however, seems to be the assumption of many early social psychologists that attitudes were simply "behaviors in miniature." In order to be able to predict behavior, all one had to do was determine the person's attitude toward the object of the behavior. The problem, then, became largely methodological—all we had to do was develop adequate measurement tools. This no doubt contributed to the large number of articles that were to begin appearing in the 1930s dealing with the measurement of attitudes.

Defining Attitudes

A cursory review of the social-psychological literature reveals that there is little consensus on the definition of *social attitudes*. Almost every user of the concept seems to develop a new definition that differs in some respect from those definitions available in the literature. Thomas and Znaniecki (1918) who, as we noted earlier, played a central role in introducing the concept, used the following definition: "By attitude we understand a process of individual consciousness which determines real or possible activity of the individual in the social world" (1918, p. 22). The most important characteristic of this definition is the notion of some underlying attitude process that determines overt behavior. As we noted earlier, this *assumed* property has contributed to the concept's popularity: by knowing one's attitudes, we can predict behavior toward the object of that predisposition. For example, if we know a person's attitude toward a minority group, we can anticipate how she or he will behave when coming into contact with a member of that minority group.

Several other widely cited definitions of *attitude* are:

> An *attitude* is a mental and neural state of readiness, organized through experience, exerting a directive or dynamic influence upon the individual's response to all objects and situations with which it is related (Allport, 1935, p. 810).
> An *attitude* can be defined as an enduring organization of motivational, emotional, perceptual and cognitive processes with respect to some aspect of the individual's world (Krech and Crutchfield, 1948, p. 152).
> *Attitude* is defined as an implicit drive producing response considered socially significant in an individual's society (Doob, 1947, p. 136).
> An *attitude* is a relatively enduring organization of beliefs about an object or situation predisposing one to respond in some preferential manner (Rokeach, 1967, p. 530).
> *Attitude* refers to certain regularities of a person's feelings, thoughts, and predispositions to act toward some aspect of his environment (Secord and Backman, 1964, p. 97).

Every one of these definitions assume that attitudes influence behavior. In addition, most of the definitions make some reference to the *multi-dimensional* nature of attitudes. For example, Secord and Backman make reference to a cognitive component (beliefs or knowledge about the attitude object), an affective component (feelings or emotional response to the attitude object), and a behavioral component (predisposition to respond in some fashion toward the attitude object). Similar components are noted in the definition developed by Krech and Crutchfield (cognition, emotion, and motivation). One of the principal tasks of researchers who employ definitions in this tradition, as we will discuss in more detail later in this chapter, is that of determining the organizational relationships between these sub-components. Is *affect* always consistent with *cognition*? If our *knowledge* about an attitude object changes, will our feelings toward that object also change? For example, what happens to the ignorant white bigot who learns (cognitive change) that blacks are *not* inherently inferior to whites? Will his or her affective or emotional responses toward blacks change in such a manner as to produce consistency?

In attempting to clarify the predisposition-to-behave component of attitudes, DeFleur and Westie (1963) have proposed that two types of definitions of *attitude* can be found in the literature. The latent-process conceptualization "postulates the operation of some hidden or hypothetical variable, functioning within the behaving individual, which shapes, acts upon, or 'mediates' the observable behavior" (DeFleur and Westie, 1963, p. 21). In such definitions, attitude is clearly a predisposition to act, operating as a motivational force within the individual. Behavior is thus "due to" attitude, which acts as an immediate and direct determinant of the behavioral response.

The second type of definition, which DeFleur and Westie feel is more consistent with the available empirical literature, employs a probability conception. *Attitude* is treated as the probability of a certain type of response in a certain type of situation. The concept is thus tied directly to observable events rather than relying on some latent process or hidden mechanism. At the same time, these definitions recognize some consistency in predisposition to behave that the individual carries from situation to situation.

Because of the confusion surrounding multiple dimensions of attitudes, several researchers prefer to define the concept as single-dimensional. Fishbein (1963) defines *attitude* simply as positive or negative affect toward some attitude object. The cognitive and behavioral components are excluded. A similar definition was used many years ago by Thurstone (1928) and is used in the widely read *Techniques of Attitude Scale Construction* by Edwards (1957). Using this approach, one's attitude toward abortion, for example, would be defined as his or her affective response to abortion. Separating attitude (affect) from belief and behavior allows the testing of the relationships between them.

In sum, although a majority of social psychologists employ definitions of *attitude* that assume it has multi-dimensional properties (usually affective, cognitive, and behavioral components), this is not true of all who use the concept. Fishbein and others prefer to treat attitude simply as positive or negative affect, thus treating the relationship between affect and belief and affect and behavior as empirical questions.

Although attitude researchers have tended to ignore the basic social-psychological theories of human behavior, behavioral psychologists have actively rejected the use of nonobservable concepts such as attitudes in attempting to explain behavior. For example, Bain, as early as 1928, argued that the study of mental processes inevitably involves useless duplication because the mental states are always inferred from the observation of behavior:

All that science can deal with are acts, behavior. Therefore, since the only way we can judge of the existence of a subjective "state" is to observe action, to say the action betrays this or that subjective state is a mere tautology, so far as science is concerned (1928, p. 946).

To prevent the tautological error made by most definitions, Bain defined an *attitude* as the "stable, overt behavior" of the individual that influences his status (Bain, 1928, p. 950). This definition is consistent with the behaviorist emphasis on observable behavior.

Doob (1947) agrees with Bain that attitude is useless as a scientific concept but laments that it will probably continue to be utilized by social scientists. He concludes with the feeling that, when the demise of attitude does occur in the far future, it will be a happy day for social science "since this event will signify the emergence of a more integrated and scientific system of human behavior" (Doob, 1947, p. 155).

More recent writers, particularly Tarter (1969, 1970), have agreed with this basic position and have argued that sociology, particularly, will become more relevant only as it heeds the principles of behavioral psychology. How these principles explain attitude formation and change will be discussed in the next chapter.

Mead (1934), one of the founders of symbolic-interaction theory, felt that attitude was central to the process of role taking. He notes that individuals appear as selves in their conduct only insofar as they take the attitude that others take toward them. On the other hand, Blumer (1969) criticizes the use of attitudes in developing a theory of human behavior from the symbolic-interactionist perspective. Basically, he rejects the assumed link between attitude and subsequent behavior as he feels it provides a "fallacious" understanding of human behavior.

> The attitude is conceived to be a tendency, a state of preparation, or a state of readiness, which lies behind action, directs action, and molds action. Thus, the attitude or tendency to act is used to explain and account for the given type of action. Further, the knowledge of the attitude enables one to forecast the kind of action which would take place if the attitude were activated (Blumer, 1969, p. 93).

Although both symbolic-interactionists and behaviorists find fault with the concept of attitude in theory, practitioners from both traditions use it in their research. This is especially true of symbolic interactionists, although the explanation of such concepts as the self provided by both theoretical positions make use of attitude-type ideas.

Given the large amount of literature in the areas of attitude organization and attitude change that employs a multi-dimensional conceptualization of attitude, we will opt for such an approach. At the same time, we need a definition that will take into account the large number of studies that have demonstrated empirically significant discrepancies between attitudes and behavior. Most of the definitions noted above fail to do this. Thus, we will employ a definition that includes elements from several writers, although it draws heavily from Secord and Backman (1964): *Attitude* refers to regularities of an individual's feelings, thoughts, and predispositions to respond to social objects that, in interaction with situational and other dispositional variables, guide and direct the overt behavior of the individual. Thus, attitude does not determine behavior; it guides and directs behavior (thus employing a probabilistic orientation). Furthermore, it guides and directs behavior in interaction with situational constraints (those factors that are present in the social situation in which the behavior is to occur) and other dispositional factors (including such things as personality characteristics of the individual respondent). Such a definition covers the major points of traditional definitions and is more consistent with recent empirical research findings. Finally, the definition applies the term *attitude* to the total system of affect, cognition, and intention and not to just one of its dimensions (Crespi, 1977).

Measurement of Attitudes

The scientific usefulness of the concept of attitude is dependent upon the ability to measure these internal states. Therefore, a principal task of students of attitude has been to develop ways to measure or assess attitudes. The literature on the measurement of attitude has probably grown even faster and larger than that concerned with its definition. Consequently, only a brief overview can be presented here.

Before describing any specific measurement techniques, it must be stressed that attitude is a *hypothetical construct.* In other words, the attitude itself cannot be directly observed; rather, it must be inferred from behavior, including self-report. We simply cannot remove the cover of the human brain and point to various attitudes. Although employing hypothetical constructs is viewed as problematic to behaviorists, other social psychologists use such concepts frequently in their research.

CONTENT ANALYSIS OF COMMUNICATIONS_____

One of the first efforts to measure attitudes was that used by Thomas and Znaniecki (1918). The method they used was basically to *infer* the attitudes they were interested in studying from different types of written documents. A wide variety of sources were used in the process, the most important one being a collection of over seven hundred letters that were mainly to or from Polish immigrants residing in America and their family and relatives still living in Poland. The researchers got the letters by advertising in an American-Polish journal, where they offered ten to twenty cents for any letter received from Poland. Other sources included copies of the Polish newspaper, *Gazeta Zwiazkowy,* that were purchased by Thomas during a visit to Poland; histories of Polish parishes and other organizations that were established by the immigrants after their arrival in America; and life histories.

As is obvious, the amount of material available to Thomas and Znaniecki was tremendous. It was their hope that common themes or *attitudes* could be identified in these materials that could then be used in understanding the behavior of the Polish immigrants. No specific tools or measurement scales were developed. As a consequence, questions of accuracy and replicability of interpretations made by Thomas and Znaniecki become critical. It is because of such questions that other social scientists sought to develop techniques that were more easily replicated and that were more easily tested for reliability and validity.

Source: W. Miller; © 1978 The New Yorker Magazine, Inc.

THURSTONE SCALING OF ATTITUDES

The first major attempt to measure social attitudes through the development of attitude scales was that of L. L. Thurstone. In his well-known paper, "Attitudes Can Be Measured," Thurstone (1928) argued that there is a *psychological continuum of affect* along which individuals can be placed. This continuum supposedly had the same basic properties as a physical continuum of weights. Operating on this assumption, Thurstone sought to develop a technique to locate individuals along this continuum.

Several scaling techniques were developed by Thurstone. The most widely used is the equal-appearing intervals method. The first step is to assemble about seventy-five statements about the attitude topic. The statements should be brief, unambiguous, and directly related to the object of concern. The statements are then reviewed by a large number of judges, usually well over one hundred. The judges are asked to sort the statements into eleven piles. A value is determined for each statement according to average ranking by all the judges. This is referred to as the *scale value* of the statement. A second measure called the *Q value* is determined for each statement by calculating an interquartile range of the distribution of judgments obtained for that statement. The Q value is really a measure of ambiguity—a high Q value indicates lack of agreement by the judges on placement of the statement; a low Q value indicates high consensus. Finally, on the basis of the scale value, the Q value, and the desire to have items that cover the range of the eleven-point scale, approximately twenty statements

Groups, professionals, and individuals, as well as social psychologists, spend a great deal of time measuring other people's attitudes.

are selected for the scale. These can then be given to the subjects to be studied, and scale scores are determined by the items with which the subjects indicate they are in agreement.

Figure 7–1 summarizes some selected items from an early attitude scale developed by Thurstone and Chave (1929) to measure attitudes toward churches. The scale values listed in the first column were determined using the procedures that are outlined above. As can be seen, the items range broadly in terms of their favorability toward the church. It was anticipated that those having positive feelings toward the church would check the items having low scale values and those who are most strongly opposed to the church would check items having the highest scores.

Several difficulties have been noted with the Thurstone equal-appearing intervals scale that have accounted for a lack of contemporary use. First, it takes a great deal of time and effort to construct, and results obtained from less complicated techniques have been very similar to those from Thurstone scales. Second, Thurstone assumed that the judges' ranking of the attitude statements would be independent of their own attitudes, but contrary evidence has been found. Early research by Hinckley (1932), Ferguson (1935), and others indicated that the attitudes of judges did not influence their placement of attitude statements. However, other studies (Hovland and Sherif, 1952; Sherif and Hovland, 1953) resulted in contradictory findings. Hovland and Sherif found that judges with extreme personal attitudes

Figure 7–1   Part of The Thurstone-Chave Attitude Toward Church Scale

SCALE VALUE	(SELECTED ITEMS)
8.3	I think the teaching of the church is altogether too superficial to have much social significance.
1.7	I feel the church services give me inspiration and help me to live up to my best during the following week.
2.3	I find the services of the church both restful and inspiring.
4.5	I believe in what the church teaches but with mental reservations.
5.4	I believe in religion but I seldom go to church.
10.5	I regard the church as a static, crystallized institution and as such it is unwholesome and detrimental to society and the individual.
8.2	The paternal and benevolent attitude of the church is quite distasteful to me.
2.6	I feel that church attendance is a fair index of the nation's morality.
11.0	I think the church is a parasite on society.
6.7	I believe in sincerity and goodness without any church ceremonies.
0.2	I believe the church is the greatest institution in America today.

Source: L. L. Thurstone and E. J. Chave. *The Measurement of Attitudes.* Chicago: Univ. of Chicago Press, 1929.

sorted a higher percentage of the statements into one category and thus biased the scale. It appears that attitudes of the judges will bias placement, but if judges with extreme attitudes are excluded the bias is minimized (Krech, Crutchfield, and Ballachey, 1962, p. 153).

LIKERT SCALING OF ATTITUDES

Shortly after the publication of the early Thurstone scales, Rensis Likert (1932) developed a scaling technique that has come to be known as the *method of summated ratings.* This method is perhaps the most widely used technique for attitude measurement. It includes some steps that parallel those used in developing Thurstone scales but is much simpler and less time-consuming to construct.

As with the Thurstone technique, one begins with a large number of statements about the attitude object of concern. However, the statements are written in such a manner that the degree of agreement or disagreement can be registered. Usually a five-point scale is used including, (1) strongly agree; (2) agree; (3) neutral; (4) disagree; and (5) strongly disagree. The group of statements and these response categories are pretested with a group of respondents, having characteristics similar to those of the population to be studied, to determine the items to include on the final scale. This is accomplished by dividing total scores of respondents into quartiles ranging from high to low (item analysis). Each individual attitude statement is then assessed in terms of whether it affords a distinction between high and low scorers. A final set of approximately twenty items is selected for the scale using this procedure.

To illustrate the procedure involved in developing a Likert scale, we can follow in brief detail the steps involved in constructing a scale to measure student attitudes toward marijuana (Frideres, Warner, and Albrecht, 1971). The researchers began by writing sixty-one statements about marijuana use and its legalization. These statements were taken from articles and reports, from interviews and discussions with students and colleagues, and from personal experience. The statements, each written in such a manner that degree of agreement or disagreement could be registered, were presented to several hundred students at a medium-sized state university. The students were chosen because of their similarity with the students at another state university where the research was actually to be conducted.

Responses by each of the students on the sixty-one items were calculated and totaled. Total scores were then ranked from high to low, and each

Table 7–1   Likert Scale to Measure Attitudes Toward Marijuana

CONTENT AREA	ATTITUDE ITEMS	RESPONSE ALTERNATIVES
Medical-Physical Harm		
	1. It has been determined by medical science that prolonged use of marijuana produces harmful physical effects	SA A N D SD
	2. Doctors have not shown that marijuana harms a person physically	SA A N D SD
	3. Doctors have shown that marijuana harms a person mentally	SA A N D SD
Deviant-Individual		
	4. A person who uses marijuana cannot be completely trusted	SA A N D SD
	5. The person who smokes marijuana is not a morally fit person	SA A N D SD
	6. Marijuana smoking is not a symbol of psychic weakness	SA A N D SD
Social Control-Exposure		
	7. I would not report another person to the police if I knew he smoked marijuana	SA A N D SD
	8. I would work on a committee to expose campus users of marijuana	SA A N D SD
	9. I would be willing to help the local police locate marijuana users	SA A N D SD
Legal-Law		
	10. I would not try marijuana even if I were certain I would not get caught	SA A N D SD
	11. Marijuana is harmless and should be sold on the open market	SA A N D SD
	12. I would sign a petition to do away with legal restrictions on the use of marijuana	SA A N D SD
	13. I would work on a committee to legalize the use of marijuana	SA A N D SD
Society-Normative		
	14. If the majority of people in my town approved of marijuana, I guess I would also approve	SA A N D SD
	15. The use of marijuana by youth threatens the stability of our society	SA A N D SD
	16. The widespread use of marijuana would be indicative of a decaying society	SA A N D SD

Adapted from Frideres, Warner, and Allorecht, (1971) P. 104.

individual statement was examined in terms of its ability to distinguish between high and low scores. Those items that best made a distinction were then considered candidates for inclusion in the final scale, which is presented in table 7–1.

One major problem of Likert scales is that they tend to be multi-dimensional, and therefore there is no systematic way to verify the results. The example presented in table 7–1 is logically separated into five dimensions: (1) medical-physical impacts; (2) individual deviance; (3) social control; (4) legal implications; and (5) society-normative impacts. The major attempt to solve the multiple-dimension problem has come from the efforts of Louis Guttman and others to develop a technique that is unidimensional.

GUTTMAN SCALING OF ATTITUDES

Guttman's scaling technique was developed by Louis Guttman and his associates in their World War II studies of the American soldier. This technique, sometimes referred to as *cumulative scaling* or *scalogram analysis,* seeks to develop a set of items for attitude measurement that will be unidimensional.

Guttman sought to develop scales in which response to any single item could be determined by a total score on the set of items. In other words, if a scale has Guttman properties, "an individual with a higher rank (or score) than another individual on the same set of statements must also rank just as high or higher on every statement in the set as the other individual" (Edwards, 1957, p. 172).

The property of unidimensionality can perhaps best be illustrated by Guttman scales of attitudes towards premarital sexual behavior. Reiss (1967) conceptualized premarital sexual behavior on a unidimensional continuum ranging from kissing to full sexual intercourse (see table 7–2).

The idea is that anyone who approves of heavy petting also approves of light petting and kissing, or any person who disapproves of light petting will also disapprove of heavy petting, oral contact, extra heavy petting, and full sexual intercourse. The unidimensionality of this scale is illustrated in table 7–3.

This example indicates perfect reproducibility (or unidimensionality). That is, the pattern of response to the complete set of items could be reproduced simply from knowledge of the total score. Reproducibility is the basis of Guttman scaling, and it is generally accepted that a set of items must have a coefficient of reproducibility of about .90 (10 percent or fewer errors). A large percentage of errors would indicate that more than one dimension is involved (that is, the scalogram in table 7–3 would show a number of $+$'s out of place). Guttman-type scales should be used if unidimensionality is critical to the problem being studied.

SEMANTIC-DIFFERENTIAL SCALING OF ATTITUDES

The semantic differential as a tool for measuring attitudes was developed by Osgood and his co-workers (Osgood, Suci, and Tannenbaum, 1955) as part of a much broader effort to study the measurement of meaning. Because the semantic differential is closely related to the issues of cognitive congruity (to be discussed later in this chapter) and language and com-

Table 7-2 Scale Measuring Attitudes Toward Premarital Sexual Behavior

1. I believe that kissing is acceptable for the male (female) before marriage when he (she) is engaged to be married.
2. I believe that kissing is acceptable for the male (female) before marriage when he (she) is in love.
3. I believe that kissing is acceptable for the male (female) before marriage when he (she) feels strong affection for his partner.
4. I believe that kissing is acceptable for the male (female) before marriage even if he (she) does not feel particularly affectionate toward his partner.
5. I believe that petting is acceptable for the male (female) before marriage when he (she) is engaged to be married.
6. I believe that petting is acceptable for the male (female) before marriage when he (she) is in love.
7. I believe that petting is acceptable for the male (female) before marriage when he (she) feels strong affection for his (her) partner.
8. I believe that petting is acceptable for the male (female) before marriage even if he (she) does not feel particularly affectionate toward his (her) partner.
9. I believe that full sexual relations are acceptable for the male (female) before marriage when he (she) is engaged to be married.
10. I believe that full sexual relations are acceptable for the male (female) when he (she) is in love.
11. I believe that full sexual relations are acceptable for the male (female) when he (she) feels strong affection for his (her) partner.
12. I believe that full sexual relations are acceptable for the male (female) even if he (she) does not feel particularly affectionate toward his (her) partner.

Agree: (1) Strong, (2) Medium, (3) Slight
Disagree: (1) Strong, (2) Medium, (3) Slight

Adapted From Riess, 1967, p. 22.

Table 7-3 A Schematic Representation of Premarital Permissiveness Gutman Scale

| PERMISSIVENESS | | ATTITUDE TOWARDS | | | | |
| | Petting | | | Full Sexual Relations | | |
	Engaged	In Love	Strong Affection	Engaged	In Love	Strong Affection	NO Affection
High Permissiveness	+	+	+	+	+	+	+
6	+	+	+	+	+	+	−
5	+	+	+	+	+	−	−
4	+	+	+	+	−	−	−
3	+	+	+	−	−	−	−
2	+	+	−	−	−	−	−
1	+	−	−	−	−	−	−
Low Permissiveness	−	−	−	−	−	−	−

Adapted from Reiss, 1967, p. 232.
+ = Agreement with Item

munication (see chapter 3), only a brief overview will be presented here.

Osgood and his associates were concerned with the basic problem of measuring the *connotative* aspect of objects or concepts. It is widely recognized that *stimulus signs* (the word used to identify an object) are not the same thing as *stimulus objects* (that which the word signifies). For example, the word *chalk* is not the same thing as the object one uses to make marks on a chalkboard. We could just as well call the object "chocolate cake," except "chocolate cake" is used to identify another stimulus object (a dessert I like to eat, despite its high calorie content).

All objects have both *connotative* and *denotative* meanings. The denotative meaning involves the "pointing to" aspect of the object. Concrete objects such as chalk and chalkboards are easy to define because we can "point to" the object and clear up any confusion. Connotative definition, on the other hand, refers to emotive meaning or the emotional response generated in the individual by the stimulus sign. Generally, it is a verbal description of the object or event. Concepts such as peace, love, and communism, being fairly abstract, create difficult denotative problems because it is hard to find a simple example illustrating the concept we have in mind. Most definitions of such concepts, therefore, are connotative, leading to greater communication difficulties.

The semantic differential was developed to tap connotative meaning. Respondents are asked to rate a series of bipolar adjectives, usually separated by a seven-point scale, to describe the object of concern. For example, the concept *police officer* would be rated on the series of bipolar adjectives as depicted in figure 7–2.

POLICE OFFICER

Good	____/____/____/____/____/____/____/____/	Bad
Worthless	____/____/____/____/____/____/____/____/	Valuable
Dirty	____/____/____/____/____/____/____/____/	Clean
Insincere	____/____/____/____/____/____/____/____/	Sincere
Foolish	____/____/____/____/____/____/____/____/	Wise
Honest	____/____/____/____/____/____/____/____/	Dishonest
Dangerous	____/____/____/____/____/____/____/____/	Safe
Weak	____/____/____/____/____/____/____/____/	Strong
Passive	____/____/____/____/____/____/____/____/	Active
Slow	____/____/____/____/____/____/____/____/	Fast
Cold	____/____/____/____/____/____/____/____/	Warm

Figure 7–2 A Semantic Differential to Measure Connotative Response to the Object Police Officer

In this particular case, the importance of connotative meaning takes on special significance. Everyone may agree that the person dressed in blue and driving through the neighborhood in a black-and-white patrol car is a police officer (the denotative, pointing-to, aspect of the concept). However, the concept *police officer* may elicit very different connotative, emotional responses in a middle-class suburb and in a central-city ghetto. The emotive response is more important in understanding the concept and the response it generates.

Connotative meaning has been found by Osgood and his associates to be multi-dimensional. They have found that three dimensions are most frequently identified: (1) evaluative (as indicated by the bad-good, worthless-valuable items); (2) potency (weak-strong items); and (3) activity (slow-fast, cold-warm). The evaluative dimension has been most widely used in the research process.

A number of uses for the semantic differential have emerged, including: (1) Studying subcultural differences in attitudes. This is illustrated by reference to the police-officer example. It may be found that emotive response to the concept *police officer* varies significantly between different groups, such as ghetto residents and middle-class suburbanites. (2) Studying sex-typed differences. Male and female respondents may exhibit different connotative responses to concepts and objects. (3) Studying self-concept. This offers one of the most interesting uses of the semantic differential. An individual may be asked to respond to the following concepts, using the same bipolar adjective set: "myself," "the average person," and "how I would like to be." Comparisons of responses to these concepts would give a good indication of how a person perceives himself or herself as compared to others or the ideal self.

Attitude Organization

As noted earlier, most social psychologists assume that an attitude is multi-dimensional; that it has cognitive (belief, knowledge), affective (emotional), and behavioral (predisposition to behave or act) properties. A critical question that emerges from this conceptualization of attitudes concerns the relationships among these three components. In addition, questions about how different attitudes are related to each other have also been explored.

Several theories of attitude organization have attempted to deal with these two questions. These different theories all have one thing in common: all are based in one way or another on the idea of cognitive consistency. That is, all assume that individuals attempt to maximize internal consistency and to avoid situations that would create cognitive inconsistency (referred to as imbalance, incongruence, inconsistency, dissonance, and so forth). Many of these theories are also related to the pioneer work of Fritz Heider (1944). Given the important contribution of Heider, we will begin with a brief overview of his balance theory of attitude organization and then will review dissonance theory as developed by Festinger and congruity theory as developed by Osgood and Tannenbaum. Although other models are available in the literature, these should give the student a good overview of cognitive consistency.

The concept of cognitive consistency is based on the assumption that an individual will strive to maximize consistency among the various components of an attitude or between two or more attitudes that are related to each other. In other words, our affective response toward some attitude object should be consistent with our knowledge and beliefs about that object, and both should be consistent with our behavior toward that object. For example, if a person strongly believes that the use of marijuana is harmful both physically and psychologically, then this individual should also express a negative emotional response to marijuana and, on a behavioral level, should not smoke it. Similarly, if a person holds two attitudes that are related to each other, these attitudes should be consistent. For example, if an individual has a positive attitude toward a teacher who openly uses marijuana, then the person should have a positive attitude towards marijuana. In either of these examples, if the components or attitudes are not consistent, then, according to the theory, the person will experience psychological stress.

Heider's balance theory focuses on sentiment as a basic component of attitude. *Sentiment* refers to how a person feels about another person or some object in the environment. Positive sentiments are seen as *liking* another person or some impersonal entity. Negative sentiments are *disliking* for the other person or the impersonal entity. Thus, if we were interested in the sentiment relationship between person (p) and another person (o) or object (x), we could refer to that relationship either as liking (L) or disliking (DL).

In addition to sentiment relationships, Heider also conceptualized unit relationships between individuals or between individuals and objects. A unit relationship simply means that two individuals or an individual and some impersonal object are related through proximity, causality, ownership, or some other unit-forming characteristic. For example, if a person (p) is engaging in a certain behavior (x) or owns an object (x), the two can be said to form a unit relationship. Relationships can be either unit (U) or not unit (NOT-U).

According to the theory, individuals will attempt to maintain a balanced state among their sentiment and unit relationships with others and with impersonal entities in their environment. A balanced state is one that is harmonious or one in which the entities comprising the situation and the feelings about them fit together without conflict or stress.

Figure 7–3 presents the classic unbalanced state in Heider's formulation.

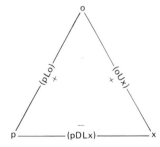

Figure 7–3 Unbalanced State in Heider's p-o-x Model. (*Persons and objects in the model:* p = person; o = other with whom person interacts in some way; x = object, event, or a third person related to both p and o. *Relationships between persons and objects:* L = sentiment relationship of liking between p and o; U = unit relationship between o and x; DL = sentiment relationship of disliking between p and x.)

As can be seen in the p-o-x triangle, three specific relationships are involved: (1) p to o; (2) o to x; and (3) p to x. Each of these three relationships has four possibilities based on the concepts of sentiment and unit relationships: L, DL, U, and NOT-U. For example, p may like o (L), o may be connected in a unit relationship with x (U), and p may dislike (DL) x. This is the type of relationship that is depicted in figure 7–3. The relationship can be said to be imbalanced because there are two positive linkages (L and U) and one negative linkage (DL). A triadic relationship, such as that depicted in the figure, will be balanced when all three linkages are positive or when there are two negative linkages and one positive linkage.

The unbalanced state depicted in figure 7–3 can be illustrated by considering an example. Suppose you (p) have positive attitudes (L) toward your college roommate (o). However, this roommate has what you find to be a very annoying habit: he refuses to ever wash his dirty dishes or otherwise clean up his share of the apartment. You are a very fastidious person and are at first annoyed and then angered by your roommate's refusal to carry out what you feel to be his responsibility as a roommate. Your roommate, then, has a unit relationship (U) with a behavior pattern that you find annoying (DL). The overall relationship is unbalanced, and the theory suggests that such an unbalanced state is stressful and creates pressures toward change.

Heider argues that the individual will try to balance the relationship. In this case, a change in any one of the individual relationships would create a balanced state. For example, a change in the first sentiment relationship would create balance. Your liking for your roommate changes to dislike, and you have a balanced state of two negative relationships and one positive relationship. You hate your roommate, you also hate an untidy housekeeper; it is natural that the two should be connected. This resolution is illustrated in part A of figure 7–4. A second alternative would be to change your attitude toward tidiness. You conclude that a dirty house is not so bad

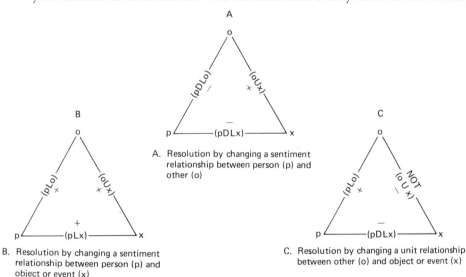

A. Resolution by changing a sentiment relationship between person (p) and other (o)

B. Resolution by changing a sentiment relationship between person (p) and object or event (x)

C. Resolution by changing a unit relationship between other (o) and object or event (x)

Figure 7–4 Resolution of Unbalanced State in p-o-x Model

after all, and, in fact, it requires far less work and hassle. Therefore, you have created a balanced state with three positive relationships. You like your roommate, you like untidy apartments, and your roommate makes sure that your apartment is always untidy (see part B of figure 7–4). Finally, balance could be created by changing the unit relationship between the roommate and his untidy behavior. In this case, you may tell your roommate that you are going to do him serious bodily harm if he does not clean up and keep things clean. Thus, the unit relationship between your roommate and uncleanliness becomes a (NOT-U) relationship, and balance is attained by two negative and one positive linkage—you like your roommate, and neither of you like dirty apartments; at least, you both keep it clean, although the motivation on the part of the roommate may come from a source other than personal attitudes. Of course, one could also eliminate the triad altogether by moving out or kicking out the roommate.

FESTINGER'S DISSONANCE THEORY

Heider's balance model suggests a tendency for consistency among relationships with other persons and with objects; dissonance theory concentrates on relationships between the components of an attitude and on the relationship between an individual's attitudes and behaviors toward the attitude object. Few theories in social psychology have created more controversy or inspired more research than has dissonance theory.

The basic ideas of dissonance theory can be found in Festinger, Riecken, and Schachter (1956), *When Prophecy Fails.* This study developed after the authors read in a local newspaper about a woman who claimed to be receiving prophecy from a planet called Clarion that foretold the destruction of the city by a flood. The messages, purportedly being received by a Mrs. Marian Keech through a process called "magic writing," told her that superior beings from Clarion had visited the earth in flying saucers and had observed fault lines that would cause the flood. Later messages extended the zone of flooding from the Arctic Circle to the Gulf of Mexico and included a major cataclysm that would also submerge the West Coast from Seattle, Washington, to Chile in South America.

Not only were the prophecies quite specific in terms of the location of the pending destruction, but they also specified a date—December 21, 1955. This specificity created a perfect situation for Festinger and his colleagues to test some emerging theoretical ideas about what happens when one holds a deep belief to which he or she is publically committed and then the belief is subjected to *undeniable disconfirmation.* The developing theory suggested that such inconsistency would lead to psychological dissonance and that such dissonance, being a noxious state, would create pressures in the individual to bring attitudes and behavior into consistency.

Festinger had several trained observers join Mrs. Keech and her followers in October to gather data about their conviction, commitment, and proselyting activities. Although the ideology that had been developed by Mrs. Keech was peculiar, Festinger was quick to note that it was not the unique raving of an isolated mad woman but was closely akin to the beliefs of numerous other groups in this country and elsewhere. She had successfully gathered around her a small but committed group of "Seekers" led by one Dr.

Armstrong, a physician working for the health services at a local university.

Between October and December, the Seekers continued to receive messages designed to buoy them up and prepare them for the events ahead. Although the commitment of some wavered, adverse publicity and peer-group support helped to strengthen the conviction of others. Public commitment and sacrifice because of that commitment was widely evident. Dr. Armstrong lost his job at the university because of his involvement with the Seekers, and other members gave up jobs and sold their possessions as final preparation.

Finally, word came that the believers were to be picked up by flying saucers at 12 A.M. on December 21 in order that they might be saved from the flood. Anticipation and excitement rose to a near frenzy as the final minutes approached and the group waited to be flown to safety. When some watches showed midnight, it was quickly agreed that the slowest was correct. This, too, soon showed midnight. The next few hours were tense ones. The promised hour had come, but the saucers and flood had not. Numerous resolutions were suggested and rejected. Finally, at about 4:45 A.M., everyone was summoned to the living room where Mrs. Keech announced a momentous message that she had just received:

> For this day it is established that there is but one God of Earth, and He is in thy midst, and from his hand thou has written these words. And mighty is the word of God—and by his word have ye been saved—for from the mouth of death have ye been delivered and at no time has there been such a force loosed upon the Earth. Not since the beginning of time upon this Earth has there been such a force of Good and light as now floods the entire Earth. As thy God has spoken through the two who sit within these walls as he manifested that which he has given thee to do (p. 169).

Festinger records the reaction to the new revelation:

> This message was received with enthusiasm by the group. It was an adequate, even an elegant, explanation of the disconfirmation. The cataclysm had been called off. The little group, sitting all night long, had spread so much light that God had saved the world from destruction (p. 169).

The message that the flood was called off because of *their* faith was readily accepted. Most went forth with renewed conviction and even continued to proselyte.

The experience of the Seekers aptly illustrates cognitive dissonance and its reduction. Clearly, there was conviction, commitment to conviction, and unequivocal disconfirmation. Festinger proposes that in such a situation there are three basic modes of resolving dissonance. The first would be to change a behavioral cognitive element. This could involve rejecting one's membership in and commitment to the Seekers and no longer participating in their meetings and activities. The second strategy would involve changing an environmental cognitive element. In this case, this could include a reinterpretation of the signs and messages received from Clarion—they were intended to have symbolic rather than literal meanings. The final strategy would be the addition of new cognitive elements. This was the strategy employed by the Seekers, who added a new revelation that resolved the dissonance by making the nonoccurrence of the flood consistent with its prior prediction. These dissonance-reduction strategies can be used in our effort to understand and explain numerous events that occur in our everyday lives.

Since the initial research by Festinger, numerous studies have been conducted using the principles of dissonance theory. In the theory, attitudes are defined as *cognitive elements.* Cognitive elements can also be any knowledge, opinion, or belief about the environment, about oneself, or about one's behavior. Various types of relationships between cognitive elements can be identified. *Irrelevant relations* exist when two cognitions have nothing to do with each other. Clearly, many of our beliefs or opinions are unrelated because they deal with issues or objects that are unrelated. For example, I know that the corn crop in Kansas is being harvested and that I am fishing in Washington. These two cognitions are irrelevant to each other. *Relevant relations,* on the other hand, are one of two types: (1) They can be *consonant,* meaning that one would naturally follow from the other. I like Jim, and Jim just did a good job repairing my car. (2) They can be *dissonant,* meaning that the obverse of one follows from the other or the two related cognitive elements are inconsistent with each other. I smoke two packs of cigarettes per day, and I believe that smoking will lead to lung cancer.

The basic proposition of the theory, as with the other cognitive-consistency theories, is that dissonance is psychologically uncomfortable and will motivate the person experiencing dissonance to reduce it. The strength of the pressure to reduce the dissonance is a function of its magnitude, which, in turn, depends on the importance of the cognitions involved. Inconsistency between two important cognitions will create more dissonance than would the same inconsistency between two marginal cognitions. Also, the number of related cognitions that are dissonant with each other contributes to the intensity of the dissonance.

Building on basic dissonance theory, several hypotheses have been developed predicting behavior under specific conditions. For example, (1) "If a person is induced to say or do something contrary to his or her attitude, he or she will tend to modify the attitude to make it consonant with his or her behavior;" and (2) "The greater the pressure to elicit behavior contrary to one's attitude (beyond the minimum necessary to elicit it), the less her or his attitude will change." The theory, in other words, proposes that the less the external justification for our behavior, the more we are likely to exhibit internal (attitude) change. If we can identify (add new elements) sufficient external justification for our behavior that is contrary to our attitudes (I was forced to do it), then there is no real need to change the attitude because dissonance has been reduced. However, if there is insufficient external justification, there is greater need for internal justification—hence, attitude or behavior changes, moving toward cognitive consistency.

A large number of experiments have been used to test the hypotheses generated by dissonance theory; we will discuss a few illustrative ones here. One of the most widely cited is the experiment by Festinger and Carlsmith (1959) in which experimental subjects spent time engaged in a very tedious task, rotating square spools in a tray and then rotating them back, over and over again. After completing the task, subjects were informed that the person who regularly served as assistant to the experimenter was unable to be there that day, and they were asked if they would be willing to fill in. Their assignment involved introducing new subjects to the task they had just completed and telling the new subjects that it was enjoyable and, in fact, "a lot of fun." In effect, they were being asked to lie for the experimenter, to falsely tell others that what they had found to be a very tedious task was, indeed, exciting. For such perjury, half the subjects were informed that they would be paid one dollar for their help, and the other half were told that they would be paid twenty dollars. The experimenters, using dissonance theory, predicted that those subjects paid one dollar would change their attitude to rate the task more favorably and those paid twenty dollars would not exhibit attitude change because the twenty-dollar bribe constituted sufficient (external) justification for lying. For the others, one dollar was not sufficient external justification, and so internal change was initiated to reduce the dissonance created: "I just told this person that the task was pleasant, I must really have enjoyed it." Dissonance theory explanations are illustrated in figure 7–5. Results were consistent with the dissonance prediction: those in the one-dollar condition rated the task as interesting and enjoyable; those in the twenty-dollar condition did not.

In another experiment (Brehm, 1960), eighth-grade boys and girls were induced to eat a vegetable they did not like. Some were then told that the vegetable had high nutrient value, and others were told nothing. As predicted, those in the high-dissonance condition (no nutrient value) exhibited the most attitude change and moved toward liking the vegetable. Those in the other condition had sufficient external justification for having eaten a vegetable that they disliked—it had high nutrient value. Without such justification, the easiest way of reducing the dissonance was to believe that maybe the vegetable was really tasty afterall—otherwise, why would one have eaten the thing?

Despite considerable empirical support, the theory has not been without its critics. Among the most important of these are Chapanis and Chapanis (1964), who have listed several major criticisms of the theory. They argue, for example, that one can easily identify alternative explanations that would

**Figure 7–5   Creation of High or Low Dissonance
by Varying External Justification for Inconsistent Behavior**

	INITIAL ACTION AS EXPERIMENTAL CONFEDERATE	PAYMENT RECEIVED	TASK RATING AFTER ACTING AS CONFEDERATE	EXPLANATION FOR TASK RATING
High-Dissonance Condition	Lying to other subjects about experimental task	$1.00	High	Internal dissonance reduction by changing evaluation of pleasantness of task
Low-Dissonance Condition	Lying to other subjects about experimental task	$20.00	Low	No need for dissonance reduction because $20.00 is sufficient external justification for behavior

account for the findings of most of the dissonance experiments. One widely cited dissonance study, made by Aronson and Mills (1959), looked at the effect of severity of initiation into a group on the liking that members would express toward that group. Aronson and Mills had college coeds go through initiations of varying severity in order to gain membership in a discussion group. The women were required to read a list of sexually stimulating words and passages to the experimenter (high-embarrassment condition), or to read a list of words that had sexual overtones but were rather innocuous (low-embarrassment), or to do nothing (no embarrassment). Then they were allowed to listen to a tape recording of a discussion by the group they were going to join. The discussion was made as boring as possible. The dissonance prediction was that those having the severe initiation would rate the discussion most highly—they had paid a high price that had to be justified, so the dissonance created by the combination of difficult initiation and dull group would be reduced by evaluating the group more highly. Results were consistent with this prediction. However, Chapanis and Chapanis note other possible interpretations: (1) maybe the women felt relief when they found the group discussion banal instead of embarrassing; (2) perhaps they were generalizing the rewarding feeling of success from having passed a difficult test; (3) the pleasure received from reading the explicit sexual materials may have carried over to future expectations—the coeds rationalized that although this particular discussion was dull, future ones would obviously get better; and (4) there is really no evidence that the women in fact evaluated the discussion as dull. This was an assumption that was untested by the researchers.

Despite the theoretical and methodological criticism of dissonance theory, adherents remain unconvinced: "The whole set of dissonance studies would require accepting a tremendous variety of alternative explanations, whereas dissonance theory alone explains a large subset of them" (McGuire, 1966, p. 493). In other words, dissonance theory can be seen as the most parsimonious theory. Perhaps the best conclusion we can reach is that the jury is still out despite the large number of studies that have been done. It is difficult to demonstrate the presence of dissonance, and few, if any, studies have dealt directly with this question. However, in those cases where one can assume that dissonance has been created, the predictions that are generated by the theory have received wide support.

OSGOOD'S AND TANNENBAUM'S CONGRUITY THEORY

Congruity theory (Osgood & Tannenbaum, 1955) is based on the same basic underlying notion—that inconsistency will create pressure toward change. However, there are important differences between congruity theory and the Heider and Festinger models. This theory is much more highly structured in that it makes very specific predictions concerning both the direction and the amount of cognitive change that will occur in order to maximize congruity or consistency. Further, although Heider's p-o-x model proposes change in one of the links to attain balance, Osgood and Tannenbaum propose that two elements that are linked together will *both* change in order to increase congruity.

To understand the concept of congruity, it is important to recognize its very direct link with an attitude-measurement technique—the semantic differential. It will be remembered that the semantic differential was developed to measure the connotative meaning of a concept by asking respondents to locate that concept between various bipolar adjectives. Congruity theory is based on the evaluative dimension of the semantic-differential scale. The underlying assumption is that when two or more objects that are located at different evaluative points on the semantic-differential scale are linked in some way, there will be pressure to change both toward a congruent state. Changes in evaluation are assumed to always be in the direction of increased congruity. Suppose you are a bright, young, politically aware female college student. During your sophomore year, you take a semester off from your studies to work in the political campaign of a candidate for the U.S. Senate. This relative newcomer to politics has, through a demonstration of hard work, commitment, and honesty, fired the imagination of thousands of people like yourself and is eventually successful in unseating a veteran incumbent. You are now convinced that many of the things you are committed to and believe in will be more strongly defended in the halls of Congress.

Let us also suppose that one of the current efforts to which you are most firmly committed is the passage of the Equal Rights Amendment. Like many of your fellow students across the country, you have dedicated many hours of labor in support of its passage. You have written letters to members of your state legislature who have voted against ratification, you have participated in debates in an effort to sway the views of others in your direction, and you have supported travel boycotts to states that have voted against ratification. You are angered and frustrated by expressions of opposition to ERA that are made by fellow students and some members of your family.

We have now identified two rather distinct attitude objects—a newly elected U.S. Senator from your state and opponents to the ERA—toward which we could measure your current attitudes. If we were to use the semantic-differential scale, it would probably be safe to predict that the Senator would fall near the +3 end of the seven-point continuum and that opponents to the ERA would fall near the other extreme point at −3.

What now happens to you when you open your morning newspaper and discover that your hero in the Senate has just cast the deciding vote *against* an extension of the time allocated for the ratification of the ERA? Two attitude objects, initially at opposite points on the attitude continuum, are now firmly and strongly linked (see figure 7–6). Your initial reaction is likely to be one of anger, frustration, and feelings of betrayal. Now that the two attitude objects are linked by the assertion in the newspaper, congruity theory predicts that the individual will experience psychological stress resulting from the incongruity and will feel pressure to bring the evaluations back to a congruous state.

Do you change your attitudes toward the Senator, deciding that you have been deceived and mislead? Or, do you change your attitude toward opponents of the ERA, accepting the belief that even those who disagree with you can do so honestly and still qualify as decent—though misguided—individuals? The theory predicts that, instead of just one attitude changing, both will change toward a more congruent state. Thus, you will judge the Senator less

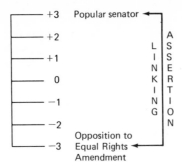

Figure 7–6 Location of Two Objects on a Semantic-Differential Scale That Became Linked by an Assertion

favorably, but you will also be less negatively inclined toward supporters of the ERA. Osgood and Tannenbaum have developed a very specific formula for predicting change:

$$AC_{oj1} = \frac{/d_{oj2}/}{/d_{oj1}/ + /d_{oj2}/} \; P_{oj1}$$

AC = Attitude Change

oj1 = Object of Judgment #1 (one of the objects toward which we hold an attitude)

oj2 = Object of Judgment #2 (the second object toward which we hold an attitude)

d = Degree of Polarization of each of the attitude objects

P = Pressure toward change or congruity (determined by the absolute difference between the two attitude objects along the evaluative dimension of the scale—the greater the polarization, the greater the pressure to change)

Returning to our example, we can now fill in the figures and make predictions of change toward congruity. If we treat the Senator as the object of judgment number 1, then our prediction of change in attitudes toward the Senator, given the assertion establishing the link with the ERA vote, would be computed as follows:

$$AC_{oj1} = \frac{/3/}{/3/ + /3/} \; 6 = 3$$

Similarly, our prediction of change in attitudes toward ERA opponents, given the assertion linking such views with the popular Senator, would be computed:

$$AC_{oj2} = \frac{/3/}{/3/ + /3/} \; 6 = 3$$

The solution to the incongruity created by the assertion linking the Senator and the ERA opposition is depicted in figure 7–7. Attitudes toward the Senator change three points on the scale, and attitudes toward ERA opponents also change three points. We now like our Senator less than we did before the ERA vote but feel less negatively toward individuals who would oppose ERA, perhaps rationalizing that there is some special reason for their beliefs and actions.

A theory stated as formally as congruity theory that yields predictions as explicit as those generated by the formula provides excellent opportunity for testing and disproving. Research by Osgood and Tannenbaum and others has indicated that our reaction when two objects at polar ends of the evaluative continuum are linked is frequently one of incredulity—we find it impossible to believe the source. The staunch right-wing Republican knows in his heart that Barry Goldwater would never advocate nationalizing private industry. Any information indicating that this had occurred would probably be rejected. Additionally, you may feel that your trusted Senator would never have voted against ERA and that the newspaper account was incorrect. Because of this, Osgood and Tannenbaum found it necessary to add a corrective factor to their formula. The correction increases with the degree of incongruity, thus limiting the amount of attitude change that is predicted. However, even with the correction factor, the evidence on congruity theory is mixed. Nevertheless, the specificity this model adds by predicting both direction and amount of change is an example of good scientific theory development.

In assessing the usefulness of these various models of attitude organization in understanding human behavior, Kiesler, Collins, and Miller (1969, pp. 168, 185) note that balance theory lacks the precision expected of a formal theory, has not stimulated much research directed at testing the theory, and, the research that has been done has not provided unequivocal support. The congruity model is more precise, although research findings are again not totally supportive, and additional modification may be required. Dissonance theory is perhaps least precise of the three despite the great amount of research it has generated. Because of this, the theory is extremely difficult to disprove, meaning that its general utility as a theory remains suspect.

Any evaluation of consistency theory eventually rests on the assumption that dissonance, inconsistency, imbalance, and incongruity are stressful and

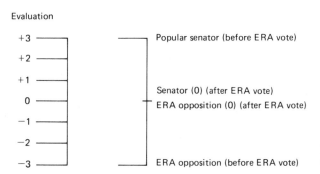

Figure 7–7 Solution to the Problem of Incongruity

will motivate change toward cognitive consistency. Each of the cognitive theories argue that if we can change a person's belief about something, we will probably also change his or her attitude (Manis, 1978); that if we change his or her attitude, we should also observe behavioral change. Predictions based on the assumption have often been impressive, but the overall empirical evidence relating to the actual measurement of dissonance or its equivalents and their supposedly motivating qualities remain core problems.

Attitudes and Behavior

For several decades, social scientists have debated the usefulness of attitudes as predictors of behavior directed toward the object of the attitude. As noted by Irving Crespi in his Presidential Address to the American Association for Public Opinion Research, "It is difficult to find any treatise by those committed to the analysis of attitudes that does not posit the existence of lawful relations between attitudes and behavior" (1977, p. 286). As we noted earlier, it was probably the belief in a direct link between attitudes and actions that inspired much of the early attitude research. In many ways, the social-psychological literature on the attitude/behavior question is exciting because of the progress that can be observed from the initial formulation of the problem to contemporary research. For general reviews of this literature, see Wicker (1969) and Liska (1974, 1975).

In 1930, a young social scientist, Richard LaPiere (see LaPiere 1934), made an automobile trip across the United States. With him on the journey was an attractive Chinese couple. Though the Chinese constituted only a small minority group in the United States at the time, anti-Chinese attitudes were assumed to be widely prevalent. During their travels, LaPiere and his friends covered approximately ten thousand miles and stopped at over sixty hotels, auto camps, and "tourist homes," and ate in over 180 restaurants and cafes. When they stopped to eat or stay for the night, the Chinese couple approached the waitress or the desk clerk while LaPiere remained in the background observing the response they received. At only one of the establishments were the travelers denied service during their journey. Upon returning home, LaPiere sent each of the establishments where they had stopped a questionnaire asking whether or not they would be willing to accept Chinese as guests. In response to his letter, 92 percent of the sleeping places and 91 percent of the eating establishments said they would not. Of the remaining, all but one indicated uncertainty, saying that it would depend upon the circumstances.

Ignoring for the moment the methodological problems in the LaPiere study, it should have given social scientists some clues as to the nature of the attitude/behavior relationship. However, LaPiere's finding of independence between attitudes and behavior was generally ignored. A few decades later, a series of other studies obtained results that closely paralleled those of LaPiere. One interesting study made by Kutner, Wilkins, and Yarrow (1952), involved two white women and a black woman who entered a number of restaurants in a fashionable neighborhood. The racially mixed group received service in each of the restaurants. Later, letters were sent to the restaurants asking for reservations for an upcoming social affair. The letters indicated that the party desiring reservations included blacks. No written answers were received to the inquiries, and a telephone follow-up resulted in a denial by a majority of the restaurants that the inquiry was ever received. At this point, the request for reservations for the mixed party was made over the telephone. Five managers made the reservations, and six refused. In a control call to each of the restaurants in which no reference was made to the racial character of the group, only one out of the eleven failed to accept reservations for the party.

These two studies clearly indicated a lack of correspondence between actual behavior and the behavior that respondents verbally indicated that they would take. Research by Minard (1952) and Lohman and Reitzes (1954) obtained similar results in different social settings. In all cases, major discrepancies appeared between how respondents said they felt about members of minority groups and how they responded to them under varying types of social conditions.

A careful review of the research that accumulated between the early La-Piere study in 1930 and the late 1960s led Wicker (1969) to conclude that, at best, attitude accounts for about 10 percent of the variability in behavior. Deutscher (1966, 1973) has gone even further in arguing that there is no theoretical reason to expect to find congruence between attitudes and behavior, and, in fact, every reason to expect discrepancies. Not all researchers agree on this point, however. In fact, Warner and DeFleur (1969) have noted that the debate has resulted in *three* rather distinct views. The first, termed the *postulate of consistency,* is based on the assumption that attitudes can be used as reasonably valid guides for prediction of the behavior that people will exhibit when confronted with the object of the attitude. This supposition has also been noted by Cohen, who claims that most investigators have viewed attitudes as precursors of behavior, "as determinants of how a person will actually behave in his daily affairs" (1964, p. 138). Although this position remains popular in some circles, there is no question that it has been seriously challenged by research.

The second position, the *postulate of independent variation,* makes the claim that there is no valid reason to assume that attitudes and behavior should be consistently related. Deutscher (1966) has rejected the assumed relationship between attitudes and behavior, and Turner (1968) has gone even further in calling the attitude concept obsolete as a predictor of action. However, support for this position has been limited. The general consensus seems to be that although empirical inconsistencies between attitudes and behavior have often been observed, the two are not entirely independent of each other.

The third position, the *postulate of contingent consistency,* combines the previous two positions. According to this postulate, behavior appears to be influenced by the person's attitude *combined* with other personality and social-situational factors. This postulate, it will be recalled, is consistent with the definition of *attitude* that we developed earlier in this chapter.

An examination of the attitude/behavior research in the three decades following LaPiere reveals that most of the studies that were done focused on attitudes alone in predicting behavior, thus ignoring the contingent-consistency idea. The results indicate that attitudes by themselves are not very good predictors of behavior. By the late 1950s, however, DeFleur and

Westie (1958) were beginning to recognize the importance of other variables in influencing the attitude/behavior relationship. In their effort to
explain the behavior of subjects who exhibited attitude/behavior inconsistency, DeFleur and Westie argue that the lack of a strong relationship between verbal attitude and overt behavior may be explained in terms of social
constraints preventing the person from acting out his convictions. For example, an individual may be extremely prejudiced against blacks but, when
introduced to a black person by his boss, responds in a gracious manner.
Although the person's attitudes predict that he would refuse to shake hands
with the black, the social constraints imposed by the presence of his boss
prevent him from acting out his attitudes.

Most contemporary attitude researchers have been influenced by this
insight and have strived to include situational constraints in understanding
attitude/behavior relationships. This has led, in turn, to the development
of two major research traditions in contemporary social-psychological research on the attitude/behavior problem. The first of these approaches has
emerged out of the work of sociologist Melvin DeFleur and his students; the
second is attributed primarily to the work of psychologist Martin Fishbein
and his associates. Both approaches have several things in common. They
have clearly moved beyond the study of a single attitude determining behavior and recognize that the problem is much more complex. Both have
combined attitude with situational and other variables and in so doing have
achieved much better prediction of behavior. In sum, both recognize the
fact that behavior in any given instance is likely to be the result of multiple
determinants, *including attitudes.*

A CONFIGURATIONAL APPROACH TO ATTITUDES AND BEHAVIOR

Melvin DeFleur has devoted nearly two decades of work to the problem of
attitude/behavior relationships (DeFleur and Westie, 1958, 1963; Warner
and DeFleur, 1969; Albrecht, DeFleur, and Warner, 1972; Acock and De-
Fleur, 1972). From this research has evolved the "contingent consistency"
approach to the studies of attitudes and behavior noted above. This approach suggests that various social constraints (such as perceived group
norms, visibility of behavior, and so on) pose contingent conditions that may
act to modify the strength of the attitude/behavior relationship. This process is demonstrated in figure 7–8.

The contingent-consistency approach, then, involves combining attitudes
with sets of individual- and social-constraint variables for the prediction of
behavior. In studies using this approach, it has been found that prediction
of behavior toward minority-group members and toward marijuana use can
be greatly improved when individual attitudes are combined with such factors as the visibility of behavior, the expectations of significant others, and
response characteristics of the individual actor, such as degree of inner or
other directedness or need for social approval. Similarly, it has been found
that attitudes formed through direct behavioral experience with the object
of the attitudes will be better predictors of later behavior than attitudes
formed through indirect experience (Fazio, Zanner, and Cooper, 1978).

One of the problems with which this approach has had to cope is deter-

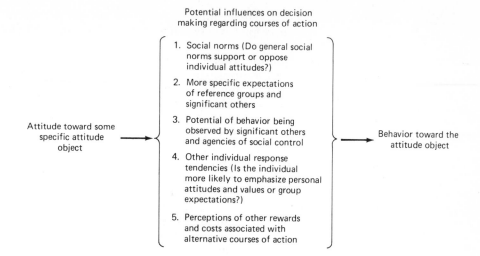

Potential influences on decision
making regarding courses of action

1. Social norms (Do general social
   norms support or oppose
   individual attitudes?)

2. More specific expectations
   of reference groups and
   significant others

Attitude toward some
specific attitude
object

3. Potential of behavior being
   observed by significant others
   and agencies of social control

Behavior toward the
attitude object

4. Other individual response
   tendencies (Is the individual
   more likely to emphasize personal
   attitudes and values or group
   expectations?)

5. Perceptions of other rewards
   and costs associated with
   alternative courses of action

Figure 7–8   A Contingent-Consistency View of the Relationship Between Attitudes and Behavior

mining which social constraints are most crucial in explaining behavior. Research completed to this point indicates that some combination of reference groups expectations and the degree of disclosure or visibility of behavior to others results in the highest prediction of behavioral outcomes.

FISHBEIN'S MODEL OF PREDICTING BEHAVIOR INTENTIONS

Fishbein and his associates (Fishbein, 1963, 1967, 1973; Ajzen and Fishbein, 1969, 1970, 1972, 1973; Ajzen, 1971; Darroch, 1971; Hornik, 1970; Carlson, 1968) have developed a theory of attitude/behavior relationships that utilizes attitudes and normative beliefs to predict behavior intentions. Three antecedent variables—attitude toward performing the behavior in question, normative beliefs about that act, and motivation to comply with these beliefs —are included in the model. The determinants of behavior intentions in this model therefore include an "attitudinal" factor and a "normative" factor. Fishbein notes that although additional variables may contribute to prediction of behavior intentions, they do so only insofar as they influence one of the specific factors in the basic model.

Considerable empirical support has been collected indicating that the model provides good predictions of behavior intentions. However, several characteristics of the model require special comment. First, Fishbein is directly concerned with predicting behavior *intentions* and not overt behavior. Fishbein notes that in many cases behavior intentions and behavior will be strongly related and that consequently his model will also be a good predictor of behavior. However, the relationship between behavior intentions and behavior is subject to the same suspicions as is the attitude/behavior relationship. In other words, what are the factors that intervene between behavior intentions and behavior to strengthen or weaken that relationship? Although the model provides impressive relationships between attitudes, normative beliefs, and behavior intentions, we still face the critical problem of the potential discrepancy between what people say they will do and what they actually do.

The second important characteristic of Fishbein's model is that it utilizes attitude toward performing a specific act under specific circumstances, not with attitude toward an object in general. In other words, Fishbein does not measure attitudes toward blacks but attitudes toward engaging in a specific act with a specific black person. One of the problems in past attitude/behavior research has been that general measures of attitude are poor predictors of specific behaviors toward the attitude object. Fishbein avoids this problem by looking at very specific attitudes toward acts. However, the measure is often so specific that the ability to generalize from the act to a range of alternative acts is severely curtailed. In other words, Fishbein's model, which he proposed to improve the predictive ability in attitude/behavior research, results in excellent predictions of specific (and frequently trivial) behaviors, but we cannot generalize from these specific behaviors to other acts in other types of situations.

A final characteristic of Fishbein's model is the measurement procedure that is utilized. Sociologists studying attitude/behavior relationships have generally used Likert-type scales to measure attitude toward an object. Fishbein, on the other hand, has used the semantic differential for measuring attitudes. For example, one study (Ajzen and Fishbein, 1972) dealt with a series of hypothetical acts, such as buying a plot of land, to which subjects were asked to respond. The act was to be rated on four evaluative semantic-differential items with the following adjective alternatives: foolish-wise, good-bad, harmful-beneficial, rewarding-punishing. The sum across these four scales was the measure of the attitude. The specificity of the attitude measure is again important. The range of behavioral acts in which one can engage in relationship to an attitude object such as buying land is almost infinite, and all the possibilities could probably never be studied using this procedure. It seems crucial that we develop measures that represent at least a part of the hypothetical range rather than just one point on it. Prediction of a very specific act may be less important than a less exact prediction of a range of behaviors (Albrecht and Carpenter, 1976).

In conclusion, the evidence suggests that human behavior in all its complexity must be viewed as a result of multiple antecedent factors (see Hartman, 1978). Recent empirical research clearly indicates the complexity of attitudes, and, in Kelman's terms (1974, p. 311), the research challenges the naive assumption that attitudes are direct indicators of behavior or that attitude assessment can serve as a cheap substitute for more elaborate studies of human behavior. For example, whether or not a person chooses to experiment with marijuana will certainly be influenced by his or her attitudes toward marijuana, but the decision will also be affected by several other considerations. If federal and state laws are harsh, the individual will probably consider the chance of getting caught and convicted. He or she will also consider the expectations of significant others. Perhaps he or she knows that his or her parents are strongly opposed to the action, but his or her friends all smoke marijuana and are pressuring him or her to join them. To continue to refuse will increase the group pressure and may eventually lead to rejection by the group. What will be the ultimate decision? Social psychology has no magic formula to perfectly predict the outcome. However, it is clear that the student of social psychology must consider a number of factors if he or she is to understand the reasons why a given course of action is chosen, and attitude is one of these factors.

Summary

Few, if any, concepts in the social sciences have received the attention that has been devoted to the study of attitudes. Almost daily, there are inquiries made regarding our attitudes toward a given consumer product, a particular political candidate, or any of a host of issues with which we are regularly confronted. Despite this attention, the concept remains poorly understood, is often ill defined, and its utility as a predictor of behavior directed toward the attitude object is still problematic.

Since the systematic study of attitudes by social psychologists began in earnest following the 1918 publication of Thomas and Znaniecki's work, numerous efforts have been made to define, measure, and utilize the concept in improving our understanding of human behavior. The record of success on all of these counts is mixed.

We defined *attitudes* as regularities of an individual's feelings, thoughts, and predispositions to respond to social objects that, in interaction with situational and other dispositional variables, guide and direct the overt behavior of the individual. This definition recognizes the multi-faceted nature of attitudes—they have cognitive (beliefs and knowledge), affective (emotional), *and* predispositional (tendency to behave) qualities.

Several efforts have been made to develop techniques for the measurement of attitudes. Among the most widely known are Thurstone, Likert, and Guttman scaling techniques and the semantic differential. The Thurstone technique involves the development of a series of attitude statements that will allow the location of an individual along a psychological continuum of affect. Likert scales are developed to establish a ranking of respondents in terms of their attitudes toward an issue by asking them to state the degree to which they agree or disagree with a set of statements dealing with that issue. Guttman scales are designed to be unidimensional so that attitudes are measured based on a single pattern of response toward an attitude object. The semantic differential is used to measure people's connotative definition of a concept or object based on their locating that object on a scale between a series of bipolar adjectives.

One set of problems widely studied by attitude researchers is that of the degree to which components of an attitude are consistent with each other, related attitudes form a consistent pattern, or attitudes are predictive of relevant behaviors. The theory of cognitive consistency argues that each of us strive to maintain some degree of balance among these various components and that imbalance is psychologically stressful and motivates us to bring about some change. There are several models based on this theory. Balance theory, coming from the early work of Fritz Heider, assumes that individuals attempt to maintain a balanced state among their sentiment and unit relationships with others. Unbalanced states are inherently unstable and motivate the individual to seek movement toward greater consistency.

Dissonance theory concentrates on relationships among the components of an attitude or on the relationship between attitudes and behavior. When one cognitive element does not follow from another related cognitive element, the result is psychological dissonance which can be reduced by changing one of the dissonant cognitive elements or by adding a new cognitive element.

Congruity theory is among the most formal of the cognitive-consistency theories and predicts that when two attitude objects that are initially at different points along an attitude continuum are linked together, both attitudes will change toward a more congruent state. This theory makes specific predictions regarding both the direction and amount of change, and, in part, because of this specificity, empirical support has been inconsistent.

A final issue concerns the utility of attitudes as predictors of behavior. Much of the early work in this area assumed that if we could properly conceptualize and measure attitudes, we could expect something approximating perfect prediction of behavior. Several decades of empirical research, however, indicate that the relationship is a contingent one—that is, the utility of attitudes as predictors of behavior is contingent upon other personal and situational factors. Attitudes may or may not be good predictors of behavior, depending upon these other factors present in any action situation.

8

attitude
change

As we can observe daily through personal experience, a great deal of human behavior is directed toward changing the attitudes of other human beings. For example, as recognition of the existence of an energy crisis has grown, millions of dollars have been spent in an attempt to change our attitudes and, hence, our consumptive patterns as these relate to the use of scarce resources. We cannot turn on the radio or television or pick up a newspaper without confronting numerous efforts to influence our attitudes —buy Brand X, vote for so and so, support your local P.T.A., and on and on. Changing attitudes toward ideal and desired family size is viewed as a step toward solving the world's population problems; changing attitudes of ethnocentrism is supposed to lead to greater international understanding and improve chances for world peace; and so on.

In chapter 7, we defined the concept of attitude, discussed ways of measuring it, dealt with how attitudes are organized, and looked at its relationship to overt behavior. In this chapter, our concern will be with the problem of attitude change. Although there is a range of alternative approaches to the study of attitude change, much of the literature that has accumulated falls within a few very broad research traditions, such as cognitive-consistency theory and reinforcement theory. Each of the major approaches will be discussed, and applications of research findings to everyday problems and experiences will be reviewed.

A great deal of time and energy are expended in trying to change people's attitudes. *Source:* Wide World Photos, Inc.

Consistency Theories of Attitude Change

As should be obvious, the cognitive-consistency theories of attitude organization that we discussed in chapter 7 also relate very directly to the study of attitude change. We will discuss briefly the way in which these theories have been applied in the attitude-change literature. Criticisms and extensions of some of the basic models will also be covered.

HEIDER'S P-O-X MODEL

It will be remembered from our earlier discussion that Heider's balance theory assumes a need in the individual to maintain a condition of cognitive balance. When two elements are out of balance, it is assumed that some psychological pressure or stress will be generated and that the individual will move toward bringing the elements back into a balanced state. Although movement toward a balanced state can involve many types of change, one of the most frequent would be a change in *attitude.* Consider the example discussed earlier. Person (p) has a positive attitude toward his college roommate (o) but a negative attitude toward his roommate's untidy housekeeping habits (x). The roommate has a unit relationship with the behavior pattern that p finds annoying. The relationship is unbalanced because of two positive linkages (p likes o and o has a unit relationship with x) and one negative linkage (p dislikes x).

Two of the modes of resolving this imbalance involve a change in p's attitude. If p changes his attitude toward his roommate from positive to negative (thus creating two negative and one positive linkages), a state of balance is attained. It should be emphasized, however, that life for p in such a condition may be even more miserable than that which existed initially. Also, if p changes his attitude toward dirty apartments (thus creating three positive linkages), balance is attained. The latter may be least costly for p because he would be living in an apartment that he liked with a roommate that he also liked. Only the third resolution (changing the unit relationship between o and x) would not involve an attitude change for p (but it would involve changing his roommate's attitude toward housekeeping).

Intuitively, the model makes a good deal of sense. We can probably all remember personal experiences that resemble the odd-couple dilemma described above. However, when one tries to identify ways to apply the model in programs designed specifically to bring about attitude change, its shortcomings become more evident. One possibility that has been reported in the literature is to get a trusted and honored leader to advocate a position that is opposed by a majority of his or her followers. By so doing, a state of cognitive imbalance is created in the followers who hopefully will resolve it by adopting the leader's position. The obvious danger here is that such a strategy may backfire. Instead of changing attitudes in the direction advocated, the followers may change their attitudes toward the leader. Thus, he or she not only has failed to bring about the desired change but has also lost the trust and respect of the group.

Kiesler, Collins, and Miller (1969, pp. 166–68) have identified a number of rather critical problems with the basic balance model. The following are among the more important of these and can be used to illustrate the difficulties associated with using the model in either a conceptual or empirical fashion.

1. Both the unit and the sentiment relationships in the model are often unclear. Kiesler, Collins, and Miller (1969, p. 166) suggest that it is difficult to specify in *advance* the existence of a unit relationship. As a consequence, although the unit relationship may be used to explain psychological events, it is not particularly useful in predicting them. Similarly, it is not often clear just what a sentiment relationship means. For example, if two good male friends (p and o, linked by a positive sentiment relationship) end up vying for the same female (both p and o have a positive sentiment linkage to the female), the model would not be particularly useful in predicting the tension that is likely to exist or its resolution.

   Perhaps the major problem is that the model is too static and, because of this, is not a useful tool for dealing with change such as that needed in this competitive example. At a later point in time, the men may dislike each other due to their rivalry, and the model could then depict the possible resolutions of the tension between them. Conversely, both may have decided that their friendship is far more important than the woman, and this balanced state would be accurately diagrammed by the two negative and one positive sentiment linkages.

2. It is unclear precisely what will occur when a state of imbalance exists. For example, which of the possible alternative changes that *could* occur *will* occur. Going back to the college roommates, it is quite clear that the tension in that relationship will create a force that will push toward balance. However, exactly how will the imbalance be resolved? Three alternatives were suggested: (a) the person can come to dislike his roommate; (b) the roommate can be convinced that he should change his housekeeping habits and keep a more tidy room; or (c) the person can change his attitudes toward the necessity for cleanliness. Any one of the three changes would resolve the problem; unfortunately, the basic model does not tell us which one to predict.

   As a partial resolution to this problem, Rosenberg and Abelson (1960) have developed a consistency theory that allows more exact prediction of where change will occur when a state of imbalance exists. Specifically, they hypothesize that the probability of adopting a particular method to restore balance is *inversely* related to the psychological effort that the method would entail. This adds the burden of measuring the "psychological effort" associated with each of the possible resolutions, but it does provide a potential solution to what is a rather thorny problem. One possible way of determining psychological effort can be derived from our discussion of a third problem area.

3. There is no provision for *degree* of balance or for *strength* of the linkages between actors and objects in the model. In the basic model, a relationship is either balanced or unbalanced; no provision for degree is made. For example, suppose that person (p) does not just like another (o) but is intensely in love with o. Suppose, in addition, that o has a habit (x) to which he or she has a very firm commitment. Thus, the unit bond between

o and x is also strong. Finally, suppose o's habit is slightly annoying to p (p DL x). According to the theory, this would represent an unbalanced state, and there should exist pressure to change. The above information would lead us to predict that the p-x link would be the one to change because "slightly annoying" does not carry as much weight as "intense love" and "firm commitment." Therefore, it would be more amenable to change.

4. There is no provision for handling complex cases. One can imagine numerous situations in which the basic balance model is of little help because of its relative simplicity. For example, consider the unbalanced situation depicted in figure 8–1. The wife, perhaps over the years, has developed what amounts to a deep hatred for her husband. The husband, however, controls a great amount of wealth that he has inherited from his family. The wife feels that because she has suffered intensely in her marital relationship she deserves access to some of that wealth. The only way she can get it, though, is to stay married and outlive him. What happens in such a case?

The basic model simply is not designed to deal with such things as complex feelings or multiple relationships between items or people within a triad or the inclusion of other persons or objects within the actors' psychological fields. It assumes greater isolation or independence in the decision-making process than is usually the case. In most situations, p must consider more than just o and x. Other actors and objects become salient, and those relationships must also be considered.

5. Finally, the empirical data have simply failed to confirm some of the predictions that have been made about unbalanced states. Failure to support theoretical predictions may be a function of the "fuzziness" of several of the concepts included in balance theory, as noted in items 1 and 3 above, or of all four problems noted.

NEWCOMB'S A-B-X MODEL

The work of Newcomb (1953, 1958, 1961) is more a theory of interpersonal attraction than one of attitude change, and we will deal with it only briefly. However, the fact that it draws so heavily upon Heider's basic model makes it an important topic of discussion for this section.

Figure 8–2 outlines the core problem with which Newcomb deals. Person

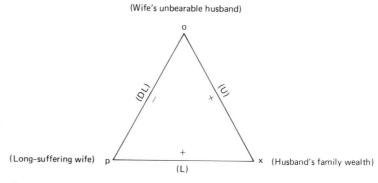

Figure 8–1 Unbalanced Relationship for Which Resolution is Difficult to Predict

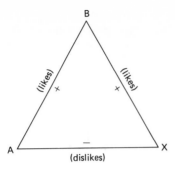

Figure 8–2 Newcomb's A-B-X Model, which Proposes a "Strain Toward Symmetry"

A likes person B, who feels positively about X (either a third person or some other object in the environment), but A dislikes X. On the basis of what we have already discussed, we would predict that the situation would be unstable and would create pressure for change in one of the connecting links. However, at this point Newcomb proposes another consideration that must enter into the resolution process. He argues that A's orientation toward B *and* toward X are not independent of each other but are, in fact, highly interdependent. In other words, one simply cannot consider one of the relationships without considering the other.

Consider the situation in which A and B (who are attracted to each other) disagree about the worth of X. This disagreement, in Newcomb's terms, will create a "strain toward symmetry." However, the amount of strain that is created will be a function of three factors: (1) the degree of A's attraction to B; (2) the intensity of A's attitude toward X; and (3) A's perception of the discrepancy between his or her opinion of X and B's opinion of X.

Newcomb proposes that the basic problem created by the state of imbalance will be resolved through the process of communication. That is, A will communicate with B regarding X, presumably to change B's attitude and restore balance. The amount of communication from A to B regarding X will be a direct function of the three factors noted above.

This process can be illustrated by a more specific example. Two close friends feel a good deal of attraction toward each other, but they disagree about the merits of a particular political candidate. Newcomb proposes that this would create a strain toward symmetry, and communication between the two would increase to eliminate the imbalance. Strain is thus reduced through communication (A convinces B that candidate X is, in fact, the best choice, or B convinces A to vote for someone else), and the old adage that we like those with whom we agree is supported.

Schachter (1951), however, has found that this increased communication will not continue indefinitely. He designed a research project in which three new members were added to established social groups. The three each played different roles. The *conformist* adopted and went along with the position of the group; the *slider* initially played a deviant role but then began to move toward the position of the group; and the *deviant* played a nonconformist role throughout. As Newcomb's model would predict, the conformist was the focus of relatively little of the group's communication. He already accepted their position, and so no strain toward symmetry was created. The slider was the focus of extensive group communication that increased as his attitude began to shift toward the group. In other words, the effort to reduce imbalance was quite obvious, and as that effort began to meet with success, it increased in intensity. The deviant, too, was the recipient of an initially high level of communication, but when he showed no change, he was eventually rejected by the group. In this case, we again see a movement toward symmetry or balance, but it is of a different nature. The group comes to dislike and reject the deviant who continues to hold a position different from their own despite their best efforts to change it. Balance is obtained with two negative and one positive linkages.

As noted above, Newcomb's concern has been more with problems of interpersonal attraction than with attitude change. However, his emphasis on the interdependence of A's attitudes toward both B and X, along with his introduction of increased communication as a mechanism for resolving a state of imbalance, adds some useful ideas and helps resolve some of the ambiguities of the basic balance model.

DISSONANCE THEORY

According to the principles of dissonance theory, attitude change can be achieved by causing one to engage in behavior that is discrepant with one's attitudes. For example, if one engages in action that is contrary to one's beliefs and attitudes, dissonance is generated. The tension associated with the resulting psychological dissonance can be reduced by changing one's attitude. In addition, attitude change thus generated is most likely to occur when the individual lacks sufficient external justification for that behavior. If someone were induced without coercion to eat grasshoppers, his or her attitude toward eating grasshoppers would probably become favorable. If the same person ate grasshoppers because he or she was threatened with punishment for failure to comply, no change in attitude would occur because there is external justification for the action (potential punishment). In the first case, the dissonance between two cognitions ("I don't like grasshoppers" and "I have just eaten grasshoppers") cannot be reduced by appeals to external sanctions. Consequently, it is likely to be reduced by a change in attitude ("I really do like eating grasshoppers after all!").

Dissonance theory has also shown that, if we choose between two attractive alternatives, our attitudes toward the rejected alternative becomes more negative (Brehm, 1956; Brehm and Cohen, 1959). Thus, if we choose a Ford over a Chevrolet, the theory predicts that our attitudes toward Fords will become more favorable and those toward Chevrolets less favorable. Listening to a proud owner of a new automobile brag about the merits of his or her choice over those of a rejected alternative seldom reveals the difficulty entailed in reaching the decision or how close the person came to making the opposite decision.

Many interesting implications can be drawn from dissonance theory. For example, if you are interested in changing someone's negative attitude toward you, the most effective means may be to get the person to do you a favor. By so doing, you will have aroused some psychological dissonance in the person ("I just did a favor for someone that I dislike"). To eliminate that dissonance, the person may change his or her attitude ("I did that for you because I really like you"). However, as noted earlier, the theory is not without its critics. Perhaps the most important issue they raise is that in a majority of studies dissonance is merely assumed to exist but is never really measured. The researcher creates a situation that is designed to arouse dissonance, and, if some attitude change is demonstrated, it is treated as a dissonance-reducing action. Dissonance, as such, is never really measured either before or after the occurrence of the change in attitude.

Dissonance experiments continue, but the utility of this theory as a general model of attitude change is questionable. No doubt, we all can recognize attitude change as a dissonance-reducing mechanism, but, if we were given the assignment of bringing about attitude change with a large audience in a nonexperimental setting, the difficulties of applying this theory would become quite evident.

DISSONANCE VERSUS SELF-JUDGEMENT

Of the many critics of dissonance theory of attitude change, one of the most widely cited is Bem (1967, 1970), who proposed a self-judgment theory. Bem evaluates dissonance experiments from the perspective of a more behaviorist background. This leads him to argue that if "external" explanations for behavior can be found, we do not need "internal" explanations, such as those proposed by dissonance theory.

Just as we observe the behavior of others and attribute motives to them on the basis of these observations (see chapter 9), so also do we observe our own behavior and attribute personal motivation for our actions. For example, an individual might attempt to determine the reinforcement received or punishment avoided as a consequence of selecting a given course of action. If that action has elicited a large reward, the individual is less likely to believe that her or his behavior is a consequence of her or his own attitudes because no justification other than the reward is necessary. On the other hand, if a small reward is associated with the action, then there is a greater probability of attributing that action to individual attitudes or preferences. The individual can then decide whether to take the more rewarding action in similar situations in the future [or can justify not changing the behavior on the basis of personal convictions]. Thus, Bem argues that we can predict dissonance outcomes simply on the basis of self-judgment of external cues without the need to rely on internal mechanisms or processes, such as dissonance reduction. In effect, then, Bem argues that dissonance experiments do not really reflect individual attitude change as a dissonance-reducing procedure. Instead, because the outcomes can be explained and predicted without reliance on internal processes, something quite different, such as self-judgment, may be happening. Although Bem's studies have supported his self-judgment explanation (Bem, 1965, 1967; Bem and McConnell, 1970), other researchers have supported more traditional dissonance explanations (Ross and Shulman, 1973; Green, 1974; Jones et al., 1968).

CONGRUITY THEORY

As is true with the other consistency theories, congruity theory can also be treated as a theory of attitude change. In this case, however, attitudes toward *both* objects—initially located at different points along the attitude continuum, but now linked by what Osgood and Tannenbaum (1955) call an "associative assertion"—change. Referring to the example we used in chapter 7, if a favorite politician endorsed a concept we oppose, the theory predicts that we would feel less favorable toward the politician but more favorable toward the concept—attitudes toward both the Senator and the issue are likely to change. Thus, our support for the Senator would likely be somewhat dampened, and our feelings toward someone who took the same position would become somewhat less negative. According to congruity theory, if two attitude objects located at different points on the continuum are linked, the attitude that we hold least strongly will change more, and the more strongly held attitude will change least. That is, strongly held views are less amenable to change, and weakly held views are more influenced by contrary opinion or information. Further support for this notion will be discussed in the section on assimilation-contrast theory later in this chapter.

The congruity model not only predicts the direction of attitude change but also specifies the amount. In this regard, it is the most precise of the more popular cognitive-consistency models. Its very precision, however, has led to the accumulation of contrary findings that cannot be explained by the initial model. In addition, the utility of congruity theory as a device for bringing about large-scale attitude change remains very questionable. Like the other cognitive consistency models, its applicability has largely been limited to small groups in research labs.

Social Learning Theories of Attitude Change

A second major orientation in the attitude-change literature grows out of the application of the reinforcement principles of classical and operant conditioning theories.

CLASSICAL CONDITIONING MODEL

As we discussed in chapter 1, the classical conditioning paradigm grew out of the early experimental work of Pavlov (1928). Pavlov presented a dog with an unconditioned stimulus (meat powder), which elicited a response (salivation). The unconditioned stimulus was then paired with a conditioned stimulus (ringing a bell), which, after a number of pairings, elicited the same response.

This initial paradigm has led to a large amount of experimental work, most of which has been conducted with animals. The ability to effect higher-order conditioning in some animals and especially in people has made the original findings even more useful. In higher-order conditioning, the conditioned stimulus eventually becomes an unconditioned stimulus, and other conditioned stimuli can be developed from this. For example, initially only the meat powder elicits salivating in the dog. If each time the meat powder is presented to the dog a bell is rung, the dog eventually associates the ringing bell with the meat powder and therefore can be made to salivate just by ringing the bell. At this point, the bell can be paired with something else (for example, a light), which, after several pairings will also become a conditioned stimulus and will also elicit the salivation response.

A series of studies by Staats and Staats (1958) is representative of the work employing the classical conditioning model to the problem of attitude change. In one of their studies, Staats and Staats sought to determine whether or not attitudes toward national names could be changed by pairing these national names with stimulus words that elicited generally positive or negative responses. They began by compiling lists of words that were found to elicit positive responses and other lists of words that led to negative responses. By using the semantic differential as a measurement tool, they found that words such as *beauty, sweet,* and *gift* led to positive reactions and words such as *bitter, ugly, sad,* and *sour* elicited negative connotative reactions. The positive words were then paired with the national name, *Swede,* and the negative words the name *Dutch.* After a series of such pairings, Staats and Staats observed that the word *Dutch* would now elicit a more negative response in their subjects, and the national name *Swede* would now elicit a positive response. Other research indicated that the same thing could be accomplished using individual names (e.g., Tom or Bill).

It is not difficult to find everyday applications of this method. Three readily identifiable examples—television advertisements that pair products with well-known and liked personalities—are depicted in figure 8–3. Note that in the third example the model is used to change attitudes toward a person. Of course, the consequences of negative pairings in these and other uses need to be considered also. Numerous politicians who were facing critical reelection battles urged Richard Nixion to stay out of their states after he came to be viewed as a serious political liability. Apparently, they recognized that being connected with a negatively evaluated stimulus could lead to a transfer of the negative response from that stimulus to themselves.

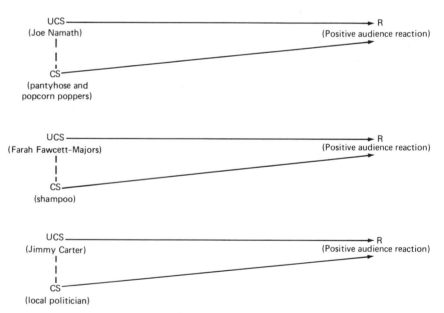

Figure 8–3 Examples of Use of Classical Conditioning Model to Influence Consumer Attitudes. (UCS = unconditioned stimulus; CS = conditioned stimulus; R = response)

The operant conditioning model is based on the assumption that behavior is a result of its consequences. That is, whether or not a response will continue to occur depends largely on the consequences that it elicits. If a response is rewarded, the person is likely to continue to make that response. On the other hand, a response that elicits negative reinforcement or punishment is likely to be discontinued. Again, a majority of the studies using this model have been conducted in small-groups laboratories or with animals. When the pigeon pecks the target and is rewarded with a kernel of corn, the probability is increased that the pigeon will again peck the target. A number of different models are employed; those most frequently used are depicted in figure 8–4.

There are several basic steps in employing the operant model of attitude change. First, the researcher needs to determine what attitude she or he wants the subjects to hold at the conclusion of the experiment. Second, the current operant level, or the present attitude held by the subjects must be determined in order to assess the amount and type of change that must be elicited. Third, an appropriate primary or secondary reinforcer or punishment must be selected. When dealing with human subjects, secondary reinforcers, such as status or approval, are frequently more effective because the needs they meet are not so easily satiated as are those met by primary reinforcers, such as sex or food. Fourth, a schedule of reinforcement must be established (see chapter 1). Although continuous reinforcement must often be used to establish a new attitude, the attitude change will be less subject to extinction if an intermittent schedule is employed. When

1. Positive reinforcement model

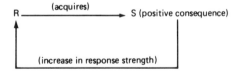

2. Negative reinforcement model

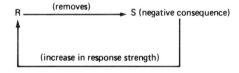

3. Punishment model

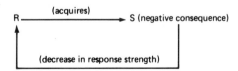

Figure 8–4 Operant Models of Reinforcement

these four steps are completed, the attitude can then be shaped in the desired direction.

This brief summary of the basic operant model should allow the student to observe ways in which it has been or can be applied to problems of attitude change. Two of the more widely cited applications to the study of attitude change are studies by Scott (1957) and Singer (1961). Scott used a debate setting to study the effect of reinforcement on attitude change. Subjects were required to defend assigned positions on important issues. At the conclusion of the debates, Scott would declare some of the debaters "winners" and others "losers." The results indicated that those declared winners changed their attitudes towards favoring the position advocated, but those who were declared losers did not exhibit attitude change. It should be recognized that although the Scott findings are cited as supportive of reinforcement theory, one could also apply a dissonance or self-judgment explanation to the results.

Singer (1961) employed a form of the F-scale (used to measure authoritarianism) and reinforced his experimental subjects by saying such things as "good" and "right" when the responses indicated a prodemocratic attitude. Control subjects were not reinforced. All subjects were then presented the E-scale (a different form of the scale to measure authoritarianism); the results indicated that the experimental subjects had significantly changed their attitudes and evinced a more prodemocratic position, but the control subjects exhibited little change.

Perhaps one of the most interesting studies that exhibits the importance of reinforcement in attitude change, although it was never conceptualized as a study to test the operant model, is Newcomb's Bennington College research. Newcomb (1958), during each of four consecutive years, compared the attitudes of junior and senior students with those of freshmen and sophomores toward a series of critical issues of the day. A majority of the women attending Bennington College during the 1930s came from well-to-do, conservative, Republican families. They brought with them to college fairly well-established family attitudes. However, at Bennington the women came into contact with a situation that was very different from their home experiences. The faculty was generally regarded as politically liberal, and expression of nonconservative attitudes came to be associated with higher status, with greater participation in various college activities, and with greater personal involvement in the college as an institution. The study revealed that a marked change occurred in the women's attitudes over the four-year college period; a majority of the students who were conservative Republicans as freshmen expressed attitudes typical of rather liberal Democrats by the time they graduated. Newcomb concludes that the change is largely a function of the reward system at Bennington. Being liberal was reinforced both by the faculty and by the older students, who already exhibited much change. Obviously, not all the women changed, and those who did not were more likely to maintain close home ties, to get little involved in college activities, and to retain their families as their primary reference groups. What is perhaps most impressive about this research is that Newcomb (Newcomb et al., 1967) was able to follow up on his subjects more than twenty years later, at which time he observed that most of the women who had developed liberal attitudes at Bennington retained these more than two decades later. The Bennington graduates were, as a whole, far less conservative than would be expected on the basis of their demographic characteristics—at least upper-middle class in terms of socio-economic level. Although Newcomb explains his results primarily in reference-group terms, the reinforcement associated with acceptance, conferral of status, and so on, has obvious importance in understanding the changes that occurred.

A large amount of research dealing with the question of attitude change has been treated as falling within the tradition of reinforcement theory; however, much of the actual empirical work is highly atheoretical (Kiesler, Collins, and Miller 1969). Nevertheless, the results of the research indicate that much attitude change is a function of the reinforcement that the change elicits. We tend to develop our attitudes through socialization processes. We tend to change our attitudes when new positions are more personally satisfying or when they are rewarded and reinforced by those who qualify as our significant others. In this regard, reference group and reinforcement principles are closely aligned. The rewards that cause us to exhibit important attitude changes are often provided by those groups and individuals whose acceptance we highly value or strongly desire.

Other Theories of Attitude Change

ASSIMILATION-CONTRAST THEORY

Assimilation-contrast theory, developed largely in the work of Sherif and Hovland, grew out of two older traditions in social psychology. First, many of the basic ideas of the theory emerged from critical analyses made by these authors of the Thurstone technique for measuring attitudes (see chapter 7). It will be recalled that one of the major steps involved in developing a Thurstone attitude scale was that of having a number of judges evaluate attitude statements in terms of their favorability or unfavorability toward the attitude object and that Thurstone assumed that the judges' evaluations of the statements were independent of their own attitudes toward the issue being measured.

A number of early studies tended to support this important assumption (Hinckley, 1932; Ferguson, 1935; Pintner and Forlano, 1937). However, research conducted by Hovland and Sherif (1952) and by Sherif and Hovland (1953) strongly contradicted these earlier findings. These authors noted that it was common practice in constructing the scales to eliminate as careless any judge who sorted thirty or more of the attitude statements into a single pile. However, they proposed that rather than being careless, such individuals simply may have had more extreme attitudes toward the object being evaluated. Therefore, their attitudes were influencing their placement of statements. To test this hypothesis, Sherif and Hovland selected several groups of judges to evaluate a series of items developed to measure attitudes toward blacks. Some of the judges were purposely selected because of potentially strong attitudes on the issue. It was found that if the criterion of eliminating any judge who placed thirty or more statements into a single pile were employed, over three-fourths of the black judges would be eliminated, as would almost as many white judges who were known to have favorable attitudes towards blacks. Judges with extreme attitudes tended to bunch statements in the categories at the end of the scale opposite their own position; black and white judges with favorable attitudes tended to place significant numbers of the items in the two or three piles at the unfavorable end of the scale. In effect, Sherif and Hovland were observing what they called a *contrast effect*—all items that contrast with an individual's position on an issue tend to be grouped or clustered together, and little discrimination is made among them.

The second tradition from which assimilation-contrast theory grew is judgment scales, in which Sherif had a long-term interest. Such scales are exemplified by his early work on the autokinetic effect (see chapter 5). Sherif concluded from this work that in conditions of physical ambiguity, individuals tend to develop reference scales to act as anchors of judgment. Therefore, individual judgments in the autokinetic-effect experiments converged toward a group mean in a series of trials and this mean in future trials acted as a reference point, a baseline against which other items or events could be assessed and evaluated.

The primary assumption of assimilation-contrast theory is that the effect of a communication designed to change attitudes on some issue will depend upon the way in which the communication is characterized by the individual who receives it. This always involves a two-stage process: (1) the recipient will make a judgment regarding the position advocated by the message relative to his or her own position on the issue; (2) based on this judgment, the recipient will either assimilate the information (supposedly by changing his or her attitude in the direction advocated by the message) or reject the communication and not change attitudes.

In considering the judgmental process involved in the first step, Sherif and Hovland propose that persuasive communications can fall within any of several theoretical "latitudes" or ranges, depending on the position advocated by the message relative to the receiver's attitude on the issue. The first of these, the *latitude of acceptance*, categorizes those positions around the receiver's attitude that she or he will judge as acceptable and will therefore agree with or endorse. Outside this latitude of acceptance is a *latitude of noncommitment*, which constitutes a residual category into which falls communication that is sufficiently different from the receiver's position that it is not readily assimilated but neither is it automatically rejected. Further away is the *latitude of rejection*, which categorizes communications judged to be intolerable or unacceptable. Because they fall outside the range of acceptance, they will bring about no attitude change. These various latitudes are outlined in figure 8–5.

The key in predicting attitude change using assimilation-contrast theory is to determine the amount of discrepancy between the current position or attitude (internal anchor point) of the recipient of the communication and the position or attitude advocated by the communication. The theory predicts that when a persuasive attempt falls within the latitude of acceptance, attitude change will occur. However, when an attempt falls outside that latitude of acceptance (and, particularly if it falls within the latitude of

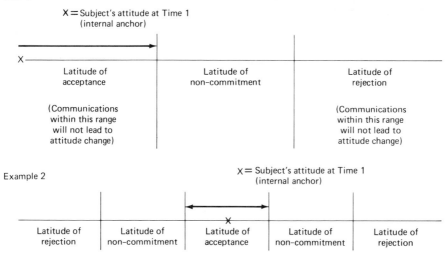

Figure 8–5 Assimilation-Contrast Theory Recipient Categories and Attitude Change

rejection) attitude change does not occur. In fact, when a persuasive attempt falls within the latitude of rejection, it may have a boomerang effect and may act to reinforce the initial position of the recipient.

The notion of latitudes also implies that the *amount* of attitude change caused by a persuasive communication will be an increasing function of the discrepancy between initial position and that advocated by the message *so long as that message falls within the latitude of acceptance.* The relationship between discrepancy and attitude change is a curvilinear relationship, as illustrated in figure 8–6.

In other words, the assimilation-contrast effect that lies behind this process operates as follows: so long as a communication falls within the latitude of acceptance, actual discrepancy between the position advocated by the message and the individual's own position is underestimated as an increasing function of the discrepancy. When a communication falls within the latitude of rejection, actual discrepancy between the position advocated and the individual's own position is overestimated as a decreasing function of the amount of discrepancy. This latter point would account for the judges' clustered placement of attitude items, discussed earlier, which is supported further by the researchers' contention that both trends are exaggerated for the highly involved subject. That is, the person who holds an extreme attitude on some topic is likely to have a relatively narrow latitude of acceptance. As a consequence, ostensibly neutral items will fall outside that latitude, will be perceived by the recipient as advocating a more extreme position than they actually do (contrast effect), and will be rejected. The usefulness of this theory as a device for eliciting attitude change is dependent upon the ability of the researcher to identify the present position (anchor point) of the subject, to determine the breadth of the latitude of acceptance, and to devise a persuasive communication that falls near the border (but not outside) the margin of that latitude.

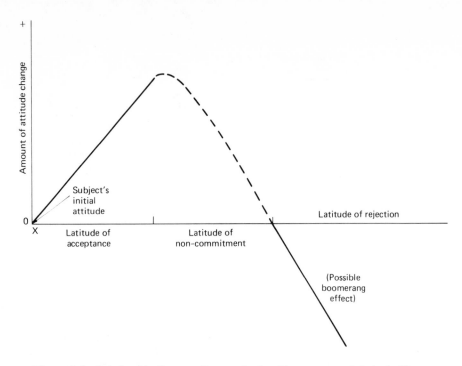

Figure 8-6 Relationship Between Communication Discrepancy and Attitude Change

ADAPTATION-LEVEL THEORY

The work of Helson (1948, 1959) on adaptation-level theory has received some attention in the social-psychology literature as a theory of attitude change. The essential concept of this theory is that what an individual experiences when exposed to a new set of stimuli will be largely a function of what he or she has already adapted to. For example, after driving 70 mph for some time on the freeway, 55 mph seems very slow. However, that same 55 mph can seem quite fast if we have been creeping along at a much slower pace because of road conditions or a traffic jam. Thus, stimuli will affect individual attitude changes differently depending on one's current adaptation level.

Other researchers have attempted to use adaptation-level theory, although their empirical applications are often quite divorced from the sophistication of Helson's original formulation. In addition, many of the studies conducted under this label can be explained as well by other theoretical perspectives, particularly reference-group interpretations. Therefore, we will touch only briefly upon some representative research studies.

The notion of adaptation can deal with the problem of conforming to social stimuli (an issue that we have discussed in greater detail in chapter 5). It recognizes specifically the role of social groups in the formation and change of attitudes. As noted earlier, probably most of the attitudes we hold can be traced at least in part to our group affiliations. Our attitudes thus reflect those of the groups to which we grant allegiance. Primary-group ties are especially important in the attitude-formation process. For example, our political attitudes and preferences usually reflect the influence of our parents; our attitudes toward our country develop through interaction with family, peers, and teachers; and so on. A change in attitudes is then seen basically as a process of *adapting* to new primary ties and to new group affiliations. Sociologists have noted that this process can often be quite conscious and have coined the term *anticipatory socialization* to account for the most conscious occurrences. Anticipatory socialization is the process of adapting our attitudes (as well as values, behavior patterns, lifestyles, and so on) to groups in which we desire to hold membership or to which we anticipate belonging at some future time. For example, the upwardly mobile individual will often change political party, religious affiliation, and various other attitudes and behavior patterns to be consistent with those of the social group in which membership is desired.

Adaptation-level theory, however, need not imply such complete and formal change. For example, we have noted that the *expression* of attitudes and beliefs is often more a function of the group setting in which it is made than of the actual position of the individual (see chapter 5). Linn (1965) accounted for much of the racial attitude/behavior inconsistency of his subjects with a similar explanation. He found that a majority of his subjects at the University of Wisconsin expressed liberal racial attitudes when responding to an attitude scale, but many were unwilling to translate these liberal attitudes into patterns of behavior supportive of racial integration. Linn argues that the *setting* of his research supported racial liberalism, and, therefore, his subjects were adapting to that perceived audience in their verbal *expressions* of attitudes. When faced with a situation requiring action, however, many reverted to a position more congruent with their actual (less liberal) personal attitudes.

As noted, much of the research that is advanced under adaptation-level theory could fit equally well under some other perspective. In addition, much of this research tends to deal more with behavioral adaptation than with attitude adaptation. A popular example of this is found in a study by Rosenbaum and Blake (1955), who asked students to volunteer to participate in an experiment. Just prior to this request, however, another student who was actually a stooge working for the experimenter was asked to participate. In fifteen cases, the stooge agreed to participate, and in fifteen he refused. Rosenbaum and Blake found that when the stooge agreed, a majority of the students agreed; when he refused, a majority of the subjects also refused.

A somewhat more complex study was conducted by Kimbrell and Blake (1958). In this case, an experimental subject and a stooge were seated together in a hall outside the room where they were supposedly going to participate in a study. In the hall, there was a water fountain, but above it had been placed a sign indicating that it should not be used. As they waited, the stooge and the subjects in two of the experimental conditions were given a bowl of crackers to eat. In one of these conditions, the crackers had been treated with a hot sauce. In half the instances, the stooge would go to the water fountain and take a drink, ignoring the sign. In the remaining cases, he would simply remain seated. If the stooge took a drink, it increased the probability that the naive subject would also take a drink. However, the nature of the crackers also had a significant independent effect on the subject's behavior. As would be expected, the subject was much more likely to drink if he had been fed crackers treated with hot sauce than if he had been given plain crackers or none at all.

Despite the interest of some of these experiments, they can perhaps better be seen in the tradition of the conformity studies discussed earlier. The utility of adaptation-level theory as a general theory of attitude change remains questionable.

FUNCTIONAL THEORIES

Functional theories of attitude change are based on the assumption that before one can change an attitude, he or she must know its role or function for the individual who holds it. Such theories have been developed by Smith, Bruner, and White (1956) and by Katz (1960), who propose that attitudes serve several important functions for the individual. According to Smith, Bruner, and White, the major functions that attitudes serve for individuals are the following:

1. *Object appraisal* or orienting the individual actor to objects in his or her social environment. For example, our attitudes toward various objects, such as family, country, and religion, serve to orient us toward these objects when we confront them. Further, these attitudes help us in assessing other social objects. Our attitude toward religion, for example, helps us in appraising our response to such things as capital punishment and abortion.
2. *Social adjustment* or facilitating and maintaining social relationships. For example, in order to attain and maintain group memberships, certain attitudes must be expressed. One would not expect a member of the Ku Klux Klan to hold attitudes favorable to integration. Having such attitudes would not be conducive to the Klan member's adjustment to this social group.
3. *Externalization,* which grows directly out of psychoanalytical theories of personality. Smith, Bruner, and White propose that some attitudes serve as defense mechanisms (see chapter 1), protecting the ego from anxiety generated by inner problems. The person who is highly prejudiced toward gays, for example, may be externalizing internal doubts and fears.

Katz proposes four basic functions that overlap significantly with those of Smith, Bruner, and White. Specifically, these include: (1) an instrumental, adjustive, or utilitarian function; (2) an ego-defensive function; (3) a value-expressive function; and (4) a knowledge function. In both cases, the primary underlying assumption is that before we can effectively bring about attitude change, we must first know the reason the person holds an attitude. The attitude-change strategy can then be geared to respond to that particular need. For example, an attitude that serves to orient the individual to his or her environment may be shifted by providing new information; an attitude that serves an ego-defensive function may be changed only when anxiety-producing internal problems have been resolved; and so on.

The functional theories grow more out of the psychoanalytic tradition than do the other perspectives discussed to this point. They have not been widely used in the research literature. However, the emphasis on knowing something about the individual's personality and the assessment of attitudes only within this context adds a useful balance to other theories, which ignore or only superficially touch upon individual personality factors in the study of attitude change.

Characteristics of the Source, the Message, and the Audience in Attitude Change

The most comprehensive and carefully detailed body of literature on attitude change that is available has emerged out of the early work conducted at Yale University by Hovland, Janis, and Kelley (1953). These researchers and many others since have examined in detail issues relating to (1) the source of the message; (2) the characteristics and content of the message; and (3) the characteristics of the recipients of the message in determining the nature and amount of attitude change that will be generated.

CHARACTERISTICS OF THE COMMUNICATOR

Suppose you are interested in the potential problems associated with the large-scale development of nuclear-power facilities. Are you more likely to be influenced by the statements of an internationally recognized nuclear scientist or by the statements of the youthful attendant at your local gasoline station? Most of us would probably respond more favorably to arguments of the former because he or she is seen as an *expert* on the topic of concern. Researchers have gathered considerable evidence that we are more influenced by an expert than we are by a layperson. Hovland, Janis, and Kelly (1953) suggest that people are likely to pay closer attention to someone who is defined as an expert than they would to someone else. Because they pay more attention, they are more likely to learn the expert's arguments and, hence, to be influenced by them. Although some laboratory evidence (Hovland and Weiss, 1951) suggests that we are as likely to *retain* information provided by low-credibility sources as that by high-credibility sources, there is support for the theory that we are more *influenced* by the expert source.

Experimental evidence on the importance of expertise is provided in a study by Aronson, Turner, and Carlsmith (1963). In the study, students who had negatively evaluated some poetry were asked to read a communication praising the poetry that was alternately attributed to T. S. Elliot or to a student at Mississippi State Teachers College. The subjects were then asked again to evaluate the poetry. As would be expected, those who thought they were reading a communication from T. S. Elliot exhibited much more attitude change than did the other group.

If someone or some entity is defined as an expert, we almost automatically assume that she, he, or it should be a source of valid and correct arguments. However, expertise is issue-specific. The nuclear physicist who knows a great deal about the advantages and disadvantages of constructing nuclear-power facilities may know relatively little about the advantages and disadvantages of alternative strategies on the football field or about specific techniques for brain surgery. Although most of us readily agree that this is

"Trustworthy" communicators, such as Judge John J. Sirica of Watergate fame, tend to be more successful in changing the attitudes of others. *Source:* Wide World Photos, Inc.

true, there are numerous instances of experts in one field of endeavor endorsing or opposing some action in another field and successfully influencing attitudes by so doing. For example, conglomerates advertise new product lines by reminding us of their expertise in unrelated fields, reasoning that any company that can make good baby foods for a century will certainly be great and trustworthy in affording geriatric health insurance.

Another very real problem in relying on experts outside of a controlled setting is that most issues in the real world are extremely complex and different experts can disagree about the relative merit of various courses of action. Returning to the nuclear-power example, there are probably equal numbers of experts on both sides of this debate. In addition, those who oppose plant construction can present credentials that are equally as impressive as those produced by scientists who favor large numbers of such facilities. The same is true with an issue such as fluoridation. Although many experts favor fluoridation of local water supplies as a means of decreasing the incidence of dental caries, there are equally expert opponents of such action that point out that fluorine is a poison. In such cases, the public tends to opt for the status quo rather than trying to choose between expert sources.

Another important characteristic of communicators that contributes to their success in influencing attitude change is *trustworthiness.* In general, trustworthiness has been treated as the characteristic of being able to establish confidence in one's intent. If we feel that we can trust a communicator, we are more likely to be influenced by that source than by a source that does not dispel all our apprehensions about being misled or manipulated. If we see strong evidence of hypocrisy between what someone says and what he or she does, then we are likely to be little influenced by his or her communications.

Trustworthiness appears to be inspired by a number of different properties. For example, if we see that a person has little to gain from his or her effort to influence us, we are more likely to define that person as trustworthy. High governmental officials are required to give up their public- and private-sector holdings to increase our trust in their legislative motives. Otherwise, we could feel that they are acting to enhance their own wealth or power rather than for the public good. Criminals imprisoned without hope of parole are successfully influencing young first offenders that crime is not a profitable pursuit; the convicts are not only experts on the subject of life in jail but are seen by the juveniles as having little to gain from the lectures.

A person who argues against what appears to be his or her own self-interest is also seen as trustworthy. Walster, Aronson, and Abrahams (1966) had a convicted criminal argue before a group of subjects in favor of a stronger police force. Because it was clear that the criminal had little personally to gain from taking this position, which additionally would be detrimental to any future illegal activities he might have planned, it was assumed that he would be highly influential. The researchers found this to be the case. Police departments now use former pickpockets or burglars, who could make more money by their crimes (barring arrest) than by their cooperation, to demonstrate how easy it is for them to apply their skills in ripping off the public. They then provide information on how to minimize the chance of victimization. Assumedly, these programs are more successful in changing attitudes and behavior than those using other communicators to present the same evidence.

However, simply appearing to argue against one's own best interest does not guarantee inspiring trust; previous information from the same source, if any, has to have proved trustworthy if the communicator wants to succeed in the present. Many people have a very difficult time believing that public utility companies are being genuine in their recent advertisements asking us to use less electricity. These people seem to feel that although such action appears to be contrary to the utilities' best interests, there must be some ulterior motive behind the messages. Perhaps loss of credibility because of such past actions as raising rates when usage drops makes the companies untrustworthy in the eyes of much of the public, and one good advertising program simply is not going to restore that lost trust.

Other communicator characteristics that are likely to impact upon the amount of attitude change that is generated include such things as *power, attraction, likableness,* and *similarity.* There are many instances in which we are more likely to be influenced by a source who has power than by one who does not (Raven and French 1958). In part, this is because the attribute of power usually affords the communicator with the ability to impose sanctions if we fail to comply with the request. Thus, we are more influenced by instructions from the boss than from someone who ranks lower than us in the organizational hierarchy. To effectively bring about change in most cases, however, the powerful source must also be visible or have the ability to monitor the degree of compliance. Otherwise, change is likely to be rather temporary—we go along only so long as our actions can be disclosed to the power agent. Remove that monitoring ability, and compliance based solely on power is likely to decrease.

The characteristics of *attractiveness* and *likableness* are probably closely related. In general, an attractive and likable communicator will have more effect on an audience than will one who is disliked or who instills hostility and anger (Mills and Aronson, 1965). The salesperson who dresses neatly and is pleasant is much more likely to make the sale than is one who is nasty, curt, and otherwise unattractive. Most highly successful salespeople have developed the ability to establish good rapport with potential customers and to present themselves in such a manner that the customers like them and define the sales relationship in positive terms.

Similarity may operate in much the same fashion (see, for example, Brock, 1965; Nesbitt, 1972). We see this used more and more in contemporary mass advertisement campaigns. For example, the housewife depicted in television commercials who hates to clean her oven can be identified with by all other housewives who similarly despise that particular job. If she has found a product that takes all of the drudgery out of oven cleaning, then obviously the same product should work for others as well. However, we do not yet know a great deal about what kind of similarity (personal appearance, situational, and so on) is most important. Is the consumer more likely to identify with and be influenced by the "average-looking" people now used in commercials or to identify with a personal ideal, such as that portrayed by perfectly dressed, beautiful actors and actresses in other ads? Additional research will be required before we can say much more about the importance of similarity in the influence process.

CHARACTERISTICS OF THE MESSAGE

What characteristics of a message cause it to be more or less successful in changing our attitudes? We will look primarily at two issues: (1) the use of fear-arousing as opposed to more rational or less emotional appeals; and (2) the content or organization of the message itself.

Fear-Arousing Appeals There are probably very few high-school graduates who did not see at some point during their high-school careers films dealing with the hazards of reckless driving, the consequences of smoking and drug abuse, and the ravages of venereal disease. Many such films have been developed, and most have been based on the assumption that if sufficient fear is aroused in an audience, they will be convinced to choose the course of action advocated by the film. Thus, some rather grisly films have been developed for use in high schools and for other audiences (such as the armed forces) that show in vivid detail such things as surgical removal of a cancer-ridden lung, highway patrol officers and ambulance personnel using plastic garbage bags to contain the remains of young people who had been killed in highway accidents caused by reckless driving, the effects of advanced venereal disease on adults and newborn babies, and so on. How effective are such techniques in influencing the attitudes of the audience? One of the authors remembers rather vividly an experiment developed by one of his high-school teachers designed to convince the members of his health class of the dangers of smoking. The teacher rigged a smoking machine that collected small amounts of almost pure nicotine. The nicotine was then fed to birds or other small animals with an eye dropper. The bird or animal shuddered a few times and then died. The experiment was frightening, but many of the boys in the class would argue over the cigarettes that were left after the conclusion of the experiment, and some would even finish the unused portions of those that had been attached to the cigarette smoking machine.

Fear-arousing appeals have been used effectively to defeat such referenda as those supporting fluoridation of the water supply (by calling it poison) and state land-use planning laws (labeled communistic). Are such emotional appeals more effective overall than more rational approaches and arguments? Early research by Janis and Feshbach (1953) dealing with appeals to practice dental hygiene found an inverse relationship between the amount of fear aroused by the communication and the influence it had in changing the behavior of the audience. An appeal that causes much fear does arouse more worry, concern, and fright in an audience, but this is less likely to be translated into attitude and behavior change than are appeals that elicit less fear and more thought. Apparently, too much fear can cause us to "turn off" the message and to react unfavorably to it. Other possibilities have also been suggested (Kiesler, Collins, and Miller, 1969). For example, highly fear-arousing appeals may be so distracting that it is difficult for the audience to attend to what is being said. Highly emotional appeals may elicit defensive reactions in the audience, or the negative aspects of the communication may cause the audience to seriously question the credibility of the communicator and to resist what is being said. These and other issues remain largely unresolved at this time.

In sum, the evidence suggests that the effectiveness of emotional or fear-arousing appeals will depend upon a number of other factors in addition to the message itself (Janis, 1967). For example, Levanthal and his colleagues (Levanthal, 1970; Levanthal and Niles, 1965; Levanthal and Singer, 1966) have found that *if* an immediate response is necessary and *if* the subject has low self-esteem, highly fear-arousing appeals are more effective. Research by Levanthal and his associates has also shown that if fear-arousing materials are followed immediately by information on how, when, and where action can be taken to alleviate the problem identified, they will be more effective.

Organization of the Message Should a persuasive message present one side of the argument or both sides? Should it draw a conclusion or leave the conclusion up to the audience? If two sides of an argument are to be presented by two different individuals, would it be more influential to speak first or second? Rather extensive research has been conducted on each of these questions, and again the conclusions drawn suggest that the answers depend upon several other factors in addition to that of message organization. For example, evidence concerning whether to present only one side of an argument or to recognize the arguments of opponents as well suggests that this depends very much on the characteristics of the audience. If the audience is well-informed and highly intelligent and likely to already know of some of the important counter-arguments, then the speaker will have more impact if he or she recognizes those counter-arguments (Hovland, Lumsdaine, and Sheffield, 1949). On the other hand, if the audience is not highly intelligent and well-informed, presenting both sides and bringing up counter-arguments may only tend to confuse them and will result in reduced success in convincing them of the validity of the position advocated. Similarly, if the audience is known to already hold an opposing position or will have the opportunity to hear from the other side, then it is better to present both sides of the argument. Apparently, to do otherwise would cause the audience to believe that the speaker either is not aware of the counter-arguments or is fearful of dealing with them.

Research evidence suggests that the importance of drawing a conclusion or not drawing a conclusion is also dependent upon other factors. The more complex the argument and the more complicated the issue, the more advantageous it is to draw a conclusion. This seems to increase the probability of the audience understanding the message and recognizing its most salient points. One of the dangers associated with allowing the audience to draw its own conclusions is that they may not draw the desired implications. Again, however, drawing conclusions is less likely to be important for intelligent and informed audiences (Thistlethwaite, deHaan, and Kamenetsky, 1955). In such cases, doing so might even have a boomerang effect or cause the initial position to be held even more strongly.

Primary versus Recency Effects There are arguments in favor of both sides of the question of whether one should speak first or last when attempting to influence an audience. For example, increased probability of retention argues in favor of recency; the audience is more likely to remember material presented last. However, the first speaker has the chance to make his or her points with sufficient impact to decrease the amount of attention the audience will pay to the arguments presented by the opponent. The key to this argument appears to be that of timing, including both the amount of time between the presentation of the two arguments, and the amount of time between the second presentation and the point at which the audience must make its decision. If there is very little time between the two presentations, the advantage seems to go to the first speaker (assuming that both speakers are equally attractive, trustworthy, and expert and that their arguments are equally well organized, rational, and so forth). In this case, absorbing the first communication seems to interfere with the learning of the second (due to fatigue, overload, and so on). On the other hand, recency effects will be more important and the audience will be able to retain more of the argument of the second communication if there is a gap between the two presentations and if a decision must be made immediately after the second presentation (Miller and Campbell, 1959). As is true with the other factors studied to this point, the results of research cannot be explained by looking just at one variable. Instead, several must be included.

CHARACTERISTICS OF THE AUDIENCE

It is quite apparent that the individual who is the focus of the persuasive appeal does not exist in a social vacuum. Certain personal characteristics of the individual are important in assessing the effectiveness of the communication, as are several group factors in large audiences.

Personality Factors Are some people more susceptable than others to attitude-change efforts? The evidence indicates that the answer to this question is yes, although there is a growing recognition that the answer is more complex than was initially assumed (McGuire, 1967). In general, people who have had a *history of success* are less likely to be amenable to persuasive appeals. Successful individuals tend to be more self-confident and so are less reliant on input from others than are those who have a history of failure. Asch-type experiments (see chapter 5) demonstrate that persons who have had greater success in responding to perception problems in earlier trials are less likely to conform to the incorrect judgments of other subjects in later trials. Subjects who are told that they have performed poorly on earlier trials are more likely to conform to the group.

Persons who have aggressive personalities are also less likely to respond to efforts to change their attitudes. Personal aggressiveness may coexist with dogmatism or closed-mindedness. A person who is absolutely convinced of the "rightness" of his or her position (closed-minded) is not likely to respond favorably to efforts to change that attitude. Other personality factors such as inner versus other directedness or need for social approval may be important, but the evidence to this point is rather inconclusive.

Group Factors Most of us do not respond directly to communicative appeals in a strict stimulus-response fashion. Rather, those appeals are usually filtered through the various group memberships and opinion leaders that play an interpretative role for us. The importance of group factors was demonstrated by early research on voting behavior (Lazarsfeld, Berelson, and Gaudet, 1948; Berelson, Lazarsfeld, and McPhee, 1954). The research showed that most voters do not respond directly to appeals made by politicians. Rather, they interpret and evaluate these appeals in terms of their memberships in organizations, such as labor unions, churches, and social clubs.

Because many of our attitudes are founded in the groups in which we hold membership, it is important to consider group factors when we evaluate efforts to change attitudes. For example, if a person is supported by a group holding similar attitudes, she or he is much more resistant to change than would be so if she or he lacked such support. On the other hand, when group ties have been broken or eroded, the person is much more amenable to persuasive appeals. This helps account for the fact that new immigrants are prime candidates for various types of extremist political and religious organizations. By pulling up their roots and moving elsewhere, migrants frequently break their major group ties with family, friends, and community. If a new group can step in and provide a new sense of identity and purpose for the migrant, it can frequently gain a convert. Radical political groups, such as the John Birch Society, have flourished in areas of southern California that are inhabited by large groups of immigrants from other areas of the country, particularly from rural areas of the Southwest. Similarly, social movements, such as the Kingdom of Father Divine, have appealed to the uprooted and to those who have left home and family behind. Thus, when group factors change, attitudes are much more amenable to change (see, for example, studies describing social movements in Toch, 1965; Cantril, 1963).

Groups are also important in that they often provide a reminder to the individual of who he or she is and, consequently, how he or she should believe and behave. In research conducted a number of years ago, Charters and Newcomb (1958) found that if their subjects' membership in the Catholic Church was made a salient issue, the subjects responded differently than when this was not the case.

Closely related to this is the fact that individuals often make *public commitments* before groups, which serve to increase the probability of a continuation of the attitude or behavior. Religious evangelists use this tactic very successfully. The potential convert or the new believer is asked to come forward a make a public commitment to a new set of beliefs or a changed life. Similarly, groups developed to help those who want to quit smoking or to lose weight rely quite heavily on public commitments. In all these ways, groups are not only important in changing attitudes but also in maintaining that change once it has been made.

Inoculation against Persuasion McGuire (1964) has demonstrated that people can be made more resistant to efforts to change their attitudes through "inoculation"—providing them with weakened counter-arguments that allow them to build up effective defenses against the persuasive effort. McGuire uses a "germ theory" of attitude change. He argues: "In the biological situation, the person is typically made resistant to some attacking virus by pre-exposure to a weakened dose of the virus. This mild dose stimulates his defenses so that he will be better able to overcome any massive viral attack to which he is later exposed, but is not so strong that this pre-exposure will itself cause the disease" (1964, p. 200).

McGuire believes that attacks on what he calls "cultural truisms" are unusually effective because we tend to feel that these beliefs are unassailable, and we have never been required to defend them in the past. A "cultural truism" is a belief that is so widely shared that we might never hear it attacked and would even doubt if an attack were possible. For example, the belief, "you should wash your hands before you eat," would be defined by McGuire as a cultural truism. By preparing the subject with watered-down versions of an attack, he or she can be made aware of the potential sources of attack as well as the basic arguments of defense. A person so prepared (inoculated) is then found to be much more resistant to persuasive appeals when they occur.

Can Attitudes Really Be Changed?

We have now reviewed numerous theories that have been advanced to account for the process of attitude change. Many of these have been used to demonstrate rather significant attitude change within the context of the social psychologist's laboratory. However, what happens outside that laboratory? Most social psychologists are now coming to admit that efforts to change attitudes in a nonlaboratory setting have not met with a great deal of success. The one major exception to this is the effort to change attitude and behavior patterns within the context of "total institutions," which we will discuss in the next section.

The basic assumption that has guided efforts to change attitudes in field settings is that if the message can be gotten across, people will change in the direction advocated by the message. Etzioni (1972, p. 45) has noted, however, "We are now confronting the uncomfortable possibility that human beings are not very easily changed after all." Etzioni uses the example of smoking behavior. Since at least 1964 when the surgeon general's report called national attention to the link between smoking and cancer, huge sums of money have been spent for advertising campaigns, including pamphlets, warning messages on cigarette packages, and mass-media efforts, to change public attitudes and behavior toward cigarettes. However, after more than a decade of such efforts, we are now consuming more cigarettes per capita than we were in 1964. Numerous similar examples could be cited, including campaigns designed to warn people of the dangers of drug abuse, programs attempting to convince the public to slow down on the highways and to use safety belts, and so on. Almost without exception, one has to conclude from such efforts that the mass media are generally ineffectual tools for profoundly changing people.

Why do we find such important differences between what some social psychologists have demonstrated in the laboratory and what we see in field studies that attempt to measure the amount of attitude change that has occurred following some persuasive appeal? Cohen (1964, pp. 129–132) suggests that there are a number of very important differences between these lab experiments and field surveys that help us to account for these differences. These include the following:

	SURVEYS	LAB EXPERIMENTS
1. Unit to be evaluated	Usually an entire program of communication, such as a compaign to change smoking habits.	Usually some specific variation in communication content or in personality of recipient; also usually limited to a single communication.
2. Time interval involved	Usually more remote, thus limiting observed impact.	Effect observed immediately or soon after exposure, thus accentuating impact.
3. Characteristics of communicator	Remote individuals; outsiders often known to espouse certain viewpoint.	Often teachers or experimenters in school setting who are lent special authority and credibility.
4. Setting	Natural environment; selective perception, reference groups, and so forth are operative.	Controlled lab; outside social-situational factors are minimized or inoperative.
5. Sample	Usually random sample of some entire population.	College students because of ready accessibility.
6. Focus of study	Socially significant attitudes to which people are highly committed.	Factors expected on the basis of theory to influence attitude change.

It is important that we understand these differences in approach. Surveys conducted in field settings usually deal with attitudes that are a direct outgrowth of the socialization experience of the individual, that are reinforced through various social relationships and group memberships, and that are very much a part of the individual's social milieu. Experimental studies, on the other hand, often deal with issues that are relatively less involving and that are more open to communicative appeals. The differences in results in the two settings should not be too surprising.

ATTITUDE CHANGE WITHIN THE CONTEXT OF TOTAL INSTITUTIONS

There are some rather dramatic examples of attitude change in nonlaboratory contexts, and these are very instructive in understanding the overall process. Synanon was initially very successful in its programs to help rehabilitate the drug addict, though there is now some evidence that "too much" control can lead to other serious problems. Alcoholics Anonymous has achieved what few other programs have been able to in rehabilitating the problem drinker. Both these programs, particularly Synanon, have operated on the principle of maintaining some control over the total environment of the individual. Synanon created a whole new social community for the addict under the assumption that only by changing the total environment can the profound change in attitude and behavior patterns required to cure the addict be achieved.

Perhaps the most dramatic change of all occurs within the context of what Goffman (1961) calls "total institutions." In the total institution, one does not just manipulate a person's existing social environment but rather removes that individual entirely from the old environment and creates a new one. This can be illustrated by what happens in such places as POW and concentration camps. The attitude changes that have occurred in such settings have been so significant that the label "brainwashing" is used to describe them. Schein, Schneier, and Barker (1961) have identified the characteristics of POW camps and communist civilian prisons that have allowed those in control to successfully "brainwash" captives:

1. Almost complete control over the system of rewards and punishments. For POW's, the captors determine when the prisoner is allowed to eat, sleep, exercise, read, or take care of other bodily functions. The systematic manipulation and disruption of daily activities and schedules can become disorienting over time and can make the victim of the manipulation less resistant and more pliable.

2. Control over communications. Within the context of total institutions, the individual does not have access to regular channels of communication. Even interaction among prisoners is often prohibited. The captors can exercise virtually total control over what is read. Only materials that are supportive of the ideology being advanced are made available, unless outside communications that will negatively affect morale can be used.

3. Total immersion of the individual in the setting. The key here is that the individual is separated from normal contacts and routines. He or she cannot leave and cannot contact anyone on the outside unless allowed to do so by the captors. The institution becomes the captive's total and only world.

4. Systematic breakup of past identities. The relatively stable self-concept and identity that the individual brought to the institution is destroyed. Symbols of past life and status are removed. Confessions of guilt are often elicited as a means of convincing the individual of the wrong of his or her past life and the need to replace it with something else.

5. Resocialization. Once one's past identity has been destroyed or severely challenged, it is rather easy to replace it with something else. A new self emerges that is rewarded within the context of the institution's environment. Trying to be what one was before is punishing and costly; being what the captors desire brings forth rewards and acceptance. In such cases, a new definition of self can and frequently does emerge.

Secord and Backman (1964) note that total institutions are often thought of in terms of alien ideologies. However, there are many parallel albeit less severe examples of such efforts in our own society. Military academies utilize virtually the same steps, although in toned-down form, to change new recruits into trained and polished cadets (see Dornbush, 1955). Mental hospitals, professional schools, convents, and monasteries all use somewhat similar procedures, although the amount of control exercised is significantly less.

The concept of total environments not only helps to account for dramatic examples of attitude change, but also helps us to explain why some efforts to change attitudes are not successful. Etzioni (1972) has noted that vast sums of money have been spent in recent years on compensatory educational programs with little demonstrated success. He argues that the most important reason for failure is that the disadvantaged child is often locked into a total environment that is almost diametrically opposed to the change that is desired. This total environment includes home and parents, neighborhood, modeling behavior of siblings and peers, and so on. When all these are pushing the child in one direction, it is clearly too much to expect that something like a compensatory educational program will be successful in significantly changing the child. Only by dealing with that total environment is change likely to occur.

In sum, the probabilities of achieving profound and immediate attitude change are not particularly great. There are too many factors in addition to the persuasive appeal itself that have to be considered. This is not to deny that an important amount of attitude change is always occurring. It is. However, much of this change is a function of new experiences, of changing group loyalties, of the attainment of new knowledge and information. Although some of these factors are open to manipulation by the change agent, others are not easily accessible. For most of us, attitudes change in much the same fashion that they are formed—slowly.

Summary

We have defined *attitude* as one of the most important concepts in the field of social psychology. One of the reasons for this prominence is that so much time, effort, and resources are spent both within and outside the academic world on the problem of attitude *change*. Advertisers hope to influence us favorably toward their products, politicians want to win us over to their camps, missionaries hope to convince us to adopt their particular religious philosophy, and so on. Changing attitudes in this country is, in short, a very big business.

Several social-psychological theories have been developed to account for the process of attitude change. Cognitive theories, such as Heider's P-O-X model, upon which most other balance theories build, view it primarily as a means to restoring balance to a cognitively unbalanced state. The dissonance model and the congruity model, both cognitive-consistency theories, see attitude change as an important stress-reducing strategy.

The second major theoretical approach we discussed is found in reinforcement theory. The classical conditioning model, based on the simple paradigm that grew out of the early experimental work of Pavlov, and operant reinforcement models, based on the assumption that a rewarded attitude will be strengthened, were seen as useful in explaining many everyday attempts at attitude change.

Although much of the research literature grows out of the cognitive-consistency and reinforcement traditions, other theoretical approaches have also been used. Assimilation-contrast theory views attitude change as a two-stage process by which attitudes are evaluated and then either assimilated, leading to attitude change, or rejected. Adaptation-level theory views attitude change simply as a mechanism for adjusting to changing group affiliations. The functional theories view attitude change as possible only when personal needs change or when more effective means of meeting them are identified because attitudes are formed to fill these needs.

A good deal of research in recent years deals with the importance of various characteristics of the source, the message, and the audience in attitude change. Communicators considered expert, trustworthy, powerful, attractive, and so on, are usually granted greater credibility and so are more effective in influencing the audience. In considering characteristics of the message, fear-arousing appeals have been found to be effective in some situations but not in others. The effectiveness of presenting both sides of the argument, drawing conclusions, and speaking first or last was also shown as varying with the audience. In assessing the audience, some individual personality characteristics and types and strengths of group affiliations must be considered. Many attitudes are firmly rooted in group memberships, and, unless the group changes, the individual is likely to be quite resistant to changes in attitudes. However, groups can be important in affecting the permanence of attitude change.

After several decades of research, we are becoming more and more aware of the difficulty of changing attitudes in natural, nonlaboratory settings. Some of the most dramatic examples of attitude change outside the laboratory have occurred in "total institutions," where such change is facilitated by a high degree of control over the individual. However, because most efforts directed toward changing attitudes in noninstitutional settings do not involve rigid control of the situation, or person, the amount of change they produce is likely to be far less dramatic.

9

person
perception

The first day of class, you are seated next to a member of the opposite sex who leans over and asks if you know the instructor and how he teaches the class. How you respond will depend on your perceptions of the other's physical appearance, motives, and the surrounding social situation. If the other person is physically attractive to you, in that he or she has a figure, hair style, and clothes of which you approve, you will probably respond in a warm and cooperative manner. The same is true if you feel that the other has asked the question because he or she finds you attractive and wishes to start a conversation. However, if you feel that the other person wants the information in order to have a head start in the competition for grades, you will probably be more closemouthed. If several other members of the class heard the request and also wait expectantly for your reply, your response will be influenced by this as well.

This example illustrates the process of person perception, which involves not only assessing observable characteristics, such as appearance, but also inferring internal states, such as emotions, personality traits, and intentions. External cues, such as appearance, body movement, facial expression, and group membership, are utilized to understand and to predict other people's behavior. The importance of accurately predicting the behavior of others in accomplishing individual goals and objectives is evident. If one of your goals in college is to date attractive members of the opposite sex, then an explanation of why the person has spoken to you and a prediction of how he or she will respond to overtures is critical information. Also, if obtaining good grades is an important goal, then predicting why the other person requested the information about the instructor may be important.

In this chapter, we will first examine three theories explaining how people use information to form impressions of those with whom they come into contact. In the second section, we will focus on how differing amounts and types of information are processed in the formation of an impression of others.

Theories of Person Perception

STEREOTYPES

Stereotypes are widely-held beliefs attributing certain characteristics to all members of a given social group. Whatever the defining traits might be, all individuals in a given category are assumed to be characterized by them and therefore to look and act very much the same as all other group members. For example, two persistant ethnic stereotypes are that the Irish are heavy drinkers who are prone to violence and that Jews are mercenary and family oriented. According to Walter Lippman (1922), the journalist who coined this use of the word *stereotype*, the number of sights, sounds, tastes, smells, feelings, and so forth that are constantly bombarding a person make it impossible for him or her to react individually to each specific stimulus. He argued that people simply cannot cope with the "blooming, buzzing confusion of reality" without the assistance of stereotypes, which afford us the comfort of recognition and save us the time and effort of interpreting masses of new stimuli hourly. Stereotypes may emerge out of long-term social interactions with others espousing these beliefs, or they may be specifically taught by others. Once stereotypes are developed, the individual places social contacts into the appropriate stereotypical category and treats members of each group in a given way. For example, a person may accept the stereotype that all people with red hair have violent tempers and should be avoided and thus would avoid or cut short *any* interaction with a redhead.

Targets of Stereotyping Theories explaining the psychological process of stereotyping have not been developed or tested as have theories pertaining to the content of stereotypes. Those studying racial and ethnic-group relations have assumed that all people use stereotypes to give order to chaos, as suggested by Lippman, and thus have been preoccupied with why certain groups have been selected as targets of stereotyping and why certain characteristics are perceived as bad, evil, or inferior and others as good, right, or superior. A rather complex theory of the selection of target groups and the content of stereotypes has been developed which summarizes the large body of research concerning stereotypes in American society (Ehrlich, 1973).

Stereotypes generally are based on physical appearance as physical characteristics are readily discernible and thus permit people to quickly categorize their perceptions of a stranger, to predict the person's behavior, and to decide how to act toward him or her. Stereotypes based on skin color have a long history in American society. At various times, black Americans have been believed to be intellectually inferior, oversexed, aggressive, superstitious, lazy, ignorant, and musical by a significant number of U.S. citizens (Karlins, Coffman, and Walters, 1969). Two stereotypes of Indian Americans have wide acceptance. The first is that all Indian Americans are like the Plains warriors who wore buckskin clothes and a bonnet of eagle feathers and rode a pinto pony. Psychologically, this stereotype portrays the Indian as being strong, silent, and having a special relationship with nature. The second stereotype, which is strongest in towns that border Indian reservations, is that all Indians are alcoholics living in self-induced poverty. The stereotype of the lazy and dirty Mexican American has been utilized by television advertisers. A deodorant commercial pictured a sweating Mexican American as a voice stated that "if this will work for him, think what it will do for you." The implication was that if the deodorant will work on a stinking and dirty Mexican American it will do wonders for others.

Stereotypes generally have norms attached to them indicating how one should behave toward a member of a particular category. For example, in the South prior to the civil-rights movement whites expected blacks, who were categorized as generally inferior and born to serve whites, to sit in the back of a bus and give up their seats to whites if the bus was crowded. Thus, when whites entered a bus they took a seat in the front, and, if those were all taken, they walked to the black person nearest the front and expected to get the seat. Having lived with these normative expectations and their own stereotypes, blacks gave up their seats. Racial stereotypes and associated behavioral norms have changed as a consequence of the civil-rights movement, but many still persist. Whatever the stereotype, there are usually norms specifying the appropriate way to act toward any member of the stereotyped group.

Stereotypes have also emerged based on hair color, height, body shape, and facial configurations. The stereotype that people with red hair are more aggressive than other people was given scientific credibility in a rather nonscientific study of the hair color of gunfighters on the American Frontier. Von Hentig (1947) reviewed the physical descriptions of Western gunfighters, including Billy the Kid and Wyatt Earp, and concluded that red-haired men were overrepresented in this group. It seems that Von Hentig ignored many nonredheaded gunfighters, and the lack of a representative sample has resulted in the rejection of his findings.

A study of college students revealed several stereotypes related to hair (Roll and Verinis, 1971). Blond hair was found to be the most desirable, and red hair the least (possibly due to the stereotype we have mentioned). People with black hair were perceived as being the most potent or powerful, which is consistent with the stereotype of darkness being powerful and dangerous. These results support the stereotype that gentlemen prefer blondes. Confirmation of the rejection of redheads of either sex and males attraction to females with light hair and skin color was reported by Feinman and Gill (1978). In a related study, it was discovered that men with an abundance of body hair were believed to be more virile and active than men with less body hair (Verinis and Roll, 1970). But recently it was found that female college students preferred clean shaven men as strongly as those with a beard (Feinman and Gill, 1977).

There is considerable evidence of a stereotype that tall men are more competent than shorter men. Feldman (1971) contends that in the United States to be tall is perceived to be good and cites two surveys reported in the *Wall Street Journal* that short men are discriminated against in the business world because of this stereotype. One survey reported that tall (6'2" and over) University of Pittsburgh graduates received an average starting salary 12 percent higher than did shorter graduates, regardless of grades and honors. The other survey reported by Feldman was conducted at the University of Michigan and involved asking 140 recruiters of college graduates to select between two applicants. The two men were equally qualified, the only difference being that one was 6'1" tall and the other only 5'. The results were that 72 percent "hired" the tall applicant, 27 percent expressed no preference, and only 1 percent chose the short applicant.

Feldman (1971) also presents anecdotal evidence supporting the tall equals competence stereotype. He suggests that the stereotype is apparent in voting behavior and points out that between 1900 and 1971 the taller presidential candidate in each race had been elected. The two presidential elections since Feldman's study indicate that the importance of height has faded as in both cases the shorter candidate won. Support for the fading importance of height was obtained in a study where men and women indicated their attraction to short, medium and tall men (Gyaziano, Brothen, and Berscheid, 1978). Female college students indicated that medium height men were the most socially desirable. Men discounted the effect of height even more as they rated short men more positive than tall men.

There is some research evidence that suggests that a person stereotypes others in terms of his or her own personality and characteristics. That is, if others have physical appearances that are similar to our own, we attribute to them those positive traits that we feel characterize ourselves. This tendency was demonstrated in a field study of hitchhiking conducted by Alcorn and Condie (1975). To determine the effect of appearance on being picked up while hitchhiking, Alcorn spent much of one summer hitchhiking in the Southwest. The two different appearances are illustrated in the photographs. During the *longhair* phase, he dressed in sandals, tie-dyed T-shirt, grubby work pants, and a railroad engineer's cap. He was unshaven, had shoulder-length hair, and carried a canteen, sleeping bag, and backpack. In the *shorthair* phase, he dressed in slacks and sportshirt, was cleanshaven, had moderately short hair, wore a windbreaker jacket, and carried a small athletic bag. In 93 percent of the cases in which Alcorn was given a ride by a "hippie" motorist, his appearance was like that of the motorist. In 67 percent of the cases in which he was picked up by a "traditional" motorist, his appearance was straight (the shorthair phase). Alcorn and Condie conclude: ". . . traditional motorists are more likely to pick up straight hitchhikers, and hippie motorists are more inclined to offer rides to their youthful counterparts on the road" (1975, p. 61).

Overall physical attractiveness has been found to be associated with pleasant personalities. In an interesting study, Miller (1970) had college students, both male and female, rate people in photographs on an adjective preference scale that included seventeen personality dimensions. The photographs were of senior students taken from the university yearbook and had previously been rated by another sample of students as to physical attractiveness (high, medium, or low). The results indicated that for fifteen of the seventeen personality traits, the highly attractive people were rated higher on the socially desirable ends of the personality scale, and the unattractive rated higher on the undesirable ends. According to Miller (1970), a consis-

Researcher in "hippie-appearance" condition of hitchhiking study.

Researcher in "middle class-appearance" condition of hitchhiking study.

tent pattern emerged in which the attractive persons were judged more positively than the less attractive. Also, sex-based stereotypes emerged, and it appeared that they influenced perceptions; men were believed to be more confident and dominant than women. Miller found that the differences between male and female stereotypes based on physical attractiveness were most prominent for the highly attractive.

The stereotype of the physically attractive possessing more socially desirable personalities was also clearly identified in a study by Dion, Berscheid, and Walster (1972). A sample of men and women were asked to rate photographs of males and females on a number of dimensions, including attractiveness and various personality characteristics. Male and female subjects gave similar ratings, and the stereotypes were similar for both the males and females in the photographs. Those individuals who were perceived as physically attractive were also perceived to be more "altruistic," "exciting," "sexually warm," "sensitive," "kind," "interesting," "strong," "poised," "modest," "sociable," and "outgoing" than those less attractive. The ratings on these individual personality traits were combined into a social desirability index, and the attractive individuals were rated significantly higher on this scale than were the average or unattractive. The subjects were also asked to predict what the future would bring to the people whose photographs they had rated. The attractive were expected to obtain more prestigious occupations, to become more competent marriage partners, and to have happier marriages than were the less attractive.

Two recent studies reported that the work of attractive people, especially females, was judged to be of a higher quality than the work of unattractive people. Anderson and Nida (1978) had college students read essays whose supposed author was identified by a photograph. The highly attractive authors received the highest rating from members of the opposite sex while medium attractive authors were evaluated highest by members of the same sex. Similar findings were reported by Kaplan (1978) as male subjects rated attractive female authors as more talented than they did unattractive authors. But female subjects did not pay attention to attractiveness in evaluating the work of female authors. Neither male nor female subjects were influenced by the attractiveness of male authors in evaluation of their work. Finally, it was discovered that judgements of psychological disturbance were also influenced by physical appearance as unattractive individuals were identified by both male and female subjects as being more likely to have been confined to a psychiatric hospital or to psychiatric counseling than attractive individuals. (Jones, Hansson, Phillips, 1978).

There is a rapidly growing literature dealing with sex-role stereotypes. For example the general stereotypes are that males are less emotional, more scientific, better suited for administrative business positions, and more stable in dealing with crises; females are more patient, sensitive, and gentle (Harrison, 1978; Minnigerode and Lee, 1978; Marini, 1978; and Schein, 1978).

The studies discussed above and many that are similar provide strong support that stereotypes exist based on physical characteristics and that specific personality traits and social characteristics are attributed to individuals seen as belonging in a specific stereotypic category. The evidence indicates that stereotypes of physical characteristics are important determinants of first impressions formed by people, and the public seems to be very much aware of this. Each year, over a billion dollars is spent on cosmetics to enhance physical attractiveness. Plastic surgery is becoming more popular as a means of enhancing physical appearance. Relatively new and functional clothing is discarded in favor of the latest fashion in order to maximize physical attractiveness.

Consequences of Stereotyping Although it is acknowledged that stereotypes do help the individual who believes them to cope with a complex social environment, most social scientists feel that stereotypes are harmful to the person stereotyped and to society in general. The major criticism against using stereotypes is that they distort reality. Hayakawa (1950) argues that stereotypes are so inaccurate as to be "widely current misinformation" and "traditional nonsense." (Surprisingly, Hayakawa years later fell victim to using stereotypes despite his warning when he commented on the impact on the poor of increased gas prices by saying that the poor don't work anyway so they don't need the gas.) The biased view of social reality provided by stereotypes is felt to interfere with a person's adjustment to his or her social environment. Stereotypes not only introduce perceptual errors, but their rigidity may prevent innovative social change.

Another reason that the use of stereotypes is seen as undesirable by social scientists is that they are frequently used to justify discrimination against members of ethnic and racial groups. For example, if the stereotype that all Indian Americans are lazy and alcoholic is accepted, then employment discrimination against them would appear to be justified. However, nonalcoholic Indian Americans, who constitute the vast majority, would be denied employment on the basis of distorted perceptions of their personal characteristics.

On the other hand, scientists have been criticized for unquestioningly assuming that all stereotypes have little basis in reality (Mackie, 1973). It has been suggested that at their root, stereotypes are based on reality and as such are a "well-earned reputation" (Zawadzki, 1948). In this case, it is argued that stereotypes are accurate descriptions of reality and are useful in predicting the behavior of stereotyped individuals. A more moderate position is that although stereotypes are largely false, they may be based on a "kernel of truth," which has long since been embellished into a largely inaccurate stereotype.

The redhead stereotype mentioned earlier is an example of a widely accepted stereotype that was rejected by scientists as inaccurate, but that later received scientific support. As mentioned earlier, Von Hentig's (1947) contention that the gunfighters of the old West included an overrepresentation of redheaded men was rejected by the scientific community and rightly so, given the study's methodological flaws. At times, it has been ridiculed as an example of absurd research. But, recent research with overaggressive children has discovered that "redheaded children are three or four times more likely than others to develop a 'hyperactive syndrome' whose symptoms include over-excitability, short attention span, quick feelings of frustration, and usually excessive aggressiveness" (*Time*, 1977a). This study, conducted in an Israeli psychiatric center, suggests that there may very well be a genetic link between red hair and aggressiveness, or that the same hereditary factors cause both—either way, the study lends support to the generalization.

The accuracy of stereotypes of various groups remains a hotly debated issue with research studies reporting cases of blatantly false stereotypes as well as cases of fairly accurate stereotypes. Regardless of the accuracy, it appears that stereotypes based on race, sex, height, hair, color, body shape, and facial characteristics are utilized by most people in explaining and predicting the behavior of others. People are categorized according to readily observable traits and are then treated on the basis of that identification.

IMPLICIT PERSONALITY THEORY

Implicit personality theory contends that each individual develops a theory of personality that describes which personality traits occur together. Therefore, when a single trait is observed in another person, those traits that are assumed to be related are automatically also inferred from the observed behavior, or are seen as implicit in the other person. For example, if I observe an individual being bold and daring, I assume that he or she is also extroverted rather than introverted. If I observe that a person is eager and inquisitive, I assume that this person is intelligent. Although many people would make these same inferences, some people would not. The word *implicit* is included in the name of the theory to differentiate it from scientific theories of personality and to stress that each person may have his or her own unique theory about what traits occur together.

Figure 9–1 illustrates implicit personality theory in a humorous example where the theory did not hold true. Dennis' implicit personality theory concluded that a polite boy named Matthew would likely be timid and an ineffectual fighter. His condition following a fight with polite Matthew indicates that timidity and incompetent fighting were not associated with polite-

"BOY! FOR A POLITE KID NAMED MATTHEW, HE COULD SURE *FIGHT!*"

Figure 9–1 An Example of a Violated Implicit Personality Theory. Dennis the Menace T.M. ® is © by Field Enterprises Inc.

ness. The cartoon illustrates how people form impressions about others and make predictions about another's behavior on the bases of one or two traits or characteristics.

Although it is acknowledged that each person may have his or her own unique personality theory, so that one person may expect an aggressive person to also be gentle in dealings with others while another anticipates him to be rough, Schneider (1973) has noted that there is a tendency for concensus in a given culture about which personality traits cluster together. In a classic series of experiments, Asch (1946) identified how people combine various personality traits they have observed in another person into an overall perception of what kind of person the other is. Asch argued that although a person may be perceived to have a large number of diverse characteristics, the observer summarizes these into a unified impression of the person. Thus, a person may be believed to be intelligent, bright, serious, energetic, patient, polite, and have a ready sense of humor, yet these characteristics produce an impression of one person. Asch demonstrated the process of combining diverse traits into a unified impression by asking college students to write a characterization of a person described in terms of a list of personality traits. An example of the list of traits is: "energetic, assured, talkative, cold, ironical, inquisitive and persuasive" (Asch, 1946, p. 260). A typical characterization is: "He is the type of person you meet all too often: sure of himself, talks too much, always trying to bring you around to his way of thinking, and with not much feeling for the other person." (Asch, 1946, p. 261). On the basis of this and similar responses, Asch concluded that the subjects had formed a unified impression of the person described. Frequently, the overall impression extended beyond the original traits as characteristics not mentioned were added to round out the impression.

Central Traits Confident that people can and do make a unified impression on the basis of several characteristics, Asch sought to determine whether some traits are more important than others in the impression-formation process. Observation suggested that certain traits were central to the impression formed while others were secondary. Asch (1946) varied two pairs of descriptive terms, "warm-cold" and "polite-blunt" in the lists of traits presented to subjects. The inclusion of "warm" or "cold" greatly influenced how the diverse traits were combined into a general impression; "polite" or "blunt" had only a modest effect. Asch concluded that the warm-cold trait is a central trait and, as such, significantly influences impression formation. A number of related experiments substantiated the centrality of certain traits but also indicated that the identification of a specific trait as central was subject to situational factors and shifted from one context to another.

A follow-up study (Wishner, 1960) refuted Asch's notion of central traits as he discovered that the so-called central traits were those that happened to be included in a list with other traits to which they were related. Wishner contended that any trait can be made central by surrounding it with other traits that are related to it. He was able to predict which traits on a check-list could make "intelligent-unintelligent" either a central or a secondary trait.

The research by Rosenberg, Nelson, and Vivekananthan (1968) did not reveal central traits but rather two theoretical dimensions around which the personality traits were clustered. Social desirability and intellectual desira-bility were the two dimensions, and according to these researchers "warm" and "cold" appeared as central traits in previous research because they are on the extremes of the social desirability scale. Support for their hypothesis was provided by Zanna and Hamilton (1972), who found that adding "warm" or "cold" to a list of personality traits affected only those traits that were strongly socially desirable or undesirable. Also, they reported that "lazy" and "industrious" affected those traits that were intellectually desir-able or undesirable. Given these findings, Schneider (1973) suggests that future research should focus on whether positive or negative traits convey the most information about the total personality of another person.

Individual Origins Three possible explanations of the origin of individual implicit personality theories have been suggested. First, it is noted that the nature of the English language may be responsible for the correlations between personality traits found in the research mentioned above. Groups of words are related by their meanings, and thus, if one word accurately describes the behavior of a person, then several others will also. For exam-ple, if a person is observed to be honest, he or she can also be described as sincere and responsible. Thus, the relationship observed between the traits of honesty, sincerity, and responsibility is a function of the English language and not the consequence of related personality traits.

The second possible explanation of the implicit personality theories is that they are the product of the imagination of the perceiver and have little to do with reality. The individual sees what he or she wants and expects to see. For example, if the person likes the individual he or she is observing, he or she is likely to perceive socially desirable traits. In this case, a "halo effect" produced by the desire for consistency in perceptions and attitudes is responsible for the observed relationship between personality traits.

Some support for the contention that the related traits are in the mind of the observer rather than in the behavior of the other is provided by Dornbusch and his associates (1965). Children at a summer camp were asked to describe the other campers and greater similarity was obtained between the descriptions made by a particular youngster of two of his friends than between the descriptions of him by his two friends. The implication is that each youngster applied his own implicit personality theory regardless of the actual characteristics of his friends.

The third possible origin of implicit personality sets is personal experience. It is suggested that because an individual has interacted with another or several others in whom certain personality traits are associated, the individual generalizes the relationship to all other people. This explanation suggests that because a person has interacted with a friend who is kind and gentle he or she assumes that all kind people are also gentle. These three explanations are not mutually exclusive, and all three probably contribute to the development of implicit theories of personality.

In summary, implicit personality theory suggests that each individual has his or her own theory about which personality traits appear together. Moreover, research has demonstrated that information about several personality traits is combined into a single overall impression of the person in question. Considerable work has been done trying to identify central traits that have greater influence than other traits on the formation of the total impression. The most recent findings suggest that implicit personality theories are organized around the two dimensions of social desirability and intellectual desirability rather than central traits. Those traits that are directly related to these two dimensions have been found to have the most impact on the impression formed about another person.

ATTRIBUTION THEORY

Attribution theory is the study of the processes a person employs in "linking events (behavior) with their underlying conditions" (Heider, 1958, p. 89). It asserts that a person links the behavior of another to underlying conditions in an effort to understand why that person acted in a certain way and to predict how he or she will act in the future. The underlying conditions or causes of behavior are of two types—basic attributes belonging to the person or to the environment. Behavior caused by a personal characteristic is seen as internally caused, and behavior linked to underlying environmental conditions is viewed as being externally caused. The objectives of the attributional processes are to describe the behavior of another, predict future behavior, and explain why (by inferring causal relations) the person behaved in a particular way.

Heider's Naive Psychology Attribution Theory The earliest formulation of attribution theory emerged in the work of Fritz Heider (1958), who was interested in how the person in the street "explained" or accounted for the behavior of others. He felt that most individuals are "naive" psychologists trying to understand the behavior of others in order to make the world more predictable. According to Heider, most individuals apply one of three possible "explanations" to the behavior of others. First, they may assume that the other person's behavior was caused by the surrounding situation. In other words, the pressures and constraints of the situation are sufficiently strong so that most people would behave in the same way. The second alternative explanation is that the behavior was unintentional and probably will not occur with any regularity in the future. The third explanation is that the individual intentionally performed the observed behavior while acting out a personal attribute. Heider was very much aware that personal attributes are most evident when the environment allows a range of alternative behaviors and when the actor has the ability to perform several different behaviors. Under these conditions, the individual has the greatest freedom, and personal tendencies will most likely be manifest. Once a personal attribute has been inferred about an individual, this information can be used to predict his or her future behavior.

Jones' and Davis' Correspondent-Inference Attribution Theory Heider's original formulation of the attribution process was modified by Jones and Davis (1965), who focused on the consequences of the behavior on which attributions are made. According to Jones and Davis, the attribution process should involve identifying the effects that are unique to each particular response in a given situation. Correspondence of inference occurs when a particular behavior produces an uncommon effect that is highly desirable to the individual. The correspondent-inference theory argues that the unique effects of an action permit inferences about behavioral dispositions.

Jones and Davis (1965) illustrate the processes of determining noncommon effects and inferring behavioral attributions with the hypothetical example of a Miss Adams who wants to get married and who has three suitors seeking her hand. As indicated in figure 9–2, the first step in the attribution process is to ascertain the probable effects of marriage, which in this example are wealth, social position, sexual enjoyment, children, and intellectual stimulation. The effects likely to accrue from marriage with each of the three suitors are identified, and then the uncommon ones for each suitor are specified in figure 9–2. Because sexual enjoyment is anticipated with any of the three suitors, it provides no useful information for making attributions about personal traits of Miss Adams. Mr. Bagby would provide wealth and social position; Mr. Caldwell promises wealth and children; Mr. Dexter offers intellectual stimulation. If Miss Adams accepts Mr. Bagby, it is inferred that she is a snob as she selected social position over children and intellectual stimulation. If Mr. Caldwell is the lucky man, then it is assumed that Miss Adams is the maternal type as she chose children. Finally, if Mr. Dexter is selected, then it is inferred that Miss Adams is an intellectual. In this example, behavior attributes of Miss Adams are inferred on the basis of her selection of a husband from three alternative suitors, each of whom promises unique effects in marriage.

Jones and Davis (1965) emphasize the importance of unique behavior as well as unique effects. According to them, culturally defined role behavior is not as informative for attributional consideration because personal traits are not as likely to be expressed. Finally, they suggest that the attribution process becomes even more complex when the involvement of the person making the attribution is considered. The normal attribution process may

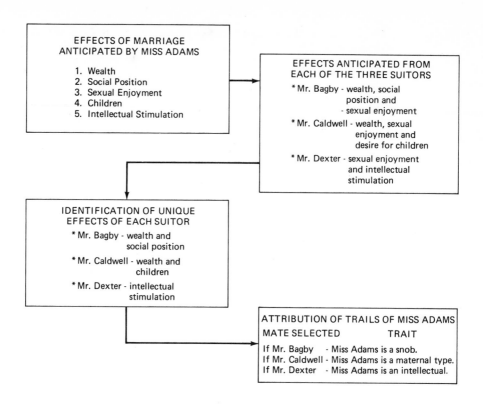

Figure 9–2 Miss Adams Chooses a Husband. Attribution of Traits to Miss Adams on Basis of Selection of Husband (Adapted from Jones and Davis, 1965, p. 231.)

be biased if the person attempting to ascertain the attributes of another is benefited by the behavior being observed.

Kelley's Co-Variation Attribution Theory The attribution theory of Kelley (1967, 1971*a*, 1971*b*) is also built on the work of Heider (1958). Kelley's attribution model or process involves the co-variation of three variables: (1) the entity being considered, that is, the person about whom an attribute is being inferred; (2) the time/modality or the conditions or situations in which the behavior occurred; and (3) the person making the attribution. Kelley argues that by holding two of these three factors constant and varying the other an individual can make correct inferences about personal attributes of others.

The principle of co-variation is best illustrated by an example presented by Shaver (1975). Shaver noted that every time he had discussed attribution theory with a particular student they ended up in an argument. Before attributing a pugnacious characteristic to the student, Shaver tried to determine if the arguments were the result of the student's argumentativeness, the result of the topic of attribution theory, or of Shaver himself. Utilizing Kelley's model, Shaver varied the time/modality (attribution theory) while holding the other two factors constant by engaging the student in conversation about other topics. The entity (the student) and the person making the attribution (Shaver) remained the same while the time/modality (attribution theory) was varied. Because an argument still occurred each time they conversed, the time/modality (attribution theory) was eliminated as the source of the arguments. Next, the entity (the student) was varied while the other two remained the same; Shaver talked to other students about attribution theory, and, because no arguments occurred, the entity (the student) was tentatively identified as the cause of the fighting. Finally, the person making the attribution was varied by having other faculty members talk to the original student about attribution theory. They also ended up fighting with the student, which eliminated the person making the attribute as the cause, and confirmed the entity (the student) as the source of the conflict. After applying the principle of co-variation, Shaver concluded that the student being observed had an argumentative personality.

Shaver's Attribution Theory Shaver (1975) combined these three early theories of attribution into a more general theory incorporating the major components of each. His formulation makes clear three assumptions about human nature on which attribution theory is based. First, attribution theory assumes that behavior does not occur randomly, but is determined and thus can be predicted. Shaver feels that at this stage of development attribution theory is not prepared to identify the ultimate causes of human behavior, but obviously assumes that personality traits or attributes play a significant part in determining behavior, along with environmental and biological factors.

The second assumption about human nature is that people have a desire to understand, to explain, and to predict the behavior of others. This assumption is important to attribution theory because making estimates about the attributes of others permits the observer to more successfully cope with his or her environment by being able to predict the behavior of others. The final assumption is that observable behavior does permit valid inferences about its underlying causes, that is, personality characteristics. The inference of a personality characteristic on the basis of observations of a limited number of acts is somewhat questionable. In our discussion in chapter 7 of the relationship between attitudes, a type of personality characteristic, and behavior, we found that the relationship is strongly influenced by situational factors and is probably true for other types of personal attributes. Most theories of attribution recognize the importance of situational pressures and realize that they can override the acting out of personal attributes. Situational factors make it risky to assume that a given behavior is always an expression of a personal attribute.

Taking these three assumptions into consideration, Shaver (1975) developed a model of attribution, which is illustrated in figure 9–3. The attribution process is illustrated with the decision that the jury had to make in determining the guilt or innocence of a fourteen-year-old Florida youth accused of killing an elderly woman. They had to determine not only if he had committed the murder, but, if he had, why. As will be seen, the jury had to link the event (behavior) with underlying conditions in determining plausible cause-effect relationships.

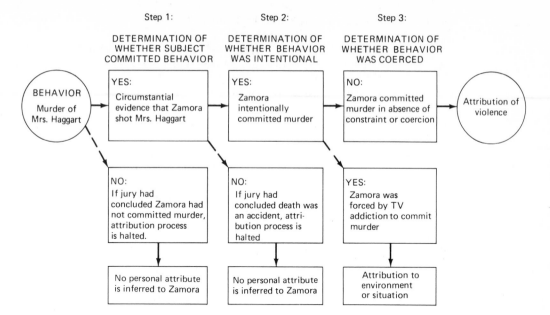

Figure 9–3 The Attribution Process. (Adapted from Shaver, 1975, p. 32.)

Step One: Determination of whether the behavior was performed. There was ample evidence that Mrs. Elinor Haggart was dead; her body had been discovered in her ransacked apartment. The first step in the attribution process of the jury was to determine if Ronald Zamora had fired the shots that killed her. If the jury had witnessed the crime, they could have more easily made this decision. Because they had not, witnesses and circumstantial evidence were presented by the prosecution to convince them that Zamora had committed the act in question. It should be noted that in contrast to juries, people in everyday life frequently accept hearsay evidence. If the jury had concluded that Zamora had not committed the homicide, then the attribution process would have terminated. If the boy had not shot Mrs. Haggart, then there was no information available about his personal attributes from this particular murder. However, because of the circumstantial evidence, the jury was convinced that the boy had fired the shots that killed Mrs. Haggart.

Step Two: Determination of whether behavior was intentional. Because the jury concluded that Zamora had performed the behavior, the second stage of the attribution process was to determine if the homicide was intentional or not. This is a critical step, as involuntary behaviors reveal little information about personal attributes. Intentions, being mental states, are extremely difficult to infer even from observed behavior. For example, the jury had to ascertain whether Zamora shot Mrs. Haggart as the result of an involuntary reflex. Was it possible that the boy was examining the widow's gun with her permission when he was startled so that he reflexively fired the gun? Also, the possibility that the death was an accident—that Mrs. Haggart was showing Zamora her gun and then dropped it causing it to discharge—had to be considered. Evaluation of the circumstances surrounding the action, such as whether Mrs. Haggart in the past had shown her gun to visitors, also provided clues as to whether Zamora deliberately shot her.

Information about the act itself frequently provides indications of intent. The fact that Mrs. Haggart was shot more than once tends to refute the reflex or accident explanations of the behavior. The person making the attribution may also utilize his or her own and others' experiences in similar situations to assess the intent of the actor. Each member of the jury probably tried to imagine how they would have acted and reacted in similar circumstances.

An important consideration in assessing intent is whether the action produced favorable consequences for the individual. In this case, $415 was stolen from the murdered women that was used to treat the accused and four friends to an exciting trip to Disney World. It also was decided that Zamora had reasonable expectations of finding money in Mrs. Haggart's apartment. The stolen Buick car and money probably helped convince the jury that the boy intentionally shot her.

If, after consideration of these factors, the determination is that the action was unintentional, then the attribution process is halted, as the behavior does not provide any information about the behavior tendencies of the observed person. In the example, the jury rejected the accidental or reflexive explanations of the homicide and decided that Zamora deliberately murdered Mrs. Haggart. The fact that the behavior was intentional implies that the individual exercised a choice in selecting between alternative actions, and, under these conditions, personal behavioral attributes are manifest.

Step Three: Determination of whether behavior was coerced. Once the jury determined that the homicide was intentional, then they proceeded to the third stage of the attribution process, which is to decide whether the action was coerced or voluntary. Coercion reduces the opportunity for personal attributes to be manifest, and thus it is important to the attribution process to ascertain that the behavior was not forced by external pressures.

The effects of coercion or constraint on the attribution process were demonstrated in an experiment by Miller and associates (1977). The subjects in the experiment were 247 male and female students in introductory psychology classes. The experimental situation involved listening to or watching a video tape of a position paper on either amnesty or abortion given by another student who was really a trained research assistant. Constraint upon the behavior of the writer or speech reader was introduced by including a statement that the amnesty essay was written by someone else and that the research assistant had been *assigned* to read it. The video-taped abortion presentation contained instructions to the research assistant to take a specific position on the issue. One-third of the subjects were *prompted* to recognize the constraints when they were asked to rate the degree of pressure on the person (research assistant) to take the position that he did.

The results are presented in table 9–1 and reveal that people making attributions of attitude place greater reliance on voluntary behavior as compared to behaviors that are constrained or coerced. The extreme attribution scores, 9.0 and 0.8, were obtained in the choice condition. Even more

Table 9–1 Mean Attribution of Attitude as a Function of Essay Direction and Constraint

ESSAY DIRECTION[a]	CONSTRAINT		
	Choice	*Assigned*	*Assigned-Prompted*
Pro	9.0[b]	8.1	6.7
Anti	0.8	2.6	3.1

[a]*The number of subjects in each condition ranges from thirty-two to thirty-seven.*
[b]*The extreme scores of 9.0 and .8 indicate the highest level of attribution.*
Adapted from Miller et al., 1977, p. 112.

important, the effect of constraint on attribution was even greater when attention was focused on the constraints in the situation, as indicated by the middle-of-the-road attributes (little attribution) made under the assigned-prompted condition.

On the other hand, research has found that, when the person behaves in opposition to constraints or coercion, attributes can be inferred with greater confidence. In a frequently quoted study, Jones, Davis, and Gergen (1961) demonstrated the importance of behavior that is counter to social norms or social roles. The experimental situation involved male subjects listening to tape-recorded job interviews. In half the interviews, the person being interviewed, a trained research assistant, gave responses appropriate to the job, but in the other half he responded in an "out of role" manner. Two occupations with specialized requirements—submariner and astronaut—were involved in the interviews. A part of the taped interviews was a description of the ideal submariner who is "obedient, cooperative, friendly, and outgoing" and a description that an astronaut should be "independent" and "not require association with others." As indicated in table 9–2, half the subjects heard the research assistant reply to the submariner interview as though he were "obedient, cooperative, friendly, and outgoing" or heard him reply to the astronaut interview as though he were "independent." The other subjects heard the assistant reply with traits opposite those desired for the ideal submariner or astronaut.

After listening to the job interviews, the subjects were asked to indicate what they felt the person was really like. The impressive results presented in table 9–2 indicate that "interviewees" who responded as expected were

Table 9–2 Mean Perceptions of Affiliation and Conformity by Social Desirability of Response

Trait	SUBMARINER INTERVIEW		ASTRONAUT INTERVIEW	
	Other Directed (in role)	*Inner Directed (out role)*	*Inner Directed (in role)*	*Other Directed (out role)*
Affiliation	12.0	8.6*	11.2	15.3
Conformity	12.6	9.4	13.1	15.9

High (15.3 and 15.9) and low (8.6 and 9.4) scores indicate higher levels of attributing the two personality traits from the observed interviews.
Adapted from Jones, Davis, and Gergen 1961, p. 307.

rated as only moderately possessing the observed trait. On the other hand, the "interviewees" who responded out of role were rated as holding the observed traits significantly more than the in-role applicants. The submariner applicant who acted out of role (inner directed) was rated lowest on affiliation and conformity, and the astronaut applicant who acted out of role (other directed) received the highest affiliation and conformity ratings. Importantly, the confidence of the in-role applicant ratings was very low, as the subjects could not decide if the interviewee was revealing real attributes or was simply role playing. The ratings of the out-role applicants were made with confidence, as the applicant had nothing to gain and a job to lose by responding as he did. The evidence strongly supports the hypothesis that when a person rejects social pressures and responds contrary to expectation he or she is perceived to have acted on his or her true disposition and the attributions are made with confidence.

In the Zamora case, the jury had to ascertain whether the boy committed the murder because of a personal attribute, such as aggressiveness, or whether the situation coerced him into performing the murder. The defense argued that television programming was responsible for the action because Zamora had become addicted to violent television shows that trained and motivated him to commit murder. The attorney contended that Zamora "was suffering from and actually under the influence of prolonged, intense, involuntary, subliminal television intoxication" (*Time,* 1977b). Therefore, because of his addiction to television violence, Zamora was powerless, as indicated by "involuntary intoxication," to prevent himself from killing Mrs. Haggart.

The defense might have argued that the boy acted in self-defense or in response to extreme provocation from the eighty-two-year-old widow. The defense attorney also could have suggested that the boy was forced by threats on his life from the four friends to commit the crime. The jury refused to accept the contention that Zamora was forced or coerced to commit the homicide. They concluded that he committed the murder, that the shooting was intentional, and that the lad was not coerced to pull the trigger. Therefore, they decided that Zamora intentionally committed a murder because of a personal attribute and that he is a violent and dangerous person.

Shaver's theory of attribution makes explicit the need for controlling the relevant factors that influence the attribution process. The influence of intent and/or coercion on attributing the cause of a particular behavior to either situational pressures or personal traits is clarified. According to Shaver, the process outlined in figure 9–3 is utilized by individuals to confidently attribute personal or situational causes to others whose behavior they have observed.

Self versus Other Attributions It has been noted in a number of studies that individuals make somewhat different attributions about themselves than they do about others. The general tendency is for the individual to infer that another person's behavior is the product of a personal attribute and to assume that their own behavior is caused by situational factors (Jones and Harris, 1967; Jones et al., 1968; McArthur, 1972; Nisbett et al., 1973; Storms, 1973).

An example of research supporting different self and other attributions is a series of three studies by Nisbett and his associates (1973). In the first experiment, undergraduate students reported that they believed that a confederate who they had observed would behave in the future in a manner consistent with the behavior they had observed. On the other hand, subjects who themselves behaved exactly as had the confederate did not believe that they would necessarily behave that way in the future. It was assumed that the subjects felt that their behavior was under situational control and that future behavior would depend on future situational factors.

In the second experiment, male undergraduates at Yale were asked to list the reasons why they liked the woman they had dated most frequently during the past year. They were also asked to list why they had chosen their particular college major. Then the students were asked why their best friend liked his girlfriend and had selected his academic major. Subjects gave twice as many situational reasons, that is, properties of the woman and the major, for their own behavior as they attributed to their best friends. The selections of the best friends were based much more on personal attributes and traits, such as "he wants to make a lot of money," or, "he needs someone he can relax with," than were reasons for their own selections.

The third experiment involved having male undergraduates at Yale identify the personality traits of themselves and four other individuals—their best friends, their fathers, an acquaintance, and Walter Cronkite. It was discovered that the subjects reported the fewest personality traits for themselves, the most for Cronkite, and a number in between for their fathers and acquaintances. The individual about whom they had the least amount of information was assumed to have the greatest number of personality characteristics, and they themselves, about whom supposedly they knew the most, were identified to have the fewest personality traits. These three experiments are good examples of different attributions being inferred about one's self as compared to other people.

The most frequently suggested explanations for this tendency to give situational attributes of one's own behavior and personal attributes for others' behaviors is that the individual has much greater knowledge about himself or herself and the reasons for the behavior (Nisbett et al., 1973). Individual actors are aware of the many situational constraints and pressures that influence their behavior. When observing the behavior of someone else, most of the situational factors are not apparent, and thus the person making the attribution credits the other person's behavioral tendencies or personality traits. Monson and Snyder (1977) reviewed a number of studies that support the contention that attributions about oneself are much more accurate than those about others because of the knowledge the person has of his or her own feelings, attitudes, and abilities.

This explanation of greater knowledge about oneself implies that because the observer knows his or her own feelings and abilities, he or she can engage in a more complete and accurate process of attributions to self. As is apparent, this explanation asserts that the person's internal states—feelings, insight, and self-concepts—will determine or mediate the causal explanation attached to the behavior. This explanation has not gone unchallenged, however. The best statement of the alternative theory of self-attribution is Bem's formulation (1967, 1972), which argues that a self-attribution employs the same process as does attributions to other people.

In essence, Bem contends that one way individuals learn about their own attitudes and emotions is by inferring them from observations of their own behavior and the circumstances in which the behavior occurs" (1972a). The proposition that self and other attributions are made in the same way has been used as an alternative to cognitive-dissonance theory in predicting attitudes. For example, a cognitive-dissonance experiment discussed in chapter 7 involved paying one group of subjects $1 to do an unpleasant task and paying another $20. It was observed that the subjects paid only $1 had attitudes more favorable towards the unpleasant task than did those paid $20. It was assumed that the dissonance between "I did an unpleasant task" and "I was only paid $1" was reduced by redefining the task as being more favorable. Bem's self-attribution proposition predicts the same outcome because the situational pressure of $1 was insignificant as compared to $20, and thus a personal attribution, such as a tolerance to this unpleasant task, was responsible for the behavior.

Also, self-attribution theory can explain behavior that cognitive dissonance has difficulty understanding. In the case of paying one group of subjects $1 and another group $20 to do a pleasant task, cognitive-dissonance theory cannot predict the individual's attitudes as no dissonance has been created. Self-attribution theory correctly predicts that the "more you pay a person to do what he would do anyway, the less favorable toward the activity his private attitude becomes" (Shaver, 1975, p. 85). This outcome occurs because the person observes his or her own behavior in light of the situational pressure of either $1 or $20, and the person paid the larger amount concludes that his or her behavior was not internally caused but rather was a consequence of the $20. Thus, he or she is less favorable about the enjoyable task.

There is not yet sufficient research to resolve the debate concerning whether self-attributions are made in the same way as those of others, but Shaver's conclusion seems warranted at this point in time. "When we are unsure of our beliefs and emotions we may well learn what we think by observing what we do" (1975, p. 92). Self-attribution research will undoubtedly continue to investigate Bem's theoretical formulations to see when and how self-attributions are similar to and differ from other attributions.

The focus of attention during the attribution process has been suggested as a second reason for the difference between self and other attribution. Jones and Nisbett (1971) contend that when making assessments of one's own behavior the individual is very much aware of the situational constraints with which he or she had to deal. However, observations of another tend to focus on the behavior and neglect the conditions surrounding it.

Support for this explanation was reported in an experiment by Storms (1973). He found that male undergraduates at Yale who participated in a conversation with another subject used more situational attributes to explain their behavior than did observers. The latter explained the behavior more in terms of personal attributes. When the subjects were later shown video tapes of their own behavior and asked to account for it, they reduced the number of situational characteristics and increased the importance of their personal attributes. Similar results were reported by Arkin and Duval

(1975), who video taped college students who had been asked to select among several art works. After making their selections, the students were asked why they had chosen a particular work of art. The choices were explained more often as being caused by the situation when the subjects reported on their actual behavior than when they were asked to explain a video tape of their actions.

Although the tendency to credit external influences for one's own behavior and internal attributes for other people's behavior has considerable empirical support, it has been noted that under certain conditions the opposite attributions emerge. Monson and Snyder (1977) reviewed a number of studies and suggest that a motivation to present a positive self-image influences the attribution process so that individuals tend to give external or situational reasons for their behavior that is inappropriate or defined as failure. For the same reason, they tend to credit internal personal attributes for success. Several studies have documented these same differences (Beckman, 1970; Featherman and Simon, 1971a, 1971b; McMahan, 1973; Gilmor and Morton, 1974; Harvey et al., 1974; Arkin, Gleason, and Johnston, 1976). The enhancement of one's self-esteem or self-concept generated by this type of attribution is apparent, as failures are blamed on bad luck or unfortunate circumstances, and success is attributed to the person's abilities and characteristics.

Featherman and Simon (1971b) discovered that the effects of success or failure on self-attribution is not as simple as originally suspected but that the relationship is mediated by expectations of either success or failure. McMahan (1973) had sixth-grade, tenth-grade, and college students solve five-letter word anagrams, such as *Frtui* (Fruit). Before they worked on each of the five different anagrams, the subjects indicated how confident they were that they could solve it. Following their effort to solve each puzzle, they were asked to indicate the reasons why they had or had not succeeded. Success was manipulated by giving half the subjects relatively easy anagrams and the other half rather difficult ones. Those subjects who anticipated success and who did succeed attributed the outcome to their ability. Those subjects who expected to succeed and who failed blamed bad luck or lack of effort for their failure. On the other hand, those who expected to fail attributed success to good luck and hard work and failure to personal attributes.

Goldberg (1976) interprets these results as the individual attempting to make his or her behavior consistent with self-concept. When the person has a positive self-concept, failure is accounted for by bad luck or situational conditions, and success, which is supportive of a positive self-concept, is attributed to personal abilities or characteristics. When the person has a negative self-concept, the opposite occurs; success is credited to good luck, and failure to personal attributes.

Although the reasons are not entirely clear, research indicates that the attribution process is different for evaluating one's own behavior as compared to another's. The success or failure of the behavior, the self-concept of the person making the attribution, feeling towards the observed other person, and expectation of performing the observed behavior in the future have all been found to influence the attribution process. It seems likely that both the information available and the motivation to maintain positive feelings about the self operate to produce the observed differences in self and other attribution.

Attribution theory has succeeded in focusing attention on a very central concern in social psychology—namely, how and under what conditions a person can assume that personal attributes or the situation caused the other's behavior. Although the basic attribution process has been supported by research, two fundamental issues must be addressed in future research.

First, the information contained in in-role behavior as compared to out-of-role behavior must be reapproached. According to attribution theory, "behavior which conforms to clearly defined role requirements is seen as uninformative about the individual's personal characteristics, whereas a considerable amount of information may be extracted from out-of-role behavior" (Jones and Davis, 1965, p. 234). Although this conclusion logically follows from research results (Jones, Davis, and Gergen, 1961; Jones and Davis, 1965), some have questioned whether these results are not more of an artifact of the research designs rather than an accurate description of what happens in the nonexperimental social world (Alexander and Epstein, 1969; Guiot, 1977).

Attribution theory's emphasis on out-of-role behavior results in perceptions of others being based on deviant behavior (Guiot, 1977). Although deviant behavior does contribute to the attribution of personality characteristics, socially expected behavior also conveys meaningful information about personal attributes. The task for contemporary attribution theory is to explain how to make valid attributions, particularly of positive traits, from socially approved behavior (Hastorf, 1970, p. 90). The inclusion of in-role or socially acceptable behavior in the attribution process is necessary if the theory is to fully account for interpersonal perception.

The second problem that should be addressed by contemporary attribution theory is how to include the perspective of the observer in the attribution process. Limited research suggests that a person's attributions of others are influenced by his or her self-identity and perceptions of the situation. For example, at the Nuremberg trials of war criminals, the judges and juries, like the jury in the Zamora case, had to decide whether the men and women indicted as war criminals were responsible for their participation in the execution of several million Jews. Zamora's behavior was inappropriate for any of the groups to which he may have belonged including U.S. society. The Nazi soldiers' and party members' behaviors, however, were appropriate for the social group to which they belonged. The role expection was that soldiers and workers should follow the orders of their superiors, even to carrying out executions. In both the Zamora and war-crimes cases, the defendants had killed; however, in the first case, the attribution was made that the boy was a violent person, but, in the second, the attribution was that the war criminals lacked moral fortitude because, rather than complying with general normative expectations binding on all members of humanity, they complied with directives from group leaders. The different attributions were the consequences of different perspectives taken by those making the causal attributions.

This example points up the need to include the perspective of the person making the attributions in the theory. As has been noted (Jones and Davis, 1965), the attribution process becomes even more complex when the characteristics of the person making the attributions are taken into account. However, complexity should not be avoided in efforts to understand social reality.

Information Processing in Impression Formation

Having discussed the major processes of impression formation, we will now examine the effects of multiple units of information, of the order of the information received, and of positive and negative information on impressions formed about others.

MULTIPLE CUES

Frequently, a person receives more than one piece of information describing another individual. Two different models, additive and averaging, have emerged out of the large body of research concerning how several units of information are integrated into an overall impression. Most of the research testing these two models has focused on feelings of liking toward another and has examined how subjects combined several units of information to obtain an overall liking score.

Additive Model The additive model of how people combine information maintains that each unit of information is assigned a weight and added in with the others to produce an overall impression of the other person. For example, in order to apply the additive model to predict how you will feel toward your new college roommate, you would be asked to weigh the importance of certain characteristics of the new roommate. In this example, you would be asked to rate your new roommate on four characteristics: Intelligence; attractiveness; responsibility; and unfriendliness, using a scale of from 1 to 10. If you had rated these four traits as intelligence = 9, attractiveness = 8, responsibility = 9, and unfriendliness = 2, these ratings would be summed to predict your overall impression or liking of the new roommate (see figure 9–4). The rating scale of from 1 to 10 is arbitrary, but illustrates how each additional positive trait increases the liking or attraction score.

Averaging Model The averaging model of information integration proposes that the ratings of the traits are averaged rather than summed. Feelings toward the new roommate are also calculated in figure 9–4 using the averaging model. The difference between the predictions of the two models is also illustrated in figure 9–4 by adding another trait, stubbornness, and observing how the overall liking scores change. If "stubbornness" is rated as being 2, then the additive liking score increases from 28 to 30, but the averaging score decreases from 7 to 6.

If the new roommate wanted to use these two models to impress you as being a person of worth, two quite different strategies would be required. The additive model would involve the new roommate providing you with a long list of his or her desirable traits and characteristics. Each additional positive trait would be expected to increase your liking of this person. On the other hand, the averaging model would suggest that he or she inform

ADDITIVE MODEL	AVERAGING MODEL	
9	Intelligence	9
8	Attractiveness	8
9	Responsibility	9
2	Unfriendliness	2
△28	Liking Score	(28) = △7 ÷ 4

CHANGE FROM ADDING STUBBORNESS

9	Intelligence	9
8	Attractiveness	8
9	Responsibility	9
2	Unfriendliness	2
2	Stubbornness	2
△30	Liking Score	(30) = △6 ÷ 5

Figure 9–4 Additive and Averaging Models for Integrating Several Units of Information into a Single Impression

you only of his or her most positive traits. Limiting information in this manner would insure a high average, which means that you would feel very positive toward the roommate.

Although the research evidence strongly indicates that people integrate information as shown by the averaging model, there are a few studies that have reported support for the additive model (Anderson, 1962; Fishbein and Hunter, 1964). Fishbein and Hunter (1964) found that subjects reported greater liking for another person who was described as having five strongly positive traits than they did for a person who was said to have only two strongly positive traits.

Anderson (1974) reviewed a number of studies designed to contrast the averaging and additive models. Most of the studies produced support in favor of the averaging model. It seems that as an individual receives additional pieces of information about another, the units of information are *averaged* together to form an overall impression.

PRIMACY VERSUS RECENCY

In his pioneering set of experiments, Asch (1946) tested the effects of varying the order in which information about another person was given to subjects. A set of six descriptive traits were presented to a group of subjects with the positive traits first: "intelligent, industrious, impulsive, critical, stubborn, and envious" (Asch, 1946, p. 270). A second group of subjects received the same traits in a reverse order: "envious, stubborn, critical, impulsive, industrious, and intelligent." The subjects wrote a brief description of the person and checked a list of personality traits for the ones they believed the person possessed. The results revealed that when the positive traits were given first, a much more favorable impression of the person was formed as compared to when the negative traits appeared first. Asch argued that this primacy effect occurred because the first pieces of information set the direction of the impression, which then influenced the interpretation of additional information.

A number of experiments since Asch have documented the primacy effect. For example, Kelley (1950) informed students in a class that they would have a guest lecture in a forthcoming class. In addition, half the students were told that the guest lecturer was a "warm" person, and the others were informed that he was a rather "cold" individual. After the man had lectured for twenty minutes, the students were asked to give their impressions of him. Even though all the students had witnessed the same lecture, those who had previous information that the man was a warm individual reported him as such, but those who expected a cold person reported him as such. Obviously, the lecturer was not warm and cold at the same time but rather was judged to be one or the other according to the initial impression. This experiment suggests that the information received first does influence the impression of an individual more strongly than does subsequent information. The importance of a primacy effect in real life is obvious as careful management of initial information can influence people to form and maintain a particular impression of another in spite of subsequent information to the contrary. One very practical example is the case of a judge or jury deciding a criminal case. If a strong primacy effect always occurs, then the prosecution has a distinct advantage as it presents its case first.

The primacy effect has been found to operate even when the later information was inconsistent with or contradicted the early information. Luchins (1957b) created two paragraphs describing a brief episode in the day of a high-school-aged boy. One paragraph described him as enjoying a walk to the drugstore; the sun is shining; he meets several friends and confidently handles a chance encounter with a pretty girl he had met the night before. The description was designed to create the impression of a friendly, outgoing, and confident young man. The second paragraph described him walking to the store and avoiding the sun, avoiding an encounter with a pretty girl he had met the night before, and seeking to be left alone in the store. This description created the impression of a shy, introverted boy. In this experiment, half the subjects received the extroverted paragraph first and then the introverted one. The other subjects received the introverted paragraph first, followed by the extroverted one. After reading the two paragraphs, the subjects were asked to describe the boy using both sets of information. A primacy effect emerged, as those who were exposed to the extroverted paragraph first described the young man as friendly and outgoing in spite of the later information to the contrary. An introverted description emerged from the subjects who had read the introverted paragraph first.

As mentioned above, one explanation of the primacy effect is Asch's "change of meaning" theory that the first information creates an initial impression that influences the interpretation of later information. An alternative explanation is that people are less attentive to later information than they are to initial information, and this is what produces a greater impact from the initial information on the impression. Boredom, fatigue, and confidence that the person in question has been adequately understood are possible reasons why attention to later information lags.

Luchins (1957a and 1958) tested the idea that lack of subsequent attention causes the primacy effect by making later information more salient. As discussed above, Luchins (1957b) used two paragraphs describing a young boy as either an introvert or an extrovert to test for the primacy effect. In a second study, he warned the subjects not to make snap judgments before he gave them the two paragraphs. This warning, which was assumed to make the subjects maintain their attention level while reading the second paragraph, produced a much reduced primacy effect as compared to when no warning was given. In a third study, the warning was made between the two paragraphs. In other words, the subjects read either the introvert or extrovert paragraph first, were then warned against snap judgments, and then read the second paragraph. In this case, not only did the primacy effect not appear but a slight *recency effect* emerged. The final study had the subjects engage in a totally unrelated task between the reading of the two paragraphs. Having the unrelated task take place between the two sets of information produced a strong recency effect. This set of experiments demonstrates that if the importance of later information is stressed, then the primacy effect is reduced and may even be replaced by a recency effect. Similar findings were reported in a later study by Stewart (1965).

It was suggested that if a long list of units of information was presented to subjects they would forget the early information and focus on the later (Anderson and Barrios, 1961). Subjects were given sixty sets of six traits upon which to base their impression of the person. Somewhat to the experimenters' surprise, a strong primacy effect appeared, although it did fade a little as the amount of information increased. This study indicates support for the primacy effect but demonstrates that additional pieces of information do gradually reduce it.

An interesting study by Hendrick and Costantini (1970) tested the effects of inconsistent information and the effects of maintaining attention to later information. A person was described to the subjects in terms of six traits, three of which were positive and three negative. One group of subjects was given a set of traits that, even though half were positive and half were negative, were reasonably consistent with each other. Another group of subjects was given a list of six traits that were inconsistent with each other. All the subjects had the six traits read to them, but to maintain attention to the entire list half the subjects were required to verbally repeat the traits to the experimenter. A strong primacy effect appeared for those subjects who did not repeat the list for both the inconsistent and consistent lists. However, a recency effect appeared for subjects who repeated the traits of either the consistent or inconsistent list. This experiment provides support for both the interpretation set and the lack of attention explanations of a primacy versus recency effect. The results demonstrated quite convincingly that whether a primacy or recency effect occurred was a function of the attention focused on the information. In addition, neither the primacy nor recency effects were affected by inconsistent information, which indicates that the more salient information, initial or most recent, does influence how other information is interpreted.

Another condition found to influence the occurrence of a primacy or recency effect is the stability of the trait, characteristic, or behavior observed. If the initial information is about a stable characteristic, such as intelligence, then a primacy effect is likely to occur. On the other hand, if a temporary characteristic, such as a depressed mood, is seen first, then a recency effect will likely shape the impression.

Jones and his associates (1968) sought to test the influence of the stability of a trait on the occurrence of a primacy or recency effect. They felt that intelligence is generally considered a stable trait and designed an experiment that created an early impression of high or low intelligence. Additional information was given later indicating that both the intelligent and unintelligent persons were actually of average intelligence. Subjects observed a confederate attempting to solve a series of puzzles. Half the subjects observed the confederate solve the first puzzles, thus suggesting intelligence, but have difficulty solving the later puzzles. The other subjects witnessed the confederate do poorly on the first puzzles but come on strong solving the later ones. In both cases, the confederate solved exactly the same number of puzzles; the only difference was that in one case success was at the start, and in the other success came at the end. Given that intelligence is generally assumed to be a stable trait, the researchers anticipated a strong primacy effect. The expected effect occurred. This experiment indicates that the stability of the trait or characteristic observed is a determinant of whether a primacy or recency effect occurs.

In summary, the order in which information is presented does influence the impression formed. However, whether impression is influenced by primacy or recency is dependent on the attention given to the information, the amount of information, and the stability of the traits or characteristics described.

POSITIVE VERSUS NEGATIVE INFORMATION

Occasionally, the information received about another person contains both positive and negative traits, characteristics, or behaviors. The averaging model predicts that the information will be weighted and averaged together to create a feeling of liking or disliking for the other person. As discussed earlier, the averaging model has been found to explain the combination of several units of information into a single impression in a wide variety of experiments. It has been discovered that immoral or unethical characteristics are usually given exceptionally heavy weights that overwhelm any positive traits or characteristics (Riskey and Birnbaum 1974). The averaging model applies, but the weights assigned to "bad" behavior or traits are so large as to completely dominate the impression (Birnbaum, 1972, 1973).

Attribution theory, as discussed earlier, has been used to explain why negative information has a greater impact than positive information on the perception of others. It is assumed that negative behaviors are generally out-of-role behaviors that are interpreted as a manifestation of a personal trait. On the other hand, "good" or positive behavior is seen as being pressured or coerced by social norms and sanctions, including the criminal justice system, and therefore does not reveal much information about personal characteristics. Within an attribution framework, negative information is considerably more valuable in making an attribution of a person's traits than is positive information. Although the research is limited, the evidence indicates that positive information *suggests* that the person has good traits, but that negative information clearly *reveals* that he or she has bad characteristics.

Summary

As people come into contact with others, they use available information to form impressions of them. These impressions are used to explain the behavior of others and, more importantly, predict how they will behave in the future. Three major theories of impression formation have emerged out of the research on person perception. The application of stereotypes, rigid and emotional descriptions applied to any member of a particular group, is a frequent means of forming an impression of another person. Stereotypes based on physical characteristics, such as skin color, hair color, weight, height, body shape, and clothing, are widely accepted in American society.

Implicit personality theory maintains that each person has an opinion about which personality traits occur together, so the observation of one trait leads to the inference of additional traits that can be used to predict the other person's behavior. Although a number of traits may be observed, they are combined to produce a unified impression of the individual. Early research suggested that the combination is affected by central traits, which appear to influence the total impression more than others, but later research suggested that impressions are organized around the dimensions of *social desirability* and *intellectual desirability*.

Attribution theory contends that people infer behavior tendencies in others on the basis of a limited sample of the others' behavior. Attributions of traits are more accurate when the observed behavior is intentional than when coerced by situational constraints, which do not permit personal attributes to manifest themselves. Significant differences have emerged concerning the attribution of behavior to others as compared to oneself. Generally, it has been discovered that people attribute their own behavior to situational pressures but attribute other people's behavior to personal traits. However, when people perform socially approved behavior, they will attribute it to positive personal traits, and they will blame failure or disapproved behavior on the situation, if they have positive self-concepts. The opposite attributions are made by people with negative self-concepts. It appears that differences in attributions made about oneself as contrasted to others are influenced by the success or failure of the behavior and the self-concept of the person making the attribution.

Frequently, several units of information are available from which to form an impression of a person. People seem to *average* rather than *add* together the information to form an overall impression. A *primacy effect* where the information received first has a greater impact on the impression than later information has been observed. Two explanations for the primacy effect are that people's attention decreases as more information is provided and the earlier information has a stronger impact on the impression, the earliest information creates an initial impression which influences how later information is *interpreted (change of meaning)*. Research suggests that both explanations operate to generate a primacy effect. On the other hand, it has been discovered that focusing attention on later information produces a recency effect so that the most recent information has the greatest influence on the impression formed. Stable traits or characteristics when observed first tend to cause a primacy effect, but a recency effect is more likely if a stable trait is learned of later. Finally, negative information appears to have a significantly stronger impact on the impression formed about another than does positive information.

10

egoism and altruism

It happens from time to time in New York that the life of the city is frozen by an instant of shock. In that instant the people of the city are seized by the paralyzing realization that they are one, that each man is in some way a mirror of every other man. They stare at each other—or, really, into themselves—and a look quite like a flush of embarrassment passes over the face of the city. Then the instant passes and the beat resumes and the people turn away and try to explain what they have seen, or try to deny it.

The last 35 minutes of the young life of Miss Catherine Genovese became such a shock in the life of the city. But at the time she died, stabbed again and again by a marauder in her quiet, dark but entirely respectable, street in Kew Gardens, New York hardly took note.

It was not until two weeks later that Catherine Genovese, known as Kitty, returned in death to cry the city awake. Even then it was not her life or her dying that froze the city, but the witnessing of her murder—the choking fact that 38 of her neighbors had seen her stabbed or heard her cries, and that not one of them, during that hideous half-hour, had lifted the telephone from the safety of his own apartment to call the police and try to save her life. When it was over and Miss Genovese was dead and the murderer gone, one man did call—not from his own apartment but from the neighbor's, and only after he had called a friend and asked her what to do.

The day that the story of the witnessing of the death of Miss Genovese appeared in this newspaper became that frozen instant. "Thirty-eight!" people said over and over. "Thirty-eight!"

. . . Austin Street, where Catherine Genovese lived, is in a section of Queens known as Kew Gardens. There are two apartment buildings, and the rest of the street consists of one-family homes—red-brick, stucco or wood-frame. There are Jews, Catholics and Protestants, a scattering of foreign accents, middle-class incomes.

On the night of March 13, about 3 A.M., Catherine Genovese was returning to her home. She worked late as manager of a bar in Hollis, another part of Queens. She parked her car (a red Fiat) and started to walk to her death.

Lurking near the parking lot was a man. Miss Genovese saw him in the shadows, turned and walked toward a police call box. The man pursued her, stabbed her. She screamed, "Oh, my God, he stabbed me! Please help me! Please help me!"

Somebody threw open a window and a man called out: "Let that girl alone!" Other lights turned on, other windows were raised. The attacker got into a car and drove away. A bus passed.

The attacker drove back, got out, searched out Miss Genovese in the back of an apartment building where she had crawled for safety, stabbed her again, drove away again.

The first attack came at 3:15. The first call to the police came at 3:50. Police arrived within two minutes, they say. Miss Genovese was dead.

That night and the next morning the police combed the neighborhood looking for witnesses. They found them, 38.

Two weeks later, when this newspaper heard of the story, a reporter went knocking, door to door, asking why, why?

Through half-opened doors, they told him. Most of them were neither defiant nor terribly embarrassed nor particularly ashamed. The underlying attitude, or explanation, seemed to be fear of involvement—any kind of involvement.

"I didn't want my husband to get involved," a housewife said.

"We thought it was a lovers' quarrel," said another woman. "I went back to bed."

"I was tired," said a man.

"I don't know," said another man.

"I don't know," said still another.

"I don't know," said others.

. . . It seems to this writer that what happened in the apartments and houses on Austin Street was a symptom of a terrible reality in the human condition—that only under certain situations and only in response to certain reflexes or certain beliefs will a man step out of his shell toward his brother.

. . . Nobody can say why the 38 did not lift the phone while Miss Genovese was being attacked, since they cannot say themselves. It can be assumed, however, that their apathy was indeed of a big-city variety. It is almost a matter of psychological survival, if one is surrounded and pressed by millions of people, to prevent them from constantly impinging on you and the only way to do this is to ignore them as often as possible.

Indifference to one's neighbor and his troubles is a conditioned reflex of life in New York as it is in other big cities. In every major city in which I have lived—in Tokyo and Warsaw, Vienna and Bombay—I have seen, over and over again, people walk away from accident victims. I have walked away myself.[1]

Egoistic and Altruistic Behavior in Contemporary Society

The incident described at the beginning of this chapter seems to have become an all too common occurrence in contemporary society. Hardly a day passes without some new story appearing that demonstrates the unwillingness of many individuals to go to the aid of someone else who is in distress. Such behavior is indicative of what can be referred to as *egoism*, or the tendency to be self-centered, characterized by a refusal to become concerned about anything but oneself and one's own interests. The opposite of egoism is *altruism*, which is the unselfish concern for the welfare of others. The issues of egoism and altruism are certainly not new. Their significance in times past is indicated by the parable of the Good Samaritan given in response to the question, "Who is my neighbor?"

But he, willing to justify himself, said unto Jesus, And who is my neighbour?

And Jesus answering, said, A certain man went down from Jerusalem to Jericho, and fell among thieves, which stripped him of his raiment, and wounded him, and departed, leaving him half dead.

And by chance there came down a certain priest that way; and when he saw him, he passed by on the other side.

And likewise a Levite, when he was at the place, came and looked on him, and passed by on the other side.

[1]Source: A. M. Rosenthal, "Study of the Sickness Called Apathy," *The New York Times Magazine*, 3 May 1964 pp. 24, 66, 69–70. © 1964 by the New York Times Company.

But a certain Samaritan, as he journeyed, came where he was: and when he saw him, he had compassion on him,

And went to him and bound up his wounds, pouring in oil and wine, and set him on his own beast, and brought him to an inn, and took care of him.

And on the morrow, when he departed, he took out two pence, and gave them to the host, and said unto him, Take care of him: and whatsoever thou spendest more, when I come again, I will repay thee.

Which now of these three, thinkest thou, was neighbour unto him that fell among the thieves?[2]

Contemporary interest in egoism can be traced almost directly to the death of Kitty Genovese. Very few incidents have attracted the continuing interest and attention of the American public to the degree that this case has.

Although it has now been more than a decade since Ms. Genovese was brutally murdered within the sight and sound of many of her neighbors, the case is still a topic of much conversation, and, whenever a similar occurrence of noninvolvement is cited, the writer or teller of the new incident almost always draws a parallel between the new event and the Genovese case. In fact, a new television movie has been made based on the death of Kitty Genovese that brings the story to the attention of another generation of viewers.

Although certainly the most celebrated, the Genovese case is far from being an isolated incident, and this is why the study of egoism and altruism have become the focus of extensive social-psychological research during the past decade. One of the most startling and disturbing of the incidents that drew research attention to this area, and an incident that demonstrated that the Genovese case was not unique, was the response of bystanders to the wreck of a bus containing a large number of school children on a major eastern highway several years ago. The bus driver lost control of his vehicle on a rain-slicked highway, and the bus tore through a guardrail and rolled down a steep embankment. A number of the children were killed, and many more were seriously injured and pinned in the wreckage. Reports indicate that many travelers on the busy highway stopped their automobiles, went to the edge, and looked over at the scene below and then hurried back to their cars to drive away. One driver went to the edge of the embankment to see the wreckage, went back to his automobile for a camera with which he took a number of photos of the tragic scene, and then returned to his automobile and drove away. In the meantime, mangled and injured children were crying for someone to come to their aid.

Another type of bizarre behavior that vividly demonstrates egoism and its consequences for others is depicted in the box below. This event not only describes the unwillingness of a crowd of onlookers to aid someone who is apparently suffering from severe emotional stress but, even more startling, describes the apparent kick they receive from seeing someone else's trouble.

[2]Luke 10:29–36.

Additional Consequences of Egoistic Behavior

The callous side of human behavior that is exhibited in failure to respond to the needs of others in emergency situations has other negative aspects as well. For example, consider the following recent incident in which the onlookers not only failed to go to the aid of the victim but, in fact, encouraged her to slash her throat with a razor blade.

Hartford, Connecticut (UPI)—A 16-year-old girl, apparently high on LSD, slashed her wrists and arms and then rushed to the steps of a Roman Catholic Church poking a razor to her throat while a crowd of 300 persons cheered and screamed, "Do your thing, sister!"

"Anything that she did that looked like it was going to draw blood, they cheered," said Police Detective William Tremont of the Friday night incident.

The girl, not identified because she is a minor, was hit by a whiskey bottle during the 45 minutes she held back police, priests and friends by threatening to cut her throat.

She finally collapsed on the steps of Immaculate Conception Church because she lost so much blood. She was treated at a Hartford Hospital and released Saturday morning.

Police called the crowd's cheering "disgusting."

"The guys [police at the scene] told me they were just like animals," Tremont said.

"They were yelling, 'Do it, sister!' 'Do your thing, sister!' 'right on!' " the officers told the detective.

"It was like they were witnessing a spectacle at a football game," Tremont said.

Friends of the girl told reporters she had taken LSD, the hallucinogenic drug. Police said she appeared to be drugged.

Three bottles were thrown by the crowd which hooted as the girl staggered on the church steps. One bottle struck the girl and the others smashed against the church and the street curb.

While the girl bled profusely, one man jumped up on the sidewalk and recited a brief couplet of doggerel verse, a witness said.

(Source: *Salt Lake Tribune*, 22 August 1976, p. A5. Permission of UPI.)

Following the publicity of these cases, much discussion seemed to focus on what was referred to as the growing impersonal, uncaring nature of modern urban society. Good Samaritanism, many argued, had died with the death of the small, personal, family-oriented, society. The large, impersonal, disinterested city that had replaced it was now inhabited by millions of persons crowded together but hardly aware of, and certainly not interested in, each other's plight or problems. However incidents like those described above have also occurred in rural communities. Urbanization, therefore, cannot be our only explanation for the responses involved. What other explanations can we advance to account for what has been called a "sickness called apathy?" Does social psychology help us in understanding and explaining this important area of human behavior?

A theory of egoistic or nonhelping behavior, to be sufficient, should also help us account for altruistic behavior as exhibited in numerous other instances in which people have gotten involved. We began this chapter by citing several instances of egoistic behavior because social-psychological research has tended to focus more on why people *do not* help others in need rather than asking why they *do*. Perhaps the negative cases have seemed to be more newsworthy, thus causing social psychologists, journalists, and others to focus on them rather than on their opposite. Nevertheless, there are numerous examples that can be cited of people making personal sacrifices in order to aid someone else. Such sacrifices clearly entail altruistic behavior.

Much of the altruistic behavior that occurs daily in this country and elsewhere grows directly out of the organized efforts of large-scale organizations developed for that specific purpose. Millions of people each year respond to such things as blood drives by the Red Cross and fund-raising efforts organized by the American Cancer Society, the American Heart Association, UNICEF, United Fund, and countless others. Altruism also appears to be a prime motivator in the actions of numerous individuals who, on their own, have gotten involved to help others, even at the potential risk of their own lives. For example, a truck driver from a small rural town in Utah was recently killed near Reno, Nevada, when he stopped his truck to help a police officer whom he noticed struggling with an assailant. Numerous others become involved as Big Brothers, Foster Grandparents, and in other voluntary associations whose purpose is to improve the life chances and opportunities of others.

How do we account for these responses? Are the differences between altruism and egoism to be found simply within the psychological makeup of the individual, or are there other explanations? It is to questions such as these that we will turn in this chapter.

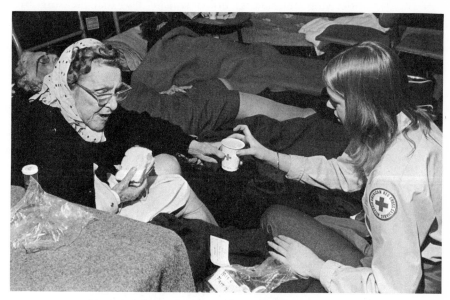

Altruistic behavior involves aiding others in a time of need.

Egoism and Altruism and Basic Human Nature

Throughout the ages, social philosophers have concerned themselves with the question of what motivates altruistic action. Without a rather healthy measure of activity directed toward the achievement of group goals (sometimes at the expense of individual goals), the successful functioning of society would become far more precarious and problematic. The motivation for group and other-directed activities has been seen by some social thinkers, such as Thomas Hobbes, as basically selfish in nature—that is, we form civil societies governed by norms and laws in order to protect ourselves from each other. Such an assumption regarding basic human nature is vastly different from that advocated by Rousseau and the Romantics of the eighteenth-century Age of Reason. From their perspective, people were perceived as innately good and motivated by such needs as those for affiliation, sympathy, and gregariousness. We cannot resolve this conflict here; the debate has continued for centuries, and arguments on both sides are still very much in evidence. Nevertheless, there are important vestiges of two long-popular theories of human nature that have some importance to the contemporary literature that require some comment.

PSYCHOLOGICAL HEDONISM

Perhaps the one theory that has most direct relevance to altruistic and nonaltruistic behavior is psychological hedonism. Although the concept of hedonism is found in the writings of social thinkers from the early Greek philosophers to the present time, its most thorough early development can be found in the work of Jeremy Bentham (1789). The primary assumption underlying Bentham's "utilitarianism" was that pleasure and pain are our "sovereign masters." Thus, people act primarily in ways that are specifically designed to secure pleasure and to avoid pain. Or, in Allport's terms, "On the occasion of every act a person is led to pursue that line of conduct which, according to his view of the case taken by him at the moment, will be in the highest degree contributory to his own happiness" (1968, p. 11).

As noted by Allport (1968), the doctine of hedonism is ultimately a doctrine of self-centeredness. Thus, the individual chooses those courses of action that are designed to maximize personal reward and to minimize punishment. If, in the course of carrying out the selected alternative action, another is helped, that is all well and good; but the decision to choose that particular course was not dictated by concern for helping another but out of the selfish concern for maximizing personal pleasure. According to this theory, then, there is probably no such thing as altruistic behavior.

However, the fact is that many people engage in actions explicitly designed to help others in times of need, and, on occasion, these actions are taken at high personal risk and without much consideration of potential future rewards. Such instances belie that the attainment of pleasure and the avoidance of pain are the primary motivating forces in human behavior. Research support for this argument is found in a study by Aronfreed and Paskal (1965), who found that children can be trained to engage in acts designed to bring pleasure to others even when doing so entails some personal loss. In the study, children were given the option of pulling one lever that activated a red light or pulling another that would result in the delivery of candy. During prior training, the experimenter hugged the children and made strong expressions of joy when they activated the light. Following the training, more of the children continued to pull the lever that brought joy to the experimenter than pulled the lever that would result in candy for themselves.

Hedonistic theory cannot really be tested in an empirical sense because there can be no negative evidence. That is, we do what is pleasurable; to some, this includes helping others. Thus, hedonistic theory cannot distinguish altruistic and egoistic behaviors if only because even behavior that results in high personal cost contributes to the altruist's happiness. Nevertheless, the evidence overall suggests that the person who stands to suffer some personal loss by engaging in altruistic behavior is less likely to engage in such behavior than would be the case if no personal loss was entailed.

THE "ALTRUISTIC GENE" THEORY

The second theory that has been resurrected by some contemporary sociobiologists has proposed the existence of an "altruistic gene" in people and other animal species (see Wilson, 1975). Such a gene serves as a device "by which individual animals curtail their own individual fitness, that is, their survivorship, or fertility, or both, for the good of group survival" (Wilson, 1975, p. 109). According to this perspective, a broad range of animal behaviors can be attributed to this inherited trait including, but not limited to, curtailment of reproduction to prevent overuse of available food source, creation of distractions to entice intruders away from one's young, warning calls (which potentially attract the predator to oneself), and food sharing.

Most social scientists tend to view the "altruistic gene" concept with a good deal of skepticism. Campbell (1972), who initially felt that altruism could perhaps be transmitted genetically, now argues that this is extremely unlikely. For example, if altruism is genetic, why not other response tendencies, such as cowardice? If such were the case, the altruistic tendency would probably soon be eliminated because the altruist would stay to fight to ensure group protection and the coward would flee to ensure self-preservation. Over a period of time, those with the dominant "altruistic gene" would be killed off faster, and those with the dominant "cowardice gene" would survive and reproduce.

There are other arguments that can be made against genetic altruism. The safest conclusion seems to be that this behavior pattern, like most others discussed in this text, is learned. As we will note below, helping behavior is an important human value that is included as part of the basic socialization experience of most humans. However, the actual operationalization of the value, even when learned, is dependent upon a number of other personal and situational factors.

The Social Norm of Reciprocity

We can begin our effort to develop a social-psychological explanation of altruistic behavior by noting that going to the aid of someone in need constitutes action that is consistent with an important and long-standing social norm. The message of the Good Samaritan implies that anyone in need of help should be regarded as our neighbor. The Golden Rule, "Do unto others as you would have them do unto you," also implies the importance of lending assistance to those in need just as we would hope that others would come to our aid when needed.

Gouldner (1960) has proposed that there exists a universal "norm of reciprocity." Supposedly, this norm makes two interrelated, minimal demands: (1) people should help those who have helped them; and (2) people should not injure those who have helped them. The norm of reciprocity also serves at least two important social functions. First, it acts as a stabilizing mechanism in society by defining individual rights and obligations. For example, if you perform some service for me or present me with a gift, then I have the *obligation* to respond in kind by doing something for you or presenting you with a gift. Similarly, if I have first performed the service for you, then I have the *right* to expect you to reciprocate. Second, it acts as a "starting mechanism" to initiate social interaction. For example, if I know that the norm of reciprocity applies, then I am more willing to initiate some action in your behalf because I know that you will willingly repay me at the appropriate time.

According to this theory, then, helping behavior is based on the idea of exchange—we do things for others at least in part because we know that they, in turn, will do things for us. Gouldner recognizes, of course, that there are many instances in which an individual or a group may provide benefits for another even without the hope of reciprocation. For example, if one person is much more powerful than another, the first may demand and receive services from the second without having to give anything (or as much) in return. A domineering husband may demand sexual favors from his wife without much concern for providing her with any particular gratification in return. Similarly, one of two partners in an exchange may have a number of alternative sources of reward or gratification while the other has none. In such a case, the other partner may be much more willing to give in order to maintain the relationship without as much concern for what is received in return. In fact, continuation of the relationship may be the only reciprocity the second person desires.

Gouldner's norm of reciprocity is somewhat reminiscent of the "system of mutual obligations" that William Foote Whyte (1943) found to underlie

"Thanks. Your bird is very nice, too."

Source: Richter; © The New Yorker Magazine, Inc.

the social organization of the Norton gang. Whyte observed that many of the actions of the group were based on the shared expectation that if one did something for someone else, the other had a clear obligation to return the favor. This system of mutual expectations was so generally accepted that no one paid attention to it *unless* someone ignored it. That is, if a member started taking advantage of others by receiving favors and not returning them, this would be forcefully called to his attention.

Social Exchange and Altruistic Behavior

The concept of social exchange that is implied in the norm of reciprocity has received extensive treatment in contemporary social-psychological literature. One of the earliest and most detailed treatments of this concept is found in the work of George Homans (1958, 1961, 1974). Homans has adopted the view that all social interaction constitutes an exchange of goods, which can be material or nonmaterial. Although two persons may involve themselves in a strictly economic exchange (for example, person A exchanges some goods for monetary payment from person B), they may also exchange nonmaterial goods (for example, A compliments B in exchange for an increase in liking from B).

Homans bases much of his theory on principles drawn from behavioral psychology. For example, he argues that the probability of the occurrence of a given action is dependent upon the extent to which that particular action has been rewarded in the past; thus, we are more likely to enter into exchanges with people with whom past exchanges have proven rewarding. Similarly, the more rewarding a past exchange has been, the more likely we are to be willing to give up more to establish such an exchange again. This principle is also applicable to group relationships. The more attractive membership in a particular group is, the more we are willing to give in order to obtain membership in that group, such as submitting to rigorous initiations in order to gain membership in a fraternity or sorority. The principle that an increasing frequency of reward leads to an increasing frequency of action holds true only to a point, however. Eventually, fatigue or satiation enter into the equation to change the reward/cost outcome.

As this implies, in addition to rewards social exchanges can also entail certain costs. In Homans' terminology, cost is equal to the value of a foregone alternative. In other words, when we choose one course of action, we frequently forego some other course of action and the potential rewards of this foregone choice become the costs of the one chosen. If we choose to spend our accumulated savings on a new automobile, for example, we are foregoing the option of using those savings for a vacation in Europe, and giving up the European vacation contains some rather obvious costs. Similarly, if we choose to ask a certain person to a dance, we are giving up the option of going alone, asking someone else, or of staying home and watching a favorite program on television. The more attractive these other alternatives are to us, the higher the cost associated with the chosen course of action. The *profit* one attains from a relationship, then, is equal to the rewards of that relationship minus these costs.

JUSTICE IN EXCHANGE RELATIONSHIPS

Homans also introduced a principle of justice that he considers important in assessing reward/cost outcomes. Basically, the principle of *distributive justice* argues that if the costs to an individual or group are high, the rewards should be high also. This principle is basically comparative in nature. In other words, if my costs are comparatively higher than yours, then my rewards should also be higher, or the rule of distributive justice is not operating. If I discover that I am putting significantly more into the relationship than you are but that your rewards are equal to or greater than mine, then I am likely to be quite unhappy with the relationship. Similarly, a person with greater responsibility should receive higher rewards than a person with less responsibility, or the rule of distributive justice is violated.

Some rather direct applications to helping behavior are obvious. Although choosing to go to the aid of a victim in distress may entail certain rewards, potential costs must also be considered. Some of the more important of these costs may involve foregone values. For example, if I stop to help you change your tire (for which you will reward me with gratitude and esteem), I may be late for an important meeting (potentially a value foregone). In considering my reward/cost outcomes, I determine that the greatest profit lies in achieving the rewards associated with getting to my meeting on time and foregoing the value associated with with your gratitude. In other words, my boss' displeasure may be far more costly than a loss of your gratitude.

In Homans' terms, most helping situations imply the notion of exchange. Although most people who stop to help a stranded motorist are probably not expecting some physical or monetary reward in return for their action, they may expect an expression of gratitude from the person aided or they may experience an increase in personal feelings of self-worth from the knowledge that they have helped someone in need. These rewards may be every bit as important as more material rewards. In fact, to many people, expressions of gratitude from others and increased self-esteem may be far more important than rewards such as monetary payments.

SOCIAL EXCHANGE AND EQUITY THEORY

Closely related to some of the basic concepts of social exchange is what Adams (1965) called "equity theory." Equity theory proposes that we seek to maintain a balance between what we give and what we receive on the one hand and what others give and what they receive on the other. If one comes out on the short end of an exchange, then pressures will develop to restore a greater measure of equity. In Homans' terms, distributive justice has not been realized, and some effort will be made for compensation, or the aggrieved party will feel frustrated and angry.

Walster, Berscheid, and Walster (1970) have applied these ideas directly to the helping behavior process. They propose that when we come upon a victim, we can seek to restore equity and balance by offering that person compensation in the form of assistance. However, we are only likely to help if the need is credible and deserves compensation. We often avoid the necessity of responding through such means as derogating the victim ("they got what they deserved and so are unworthy of my help"), or through such other means as denying any personal responsibility ("someone else must compensate to restore equity"), or by minimizing the loss that the victim has experienced. In each case, however, we attempt to restore equity to what appears to be an inequitable situation.

RESEARCH ON COSTS AND REWARDS AND HELPING BEHAVIOR

Walster and Piliavin (1972), Gergen, Gergen, and Meter, (1972), and others have noted that individual perceptions of reward and cost outcomes are critical in determining whether they intervene in an emergency or not. Inaction may include such costs as feelings of guilt for not helping someone in need. However, action may lead to personal danger and injury, the possibility of lawsuits, and so on. The primary reward for helping behavior may simply be feeling good for having assisted someone in need. The rewards for inaction may include avoiding the potential negative consequences, not losing the time it would require when one should be doing something else, and so on. Latane and Darley (1976) note that most of these factors may be weighted in favor of *inaction*.

Pomazal and Jaccard (1976) note that it is primarily an evaluation of the *costs* or negative consequences of action that determines behavior in a helping situation. In a study of blood donors and nondonors, these researchers found that both groups believed that donating blood would result in positive outcomes. However, those who did not donate were much more likely to believe that giving blood would have negative personal consequences.

In another study of blood-donor behavior, Condie, Warner, and Gillman (1976) found that the two variables most closely related to donorship were the provision of incentives (for example, providing public recognition for donors or providing information to the donor about blood type) and considerations of cost (such as fears about pain and discomfort, loss of time, or inconvenience). Other measures, such as feelings of humanitarianism, were among the least influential in accounting for donorship.

These studies clearly fit within the exchange framework and imply that before taking action many people carefully consider the potential consequences of alternative courses of action. If personal costs are evaluated as being higher than potential rewards, a decision not to become involved is usually the outcome.

TIME AS A COST FACTOR IN HELPING SITUATIONS

In an effort to replicate what they felt were some of the more relevant characteristics present in the Good Samaritan parable, Darley and Batson (1973) conducted an innovative experiment using seminary students as subjects. The researchers proposed that two situational variables were relevant to the actions of the participants in the parable or any helping situation: (1) the content of one's thinking; and (2) the amount of hurry in one's journey. Both the Priest and the Levite should have had their minds occupied with religious matters because they were both religious functionaries.

At the same time, because they were important individuals (at least in terms of self-definition), they may have been in a greater hurry to reach their destination.

To test the influence of these factors in helping behavior, Darley and Batson asked seminary students to assist in a study on religious education and vocations. Subjects began the study in one building but finished it in another. While in transit between buildings, each subject passed a "victim" slumped in an alley. The purpose for going to the second building was to record a talk on one of two assigned subjects: (1) jobs in which seminary students would be most effective; or (2) *the parable of the Good Samaritan.*

Three conditions of "hurry" were employed. In the first, the seminary student was told that he was already late, and the person recording the talk would be waiting. In the second, the student was told that the assistant was ready, but no mention was made of being late. In the final condition, the subject was told that the assistant would not be ready for a few minutes but to go on over anyway.

Darley and Batson described the potential helping situation as follows:

> When the subject passed through the alley, the victim was sitting slumped in a doorway, head down, eyes closed, not moving. As the subject went by, the victim coughed twice and groaned, keeping his head down. If the subject stopped and asked if something was wrong or offered to help, the victim, startled and somewhat groggy, said, "Oh, thank you (cough) . . . No, it's all right. (Pause) I've got this respiratory condition (cough) . . . The doctor's given me these pills to take, and I just took one . . . If I just sit and rest for a few minutes I'll be O.K. . . . Thanks very much for stopping though (smiles weakly)." If the subject persisted, insisting on taking the victim inside the building, the victim allowed him to do so and thanked him (1973, p. 104).

As would perhaps be expected, subjects in a hurry were less likely to offer help to the victim than subjects not in a hurry. Of those, who were least hurried, 63 percent offered help. This dropped to 45 percent in the intermediate condition, and to 10 percent in the most hurried condition. However, the subject's topic of speech did not significantly affect his helping behavior. These authors conclude:

> A person not in a hurry may stop and offer help to a person in distress. A person in a hurry is likely to keep going. Ironically, he is likely to keep going even if he is hurrying to speak on the parable of the Good Samaritan, thus inadvertently confirming the point of the parable. (Indeed, on several occasions, a seminary student going to give a talk on the parable of the Good Samaritan literally stepped over the victim as he hurried on his way!) (Darley and Batson, 1973, p. 107.)

Although we tend to think of the expenditure of personal time as a major cost factor only to those in modern industrialized society, apparently this is not so. If intervention to help others will take time, or if it entails personal cost of some other nature, we are clearly less likely to intervene. However, other factors are also important in influencing that decision.

Diffusion of Responsibility and Failure to Help Others

As noted earlier, social-psychological interest in the issues of altruistic and egoistic behavior was promoted, at least in part, by the occurrence of a series of events that were puzzling and problematic. The common property that seemed to run throughout many of these events was the fact that in all cases, there were a number of witnesses. That is, not just one neighbor but many observed the plight of Kitty Genovese. The schoolbus crashed not on an isolated highway but on a busy interstate. Could it be that the number of witnesses was one of the important explanations for those instances in which people have refused to go to the aid of a victim? Following the Genovese murder, a growing number of studies have been conducted on the relationship between the number of witnesses present and the incidence of helping behavior.

One of the first studies to examine this effect was conducted at Columbia University by Latane and Darley (1968). Subjects (male undergraduates at Columbia) were invited to participate in an interview where they would discuss some of the problems of adjustment at an urban university. The students were asked to take seats in a small waiting room and to fill out a questionnaire while they waited for the interview to begin. Shortly after being seated, smoke began to pour into the waiting room through a vent in the wall. Although the condition in which the subjects found themselves was somewhat ambiguous, it certainly presented a potentially dangerous situation. The smoke continued to pour into the room during the next few minutes so that, by the end of the experiment, vision in the room was obscured.

Latane and Darley were interested primarily in the effect of the presence of others on the response of the subjects to the potential crisis situation. To accomplish this, three experimental conditions were employed. In the first condition, the subject was alone in the waiting room. In the second condition, two confederates who were instructed to notice the smoke but remain indifferent to it were seated in the waiting room with the experimental subject. The confederates would simply look up when the smoke began, shrug their shoulders, and return to the task of completing the questionnaire—occasionally waving their hand to get the smoke out of the way. In the third condition, subjects were taken into the waiting room in groups of three, but in this case all three members were naive subjects. Thus, when the smoke started pouring through the vent, they were free to discuss it, run for help, jointly decide upon an appropriate course of action, or whatever. In all cases, the smoke was allowed to come into the room for six minutes. If the respondent(s) had done nothing by that time, the experiment was terminated.

Latane and Darley found the respondents who were by themselves behaved rather reasonably. They would typically appear rather startled when the smoke first started coming into the room, would usually investigate the matter more closely, and then would leave the room and find someone else to whom they would report the incident. A total of 75 percent of the respondents who were in the room by themselves reported the incident within the six-minute period. Most did so within two minutes of the first appearance of the smoke.

However, in only 10 percent of the cases in which the subjects were in the presence of the passive confederates did they report the smoke. The others remained in the room filling out the questionnaires, coughing, and waving the smoke out of their eyes.

In the third condition, three naive subjects were present, any one of whom was free to report the smoke. Therefore, in this case the results had to be treated somewhat differently to avoid bias. For example, if one member responded immediately, the other two could assume that the situation had been handled and so could be expected not to do anything themselves. To overcome this problem, the researchers calculated what they called the *effective individual probability* of helping. The results were almost equally dramatic to those in the second condition, as the probability of helping was only 15 percent.

This study clearly demonstrates the importance of numbers in determining individual response to crisis situations. However, it really does not tell us a great deal about the diffusion of social responsibility that may be implied because we could just as well be observing conformity or modeling effects. We noted in chapter 5 that the probability of conformity often increases in ambiguous situations. The naive subjects could simply have been looking to others for cues as to appropriate or inappropriate response in an ambiguous setting. Because the role models were unconcerned, the naive subject seemed to define this to be the appropriate response to the situation. However, the importance of diffusion of responsibility became more obvious in other experiments conducted by these researchers.

As the data from this first study indicate, single subjects were much more likely to respond to the potential threat than were subjects in groups. However, the smoke carried with it the potential danger of personal harm, and consequently subjects may have felt that there was safety in numbers. To test this, a second experiment was developed in which the threat of personal harm or danger was eliminated (Latane and Rodin, 1969).

Student subjects were invited to participate in a marketing research study dealing with game and puzzle preferences. Subjects were met at the door by a woman who indicated that she was a representative of the testing company. They were then led to the testing room, which contained a variety of games and puzzles. After some initial instruction, the young lady provided the subjects with a game preference questionnaire and then went into an adjoining office separated from the game room by a collapsible curtain. The subject filling out the questionnaire could hear the representative working at the desk in the adjoining office. After several minutes, she could be heard climbing on a chair to reach some papers atop a bookcase. At that point, there was the sound of a loud crash and a scream as the chair collapsed. This was followed by her saying: "Oh, my God, my foot. . . . I . . . can't move . . . it. Oh . . . my ankle . . . I . . . can't get this . . . thing . . . off me." The cries and moans then continued for about another minute.

Four experimental conditions were employed in assessing whether or not the subjects took action to go to her aid. In the first, the subject was in the testing room by himself filling out the questionnaire when the supposed accident occurred. In the second, a confederate who was instructed to act as passively as possible to the sounds coming from the adjoining office was also present. The third and fourth conditions also involved pairs of subjects, but in these instances both were naive participants. In the third condition, pairs of strangers were filling out the questionnaire when the accident was staged. In the fourth, the two were friends.

Again, the results indicate the importance of numbers in subject response. A total of 70 percent of the subjects who heard the crash while alone went to the aid of the victim. At the opposite extreme, only 7 percent of those who were with the passive confederate intervened. The researchers noted that the subjects in this condition frequently appeared upset and confused and kept glancing at the confederate. However, when the confederate did nothing, 93 percent of the subjects did nothing.

Pairs of strangers were somewhat more likely to respond. The effective individual probability of responding (correcting for the fact that *two* could respond) was 23 percent. However, this is much lower than was true for subjects *alone*. Pairs of friends were more likely to respond than were strangers (45 percent effective individual probability), but again this was much lower than in the first condition.

Latane and Darley (1976, p. 13) have proposed that in emergency situations, the presence of other people can alter the cost of *not* acting. A person alone at the time of an accident cannot assume that others will do something about it and therefore carries the full burden of acting or not acting to relieve the distress. However, if others happen to be present, "the onus of responsibility is diffused, and the individual may be more likely to resolve his conflict between intervening and not intervening in favor of the latter alternative." Responsibility, in other words, is shared when more than one person is present and is not unique to any one. The consequence is that "each may be less likely to help."

This suggests that the more individuals that are present in a crisis situation, the less likely any one of them is to intervene. Darley and Latane (1968) tested this idea by having subjects experience a crisis by themselves or in the presence of up to four others. Subjects were to discuss with others the problems faced by college students in adjusting to high-pressure, urban environments. The discussions were to occur via an intercom system, supposedly to guarantee anonymity and encourage free and open response. Subjects were to take turns talking, and then each would comment on what the others had to say.

In reality, the experimental subject was the only one present. Responses heard by this subject were always tape recordings made to give him the impression that there were one or more others present. In all cases, the future victim spoke first (actually, a prerecorded tape segment). This individual indicated his problems of adjustment to urban life, and, with very obvious embarrassment, indicated that he had a problem with seizures, especially during pressure situations, such as at exam time. Other respondents took their turn speaking, but when it came back to the victim for a comment, it became quite obvious that he was experiencing some type of problem. The recorded segment heard by the experimental subject went as follows:

I-er-um-think I-I need-er-if-if could-er-er-somebody er-er-er-er-er-er-er give me a little-er-give me a little help here because-er-I-er-I'm-er-er-h-h-having a-a-a real problem-er-right now and I-er-if somebody could help me out it would-it would-er-er s-s-sure be-sure be good . . . because-er-there-er-er-a cause I-er-I-

uh I've got a-a one of the-er sei—er-er-things coming on and-and-and I could
really-er-use some help so if somebody would-er give me a little h-help-uh-er-
er-er-er-er c-could somebody-er-er-help-er-uh-uh-uh (choking sounds) . . . I'm
gonna die-er-er-I'm . . . gonna die-er-help-er-er-seizure-er-(chokes, then quiet)
(Darley and Latane, 1968, p. 379).

As noted, the major independent variable being tested was the number
of others the experimental subject believed were also listening to the plight
of the victim. In the first condition, the subject had been led to believe that
he or she was alone and that no one else could be aware of the seizure being
experienced by the discussion partner. The second condition involved one
additional person; that is, the experimental subject believed that there were
two others present (one of whom experiences the seizure). In the final
condition, the naive subject believed that the person experiencing the seizure and four others were also in the discussion group.

The results of this interesting experiment clearly demonstrate the diffusion effect. In 85 percent of the cases in which the subject thought he or she
was alone in hearing the plight of the victim, the seizure was reported before
the victim's mike was cut off. The other 15 percent did so soon after. On
the other hand, only 31 percent of the subjects who believed that four others
could also hear what was happening reported the seizure before the victim
was cut off, and 62 percent did eventually. Subjects who believed that one
other person could hear the seizure fell about halfway between these two
extremes.

Each of these three studies shows that the presence of others generally
inhibits our response in emergency situations. The fact that we do not face
the situation alone allows us to share the responsibility for what is happening, to rationalize by saying that someone else will take care of the problem,
or to justify our own inaction by saying that if it was really an emergency,
others would have responded accordingly. The important *social* issue in all
of this, however, is whether *anyone* helps. From the victim's point of view,
it probably matters little who helps so long as someone does.

The diffusion-of-responsibility concept is appealing because, on the surface, it offers the potential of serving as *the* major variable in explaining
helping and nonhelping behavior. However, as research on this concept
continued, contrary evidence soon appeared. Perhaps most important of
this evidence is an interesting study by Piliavin, Rodin, and Piliavin (1969).
To test the diffusion-of-responsibility concept, these researchers conducted
studies using the New York subway as their experimental lab. An accomplice
of the experimenters would enter the subway car and move to a central,
conspicuous position. After standing there for a few moments, the accomplice would stagger and collapse on the floor of the train. The victim would
then remain motionless on the floor of the train staring at the ceiling until
someone volunteered aid. This simple event was repeated over a hundred
different times under a number of different conditions.

In most instances, the researchers observed that someone would rush to
the aid of the victim almost immediately. This was especially likely to be
true if the accomplice was defined as ill. Under this condition, help was
offered almost immediately in over 95 percent of the trials. Even when the
victim appeared to be drunk (he carried a bottle of liquor in his hand and

smelled strongly of alcohol), he received immediate help about half of the time.

The important observation in terms of diffusion of responsibility, however, was that helping behavior on the subway car *was* affected by the number of witnesses but in the direction contrary to what the hypothesis would predict. That is, in those instances in which there were seven or more witnesses in the immediate area, help was received more quickly than when there were only one to three witnesses. Thus, there simply was not a diffusion effect caused by an increasing number of persons in the immediate vicinity of the victim.

When testing social-psychological theory, contrary evidence that is not a result of measurement or other systematic experimental error requires that the initial theory be revised. On the basis of these experimental findings, Aronson (1976) has proposed that diffusion of responsibility works *except when:* (1) witnesses share a common fate with the victim; or (2) witnesses are caught in a face-to-face situation with the victim that they cannot escape. The first exception implies that we will help others with whom we identify even when there are others present with whom we could theoretically share the responsibility for action. The second implies that when we are in an enclosed environment, such as on a subway train, where we must either go to the aid of the victim or stand there and stare at him or her for the duration of the journey, we are more likely to help. In summary, although the diffusion concept helps us to understand helping and nonhelping behavior, there are other factors that must be considered as well.

Blaming the Victim or Believing the World Is Just

There is growing empirical evidence that a significant percentage of us tend to believe that if someone is victimized he or she must be responsible for what has happened. For example, rape victims are often hesitant to report the crime because of the widely reported experiences of some women that indicate that the ordeal of pressing charges may be more traumatic than the rape itself. Although admissible evidence laws are changing, it used to be that the victims' past was carefully scrutinized ("Is there any evidence of past immoral activity?"), and their behavior prior to the act was closely examined (Why were they alone in such a place? Why were they wearing "suggestive" clothing if they weren't looking for trouble anyway?). Following the television film "Cry Rape," the number of rapes reported to the police actually decreased, apparently because many victims feared that they would be blamed for what happened to them as was the victim in the film. Following the assassination of Martin Luther King, almost a third of the respondents in a representative sample of Americans expressed the belief that King had "brought it on himself" (Rokeach, 1970).

This tendency to blame the victim would often account for the failure to aid someone in a time of need. Lerner (1965, 1966, 1970) has proposed that the tendency to blame the victim for his or her troubles results from a need to see the world as just. According to this view, there is a "fit" between what people do and what happens to them. Thus, if two people work equally hard on some task but one of the two, by a flip of the coin, receives a large reward and the other receives nothing, observers of this outcome are likely to express the belief that the one who was rewarded actually worked harder. To believe otherwise would be to believe that the world is fickle and capricious and that there is no real justice.

This prevalent tendency to blame the victim because of the need to view the world as just often takes some strange twists. For example, newspaper accounts indicate that David Berkowitz, the confessed "Son of Sam" killer in New York who brutally gunned down several victims, receives a huge volume of mail and gifts. Many of the letters suggest that the victims were probably all "whores" who richly deserved what Berkowitz did to them. James Michener (1971) reports that following the shooting of students by National Guardsmen at Kent State University, rumors quickly spread through the community that the two women killed were pregnant, that the bodies of all four were covered with lice, and that they were all so inflicted with syphillis that they soon would have been dead anyway. Thus, the world remains just, and the fate of the victims was clearly deserved.

Other Personal and Situational Factors and Helping Behavior

The early work on bystander intervention has led to a large number of studies concerned with the more general problem of helping behavior. Many of these studies have dealt with the types of personal and situational characteristics that are most likely to contribute to or impede helping other people in times of need. These studies make it quite clear that there are a large number of variables that can be important in influencing an individual's decision to aid or ignore a person in need. We will discuss briefly the findings of several of these studies in identifying some of the more important individual and situational variables that influence helping behavior.

PERSONAL CHARACTERISTICS AND HELPING BEHAVIOR

What types of individuals are most likely to come to the aid of someone in distress? Suppose you have automobile trouble and are sitting beside the road waiting for help. Who is most likely to stop and offer aid? We should be immediately aware that the answer to this question depends upon a number of factors, and that many of these factors interact with each other. For example, if you happen to be a nicely dressed young woman, the probability of someone stopping to offer aid as well as the characteristics of the person will likely differ somewhat than if you are an older woman, a man, or someone who looks slovenly or eccentric.

Our discussion on the diffusion of responsibility suggests that the probability of someone stopping to offer help will in part be a function of the number of persons who are available to offer aid. Several other individual variables have also been identified as important.

Perceptions of Consequences and Personal Responsibility An interesting series of studies has been conducted by Schwartz (1968a, 1968b, 1970, 1977) that has direct relevance to the question of helping behavior. Much of Schwartz's work evolved out of an interest in understanding why or why

Characteristics of the participants are often important in understanding helping behavior. In this 1943 photo, a New Guinea tribesman aids a blinded Australian soldier. *Source:* George Silk, Life Magazine © 1943 Time Inc.

not human behavior could be predicted from the study of verbal attitudes (see chapter 7). According to Schwartz, in order for an attitude or norm to influence behavior, that attitude or norm must be activated and perceived as relevant to the action situation. Behavior may be inconsistent with a norm simply because the norm has not been activated or made relevant for the individual in the particular situation at hand.

Schwartz is specifically concerned with what he calls moral norms or those norms that are applied to actions that have consequences for the welfare of others. A norm suggesting that I have some responsibility to come to your aid if you are in serious distress, then, would be considered a moral norm. According to Schwartz, "The necessary conditions for the activation of moral norms . . . are: (a) the person must have some awareness that his potential acts may have consequences for the welfare of others, and (b) he must ascribe some degree of responsibility for these acts and their consequences to himself" (1968b, p. 233). The first of these factors is labeled "awareness of consequences" or AC, and the second is referred to as "ascription of responsibility" or AR. AC, as a personal orientation, refers to a disposition on the part of the individual to become aware of the potential consequences of his or her acts for the welfare of others. Some persons, in other words, exhibit greater levels of empathy or understanding of the problems of others and are willing to recognize the consequences that will befall such others unless some action is taken. AR refers to the willingness on the part of the individual to personally assume responsibility for the consequences that are likely to follow from his actions. ("If I fail to aid the person in distress, then I am at least partially responsible for whatever negative consequences that person suffers.")

Schwartz measures subject AC through the use of projective tests in which the subject describes the "thoughts and feelings that might run through the minds of people facing a series of decisions with interpersonal consequences" (1968b, p. 236). AR is measured by reactions to such items as the following:

> You can't blame basically good people who are forced by their environment to be inconsiderate of others.
>
> Being very upset or preoccupied does not excuse a person for doing anything he would ordinarily avoid.
>
> If a person is nasty to me, I feel very little responsibility to treat him well (1968b p. 235).

Schwartz argues, "It is only when there is both awareness of interpersonal consequences and acceptance of responsibility for them that norms governing these consequences are likely to be experienced as applicable and to influence behavior, except insofar as other pressures supporting them are brought to bear (e.g., they are invoked by someone else in the situation)" (1968b, p. 234). Overall, Schwartz' data have been highly supportive of his hypotheses. Subjects have been more willing to volunteer to engage in actions that will benefit others when they have been made aware of the consequences of their decision and when they have been willing to assume some personal responsibility for those consequences.

Personal Skill to Aid the Victim Other personal characteristics have been studied or intuitively seem to be possible candidates as explanations of altrustic behavior. For example, skill may be a key determinant of who stops to help someone in distress. If one does not know the difference between a tire jack and a carburetor, stopping to aid a motorist with engine trouble may be an exercise in futility. Thus, the thinking that someone else will come along who can truly offer meaningful help is probably more than a mere rationalization in many instances. Similarly, many people feel that it would do no good for them to go to the aid of accident victims because they know nothing about first aid, and they tell themselves they will stop at the next town and call an ambulance. It may be difficult to distinguish between rational action and rationalization in such situations; nevertheless, if the individual defines the situation as one in which he or she could be of little help anyway, he or she is quite unlikely to get involved.

The difficulty here, of course, is that helping behavior becomes situation-specific—those with mechanical skills are more likely to help people with stalled cars, those with medical skills are more likely to help accident victims, and so on. The question remains, however, if there are some types of people who are more likely to stop and help *across* situations. More than once, the authors have been stuck with car troubles, and others have stopped who knew even less about the car. Skill, therefore, may be a contributing factor but probably does not account for a great deal of the variance in helping behavior.

Benefactor/Victim Similarity Emswiller, Deaux, and Willits (1971) have found that the more similar in appearance the person needing help is to the possible benefactor, the more likely the possible benefactor is to offer the needed aid. This finding was replicated more recently by West, Whitney, and Schnedler (1975), who found that black victims were helped faster in black neighborhoods, and white victims were helped faster in white neighborhoods. This would suggest that minority-group members are more likely to help others of their groups, the middle class are more likely to aid the middle class, and so on. Although this may be true in some instances (for example, campers are more likely to help other campers in distress, and C.B. owners to help other C.B. owners), the degree to which such observations would hold overall must still be subjected to additional empirical test.

Further evidence that victim/benefactor similarity is not the only key can be found in numerous studies that have observed that female victims receive nearly twice as much help as males (Howard and Crano, 1974). Young, attractive women appear to be more likely than any other group to benefit from a willingness to go to the help of someone in need (Pomazal and Clore, 1973). However, Kitty Genovese was young and attractive; other factors are involved.

SITUATIONAL DETERMINANTS OF HELPING BEHAVIOR

As already noted, one of the most important situational determinants of helping behavior is the number of others present in the helping situation. If there are others present so that there is a diffusion of responsibility, each person is less likely to get involved. A crowd also offers anonymity. If you do not help, no one is likely to notice, and besides, someone else will take care of the problem who is more qualified or less busy than you are anyway.

Modeling and Helping Behavior Other people present in a situation frequently act as models for the behavior of the individual. Thus, the presence of a passive bystander tends to inhibit attempts by another to rescue an accident victim (Latane and Rodin, 1969), a generous model increases the frequency that others will themselves make charitable contributions (Bryan and Test, 1967), and so on. Gross summarizes several possible explanations for this imitative effect in helping behavior: "(1) the model may define what is possible, right, permissible, or normative especially in ambiguous or unusual circumstances. (2) Positive or neutral consequences experienced by the model may reduce restraints against helping in an observer. (3) The model may simply call attention to a situation where helping is already a strongly prescribed behavior. In the last case the behavior of the model may be irrelevant as long as the observer is confronted with a helping possibility that he himself feels is appropriate" (1975, p. 45). Gross found that generous models and models engaging in behaviors that the possible benefactor could define as legitimate were more likely to trigger helping behavior in subjects than were models having the opposite characteristics.

Perceived Need for Help Other studies have found that *dependence* of the recipient on the prospective benefactor is important in determining helping behavior (Berkowitz and Daniels, 1963). Perceived *seriousness* and *legitimacy* of need are closely related to this (West and Brown, 1975). For example, if a collapsed victim is defined as ill, he or she is more likely to be assisted than if defined as drunk.

Confirmation for the importance of an awareness of need for help is found in research by Clark and Word (1972). Using an experiment that was similar to Latane and Rodin's "lady in distress" study, these researchers found that when the situation was unambiguous—that is, when it was obvious that the victim really did need help—all subjects intervened even in the presence of a passive confederate. However, when the staged emergency was more ambiguous, the percentage of subjects who went to the aid of the victim was much smaller.

Several of the neighbors of Kitty Genovese who observed her plight from the safety of their apartments rationalized their failure to aid her by saying that they thought it was simply a lover's quarrel and that they had no business to intervene. At any rate, it is quite obvious that we will not go to the aid of someone in distress unless we truly define the situation as one of need.

Urban and Nonurban Settings Numerous social thinkers in the past have lamented the demise of rural, agrarian, primary communities and their replacement by the complex, heterogeneous, and impersonalized urban society of today. The German sociologist Ferdinand Tönnies (1887) contrasted what he called *gemeinschaft* and *gesellschaft* relationships. In the gemeinschaft society, relationships tend to be personal and informal. Behavior is governed by traditions and folkways that are handed down from the past. Most of the individual's daily encounters occur in primary groups or in groups in which he or she is known, understood, and cared about.

Gesellschaft societies are characterized by relationships that are impersonal, utilitarian, and more formal or contractural in nature. Many of the individual's daily actions occur in the context of secondary groups in which one interacts more with the role than with the individual actor who happens to occupy the role. Rather than sharing common interests, traditions, and values, the gesellschaft society is composed of an aggregation of largely anonymous individuals whose ties to each other are largely utilitarian instead of personal.

According to this perspective, the inhumanity noted in several of our examples is largely a function of the fact that contemporary urban societies are becoming more and more gesellschaft in their nature. As we experience a breakdown in our traditional small community and primary-group ties, we become more unknowing and uncaring about the needs of others.

We have already noted that not all instances of nonhelping behavior occur in urban settings, but there seems to be a preponderance of those that do. More recently, there has developed an increasing amount of experimental evidence indicating that rural societies tend to retain more of the characteristics of gemeinschaft society than do urban societies and that "victims" are significantly more likely to be assisted in rural than in urban settings.

Korte and Kerr (1975), for example, tested what they refer to as the "urban incivility" hypothesis, which states that "interaction between strangers is less civil, helpful, and cooperative in urban environments than in nonurban environments." This hypothesis was tested by collecting data in Boston and in several small towns in eastern Massachusetts. A number of situations were created that involved such things as requests for assistance by wrong-number telephone callers, overpayments to store clerks, and "lost" postcards. They found that for each of their dependent measures, the likelihood of receiving help from strangers was greater in the nonurban setting than in the city.

In a study of "good Samaritanism" in rural and urban settings, McKenna

(1976) found that rural residents were much more likely to assist a stranded female motorist than were urban dwellers. McKenna cautions that urban subjects may have been less willing to help because, "hardened by a cynical but healthy mistrust of others," they were more likely to doubt the legitimacy of the request for help. No empirical evidence to support this alternative explanation of his findings was found, however.

Not all experimental results are consistent with the hypothesis that helping behavior is less likely to occur in urban settings. Lesk and Zippel (1975) found that helping behavior obtained in a large urban area matched that for smaller communities, casting doubt, in their minds, on the idea that people in large cities are more heartless than those in smaller ones. Korte, Ypma, and Toppen (1975), in a study of helpfulness in Dutch society, found no difference between cities and towns nor between four different neighborhoods in Amsterdam that had different stereotypes of friendliness.

It should be noted that the dependent variables and the research designs employed varied rather significantly in these different studies. Therefore, it is probably safe to conclude that all the evidence is not yet in on the question of the importance of urban versus rural settings in helping behavior. Many social philosophers have exhibited an anti-urban bias in decrying the vices of industrialized societies in contrast to the virtues of more traditional, rural, folk communities. Perhaps some social-psychological researchers have exhibited these same biases. However, additional research must be done before this question can be finally resolved.

Other Factors Several other variables have been found to influence the probability of the occurrence of helping behavior. We have already noted that attractive, young women are perhaps more likely than any other group to receive offers of aid during times of need. The attractiveness of the person needing help seems to be an even more general concept, however, in assessing helping behavior. For example, Gross, Wallston, and Piliavin (1975) varied the attractiveness of an experimental assistant by having her respond in a very cordial and supportive fashion to the subject or by having her respond with considerable irritation and curtness. When asked later by someone else to do a favor for the assistant, the subjects were almost twice as likely to respond to the request for help for the pleasant as for the unpleasant assistant.

Nelson and Dynes (1976) have found that church attendance is a good predictor of altruistic behavior. However, the primary effect of church attendance on *emergency* helping behavior was found to be largely through the church's provision of organizational means for participation. In other words, the church provides the individual with the opportunity to make a contribution or to otherwise engage in helping behavior. Those who do not attend church do not have this organizational encouragement to contribute provided to them.

Helping Behavior as a Decision-Making Process

On the basis of the evidence we have been able to present to this point, it is quite clear that we are dealing with an extremely complex phenomenon. All the factors reviewed above, as well as others, appear to be of some importance in our understanding of altruistic and egoistic behavior. The number of variables found to be important indicates the complexity of the problem. It still remains for some future social psychologist to pull together these various empirical findings into a comprehensive theory that will allow us to explain with greater confidence this fascinating and important area of social behavior. Let us summarize by noting that we are probably dealing with a rather complex decision-making process. In fact, Latane and Darley (1976, pp. 3–4) have concluded that intervention in an emergency involves not just one but a whole series of decisions.

1. First, the bystander must recognize that something is happening and that this event can be defined as an emergency, or at least as a situation of need, in which someone could benefit from the assistance of someone else. If a situation is not defined as an emergency, we could obviously not expect the individual to respond as if it were.

2. Once the bystander has recognized that an emergency situation exists, he or she must next make some decision regarding whether or not to intervene. It is at this level that many of the variables that we have discussed in this chapter come into play. For example, in making this decision the actor is probably going to give some consideration to the potential costs and rewards that would be associated with intervention. How much time would it take? Do I have the necessary skills to make a useful contribution, or would it simply be an exercise in futility? What are the characteristics of the victim? Is he or she like me in some important way? Are there others present who will probably intervene? What is my personal responsibility for action? All these factors and more will probably be considered (although they certainly need not all be considered in each individual case) before the final decision to go or not to go to the aid of the victim is made.

3. If the bystander has decided that he or she does have some responsibility to respond to the emergency situation, that the costs of inaction would be higher than the costs of action, and that the responsibility cannot be diffused to others, he or she must then decide upon the form of assistance that will be offered. For example, should one offer personal aid or rush off to find someone more qualified to respond to the needs of the victim? This decision is probably not nearly as critical as that of whether to intervene or not, but it can still have rather important consequences for the victim.

4. Finally, Latane and Darley proposed that a decision must be made regarding how to implement the course of action decided upon. What type of assistance is most needed? Where is the nearest doctor?

Each of these decisions carries important implications for the bystander as well as for the victim. Latane and Darley note that the rewards and costs for action or inaction are often biased in favor of the latter. "All the bystander has to gain . . . is a feeling of pride and the chance of being a hero. On the other hand, he can be made to appear as a fool, he can be sued, or he can even be attacked and wounded" (1976, p. 4). This weighting, no doubt, contributes to the frequency of the occurrence of egoistic incidents. It increases the probability that egoism will win out over altruism.

Effects of Helping Behavior on Recipients

Although extensive research has been conducted on factors that affect helping behavior, much less has been done on the reaction of the recipient to the aid received. Popular wisdom has suggested for years that aid can often have negative consequences for the recipient. For example, he or she may become "dependent" upon others and less able to provide for his or her own needs; self-esteem may suffer because he or she must rely on handouts from others; and so on. All have been used as arguments against public and private welfare programs.

In looking at effects of aid on recipient self-concept, Nadler, Fisher, and Streufert have recently suggested that "situational conditions determine whether aid conveys a predominantely supportive message (e.g., elements of caring and concern) which leads to favorable self-perceptions, or a predominately threatening message (e.g., elements of inferiority and dependency) which leads to negative self-perceptions" (1976, p. 392).

Additional recent research by these authors suggests that receiving aid from a donor who is similar to oneself is often a threatening experience. However, receipt of aid from someone different from oneself is less threatening. Certainly, when one's life or person are threatened by an assailant, the status or similarity of a potential helper is probably quite irrelevant. However, in situations that are less critical, it can apparently be quite important. In other words, aid that provides the recipient an opportunity to overcome stress without threatening feelings of self-esteem is likely to be positively received, but aid that emphasizes the failure and relative inferiority of the recipient will probably be received less favorably and will result in more negative consequences.

As noted by Fisher and Nadler (1974), because numerous public and private agencies in the United States and elsewhere are engaged in handing out billions of dollars annually to various welfare programs, it is somewhat surprising that more research has not been devoted to the study of the consequences of such programs. Additional research in this area is needed before we will be able to identify fully the consequences of aid for those who receive it.

The Modern "Good Samaritan"

We have now discussed a rather extensive body of research on helping behavior. In conclusion, let us come back to the issue of the Good Samaritan who is willing to suffer potential personal loss, including injury and death, in order to help the victim in distress. The efforts of the Good Samaritan in the parable clearly were made to help the sufferer because one should be willing to suffer personal inconvenience in order to assist someone in need of help, whoever that other person happens to be. However, recent research by Huston, Geis, and Wright (1976) suggests that the motivation of some modern "Good Samaritans" may be quite different.

In 1965, the State of California enacted a Good Samaritan law that is designed to compensate private citizens for injuries they receive while attempting to prevent a crime, capture a criminal, or go to the aid of someone in an emergency situation. Huston, Geis, and Wright noted that by January 1976 the California State Board of Control had awarded money to seventy-one Good Samaritans. Extensive interviews were conducted with as many of these individuals as could be located in an effort to learn more about what motivates willingness to become involved in the plight of others. None of the Good Samaritans had been aware of the California law prior to their action, so the existence of the law as an "insurance policy" must be ruled out as a motivator.

The overall picture is an interesting one. The authors state, "Our impression now, after interviewing half the group, is that most of the Samaritans are risk-takers, men on familiar and rather amiable terms with violence. . . . We have been struck by the number of Samaritans who verbally put down anyone else who tried to help during the incident in which they were injured. They usually see themselves as preeminently qualified to provide assistance, and appear jealous when others invade the limelight" (1976, p. 64).

In other words, the picture of what motivated this group of individuals to get involved appears to have little to do with the *victim*. "We . . . sense that the Samaritan's prime motive for intervention is often anger against the criminal rather than concern for the victim. Many Samaritans seem unsympathetic toward the victims, maintaining that they brought the trouble on themselves through stupidity. They seem to see their intervention as a *contest* between them and the criminal, with the victim almost a side issue—the occasion rather than the reason for action" (Huston, Geis, and Wright, 1976, p. 64).

What a contrast this creates. Remember that in the parable, the two primary actors are the Samaritan and the victim. If the preliminary data collected by Huston, Geis, and Wright are substantiated, the contemporary version of the event would be rather different. Upon finding the wounded and bleeding victim by the roadside, the Samaritan would immediately run

off in hot pursuit of the robbers, leaving the victim to perhaps suffer and die unless someone else should come to his aid.

This type of contemporary "Good Samaritan" was depicted by Charles Bronson in the movie "Death Wish." The "hero," after his wife was killed and his daughter raped by muggers, spends all his time looking for similar instances of crime, *not* so that he can aid the innocent victim but so he can pit his own skills of violence against those engaging in the crimes.

We would anticipate that "altruism" of this nature is probably rather atypical overall although we have no empirical evidence at this time to support the contention. In fact, Huston, Geis, and Wright's data may apply only to individuals who go to the aid of victims of violence or who, in giving aid, make themselves vulnerable to a violent counterattack. Nevertheless, their observations are provocative and call for additional research.

Summary

Egoism can be defined as self-centered behavior or behavior engaged in out of concern for self-interests rather than for the interests of others. *Altruism* is defined as the unselfish concern for the welfare of others. Despite the numerous cases of altruism and helping behavior that we could cite, greater attention has been paid in recent years to egoistic incidents. Attempts to account for egoistic and altruistic behavior relate rather directly to the long-standing debate regarding basic human nature. Psychological hedonism, a concept that goes back to early Greek thinkers, is clearly an egoistic theory of human nature and assumes that we act in ways that are designed

The movie "Death Wish" involved a character depicted by some as the modern Good Samaritan. *Source:* Culver Pictures, Inc.

to maximize the attainment of pleasure and the avoidance of pain. Such a theory virtually eliminates the existence of altruistic behavior because it assumes that even actions designed to help others are, at base, self-centered and selfish. That is, we help others only when it would be more costly not to do so.

A second view of human nature argues that altruism is genetic. From this perspective, actions that curtail the opportunity for personal survival in favor of group well-being are attributable to the existence of an inherited "altruistic gene." Evidence in support of such a contention is, at best, unimpressive. In fact, this theory can be seen as a step backward several decades to the time when some social psychologists attempted to attribute all human behavior patterns to biological instincts.

It can be argued that aiding someone in need is normative behavior in the sense that it entails conformity to a social norm of reciprocity. This proposes that we have an obligation to help those who help us. Social-exchange theory proposes that all social behavior involves an exchange of material or nonmaterial goods. Satisfaction with an exchange is usually determined by a consideration of the costs and rewards that are present in that exchange. A decision to aid someone in need may be a function of a weighing of the rewards to be received from such action and the costs to be incurred. Among the other explanations that have been advanced, that of the *diffusion of responsibility* has been one of the most popular. This theory proposes that the key in accounting for intervention or nonintervention in a time of need is the number of other witnesses that observe the event because the responsibility to help is spread across those present.

Although an impressive amount of empirical evidence has accumulated in support of the importance of diffusion of responsibility, a number of other situational and personality factors have also been identified as crucial to our understanding of the problem. Among these are: (1) an awareness of the consequences of not helping and a willingness to assume personal responsibility for those consequences; (2) personal skill of the potential benefactor to really be able to provide meaningful assistance to the victim; (3) the similarity of the victim to the benefactor; (4) the behavior of models; (5) the perceived legitimacy of the need for help; and (6) whether the setting is rural or urban.

Recent research has begun to concentrate on the effects of helping behavior on the victim. The person who is severely threatened probably is not concerned with who helps or why, but in less critical situations, the receipt of aid apparently can effect the self-esteem of the recipient. Additional research in this area is needed, however.

Finally, some recent evidence has shown that the contemporary Good Samaritan is less concerned with the victim than he or she is angry with the criminal. In fact, the victim often becomes little more than the occasion rather than the reason for intervention.

Much of the research in this important area of human behavior is rather recent. As additional data are accumulated, some of the findings and observations of this chapter may require further clarification and interpretation. The one conclusion that seems clear is that this is an extremely complex issue, and if we expect simple explanations or single variables to account for all of the observations obtained, we are certain to be disappointed.

aggression
and
violence

In August 1973, Elmer Wayne Henly, Jr., led police to mass graves containing the bodies of twenty-seven teenage boys. He confessed to one of the largest and perhaps the most grisly mass murder in modern American history. The confession revealed shocking details of how he had conducted homosexual orgies, brutal torture, and cold-blooded murder.

During the 1975 Christmas holidays, a bomb planted at New York City's La Guardia Airport exploded and killed eleven people and wounded fifty-one others. The bomb was set to go off during the time of heaviest traffic and in the busiest part of the airport to insure maximum injury. The blast hurled pieces of metal and glass that cut through the crowd, virtually shredding some of the victims; witnesses reported that a woman's severed head came to rest on a ledge. A young Marine lost one foot in the blast and the other by amputation at the hospital. The reason behind this slaughter is not known, and a perpetrator has not been apprehended.

In the summer of 1976 in Northern California, twenty-six children and their schoolbus driver were kidnapped, locked in a large truck, and buried six feet underground. Even though food and water were available, the victims faced the real possibility of suffocation. Tragedy was averted by the quick action of the driver and some of the older boys who climbed on piled-up mattresses and pushed away the heavy steel plate covering the entrance.

In the 1960s, urban disturbances, such as the riots in Detroit, Watts, and Newark, inflicted over eight thousand casualties and two hundred deaths. In the 1970s, similar civil disturbances have occurred in northern cities over the issue of school integration.

Successful and attempted political assassinations during the past two decades have shocked the nation. President John F. Kennedy, Martin Luther King, Senator Robert Kennedy, and presidential candidate George Wallace have all been shot. Two assassination attempts were made on President Gerald Ford during the brief time he served in office.

Spiraling crime rates, especially for personal injuries, testify to the increasing level of violence in American society. Movie and television screens are filled with assault, rape, torture, and homicide. Violence in the opinion of many has risen in athletic contests and among spectators at all levels from elementary school to professional sports. Many teams have "enforcers" who are quick to use their fists to intimidate members of other teams.

These widely publicized examples of violence in U.S. society raise questions concerning why individuals and groups commit such actions. Political leaders have attempted to find answers to these questions by creating several national commissions to explore why violence has been increasing and to suggest strategies to alleviate the problem. The National Advisory Commission on Civil Disorders was appointed in 1968 to assess the reasons for the urban civil-rights riots of the 1960s. The President's National Commission on the Causes and Prevention of Violence was organized in 1969 to study why the occurrence of violence in U.S. society had increased so dramatically. Congress requested in 1969 that the Department of Health, Education and Welfare study the effect of television violence on the attitudes and behavior of children, and, in response, the Surgeon General's Scientific Advisory Committee on Television and Social Behavior was created. An overview of the findings of this committee reported that "the most striking impression left by the studies in this volume is of the intractability of violence in commercial television entertainment in the United States. . . . Violence is a staple of all mass media . . ." (p. 25). The President's Commission on Campus Unrest (1970) examined the student protest associated with the civil-rights movement and the anti-war movement and concluded that a "nation driven to using weapons of war upon its youth is a nation on the edge of chaos."

Social psychologists working as individual scientists and as members of various commissions have developed theories of why people and/or groups engage in aggressive behavior and have attempted to test them. The first step in generating and testing theories of aggression is to define it. We will review several popular definitions of aggression and then discuss the major theories.

Definition of *Aggression*

A difficult and important problem faced by the commissions and social scientists who have attempted to explain violence is defining *aggression* logically yet in a way that can be empirically studied. Everyone has a common-sense notion that aggression involves one person injuring another. Some social scientists have accepted a simplified definition of *aggression* that focuses only on the act itself. For example, Buss (1961, P. 3) defines *aggression* as "a response that delivers noxious stimuli to another organism."

Other scientists contend that not only the act of hurting someone but also the intent of the person behaving is important. Berkowitz (1975, p. 215) provides an example of this type of definition, as he defines *aggression* as "the intentional injury of another." According to this definition, aggression is behavior that not only injures another but also is intended to do so. In the case of Claudine Longet and the shooting of Vladimir "spider" Sabich, she admitted holding the gun and squeezing the trigger that fired the bullet into Spider Sabich's body, killing him, but the courts and the general public wanted to know if she *intended* to harm him or if the shooting was accidental. Including intention creates a rather different definition.

There is an enormous difference between an injury resulting from an accident and an injury intentionally inflicted upon another person. The difference between an accidental shooting and a deliberate shooting is manifest in the different punishments associated with manslaughter (accidental) and homicide (intentional). The obvious problem of including intent in a definition of *aggression* is that it is extremely difficult to ascertain. In the trial of Longet, the jury had a stormy time trying to decide whether she had intended to shoot Sabich. They eventually convicted her of negligent homicide, meaning that the jury concluded that she did not intend to shoot him but that she was negligent and careless in how she handled the gun.

All definitions of *aggression* stress the injury—social, psychological, or physical—of one person or group by another person or group. In some theories of aggression, intent is irrelevant; in others, it is of central concern. As the theories are outlined, the role of intent in explaining aggressive behavior will be discussed.

Biological Explanations of Aggression

INSTINCT THEORIES

Although there are many different definitions of *instinctual behavior,* most contain the idea that an instinct is an inherited readiness to detect and react to certain objects in the environment, if these objects make their appearance at the appropriate time (McDougall, 1923; Thorpe, 1956; Lorenz, 1958). William McDougall, a pioneer in instinct theory, conceptualized an instinct as an inborn, unlearned principle of action that is expressed as an *idea,* a *felt urge,* and an *emotional state.* For example, the aggression instinct involves an idea of a violent act, the urge to aggress, and the emotional excitement of anger. The importance of learning in determining the specific manifestation of an instinct is acknowledged by most instinct theories. The influence of learning on the expression of an aggression instinct is illustrated by the various means used in different societies to act out aggressive impulses. For example, in some societies athletic contests are utilized to express the aggression instinct, but in others warfare or defiance of authority give it expression.

Intentions are of little interest to instinct theories because, although the intent to hurt someone is assumed to be present, it is irrelevant in explaining why the behavior occurred. According to this theory, the purpose of such aggression is to reduce the psychological tension created in the individual by the aggression instinct.

PSYCHOANALYTIC THEORY

Psychoanalytic theory as originally developed by Sigmund Freud (1924, 1959) is one of the earliest theories of an aggressive instinct. Freud contended that the personality is powered by psychic energy derived from instincts. Freud never identified how many human instincts there are but did argue that they all belonged in two categories: life instincts and death instincts. The life instincts of survival, hunger, thirst, and sex were critical to Freud's theory of human behavior and were discussed at great length, but he said little about the death instincts other than that they eventually succeed. Freud felt that the life and death instincts are continually struggling against each other's expression. A person engages in an aggressive behavior toward others because his or her death instinct is blocked, and by attacking others he or she reduces the internal tension striving for his or her own death. Freud's career ended before he had an opportunity to fully develop the theory of instinctive aggression, but other psychoanalytic theorists have built upon his ideas and have created elaborate aggression instinct theories (Freud, 1949; Hartmann, Kris, and Loewenstein, 1949).

ETHOLOGICAL THEORIES

Ethology, often referred to as behavioral biology, is the scientific study of animal behavior. Several leading ethologists have gathered support for instinctual aggression in animals and then generalized this to humans. They argue that because most species of animals have a killer instinct and because humans are animals, they, too, must have a similar instinct. Konrad Lorenz, who received a Nobel Prize in 1973 for his work in behavioral biology, presented an articulate statement of the human aggression instinct in his book, *On Aggression,* which has had considerable impact on the general public. Other books by ethologists that posit an aggression instinct are *African Genesis, Territorial Imperative,* and *The Social Contract,* by Robert Ardrey; *Adventures with the Missing Link,* by Raymond Dart; *The Naked Ape* and *Human Zoo,* by Desmond Morris; and *Human Aggression* and *Human Destructiveness,* by Anthony Storr.

Lorenz reports that he was originally very critical of Freud's theory of an aggressive instinct but that when he treated it as a working hypothesis he "came to understand much in Sigmund Freud's theory that he had previously rejected as too audacious" (1966, p. x). Based on observations of the fighting behavior of different species of animals, Lorenz modified Freud's theory by shifting aggression from the death instinct and making it a part of the life instinct. Lorenz argues that, although at times aggression instincts may appear destructive, in the long run they are functional to the survival of the species, and he identifies the positive functions of fighting between members of the same species and between members of different species. According to Lorenz, the most important function of intraspecies fighting is that it tends to spread the members of the species over the available habitat. This spatial distribution helps to prevent exhaustion of food resources. It is suggested that this is one reason for the human tendency to settle new lands, which has made available more of the earth's natural resources. A second function of intraspecies fighting is that it facilitates mating between the strongest and/or most cunning members of the group, which strengthens the genetic traits of the species. Finally, Lorenz contends that intraspecies duels train an aggressive family defender to be capable of protecting the young.

According to Lorenz, animals who are equipped with claws and canine teeth that enable them to kill quickly have evolved inhibitions against indiscriminate injuring and killing. Ritualistic fighting that inflicts little injury has replaced actual combat and includes appeasement gestures, which are per-

Aggression between animals of two different species. *Source:* John Dominis, Life Magazine © 1965 Time, Inc.

formed by the "defeated" animal to terminate the aggression of the victor. For most of our history, people have not possessed a quick means of killing, and thus we have not developed the inhibitions against aggression. Lorenz feels that the aggression instinct was extremely functional to people until we developed weapons, giving us the ability to kill easily. At this point, the aggression instinct became "exaggerated, grotesque, and inexpedient" because we have not developed inhibitions to control it.

Lorenz argues that the knowledge that the aggression is caused by an instinct should enable society to realize its potential danger to people, and that failure to recognize instinct as the real cause renders ineffective most attempts to reduce it. He suggests that acceptance in American society of the idea that children would grow up less aggressive if they were spared all disappointments (frustration) and indulged in every way is an example of a futile attempt to reduce aggression because of ignorance of its origin. The results were the "countless, unbearably rude children who were anything but nonaggressive" (Lorenz, 1966, P. 50). He does not advocate accepting aggression as inevitable but rather feels once the aggression instinct is recognized society can identify the ways of discharging it in nondestructive ways. He is optimistic that the aggression drive can be channeled into activities functional to our survival.

Surprisingly, the theory of innate human aggression has been uncritically accepted by many scholars and laymen and has frequently been presented to the public as scientific truth. Figure 11–1 is an advertisement for a four-hour television special about the killer instinct based on the work of Lorenz, Ardrey, and other ethologists. This and similar materials have contributed to the belief that people are by nature brutal and aggressive.

The killer theme has also been disseminated by novelists and dramatists. The novel, *A Clockwork Orange,* by Anthony Burgess was produced as a violent movie by Stanley Kubrick. Advertisements for the movie intimated the rape, sexual sadism, and violence contained in the movie. Kubrick, who acknowledged being influenced by Ardrey, portrayed people as ignoble, savage, irrational, and brutal (Montague, 1976, p. 29). Malcolm McDowell, the star of the movie, agreed with Kubrick and stated in a letter to the *New York Times* that "people are basically bad, corrupt. I always sense that man has not progressed one inch, morally, since the Greeks" (Burke, 1972, p. D13).

Novels, movies, and television have all contributed to the acceptance of the belief that people are aggressive by nature when such a belief has very little basis in fact. Unfortunately, acceptance by many of the theory of innate aggressiveness has been used as justification of people's inhumanity to other people and has directed attention away from seeking other causes of aggression.

The convincing rhetoric of Lorenz, Ardrey, and other innate aggressionists cannot hide the serious flaws in their logic and the failure of empirical observation to verify the theory. The universal fighting and territorial nature reported by ethologists has been challenged by the observation of several species of animals who are not aggressive. If species such as the gorilla are exceptions to the aggression instinct, there is little logic in generalizing the trait to people.

The most persuasive criticism of the instinct theory of aggression is set

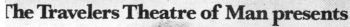

The Travelers Theatre of Man presents

"Primal Man: The Killer Instinct"

Tonight, this first of four specials titled "Primal Man" explores
the origins of aggression and what it is that provokes us to violence.
A David L. Wolper Production. Sponsored by The Travelers
Insurance Companies and their agents and brokers everywhere.

ABC Special 6:30PM 8

Figure 11–1 This television special is an example of the popularization of theories of innate instinctual aggression. (Source: *Daigon* 1975, p. 14.)

forth by Ashley Montague in *The Nature of Human Aggression* (1976). Montague carefully examines the evidence collected by several scientific disciplines and point by point refutes the arguments for innate aggression. He
notes that there are a number of societies, such as the Tasady of Mindanao,
the Ifaluk of the Pacific, the Pygmies of the Ituri Forest, and the Semang of
Malay, that display little or no aggression (1976, p. 317). Montague concludes:

> The writings of the innate aggressionists leave one with the impression that
> man is little more than a mechanism driven by innate instincts ineradicably
> inherited from ancestral "killer" apes. It is a dreary picture they have painted,
> and were it true the future of the species would, indeed, be dark and unpro-
> mising. In the preceding pages I have endeavored to examine the views of
> these writers in the light of the scientific evidence, and I hope I have suc-
> ceeded in showing that on every one of the fundamental claims they have

made concerning man's allegedly instinctive aggressive drives they are
demonstratively wrong (1976, p. 300).

The theories that we engage in aggressive behavior because of an innate
instinct have not been supported by scientific evidence. Thus, the search for
explanations of why people sometimes injure each other that will allow the
prediction and control of such behavior focuses on other reasons.

HORMONE THEORIES

Two types of hormones that have been found to increase aggression in
humans are adrenalin and sexual hormones. The ability of adrenalin to
assist the body to accomplish greater feats of strength and speed in tense
or threatening situations is well-documented. In controlled laboratory studies, when adrenalin was injected into human subjects who were then exposed to an anger-producing situation, they were significantly more hostile
than subjects injected with salt water (Schachter and Latane, 1964).

The effect on aggressive behavior of reducing male sexual hormones is
well-known as for centuries castration has been utilized to help make male
animals gentle. After castration, wild stallions are more gentle, savage bulls
become docile steers, and aggressive dogs become passive house pets. Experiments with animals reveal that fighting behavior can be greatly reduced
by castration and then reinstated by injecting male hormones into the
bloodstream of the animal (Beeman, 1947).

Therapeutic castration of human subjects has been reported to produce
a reduction of aggressive behavior. Le Maire (1956) indicates that in Den-
mark therapeutic castration of convicted criminals, primarily sexual offenders, has led to a "general pacification" and a relatively low occurrence of
violent sexual crimes after release. The impact on nonsexual aggressive
crimes is not as clear, although Le Maire quotes a researcher who concluded
from the Danish experience that it has reduced all violent crimes. Le Maire
(1956) argues that the reduction in both sexual and nonsexual crimes justifies castration as a potential treatment for given criminal offenses and
provides support for the hormone theory of aggression.

Women's aggressive behavior also appears to be related to hormonal
imbalance, as the premenstrual period is frequently associated with heightened tension, irritability, and hostility (Hamburg, 1966). In an early study
of prison records, it was discovered that among women imprisoned for
crimes of violence over 60 percent had committed their crimes during the
premenstrual time as compared to only two percent at the end of the
monthly period (Morton et al., 1953). Similar findings are reported by
Dalton (1964) who found that 49 percent of all crimes were committed by
women during the menstrual or premenstrual period. The 61 percent of
women convicted for violent crimes and 49 percent of all crimes reported
in these two studies are significantly greater than the 29 percent that would
have been committed during this eight-day period if the crimes had been
equally distributed over the month.

The intention of aggressive acts that occur as the consequence of a specific level of a particular hormone or because of an imbalance between
hormones is irrelevant to explaining why it occurred. The person behaved

aggressively because of his or her biological characteristics and not because they wanted to injure others.

Although the evidence is limited, it does appear that hormones contribute to the occurrence of aggressive behavior. They obviously do not account for all aggressive behavior, but they are important in understanding why such behavior emerges under certain conditions.

BRAIN-DAMAGE THEORIES

Research has demonstrated that certain areas of the brain are associated with aggressive behavior. Severing or destroying some sections of the brain and stimulating others has reduced the aggression of different species of animals. For example, lesions in the temporal lobes of the brains of wild monkeys eliminated their aggressive behavior and even made them playful (Kluver and Bucy, 1937). Lobotomies, or the severing of the frontal lobes of the brain, have been used in the past to pacify violent mental patients. Because of other side effects and the irreversible nature of the procedure, lobotomies are currently outlawed in the United States except under very unusual circumstances in some states.

Electrical stimulation of certain areas of the brain has been found to produce violent behavior in animals. For example, violent attack and killing behavior in animals has been elicited by stimulating the hypothalamus section of the brain. Cats, who normally behave peacefully towards rats, become alert and start to prowl when the hypothalamus is stimulated at a very low intensity. An increase in the electrical stimulation results in the cat pouncing on the rat and viciously biting it on the back of the neck, usually killing it (Flynn, 1967). This type of aggression appears to be relatively unemotional, but if the stimulation is shifted to a different part of the hypothalamus the cat responds with wild emotional attacks on any available object. These attacks are accompanied by dilated pupils, an arched back, hair standing on end, hissing, and urination, which indicate a violent rage (Egger and Flynn, 1963). The hypothalamus has also been stimulated with certain drugs, which have produced similar results (Smith, King, and Hoebel, 1970).

Johnson (1972) reviewed the research concerning brain stimulation producing aggression and concluded that "every individual has the neural machinery to engage in violent aggressive behavior." He also concluded that there is not a single "aggressive center" in the brain. Although aggression research has concentrated on the hypothalamus, violence and killing have been elicited from a number of widely separated portions of the brain.

The brain-damage theory of aggression has been supported by cases in which normally peaceful individuals have become aggressive following brain damage. A frightening example is the change in people who have contracted rabies, which literally means "rage." The viral infection attacks a section of the brain and turns the most peaceful individual into one characterized by uncontrollable rage and violence.

A well-known case of brain damage and subsequent aggression is that of mass murderer Charles Whitman. A short while before his murderous escapade, Whitman had sought psychiatric help and confided uncontrollable violent impulses. He never returned after the initial two-hour session but attempted in his own words to "fight my mental turmoil alone" (Johnson, 1972, p. 78). On the eve of July 31, 1966, he decided to kill both his mother and wife as painlessly as possible in order to spare them the embarrassment his actions would cause them. The next morning, he shot thirty-eight people, killing fourteen, from the top of a tall building on the University of Texas campus with a high-powered hunting rifle equipped with a telescopic sight. He was shot by the police, and a post-mortem examination of his brain revealed a large tumor (Sweet, Ervin, and Mark, 1969).

The Whitman case received wide publicity because of the number of people killed and injured, but the case is not rare. It was estimated that in 1970 over 10 million Americans had obvious brain damage and another 5 million had less obvious damage (Mark and Ervin, 1970). Although not all of these individuals express aggressive behaviors, it is suspected that a substantial proportion do.

In a study of eighty-three self-referred patients with violent impulses and eighty inmates of a prison, it was found that about half of both the patients and the prisoners had symptoms indicating brain abnormalities, which is much higher than occurs in the general population (Mark and Ervin, 1970). These findings tentatively suggest that some criminals may have committed violent crimes over which they had limited control because of brain damage. More importantly, incarceration does not correct the brain damage, and similar crimes will probably follow release. Johnson (1972, p. 80) feels that much innocent suffering by both law breakers and their victims could be prevented by greater recognition of brain damage as a cause of violent crime and by devoting more resources to its identification and treatment.

People suffering from brain damage are often not able to control their behavior, and thus intentions are irrelevant. The violent behavior usually occurs as uncontrollable rage, and not because the person intended or wanted to harm other people.

Recent advances in medical technology now make treatment of brain damage much more successful. Stereotoxic surgery, the precise locating of small electrodes in the damaged area of the brain, can identify the affected part of the brain and destroy it. The following is an example of the potential of stereotoxic surgery to destroy damaged brain tissue and reduce aggressive behavior:

At the age of 33, Clara T. slipped on a patch of ice and sustained a head injury which soon led to temporal lobe epileptic seizures. Despite anti-seizure medication the frequency and intensity of her seizures increased during the following 29 years. She became more physically assaultive, attacking her mother-in-law, her husband, and many visitors. After being hospitalized, she stabbed a nurse with scissors during one violent episode. It took six people 45 minutes to subdue this 62 year old woman who weighed only 86 pounds.

Neurological examinations showed that Clara had extensive damage in her temporal lobes, and stereotoxic surgery was performed in which a bank of 40 electrodes was implanted in and around the amygdala. The electrodes were kept in place for several months during which extensive tests were carried out. Abnormal brain waves were discovered in recordings through certain electrodes, and when weak electrical stimulation was applied at these points Clara began having a seizure. Using radio frequency current, heat was then generated through these electrodes to destroy the cells around the electrode tips. The electrodes were then withdrawn and Clara's behavior was closely observed. She continued having epileptic seizures, but they were much milder and decreased in frequency. For six years following the operation there was a total absence of rage or unprovoked assaults, and once again she was able to resume her normal family and community life (Johnson, 1972, p. 84, reprinted by permission of publisher).

Although brain surgery often produces dramatic results, the process is not reversible, and thus other treatments, such as drugs or psychiatric therapy, generally are attempted first. In cases in which conventional treatment has failed, surgery appears to have great potential for treating brain damage and controlling aggressive behavior related to it. The remarkable success of some brain stimulation and surgery suggests that brain damage is a probable cause of *some* aggressive behavior.

CHROMOSOME-ABNORMALITY THEORY

The genetic inheritance of an individual is contained in twenty-three pairs of chromosomes. One of each pair is provided by the mother, and one by the father. Twenty-two pairs are identical for both males and females, the sex chromosomes differ—the female has a matching pair (XX), and the male has one female chromosome (X) and one male chromosome (Y). The male XY pair is responsible for the masculine characteristics that develop in men. Recent technology has allowed the observation of chromosomes and certain abnormalities have been identified. A supermale syndrome (XYY) has been discovered and linked to heightened aggressiveness and criminality. A sampling of the criminally insane discovered that inmates are twenty times more likely to have the extra Y chromosome than are members of the general population (Court-Brown, 1967). Studies of large populations have attempted to determine the frequency with which the XYY pattern occurs in the general population. The best estimate is that one out of every 550 men has this chromosome abnormality, which means that there are over 400,000 such men in the United States (Shah, 1970).

Although the supermale syndrome does occur quite frequently, there is very little support for the theory that it causes aggressive or criminal behavior. For example, Shah (1970) reported that individuals with the XYY anomaly are not more aggressive than matched offenders with normal chromosome constitution. In spite of this lack of support for the XYY-pattern aggression theory, it has been utilized in the courts as a defense for violent crimes. A convicted murderer was given a reduced sentence by a Paris court in 1968 because of his XYY chromosome pattern. This is an example of the public accepting as scientific fact a rather speculative theory that later turned out not to be entirely correct. At present, available evidence suggests that the theory should be rejected.

PAIN-AGGRESSION REFLEX THEORY

Reflexive aggression, like other reflexes, is elicited by an external stimulus and is involuntary. Reflexive aggression is differentiated from instinctual aggression, in that it is elicited by an external stimulus rather than an internal stimulus, and from learned aggression, in that its consequences do not effect its occurrence. Experiments with a number of different species of animals have demonstrated that a painful stimulus, including an electrical shock, a heated floorplate, a physical blow, and a pinched tail, elicit reflexive fighting behavior. For example, monkeys responded to electrical shock of their tails by attacking an inanimate ball (Azrin, Hutchinson, and Sallery, 1964). When two rats that peacefully coexisted in a common pen were given foot shocks, the rats turned and attacked each other (Azrin, 1964). Reflexive fighting has been elicited in rats that have been raised in social isolation, which indicates that such behavior is innate rather than learned (Hutchinson, Ulrich, and Azrin, 1965). Consistent with other reflexes, such as salivation and blinking, aggression reflexes have been classically conditioned so that stimuli other than pain elicit the fighting reflex. A combination tone/light stimulus elicited the fighting behavior in rats after it was paired with foot shock (Farris, Gideon, and Ulrich, 1970).

Azrin and Holtz (1966), who have conducted several of the pain-aggression experiments, concluded that "reflexive fighting . . . appears to be a general response to aversive stimulation" (p. 443). They stress that this indiscriminate reflexive aggression is socially maladaptive because nonpunitive individuals are frequently attacked. Thus, reflexive aggression "can be expected to disrupt or terminate social relations that are in no way punitive."

Although the evidence supporting the pain-aggression reflex is convincing for several species of animals, there is little support for generalizing such a reflex to humans. Casual observation reveals that pain generally does not elicit fighting in humans. Rather it appears that men inhibit their reaction while ascertaining who is causing the pain and why the pain is occurring before reacting to it. For example, the doctor or dentist who is inflicting pain on a patient while correcting a medical problem usually is not the recipient of reflexive fighting responses.

Biological theories of aggression are clearly in the realm of psychology but it should be recognized that these theories do not provide a complete explanation of aggression and thus social factors must be considered. In addition, aggression is frequently the result of an interaction between biological, psychological and social factors. This interaction is evident in that several of the biological theories acknowledge that social learning influences the manifestation of biologically-induced aggression.

Other Theories of Aggression

FRUSTRATION-AGGRESSION THEORY

The frustration-aggression sequence (Dollard et. al, 1939) is illustrated in figure 11–2. The theory contends that interference with goal-seeking behavior generates frustration and instigation to aggression. The level of *frustration* and *instigation* to aggression is contingent on the strength of the goal-seeking response (how strongly the individual desired the goal), the degree of interference (complete blocking of the goal-seeking response, partial blocking, or only a delay), and, finally, the number of goal-seeking responses that are interfered with.

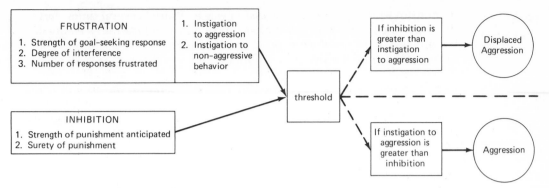

Figure 11–2 Frustration-Aggression Sequence

The amount of *inhibition* against aggression is determined by the surety and strength of the punishment anticipated for aggressive behavior. If the inhibition is greater than the instigation, the latter will be displaced to other activities or to an alternative target in a different situation. On the other hand, if the instigation is greater, aggressive behavior will occur against the source of frustration. The theory maintains that if frustration continues, eventually it will surpass the inhibition threshold and aggression will invariably occur. "In other words, a sufficiently 'infuriated' (frustrated) person will 'throw caution to the winds' and attack the frustrating agent" (Dollard et al., 1939, p. 38).

The frustration-aggression theory is based on psychological principles but does include social factors in explaining why and when aggressive behavior appears. The blocking of social goals, such as gaining acceptance or prestige, may generate frustration and subsequent aggression. Also, inhibitions that hinder the expression of aggression under certain conditions generally reflect behavior that is disapproved in a given group.

Numerous studies have demonstrated the relationship between frustration and aggression. For example, second-, third-, and fourth-grade students were promised a prize for successfully pushing marbles through holes in a box (Haner and Brown, 1955). Frustration was created by terminating the opportunity to win the prize before the student could complete the task. It was assumed that the closer the student was to completing the task when stopped, the greater would be the frustration. A loud buzzer signalled that the student had taken too long to finish the task and had to start over. The student had to push a plunger to turn the buzzer off and the pressure exerted against it was used as a measure of aggression. Although it is a rather weak measure of aggression, the pressure on the plunger was significantly greater the nearer the students were to completing the task and winning the prize. The results provide support for the hypothesis that frustration leads to aggression.

Very convincing evidence for the frustration-aggression theory was obtained by Hamblin and his associates (1963) in an experiment with college students. Two ROTC cadets were asked to help a senior cadet (in reality a confederate of the experimenter) to solve a difficult puzzle. The puzzle was part of a game the group played at which they could win money. The senior cadet refused to accept the obvious and correct solution, which blocked them from winning money. Aggression was measured several times during the experiment by asking the subjects to rate the senior cadet's leadership potential. The subjects were promised that their individual rating would never be shown to the senior cadet but that his average from several groups would significantly affect his promotion in the ROTC program. The results were very impressive as aggression increased in a lawful way as a function of frustration.

As shown in figure 11–2, when inhibitions exceed instigation to aggression, the individual will probably displace the aggression against an alternative target rather than attacking the source of the frustration. The typical example used to illustrate the displacement of aggression is that of the employee who is imposed upon (frustrated) by her boss. The employee, fearing for her job, does not aggress against the boss but when she arrives home after work, attacks her husband. He is bewildered by her sudden abuse of him when he had done nothing to warrant such treatment. The displacement of aggression may be repeated as the husband fears his wife's wrath and thus he displaces his instigation to aggression to their children. Finally, the children displace their aggression to the family dog, who then goes looking for the neighborhood cat.

Hovland and Sears (1940) conducted an interesting test of the displaced-aggression hypothesis on the societal level. Their study illustrates how psychological processes influence patterns of social behavior. They explored the relationship between economic conditions and lynching for the forty-nine-year period 1882 to 1930. Black Americans and criminals, the usual victims of a lynching, were not responsible for the frustrations of a declining economy but were innocent targets of displaced aggression. General economic conditions for the nation as a whole were determined by a scale combining statistics about production, construction, imports, exports, prices, and consumption. Because over 70 percent of the lynchings had a black victim and occurred in the South, a special economic index related to cotton production was calculated for the fourteen southern states. The authors identified 4,761 cases of lynching during this period. The results revealed that in good economic times there tended to be a low level of lynching, which increased when economic conditions worsened. The relationship was significant for both the South and the entire United States. The authors interpreted these findings as support for the frustration-displaced aggression theory.

The many experiments and field studies testing the frustration-aggression theory have found that it is not nearly as general as the original authors claimed. Research has confirmed that frustration produces instigation to behaviors other than aggression and thus frustration does not invariably lead to aggression. Also, it has been demonstrated that aggression frequently occurs in the absence of frustration when individuals use aggression as a goal-seeking tactic.

SOCIAL-LEARNING THEORY

The social-learning theory of aggression contends that people learn to perform aggressive behaviors and that they learn under what conditions such responses are likely to be successful in obtaining desired goals. Although a person may be emotionally aroused (angry) when performing learned aggression, frequently such behavior is used in a dispassionate fashion. The aggressive behavior of a door-to-door salesman who attempts to intimidate in order to sell a product is displaying nonanger learned aggression.

The social-learning model (adapted from Bandura, 1973) is illustrated in figure 11–3. The social-learning model combines social and psychological factors into an impressive social-psychological theory of aggressive behavior. According to this theory, the individual or group learns aggressive responses by direct instruction, by accidental trial-and-error learning, or by observational learning or modelling. An example of social learning is a soldier who is taught to use weapons of destruction in the expectation that he will behave aggressively in combat situations. In this example, the individual is taught aggressive behaviors to be used only under conditions of war, but once such behaviors are mastered they can then be used in other situations. Also, sometimes the training is more general as people are taught to be aggressive in a wide variety of social situations. Today, many people are taking assertiveness training to learn how to be more aggressive in interpersonal relationships.

Observation of others is frequently a source of learning aggressive behaviors. A child may witness an older boy intimidate a third child and take his lunch away from him. A business executive observes that a ruthless business deal by a colleague earned the latter's company a substantial profit and the colleague a raise in salary. In each of these cases, the individual witnessed an aggressive act, noted how to perform it, and observed that the behavior was rewarded by others. This experience greatly increases the probability that the observer will try aggressive behavior.

Finally, people learn aggressive responses by trial-and-error learning. For example, a child is attacked by another, and because he is confined and cannot flee he counterattacks and defeats his assailant. When attacked in the future, the child will probably fight rather than run and may learn that aggressive behavior obtains important goals, so that eventually the child initiates conflict.

Once an individual has learned an aggressive response, the theory suggests that he or she probably will not use it in an indiscriminate way. As indicated in figure 11–3, instigators signal the appropriate time and place for aggression. Bandura (1973) identified five types of events that inform the person that aggression will probably have favorable consequences. Unpleasant, painful, or frustrating experiences not only emotionally arouse the

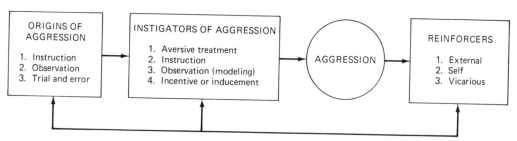

Figure 11–3   Instrumental Aggression Model. (Adapted from Bandura, 1973.)

person but signal that aggressive behavior is socially acceptable—that it may even be the socially approved reaction to such treatment. The Milgram studies (1963, 1964, 1965) discussed in chapter 5 illustrate how instructions can signal people that now is an appropriate time to be aggressive. A significant number of mature adults were willing to administer very severe and dangerous electrical shocks to a fellow subject when instructed to do so by the experimenter despite the victim's desperate pleas for mercy. These adults obeyed instructions not only from a legitimate scientist in a university laboratory but also obeyed to nearly the same extent a person conducting an experiment in an old warehouse. Some subjects continued to administer the severe shock even when the victim was in the same room and pleaded to be spared further shocks because of the pain.

Bandura (1973) quotes Smith (1961, p. 24) to illustrate the impact of instructions by political leaders on the occurrence of violence: "When you think of the long and gloomy history of man, you will find more hideous crimes have been committed in the name of obedience than have been committed in the name of rebellion." Experiments such as Milgram's provide some measure of understanding of why basically "good" people commit atrocities.

The third instigator discussed by Bandura (1973) is the observation of other people performing aggressive acts. In this situation, the person is not learning an aggressive response from the model but is learning under what conditions such behavior is appropriate. Considerable research has demonstrated that people are more aggressive after witnessing aggression in others. Subjects who have witnessed a film segment portraying violence (prize fight, war scene, and so on) have expressed significantly more subsequent aggression than those who watched equally long and exciting nonaggressive films.

The fourth type of instigator is the anticipation of incentives or potential rewards anticipated from the aggressive behavior. The person decides that aggression is the best means to accomplish a desired goal and performs the aggressive behavior in a cool and dispassionate way. Usually, people do a pretty good job of estimating the potential rewards and punishments likely to follow an aggressive act, but occasionally the positive or negative consequences are over- or underestimated. When the rewards are overestimated and the negative consequences underestimated, the functional aspect of learned aggression is not readily apparent and in fact it may appear to be rather stupid or irrational behavior. What may appear to an observer as an impulsive irrational act may have been the consequence of faulty judgment that at the time showed aggression as the most rational response to the person. For example, it has been discovered that habitual criminals frequently overestimate the rewards associated with a given criminal action and underestimate the probability that they will be caught (Claster, 1967).

The discussion of the acquisition of aggressive responses has stressed the importance of the consequences of such responses to how quickly they are learned and how frequently they are utilized. This is consistent with the large body of evidence that behavior is primarily controlled by its consequences. Those behaviors that are reinforced will occur more frequently, those that are ignored will gradually disappear (be extinguished), and those that are punished will quickly cease. The social-learning model illustrated in figure 11–3 identifies three forms of reinforcement: external reinforcement, self-reinforcement, and vicarious reinforcement.

External reinforcement includes tangible rewards, social approval, social status, removal of painful experiences, and expressions of injury in the victim. The power of tangible and social reinforcement to maintain aggressive behaviors is illustrated by the rewards offered for killing North Vietnamese in the Vietnam war (Bandura, 1973). A U.S. infantry battalion rewarded soldiers for killing with "Kill Cong" emblems to be worn on their uniforms as well as rest-and-recreation leaves. In order to document the killing of the enemy, a soldier had to present the ear of the dead person as evidence, and a string of ears was proudly displayed as a tribute to the effectiveness of the battallion.

Self-reinforcement occurs when the person "feels good" about the ag-

The training of aggressive behavior. *Source:* U.S. Army.

gressive behavior just performed. He or she may feel "proud" that he or she stood up to a threat or defended family or country even though he or she suffered pain and deprivation in the process. Some men may feel "masculine" after participating in male-oriented activities such as fighting; also, feelings of "remorse" or "shame" may accompany the failure to act aggressively under certain conditions. Although self-reinforcement is difficult to observe, it can be a very powerful reinforcer as evidenced by the number of men and women who have suffered pain and death rather than experience the "shame" or "guilt" associated with surrender.

Vicarious reinforcement is the psychological sharing with an aggressor the consequences of aggression. A person may feel proud when a football team soundly beats another team or when the country's army inflicts injury on the enemy. On the other hand, the individual may experience shame when someone he or she identified with fails to be aggressive in the appropriate situation. Although vicarious reinforcement is not as powerful as external or self-reinforcement, it is sufficient to strengthen and maintain aggression responses. The influence of reinforcement on both the learning and the utilization of aggression is illustrated by the arrows at the bottom of figure 11–3. The interaction between the learning of aggressive responses, the learning of the appropriate times and places to perform them, and the reinforcement obtained from them are also apparent.

SUBCULTURE-OF-VIOLENCE THEORY

The subculture of violence theory is a special case of the social learning theory as the group teaches such behavior and reinforces members in utilizing it. American society has a tradition of violence, which grew out of the experience of a revolutionary war, a civil war, participation in two world wars and several small wars, police actions, and undeclared wars. The settlement of the West with the Colt revolver is one of the most revered segments of American history. The tradition of violence in American culture is viewed as one reason why American society has a rather high level of such behavior.

Observation of juvenile gangs have revealed that such groups frequently engage in aggressive and violent behavior, and it has been suggested that this behavior is the result of unique cultural values and behavior patterns that support and encourage violence (Wolfgang, 1958; Wolfgang and Ferracuti, 1968). The values of these violent subcultures conflict with the values of the dominant culture but their influence on members of the group is substantial. The senseless, almost random killing that occurred in the streets of San Francisco in 1974 was attributed by many to a blood cult that required would-be members to commit a murder as their initiation. At least ten deaths with the same apparent lack of motivation occurred in a four-month period, but the killers were never apprehended, so the existence of a violent subculture was never confirmed or discounted.

Research attempting to identify a violent subculture in delinquent gangs has not supported the theory, as most studies have found that delinquent gangs reflect lower-class values and behaviors (Short and Strodtbeck, 1965; Jansyn, 1966; Miller, 1966). The extremely violent gang sometimes gives status to those with fighting skills and experience, but a subculture of violence is absent.

Juvenile gangs at war as portrayed in the movie *The Warriors* such gangs exemplify the learning of aggression and its instrumental use to obtain valued goals. *Source:* Culver Pictures, Inc.

The study of adult subcultures of violence, although limited, also has failed to discover values supportive of violence. The President's Commission on the Causes and Preventions of Violence obtained questionnaire data from a national sample about approval for using violence in five specific situations (Baker and Ball, 1969; Stark and McEvoy, 1970; Ball-Rokeach, 1973; Erlanger, 1974). A very low level of approval for the use of violence was found, and more importantly none of the social-class or racial subgroups studied evidenced support for violence.

Although the subculture of violence has been accepted by many as an explanation for the violence of certain delinquent and lower-class subgroups, there is little empirical support. There is no doubt that such subgroups evidence more aggressive behavior than others, but the violence is not the product of supportive values.

The social-learning theory of aggression has received a great deal of support in the laboratory and in natural settings (such as schools). Hyperaggressive children have greatly reduced their aggressive behavior when reinforcement contingencies do not reinforce such behavior (Hamblin et al., 1971).

This review of the major theories of aggressive behavior has documented that there may be several different types of aggression, including unemotional, directed aggression and angry, undirected rage. More important, it seems that there is not a single determinant of aggressive behavior, but that it can be and is caused by a variety of events and conditions. The research evidence indicates that the biological characteristics of hormonal imbalance and brain damage cause aggressive acts. However, these are not the only determinants of aggression. Under certain conditions, frustration has been repeatedly demonstrated to be a causal antecedent of aggression. Finally, the learning of aggressive responses and their instrumental use has been well-documented. Frequently, several of these factors interact to cause an individual to engage in aggressive behavior.

It is important to recognize the multiple determinants of aggression, as any attempt to reduce violence that focuses on only *one* of the many potential causes is destined to limited success. If American society and its elected representatives are serious about reducing aggression and violence, programs that work with several or all the variables identified will be necessary to produce a significant impact on this type of behavior.

Violence in Society

The rising crime rates, urban riots, campus protests, and political assassinations of the 1960s inspired President Lyndon Johnson to create the National Commission on the Causes and Prevention of Violence. This commission, under the direction of Chairman Milton S. Eisenhower, was to assess the reasons for mounting violence in society and to conduct public hearings. Commission task forces explored the problems of violent crimes, group violence, civil disobedience, assassinations, law enforcement, firearms, and television programming, but space does not permit a review of each task force's report. The end product was fifteen volumes on specific aspects of violence in American society and a summary report, *To Establish Justice, To Insure Domestic Tranquility.*

VIOLENT CRIME

Analysis of the information collected by police departments reveals a rather startling increase in the rate of violent crime in America. Figure 11–4 illustrates how violent crime against persons increased 47 percent during the

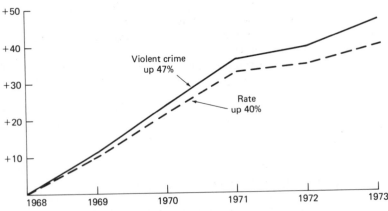

CRIMES OF VIOLENCE
1968-1973
PERCENT CHANGE OVER 1968

LIMITED TO MURDER, FORCIBLE RAPE, ROBBERY AND AGGRAVATED ASSAULT

Figure 11–4 Increase in Number and Rate of Violent Crimes From 1968 to 1973. (Source: *FBI Uniform Crime Reports,* 1974, p. 4.)

five-year period 1968–1973. When the effects of population growth are taken into account, violent crimes increased by 40 percent during this time. Since 1973, the homicide and robbery rates have decreased while the rates for rape and aggravated assault have increased. Overall, the trend for violent crime between 1973 and 1977 has been a slight increase but not nearly as large as between 1968 and 1973. The crime clocks prepared by the FBI (see figure 11–5) revealed that in 1977 a violent crime occurred every thirty-one seconds, a forcible rape every eight minutes, a murder every twenty-seven minutes, a robbery every seventy-eight seconds, and an aggravated assault every minute. Violent crimes have increased in frequency despite the control attempts by increasingly sophisticated police personnel and equipment.

These statistics on rising crime rates are not confined to decaying large cities, as illustrated by the experiences of a small, rural high school in southern Missouri. A wave of burglaries at the school was finally attributed to six of the school's star athletes (*Newsweek*, 1975). The track coach's car was stolen, overturned, and burned by a group of students. The social-science teacher was shot at twice, the chemistry teacher was assaulted in the hall by a student he had never taught, and the basketball coach was attacked

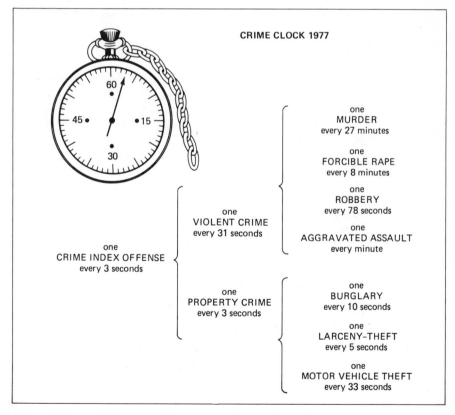

Figure 11–5 Crime Clock Indicating the Frequency with which Violent Crimes Occur in American Society. (Source: *FBI Uniform Crime Reports,* 1978, p. 6.)

by a coed with a butcher knife. Violence in schools has been increasing across the nation as students' attacks on other students have risen 3,000 percent during the past decade and assaults against teachers have increased 7,000 percent (*Newsweek,* 1975).

TELEVISION VIOLENCE

The dramatic increase in violence in American society and the amount of force, fighting, and killing shown in television programming has raised the question of whether there is a relationship between the two. Concern has been expressed that the violence portrayed on TV teaches and encourages violent acts to millions of viewers. It is estimated that 96 percent of the households in this country have a television set that is played an average of six hours each day (Gerbner, 1972). The potential impact of television is evident when it is realized that 81 million people are exposed to television each and every day. Half this audience are children between the ages of two and eleven who, by the time they are twelve, have logged 13,500 hours of television viewing, twice the number they have spent in the schoolroom (Steinfeld, 1973). As television has become an integral part of the daily life of most Americans, interest in the impact of television programming on the behavior of the viewer has increased. Specifically, the relationship between television violence and violence in society has become a topic of growing concern and controversy.

TELEVISION VIOLENCE AND JUVENILE DELINQUENCY

One of the first government bodies to investigate the impact of television violence on the aggressive behavior of the viewing public was the Senate Subcommittee to Investigate Juvenile Delinquency (1954). This subcommittee attempted to discern if the violence portrayed on television was contributing to the increase in juvenile delinquency. During public hearings, spokespeople for television contended that there was very little violence on television and, more importantly, that television programming was not responsible for delinquent behavior. According to Golden the hearings were similar to "an argument about which straw broke the camel's back, industry spokesmen claiming the straw they added to the burden should not be blamed, their opponents arguing that it should not be exonerated" (1976, p. 141). The subcommittee concluded that exposure to television violence was "potentially harmful" to young viewers, as it may predispose delinquent activities. The television industry rejected this conclusion, but did agree to reduce the violence. Ten years later, the subcommittee again examined the degree of fighting, injury, and killing on television and discovered that, contrary to industry claims, violence had not decreased but had actually increased (Subcommittee to Investigate Juvenile Delinquency, 1965).

TELEVISION VIOLENCE AND MENTAL ILLNESS

The most critical examination of television's impact on aggression was initiated by Senator John O. Pastore, chairman of the Communications Subcommittee of the Committee on Commerce. Pastore wrote to the newly

Example of applauded aggression shown on television. *Source:* E. Stanford.

appointed Secretary of Health, Education and Welfare, Robert Finch, in March 1969 requesting the appointment of a scientific advisory committee to assess the link between television violence and *mental illness.* The suggestion was to follow the precedent of the Surgeon General's study of smoking and cancer. In June 1969, the Surgeon General's Scientific Advisory Committee on Television and Social Behavior was created and directed to report on the link between television violence and mental illness.

A very high level of violence was documented by the Committee. It was discovered that two out of every three leading characters on television were involved in violence, and half the leading characters were committing aggressive acts. The use of violence to hurt or kill was found to occur at a rate of eight such events per hour (Gerbner, 1972). Because of the concern generated by this type of research, the incidence of killing on television has decreased considerably, but rape, assault, injury, and other forms of nonlethal aggression have remained at the same high (or even higher) level. One area of programming where violence has continued to increase is children's cartoons. In defense of the saturation of violence, television personnel have replied that television is filling an important psychological need. They contend that television violence is a socially acceptable outlet for instinctual aggression (Baldwin and Lewis, 1971, p. 314).

> Psychologists would say that if we didn't give people violence on TV, they would seek it elsewhere. These action shows, they say, fulfill a need. If TV does not provide escape, the audience will find escape elsewhere. [Producer]

> People need to watch a certain amount of aggressive action to get release and escape. Note that now violence has been soft-pedaled in television drama, it has come out more strongly in films for theatre showing. [Director]

Although it was fairly easy to document the degree of violence on television, it was much more difficult for the committee to determine whether there was a causal link between the TV violence and inappropriate social behavior. Numerous cases of people apparently imitating crimes witnessed on television or in the movie theater have been reported. For example, in 1973 a young woman in Boston was soaked with gasoline and set afire by a gang of youths the day after a TV movie had shown the murder of a derelict in precisely the same way. Three men who committed a robbery in Ogden, Utah, in 1974 attempted to kill the witnesses by forcing them to drink lye, in direct imitation of the movie *Magnum Force,* which they had seen several times. In another case in Ogden, a young mother watched a television movie involving aliens from outerspace who impregnated all the women in the small town. The babies born to these women all had glassy eyes that tended to glow or shine in the dark. A short time after the show, the mother, while under the influence of drugs, was awakened by the crying of her one-year-old son. As she entered the child's room, she perceived that he had glassy eyes and immediately drowned him in the bathtub. The mother had previously sought psychiatric counseling and was under the influence of drugs, but the idea that her child might have shining eyes and should be drowned was suggested by television.

The national Parent Teacher Association held hearings across the nation during late 1976 and early 1977 at which hundreds of examples of apparent television-inspired violence were reported. One mother told how her four-year-old son tried to smother the family dog with a pillow while watching the Sunday Night Mystery Theatre. The boy had just watched a corrupt policeman try to smother a victim with a pillow. These cases illustrate the suggested modeling effect of violence but certainly do not document a causal link between television programming and violent social behavior. The supposed link between television and violence was interjected into the murder-trial defense of 14-year-old Ronald Zamora (see chapter 9). The jury did not accept the contention that Zamora was addicted to television nor that television violence motivated his action.

To test the relationship between television and real-life violence, several experimental studies that manipulated exposure to aggressive films and television shows, primarily cartoons, and watched for changes in aggressive behavior were reviewed by the committee. An example is an experiment with four- and five-year-old boys in a Sunday-school kindergarten (Hanratty et al., 1969). Half the boys were shown a two-and-a-half minute color and sound film in which an adult male model aggressed against a young woman dressed up as a clown. The aggression portrayed in the film involved verbal assaults, shooting with a toy machine gun, and hitting with a plastic mallet. Half the boys who had seen the film and half those who had not were then left alone in a room containing a three-foot inflated plastic Bobo doll. The boys were left alone for ten minutes, during which time their aggressive behavior toward the doll was recorded. Because such inflated dolls are frequently used as punching bags, it is not surprising that almost all the children punched or kicked the doll. However, those who had viewed the film of the aggressive model did so to a greater extent. The other subjects were placed in the room with a young woman dressed as a clown who stood idly in the corner. Several of those who had witnessed the film imitated the aggressive behavior against the clown; none of the other children did so. Although the evidence of such experiments is impressive, it should be noted that most have used children as subjects, which limits the generalizability to the general population. Also, these studies usually test the effect of only a single segment of television programming, which neglects the cumulative effect of having witnessed hours of violent viewing. Finally, these experiments focus only on the short-range effects of television programming as they usually last only a few minutes, hours, or a few days at the most. Obviously, such experimental procedures cannot assess the long-range impact of television violence.

A large number of correlational studies that measure television viewing and violent behavior at only one point in time have been conducted. These studies generally support the link between television violence and aggressive behavior. Obviously, a casual relationship is hard to infer from this type of data. A longitudinal study of 900 children in a rural New York county provides more impressive correlational support for the relationship (Lefkowitz et al., 1971). The students were first studied in 1963 while they were in the third grade, and it was discovered that the amount of television that boys watched was significantly related to peer ratings of aggressive behavior in the classroom. Ten years later, 400 of the youngsters were located and interviewed, and it was found that the television violence watched in the third grade was related to peer ratings of aggression at age nineteen. Obtaining data at two points in time, ages nine and nineteen, provides stronger support that television viewing and aggression are related, but it is still difficult to infer that one caused the other.

Given the lack of strong evidence relating television violence to aggressive behavior, the committee issued a noncommittal final report. The report states that there is a "tentative indication" of a casual relationship between television violence and aggression but then qualifies the relationship even more by stating that it operates "only on some" children and "only in some" environmental situations.

The reactions to the report were extremely critical, and several of the scientists who had worked for the committee stated that their research had been misinterpreted, if not misrepresented. Testimony in public hearings revealed that several irate scientists had written Senator Pastore's Subcommittee on Communication to protest the playing down of "their findings that aggressive TV increased the aggressive behavior of half of the children they studied, and that aggressive programs had deleterious effects on the children's ability to exert self-control and to tolerate minor frustration" (Murphy, 1972, p. 10). They made the point that "half" is considerably more than "only some" children. The bitter denunciation of the committee's report and the challenge of its integrity is illustrated in a letter written to the Senate Subcommittee on Communication by Albert Bandura:

The combined findings of laboratory experiments, controlled field studies, and correlational investigations provide substantial testimony that televised violence, through its instruction and sanction of aggressive methods, reduces restraints over behaving aggressively and shapes its form. Exposure to televised violence increases the likelihood that some viewers will behave aggressively in the face of other inducements. The irate researchers whose findings were irresponsibly distorted in the Surgeon General's Report are fully justified in the objections they have raised. In addition to distorting research evidence, some highly pertinent studies demonstrating that violence viewing causes children to behave aggressively are not even mentioned, a double standard is used in evaluating individual studies depending on how their findings relate to the industry viewpoint, questionable assumptions about the determinants of aggression are presented as established facts, and the very methods by which knowledge on this issue can be advanced are cavalierly misrepresented (1972, p. 19).

A year or so after the committee submitted its report, Surgeon General Steinfeld took an unequivocal stand that television violence is harmful (Steinfeld, 1973, p. 38). He concluded that "we can no longer tolerate the present high level of television violence that is put before children in American homes."

Although the majority of the studies do support a link between television violence and aggressive behavior, there are some that support the view that television violence does not facilitate aggression and may even reduce subsequent aggressive behavior. One example is an innovative field experiment sponsored by CBS, which was conducted in New York City (Milgram and Shotland, 1973). Because CBS was involved, the researchers had access to the network's television offerings to use as a stimulus in the study. *Medical Center* was chosen, and a special episode was produced that had three different endings. The show involved a young white male named Tom Desmond, who worked as an attendant at Medical Center. Tom was married and had recently become a father. He quit his job at the center, then realized that this was a mistake and asked for his job back—but Dr. Gannon would not rehire him. Tom's wife became ill, the bills mounted, and he was forced to give up a small sailboat to which he was deeply attached. At this point, Tom entered a bar where he saw Dr. Gannon participating in a fundraising telethon. A collection box for the telethon was visible on the bar.

The first ending portrayed antisocial behavior followed by punishment. In this version, Tom called the telethon and was extremely abusive. He then grabbed a bludgeon off the wall of the bar, smashed the collection box, gathered the money, and fled out into the street. He sought out four other collection boxes and burglarized them as well. Tom was captured by police and sent to jail; additional punishment came to Tom when his wife divorced him.

The second scenario was very similar except the antisocial behavior was not followed by punishment as Tom escaped to Mexico and was later joined by his wife. The third version had Tom consider the antisocial behavior but at the last minute reconsider and, rather than smash the collection box, deposit a coin in it.

The three different versions of the show and a neutral Medical Center episode were shown to four sets of male subjects, recruited by newspaper advertisements, in a special preview held in the National Preview Theatre. They were promised a transistor radio if they would preview a segment of a popular television show. After previewing one of the four segments of the show, they were instructed to go to the office of Bartel World Wide, who was distributing the radios, to pick one up.

The office was located on the twenty-third floor of a commercial office building. When the subjects arrived to pick up their radios, they found the office open, but there was no one present and the following handwritten notice was on the counter: "We have no more transistor radios to distribute. This distribution center is closed until further notice." In order to provide the subject an opportunity to aggress in a manner similar to the television model they had viewed the week before, a collection box for a well-known charity was fastened to the wall. The poster depicted a doctor administering to a sick girl lying in a hospital bed. The message was: "Where there is Hope, there is Life. PROJECT HOPE. A People-to-People Program of Medical Education and Treatment for Developing Nations." The clear plastic canister contained a ten-dollar bill, four singles, and some change. The edge of one of the dollar bills was sticking out of the canister so that it could be removed without much difficulty. The subject's behavior towards the charity collection box was observed and videotaped by hidden observers and cameras. Thus, subjects had been shown an aggressive model, had been frustrated by blocked efforts to obtain a promised radio, and were given an opportunity to imitate the model. The results are presented in figure 11–6, which indicates that the aggressive model did not generate imitated aggression. If anything, exposure to the model reduced the occurrence of aggression. Statistical analysis revealed that none of the differences between the four groups of subjects were significant, so the authors concluded that the television aggression had no impact on subsequent aggression. The study was later modified and replicated in St. Louis with similar results. The authors summarize the contribution of their study to the television-violence controversy by advocating patience in reaching final conclusions:

> It is possible that people have been entirely too glib in discussing the negative social consequences of the depiction of television violence. Personally, the investigators find the constant depiction of violence on television repugnant. But that is quite different from saying it leads to antisocial behavior among its viewers. We have not been able to find evidence for this; for if television is on trial, the judgment of this investigation must be the Scottish verdict: Not proven (Milgram and Shotland, 1973, p. 68).

Although this is very innovative research, it suffers from the same weakness as do those that support the link between television violence and aggressive behavior. The segment of Medical Center was only *one* very mild dose of violence and its impact was viewed for only one brief period, and the subjects' aggressive behavior was observed for an even briefer period. The cumulative influence of watching violent show after violent show remains unknown.

An innovative study by Loye (1978) used cable television to control the shows available in 183 homes for one week. The study focused on the husbands, who filled out a check list of their moods before and after each show they viewed. The wives also recorded their husbands behavior for the week. Prosocial television shows such as the Waltons significantly decreased aggressive moods. Although violent television did not heighten aggressive

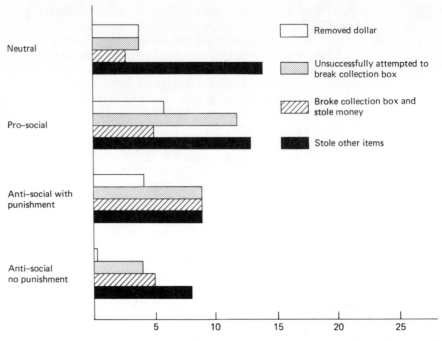

Figure 11–6 Percentage of Subjects Performing Anti-Social Acts (Adapted from Milgram and Shotland, 1973 p. 20.)

moods, it did increase the level of aggressive behavior, such as breaking objects and driving while drunk, as recorded by the wives.

A six year study of 1,500 teenage boys in London attempted to separate out the effects of non-television factors on the boys' violent behavior, thus hoping to identify the effects of viewing television violence. The study concluded that, other things being equal, the long range effect of television violence was an increase of violent behavior (Belson, 1978).

A related finding to emerge out of the study of television programing and violence was that people who were heavy television watchers see the world as more dangerous and are less trusting than light or moderate viewers (Gerbner and Gross, 1976a). According to this study, violence viewed on television alters perceptions of the real world of the heavy watchers and they overestimate the violence occuring around them. Gerbner and Gross suggested that the fear generated by television violence is partially responsible for the flight from the inner city to the suburbs. A later study (Doob and Macdonald, 1979) reported that when the level of actual crime in a person's neighborhood was controlled, the relationship between television viewing and fear of being a victim of crime disappeared. In other words, people living in the inner city are aware that they are in a high crime area, regardless of how much television they watch, and they move to the suburbs to escape.

Wurtzel (1977) reviewed a number of studies testing the link between television violence and aggressive behavior and concluded that although the findings have not been unanimous they have established a relationship between violent programs and aggressive behavior. The same conclusion was reached by Comstock and his associates (1979) in an extremely thorough review of over 2,500 scientific studies or reports.

As is apparent, the controversy about the impact of television programming on real-life violence continues. It does appear that the weight of the evidence appears to support the hypothesis that what is viewed on television contributes to the problem of increasing violence in American society.

In spite of the committee's report, the public hearings, and all of the research, very little change has been made in television programming. A follow-up study documenting the degree of violence on television found the number of violent acts has remained fairly constant between 1967 and 1976 (Gerbner and Gross, 1976b). The viewing period with the most violence was the weekend daytime hours, which have a very high rate of children viewers. Thus, those likely to be the most susceptible to any effects of television violence are receiving the largest doses. The Federal Communication Commission and the broadcasting industry did jointly agree to create a "family viewing time." Their solution to the violence on television was to designate the time period between 7:30 p.m. and 9:00 p.m. as family viewing time and to reduce the adult content (violence and sex) portrayed during this time. This policy took effect in September 1975, but differences in time zones and the length of movies and two-hour programs have frequently resulted in the violation of the rule. In spite of the family hour, researchers at the University of Pennsylvania concluded that television violence increased on the three major networks during 1976, making it the most violent since 1967. This same high level of violence appears to have persisted to the present.

URBAN RIOTS

Urban riots are cases of collective or group violence that at times have threatened the stability of U.S. society and generated great concern among U.S. citizens. Generally, urban riots have occurred because social conditions have triggered the psychological processes resulting in aggressive behavior of large numbers of people simultaneously. Social contagion and social approval of riotous behavior spread its occurance. During the 1960s, nearly two hundred cases of rioting occurred in which 200,000 citizens participated (Violence Commission, 1969). Hundreds of thousands of citizens of this country openly and violently defying the government came as a great shock to society. President Johnson appointed the National Advisory Commission on Civil Disorders (1968) to study the conditions and events leading to violent outbursts and to make recommendations for preventing future riots and for healing the wounds created by those that had already occurred. The descriptions of the major riots discussed below were obtained from the reports of this commission.

Harlem The 1964 Harlem riot started when a group of young blacks walking to summer school became involved in a dispute with a white building superintendent. An off-duty police officer intervened, and, when a fifteen-year old youth attacked him with a knife, he shot and killed the youngster. A crowd of teenagers gathered and started to smash windows and a large detachment of police was required to disperse the crowd. The next day a Marxist group, the Progressive Labor Movement, passed out inflammatory leaflets charging police brutality. A "peaceful" protest march to the police station turned into an uncontrollable mob that started looting and turning in false fire alarms. This pattern of "peaceful" protest marches or meetings turning into violent confrontations with the police and accompanying looting repeated itself for several days before order was restored.

Watts   In the summer of 1965, rioting occurred in the Watts section of Los Angeles when a highway patrolman stopped a young black male driver for speeding. The man appeared to be drunk and refused to cooperate with the police. A crowd gathered, and, when the highway patrolman mistakenly struck a bystander with his night stick, the riot erupted. Blacks stoned white motorists and beat the drivers of cars that stopped. The next day, there was looting, which the police ignored, hoping things would die down. Because the police did not respond, the looters became much bolder and openly left stores with their arms loaded with stolen merchandise. As police attempted to halt the subsequent looting, snipers fired at them, they responded, and the conflict escalated. Eventually, the National Guard was mobilized to help stop the conflict. By the time the fighting was over, thirty-four people had been killed, and $35 million in property destroyed.

Newark   The Newark riots in 1967 grew out of conflict between the city and the black community over a number of issues, including the relocation of black families to provide a 150-acre site for a medical school. The police and black community also had a long history of conflict. These bitter feelings came to a head when a cab driver was stopped for a traffic violation, was found to have a revoked license, and several blacks witnessed the cabbie being "dragged" into the police station. A rumor that the police had beat him was quickly spread by cab drivers over their C.B. radios. A large crowd gathered across the street from the police station, and as they milled about cursing the police they were showered with rocks. It is suspected the rocks were thrown by teenagers in a nearby black housing development. The provoked crowd started to smash windows, began looting, and torched an old car. When the police attempted to disperse the crowd, the fighting and violence escalated. The conflict continued for several days, and the National Guard was called in to assist the police. The police and National Guard claimed that snipers were firing at them, and they were forced to return the fire. Also, the looting had reached such proportions that the decision was made to shoot looters. The action resulted in several innocent bystanders being shot and killed by the police and Guardsmen. It was reported that stores with "Soul Brother" signs in the window, which had been spared by looters, were destroyed by gunfire from the police and National Guard. The property damage was so extensive that it has never been fully repaired; many families and businesses fled the city instead.

Detroit   The Detroit riot in 1967 followed the familiar pattern of conflict and tension between the police and black community. A precipitating event was a police raid on an after-hours drinking and gambling spot. A crowd gathered in the early morning hours as the police escorted the arrested individuals to the police station. As the crowd grew, looting began, as did fire bombings, false fire alarms, police dispersion of crowds, and sniper fire. In this riot, the looting appeared to be excessive and more organized than that in previous riots. Several cars were used to make repeated hauls of stolen goods. The conflict ebbed and flowed for several days, and finally the National Guard was called in to bolster the battered police force.

New York City A somewhat different case of rioting occurred in New York City in July 1977. Previous riots had been based on strong feelings of injustice and were designed to protest such treatment. This was not the case in New York City as the material goods obtained appeared to be the primary motivation for looting. At 9:34 p.m. on July 13, 1977, the city's electricity was interrupted when lightning struck two transmission towers in upstate New York; there was no power for up to twenty-four hours. During this time, tens of thousands of blacks and Hispanics poured out of the ghettos and vandalized and looted (*Time,* 1977, pp. 12–25). Over one thousand fires were reported, six times the normal number, along with 1,700 false alarms.

Four people were killed—three in fires and one shot by a storeowner—and the property damage was staggering. Over two thousand stores and shops were plundered. People were reported to have chanted "it's Christmas time, it's Christmas time" as they systematically looted clothing stores, furniture stores, supermarkets, and liquor stores. One Pontiac car dealer lost fifty new cars to looters who hot-wired them and drove them away (*Time,* 1977, p. 12). According to the police, the looters utilized "trucks, vans, trailors, and anything that would roll" to haul away the booty. The police at times attempted to curb the looting, and they arrested 3,500 people, but because of the large numbers the usual strategy was to chase the looters away from the store or shop they were attacking. Most looters simply ran to a store in the next block and resumed their pilfering.

Those who observed the looting reported that the outburst of vandalism and looting was not characterized by statements of ideology and was not seen by the participants as a protest against injustice. Rather, the activity was characterized by a general feeling of "we have wanted these things but couldn't afford them and now we can have them for nothing" (*Time,* 1977,

Looting of shoe store in Harlem during the 1977 blackout in New York City illustrates social learning of aggressive behavior. *Source:* Wide World Photos, Inc.

p. 17). It was speculated that the blacks and Hispanics felt frustrated in their pursuit of the American dream, and the vandalism and looting provided a means for reducing their frustration. The vandalism allowed the expression of aggression against "the Establishment," the perceived agent of frustration, and the looting provided previously denied desired goods.

These urban riots exemplify elements of both the frustration-aggression sequence and the learned-aggression theory. Several researchers have noted the underlying frustration that sustained the disruptive behavior. The National Advisory Commission on Civil Disorders (1968) reported that the black community's greatest source of frustration was harrassment by the police. Police practices were followed by problems of employment, inadequate housing, limited education, inadequate recreational facilities, exclusion from the political structure, white prejudice, unequal administration of justice, limited participation in federal programs, and inadequate municipal services as sources of frustration to ghetto residents. The acts of discrimination, exclusion, and neglect directly affected the lifestyle of black Americans and interfered with their pursuit of the good life, generating a high level of frustration.

In a study of both Newark and Detroit, rioters were found to perceive greater blockage of their educational, employment, and housing opportunities than did nonrioters (Caplan and Paige, 1968). The same finding was reported by Ransford (1968) in his study of the Watts Riot. He found that those who were willing to engage in a riot felt that they had been the victims of discrimination to a greater extent than had those who expressed an unwillingness to be involved. Ransford discovered that the frustration was heightened by feelings of powerlessness so that the potential rioters were not only frustrated, but felt powerless to change conditions to reduce the frustration. The results appear to be a blind rage and lashing out at any available targets.

The instrumental qualities of riots can be seen in the attempts by militant groups to use violence to focus public attention on certain situations and to force political leaders to make concessions. Investigation has revealed that small, organized groups attempted to instigate rioting because of the anticipated consequences. As already noted, the Progressive Labor Movement passed out inflamatory pamphlets hoping to generate violent conflict, thus further polarizing whites and blacks to increase the movement's membership and to embarrass the government. But it is doubtful that without the underlying frustration such attempts would have met with much success. This is not meant to imply that most or even a majority of riot participants did so because they felt that such violence would bring desired social change but rather that some militant groups have attempted to encourage conflict between ghetto residents and the police for their own ends.

On the individual level, the looting that frequently accompanied rioting provided food, liquor, clothing, appliances, and other objects that many people had desired but had been unable to afford. Probably, some actively participated in rioting not because of any deep feeling of frustration but because they perceived the riot as an opportunity to loot with little chance of legal reprisal. In a review of civil disturbances including urban riots, Dynes and Quarantelli (1968) reported that in the riots individuals and groups looted more for profit than for ideology. They concluded that many rioters saw the outburst as a chance to redistribute the property and wealth in their community in a way to benefit themselves.

Both the Riot Commission and the Violence Commission made recommendations for alleviating the conditions responsible for such violent outbursts. The Riot Commission (1968, p. 413) recommended that institutional discrimination, which restricts minority individuals' choice of housing, employment, and education, be eliminated. The commission encouraged public and private institutions, businesses, churches, government agencies, and so on to help minorities to solve their economic problems, thus alleviating the feelings of frustration and powerlessness.

The Violence Commission (1969, pp. 271–82) made a large number of recommendations for dealing with specific types of violence. They, too, strongly recommend programs to reduce the frustration of the disadvantaged in American society. The commission suggested a cut in the defense budget and a massive increase of $20 billion in social-welfare expenditures. The intent was to reduce the level of frustration associated with poverty. Related to this goal was the recommendation of providing meaningful jobs to all able to work and providing adequate housing to all citizens.

Several social-control recommendations were made to increase inhibitions against aggression. These included more and better trained police officers and crowd-control equipment. Also, more sure punishment for violent behavior was suggested to reduce instrument aggression such as looting. The commission made a large number of specific recommendations for strengthening the police, courts, and correctional institutions.

At the individual level, citizens were encouraged to become personally involved in violence prevention by supervising the television their children watched, to seriously consider if they needed a hand gun—a suggestion intended to reduce the number of hand guns available in society, and to try to bridge the "generation gap" and open communication between the young and old.

The Control of Aggression

Aggression is a part of the American way of life and it is doubtful that many Americans would want to completely eliminate such behavior. Spirited competition between businesspeople, basketball teams, scientists and a reluctant environment or killer virus, students in the classroom, have contributed to the development of the extended personal freedoms and the high standard of living available in this country. But, the fact that society has made a wide range of aggressive behaviors "crimes" and provided for the capture and punishment of offenders reveals its desire to control destructive aggression. Also, public opinion polls, support for law-and-order candidates, and the establishment of government commissions indicate a desire to reduce the escalating violence. It seems that there is a fairly high degree of consensus among Americans that although not all aggressive behavior is "bad" or 'wrong," the more destructive forms are and should be prevented or controlled. The first step in designing programs to prevent and control violence is to recognize that aggression can be the product of a wide variety of causes.

BIOLOGICAL CONTROL TECHNIQUES

The evidence that aggression can be caused by brain damage and hormone level dictates that research be conducted to develop more accurate means of identifying these causes. Also, research needs to be done to discover ways of correcting or controlling brain damage and hormone imbalance. Finally, current techniques of identification and treatment should be implemented and made available to the general public. Children, when they receive their school checkup, could be examined for the above-mentioned conditions and medical treatment made available to those who require it.

SOCIAL-LEARNING CONTROL TECHNIQUES

The greatest potential for altering aggressive behavior is provided by the social-learning model of aggression. People can be taught nonaggressive behavior patterns, be taught to use aggression only in specific situations, and be reinforced for performing appropriate behavior and punished for inappropriate behavior.

Parents can be encouraged to use child-rearing practices that emphasize cooperation and negotiation rather than conflict. Television, movies, and other forms of mass media can be invited to not only reduce the violence contained in their presentations but also to present nonaggressive models in a more favorable light. Cooperation and kindness can replace toughness as characteristics associated with social approval and getting ahead in American society.

The judicial system can be overhauled to ensure those accused of crimes a speedy trial and those who are found guilty sure punishment. We are not advocating negating any of the personal-freedom safeguards in the judicial system but rather are advocating the creation of more courts and appointment of additional judges so that the weeks, months, and even years of delay between arrest and trial are shortened.

Prison reforms that emphasize preparation for legitimate participation in society would probably reduce the recidivism rate. Most prisons are overcrowded, understaffed, and inadequately financed so that they end up providing custodial care for prisoners and leave their education to other prisoners. The result is that prisons frequently are vocational schools for criminals.

FRUSTRATION-AGGRESSION CONTROL TECHNIQUES

The frustration-aggression theory suggests that programs be designed to alleviate poverty and racism, two major sources of widespread frustration in American society. Although the War on Poverty of the 1960s was no more successful than was the concurrent war in Southeast Asia, this should not discourage policy makers from seeking better solutions to the problems of inequity. Highest priority should be given to programs that prepare the poor for greater participation in society and that create opportunities for them to become a part of the mainstream. On the other hand, it is recognized that there will always be a segment of population who, because of physical, mental, or social handicaps, are unable to provide for themselves. The assurance of an adequate standard of living for these individuals would greatly reduce personal frustration.

Finally, support for community mental-health facilities and public education on availability of mental-health counseling would provide assistance for those who feel pressure to engage in violent behavior. Public-education programs could teach the symptoms of violent behavior so that family and friends could recognize when a person is moving toward a violent outburst.

None of these suggestions are the ultimate answer to violence in U.S. society, but all have the potential to make a significant contribution to reducing the violence and its attendant suffering.

Summary

The increase in violence in American society as evidenced by violent crime, terrorism, conflict in the public schools, and urban riots has prompted demands for the study of aggressive behavior. It is assumed that once the causes of aggression have been identified, programs to control such behavior or to channel it into less-destructive activities can be developed.

There are many different definitions of *aggression,* but all involve the injury of another person. One group of definitions focuses only on whether someone was harmed; another includes intent, thus eliminating accidents but making the study of aggression more difficult because of the problems in determining why someone committed an act that injured another.

There are many theories put forth concerning what causes aggression. We discussed several explanations, including biologically based psychoanalytic and ethological instinct theories, hormone-imbalance theories, brain-damage theories, and chromosome-abnormality theory; pain-aggression reflex theory; frustration-aggression theory; and social-learning aggression theory. Research support for each varies, showing that none of these explanations should be taken on faith to be true as has often been the case in the past. In fact, it appears that there is not a single cause of aggressive behavior; rather, the evidence indicates that hormones, brain damage, frustration, and learning can each produce aggressive behavior and that frequently more than one of these factors combine to cause a particular aggressive act.

Crime ranging from physical, individual violence to urban riots has been identified as the manifestation of a violent society that is becoming even more violent. Presidential commissions, citizen organizations, law-and-order associations, and research into the causes of violence have all been initiated to help combat this problem.

Two federal commissions were organized to investigate the degree of violence on television and its relationship to viewer behavior. In the 1950s, one discovered a high level of violence on television and concluded that exposure to such programs may predispose delinquent acts. In the 1960s, another found an even higher rate of violence and concluded that the heavy dose of violent viewing has an influence "only on some children" and "only in some" situations. This conclusion has been challenged by several scientists as not being strong enough, including some who worked on the committee and on whose research the conclusion rests.

During the 1960s, violent urban riots occurred in Harlem, Watts, Newark, and Detroit. The underlying frustration, caused by several different types of discrimination, exclusion, and neglect, experienced by black Americans in urban ghettos was identified as one of the principal causes of such outbursts. Considerable socially learned aggression in the form of looting was also documented. The National Advisory Commission on Civil Disorders studied the events and conditions leading to the riots and made recommendations to reduce the level of frustration of ghetto residents in hopes of preventing future riots.

The concern of many citizens as well as government officials about the degree of violence in society necessitates an overall attempt to reduce violence to an "acceptable" level. Research to discover ways to identify and correct hormonal imbalance and brain damage can have a significant impact, especially if the techniques of identification and treatment are made available to the general public. Learned aggression can be reduced by encouraging the use of nonaggressive behavior such as cooperation and negotiation. Television programs and movies could not only show less violence but also portray nonaggressive models in a more favorable light. Finally, programs to alleviate poverty and racism can reduce the frustration experienced by a significant proportion of the American public. This would reduce their instigation to aggression and in turn would decrease their participation in violent activities.

12

collective
behavior

Introduction

To this point in our discussion of the field of social psychology, most of the concepts we have studied are used to explain the existence of stability and order in human social interaction. In an effort to understand the consistency and predictability of human behavior, the social psychologist employs concepts such as norm, conformity, role, status, social system, self, attitude, and personality. These concepts help us realize the extent to which most of our actions, as well as the actions of others around us, are governed by established norms that have been learned during the socialization experience and are applied as individuals occupy different positions and roles during the course of their lives.

However, there are numerous examples of human behavior at the group level that appear, at least at first glance, to be contrary to the notion of social order. The label "collective behavior" has been generally applied to these events and refers to "group behavior which originates spontaneously, is relatively unorganized, fairly unpredictable and planless in its course of development, and which depends on interstimulation among participants" (Milgram and Toch, 1969, p. 507). Examples of collective behavior include panics, revolutions, riots, lynchings, manias, crazes, and fads. All these actions appear to be nonnormative and contrary to expectations of social order, at least in terms of traditional definitions and expectations.

The study of collective behavior has attracted the interest of the social psychologist for many years. The first textbook published under the title *Social Psychology* (Ross, 1908) devoted extensive attention to the description and analysis of crowds. The periodic occurrences of race riots, destructive and deadly panics, lynchings, and revolutions have continued to sharpen the interest of the student of human behavior and have challenged his or her abilities to place these events within the larger context of everyday interaction.

Traditional approaches to the study of collective behavior have emphasized the importance of emotion, suggestability, and irrationality in the understanding of collective episodes. In the early work of LeBon (1896) and Freud (1922), crowd participants were viewed basically as creatures of passion who act on impulse and are unable to control their own actions basically because the power of control has been given over to the collectivity, what LeBon called the "group mind." Crowd actions are seen as spontaneous and noninstitutionalized, lacking in structure and stability.

More recent studies of collective behavior, however, have taken a rather different approach. In their review of the literature of the late 1960s and 1970s, Marx and Wood (1975) note a growing belief that collective behavior can be studied within the same framework that is used to study more conventional behavior. For example, in a study of a confrontation between students and administration at Northwestern University, Berk (1974) began with the assumption that crowd participants (1) exercise a substantial degree of *rational* decision making rather than being strictly creatures of passion and irrationality; and (2) should *not* be defined a priori as less rational than in other contexts. Berk (1974), Raiffa (1970), Schelling (1963), and others have applied a gaming-theory approach to the study of collective behavior, which assumes a highly rational conscious weighing of payoffs that participants associate with alternative courses of action. This approach describes decision-making processes in crowds as follows: ". . . each individual in the crowd is faced with a series of decisions. Options for actions are noted, the likelihood for various events assessed, preferences are constructed and eventually the 'best' outcome selected. In a group context, all these processes depend on others in the crowd. Hence, one can view milling before concerted action as a period in which these assessments are made and in which payoff matrices are communicated, alternative action suggested and negotiated settlements reached. Crowds will continue to mill until mutually satisfactory solutions occur and are widely known" (Berk, 1974, p. 364).

Studying Collective Behavior

Much of the empirical literature on collective behavior is constrained by problems that are endemic to work in this area (Berk, 1972). For example, early studies tended to rely heavily on accounts provided by interested observers and bystanders of collective episodes. Researchers have always recognized the problems associated with the fact that collective outbursts are not highly predictable and, therefore, do not always occur at a time or place that is convenient for collecting data. Thus, the tendency has often been to rely on secondary sources, such as newspaper accounts and historical records, or on narratives provided after the fact by participants or observers. Narratives rely on the reconstruction of events based upon recall, and in most instances the sources are untrained in social-science research methods.

Despite these difficulties, a number of approaches have been used by researchers in attempting to study the phenomenon of collective behavior. In combination, these approaches have tempered some of the distorted views of crowds and other collective episodes that characterized the early literature in the field. The major approaches to the study of collective behavior are summarized below (see also Milgram and Toch, 1969).

SURVEY METHODS

Social scientists have used both questionnaires and personal interviews as survey methods in studying collective-behavior episodes. Usually, these surveys are taken after the fact and participants are requested to recall their involvement as well as their feelings, perceptions, and observations. However, other studies have used survey techniques to examine collective behavior as it is occurring. For example, Mann, Nagel, and Dowling (1976) studied an economic panic in Adelaide, Australia, even as it was occurring by systematically sampling and interviewing persons standing in lines to withdraw their savings from a financial institution that they believed was failing. Although secondary accounts from the news media may have led one to believe that this was a wholesale economic panic, their interviews with actual participants led the researchers to conclude that there was "little evidence of panic in the popular sense, that is, incoordination, destructive competitiveness, and mob-like behavior. Most withdrawers were very anxious, but they waited patiently in well ordered, self-regulated queues" (p. 229). There are some obvious limitations in using survey research methods to study some types of collective behavior. For example, members of a murderous lynch mob are hardly likely to submit to an interview and the person fleeing a burning building cannot be expected to pause and fill out a questionnaire. Nevertheless, this method has important applications in increasing our understanding of collective-behavior phenomena.

CONTENT ANALYSIS

Numerous secondary sources are available that provide a rich pool of information for the researcher who is interested in particular collective-behavior episodes. For example, if one were interested in studying the riots and violence that occurred at the Democratic Convention in Chicago in 1968, one could turn to the hours of television footage that were shot at the time; to the hundreds of interviews that were conducted with elected officials, with policemen, and with participants in the demonstrations; to the analysis that was conducted by a presidential commission appointed to determine the causes of this and similar disturbances in other American cities in the late 1960s; to the writings of the leaders of the Yippies and other quasi-revolutionary groups that played crucial roles in the disturbance; and so on. All these sources would allow the researcher to develop a broad and comprehensive picture of this particular historical event. Similarly, numerous sources are becoming available if one is interested in studying the mass suicides in Jonestown, Guyana in 1978. From these sources, one could piece together a rather comprehensive picture of the events that led to this tragedy and place them within the context of other cult movements. Content analysis provides an after-the-fact method of studying collective-behavior episodes but is useful in increasing our understanding of these events.

OBSERVATIONAL TECHNIQUES

As noted, one of the problems in studying collective behavior has been the fact that such episodes are difficult to predict and do not always occur at a time or place that affords direct access to the events as they are happening. Nevertheless, there are a growing number of instances in which social scientists have been present and have been able to become direct observers of the action. For example, Berk (1974) and several of his students became participant observers in a confrontation between students and university administrators. Each of the participant observers collected extensive field notes that, along with other sources, became the materials used to test a gaming theory of crowd behavior. The carefully trained observer can collect data that are extremely useful in testing specific research hypotheses. In fact, data collected this way by trained researchers have contributed greatly to the erosion of stereotypical views of collective behavior that characterized the literature for many years.

EXPERIMENTAL APPROACHES

Several researchers have attempted to study collective behavior by developing lab experiments that test relevant theoretical variables. Although it is amply clear that the conditions that give rise to authentic collective behavior episodes are not easily reproduced in the laboratory (Milgram and Toch, 1969), some innovative studies have appeared periodically in the research literature. For example, an early study by French (1944) attempted to simulate panic conditions in order to assess the differential reactions of organized and unorganized groups. Groups that had either been organized and structured beforehand or had been left unorganized and unstructured were placed in a locked room and were led to believe that a fire had started in the building. To simulate conditions that might lead to panic, fire bells were sounded and smoke poured under the door of the locked room. No panic occurred among the participants although the previously organized groups tended to react in a more orderly way than did the previously unorganized groups.

Mintz (1951) had a group of subjects stand around a bottle with a narrow neck and had each hold a string attached to a cone in the bottle. If drawn out one at a time in an orderly fashion, each cone could easily be removed from the bottle. However, if more than one cone was drawn out at a time, jamming occurred. To simulate a panic situation, Mintz would have water rise slowly in the bottle, and subjects were rewarded if their cones stayed dry and fined according to what extent their cones got wet. Mintz found that the reward structure was important in determining whether or not the subjects removed their cones in an orderly fashion or panicked and caused jamming. Also important was whether group members developed a cooperative or a competitive orientation.

Although important theoretical aspects of gaming theory and decision theory have been tested or proposed for study in the experimental lab (see Berk, 1974; Buckley, Burns, and Meeker, 1974; Johnson, Stemler, and Hunter, 1977), much work still remains to be done before this literature is entirely convincing. Milgram and Toch proposed several years ago: "There is no really satisfactory experiment on collective behavior. The best is still that of Mintz, but it stands in relation to actual panic as the game of Monopoly does to high finance" (1969, p. 582).

In summary, many different tools and techniques are available to the researcher interested in studying collective behavior. However, it must be recognized that this area presents problems that differ in important ways from other research areas discussed in this book. As we have noted, persons fleeing in panic from a burning building are not amenable to the same research techniques that one might use in studying the decision-making process and communication patterns that occur in a lodge meeting. Lynchings and revolutions cannot be reproduced in the lab. Nevertheless, the imaginative student of collective behavior can develop techniques and procedures that will increase our knowledge and understanding in this important area of behavior.

Types and Examples of Collective Behavior

The term *collective behavior* has been applied to a broad range of group activities ranging from the rather spontaneous and short-lived actions of a crowd to the more organized, structured, and long-term experiences of a major social movement. We will discuss for illustration several types of collective behavior in this section. Other examples will be covered in our discussion of theoretical approaches to the study of collective behavior and a more detailed section on social movements.

THE CROWD

We ride the busy subway or bus to and from work; we attend the theater and athletic events with large numbers of other people; we join in a mass political demonstration in an effort to change the direction of our nation's domestic or foreign policy; we rally with others to seek improved rights for an oppressed minority group. Each of these actions could be viewed as crowd behavior. *"Crowd* is a generic term referring to highly diverse conditions of human assemblage: audience, mob, rally, and panic all fall within the definition of crowds. Common to these terms is the idea of human beings in sufficiently close proximity that the fact of aggregation comes to influence behavior" (Milgram and Toch, 1969, p. 509).

Unfortunately for the researcher, crowd incidents do not seem to follow any recurrent and predictable pattern. The riot and panic that led to the deaths of several hundred spectators following a soccer match in Lima, Peru, clearly differs in important ways from the huge crowds that gathered in Rome for the coronation of Pope John Paul II.

Roger Brown (1954) developed a taxonomy of crowds that attempts to provide some structure to the field. Following the earlier work of Park and

A common example of collective behavior: an estimated 200,000 pack a southern California racetrack for a rock concert. *Source:* Wide World Photos, Inc.

Burgess (1921), Brown classifies crowds as either active or passive. Passive crowds are given the label *audiences* and can be either casual (a group pausing on a street corner to observe some stimulus event) or intentional (spectators at an athletic event) in nature. Active crowds are called *mobs* and include aggressive collectivities, such as rioters and lynch mobs, panics of escape and acquisition, and expressive crowds.

Using a somewhat similar typology, Blumer (1951) refers to crowds as either *acting* or *expressive.* Acting crowds are those that seek, in one way or another, to change their social environment. Expressions and behavior are directed outward toward some event or target. It is the active crowd that engages in more violent forms of behavior that may focus on property, as in a riot, or a person or persons, as in a lynching. Although in their more visible and publicized forms acting crowds tend to be hostile and violent, this need not be the case. For example, acting crowds at athletic events can be a source of emotional support for their team and can be a source of comfort during times of disaster.

Expressive crowds exist to give expression to the feelings of individual members. Thus, the subjective experiences of the individual members are of primary interest and concern, such as in the highly emotional religious revival or the group of teenagers caught up in euphoric adoration of their latest rock idol.

Within the context of the expressive crowd, traditional norms and social constraints are no longer relevant. The goal of the participant is often to really "let go" and to experience new emotional or spiritual "highs." In such a context, Turner and Killian note that "the emergent definition . . . is one which makes behavior sensible that would normally be regarded as eccentric or immoral. It gives significance to subjective sensations which would otherwise be meaningless or disturbing" (1972, p. 102). Inhibitions are lowered and the individual frequently engages in acts that, when reflected upon later, will cause feelings of embarrassment or even guilt.

In addition to these two major types, other crowds have been defined by Blumer as *casual* (made up of individuals who come together largely spontaneously for a brief period of time while their attention is focused on a common event or object) and *conventionalized* (made up of a group of persons who assemble for a specific purpose, such as to view a theater production or a movie). Some analysts distinguish audiences from crowds, but in Blumer's terms the audience would probably be considered a type of conventionalized crowd.

Whatever the preferred method of classifying crowds, it is important to consider the question of what actually "causes" the individual crowd member to begin to act out a form of behavior that is probably different from what would occur without the collectivity.

Berk (1974) suggests that one of the key determinants is perceived support from other actors. *Support* is defined as "actions by crowd members which decrease the anticipated costs for a given individual" (p. 366). Indicators of support include the following: (1) the actual *number* of other people acting in ways that are consistent with the desired action of the individual; (2) the visibility of the actions of others, which allows the individual crowd member to be aware of their support; (3) the ease of interpreting the actions of others as supportive; and (4) the proximity of acting others. Support from other participants obviously increases the potential rewards and decreases the potential costs of the individual actor in a crowd situation.

Similarly, Granovetter (1978) argues that individuals have different "thresholds" at which they will be willing to engage in an act such as a strike or a riot. A *threshold* is defined as the number or proportion of others who must make the commitment to act before a given actor is willing to do so. Thus, a "radical" might have a low threshold and be willing to riot even when no one else does so. Someone else might have a 90 percent threshold, entering the fray only when 90 percent of the other people present have already entered. Like game theory and decision theory, the threshold model assumes rational actors who have complete information. What accounts for outcomes is the simple principle of aggregation—as each individual joins the action, the way is paved for others to join because their individual threshold has now been reached.

Experimental evidence tends to support these ideas in that it has been shown that the initial size of a crowd has a clear effect on the probability of others adopting the behavior of the crowd (Milgram, Bickman, and Berkowitz, 1969). For example, although only 4 percent of the passersby stopped alongside a single individual staring toward the upper floors of a neighboring building, 40 percent stopped alongside a stimulus crowd of fifteen.

An Unresolved Issue in Studying Crowds: The Unit of Analysis There is some confusion as to whether the proper unit of analysis in describing crowds should be the individual or the collectivity. Zimbardo (1969), in an excellent discussion of a broad range of antisocial behaviors, opts for an emphasis on the individual. Zimbardo calls the process through which normally unanticipated behaviors begin to appear in emerging groups as "deindividuation."

He defines *deindividuation* as "a complex, hypothesized process in which a series of antecedent social conditions lead to changes in perception of self and others, and thereby to a lowered threshold of normally restrained behavior. Under appropriate conditions what results is the 'release' of behavior in violation of established norms of appropriateness" (Zimbardo, 1969, p. 251). He also notes that such conditions permit the expression of such antisocial behaviors as selfishness, greed, hostility, lust, power seeking, and so on.

Conditions that Zimbardo identifies as releasing spontaneous, impulsive behaviors on the part of the individual are similar to those we discussed earlier from Berk, and include: (1) anonymity—others cannot identify the actor or evaluate, judge, or punish his or her performance; (2) *responsibility* is made insignificant or is shared with others (see chapter 10); (3) the presence of others aids anonymity and shared responsibility but also contributes a *modeling* effect; (4) *time perspectives* change such that the individual forgets past and future obligations and "lives for the moment;" and (5) individual *arousal* is often stimulated or induced through preparatory actions, such as singing, chanting, and shouting. In addition, behavior is often less restrained in novel or unstructured situations and when states of consciousness have been altered through taking drugs or drinking alcoholic beverages.

In summary, deindividuated behavior is emotional, impulsive, irrational, and atypical. It also tends to be unresponsive to features of the situation that would normally evoke a more rational, constrained response.

Weller and Quarantelli (1973) prefer the collectivity as the proper unit of analysis. They feel that the theoretical separation between collective behavior and other areas of sociology is artificial, unnecessary, and unfruitful. A more theoretically meaningful approach, from this perspective, would be to not only search for the social conditions that lead to collective behavior episodes and the social consequences that result but also to define the problems of analysis at the social level.

Traditional sociological models of institutional behavior tend to treat individual behavior as unproblematic, governed by social norms that, in turn, are affected by socialization, anticipation of sanctions, exchanges of valued commodities, and power relationships (Weller and Quarantelli, 1973; p. 673). Taken this as a given, the focus of the sociologist has then been concentrated on a consideration of social patterns that develop in the group. Using this same orientation, a more sociological approach to the study of collective behavior would emphasize two major aspects of social organization: social norms and social relationships. Collective-behavior episodes can then be studied and understood in terms of emerging or enduring systems of social relationships. The characteristics of individual actors, although important, become secondary to the patterns of social organization that exist or develop in the collectivity.

A social-psychological approach to the study of collective behavior looks both at the characteristics of the individual and the patterns of the collectivity. Therefore, methodological and theoretical advances that develop from either or both of these traditions will aid the student of social psychology in improving his or her understanding of collective-behavior phenomena.

Communication in the Crowd: Rumors Most analysts of crowd behavior argue that the dispersal of information through rumors is one of the most important and significant processes underlying the whole phenomenon. In order for a mass of individuals to join together in a common course of action, such as a riot, panic, or lynching, they must usually develop something approximating a common definition of the situation. A target must be identified; cause must be attributed; appropriate responses must be defined; and so on. The development of this common definition often occurs through the rumor-dissemination process.

Turner and Killian (1972, p. 32) have noted that rumor is the characteristic mode of communication in collective-behavior episodes. It is the mechanism by which meaning is applied to what is otherwise likely to be an ambiguous situation. This conception is clearly implied in Shibutani's definition of *rumor* as "communication through which men caught together in an ambiguous situation attempt to construct a meaningful interpretation of it by pooling their intellectual resources" (1966, p. 17). Thus, rumors play an important problem-solving role; they allow people to deal with the complexities and uncertainties of life by providing meaning and structure. The classic statement in this regard has been provided by Allport and Postman

(1947) who argue that importance and ambiguity are the key ingredients in the rumor process. When clear explanations of some phenomenon are not directly available, the tendency is to fill the information gap with rumors, which then relieve the tensions of uncertainty.

Growing awareness of the importance of the rumor process in contributing to such collective actions as riots is illustrated by organized efforts to control rumors through informing citizens about the facts in crisis situations (Ponting, 1973). During the urban riots in the late 1960s, rumor-control centers were established in many cities with the explicit purpose of combatting the rumors that developed out of and in turn fed the crises that were occurring. Although the effectiveness and success of these programs varied from city to city, it is worth noting that the President's National Advisory Commission on Civil Disorders cited the rumor-control center in Chicago for its role in preventing the outbreak of civil disorders in that city.

As noted above, rumors are most likely to develop in situations that are characterized by both *ambiguity* and *stress*. Experimental evidence is particularly supportive of the importance of ambiguity in fostering rumors (see Schachter and Burdick, 1955; Anthony, 1973), and a recent analysis of rumors of mass poisoning and other atrocities in Biafra supports the importance of stress (Nkpa, 1977). If the situation were unambiguous, there would be no direct need for the development of rumors to provide meaning and structure. Stress increases the *immediacy* of need for meaning. Thus, when our personal welfare appears to be threatened in some way and there is no clear definition of what is happening or why, rumors are likely to run rampant. Rumors are generally passed by word of mouth from one person to another, and, during periods when large groups of people are milling together, the speed of the transmission is greatly facilitated. Few recipients of the rumor are likely to be interested in establishing its authenticity, and so the information that is passed from one person to another is likely to be accepted at face value.

Because of the absence of interest in checking on the validity of rumors at the time of transmission, the information that is disseminated is likely to be highly distorted. This distortion can take a number of different forms. For example, although early social-psychological theory suggested that rumors "grow," this appears to be true only in a certain sense of the word. Rumors grow in that, up to a point, an ever-expanding *number of persons* are consumers or recipients of the message. However, in terms of *content,* the opposite trend is usually observed. That is, any given body of information, whether it be fact or fiction, is subject to shrinkage as information is lost through successive transmittals (Campbell, 1958; Fliegel and Kivlin, 1974). An important consequence of this loss of information is that the relative importance of any given piece of information retained may take on a very different meaning (Fliegel and Kivlin, 1974, p. 6).

This altering tends to follow three patterns (DeFleur, 1962; Rosnow and Fine, 1976): (1) leveling, or the process by which the rumor grows shorter, more concise, and more easily grasped and told; (2) sharpening, or the process through which certain details remain and become the dominant theme of the rumor while others drop out; and (3) assimilation, which involves distorting the rumor in the direction of established norms and conventions. Both the leveling and sharpening move the rumor in a direction that is consistent with the primary needs, values, and concerns of the group.

Through these processes, as information is passed through a group both shrinkage and distortion occur. *Distortion* has been defined as changes that "occur in message content as a function of the 'normal' communication process" (Fliegel and Kivlin, 1974, p. 9). This concerns primarily the imperfect reproduction of a message in successive transmissions in a social network. Distortion, like shrinkage, takes on less of a negative connotation in this view and is seen as a rather natural process associated with practically any information transmittal.

Rumors play a critical role in most episodes of collective behavior. Through providing meaning in situations of ambiguity and stress, they provide an orientation for the potential actors by helping them develop a common or shared definition of the situation. This, in turn, aids in the mobilization of the participants for action by identifying a target in a riot or lynching, by attributing cause for problems and failures, and by defining what would be an appropriate course of action.

The 'Death' of Paul McCartney A fascinating example of the rumor development and transmission process can be found in Barbara Suczek's (1972) study, "The Curious Case of the 'Death' of Paul McCartney." In late 1969, a series of rumors developed relating to the alleged death of Beatle Paul McCartney. Within a very short time of the appearance of the first rumors, major segments of the news media were actively involved in reporting and researching the phenomenon. Whatever its source and purpose, the rumor spread quickly throughout much of the world. Thousands of fans apparently remained glued to their radios hoping to receive additional information, mourners began to gather outside the McCartney home in London, and letters and phone calls were being received nonstop by the offices of Beatle publicists. By November, the story had received sufficient interest that *Life Magazine* carried "the Case of the Missing Beatle" as its cover story, thus carrying the rumor to the remote outposts of the literate world.

The gist of the McCartney rumor was as follows:

> Paul McCartney was allegedly killed in an automobile accident in England in November 1966. The remaining Beatles, fearing that public reaction to the news would adversely affect the fortunes of the group, agreed among themselves to keep the matter a secret. Since it was obvious that Paul could not simply disappear from their midst without rousing a storm of embarrassing questions, they hit upon the idea of hiring a double to play his part in public, a role that was filled to perfection by the winner of a Paul McCartney Look-Alike Contest, an orphan from Edinburgh named William Campbell. By an astonishing stroke of good luck, it turned out that Campbell not only bore a striking physical resemblance to McCartney, but was also endowed with similar musical abilities so that, with a bit of practice, he was able to sustain a performance that completely deceived an attentive and discriminating audience for almost three years. A slight awkwardness developed when a private affair intruded upon the public image: "Campbell" married the lady of his own choice, Linda Eastman, causing a short-lived flurry of consternation among Beatle fans who had for some time been expecting Paul to marry British actress Jane Asher. Miss Asher, the story goes, was paid a handsome sum to be quiet (Suczek 1972, p. 63).

However, Suczek notes that for some unspecified reason, the plot that had been hatched took an important qualitative change and, at least for John Lennon, it developed into an all-encompassing religious vision. This was manifested by his insertion of messages relating to McCartney's death into the lyrics of Beatle songs and onto the decorations of the album covers. Suczek notes that the catalog of such "buried" clues that continued to feed the rumor was both lengthy and ingenious. For example, on the cover of "Magical Mystery Tour," the other three Beatles are pictured wearing red carnations, but McCartney's is black. Similarly, on the centerfold of "Sgt. Pepper," McCartney is pictured wearing an arm patch reading "O.P.D.," which supposedly stood for "officially pronounced dead." Finally, it was said that if the song "Revolution Number 9" is played backwards, a voice seems to say, "Turn me on, dead man!"

Such clues were reinforced by other rumors that supposedly supported the story. For example, a professor at the University of Miami is reported to have applied scientific voice detectors to some of the Beatle records and concluded that at least three different voices were attributed to Paul McCartney. And so it goes.

Rumors are an important mechanism of information transmittal in most societies and, as noted, their significance is increased dramatically during periods of stress or crisis. It is difficult to imagine any major episode of collective behavior taking place without the occurrence of rumors to fuel the fires, to identify targets, and to provide structure and meaning for past, ongoing, and anticipated events. Thus, in a very real sense, rumors can be seen as the principle "collective problem-solving mechanism" (Turner and Killian, 1972) in most collective behavior events.

The Role of Leadership in a Crowd The triggering of activity in many collective-behavior episodes can often be attributed to the actions of one or more persons who assume a leadership role. This emergent leadership often acts as a stimulus in that it does first what the others will do subsequently (Brown, 1965). It is emergent in that although there will be leaders, they tend not to be selected in accordance with traditional or established practices. Rather, they emerge out of the course of group interaction, and, after the episode has run its course, they often disappear back into the crowd. The major exception to this is the development of leadership in major social movements. Many of the important political personalities of the last few decades gained their status and achieved worldwide recognition through their emergence as leaders of social movements. Examples include Ghandi, Ho Chi Mihn, Fidel Castro, Mao Tse Tung, and others. However, in more short-lived collective outbursts such as riots and lynchings, the persons who have occupied leadership positions usually merge back into the mass once the fury of the group is spent and the event has run its course.

Conventional leadership in normal day-to-day interactions tends to fall to those who best exemplify and most clearly follow conventional norms; leadership in a mob that is engaging in the violation of conventional norms tends to fall to those among whom the norms are the weakest (Brown 1965; p. 758). In many of the more violent mob activities directed against blacks around the turn of the century, a majority of the participants had lower-class backgrounds, and many of the leaders emerged from the very bottoms of the status hierarchy. For example, the acknowledged leader of the brutal Leeville lynching that occurred in 1930 was a man who could not read nor write, was without a regular occupation, drank heavily, and had been charged with bootlegging. At least eleven of the most active participants had previous police records (Cantril, 1963). Many of the conventional leaders of the community were opposed to what happened but dared do nothing about it.

Raper (1933) has made an important distinction in the type of leadership that appears in different forms of mob action. For example, he notes that many of the lynchings that occurred in the old South could be classified as either *proletariat* or *Bourbon* lynchings. The proletariat lynchings more clearly fit within our definition of collective behavior and were characterized by emergent and usually lower-class leadership. Such lynchings usually occurred in areas where blacks were the minority, where there was direct competition between blacks and lower-class whites, and where the object of the mob appeared to be more to persecute a race rather than a particular individual (Cantril, 1963). The proletariat lynching tended to be brutal, and frequently, at the encouragement of its leadership, the mob turned on other accessible minority group members after disposing of its first victim.

The Bourbon lynching was frequently organized and led by the leading citizens of the community and often occurred with the concurrence of local law-enforcement officials. Its object was to punish a specific individual for a specific crime, and once the action had been completed the group would be quickly disbanded. In this case, the leadership was neither emergent nor lower class. However, the Bourbon lynching was so highly organized and so institutionalized that it perhaps does not even fit within our definition of collective behavior.

Myrdal (1944), in his classic study of race relations in the United States, made a distinction that closely parallels that of Raper by discussing "vigilante" and "mob" lynchings. The former constituted almost an institutionalized mode for maintaining white supremacy; the latter was violent, unstructured, and less identifiable in terms of specific purpose. Again, one important distinction was the type of leadership for each.

The critical importance of leadership in most collective-behavior occurrences can best be summarized by reviewing the roles the leader plays. First, the leader helps build and increase the emotional tensions of the group. Anyone who has attended a religious revival can recognize this process. The revivalist uses approaches that arouse feelings of fear and guilt in the audience and then provides the opportunity for emotional catharsis by inviting the audience to come forward and confess Jesus. The leader of the lynch mob reminds his audience of the horror of the crime that has been committed (usually greatly exaggerated) and of the importance of their responsibility to right the wrong.

Second, the leader suggests a course of action that will relieve the built-up emotion. In the religious revival, this may be a confession of guilt and a public commitment to mend one's ways. In a lynch mob, this often involves the identification of a target and the specification of action that should be taken to right the wrong that has been committed.

Johnson (1974), on the other hand, attributes group action to what he refers to as a group-induced shift rather than to individual leaders. Numerous research studies in the past few years have found that in decision-making situations groups often tend to select courses of action that are more daring and risky than do individuals acting alone (see for example Cartwright, 1971; Pruitt, 1971; Silverthorne, 1971). However, Johnson argues that some group decisions are actually in a conservative direction; therefore, the label "group-induced shift" more adequately describes what happens. In many group or collective-behavior situations there will be a number of individuals with predispositions toward risk-taking or other more extreme behaviors. These individuals may act as models in creating a group-induced shift toward this more extreme or deviant pattern. The presence of the group allows the individual to be released from normal social constraints and to move toward a higher level of risk-taking. However, the group-induced shift in other situations may be in a more conservative direction, and the group may break up or engage in other more normal, traditional modes of action.

Finally, the leader justifies the specified course of action as being "right." For the timid, for the more rational, for those who hesitate, this is the final conversion process. The wrong *must* be righted; the sins *must* be confessed if salvation is ever to come; the member will never be able to feel right if the victim is not punished; and so on. In these ways, the leader helps mold and direct the emotions and actions of the gathered mass. If no one stepped forward to play these roles, the outcome would probably be far different than it otherwise is.

However, as is so often true in collective-behavior episodes, things are not always as they seem. In his study of social movements, Marx (1974) notes that some activists and even some leaders of social movements are actually "agent provocateurs" or informants who have been planted by authorities to create internal dissension, gain information on the group, and provoke the group to engage in illegal actions that would then justify a harsh response and negatively affect public opinion. Using Goffman's (1959) terminology, the informant and the agent provocateur are playing discrepant roles. However, this fact does not diminish their potential influence on the group nor their unique status as group leaders.

PANICS AS A TYPE OF CROWD BEHAVIOR

Some of the more dramatic episodes of crowd behavior that are discussed in the literature can be referred to as panics. Although panics tend to emerge from crowd situations—for example, spectators at a theater panic when someone yells "fire"—they can also occur in instances lacking one of the key properties of a crowd as determined by our earlier definition—close proximity. Economic panics can occur among persons who are widely dispersed (sometimes referred to as a mass in contrast to a crowd) if they come to apply a similar set of definitions to a common situation. Some stimulus is required to prompt the action of the dispersed participants, such as a television or radio report of a pending bank failure or of an invasion of aliens. The presence of a crowd, however, probably facilitates the panic reaction.

Crumbling Before the Juggernant:
Panic in Wartime

As American involvement in the Vietnam War wound down, dozens of field reports indicated that the public response to the dangers associated with the advance of Viet Cong and North Vietnamese troops frequently led to wide-scale panic. The following accounts describe the final days before the fall of the City of Danang:

At first there seemed to be no sense of impending disaster, no awareness of the mortal enemy gathering strength in the dark outside the city. Restaurants, cinemas and pool halls remained open and crowded; the seedy waterfront bars, lit with garish neon, and the French-style cafes were packed with people, especially the young. . . .

Even the refugees who flowed unendingly into the city showed few tears and little panic. From the old imperial capital of Hue, 50 miles to the north, the lines moved in silence, sometimes edging forward down the packed roads at the frustrating rate of only 20 miles a day. In all, 500,000 people swarmed into the city, doubling Danang's population in a matter of days. Amazingly, most of them were swiftly absorbed off the streets, out of the makeshift sidewalk shelters and shanties. . . . Though some emergency rice arrived from volunteer relief groups, the refugees' survival was largely in their own hands. Somehow it worked—for a while.

But soon, as the word spread that not only were district towns giving way but also capital cities and whole provinces, a desperate unease gripped Danang. With it came a growing hatred and confusion that are new even to this war. Gradually the city realized that it might not be safe after all, that the war was going much worse than anyone had feared. The news of the fall of Hue, which everybody expected the government to defend, came as a severe shock. Equally frightening, the dusty buses pathetically crowded with refugees were no longer coming in only from the northern provinces; they were arriving from the south as well, bringing with them the terrible news that the escape route down the coast was cut. Danang was sealed off. There was no way out except by sea or by air.

Quicky the mood of the city turned frightened and ugly. Banks simply ran out of cash as people rushed to withdraw their money. More and more disbanded soldiers, their guns slung carelessly over their shoulders, crowded the streets; some of them were raucously drunk. At the harbor, the troops withdrawn from Hue disembarked in mixed units, arriving in the confused state of a total rout. Enlisted men and officers alike dispensed with the niceties of rank or discipline. No one saluted, no one marched or regrouped. They just got off and wandered into town with their friends. . . .

By midweek the unease, the anger and the frustration had all boiled over into undisguised panic. One morning several rockets aimed at the airport fell short, striking the adjoining hamlet; six were killed and 36 wounded. With company-level engagements taking place just a few kilometers away, it was all too evident that the city was desperately vulnerable. Food was running low, and nobody knew how many more shipments would come in before it ran out altogether.

Many began frantically trying to find some way out of Danang by air. In one day, the price of a single one-way air ticket to Saigon on the black market jumped from $51 to $140. The traffic halted only when the military took control of the Air Viet Nam flights to provide for their own families. Then came the welcome promise that the U.S. would begin an airlift to take 10,000 people a day to Cam Ranh, a half-hour's trip by air some 200 miles to the south. But still there was panic. Even the so-called priority evacuation flight, limited to Americans and Vietnamese with proven U.S. connections, brought hundreds of people stampeding to the gleaming white U.S. consulate. Mimeographed consulate passes were photocopied and the forgeries passed on or sold to close friends or relatives. Even access through the guarded entrance to the airport became subject to bribes. By the morning of the priority flight, thousands of Vietnamese were besieging planes on the landing strip. The airport was described as "insecure," and not because of the enemy. Under these conditions it was hard to imagine a single Vietnamese civil servant willing to stay on the ground and organize the promised U.S. evacuation, much less how it could possibly be organized. . . .

In Danang, the day before the city fell, some 400 Vietnamese air force men firing pistols and grenades forced their way past women and children onto a World Airways 727 chartered to fly refugees from the city. Several people were crushed as the plane took off; others fell to their deaths after trying to cling to the still open stairs and wheel wells. The incident and the unruly mobs at the airport caused the U.S. to suspend its program of evacuating refugees by air. The chaos and hopelessness in Danang moved President Ford to order four U.S. Navy transports to stand off the Vietnamese coast to pick up refugees and take them to safety. "I have directed that U.S. Government resources be made available to meet humanitarian needs," declared the President. He also called upon "all nations and corporations that have ships in the vicinity" to help with the evacuation.

The panic later spread to Saigon itself, and, in their final evacuation of the city, American troops often used rifle butts to club panicking Vietnamese who were storming the American embassy. When the last escape routes by air and ground had been severed, tens of thousands of Vietnamese put out to sea in rafts, sampans, and fishing boats. For two days, many of the ships of the U.S. armada lingered off the coast to pick up survivors. Reports indicated that at night so many candles and lanterns burned on the water that from the air the offshore waters appeared to be a densely populated city. Some of these refugees were so afraid of being left behind that they set their small fishing boats ablaze in the hope of being picked up immediately.

(Source: *Time,* 7 April 1975, pp. 30–34. Reprinted by permission.)

Even in panic situations, however, not all individuals respond equally. In the economic panic in Adelaide, Australia, that was triggered by the rumored financial problems of a savings institution, some members of the crowd were actually there to *deposit* rather than *withdraw* funds (Mann, Nagel, and Dowling, 1976).

In the simplest sense, panics involve competition for something in short supply. This may be economic resources, products, social status, or exits. Economic panics occur when money or some other commodity is believed to be in short supply and may result in such behaviors as a run on a bank or a selling run on a stock exchange. Other panics may occur when groups of people believe that there are insufficient escape routes in a dangerous situation, such as when a building is on fire. Many of the 602 deaths that occurred in the Chicago Iriquois Theater fire in December 1903 were not caused by the fire itself but by the panic reaction of the audience who, in their competition for the short supply of exits, blocked and trampled each other, resulting in far more deaths than were necessary (see Brown, 1965).

Simulated panic situations have been created by French (1944), Mintz (1951), Kelley et al. (1965), and Guten and Allen (1972). From this experimental literature, the conclusion has developed that the individual's definition of the potential panic situation in terms of expectations about the likelihood of escape and probability of danger is crucial. For example, in

Guten and Allen's experiment, subjects were punished through the use of electrical shocks if they failed to "escape," and it was found that intensity of escape attempts was related curvilinearly to likelihood of escape. That is, subjects tried harder to escape if they were unsure that they would be able to do so. These results would help to explain why panics usually do not occur when danger is very high but probability of escape is very low, such as the case when men are trapped in a mine cave in. On the other hand, ambiguity about the degree of danger *and* the probability of escape increase the probability of panic behavior.

Expanding upon this experimental literature, Fritz and Williams (1957; p. 44) conclude that panics are most likely to occur when the following conditions exist:

1. Individuals perceive an immediate and severe danger, whether to life and limb or to one's financial security, social status within the community, and so on.
2. People believe that there is only one or a limited number of escape routes, or any other applicable form of "short supply." If there were a large number of escape routes that would easily accommodate all those in need, there would be no need for competition and, hence, panic.
3. People believe that the existing escape routes are closing, so that if one does not get out in a hurry, there will be no escape at all. If the escape routes are not closing, there should be ample time for everyone to make an escape, and panic will likely not occur.
4. Finally, there is either a lack of information or the existing communication channels are unable to keep everyone adequately informed on the issue. This leads to ambiguity and greater urgency in the situation.

We can briefly contrast two situations in order to demonstrate the operation of these factors. When American forces in Vietnam were still providing largely support functions rather than involvement in actual combat, a large group of South Vietnamese soldiers had been involved in close combat with a well-equipped contingent of Viet Cong for several days. Casualties inflicted on the South Vietnamese were high, and supplies were running low. Finally, the South Vietnamese soldiers found themselves virtually surrounded by the enemy. About this time, several American support helicopters were flown into the area to deliver supplies and to pick up the wounded and fly them out for medical assistance. The helicopters landed and unloaded their cargo under heavy enemy fire. Wounded South Vietnamese soldiers were taken aboard, and the helicopters were about ready to begin their departure. Suddenly, the remaining South Vietnamese rushed the copters and attempted to climb aboard. Some of them hung on the rotor blades and the landing gear. In order for the helicopters to lift off, it became necessary for South Vietnamese officers and their American advisors to turn their guns on their own soldiers and kill a number of them.

One can readily perceive the existence of an immediate and severe danger in this situation. Many of the soldier's comrades had already been killed. The survivors were surrounded by a relentless enemy that seemed to be closing in from all sides, cutting off routes of escape and retreat. By this time, the escape routes were clearly limited and, for many of the panicking soldiers, had now apparently further been narrowed to the departing heli-copters. Further, this final escape route was closing—if the men could not board the copters, they perceived that there would probably be no escape. By this time, the communication channels had broken down completely, and the officers were unable to influence the actions of their troops.

Contrast this situation with another that was personally experienced by one of the authors who with several friends, was occupying a small apart-ment near the Waikiki Beach in Oahu. At about 2:00 A.M., the group was awakened by loud knocking on the door. The apartment owner was inform-ing all residents that a severe earthquake had occurred somewhat earlier near Japan and that a large tidal wave was expected to hit the area within the next couple of hours. An earlier, similar experience had resulted in a great deal of damage and the loss of many lives. To avoid the reoccurrence of the earlier tragedy, the decision had been made to evacuate all from the low-lying areas that stood in the path of the tidal wave.

The situation was ripe for a panic response. The danger was defined as severe and potentially immediate. Many people had to be awakened, gotten out of their homes and apartments, and transported to higher ground. Thousands of people rushing to their cars at 2:00 A.M. to flee an area certainly creates at least the potential for a major panic. Escape routes at the time were still open, but they could be closed off rather quickly. However, there was no panic. Instead, the large area was evacuated quickly and effi-ciently. The primary difference between this example and the first seems to be that through the use of effective communication, the participants were kept fully informed at all times of existing conditions. Everyone was assured that although the potential escape routes were somewhat limited due to the limited number of highways out of the area, they were sufficient to meet the needs of the people. Authorities further assured everyone that the escape routes would not close unless everyone did panic. Law-enforcement officers and volunteers were out at all major intersections to assure a steady and continuous movement of the populace from the area. Drivers moved out as quickly as possible but retained a high degree of civility and cooperative-ness. Although the possibility of a panic was certainly present, it did not occur.

FASHIONS AND FADS

The examples of collective behavior discussed to this point tend to be dramatic and unconventional. There are other types that tend to be more trivial in terms of their total impact on individual lives, but they are also included under the umbrella of collective behavior. Two such types are *fads* and *fashions*. Unlike many collective episodes, which tend to be "crowd" phenomena, fads and fashions do not depend upon the physical proximity of participants and can affect the behavior of individuals in widely dispersed circumstances.

A fad can be defined as some short-lived variation in patterns of speech, behavior, or decoration. Its occurrence is quite unpredictable, but its life can be expected to be short. A recent example was the fad of "streaking" that appeared primarily on university campuses in the summer of 1974. Very few campuses did not experience at least one case of male and/or female stu-

What is fashionable in other cultures may seem strange in our own. A Ubangi woman with fashionably enlarged lips.

dents disrobing and racing through some public place. Often, huge crowds would gather at specified spots on campus as word circulated that some daring streakers would make their appearance at a specified hour.

The streaking phenomenon points out clearly the importance of the mass media in fad behavior (Anderson, 1977). Had not the television networks practically fallen over themselves to obtain footage on the events and interviews with the participants, it is extremely unlikely that the behavior would have spread as quickly and as generally as it did. This is true of other fads, such as speech patterns ("sit on it") and behaviors (Hula-Hoops and skateboards). The transmission of these patterns from one area to another is largely a function of the media, although in a mobile society such as ours they may also be carried more directly by individual actors.

Fads typically grow very rapidly, peak over a short period of time (everyone seems to be doing it), and then decline again almost as rapidly. However, some fads may stay on the scene for longer periods, and some even become a part of the culture and are passed from one generation to the next.

Fashions tend to be longer-lived than fads. However, fashion is a *process,* which means that it is a continuing state of change. Blumer (1968, pp. 341–42) notes that when we talk about fashion, we are dealing with "a continuing pattern of change in which certain forms enjoy temporary acceptance and respectability only to be replaced by others more abreast of the times."

When most of us think of fashions, we tend to think of hemline length, lapel width, hair lengths, the style of eyeglasses, and so on. However, the term applies to many other areas as well. When Jimmy Carter was first elected president, the "style" of leadership in Washington changed noticeably from the Nixon era. It became "fashionable" to be less formal and more open.

Traditionally, it has been assumed that fashions were introduced by people of high social status and that they then filter downward. In many instances, this is true, but the filtering also goes in the other direction as well. For example, some contemporary speech patterns, styles of dress, and food preferences (such as ethnic foods) originated in the lower social classes and then filtered upward.

Although fads and fashions tend to be more trivial than many of the other types of collective behavior covered in this chapter, they are nonetheless important. We can observe patterns of diffusion and influence in their transmission throughout a society, we can learn something about the formation and change in social norms and about conformity to those norms, and we can often find in fads and fashion important reflections about current changes and concerns in a society.

Short-lived but popular fads of the 1950s:3-d movie-goers and hula-hoop participants. *Source:* J.R. Eyerman, Life Magazine, © 1958 Time Inc. and Ralph Morse, Life Magazine, © 1952 Time Inc.

Theoretical Approaches to the Study of Collective Behavior

Numerous theoretical approaches have been taken to the study of collective behavior. The most fully developed early work was that of Gustave LeBon (1896), who, in his work on crowds, postulated that individuals undergo a radical transformation in crowds in which the "veneer" of civilization is stripped away and more primitive, irrational elements emerge. Through this transformation, a "mental unity" develops in the crowd, and the individual loses self-control and personal responsibility for action. The crowd is characterized by a very high level of emotion, and members display impulsive and extreme behaviors.

Although LeBon's work was influential for many years, its shortcomings as a general theory of collective behavior have been identified by several writers. For example, Milgram and Toch (1969) summarize the following major problems:

1. LeBon's generalizations are based on anecdotal and unsystematic evidence.
2. The irrationality of crowds is contrasted with the model of the normal, isolated individual. However, individuals also exhibit irrational and emotional behavior, even when alone.
3. LeBon's writings reflect the prejudices of his era, and his own racist views color many of his observations and conclusions.
4. Images of masses of people responding uniformly and uncritically simply are not supported by the available empirical data.

Early psychoanalytic theories of collective behavior, particularly those developed by Freud (1922), were highly influenced by LeBon's observations. In effect, Freud attempted to extend his psychoanalytic theory of individual behavior to group processes. Thus, primary emphasis was placed on irrational and unconscious motivation in crowd settings. In Freud's scheme, the ties that bind followers and leaders are critical and help account for violence in crowds. The individual participant comes to depend on the conscience of the leader and is no longer checked by his own superego.

More recently, gaming and decision-making theories have been applied to collective behavior by Brown (1965), Berk (1974), Raiffa (1970), Buckley, Burns, and Meeker (1974), and others. These approaches assume a much higher level of rationality among participants in crowds and downplay emotionalism, irrationality, impulse, and passion. Individual actors are seen as rational beings adopting prescriptive strategies designed to maximize personal rewards and minimize personal costs. Beliefs and actions are assumed to be well-grounded in reality rather than "lost" to some higher force such as a "group mind."

Though not applicable to all collective-behavior episodes (see Mann, Nagel, and Dowling, 1976), there is evidence that these more rational models better describe crowd actions than do images based on psychoanalytic or group-mind theories. However, they also face important difficulties in reducing extremely complex phenomena to theories growing largely out of two-person games, in assuming that individual decisions are not contingent on a prior decision made by others and in assuming simultaneous decision-making by actors (for a general critique, see Granovetter, 1978).

Although each of these theoretical approaches has some importance (and, decision-making theories particularly have a growing importance), the major theoretical orientations of the past two decades have been summarized under the general headings of contagion, convergence, and emergent norm theory. Each of these will be described in somewhat more detail below. In addition, Smelser (1963) has developed a general sociological theory that deals more with the *process* through which collective-behavior episodes emerge. We will use Smelser's theory in discussing a particular incident of collective behavior.

CONTAGION THEORY

Historically, contagion theory has probably been the most widely adopted approach in efforts to understand such phenomena as riots, panics, and other noninstitutionalized crowd actions. Theories of collective behavior based on contagion "explain collective behavior on the basis of some process whereby moods, attitudes, and behavior are communicated rapidly and accepted uncritically" (Turner, 1964, p. 384). As noted by Turner, the focal point of the theory has been to attempt to explain how people in a collectivity come to behave (1) uniformly; (2) intensely; and (3) at variance with their usual patterns.

Contagion theory grows out of the classic work of LeBon (1896) discussed above. LeBon sought to understand how groups of individuals could come to present characteristics that were both different and unpredictable from the characteristics of the individuals composing the group. LeBon's explanation came to be referred to as the "law of the mental unity of crowds." This proposed that under the right set of circumstances, the sentiments and ideas of all persons in a group would take one and the same direction, and individual initiative and personality would vanish. In such circumstances, the behavior that resulted would be unique to the group setting in that one could not predict its occurrence simply from the study of the individuals comprising the group.

Contagion theory relies heavily on such ideas as stimulus-response and emotional contagion. Supposedly, as a crowd mills about and interacts, emotions are transmitted quickly from one individual to the other, and each individual becomes transformed as he comes more and more under the influence of the group. This transformation, according to Blumer (1951), is facilitated through "circular reaction" or "a type of interstimulation" whereby one individual reproduces the stimulation that has come from another and when reflected back to this individual, reinforces the original stimulation.

The image of people held by the contagion theorist is not necessarily a negative view. People do not, through the exercise of individual free will, choose to engage in activities such as riots and lynchings. Rather, the individual is subject to the group and in certain types of crowd situations can totally lose personal individuality and become a part of a larger entity, which now makes the decisions and determines the course of action that is to be pursued.

Although the contagion view has remained popular in some circles, Turner (1964, pp. 386–87) has noted several problems with it as a general approach to the understanding of collective behavior. First, he notes that the theory seems to rely heavily on extreme and rare instances of behavior that attract much popular attention and interest but are not observed directly by the social scientists. Most of the accounts are historical and have been written by untrained and, often, not uninterested observers. However, even if the observations tend to be correct, Turner argues that it would be unwise to adopt such exceptional occurrences as the model for collective behavior as a whole.

Second, Turner is uncomfortable with the assumption that crowds require a level of psychological explanation that is different from that of other organized groups. The assumption that the social scientist who is interested in studying collective behavior must throw out the theories and tools that have been developed for the analysis of other types of behavior and begin anew is not acceptable.

Third, those factors that are advanced to explain contagion are not amenable to empirical verification, and, if they cannot be studied and submitted to test, they are of little value to the scientist. As Turner notes, "There may well be some contagiousness about a state of excitement, but it is doubtful that specific emotions are transmitted apart from some awareness of a situation to which they are appropriate responses." In other words, there may be some factors even in a situation of emotional contagion that can be identified and measured by the researcher. As currently conceptualized, the theory does not provide these.

Fourth, contagion theory does not provide a basis for predicting shifts that occur in most episodes of crowd behavior. For example, what determines the direction of the shift, and why is there a shift in one instance but not in another? Finally, contagion theory is not helpful in offering clues for the study of the organization of collective behavior. How does a division of labor develop? What is its function in crowd instances? All these problems combined make contagion theory problematic as a general explanation of collective behavior.

A recent critical test of contagion theory has been provided in a case study of a "monster" sighting in a rural community in Illinois (Miller, Mietus, and Mathers, 1978). The authors note that although some media accounts of the event would lead one to accept such contagion notions as rapid mobilization and unanimity of opinion among area residents in response to reported monster sightings, in reality things were quite different. Among area residents it was found that the type as well as the extent of participation varied significantly. Mobilization, to the extent it did occur, was less dependent upon emotional contagion and more dependent upon such rational processes as availability—that is, participants had some "uncommitted time," —whether notification of the event had occurred (see also McPhail and Miller, 1973), and institutional demands.

Let us conclude that there is no doubt some emotional contagion in any collective behavior outburst and that this emotional contagion is rather critical in stimulating the crowd to action. However, other factors must also be considered in developing a more comprehensive theory of collective behavior.

Convergence theory of collective behavior offers a very different explanation for the events that occur in instances such as riots and lynchings. This is so primarily because the theory is based on a very different image of people. According to contagion theory, the individual in a crowd situation loses himself or herself to the emotion of the crowd and does something that could not be predicted on the basis of individual characteristics. Convergence theory, on the other hand, argues that participants, particularly in violent collective episodes, were already *predisposed* to engage in such actions —the crowd simply offers them the excuse. Thus, collective behavior is explained on the basis of the simultaneous presence of a number of people who share the same predispositions, which are activated by the event or object toward which their common attention is directed. The problem becomes (1) to identify the relevant latent tendencies; (2) to note the circumstances bringing people with similar latencies together; and (3) to determine the kinds of events that will trigger these tendencies into action (Turner, 1964, p. 387).

According to convergence theory, then, the presence of the crowd is not the casual factor in collective outbursts. Rather, it simply provides an excuse for people to do what they were already predisposed to do anyway. According to Allport, nothing new is added by the crowd situation "except an intensification of the feeling already present, and the possibility of concerted action" (1924, p. 295).

As is true with contagion theory, Turner notes that there are several important problems with convergence theory as a general explanation of collective behavior. First, it is again difficult to explain shifts in the behavior of crowds using this approach. For example, if the behavior of a crowd reflects the common predisposition of the members of that crowd, how does one account for changes in the direction of the crowd's behavior? Has another latent predisposition surfaced? This is a difficult problem in any study of crowd behavior, and convergence theory does little to help us resolve it.

Second, as was also true with contagion theory, convergence theory gives us little help in studying organization in crowd situations. How does a leadership structure emerge? How does one account for the role differentiation that occurs in most episodes of crowd behavior?

Third, and closely related to the first point, if we grant that individuals probably have several and perhaps many latent tendencies rather than just a single one, how can we predict which of the latencies will make its appearance? Finally, if we accept the dictum that people respond to situations in terms of how they define those situations, and that in episodes of crowd behavior the definition of the situation may emerge through the process of group interaction, this leaves little room for the concept of latent predispositions. In other words, if the definition of the situation is a group product, it could very well be contrary to the supposed latent tendencies of many members of that group. Obviously, these are important empirical problems that are extremely difficult to resolve.

Recent empirical evidence is also highly critical of a convergence explanation for collective behavior. For example, in a study of a group of students building a barricade as part of a confrontation with administrators, Berk (1974) found that student participants held a variety of views about the situation, and rarely did one belief predominate. Participants were complexly motivated and often ambivalent, as was the case in the bank run in Australia (Mann, Nagel, and Dowling, (1976), when some people in line were actually there to *deposit* funds.

EMERGENT-NORM THEORY

Unlike the other two theoretical approaches, emergent-norm theory proposes that in our effort to study collective behavior we do not need a new set of tools or a new set of concepts at all. Rather, we can employ many of the same basic tools and concepts that we use to study other types of human behavior. For example, just as most other types of behavior that we have studied in this book are governed by a social norm, so is collective behavior. However, collective behavior is regulated by a social norm that arises specific to the given situation. Consider participants in the looting that occurred during the New York City blackout in the summer of 1977. Most of these looters would probably have felt that they were engaging in *normative* behavior; that is, as they observed events around them everyone else appeared to be doing what they were doing and so *not to* would have appeared deviant. However, this norm is an emergent norm—it was specific to the situation. Lynching can be defined as normative in the emotion of the immediate situation, and persons who argue against such actions are often punished or otherwise sanctioned just as they would be for refusing to behave in a manner that is consistent with other important norms. However, the lynching norm is situation-specific; it emerges in a particular situation in response to a particular need. Once the act has been completed, most participants would probably go back to acceptance of another more general norm such as "thou shalt not kill."

The emergent-norm approach as initially developed by Turner and Killian (1957) argues that observers of collective-behavior episodes have tended to get so caught up in the emotion of the situation that they fail to make important observations of what actually is happening. Thus, they fail to notice the definitional process that is often occurring. "The shared conviction of right, which constitutes a norm, sanctions behavior consistent with the norm, inhibits behavior contrary to it, justifies proselyting, and requires restraining action against those who dissent. Because the behavior in the crowd is different either in degree or kind from that in noncrowd situations, the norm must be specific to the situation to some degree—hence emergent norm" (Turner, 1964, p. 390). Bystanders, influenced by the emotion of the situation, often fail to observe this process.

Emergent-norm theory differs in several important respects from the other two approaches. For example, rather than attributing crowd action to the "spontaneous induction of emotion," greater emphasis is placed on group conformity through the imposition of a social norm. The crowd suppresses incongruous feelings and actions of its members and provides direction and meaning. In addition, limits on the direction and degree of crowd action are more readily explainable by emergent-norm theory than by the other two. The crowd defines certain behaviors as appropriate to the situation, but other behaviors may remain defined as inappropriate. The individual who goes beyond these limits is often chastised and sanctioned. For example, during a student take over of a university administration building following the Kent State shootings during the late 1960s, the group defined the takeover as appropriate but the breaking of windows and other malicious damage as inappropriate. Crowd members who began engaging in such actions were quickly sanctioned by the larger group. The emergent norm defines certain actions as normative that may not previously have been so defined, but other actions still remain forbidden.

The emergent-norm theory also allows us to avoid extremes in long-standing controversies over the importance of the group versus the individual. Convergence theory emphasizes the latter; each participant in the collective episode is responding to a personal latent tendency or predisposition. The group context of the action is simply a function of the coming together of many separate individuals with similar latent tendencies. Contagion theory argues for the preeminence of the group. The group creates in its members certain attitudes, motives, and modes of behavior that have no counterparts in any of the individual participants by themselves. Emergent-norm theory does not require an either/or view. Emotions may be heightened through group stimulation, causing some persons to behave contrary to internalized personal norms at the same time other actors with latent fears and frustrations may be able to act these out. In other words, both individual actor and group context are important.

For the student of social psychology, the primary advantage of the emergent-norm perspective is that it allows the application of already learned concepts to the study of collective action. The continuity between group behavior and crowd behavior is stressed rather than minimized: "Just as behavior in normal groups gives rise to, and is governed by, norms, so the crowd generates and is governed by normative control" (Turner, 1964, p. 392). A basic problem of emergent-norm theory is that Turner and Killian never systematically address the actual *source* of the emergent norm (Berk, 1974). Gaming theory offers some potential solutions in this regard.

Important continuities between collective behavior and institutional behavior have been noted by others as well (Couch, 1968, 1970; Weller and Quarantelli, 1973). These authors agree with Turner that until we recognize these continuities, adequate and valid theories of collective behavior will not be developed. Although collective episodes may be exciting, frightening, dangerous, or whatever, they still involve the behavior of human beings that are responding, in one way or another, to normative definitions.

We would concur that the social scientist should not ignore the areas of continuity between more traditional types of group behavior and crowd behavior, but that the other side of the case should not be ignored or understated either. Social psychologists typically spend their time studying the regularities of human behavior, and, as we have noted, most of their concepts have been developed to describe and understand these regularities. However, even though many of the events that occur in collective outbursts may be normative (at least in the sense that they are guided by an emergent norm), the behaviors associated with the event tend not to be conventional or traditional. Therefore, the questions that are asked are rather different questions, and the social and psychological factors that come into play tend to be rather atypical from those that guide the more "normal" course of human interaction. The student of collective behavior should be aware of these differences and should examine this topic both for its continuity and for its uniqueness.

SMELSER'S VALUE-ADDED THEORY

One of the more thorough efforts at developing a formal sociological theory of collective behavior can be found in the work of Neil Smelser (1963). In effect, Smelser combines ideas from economics with the work of sociologists in developing what he refers to as a "value-added" theory. Smelser's theory seeks to provide answers to two basic questions (Milgram and Toch, 1969, p. 556): (1) What are the factors that determine whether or not a collective-behavior episode will occur? and (2) What determines whether one type (for example, panic as opposed to a riot) rather than another will occur? Smelser's "value-added" notion implies that the development of a collective-behavior episode, whether it be a panic, a craze, a riot, or a social movement, involves a *process* and that each stage in that process adds its value to or influences in an important way the final outcome or product. More specifically, Smelser sees six stages as necessary before collective actions of the nature discussed above will occur. These six stages occur in sequence, and all are necessary, or the developing episode will terminate. The six stages in Smelser's theory include (1) structural conduciveness; (2) structural strain; (3) growth and spread of a generalized belief; (4) a precipitating event; (5) mobilization of the participants for action; and (6) an absence of sufficient social control. Let us look briefly at a classic case of collective behavior and then apply Smelser's theory in attempting to explain what has occurred.

The Leeville Lynching Hadley Cantril (1963) has provided a detailed study of a brutal lynching that occurred in the small town of Leeville, Texas, in the spring of 1930. On a Saturday morning on the day in question, a black laborer on a white man's farm went to his employer to collect some wages that were due him. The farmer was not at home, and supposedly the laborer left but returned a short time later with a shotgun to demand his money. The farmer's wife, fearing the man, backed through a hall into a bedroom, where she was attacked and raped. She was then tied to the bed, and the attacker fled. The woman eventually freed herself and phoned the sheriff from a neighbor's house. A deputy sheriff came to the scene and arrested the black man, who supposedly pleaded guilty, and took him to a jail in a neighboring town.

Although medical evidence indicates that sexual relations had occurred between the pair, there is a good deal of controversy over whether or not rape was a factor. Most blacks and a good many whites in the area believed that the woman had invited the relationship and then had become frightened and phoned the sheriff. Whatever the actual events, by the following Friday when the trial was to be held, many exaggerated versions of the incident were being passed about, and a large crowd had gathered from the local town and from neighboring communities. As the crowd around the courthouse grew larger and more belligerent, an important rumor began circulating that the four Texas Rangers who had been assigned the responsibility to guard the courthouse had received instructions from the governor not to shoot anyone while attempting to protect the prisoner. Although untrue, this rumor made the crowd bolder and more violent.

According to Cantril, the event that turned the huge crowd into a vicious mob "was the bringing of the woman from the hospital to the courthouse in an ambulance and carrying her on a stretcher through the crowd into the courtroom" (p. 99). At that point, the mob went wild. It repeatedly broke into the courthouse, from which it was driven back by the rangers with drawn guns and teargas. Finally, unable to obtain the prisoner by other means, the crowd set the building afire. The prisoner was placed in a fire-proof vault room on the second floor of the courthouse, and the Rangers and the other court officials fled the burning building. Efforts by firemen to extinguish the blaze were thwarted by the mob, and by evening the only thing that remained standing in the courthouse square was the steel and cement vault.

During the evening hours numerous efforts were made to enter the vault. Finally, a hole was cut with an acetylene torch, and the leader of the mob entered and threw the prisoner, who was by then dead, out. The corpse was drawn up to the limb of a tree so everyone could see it and then was tied to an automobile and dragged to the black section of town. At that point, "About five thousand howling, yelling people fell into a midnight parade behind the corpse. Someone struck up the strains of 'Happy days are here again,' and soon hundreds joined in with 'Let us sing a song of cheer again, happy days are here again.' Motorists tooted their horns. The city police tried to direct traffic (p. 102).

Collective behavior carried to its extreme: Accused in 1937 of murdering a white in Mississippi, this black man was tortured with a blow-torch and then lynched.

After dragging the body to the black section of town, it was drawn up to the limb of another tree, and a fire was set beneath from materials stolen from ransacked black-owned businesses. The crowd cheered as the body, still in a semicrouched position and dangling from a chain, began to burn.

Fourteen men and boys were eventually indicted for the crime that occurred in Leeville that night, but thirteen of these were never tried. The fourteenth was eventually sentenced to a two-year prison term for arson, but only after he had gotten into additional trouble with the law. However, even in this case, the man was released by the governor before finishing his term in response to a petition from the Leeville citizens.

Looking back at a historical event, it is often difficult to understand how such a thing could ever have occurred. In this case, Smelser's value-added theory helps us to understand what happened that day in Texas.

Structural Conduciveness The concept of structural conduciveness implies conditions that are permissive of a particular sort of collective behavior. That is, general conditions in a given society are such that they would enable or allow a particular form of collective behavior. At the time of the Leeville lynching, Texas ranked third among all states in terms of the number of lynchings committed. Only Georgia and Alabama had had a greater number of lynchings. Twenty other lynchings occurred in the Southern States during this same year; since the late 1800s, lynching had become more and more accepted as a method of meting out justice to blacks accused of any of a broad range of crimes (see table 12–1). Thus, social conditions in the Leeville area as well as in many other areas of the South were conducive to this type of behavior. The lynching of a black man for allegedly engaging in a crime such as rape was not only condoned, it was even expected. This is dramatically illustrated by the contents of a newspaper editorial in another community following the lynching of a black youth for attempting to rape a white girl: "That the feeling of a people should be aroused is natural and we find ourselves, despite our views on lynching, not too greatly disturbed. . . . We find ourselves calmly accepting the crime last night as inevitable" (quoted in Cantril, 1963, p. 96). The conduciveness of the situation in the Leeville area is reflected in the facts that only one of the participants in the Leeville lynching was ever tried for the crime and that the location of the trial had to be changed to the state capital because the judge in the local area was unable to obtain a jury panel who would agree

Table 12–1   Lynchings in South: 1882–1940

DECADE	WHITES	BLACKS	TOTAL
1882–1889	669	534	1,203
1890–1899	429	1,111	1,540
1900–1909	94	791	885
1910–1919	53	568	621
1920–1929	34	281	315
1930–1939	11	119	130

Adapted from Guzman 1969, pp. 56–59.

to convict the defendant *even if proven guilty*. Further, witness after witness at the trial conveniently could not remember having recognized anyone among the thousands of participants in the lynching.

Structural Strain The conditions that were conducive to lynching behavior apparently were present throughout much of the South for several decades, yet such episodes were fairly irregular occurrences. According to Smelser's theory, the next stage in the development process involves the emergence of specific strains within the system. More specifically, structural strain refers to certain aspects of a system that are "out of joint" with each other. At the time of the Leeville lynching, about 10 percent of the county population was black. Although blacks tended to be located at the bottom of the socioeconomic ladder, they were joined there by a large element of property-less whites. Cantril also noted that during the decade preceding the lynching, the population of the county decreased by over eight thousand people at the same time that the state's population increased nearly 25 percent. Railroad shops had moved away, and the area's two small colleges had closed. Thus, the entire area was feeling the pinch of economic decline. One of the consequences of this economic picture was that the lower-class whites were thrown into direct competition with lower-class blacks for jobs and other economic benefits. This resulted in growing stress and strain among these elements of the population. Support for the importance of these factors in accounting for the events of the lynching can be found in the fact that approximately 55 percent of the actual mob members were either unemployed or were classified as common laborers.

The Growth and Spread of a Generalized Belief The third phase in the development process involves the development among the potential participants of a generalized belief regarding the causes for the strain that exists and some means by which it may be eliminated. In other words, the developing belief that comes to be accepted by members of the group identifies the source of the strain, attributes certain agreed-upon characteristics to this source, and then makes some recommendation about how the strain can be relieved. Particularly among lower-class whites in the South at the turn of the century and for several years thereafter, there existed the widespread fear that blacks must be kept in their place. Apparently, fears regarding sexual contact between black men and white women were especially prevalent. Thus, the generalized belief was quickly accepted that if the black man was not kept in his place, no one (particularly white females) could be considered safe. Violent physical attacks were accepted as one means of such suppression.

Precipitating Factor The precipitating event is the incident or action that sets off the collective episode. Because of conduciveness, strain, and the development of a generalized belief, the situation is now ripe for an explosion. All it needs is the spark that will set it off. In the Leeville lynching, the precipitating event is rather easy to identify. On the day of the trial, a huge curious crowd gathered from the surrounding area, but that crowd was not yet a mob. However, bringing the "victim" to the courthouse in an ambulance and carrying her on a stretcher into the courtroom was all that was needed. This obviously could be seen as an effective ploy by the prosecuting attorney to sway the sympathies of a jury, but the consequences in Leeville were far more lethal.

Mobilization of Participants for Action Now all that is needed is for the gathered participants to mobilize. The mobilization is largely a function of two forces—leadership and communication. Before the milling and largely disorganized crowd can begin to take some coordinated action, some form of leadership must be provided. This emergent leadership then communicates direction to the crowd—for example, the target for the hostilities is defined, appropriate actions are specified, a division of labor may even be established, and so on. At this point, a full-fledged collective episode is underway.

The Operation of Social Control The sixth factor in the process is somewhat unique from the others. Up to this point, we have argued that the factors identified must be present or the collective action will not occur. Now, however, we are dealing with a factor whose *absence* is the key to the final outcome. In other words, social control is really a counter-determinant. In the case of the Leeville lynching, four Texas Rangers were assigned the responsibility of protecting the proceedings from the attack of approximately five thousand frustrated and angry mobsters. Although there were additional local and county law-enforcement officers in the area, there is evidence that at least some of them were in sympathy with the mob. As a consequence, the forces of social control were simply unable to control the crowd. According to the theory, had there been a sufficient show of force at this point, the collective episode would not have occurred even with the presence of the other five elements in the process. After killing the prisoner, the mob continued its activity in attacking other blacks and black-owned businesses until several hundred National Guardsmen were sent into town. Only after the arrival of the soldiers with machine guns, rifles, and tear gas did the mob begin to disperse. The mob continued to engage in violent collective action until the factor of social control became sufficiently operative to terminate the behavior.

Smelser's value-added theory has probably received more empirical test than any theory of collective behavior. For example, it has been used to study the rise of a right-wing political party in Canada (Pinard, 1971), an antipornography movement (Zurcher et al., 1971), the Kent State tragedy (Rudwich and Meier, 1972; Lewis, 1972), hysterical contagion growing out of the belief of being bitten by a poisonous insect (Kerckhoff and Back, 1968), an economic panic in Australia (Mann, Nagel, and Dowling, 1976), and so on.

The major criticism growing out of this research has focused on Smelser's discussion of generalized beliefs because of this idea's failure to consider the heterogeneity among participants and leaders in a collective behavior episode (Marx and Wood, 1975). Researchers have also noted difficulty in operationalizing the concepts of structural conduciveness and structural strain. Nevertheless, the approach has been found very useful and will no doubt continue to receive attention in the literature.

The contagion, convergence, and emergent-norm approaches and Smelser's value-added work constitute the major theoretical efforts in the study of collective behavior to this point. All have advantages and shortcomings. However, none approaches the sophistication and formality one would hope to achieve in theory construction. This shortcoming is largely a function of the topic at hand. When a topic is not readily amenable to a controlled experimental analysis, it is difficult to develop theories about it that can be tested and verified.

Social Movements

Although social movements are generally treated as a type of collective behavior, they differ in important ways from such other collective episodes as panics, riots, and mobs. *Social movements* have been defined by Blumer (1971) as "collective enterprises to establish a new order of life." The collective element is important to such a definition, but the notion of an organized effort to establish a new order of life implies much more structure and much less transiency than one observes in panics, riots, and other collective episodes discussed to this point.

The recent empirical literature on social movements also notes additional important conceptual differences between social movements and other types of collective behavior. "The fundamental difference between these two types of behavior is the existence of bonds of positive solidarity that makes it possible for social movements to generate common ideology, internal organization, continuity of leadership and a sense for strategic necessity. The elementary forms of collective behavior lack these traits because they lack the cohesiveness and staying power that depends on a sense of common destiny among members" (Traugott, 1978, p. 43). In other words, important, positive bonds are an essential ingredient to the development of social movements, although unnecessary for the development of most other types of collective behavior we have discussed. For example, panics presume no bonds of solidarity among participants but rather are characterized by virtually the opposite in that each person tends to revert to action that is based on individual interest as contrasted with collective good (Traugott, 1978). Traditional definitions of *collective behavior* have emphasized their spontaneous and ephemeral character; they are noninstitutionalized and lack structure and stability. However, social movements tend to develop highly defined structure and organization.

TRADITIONAL APPROACHES TO THE STUDY OF SOCIAL MOVEMENTS

Much of the literature of the past two decades can be characterized by the common assumption that social movements emerge out of the shared grievances and discontent that are present in a given population. The movement itself develops as a vehicle to reduce these grievances or to change the negative social conditions that gave it birth. McCarthy and Zald (1977) note that the three most influential approaches to the study of social movements of the past several years (those of Gurr, 1970; Turner and Killian, 1972; and Smelser, 1963) share this assumption, even though they differ in other important respects.

The traditional literature has also emphasized that social movements tend to follow a recurring life cycle (Killian, 1964; King, 1965; Zald and Ash, 1966; Mauss, 1971). The *genesis* of the movement, as noted, is usually found in pockets of frustration or dissatisfaction with the present social order or with the course of history that social order seems to be pursuing. In Blumer's terms, the motive power of the movement derives from dissatisfaction with current conditions and hopes for a better scheme of living. In this regard, millenarian movements such as religious cults frequently decry the negative characteristics of this worldly life and look forward to the establishment of a more divine order sometime in the future.

Cameron (1966, p. 10) identifies more specifically the societal conditions that lead to the genesis of social movements. These include: (1) a recognition of dissatisfactions and a sharing of these with others; (2) a belief in the ability to influence and reshape the course of events; and (3) an existence of social conditions "in which the banding together to change something is both possible and plausibly effective." As this implies, shared frustrations with the current social order are not enough. There must also develop the belief that a different state of affairs is both desirable and possible if a full-blown social movement is to emerge. If a problem is not defined as remediable, as in the case of inmates in a concentration camp who have been drained of physical energy and hope or of medieval peasants who regard their misfortune as divinely ordained (Milgram and Toch, 1969), then a movement to change conditions is unlikely to develop.

Out of the growing beliefs that a better state of affairs is possible, the social movement frequently evolves as an "enduring organization devoted to the attainment of this vision" (Killian, 1964, p. 433). Values and goals are

Visible collective behavior in the form of a supporting demonstration is a very important part of a social movement. *Source:* Wide World Photos, Inc.

defined into a group ideology, a structure emerges with its role definitions and division of labor, and the movement enters the phase of its career during which its impact on the larger social order is likely to be at its highest peak. During this phase, membership in the movement is likely to be increasing at an accelerating rate, and many members are filled with feelings of exhiliration growing out of the belief that the desired end state is on the verge of being achieved. Such beliefs are very often unrealistic when one objectively compares the realtive strength and size of the emerging social movement with the larger society from which it has emerged. A small, relatively unorganized group that complains about conditions is likely to be viewed with a good deal of "benign neglect" or may even be humored by the larger society, but, as that movement grows larger and more powerful, opposition forces frequently come into play.

It is in part because of this potential emergence of strong opposition that the road from this juncture on is usually one of decline. One particular strategy often employed by host societies is to coopt the movement or certain portions of it. When the larger society against which the movement has directed its attention suddenly adopts some of the platforms of the movement, its reason for existence is threatened. On the other hand, the movement may be vigorously suppressed by the host society. This is particularly likely to occur in totalitarian societies but can occur in more democratic societies if the emerging movement is defined as a dangerous threat to important values in the host society. In other instances, the original momentum of the movement may simply be lost and, though the movement itself may continue to survive, its influence becomes virtually insignificant.

RESOURCE-MOBILIZATION APPROACH TO SOCIAL MOVEMENTS

Recent theorists have begun to question some of the assumptions that guided traditional analyses of social movements. The new approach is generally referred to as a resource-mobilization theory of social movements and is most fully articulated by McCarthy and Zald (1973, 1977), but it is also evident in the work of Oberschall (1973), Wilson (1973), Tilly (1973, 1975), Gamson (1968), 1975), and others.

These writers argue that recent empirical work questions "the assumption of a close link between preexisting discontent and generalized beliefs in the rise of social movements" (McCarthy and Zald, 1977, p. 1214). Instead, there has been little empirical support found for the hypothesized relationship between objective and subjective deprivation and the emergence of social movements. This has led Tilly (1973) to argue that social movements grow directly out of the central political processes evident in a society rather than out of occasionally heightened strains and discontent.

McCarthy and Zald (1977) further deemphasize the importance of grievance and discontent as a necessary precondition for the emergence of social movements by noting that there may *always* exist enough discontent in a society to supply the grass-roots support for a movement, and, even if this is not the case, it may be created by entrepreneurs and organizations. Thus, full-scale social movements might be mobilized by purposive actors within the system; they may not grow directly out of existing grievances but out of the organizational abilities and efforts of some set of individuals or established elite groups.

Central to the resource-mobilization theory of social movements are the following (McCarthy and Zald, 1977, p. 1216):

1. Because resources must be aggregated for the engagement in social conflict, the processes by which money and labor are accumulated becomes a major focus of concern.
2. Because the aggregation of such resources as money and labor requires some minimal social organization, the development and maintenance of organizational structure within the social movement becomes a key issue.
3. The role of individuals and organizations outside the movement is of major concern. For example, the mobilization of elderly people to lobby for Medicare was largely the result of efforts by the AFL-CIO.
4. There is increased sensitivity to the importance of costs and rewards in explaining the involvement of individuals and organizations in social movements.

As is true of efforts to apply gaming and decision theory to other types of collective behavior, the development of resource-mobilization theory in the study of social movements can be seen as a direct effort to: (1) establish an approach that is more consistent with the available empirical evidence; and (2) locate this area of study within rather than outside the major techniques and theories that are used to understand other, more institutionalized, areas of human social behavior. As social scientists come to rely more on their own empirical studies of social movements and less on journalistic and historical accounts, it appears that greater emphasis will be given to more rational and structural explanations such as that embodied in resource-mobilization theory.

TYPOLOGIES OF SOCIAL MOVEMENTS AND THEIR MEMBERS

There are numerous ways of classifying social movements, and many of the classification schemes are indicative of the range of collective activities that can be subsumed under the heading of social movements. Blumer (1951) made a distinction between *general* and *specific* social movements, which differ primarily in terms of the specificity of the issues upon which they focus and their degree of organization. General movements are likely to be characterized by rather vague and ill-defined goals; the objectives of a specific social movement tend to be well-defined. In addition, Blumer distinguishes between *expressive* movements on the one hand and *nationalistic* or *revival* movements on the other. Expressive movements emerge out of and seek to cope with personal and social discontinuities. They may include certain religious movements that focus on changing individual lives without necessarily changing external social conditions. Nationalistic or revival movements, on the other hand, seek to change society. The notion of revival comes from the fact that such movements often seek to impose on present-day society idealized values from the past.

Smelser (1963), in his comprehensive and detailed discussion of collective behavior, makes a distinction between types of social movements that parallels in several ways Blumer's typology. Smelser's primary distinction is between *value-oriented* movements and *norm-oriented* movements. Value-oriented movements tend to be comprehensive in their outlook and seek to bring about major changes in society. Mauss (1975) indicates that they include "many of the religious movements of history, especially those that have swept whole societies and continents, and probably all of the movements based on the great 'isms,' such as Communism, Fascism, millenarianism, and the like, which attempt to reorder entire ways of life" (p. 46).

Smelser's norm-oriented movements, on the other hand, are not concerned with a major reorientation of the larger society nor are they interested in bringing about basic changes in social value structure. Rather, their focus is upon attempts to bring about change in more specific social relationships within the broader society. As the name implies, norm-oriented movements would be quite satisfied with changing rather specific norms, such as those dealing with the sale and consumption of liquor. The Women's Christian Temperance Union would be an example of such a movement. Their concern was not with a dramatic overturn of all major social institutions but focused quite specifically upon what they defined as the evils of alcohol consumption. The goals of a group such as the WCTU can be contrasted with those of a Marxist-oriented revolutionary movement that seeks to overturn all the major institutions in a given society and replace them with a rather different political, economic, and social order.

Aberle (1966), in his research on the Peyote cult among the Navajo Indians, has developed a typology of social movements based on the two dimensions of the locus (individual or social structure) and amount (partial or total) of change desired. This typology is summarized in figure 12–1.

An alternative movement seeks partial change in the individual actor, while a redemptive movement seeks to bring about total change in the individual. At the societal level, a reformative movement seeks partial change while a transformative movement seeks total change. Overall movement impact would be least for an alternative movement and greatest for a transformative movement.

More recently, McCarthy and Zald (1973) have argued that the increased funding made available by churches, foundations, governmental agencies, and other organizations has led to the development of a professional class who base their careers on social-movement leadership. This has led to the development of the "professional social movement" characterized by highly trained, full-time leadership and a fairly large and dependable resource base.

Whatever classification scheme one prefers, one must still deal with ques-

LOCUS OF CHANGE DESIRED

		Individual	Social Structure
AMOUNT OF CHANGE DESIRED	Partial	Alternative Movement	Reformative Movement
	Total	Redemptive Movement	Transformative Movement

Figure 12–1 Aberle's Typology of Social Movements

tions of mobilization and recruitment. The first question deals with how a *potential* movement is transformed into an *actual* movement. Recent emphasis has focused on the role of leaders in the mobilization process; McCarthy and Zald (1973) call them "social movement entrepreneurs" and feel they organize resources and personnel and focus these in a particular direction. However, Marx and Wood (1975) argue that much work still must be done on the relationship between leaders and masses in the mobilization process.

The second question of recruitment is related to that of mobilization but is more directly concerned with who actually joins a developing or existing movement. As noted by Milgram and Toch (1969), spectators may get the impression that those engaged in social-movement activities are a distinct human breed—unwashed malcontents or right-wing radicals. The empirical evidence suggests a broad range of individuals can be found in most social movements. For example, extensive research on the student movement of the 1960s (see Flacks, 1967; Mankoff and Flacks, 1971) suggests that early participants tended to be from upper-middle class backgrounds but by the later phases of the movement, the social-class base had broadened.

Even among recruits, significant differences occur in the level and type of involvement. Some members become true ideological converts while others occupy a much more peripheral role. For example, Harrison's (1977) study of participants in a Catholic Pentecostal movement found that there were numerous dimensions of involvement among those who were considered to be members. Some organized their entire daily routine around the movement, while others exhibited lower levels of commitment.

The amount of knowledge available on recruitment is increasing but needs now to be extended from research on the student- and civil-rights movements to other areas in order for more general theories to be developed.

MILLENARIAN MOVEMENTS: AN EXAMPLE

Some of the most frequently studied types of social movements are those which share a millenarian vision, or, in Zygmunt's (1972) terms, "a collective conviction that a drastic transformation of the existing social order will occur in the proximate future through the intervention of some supernatural agency" (p. 245). One factor that has made millenarian groups the focus of frequent research by the social psychologist is continuing interest in the question of how groups are able to sustain their beliefs in supernatural intervention in the face of disconfirming evidence. In an earlier chapter we discussed Leon Festinger's study as a specific example of response to dissonance engendered when strongly held beliefs are disconfirmed. As Zygmunt notes, "idological crisis born of prophetic failure is a virtually universal feature of the careers of millenarian groups" (p. 245). In this section, we will draw from Zygmunt's work on millenarian movements in an effort both to increase our understanding of this process and as a means of rounding out our analysis of this important area.

Most millenarian prophecies, such as the message of Mrs. Keech, are couched in terms that make them amenable to confirmation or disconfirmation. The event either happens at the appointed time and place or it does not. There is really no middle ground. The specificity of such events makes response to their disconfirmation more open to empirical analysis. However, not all millenarian prophecies are so clearly defined. Those that make reference to supernatural personages, events, or agencies that are not temporarily tied are less open to disconfirmation and can insulate their adherents from more empirically based logics of proof and disproof.

The organizational dimensions of the millenarian movement are also rather crucial in evaluating the response of believers to diconfirmation. Loosely organized groups who rely heavily on emotional contagion, rumor creation, intensifying excitement, and inflating enthusiasm, are likely to be seriously affected by disconfirming evidence. On the other hand, more organized collectivities that are characterized by more stable leadership, more fully developed ideologies, rituals, and the like are better able to handle the failure of specific prophecies. In fact, with highly organized and structured groups, disconfirmation is not likely to be seriously damaging to the continuity of the movement. As Zygmunt notes, failures can be rationalized, explained, reinterpreted, or denied, leaving millennial hopes still intact.

Millenarian movements exhibit a number of different patterns of action. Zygmunt identifies four major types:

1. *Expressive activities.* Expressive activity by the group appears to be virtually a universal feature of the early stages of millenarian movements. Such expressive activity involves the development and spread of emotional contagion, which is aroused by prophetic declarations and rumors of impending change. Although the development of passionate commitment to the movement can be aroused through such activities, it can also be dangerous because of the increased potential for serious disappointment and defection when the highly inflated expectations fail to be realized.

2. *Agitational activities.* As the movement moves toward greater organization, agitational activity usually emerges. In Zygmunt's terms, this involves efforts by the leaders and converts to disseminate their prophetic message by proselyting among those who have not yet heard or accepted it. As is true with expressive activities, however, agitational activities also contain the potential of being double-edged. For example, proselyting can increase membership, but it also exposes the faith to public scrutiny and proselytization can open the group to ridicule and discreditation, especially in the case of prophetic disconfirmation.

3. *Preparational activities.* The acceptance of millenarian beliefs usually also entails engagement in some sort of preparatory action. The believers must prepare for the prophecied future. In Festinger's study, the believers had to prepare by divesting themselves of worldly possessions, by removing all metal objects from their personal clothing, and so on. It may be necessary that food supplies be stocked and that other personal preparations are made to be ready for the event. The willingness to make the sacrifices that are included in the preparatory activities is sometimes used as an indication of the degree of personal commitment that a person has made to the movement.

4. *Interventional activities.* Although many millenarian groups depend heavily upon superhuman intervention to bring about the desired new state of affairs, some groups engage in acts designed to actually implement the

millenarian vision or to facilitate its realization. As noted by Zygmunt, "acts of prophecy-fulfilling intervention have by no means been rare among millenarian groups. Some have developed definitions of themselves and of their collective missions which prompt them to try to play more active roles in ushering in the new order. Conceiving of themselves as the earthly instruments of supernatural forces, entrusted with special mandates to act as liquidators of the old system or as vanguards for the establishment of the new, some movements have engaged in acts of rebellion, warfare, pillage, and the like" (p. 256). However, this route to prophetic fulfillment has usually been characterized by disaster. The response has usually been strong repressive action from the host society, whose power, in comparison with that of the fledging social movement, is generally overwhelming.

But what happens when disconfirmation occurs? Zygmunt notes the disintegration and collapse of the movement will follow unless it is able to cope effectively with the strains associated with disconfirmation. Several coping strategies include: (1) *Acknowledgment of error and organizational recycling.* Basically, this involves an acknowledgment that the group was in error in terms of some specific prophecy, but the foretold event is still to occur sometime in the future. The movement is simply recycled around the same basic belief projected into the future. (2) *Assignments of blame and organizational redirection.* In this mode of adaptation, explanations are constructed that typically assign responsibility to some natural or supernatural agency. The members may not have been spiritually ready, there needs to be more self-purification, external agencies may have worked to obstruct the predicted events, and so on. (3) *Assertion of prophecy-fulfilling claims and organizational transformation.* Rather than admit personal errors of interpretation or the assignment of blame for the nonoccurrence of prophesied events, the movement may simply fail to concede or recognize that a failure has occurred. A group may simply assert that announced prophecies have occurred. However, such announcements must be defined as credible within the framework of the group to be successful.

Although this discussion applies specifically to millenarian movements, the general outline of activities and responses appears applicable to other types of social movements as well. For example, a movement that is more concretely oriented, such as the feminist movement, may explain or justify its successes and failures by adopting rationalizations that closely parallel those noted above.

The importance of social movements rests largely in the impacts that they have on society. "The significance of social movements . . . lies not in their careers but in their consequences for the larger society and its culture. Unless a social movement results in significant social change, it becomes merely an interesting sidelight to history, a curiosity" (Killian, 1964, p. 452). The fact is that entire societies have been altered in rather dramatic fashions by various types of social movements. In our own society, many important social changes have occurred in the past two decades as a result of the efforts of the civil-rights movement, the anti-Vietnam war movement, the environmental movement, and the women's liberation movement. The significant nature of the change that is reflected in many of our important social institutions as well as in the life styles of our society's citizens testifies of the importance that can be attached to this interesting form of collective behavior.

Collective Behavior and Social Change

Few episodes of collective behavior leave the society in which they have occurred untouched or without some lasting impact. A large urban riot can leave a major city scarred for years to come. At the same time, it can prompt the larger society to develop social programs that may help to alleviate the ills and frustrations that spawned the riot in the first place. Panics can leave long-term emotional and psychological scars on those who survive as well as on the family and friends of those who do not. Participation in a mass religious revival may have life-long effects on the behavior of individual participants as well as on whole communities and societies. Social movements may leave few of societies' major institutions untouched, and successful revolutionary movements may overturn existing institutions and dramatically affect relationships in all facets of life.

In all these senses, then, there is a rather direct and important link between collective behavior and the larger issue of social change. Many collective-behavior episodes play a direct role in facilitating the process of social change in the larger society. We have noted that the specific goal of many social movements is to change the society from which they emerge, and many movements have done that in rather dramatic fashion.

It is true, however, that not all collective-behavior episodes have measureable or long-term impacts, particularly if we only treat impacts at the societal level. However, even those that leave the larger society relatively untouched may have both major and long-term effects on the lives of individual participants. This second level has often been ignored by writers who argue that most collective-behavior episodes are little more than curiosities.

We should also not forget that the specific function of some collective-behavior episodes is to resist change and to promote the stability of existing arrangements and institutions. Resistance movements develop in most societies in opposition to developing trends. For example, the Right to Life Movement in the United States has emerged in response to legal and other changes that facilitate the practice of abortion, which this group opposes. Some movements not only seek to stop the clock of social change, they would like to turn it back to an earlier, idealized period. The Ghost Dance movement among American Indians several decades ago was such a movement. It was based on the dream that time could be turned back to when the Indians controlled a land inhabited by ample herds of buffalo and other game and the white man and the destruction he perpetrated was not on the scene.

We should also not ignore the role of collective behavior in defining social problems. Recent arguments have been developed by Blumer (1971), Mauss (1975), and others that social problems cannot be located in objective social conditions. Rather, they have their being in a process of collective definition. In this view, what a society defines as a "social problem" is largely a function of the efforts of organized collectivities who legitimate an existing set of objective conditions as deserving of the label "social problem."

Not enough is known at present about the relationship between collective behavior and social change. Nevertheless, there is little question that an important link exists, and the development of further knowledge and understanding of this link awaits the effort of the student of social psychology.

Summary

The label "collective behavior" has been applied to that broad range of group actions that originate spontaneously, are relatively unorganized, tend to be quite unpredictable in their course of development, and are affected by interstimulation among participants. Examples include panics, revolutions, riots, crazes, fads, and social movements. Although traditional approaches to the study of collective behavior have stressed the importance of emotion, suggestability, and irrationality, contemporary approaches deemphasize the differences between collective and conventional behavior and argue that empirical evidence fails to support the traditional view.

Unique problems must be overcome in studying collective behavior; nevertheless, a broad range of tools and methods are available. These include survey methods, content analysis, observational techniques, and experiments in which relevant elements of collective behavior are simulated.

The generic term *crowd* has been applied to a diverse set of human assemblages that qualify as collective behavior. Crowds can be classified as either active or passive. Active crowds include aggressive collectivities, such as rioters, as well as panics and expressive groups, such as large religious revivals. Examples of passive crowds include casual or intentional audiences.

However we choose to classify crowds, it is important to consider what actually "causes" the individual crowd member to "act out." Support from others as indicated by numbers, visibility, ease of interpretation of actions, and proximity is clearly a key factor. Individuals will join in the action of the crowd when their own threshold is surpassed. In studying crowds, some researchers have focused on the individual and have attempted to determine the process through which individual actors develop a lowered threshold of normally restrained behavior. Others prefer the collectivity as the proper unit of analysis and focus on the social patterns that develop in the group and that in turn influence the direction of group behavior. The study of social psychology draws from both perceptions.

Rumors, the primary means of information dispersal in crowd settings, are most likely to develop in situations characterized by ambiguity and stress. They are usually passed by word of mouth and are important in mobilizing crowd participants for action, defining a target, and specifying the course of action to be taken in relationship to the target.

The role of leadership is primarily that of triggering the activity of the crowd. Leaders frequently do first what others will do later. However, in most collective behavior events, the leadership is emergent and conventional leaders usually play insignificant roles.

Large-scale panics, among the more dramatic episodes of crowd behavior, usually involve competition for something in short supply and tend to occur when there are perceptions of immediate danger, potential escape routes when there are perceptions of immediate danger, potential escape routes are both limited and closing, and there is a breakdown in communication.

Fads and fashions are far more trivial types of collective behavior. Fads usually involve some short-lived variation in speech, behavior, decoration, or similar items; they spread rapidly, reach a peak, and then decline almost as rapidly. Fashions involve a continuing process of change as reflected in clothing styles, hair length, and so on.

Several theoretical approaches have developed for the analysis of collective behavior. Early work that postulated that individuals undergo a radical transformation in crowds and more primitive, irrational and unconscious motivation emerges in crowd settings, was replaced more recently by gaming and decision-making theories that have provided a more rational, less emotional view of collective behavior.

The major theoretical approaches of the past several decades are generally summarized under the concepts of contagion, convergence, emergent norm, and value-added. The fewest empirical problems exist with emergent-norm and value-added theories, which also allow us to study collective behavior without developing separate concepts that do not apply to other phenomena.

Although generally included under the label of collective behavior, social movements differ in important ways from the other examples covered in that they involve collective enterprises that are developed to establish a new order of life and tend to be less spontaneous, more organized, and more enduring than most other types of collective behavior. Many social movements such as the civil-rights movement, the anti-war movement, and the feminist movement, have had major impacts on the larger society from which they have emerged.

Finally, one of the reasons for the importance of the field of collective behavior to the student of social psychology is found in the relationship between collective behavior and the larger issue of social change. Some of the world's major social movements have been the driving force behind the great and revolutionary changes that have occurred in many areas of life over the past centuries. Other collective-behavior events are more trivial, and their impact on the larger society is virtually nonexistent. However, even in cases such as these, few collective episodes leave the lives of their participants untouched and unchanged.

13

research

methods

in

social

psychology

In the preceding chapters of this book, we have discussed a rather broad array of topics including such things as the development of the self, the importance of social roles, aggressive and altruistic responses, conformity to social norms, and so on. Although many of our *observations* about these phenomena have come from personal experiences or from what we see others experience, most of our *knowledge* about them comes from information that is accumulated through research. For example, most of the materials that we presented on how language develops in humans and infrahumans, data on the causes and consequences of human aggression, and information provided on the ways in which the individual responds after having engaged in an attitude-discrepant behavior come from research studies conducted by social psychologists and other scientists interested in these important questions. In an effort to understand and explain social behavior, social psychologists utilize a range of research tools. These vary from fairly unsystematic observation of everyday events to the careful measurement of explicitly defined variables within a highly controlled experimental laboratory. In this final chapter, the methods and issues that are important in the development of social-psychological knowledge will be discussed.

Language of Research

VARIABLE

In order to discuss the research process, it is necessary to define a few scientific and research concepts. Most research projects begin as hypotheses or propositions linking two or more *variables.* Hypotheses may be derived from a theory or may be suggested by observation of a given social behavior. An example of the latter is the Kitty Genovese murder which was witnessed by thirty-eight people who not only did not help her, they did not even call the police. This observation suggested to some researchers that if several people witness a person in distress, each assumes someone else will offer aid. The "diffusion of responsibility" hypothesis that emerged from these observations states that the greater the number of people present in a crisis situation the less likely it is that any single individual will offer assistance. The two variables linked by the hypothesis are the number of people present and the rendering of aid. Since the primary interest of the social psychologist in this particular example is in people helping others, the giving of aid is the *dependent variable. Independent variables* are those things that explain or predict the dependent variable. In this case the independent variable is the number of people present. Frequently there is more than one independent variable because social behavior tends to be fairly complex.

OPERATIONAL DEFINITIONS

An operational definition is a specific set of instructions explaining how the variables are measured. In one test of the diffusion of responsibility hypothesis, an experiment was conducted where "assistance"—the dependent variable—was operationally defined as the subject going from one room to the next and offering aid to a young woman who had pretended to have fallen from a chair upon which she was standing (Latane and Rodin, 1969). The experimental procedure allowed the subject two minutes to respond to the crashing sound in the adjoining room. The independent variable was operationally defined as the number of people present when the "accident" occurred. The experimenter controlled the number present by having more than one subject arrive at the same time or by using confederates who pretended to be subjects. Operational definitions must be clear and specific so that others can tell exactly how the variables are measured and whether they are good indicators of what is being studied. The operational definitions must be specific enough that other scientists can replicate the research.

RELIABILITY_____

Reliability refers to the consistency or stability over time of measurements from a given operational definition. Reliable operational definitions will yield the same results for different investigators if all other things are equal. The reliability of operational definitions involving observations can be assessed by having two or more observers independently record the same set of events. The comparison of the results reveals the degree of reliability of the observations. Generally, if the observers agree on 80 to 85 percent of the observations, they are accepted as being reliable.

VALIDITY_____

Validity deals with the issue of whether the operational definition has actually measured what it was supposed to measure. In other words, is the operational definition a "real" indicator of the theoretical variable? Validity is extremely difficult to assess. The few studies that have been done to measure this have compared different indicators of the same theoretical variable and usually have rather substantial differences as results. For example, during World War II, a sample of people who according to government records had redeemed war bonds, were interviewed (Hyman, 1944). Seventeen percent denied that they had actually cashed their war bonds, an act that was generally defined as unpatriotic. This high rate of giving invalid answers casts serious question on the validity of self-reported behavior, especially when the behavior is contrary to accepted values.

There are several techniques to assess the validity of operational definitions, but they tend to be either extremely difficult to apply or are inconclusive in demonstrating validity. The best technique is to use an alternative source of information, as in the case of the war bond study. Unfortunately, multiple indicators are usually not available for most variables. Even when there is more than one indicator of a variable, it may not be possible to determine with certainty which of the different indicators is the most valid or the closest to reality. In some cases the difference is very small and the researcher feels confident that either measure is a valid indicator of a particular variable. But frequently the different operational definitions produce radically different estimates of reality.

Whatever technique is used to assess validity, the final judgment remains an opinion of the researcher. In effect, he must satisfy himself as best he can that his operational definitions are valid, and then proceed as if they are. He

"Basinski is into very, very basic research."

hopes that those who review his research will also be persuaded that the measures of his variables are sound, or that they, through additional research, will develop more valid indicators.

CAUSALITY

Whether or not all social behavior has a "cause" or whether social scientists can clearly identify causal relationships has been debated by scientists for many decades (Braithwaite, 1960). While it is difficult, if not impossible, to completely "prove" that one event or condition causes another, science has made startling progress because it *has* assumed causal relationships. The assumption that identifiable germs cause specific diseases has permitted medical researchers to control many formerly deadly illnesses. Physicists, assuming that the laws of physics specify cause-and-effect relations, have been able to construct rocketships which have carried men to the moon. Social scientists, while not yet duplicating the feats of their physical and medical science colleagues, have contributed to mankind's well-being by accepting the causality assumption in their research. Thinking in terms of causal relationships, social scientists should be able to discuss the "laws" of human behavior. These can then be used to create more humane societies and to ameliorate social problems such as crime, mental illness, suicide, and so on.

The major problem in identifying causal relationships is the elimination of alternative explanations of the behavior being studied. The failure to eliminate alternative explanations is vividly illustrated in the Hawthorne studies, a series of experiments designed to determine factors that affect productivity in factory work environments (Roethlisberger and Dickson, 1939). The Hawthorne studies, conducted in 1927–1932, involved testing the effects of various work conditions such as light intensity, the frequency and length of rest periods, and the type of supervision (independent variables) on work performance (dependent variable). Female employees were selected for the studies and were relocated in a special observation room. For two years, the lighting, rest periods, and supervision were varied; and much to the researcher's delight, each change "caused" production to increase. Eventually, however, it became apparent that it was the attention of the researchers and not the light, rest periods, or supervision that was causing the increase in production.

Despite the fact that a recent statistical reinterpretation of the Hawthorne data suggests that the experimental variables *did* account for most of the variability in quantity and quality of output (Franke and Kaul, 1978), the problem of accounting for the effect of unmeasured variables in the research setting remains an important one. A recent example of this can be found in the widespread acceptance of a causal relationship between individual biorhythms and various behaviors. It has been assumed, with some scientific evidence, that each individual goes through reoccurring intellectual, emotional, and physical cycles on a monthly schedule. Also, it has been assumed that these cycles can affect the daily experiences of the individual, including such things as the probability of an accident or an inferior or superior performance. Industrial psychologists reasoned that if they identified their employees' cycles they could pinpoint those days when each employee would be most creative and productive (all three biorhythms at their high points) and the days when each employee would have a bad day (all three biorhythms at their low points). Using biorhythm charts, industrial psychologists have "flagged" the time cards of employees on the day immediately before their "bad day." Thus, when a worker's biorhythm predicted a bad day, this was called to his or her attention by a little red flag on the time card. The individual was encouraged to be especially careful on that day and the results have been amazing—up to 60 percent reduction in industrial accidents. But more controlled research has demonstrated that it was not the biorhythms that reduced the industrial accidents. Rather, it was the attention given to "being careful" that produced the effect (Shaffer et. al., 1978; and Louis, 1978).

Accepting the assumption that it is possible to identify causal relationships where the independent variable causes or produces the dependent variable does not mean that these are the only relationships studied by social scientists. It is also useful to study non-causal, "correlational" or "associational" relationships as well. An example of using a correlational relationship to predict behavior is the use of admittance or screening tests by universities, private businesses, and other similar organizations. The score on a given test such as the Graduate Record Examination (GRE) has been found to correlate very highly with performance in graduate school. There is no actual causal relationship between the test experience and graduate school performance. Both are probably caused by some unmeasured characteristic such as "intellectual ability." The point is that much of the research conducted by social psychologists has focused on non-causal relationships and this research has applied as well as theoretical significance.

It is crucial that correlational relationships be clearly labeled as such and not be presented as though they are cause-and-effect. Some research reports have not been sufficiently specific on the nature of the relationships observed, and those responsible for social action programs have accepted correlational relationships as causal. Programs have been designed which controlled or manipulated certain variables and the architects of these programs have been extremely disappointed when the particular behavior did not exhibit significant change. The War on Poverty of the late 1960s included a large number of social programs designed to improve academic performance, increase vocational training, reduce unemployment, curtail delinquency and crime, decrease alcoholism, strengthen family life, and ameliorate other problems associated with poverty. New programs were designed using the results of correlational studies, and, as a consequence, the outcomes of these programs have usually been less than impressive. While correlational relationships do permit prediction, they cannot be used to control behavior.

TESTS OF SIGNIFICANCE

Social psychological studies usually present their findings in terms of "significant differences" or "significant relationships." In this case, *significant does not mean important;* rather it means that the particular relationship did not occur by chance. For example, suppose we are interested in determining whether observing aggressive behavior on the part of others increases the probability of aggression on the part of the observer. We might design a study in which we have half of our subjects watch an extremely violent television program while the other half spends an equal amount of time listening to quiet music. Suppose we then measure the frequency of occurrence of aggressive acts engaged in by members of the two groups during the 30 minutes following the television program or musical interlude and find that the television group commited three times more aggressive actions. A test of significance of difference computed for the two groups would tell us whether the observed difference is "real", that is, whether observing aggression actually leads to more aggression or whether the difference is such that it could have occurred simply by chance.

A test of significance is usually stated as the number of times out of one hundred that the observed difference would appear by chance. The .05 level means that the relationship would happen by chance five times out of one hundred. Normally the .05 level is accepted as the cut-off point in the social sciences and is accepted as being evidence of a real relationship.

The significance test does not provide any information about the magnitude or strength of the relationship. When the number of subjects is large, say over 200, very small and trivial differences may be statistically significant. The problem in equating significance with importance is obvious when a significant, but very weak, relationship is used to predict or control a specific behavior. Inaccurate predictions and very little control will be the result. This does not imply that tests of significance are unimportant. In analyzing the data testing a hypothesized relationship, the first step is usually to determine if the relationship is significant (real), and then to determine its strength.

MEASURES OF ASSOCIATION

Measures of association indicate the strength of a relationship between variables. The level of explained variance is one of the most popular ways to report the strength of a relationship. This refers to how much of the variation in the dependent variable can be predicted or controlled by the independent variable. Results are usually expressed as a percentage. For example, it may be reported that the number of people present (independent variable) explained 75 percent of the help given to a stranger in distress (dependent variable). In this case, knowledge of the independent variable would permit a reasonably accurate prediction of the dependent variable.

Just as significant relations can be very weak, it is possible for a very powerful relationship (75–80 percent explained variance) to be a chance relationship, especially when the number of subjects or respondents is small, say twenty or less. In this case, applying the findings will result in random consequences. The analysis of social psychological data should include a test of significance and a measure of association, assuring the reader that the relationship is significant (real) in a probabilistic sense and indicating how strong it is.

SAMPLING

The objective of science is to discover principles that can be generalized to all humans or at least to significant segments of human-kind. Some researchers may wish to identify principles that apply to all members of a society while others wish to generalize only to males, to married couples, to second graders in public schools, and so on. It is often not feasible or necessary to test the proposed principle on every individual in the population to which he or she wishes to generalize. If properly conducted, a sample can be selected from a larger group to serve as research subjects, and the results then applied to the entire group.

The most frequently used sampling procedure is to draw a simple random sample where every individual in the population has an equal chance to be selected as a research subject. This procedure sounds easy to execute but this is not the case. Often a roster of everyone in the population is not available. For example, there are seldom complete lists of the residents of towns and cities and almost never complete lists of residents of counties or states. Phone books, utility users lists, city directories, dwelling units in census tracts, and similar lists are frequently used to compile a roster of the individuals in the population, though each of these will be incomplete to one degree or another.

Once a roster is obtained and a sample drawn, the researcher has the difficult task of locating the selected subjects, convincing them to participate, and either traveling to each person's home or bringing him or her to the research site in order to collect the required data. The latter is a very serious problem for experimental research, as the costs of bringing a random sample of a large area to a given research site is prohibitive. Because of these difficulties, those conducting experiments frequently use college students who are available and who can be "encouraged" to participate in the experiment with promises of extra classroom credit or points. This makes it difficult to generalize to the larger and more diverse population. No matter what kind of research is being done, all three of the above-mentioned problems result in a percentage of the sample not being included in the study, which greatly influences the generalizability of the results to the larger population. If a large percentage of the sample does not participate or if those who do are not unique in some way, then generalization is risky.

Types of Research Methods

While the various research methods available to the social psychologist all have specific advantages and limitations, their similarities and differences can be better understood by asking two questions of each method: (1) what degree of control over the critical variables does the method allow, and (2) to what degree are the research findings generalizable to the real world?

The laboratory experiment affords the greatest amount of control which facilitates the testing of causal relationships. But, unfortunately, it is low on generalizability to the real social world. The field experiment increases the general applicability of the results by having the experiment conducted in a natural setting (school, factory, or hospital), but in such a setting the researcher loses some control over the variables and, consequently, loses some of the ability to test for causality. On the other hand, survey studies where questionnaires or interviews are administered to random samples of the population permit generalization to the total population, assuming that the sampling procedures have been adequate. But the researcher has very little, if any, control over the variables, and this makes it exceptionally difficult to demonstrate cause-and-effect relationships.

There is no simple procedure for selecting one research design over another. The decision usually involves making a series of trade-offs. The researcher must decide the objective of his research, consider his resources, and then carefully weigh the advantages and disadvantages of the different research designs in deciding which to employ.

EXPERIMENTAL RESEARCH

Experimental research generally involves the creation of a setting in which the independent variable can be systematically varied while the dependent variable is carefully measured. The independent variable is under the experimenter's control so he or she can regulate the timing and quantity of its introduction into the experimental setting. Also, extraneous variables can be controlled by dividing subjects into experimental and control groups. This control over the relevant variables maximizes the opportunity to demonstrate a causal relationship between the independent and dependent variable.

Laboratory Experiments offer the greatest control over the relevant variables because the researcher can determine factors such as the time of day the study is conducted, the temperature in the experimental room, the color of

Tom K. Ryan © 1975 United Feature Syndicate.

the walls, the type of furniture, the number of people present, the information given subjects, and so on. The independent variable can be manipulated so that changes in the dependent variable can be observed while holding other variables constant. Obviously the laboratory experiment must cope with the problem of bringing the real world into the laboratory, which, for certain research hypotheses, is very difficult to do.

A popular experimental design known as the Solomon Four Group Design is illustrated in Figure 13–1. Subjects are randomly assigned to one of four groups, two experimental and two control. Groups I and II (one control group and one experimental group) are observed or tested on the dependent variable at Time 1. For example, in a study testing the effects of leadership styles on productivity, the subjects were observed at Time 1 to determine their initial rate of building complex Tinker Toy models according to blueprint plans (Day, 1971). At Time 2, the two experimental groups, Group I and III, were exposed to the independent variable defined as leadership "style." In this example, the task leader used punative leadership by berating the ability and performance of the subjects for twenty minutes. The performance of all four groups on building the models was then observed at Time 3. Since models were built faster in Groups I and III at Time 3, it was concluded that punative leadership increased work productivity.

Campbell and Stanley (1963, pp. 5–12) identify a series of extraneous factors that may be the actual cause of any change observed in the dependent variable in an experiment, and point out how these can be assessed by a good experimental design such as the Solomon Four Group Design.

A *history effect* involves the subjects' exposure to events other than the

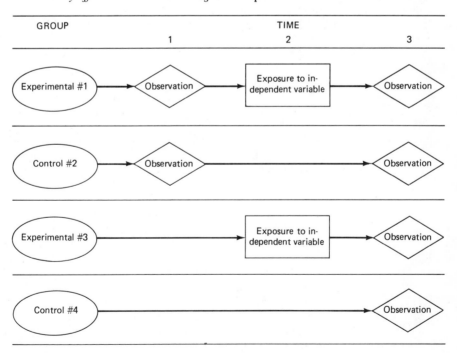

Figure 13–1 Solomon Four Group Experimental Design

independent variable that have the potential to affect the subjects' behavior on the dependent variable at Time 3. An earthquake, a flood, or a power outage might have occurred which greatly affected the subjects' behavior. While these are extreme cases, events can and do occur which influence experimental results.

The experimental design in Figure 13–1 controls for the effects of history by including two control groups. If a historical event occurred during the experiment, the impact would appear in the behavior of both the experimental and the control groups.

The effects of *maturation* are most apparent in long-term experiments such as the Pygmalion in the Classroom study which lasted an entire school year (Rosenthal and Jacobson, 1968). The study tested the effects on academic performance of labeling student as "bright." For many of the subjects, the improvement in academic performance was rather dramatic. While much of this was directly attributable to the "labeling" process, academic performance also increased as a function of age. That is, the students matured during the year and the increased attention span, the greater emotional control, the increased physical coordination, and the practice of academic skills contributed to improved school performance. Even in brief experiments of less than an hour, maturation can have an impact as subjects become hungry, fatigued, and so on. The impact of maturation can be separated from that of the independent variable by comparing the results of Experimental Group I and Control Group II in Figure 13–1. Maturation will affect the behavior of both groups equally, so that a difference between them may be attributed to something other than maturation; hopefully the independent variable.

Testing Effects occur because subjects are exposed to the initial observations at Time 1, which may have an important effect on their response at Time 3. A testing effect may be mistaken for an effect of the independent variable. Earlier we discussed the Hawthorne Effect phenomenon, which has been used to describe cases where the very fact that the subjects had been observed had a greater impact on their behavior than did the independent variables that had been manipulated by the researchers. The experimental design outlined in Figure 13–1 identifies the testing effect by contrasting the results for Experimental Group II and Control Group IV, neither of which was exposed to the initial observation at Time 2. Also, Experimental Group I can be compared to Experimental Group III and Control Group II to Control Group IV, to determine the testing effect since in each pair only one group of subjects was exposed to observation or testing at Time 1.

Instrumentation refers to changes in behavior observed between Times 1 and 3 due to alterations in the instrument that is used to make the observations. Frequently in social research, the observations are made by human observers who may change their techniques and, because of this, inadvertently affect the results. The observer may become tired or experience a change in mood that influences his sensitivity to the dependent variable.

Statistical Regression in experimental research refers to the fact that upon subsequent testing, individuals with the most extreme scores on initial measurements are likely to regress toward the mean on the basis of chance alone. In some instances, change attributed to the independent variable would be a function of such chance processes. The Solomon Four Group

Design controls for the regression effect by comparing the Experimental Groups I and III to the Control Groups II and IV. Both experimental and control groups would evidence a regression effect.

The *selection of experimental subjects* is important since this strongly influences the groups to whom the findings can be generalized. An ideal group of subjects might be a random sample of the adult population of the United States. The results could then be generalized to the entire adult population of the country. If the experiment concerned the behavior of a specific group such as children, the aged, or a minority group, then a random sample drawn from all members of that group would be the ideal set of experimental subjects. Unfortunately, motivating people to participate in an experiment is difficult. People are suspicious of social experiments and also tend to be too busy for social research. Because of the problems of interest and money, social scientists usually utilize subjects who are already gathered together and over whom they have some degree of control, such as the college sophomore who is participating as a class requirement or to earn extra credit. The proportion of social psychological experiments that use college sophomores as subjects has led to the concern that American psychology is really the psychology of the college sophomore. This is an important and legitimate criticism of social psychology, as it is risky to generalize principles of behavior that have only been tested with college students to the general population. While it is difficult, time consuming, and expensive, researchers conducting social psychological experiments should make every effort possible to obtain more representative samples of subjects.

Field Experiments As mentioned earlier, one way to make experiments more realistic is to conduct them outside the laboratory in a natural setting. As with any research design strategy, the decision to conduct the research "in the field" instead of the laboratory will require a trade-off of advantages and disadvantages. The researcher must determine if the benefits accruing from the natural setting and the ability to generalize to the real world will offset the disadvantages of the loss of some control of the relevant variables. The decision has to be made by carefully considering the basic purposes of the research. If the social psychologist's intent is to carefully test causal relations among variables implied by his theory, he would likely opt for a laboratory experiment. However, if he needs to determine by his investigation whether a given manipulation of an independent variable will make a difference in the "real world," he most likely would decide on a field experiment.

A good example of a field experiment is the Federal government's testing of Income Maintenance or Negative Income Tax (Kershaw, 1972). In 1968 an experiment sponsored by the government was designed to test whether families who were assured a certain level of income through negative income tax payments (independent variable) would reduce their incentive to work (dependent variable). Thirteen hundred poor families were selected in four cities in New Jersey and one in Pennsylvania and then randomly divided into an experimental group which received the guaranteed annual income, and a control group which did not. The amount paid to the families in the experimental condition ranged from $1,650 to $4,125, while the control group received nothing. In order to encourage people to work, the amount of the government payment was only gradually reduced as the families' income rose. Even though the government payment was reduced by a given percent, any one family could increase its total income by getting higher-paying jobs or having more family members work.

The results showed that there was no difference between the control and experimental groups. Those families with the guaranteed annual income were just as likely as the control group to try to improve their incomes. The guaranteed income did not result in lowered work incentive, although there was some suggestive evidence that those with guaranteed incomes were more discriminating in the jobs they accepted. This field experiment repudiated much more convincingly than a laboratory experiment could that guaranteed incomes for the poor result in loss of work incentive.

While the initial study showed no differences between experimental and control groups, later experiments in Gary, Indiana; Seattle, Washington; and Denver, Colorado showed important impacts of guaranteed income on family structure and marital disolution, and secondary workers tended to reduce their participation in the labor force with income maintenance (Hannan, Tuma, and Groeneveld, 1977, 1978).

Natural Experiments Certain independent variables in which the researcher may be interested simply are not open to manipulation in the laboratory. The variable may not be controllable by current technology; for example, how does one create a full-size tornado in order to study its effects on social interaction? Also, ethical, moral, or legal constraints may prevent the manipulation of an independent variable which might possibly harm subjects. Contagious diseases, failure in school, the death of a loved one, the firing of a worker, and similar events obviously cannot be caused by the experimenter simply in order to observe how people respond. A natural experiment is conducted by letting nature and/or other social conditions cause such a given change, and then data is collected.

One problem with naturally occurring events is the suddenness with which they frequently occur, thus limiting opportunities to pretest the affected population or to develop instruments to collect the desired information. One strategy to overcome this problem is the creation of disaster research centers, which have obtained pre-experimental measures of certain dependent variables and have a trained staff prepared to go where a natural disaster occurs to collect the post-experimental data.

Natural disasters are not the only type of natural experiment. Advanced notice of "naturally occurring" events such as the shutting down of a factory, or the dispensing of failing grades by a teacher, permit the experimenter to obtain pre-experimental measures of a relevant dependent variable before and after the event occurs. For example, Lieberman (1956) learned of pending changes in factory workers' status and used this as an experiment to test the effect of role-change (independent variable) upon workers' attitudes toward the company (dependent variable). Some workers were going to be promoted to foremen while others were to be selected as union shop stewards. He measured workers' attitudes toward management and labor unions before the promotions occurred. Approximately one year after the change in work status, he again assessed the employees' attitudes. He compared those who had become foremen or union stewards with a matched sample of factory workers who had not been promoted. The control group showed no change in attitude, while the union shop stewards had become more pro-union and the foremen had become more anti-union/pro-management. A little over a year after Lieberman's initial study, natural conditions again altered the independent variable of job status. A recession required a cutback at the factory, resulting in about one-third of those who had previously been made foremen being demoted back to their former jobs. Lieberman discovered that those who remained as foremen became even more pro-management while those demoted adopted attitudes similar to the typical worker.

Advantages. The great advantage of experimental research is that it can test cause-and-effect relationships. Experimental research has been the primary means of establishing principles of human behavior that have been utilized by teachers, social workers, government officials, city planners, parents, and others to attempt to create a humane and individually satisfying society, city, or home. Because of the ability to test causal relationships, experimental research will probably remain the dominant research strategy in social psychology, in spite of the problems.

Disadvantages. There are several major disadvantages or problems of experimental research which must be wrestled with each time an experiment is designed. The first is the ethical and legal responsibility for what happens to experimental subjects. In an experiment, the researcher causes or manipulates an independent variable that is predicted to have a specific effect on the research subjects. There is always the potential of unanticipated, harmful effects such as feelings of depression or shame, loss of confidence, a mental breakdown, a heart attack, or even suicide. Even when the experimenter has done all that he can to insure that such things do not happen, there is always the possibility that they will occur.

The second major disadvantage is that of generalizability. As mentioned, some topics or variables or situations cannot be created in the laboratory and the closest approximation may be so sufficiently different that generalizing from the experiment to the real world is not justified.

One other problem of experimental research in social psychology is that human beings differ significantly from rats, pigeons, germs, plants, and chemical compounds which are the subjects in other sciences. The social psychologist's subject knows that he is participating in an experiment and this knowledge of self as experimental subject may affect the outcome of the research.

SURVEY RESEARCH

Survey research involves obtaining information from a sample of people or groups who represent a larger population. Survey research collects data using one of two basic techniques: interviews or questionnaires.

Interview Studies Interview surveys involve carefully trained interviewers asking a sample of respondents a series of questions and then recording their answers. An example is a multi-state study conducted by one of the authors to assess the social and social psychological impacts that are occurring in the contemporary western "boom towns" created by the large-scale development of energy resources. By interviewing samples of community

"HELLO, FDA?...I'D LIKE TO REPORT RESEARCH THAT DIRECTLY LINKS CHEESE WITH DEATH IN RATS."

© 1977 Wayne Stayskal, Chicago Tribune.

residents, the research team sought to test hypotheses concerning individual and group adjustment to rapid social change, sources of social conflict and cleavage resulting from the mixing of groups with very different cultural traditions and lifestyles, and whether rapid industrial and economic growth increases or decreases the amount of social and economic inequality that already existed in the study community prior to the development.

Questionnaire Studies The second data collection technique is the self-administered *questionnaire.* In this type of survey, a questionnaire is delivered to a respondent who reads the questions and then checks or writes his responses to them. A popular form of questionnaire research is the mail questionnaire survey which allows large samples of people to be contacted

Blondie ® is © by King Features Syndicate, Inc.

for a relatively small cost. For example, a study of divorce conducted by two of the authors in eight western states obtained over 4,000 completed questionnaires from a random sample drawn from the phone books for the eight states. Each respondent was mailed the questionnaire along with a cover letter explaining the purpose and importance of the study. Those that did not return the questionnaire were then sent a postcard reminder. Two additional mailings, including another copy of the questionnaire, were sent to those who still failed to respond. Even with four separate mailings the cost was less than one dollar per completed questionnaire as compared to an average cost of many times that amount for a completed interview. The study revealed important information about the experiences of males and females who go through a divorce.

Advantages An important advantage of survey research is the great variety of topics which can be studied. Some issues of vital concern to social psychology cannot be studied in the experimental laboratory, but can be studied using survey techniques. What proportion of voters favor the Democratic candidate over the Republican candidate in the coming election? What proportion of college students have participated in premarital sexual relations? Is the rise of the women's liberation movement associated with widespread changes in sex roles in the U.S.? Does the highly publicized execution of a convicted murderer increase or decrease the people's rejection of capital punishment? No matter how ingenious the social psychologist may be in designing innovative experiments, topics like these cannot be taken into the laboratory.

A second advantage of survey research is that it can approximate real life situations. Survey research can ask the person or group to reveal experiences or feelings about real situations, and the findings can be made relevant to real life behavior.

One additional advantage of survey research is its ability to obtain information from samples which permit generalizing the results to larger populations. A researcher can collect data from a relatively small group of individuals and can then make fairly accurate statements about the attitudes and behavior of a much larger population from which the group was selected.

Disadvantages Since the researcher cannot control for all the potentially relevant variables and since he usually collects data at only one point in time in survey research, any causal inferences are tenuous. Collecting data at only one point in time makes it difficult to tell which variable occurred first, and the order in which the variables occur is critical in determining cause-and-effect relationships. It is obvious that an event could not have been the cause of another event which has already happened. Sometimes it is possible in survey research to establish the time sequence of variables by asking the respondents to indicate which occurred first.

A technique used in trying to trace causal inferences from survey research is the utilization of a well-developed theory. If the results are consistent with a theoretical prediction of a causal relationship, the researcher is more confident in suggesting one. Also, the "changeability" of variables can be used to assess whether the relationship between two variables might be causal. If one of the variables can't change, then it is treated as a cause rather than an effect. For example, suppose a relationship is discovered between sex and movie attendance where girls go to the movies more often than boys. In this case sex would be assumed to be the cause since there is no way movie attendance can change boys into girls and girls into boys.

Even when the changeability of the variables and the time sequences are established and the results are consistent with theory, it is still very risky to infer a cause-and-effect relationship from survey research. If possible, cause-and-effect relationships suggested by survey research should be tested in experimental research.

There is also the concern in survey research about whether respondents tell the truth. A failure to remember what really happened, a fear of the consequences of revealing certain behaviors, a desire to appear in a socially approved light, and a desire to tell the researcher what he wants to hear, may all contribute to the respondent distorting reality. Validity is an especially serious problem when the focus of the study is on an illegal, immoral, or disapproved behavior such as drug abuse, homosexual behavior, child abuse, etc. Survey researchers have developed a number of strategies to try to increase the truthfulness of response. Promises of anonymity or confidentiality, lie scales, and/or asking the same question in two or three different ways are used to encourage people to respond with truthful or valid answers. The success of these strategies seems to vary from study to study and this indicates that the social psychologist needs to be aware of the problem and do all he can to insure validity.

It is apparent that the strengths of survey research match the weaknesses of experimental research and that the weaknesses of survey research are the strengths of experimental research. Social psychology requires both research methods in order to continue to accumulate knowledge about human behavior.

QUALITATIVE RESEARCH

The basic strategy of qualitative research is for the researcher to *experience* the behavior being studied (Filstead, 1970). For example, a qualitative researcher interested in prison life, would have himself "sentenced" to a prison and experience incarceration firsthand. The basic assumption of qualitative research is that *experience is knowledge.*

Qualitative research rejects to a large degree the "scientific research methods" that have been discussed in this chapter. Hypotheses, operational definitions, and quantitative measurements are felt to distort reality by forcing it into preconceived categories. In theory, the qualitative researcher approaches the behavior in question as a highly trained, yet blank, sheet of paper that is able to record whatever is happening. Qualitative researchers sometimes compare themselves to artists, who paint reality as they experience it with their trained senses while the quantitative researcher is the commercial artist who sketches out a design forced on him by someone else. Different artists, or even the same artist, may paint several different pictures of a given mountain scene. All would represent reality and yet they would not look alike.

Qualitative research stresses that the behavior being studied should be examined through the eyes of those who perform it. For example, according to qualitative research, prostitution should be studied from the perspective of the prostitute and her client, rather than from that of the police, the social worker, or government official. Related to this concern is the accusation by some qualitative researchers that scientific research is controlled by the "establishment," meaning big business, the military, and government (Lee, 1970). These individuals argue that The Establishment uses scientific research to find ways of controlling people who engage in what it considers to be "inappropriate behavior." To a limited degree, this is correct, as considerable research is directed at reducing "social problems" including drug abuse, alcoholism, mental illness, poverty, crime, delinquency, divorce, child abuse, and so on. The intent of most of the research directed at social problem type behavior is to prevent or to rehabilitate those who commit it.

An example of qualitative research is a study of cab drivers' gambling behavior (Henslin, 1967). Henslin, while a graduate student in St. Louis, took a job as a cab driver and immersed himself in the social world of the cabbie. While waiting to check their cabs in and out of the company barn, the drivers would play craps. Henslin not only watched their gambling, but he gambled with them, as one of them. He tried the same techniques that they did to influence the dice. He talked to the dice, blew on them, threw them in certain ways and rubbed them to experience what he suspected other cab drivers were experiencing. From the experience Henslin contended that seemingly irrational behavior becomes rational and predictable. Qualitative studies have been the source of many interesting and inciteful hypotheses which have then been tested using other research techniques.

Participant Observation is basically qualitative research but it usually involves some traditional scientific research methods such as the testing of hypotheses, standardized questions, or behavior code sheets. Participant observation ranges from complete participation with total secrecy about the real identity of the researcher to fairly limited participation with the researcher's purpose known to leaders or officials of the group to be studied. There are several classic participant observation studies in sociology and social psychology including William Foote Whyte's *Street Corner Society* (1943), Howard Becker's et al. *Boys in White* (1961), Elliot Liebow's *Talley's Corner* (1967), Laud Humphreys' *Tearoom Trade* (1970), John Howard Griffin's *Black Like Me* (1961), and Leon Festinger et al.'s *When Prophecy Fails* (1956).

Advantages The major advantage of qualitative research is the rich detail it provides. The researcher is able to experience and to observe the day to day activities of the group being studied and thus discover insights and details glossed over by experimental and survey research.

Qualitative research generally has no problem about the behavior being real. The researcher and the individual or group he or she is studying are in the real world, engaging in real life behavior. The only exception to this is when it is necessary to inform some members of the group that the researcher is not really a member but is there to observe them. As discussed before, when people know they are being studied they frequently alter their behavior. The more people who know the researcher's purpose, the greater the possibility of role playing by the individuals in the group. For example, if the researcher wants to be committed to a mental hospital, it would probably be necessary to obtain the cooperation of the director or head psychiatrist. If only this individual knew of the researcher's intent, the doctors, staff, and patients would probably behave as usual. But if the doctors and staff members learn the researcher's identity, then they would probably alter their behavior, which in turn would influence the patients' behavior and give an unreal or distorted picture of the mental hospital.

In spite of the problems involved, qualitative research provides an indepth exposure to the research topic that no other type of research is capable of. It provides the researcher with insights that may never emerge with alternative research methods.

Disadvantages The disadvantages or problems of qualitative research are similar to those of experimental research in that the researcher has an impact on the lives of the research subjects. There is the very real danger that the group being studied will have their behavior altered by their association with the researcher. He may introduce new behavior patterns, or the group may come to depend on the researcher, which will leave a void when he leaves the group at the study's conclusion.

The person doing qualitative research runs the risk of becoming involved in illegal or unethical activities. For example, research on a delinquent gang, a group of safe crackers, a prostitution ring, or a drug culture may involve the researcher in activities that are clearly outside the law. Qualitative research in a polygamous commune, an anti-nuclear power plant protest group, or a rock concert tour may place the researcher in a position where he must violate his own personal moral values in order to experience the life of the group he is interested in.

There is also the danger that the researcher may "go native" and become so well-socialized into the group that he or she rejects the life of a social psychologist and becomes a permanent part of the study group. A less severe form of going native occurs when the social psychologist identifies with those being studied to the point that the research findings become biased.

Perhaps the most serious disadvantage of qualitative research is the problem of generalizability. While the description of a particular group may be insightful, it is a description from the perspective of only one person and is a description of only one group. It is extremely difficult to generalize from the experiences of the researcher to other members of the same group, let alone to other groups.

Qualitative research appears to make its greatest contribution to social psychology by suggesting hypotheses that can then be tested by more rigorous scientific methods. Also, it can provide detail and background information which facilitates the interpretation of experimental or survey research findings.

Problems Unique to the Science of Human Behavior

Each data-collection method that is used by social psychologists in their research efforts carries with it certain specific advantages and disadvantages that must be considered as one designs a particular study. In addition, there are some other very important problems that must be considered that are somewhat unique to the subject matter of the social scientist. These problems evolve around the very fact that social psychology involves acting, thinking, and feeling human beings studying other acting, thinking, and feeling human beings.

REACTIVITY IN SOCIAL PSYCHOLOGICAL RESEARCH

Reactivity occurs because research subjects are human beings, and this very fact may alter the nature of the observations obtained. In other words, because one is being observed, one may change, either consciously or unconsciously, the nature of the action in which one engages or the responses one gives to a question. In recent years, social psychologists have become aware that the characteristics of the experiment itself influence its outcome. Some of these factors include: the experimental setting; the behavior of the experimenter; experimenter expectations; and role attributions of the experimental subject. These factors have all been shown to have important effects on the research findings.

In addition to the experimental setting, the expectations of the experimenter as well as other characteristics and behaviors that he or she brings to the experiment may affect research results. Rosenthal (1964, 1966, 1969) suggests that experimenters often influence their subjects in ways that tend to confirm their research hypotheses.

Interviewers engage in interaction with the subjects, and the interview may be influenced, to one degree or another, by this interaction. For example, the study of white prejudice toward blacks and blacks' attitudes toward civil-rights activities have been found to be influenced by the race of the interviewer as compared to the race of the subject.

How does the researcher overcome the problems associated with reactivity? The answer to this question is not simple. However, Webb et al. (1966) have proposed two basic procedures.

First, they propose the development and use of nonreactive measures or measures that eliminate direct interaction between the researcher and the subject through which the response of the subject could be influenced. For example, rather than asking subjects about their drinking behavior, one might count the liquor bottles in their trash cans.

The second strategy proposed by Webb and his colleagues is to use a process referred to as *triangulation*. In social-science research, this refers simply to the utilization of more than one operational definition using different research strategies to test the research hypotheses or theory. Triangulation is based on the assumption that the strengths of one method may be the weakness of another. Thus, as Deutscher (1973, p. 133) has noted, if we have convergence of conclusions derived from a series of measures using different techniques—for example, a survey, a field study, and an experiment—each of which have their own peculiar form of reactivity, then we can grant more credibility to the researcher's conclusion.

ETHICS

The story is told of an eminent entomologist who had spent much of his life developing a complete category system for all insects. Shortly after his work was finished, as he was walking home one evening, he noticed a very unusual-looking insect crawling along the side of the walkway. Upon careful observation, he concluded that it was indeed a unique insect—one that did not belong to any of the classes of insects he had worked to create. Question: What did the scientist do? Answer: He stepped on it.

Questions of ethics have been at the heart of science since its inception. Virtually all scientific societies prepare ethical guidelines that outline in general terms the behavior expected of any member. In general, science requires ethical presentation of data, accurate credit given for use of any material or ideas, acknowledgement given to all involved in collaborative efforts, and disclosure of sources of financial support. When departures from these rules of ethical scientific conduct occur, scientific societies feel duty-bound to investigate and censure those violating the principles.

The social psychologist has had to face ethical problems not faced by many other scientific disciplines. Because the subject matter of social psychology is human behavior, the social psychologist undertaking research *must* be concerned for the welfare of his research subjects. Unlike the chemist in his laboratory, the social psychologist cannot expose the research elements to any combination of forces he wishes in order to study the resultant changes. The chemist may wish to see which substance will radically change the composition of the compound under study; the social psychologist must make sure that what he does does *not* result in any *permanent change,* damage, or injury in the human research subject.

In the face of the need to protect the rights of human subjects, universities have created special committees to carefully evaluate all research before it is undertaken. The federal government requires that any project involving human beings as subjects that receives federal funds be approved by the appropriate Human Subjects Review Committee.

At first glance, all this formality may appear to have sufficiently handled the ethical problems. Such is not the case. In 1973, the American Psychological Association published a revised edition of *Ethical Principles in the Conduct of Research with Human Participants.* This was the result of several years of committee work as well as careful analysis of suggestions and criticism from thousands of individual psychologists. This statement of ethical canon in effect said that the researcher had the responsibility of advising subjects in advance of any aspects of the research that might influence the decision to participate. In short, the subject had to be able to give "informed consent." In addition, the researcher must be forthright and honest in dealing with the subject and must protect him or her from mental and physical stress. This is a forthright statement against deception in research and a strong stand against the invasion of privacy or otherwise inflicting stress or pain upon the subjects.

Deception in Research Social psychologists are aware of the fact that most research in social psychology employs some deception. This is done in order to ensure realism (Aronson, 1976, p. 292). Because the researcher wishes his or her subjects to act as they would naturally or to tell their true feelings and behavior, he or she frequently does not divulge the real purpose of the research. If subjects knew the focus of the study, they might overreact trying to be good subjects and give the researcher the kind of behavior or answers they feel are wanted. By knowing the purpose of the study, the subject may also employ his or her own normative standard about what he or she feels people ought to do and then behave according to this standard or report that he or she behaves this way rather than the way he or she actually does.

Was the knowledge coming from the oft-quoted Milgram research on obedience worth the price of deceiving the subjects? Somewhat ironically, answers to this question can only be given by accepting for oneself a given set of ethical standards. If one believes that one should not lie; that deception is degrading to both the deceiver and the deceived; and that ultimately deception is an invasion of privacy because the deceived can never give "informed consent," then such social psychological research is not worth the costs. For others, who believe that society has a right to know about the very real possibility of the dangers of excesses of obedience to authority, such as occurred in Nazi Germany, and that adequate debriefing of subjects diminishes the danger, the benefits outweigh the costs. It is informative to know that when the Milgram research was completed, 84 percent of the subjects, after learning of the real nature of the experiment, said they were glad to have been in the experiment, 15 percent were neutral, and only 1 percent were sorry. Seventy-four percent felt they had benefitted from the experience (Samuel, 1975, p. 58).

Although the cost/benefit ratio derived from any research involving deception may be hard to evaluate, there is one consequence that is of major concern to social psychologists. This is the fact that wide-scale deception in research is producing a generation of college students who are not naive about research deception. This in and of itself is threatening to the discipline of social psychology. If deception works the first time, forever after that subject will realize that the researcher likely has something else as the real purpose. There is no ready-made or easy solution to the problem of deception.

Protecting Privacy Next to the issue of deception, privacy is the ethical problem most troublesome for the social psychologist. The two problems are not independent of each other. Deception often opens up the very real

possibility of invasion of privacy. To become angry, fearful, frustrated, or otherwise extremely tense are often very private emotional reactions. If the researcher, unknown to the subject, constructs the research setting to elicit these emotions and then carefully observes the subject's reactions without the informed consent of the subject, this by anyone's definition is an invasion of privacy.

Laboratory experiments are not the only research designs that force a face-to-face confrontation with the privacy dilemma. Field experiments, natural experiments, participant observational studies, private interview studies, and questionnaire surveys are all likely to elicit private information. The basic resolution is not an easy one to make, and different segments of the population resolve the issue differently. Nixon believed the Watergate tapes to be private material, but the courts eventually decided that they were public documents.

One research report some years ago that highlighted the privacy issue is *Tearoom Trade: Impersonal Sex in Public Places,* by Laud Humphreys (1970). Humphreys chose to study homosexual behavior in public restrooms. In order to carry out the observational research, he became a participant observer. This was made possible by Humphreys playing the role of the "watchqueen." In homosexual jargon, this is the third man who watches to warn of the approach of a nonhomosexual while the other two are engaging in homosexual activity. If a stranger comes, the watchqueen coughs or otherwise signals that a stranger is approaching. By so acting, Humphreys was able to record hundreds of homosexual acts. Participant observation provided an excellent measure of the dependent variable, homosexual behavior, but did not permit the researcher to obtain information about independent variables such as age, education, occupation, income, and marital status. In order to collect this information, Humphreys recorded the men's automobile license plate numbers without their knowing it. These numbers were then used to obtain the men's names, addresses, and additional information available in state motor vehicle records. Using the addresses, Humphreys visited the neighborhoods of these men and observed the type of neighborhood, the type of house, and other indicators about the life style of the individuals being studied. One year later he disguised himself by changing his hair style, driving a different automobile, and wearing different attire and then interviewed each of these men in their homes as a social scientist doing a study of "health care." Admittedly, Humphreys had invaded these men's private lives and had recorded information that made them liable to criminal prosecution, embarrassment, or blackmail. Is such "unethical" behavior of the researcher justifiable?

Obviously, the question will be answered differently by different people according to their own set of ethics. Humphreys wrote: "You do walk a really perilous tightrope in regard to ethical matters in studies like this, but . . . someone (must) walk it. . . . The methods I used were the least intrusive possible. Oh I could have hidden in the ceiling as the police do, but then I would have been an accomplice in what they were doing" (cited in von Hoffman, 1970, p. 5). Because Humphreys went to great lengths to protect the men he was studying, even accepting arrest rather than divulge the names and actions he had recorded, he feels that he protected the rights of the men he studied.

Von Hoffman (1970) arrives at a different answer to the ethical question. He agrees that increased knowledge of human behavior is beneficial, but for him it does not outweigh the problems associated with loss of privacy.

So after all we have said about the ethical dilemma facing social psychology researchers, where do we stand? The researcher must balance the two goods, the right to know against the right to privacy, and in general it seems that preserving the right to privacy is currently given greater weight than the right to know. This follows from the position that the social psychologist has a *vested* interest and will very likely be unable to objectively make such a decision. Because society's norms at present dictate that the researcher is basically the one who must make this decision, we see greater harm occurring from *excess* on the part of the researcher compared to the information lost because the research is not done.

It seems that social psychologists in general are very much concerned about violation of general ethical standards of objectivity and integrity in research. However, not only must the social scientist be concerned about the welfare of his research subject, he must also be honest and ethical in how he analyzes and reports research findings. It appears from the absence of evidence to the contrary that generation of false data, using others' material and ideas, or reporting data in a less than honest manner, rarely occurs. But a sufficient number of violations have become public to demonstrate that they do exist. Social psychology in particular and humanity in general will be the losers if lack of integrity on the part of researchers undermines society's trust in the discipline.

references

ABERLE, D. F. 1966. *The peyote religion among the navaho.* Chicago: Aldine.

ACOCK, A. C., and DeFLEUR, M. L. 1972. A configuration approach to contingent consistency in the attitude-behavior relationship. *American Sociological Review* 34:714–726.

Ad Hoc Committee on Ethical Standards in Psychological Research. 1973. *Ethical principles on the conduct of research with human participants.* Washington, D.C.: American Psychological Association.

ADAMS, J. 1965. Inequity in social exchange. In *Advances in experimental social psychology,* vol. 2, ed. L. Berkowitz, pp. 267–299. New York: Academic Press.

AINSWORTH, M. P. S. 1973. The development of infant-mother attachment. In *Review of child development research,* vol. 3., ed. B. M. Caldwell and H. N. Riccuiti, pp. 1–94. Chicago: University of Chicago Press.

AJZEN, I. 1971. Attitudinal vs. normative messages: an investigation of the differential effects of persuasive communications on behavior. *Sociometry* 34: 263–280.

_____, and FISHBEIN, M. 1969. The prediction of behavioral intentions in a choice situation. *Journal of Experimental Social Psychology* 6: 400–416.

_____ 1970. The prediction of behavior from attitudinal and normative variables. *Journal of Personality and Social Psychology* 6: 466–487.

_____ 1972. Attitudes and normative beliefs as factors influencing behavioral intentions. *Journal of Personality and Social Psychology* 21:1–9.

_____ 1973. Attitudinal and normative variables as predictors of specific behaviors. *Journal of Personality and Social Psychology* 27:41–57.

ALBRECHT, S. L.; DeFLEUR, M. L.; and WARNER, L. G. 1972. Attitude-behavior relationships: a reexamination of the postulate of contingent consistency. *Pacific Sociological Review* 15: 149–168.

ALBRECHT, S. L., and WARNER, L. G. 1975. Situational and personality factors: interactive effects on attitude-action consistency. *Youth and Society* 6:344–364.

_____, and CARPENTER, K. E. 1976. Attitudes as predictors of behavior vs. behavior intentions: a convergence of research traditions. *Sociometry* 39: 1–10.

ALCORN, D. S., and CONDIE, S. J. 1975. Who picks up whom: the fleeting encounter between motorist and hitchhiker. *Humboldt Journal of Social Relations* 3:56–61.

ALEXANDER, C. N., JR., and EPSTEIN, J. 1969. Problems of dispositional inference in person perception research. *Sociometry* 32:381–395.

ALLEN, V., and LEVINE, J. 1971. Social support and conformity: the role of independent assessment of reality. *Journal of Experimental Social Psychology* 7:48–58.

ALLPORT, F. H. 1920. The influence of the group upon association and thought. *Journal of Experimental Psychology* 3:159–182.

–––––– 1924. *Social psychology.* Boston: Houghton Mifflin.

ALLPORT, G. W. 1935. Attitudes. In *A handbook of social psychology,* ed. C. Murchinson, pp. 798–844. Worcester, Mass.: Clark University Press.

–––––– 1968. The historical background of modern social psychology, In *The handbook of social psychology,* vol. 1, 2nd ed., ed. G. Lindzey and E. Aronson, pp. 1–80. Reading, Mass.: Addison-Wesley.

––––––, and POSTMAN, L. J. 1947. *The psychology of rumor.* New York: Holt, Rinehart and Winston.

ALPERT, J. L. 1975. Teacher behavior and pupil performance: reconsideration of the mediation of pygmalion effects. *Journal of Educational Research* 69:53–57.

ANDERSON, N. H. 1962. Application of an additive model of impression formation. *Science* 138:817–818.

–––––– 1965. Averaging versus adding as a stimulus combination rule in impression formation. *Journal of Experimental Psychology* 70:394–400.

–––––– 1974. Cognitive algebra: integration theory applied to social attribution, In *Advances in experimental social psychology,* vol. 7, ed. L. Berkowitz, pp. 1–101. New York: Academic Press.

––––––, and BARRIOS, A. A. 1961. Primary effects in personality impression formation. *Journal of Abnormal and Social Psychology* 63:346–350.

ANDERSON, R., and NIDA, S. A. 1978. Effect of physical attractiveness on opposite- and same- sex evaluations. *Journal of Personality* 46:401–413.

ANDERSON, W. A. 1977. The social organization and social control of a fad: streaking on a college campus. *Urban Life* 6:221–239.

ANTHONY, S. 1973. Anxiety and rumor. *Journal of Social Psychology* 89:91–98.

APPLETON, T.; CLIFTON, R.; and GOLDBERG, S. 1975. The development of behavioral competence in infancy. In *Review of child development research,* vol. 4., ed. F. D. Horowitz, pp. 101–186. Chicago: University of Chicago Press.

ARDREY, R. 1961. *African genesis.* New York: Atheneum.

–––––– 1966. *The territorial imperative.* New York: Atheneum.

–––––– 1970. *The social contract.* New York: Atheneum.

ARKIN, R. M., and DUVAL, S. 1975. Focus of attention and causal attributions of actors and observers. *Journal of Experimental Social Psychology* 11:427–438.

ARKIN, R. M.; GLEASON, J. M.; and JOHNSTON, S. 1976. Effects of perceived choice, expected outcome, and observed outcome of an action on the causal attribution of actors. *Journal of Experimental Social Psychology* 12:151–158.

ARONFREED, J. 1969. The concept of internalization. In *Handbook of socialization theory and research,* ed. D. A. Goslin, pp. 263–324. Chicago: Rand McNally.

––––––, and PASKAL, V. 1965. Altruism, empathy, and the conditioning of positive affect. Unpublished manuscript. Philadelphia: University of Pennsylvania.

ARONSON, E. 1969. The theory of cognitive dissonance: a current perspective. In *Advances in experimental social psychology,* vol. 4, ed. L. Berkowitz, pp. 1–34. New York: Academic Press.

–––––– 1976. *The social animal.* San Francisco: Freeman.

––––––, and MATTEE, D. R. 1968. Dishonest behavior as a function of differential levels of induced self–esteem. *Journal of personality and social psychology* 9:121–127.

ARONSON, E., and MILLS, J. 1959. The effects of severity of initiation on liking for a group. *Journal of Abnormal and Social Psychology* 59:177–181.

ARONSON, E.; TURNER, J. A.; and CARLSMITH, J. M. 1963. Communicator credibility and communication discrepancy as determinants of opinion change. *Journal of Abnormal and Social Psychology* 67:31–36.

ASCH, S. E. 1946. Forming impressions of personality. *Journal of Abnormal and Social Psychology* 41:258–290.

———— 1951. Effects of group pressure upon the modification and distortion of judgment. In *Groups, leadership, and men,* ed. H. Guetzkow, pp. 177–190. Pittsburgh: Carnegie.

———— 1952. *Social psychology.* Englewood Cliffs, N.J.: Prentice-Hall.

———— 1956. Studies of independence and conformity: a minority of one against a unanimous majority. *Psychological Monographs* 70:1–70.

AUSUBEL, D. P. 1952. *Ego development and the personality disorders.* New York: Grune and Stratton.

AZRIN, N. H. 1964. Aggressive responses of paired animals. Paper read at symposium on medical aspects of stress, Walter Reed Institute of Research, Washington, D.C.

————; HUTCHINSON, R. R.; and SALLERY, R. D. 1964. Pain-aggression toward inanimate objects. *Journal of Experimental Analysis of Behavior* 7:223–227.

AZRIN, N. H., and HOLZ, W. C. 1966. Punishment. In *Operant behavior: areas of research and application,* ed. W. K. Honig, pp. 442–443. Englewood Cliffs, N.J.: Prentice-Hall.

BAIN, A. 1868. *Mental science.* New York: Appleton.

BAIN, R. 1928. An attitude on attitude research. *American Journal of Sociology* 33: 940–957.

BAKER, R. K., and BALL, S. J. 1969. *Mass media and violence: report to the national commission on causes and prevention of violence.* Washington, D. C.: U.S. Government Printing Office.

BALDWIN, T. F., and LEWIS, C. 1972. Violence in television: the industry looks at itself. In *Television and social behavior, reports and papers.* Vol. 1: Media content and control, Surgeon General's Scientific Advisory Committee on Television and Social Behavior. Washington, D.C.: U.S. Government Printing Office.

BALES, R. F. 1950. A set of categories for the analysis of small group interaction. *American Sociological Review* 15:146–159.

BALL-ROKEACH, S. J. 1973. Values and violence: a test of the subculture of violence thesis. *American Sociological Review* 38:736–749.

BANDURA, A. 1969a. Social learning theory of identificatory processes. In *Handbook of Socialization Theory and Research,* ed. D. A. Goslin, pp. 213–262. Chicago: Rand McNally.

———— 1969b. *Principles of behavior modification.* New York: Holt, Rinehart and Winston, Inc.

———— 1972. Letter to subcommittee on communication committee on commerce. *Hearings on the surgeon general's report by the scientific committee on television and social behavior,* March 21, p. 19. Washington, D.C.: U.S. Government Printing Office.

———— 1973. Social learning theory of aggression. In *The control of aggression,* ed. J. F. Knutson, pp. 201–250. Chicago: Aldine.

———— 1977. *Social learning theory.* Englewood Cliffs, N.J.: Prentice-Hall.

————, and WALTERS, R. H. 1963. *Social learning and personality development,* New York: Holt, Rinehart & Winston.

BASSO, K. H., and ANDERSON, N. 1973. A western apache writing system: the symbols of Silas John. *Science* 180:1013–1022.

BATES, F. L. 1956. Position, role and status: a reformulation of concepts. *Social Forces* 34:313–321.

BAUMRIND, D. 1967. Child care practices anteceding three patterns of pre-school behavior. *Genetic Psychology Monographs* 75:43–88.

―――― 1971. Current patterns of parental authority. *Developmental Psychology Monographs* 4, pt. 2.

BAVELAS, A.; HASTORF, A. H.; GROSS, A. E.; and KITE, W. R. 1965. Experiments on the alteration of group structure. *Journal of Experimental Social Psychology* 1: 55–70.

BECKER, F. D. 1973. Study of spatial markers. *Journal of Personality and Social Psychology* 26:439–445.

BECKER, H. S. 1963. *Outsiders.* New York: The Free Press.

――――; GEER, B.; HUGHES, E. C.; and STRAUSS, A. L. 1961. *Boys in white; student culture in medical school.* Chicago: University of Chicago Press.

BECKER, W. C. 1964. Consequences of different kinds of parental discipline. In *Review of child development research,* vol. 1., ed. M. L. Hoffman and L. W. Hoffman, pp. 169–205. New York: Russell Sage.

BECKMAN, L. 1970. Effects of students' performance on teachers' and observers' attributions of causality. *Journal of Educational Psychology* 61:76–82.

BEEMAN, E. A. 1947. The effect of male hormone on aggressive behavior in mice. *Physiological Zoology,* 20:373–405.

BELLAK, L. 1971. *The TAT, CAT, and SAT in clinical use.* New York: Grune and Stratton.

BELSON, W. 1978. *Television violence and the adolescent boy.* Farnborough: Saxon House.

BEM, D. J. 1965. An experimental analysis of self-persuasion. *Journal of Experimental Social Psychology* 1:199–218.

―――― 1970. *Beliefs, attitudes, and human affairs.* Belmont, Calif.: Brooks/Cole.

―――― 1972. Self-perception theory. In *Advances in experimental social psychology,* vol. 6. ed. L. Berkowitz, pp. 1–62. New York: Academic Press.

――――, and McCONNELL, H. K. 1970. Testing the self-perception explanation of dissonance phenomena: on the salience of premanipulation attitudes. *Journal of Personality and Social Psychology* 14:23–31.

BEM, S. L. 1975. Sex-role adaptability: one consequence of psychological androgyny. *Journal of Personality and Social Psychology* 33:48–54.

BENTHAM, J. 1879. *An introduction to the principles of morals and legislation.* Oxford: Clarendon Press.

BERELSON, B. R.; LAZARSFELD, P. F.; and McPHEE, W. N. 1954. *Voting.* Chicago: University of Chicago Press.

BERK, R. A. 1972. The controversy surrounding analyses of collective violence: some methodological notes. In *Collective violence,* ed. J. F. Short, Jr., and M. E. Wolfgang, pp. 112–118. Chicago: Aldine.

―――― 1974. A gaming approach to crowd behavior. *American Sociological Review* 39:355–373.

BERKO, J. 1958. The child's learning of english morphology. *Word* 14:150–177.

BERKOWITZ, L. 1975. *A survey of social psychology.* Hinsdale, Ill.: Dryden.

――――, and DANIELS, L. R. 1963. Responsibility and dependence. *Journal of Abnormal and Social Psychology* 66:429–436.

BERSCHEID, E., and WALSTER, E. 1974. Physical attractiveness. In *Advances in experimental social psychology,* vol. 7, ed. L. Berkowitz, pp. 157–215. New York: Academic Press.

BIDDLE, B. J., and THOMAS, E. J. 1966. *Role theory: concepts and research.* New York: Wiley.

BIESANZ, J., and BIESANZ, M. 1969. *Introduction to sociology.* Englewood Cliffs, N.J.: Prentice-Hall.

BIRNBAUM, M. H. 1972. Morality judgments: tests of an averaging model. *Journal of Experimental Psychology* 93:35–42.

―――― 1973. Morality judgments: tests of an averaging model with differential weights. *Journal of Experimental Psychology* 99:395–399.

BLAU, P. M. 1964. *Exchange and power in social life.* New York: Wiley.

BLOOM, L. 1973. *One word at a time: the use of single word utterances before syntax.* The Hague: Mouton.

BLUMER, H. 1951. Collective behavior. In *New outline of the principles of sociology,* ed. A. M. Lee, pp. 168–169. New York: Barnes & Noble.

_____ 1966. Sociological implications of the thought of George Herbert Mead. *American Journal of Sociology* 71:535–544.

_____ 1968. Fashion. In *The international encyclopedia of the social sciences,* ed. D. L. Sills, pp. 341–342. New York: Macmillan and Free Press.

_____ 1969. Attitudes and the social act. In *Symbolic interactionism: perspective and method.* Englewood Cliffs, N.J.: Prentice-Hall.

_____ 1971. Social problems as collective behavior. *Social Problems* 18:298–306.

BOGARDUS, E. S. 1925. Measuring social distances. *Journal of Applied Sociology* 9:- 299–308.

_____ 1925. Social distance and its origins. *Journal of Applied Sociology* 9:216–226.

BORGATTA, E. F.; COUCH, A. S.; and BALES, R. F. 1954. Some findings relevant to the great man theory of leadership. *American Sociological Review* 19:755–759.

BORNSTEIN, M. 1975. Qualities of color vision in infancy. *Journal of Experimental Child Psychology* 19:401–419.

BRAITHWAITE, R. B. 1960. *Scientific explanation: a study of the function of theory, probability and law in science.* New York: Harper Torchbooks.

BRAZELTON, T. B. 1976. Early parent–infant reciprocity. In *The family—can it be saved?,* ed. V. C. Vaughan, III, and T. Brazelton, pp. 133–142. Chicago, Ill.: Year Book Medical Publishers.

BREHM, J. 1956. Post decision changes in the desirability of alternatives. *Journal of Abnormal and Social Psychology* 52:384–389.

_____ 1960. Attitudinal consequences of commitment to unpleasant behavior. *Journal of Abnormal and Social Psychology* 60:379–383.

_____, and COHEN, A. 1959. Choice and chance relative deprivation as determinants of cognitive dissonance. *Journal of Abnormal and Social Psychology* 58:383–387.

BRIM, O. G., and WHEELER, S. 1966. *Socialization after childhood: two essays.* New York: Wiley.

BROCK, T. 1965. Communicator–recipient similarity and decision–change. *Journal of Personality and Social Psychology* 1:650–654.

BRONFENBRENNER, U. 1977. Who cares for America's children? Paper read at 6th Annual Family Research Conference, February 1977, at Brigham Young University, Provo, Utah.

BROOKOVER, W. B.; LePERE, J. M.; HAMACHEK, D. E.; THOMAS, S.; and ERICKSON, E. L. 1965. *Self concept of ability and school achievement II.* East Lansing, Mich.: Bureau of Educational Research Services, College of Education, Michigan State University.

BROWN, R. 1954. Mass phenomena. In *Handbook of social psychology,* vol. 2, 1st ed., ed. G. Lindzey, pp. 833–876. Cambridge, Mass.: Addison-Wesley.

_____ 1965. *Social psychology.* New York: Free Press.

_____ 1973. *A first language: the early stages.* Cambridge, Mass.: Harvard University Press.

_____ 1976. In memorial tribute to Eric Lenneberg. *Cognition* 4:125–154.

_____; CAZDEN, C.; and BELLUGI, U. 1969. The child's grammar from I to III. In *Minnesota symposia on child psychology,* ed. J. P. Hill, pp. 28–73. Minneapolis: University of Minnesota Press.

BROWN, R., and HANLON, C. 1970. Derivational complexity and order of acquisition in child speech. In *Cognition and the development of language,* ed. J. R. Hayes, pp. 11–53. New York: Wiley.

BROWN, R., and LENNEBERG, E. H. 1954. A study in language and cognition. *Journal of Abnormal and Social Psychology* 49:454–462.

BRYAN, J. H., and TEST, M. A. 1967. Models and helping: naturalistic studies in aiding behavior. *Journal of Personality and Social Psychology* 6:400–407.

BUCKLEY, W.; BURNS, T.; and MEEKER, L. D. 1974. Structural resolutions of collective action problems. *Behavioral Science* 19:277–297.

BURGESS, R. L. 1968. Communication networks: an experimental reevaluation. *Journal of Experimental Social Psychology* 4:324–337.

BURKE, T. 1972. Malcolm McDowell: the liberals they hate "clockwork." *New York Times* 30 January, p. 13.

BUSS, A. H. 1961. *The psychology of aggression.* New York: Wiley.

BUTLER, J. M., and HAIGH, G. V. 1954. Changes in the relation between self-concepts and ideal concepts consequent upon client-centered counseling. In *Psychotherapy and personality change,* ed. G. R. Rogers and R. F. Dymond, pp. 55–75. Chicago: University of Chicago Press.

CAFFEY, J. 1946. Multiple fractures in the long bones of infants suffering from chronic subdural hematoma. *American Journal of Roentgenology and Radium Therapy* 56:163–173.

CAMERON, W. B. 1966. *Modern social movements.* New York: Random House.

CAMPBELL, D. T. 1958. Systematic error on the part of human links in communication systems. *Information and Control* 1:334–369.

——— 1972. On the genetics of altruism and the counterhedonic components in human culture. *Journal of Social Issues* 28:21–37.

———, and STANLEY, J. C. 1963. Experimental and quasiexperimental designs for research on teaching. In *Handbook of research on teaching,* ed. N. L. Gage, pp. 171–246. Chicago: Rand-McNally.

CANNELL, C. F., and MacDONALD, J. C. 1956. The impact of health news on attitudes and behavior. *Journalism Quarterly* 33:315–323.

CANTRIL, H. 1963. *The psychology of social movements.* New York: Wiley.

——— 1940. *The invasion from mars.* Princeton: Princeton University Press.

CAPLAN, N., and PAIGE, J. M. 1968. A study of ghetto rioters. *Scientific American* 219:15–21.

CARLSON, A. R. 1968. *The relationships between a behavioral intention, attitude toward the behavior and normative beliefs about the behavior.* Unpublished doctoral dissertation. Urbana: University of Illinois.

CARTWRIGHT, D. 1971. Risk-taking by individuals and groups: an assessment of research employing choice dilemmas. *Journal of Personality and Social Psychology* 20:361–378.

CAZDEN, C. 1965. *Environmental assistance to the child's acquisition of grammar.* Unpublished doctoral dissertation. Cambridge: Harvard University.

CHAPANIS, N., and CHAPANIS, A. 1964. Cognitive dissonance: five years later. *Psychological Bulletin* 61:1–22.

CHARTERS, W. W., and NEWCOMB, T. M. 1958. Some attitudinal effects of experimentally increased salience of a membership group. In *Readings in social psychology,* ed. E. Maccoby, T. M. Newcomb, and E. L. Hartley, pp. 276–280. New York: Holt, Rinehart, & Winston.

CHOMSKY, N. 1959. A review of verbal behavior by B. F. Skinner. *Language* 35:26–58.

——— 1968. *Language and mind.* New York: Harcourt Brace Jovanovich.

——— 1975a. *Reflections on language.* New York: Pantheon.

——— 1975b. *Syntactic structures.* The Hague: Mouton.

CLARK, B. B., and TROWBRIDGE, N. T. 1971. Encouraging creativity through in-service teacher education. *Journal of Research and Development in Education* 4:87–94.

CLARK, K., and CLARK, M. P. 1952. Racial identification and preference in negro children. In *Readings in Social Psychology,* ed. G. Swanson, T. M. Newcomb, and E. L. Hartley, pp. 551–560. New York: Holt, Rinehart & Winston.

CLARK, R. D. III, and WORD, L. E. 1972. Why don't bystanders help? Because of ambiguity? *Journal of Personality and Social Psychology* 24: 392-400.

CLASTER, D. S. 1967. Comparison of risk perception between delinquents and nondelinquents. *Journal of Criminal Law, Criminology and Police Science* 58:80–86.

CLAUSEN, J. R. 1966. Family structure, socialization, and personality. In *Review of child development research,* vol. 2, ed. M. L. Hoffman and L. W. Hoffman, pp. 1–54. New York: Russell Sage.

COHEN, A. 1964. *Attitude change and social influence.* New York: Basic Books.

COLEMAN, J. S.; CAMPBELL, E. Q.; HOBSON, C. J.; McPARTLAND, J.; MOOD, A. M.; WEINFELD, F. D.; and YORK, R. L. 1966. *Equality of educational opportunity.* Washington, D.C.: U.S. Government Printing Office.

COMSTOCK, C.; CHAFFEE, S.; KATZMAN, N.; McCOMBS, M.; and ROBERTS, D. 1978. *Television and human behavior.* New York: Columbia University Press.

CONDIE, S. J.; WARNER, W. K.; and GILLMAN, D. C. 1976. Getting blood from collective turnips: volunteer donation in mass blood drives. *Journal of Applied Psychology* 61:290–294.

COOLEY, C. H. 1902. *Human nature and the social order.* New York: Charles Scribner's Sons.

COOPERSMITH, S. 1967. *The antecedents of self-esteem.* San Francisco: Freeman.

COTTRELL, L. S. 1969. Interpersonal interaction and the development of the self. In *Handbook of socialization theory and research,* ed. D. A. Goslin, pp. 543–570. Chicago: Rand McNally.

COUCH, C. J. 1968. Collective behavior: an examination of some stereotypes. *Social Problems* 15:310–322.

———— 1970. Dimensions of association in collective behavior episodes. *Sociometry* 33:456–471.

COURT-BROWN, W. M. 1967. *Human population cytogenetics.* New York: Wiley.

CRESPI, I. 1977. Attitude measurement, theory, and prediction. *Public Opinion Quarterly* 41:285–294.

CROWNE, D. P., and MARLOWE, D. 1964. *The approval motive.* New York: Wiley.

CRUTCHFIELD, R. S. 1955. Conformity and character. *American Psychologist* 10:191–198.

CUNNINGHAM, R. 1973. *The place where the world ends.* New York: Sheed & Ward.

CURTISS, S. 1977. *Genie: a psycholinguistic study of a modern-day "wild child."* New York: Academic Press.

CUZZORT, R. P. 1969. *Humanity and modern sociological thought.* New York: Holt, Rinehart, and Winston.

DAGER, E. L. 1964. Socialization and personality development in the child. In *Handbook of marriage and the family,* ed. H. Christensen, pp. 740–781. Chicago: Rand McNally.

Daily Herald. 1976. Courts ordered in beating death. 29 April: 20. Provo, Utah.

DALTON, K. 1964. *The premenstrual syndrome.* Springfield, Ill.: Charles C. Thomas.

D'ANDRADE, R. G. 1966. Sex differences and cultural institutions. In *The development of sex differences,* ed. E. E. Maccoby, pp. 170–204. Stanford, Calif.: Stanford University Press.

DARLEY, J. M., and BATSON, C. D. 1973. From Jerusalem to Jericho: a study of situational and dispositional variables in helping behavior. *Journal of Personality and Social Psychology* 27:100–108.

DARLEY, J. M., and LATANE, B. 1968. Bystander intervention in emergencies: diffusion of responsibility. *Journal of Personality and Social Psychology* 8:377–383.

DARROCH, R. K. 1971. *Attitudinal variables and perceived group norms as predictors of behavioral intentions and behavior in the signing of photographic releases.* Unpublished Doctoral Dissertation. Urbana: University of Illinois.

DART, R. 1959. *Adventures with the missing link.* New York: Harper & Row.

DASHIELL, J. F. 1930. An experimental analysis of some group effects. *Journal of Abnormal and Social Psychology* 25:190–199.

DAVIDSON, D. 1976. Discussion. *Annals of the New York Academy of Sciences* 280:42–45.

DAVIS, J. A. 1975. Communism, conformity, cohorts, and categories: American tolerance in 1954 and 1972–73. *American Journal of Sociology* 81:491–513.

DAVIS, J. B. 1930. The life and work of Sequoyah. *Chronicles of Oklahoma* 8:159–162.

DAVIS, K. 1940. Extreme social isolation of a child. *American Journal of Sociology* 45:554–565.

———— 1947. Final note on a case of extreme isolation. *American Journal of Sociology* 52:432–437.

———— 1966. Foreword. In *Wolf children and feral man*, J. A. L. Singh and R. M. Zingg, pp. xxi–xxiii. Hamden, Conn.: Archon Books.

DAY, R. C. 1971. Some effects of combining close, punitive and supportive styles of supervision. *Sociometry* 34:303–327.

DEFLEUR, M. L. 1962. Mass communication and the study of rumor. *Sociological Inquiry* 32:51–70.

———— 1970. *Theories of mass communication*, 2nd ed., New York: David McKay.

————, and BALL-ROKEACH, S. 1975. *Theories of mass communication*, 3rd ed. New York: David McKay.

DEFLEUR, M. L., and WESTIE, F. R. 1958. Verbal attitudes and overt acts: an experiment on the salience of attitudes. *American Sociological Review* 33:667–673.

———— 1963. Attitude as a scientific concept. *Social Forces* 42:17–31.

DENZIN, N. K. 1977. *Childhood socialization*. San Francisco: Jossey-Bass.

DEUTSCH, M. 1949. An experimental study of the effects of cooperation and competition upon group processes. *Human Relations* 2:199–232.

————, and GERARD, H. 1955. A study of normative and informational social influences upon individual judgment. *Journal of Abnormal and Social Psychology* 51: 629–636.

DEUTSCHER, I. 1966. Words and deeds: social science and social policy, *Social Problems* 13:235–254.

———— 1973. *What we say/what we do: sentiments and acts*. Glenview, Ill.: Scott Foresman.

DEWEY, R. 1922. *Human nature and conduct: an introduction to social psychology*. New York: Henry Holt.

DION, K. K.; BERSCHEID, E.; and WALSTER, E. 1972. What is beautiful is good. *Journal of Personality and Social Psychology* 24:207–213.

DOLLARD, J.; DOOB, L.; MILLER, N. E.; MOWRER, O.; and SEARS, R. 1939. *Frustration and aggression*. New Haven: Yale University Press.

DOLLARD, J., and MILLER, N. E. 1950. *Personality and psychotherapy: an analysis of learning, thinking, and culture*. New York: McGraw-Hill.

DOOB, A. N., and MACDONALD, G. E. 1979. Television viewing and fear of victimization: is the relationship causal? *Journal of Personality and Social Psychology* 37: 170–179.

DOOB, L. W. 1947. The behavior of attitudes. *Psychological Review* 54:135–156.

DORNBUSCH, S. M. 1955. The military academy as an assimilating institution. *Social Forces* 33:316–321.

————; HASTORF, A. H.; RICHARDSON, S. A.; MUZZY, E. R.; and VICELAND, R. S. 1965. The perceiver and the perceived: their relative influence on the category of interpersonal cognition. *Journal of Personality and Social Psychology* 1: 434–440.

DYNES, R., and QUARANTELLI, E. L. 1968. What looting in civil disturbances really means. *Trans-action* 5:9–14.

EDWARDS, A. L. 1957. *Techniques of attitude scale construction*. New York: Appleton-Century-Crofts.

EGGER, M. D., and FLYNN, J. P. 1963. Effect of electrical stimulation of the amygdala on hypothalamically felicited attack behavior in cats. *Journal of Neurophysiology* 26:705–720.

EHRLICH, H. J. 1973. *The social psychology of prejudice.* New York: Wiley.

EIBL-EIBESFELDT, I. 1970. *Ethology: the biology of behavior,* trans. by E. Klinghammer. New York: Holt, Rinehart, & Winston.

EKMAN, P.; FRIESEN, W. V.; and ELLSWORTH, P. 1972. *Emotion in the human face.* Oxford: Pergamon.

EKMAN, P.; SORENSON, E. R.; and FRIESEN, W. V. 1969. Pan-cultural elements in facial displays of emotions. *Science* 175:911–912.

ELKIN, F., and HANDEL, G. 1978. *The child and society: the process of socialization,* 3rd ed. New York: Random House.

ELMS, A. C. 1972. *Social psychology and social relevance.* Boston: Little, Brown.

_____, and MILGRAM, S. 1966. Personality characteristics associated with obedience and defiance toward authoritative command. *Journal of Experimental Research in Personality* 2:282–289.

EMSWILLER, T.; DEAUX, K.; and WILLITS, J. E. 1971. Similarity, sex and requests for small favors. *Journal of Applied Social Psychology* 1:284–291.

EPSTEIN, S. 1973. The self-concept revisited: or a theory of a theory. *American Psychologist* 28:404–416.

ERLANGER, H. 1974. The empirical status of the subculture of violence thesis. *Social Problems* 22:280–292.

ETZIONI, A. 1972. Human beings are not very easy to change after all. *Saturday Review* 55:45–47.

EXLINE, R. 1963. Explorations in the process of person perception: visual interaction in relation to competition, sex, and need for affiliation. *Journal of Personality* 31:1–20.

_____ 1972. Visual interaction: the glances of power and preference. In *Nebraska symposium on motivation,* vol. 19, ed. J. Cole, pp. 163–206. Lincoln, Neb.: University of Nebraska Press.

_____, and WINTERS, L. C. 1965. Affective relations and mutual glances in dyads. In *Affect, cognition and personality,* ed. S. S. Tomkins and C. E. Izard, pp. 319–50. New York: Springer.

FARRIS, H.; GIDEON, E.; and ULRICH, R. F. 1970. Classical conditioning of aggression: a developmental study. *The Psychological Record* 20:63–67.

FAZIO, R. H.; ZANNA, M. P.; and COOPER, J. 1978. Direct experience and attitude-behavior consistency: an information processing analysis. *Personality and Social Psychology Bulletin* 4:48–51.

FEATHERMAN, N. T., and SIMON, J. G. 1971a. Attribution of responsibility and valence of outcome in relation to initial confidence and success and failure of self and other. *Journal of Personality and Social Psychology* 18:173–188.

_____ 1971b. Causal attributions for success and failure in relation to expectations of success based upon selective or manipulative control. *Journal of Personality,* 39:527–541.

Federal Bureau of Investigation. 1974. *F.B.I. uniform crime reports: crime in the United States 1973.* Washington, D.C.: U.S. Government Printing Office.

_____ 1978. *F.B.I. uniform crime reports: crime in the United States 1977.* Washington D.C.: U.S. Government Printing Office.

FEIN, G.; JOHNSON, D.; KOSSON, N.; STORK, L.; and WASERMAN, L. 1975. Sex stereotypes and preferences in the toy choices of 20 month-old boys and girls. *Developmental Psychology* 11:527–528.

FEINMAN, S., and GILL, G. W. 1977. Females' response to males' beardedness. *Perceptual and Motor Skills* 44:533–534.

_____ 1978. Sex differences in physical attractiveness preferences. *Journal of Social Psychology* 105:42–52.

FELDMAN, S. D. 1971. The presentation of shortness in everyday life—height and heightism in American society: toward a sociology of stature. Paper present-ed at the annual meeting of the American Sociological Association, Boston, Mass.

———; NASH, S. C.; and CUTRONA, C. 1977. The influence of age and sex on responsiveness to babies. *Developmental Psychology* 13:675–676.

FERGUSON, L. W. 1935. The influence of individual attitudes on construction of an attitude scale. *Journal of Social Psychology* 6:115–117.

FESTINGER, L., and CARLSMITH, J. M. 1959. Cognitive consequences of forced com-pliance. *Journal of Abnormal and Social Psychology* 58:203–210.

FESTINGER, L.; RIECHEN, H. W.; and SCHACHTER, S. 1956. *When prophecy fails.* New York: Harper Torchbooks.

FILSTEAD, W. 1970. *Qualitative methodology: firsthand involvement with the social world.* Chicago: Markham.

FISHER, J. D., and NADLER, A. 1974. The effect of similarity between donor and recipient on recipient's reactions to aid. *Journal of Applied Social Psychology* 4:230–243.

FISHBEIN, M. 1963. An investigation of the relationships between beliefs about an object and the attitude toward that object. *Human Relations* 16:233–240.

——— 1967. Attitude and the prediction of behavior. In *Readings in attitude theory and measurement,* ed. M. Fishbein, pp. 477–492. New York: Wiley.

——— 1973. The prediction of behaviors from attitudinal variables. In *Advances in communication research,* ed. D. C. Mortensen and K. K. Sereno, pp. 3–31. New York: Harper and Row.

———, and HUNTER, R. 1964. Summations versus balance in attitudinal organiza-tions and change. *Journal of Abnormal and Social Psychology* 69:505–510.

FLACKS, R. 1967. The liberated generation: an exploration of the roots of student protest. *Journal of Social Issues* 23:52–75.

FLIEGEL, F. C., and KIVLIN, J. E. 1974. Fidelity of information transmission in local campaigns on water issues. Unpublished manuscript. Urbana: University of Illinois Water Resources Center, April.

FLYNN, J. P. 1967. The neural basis of aggression in cats. In *Neurophysiology and emotion,* ed. D. C. Glass, pp. 40–60. New York: Russell Sage and Rockefeller University Press.

FODOR, J. A. 1975. *The language of thought.* New York: Crowell.

FRANKE, R. H., and KAUL, J. D. 1978. The Hawthorne experiments: first statistical interpretation. *American Sociological Review* 43:623–643.

FRANKS, D. D., and MAROLLA, J. 1976. Efficacious action and social approval as interacting dimensions of self-esteem: a tentative formulation through con-struct validation. *Sociometry* 39:324–40.

FREEMAN, J. 1970. Growing up girlish. *Trans-action* 8:36–43.

FRENCH, J. R. P. 1944. *Organized and unorganized groups under fear and frustration.* Iowa City: University of Iowa Press.

FREUD, A. 1949. Aggression in relation to emotional development: normal and pathological. *The Psychoanalytic Study of the Child* 3–4:37–42.

FREUD, S. 1922. *Group psychology and the analysis of the ego.* London: Hogarth.

——— 1924. *Collected papers,* ed. E. Jones. London: Hogarth.

——— 1959. *Beyond the pleasure principle.* New York: Bantam.

——— 1963. *General psychological theory: the collected papers of Sigmund Freud.* New York: Collier Books.

FRIDERES, J. S.; WARNER, L. G.; and ALBRECHT, S. L. 1971. The impact of social constraints on the relationship between attitudes and behavior. *Social Forces* 50:102–112.

FRITZ, C. E., and WILLIAMS, H. B. 1957. The human being in disasters: a research perspective. *Annals of the American Academy of Political and Social Science* 309:42–51.

FROMKIN, V.; KRASHEN, S.; CURTISS, S.; RIGLER, D.; and RIGLER, M. 1974. The development of language in genie: a case of language acquisition beyond the critical period. *Brain and Language* 1:81–107.

FUCHS, E., and HAVIGHURST, R. J. 1972. *To live on this earth.* Garden City, N.Y.: Doubleday.

FULLER, L. L. 1963. Collective bargaining and the arbitrator. *Wisconsin Law Review* 3–46.

———— 1971. Mediation—its forms and functions. *Southern California Law Review* 44:305–339.

GALLUP, G. C. 1972. *The gallup poll: public opinion 1935–1971.* New York: Random House.

GALLUP, G. G.; BOREN, J. L.; GAGLIARDI, G. J.; and WALLNAU, L. B. 1977. A mirror for the mind of man, or will the chimpanzee create an identity crisis for Homo Sapiens? *Journal of Human Evolution* 6:303–313.

GAMSON, W. A. 1968. *Power and discontent.* Homewood, Ill.: Dorsey.

———— 1975. *The strategy of protest.* Homewood, Ill.: Dorsey.

GECAS, V. 1979. The influence of social class on socialization. In *Contemporary theories about the family,* vol. 1 ed. W. R. Burr, R. Hill, I. L. Reiss, and F. I. Nye, pp. 365–404. New York: Free Press.

GERBNER, G. 1972. Violence in television drama: trends and symbolic functions. In *Television and social behavior, reports and papers.* vol. 1: Media content and control, Surgeon General's Scientific Advisory Committee on Television and Social Behavior. Washington D.C.: U.S. Government Printing Office.

———— GROSS, L. 1976a. The scary world of TV's heavy viewer. *Psychology today* 9:41–45, 89.

———— 1976b. Living with television: the violence profile. *Journal of Communication* 26:173–199.

GERGEN, K. J.; GERGEN, M. M.; and METER, K. 1972. Individual orientations to prosocial behavior. *Journal of Social Issues* 28:105–130.

GEWIRTZ, J. L. 1969. Mechanisms of social learning. In *Handbook of socialization theory and research,* ed. D. A. Goslin, pp. 57–212. Chicago: Rand McNally.

GILMOR, T. M., and MORTON, H. L. 1974. Internal versus external attribution of task performance as a function of locus control, initial confidence and success-failure outcome. *Journal of Personality* 42:159–174.

GOFFMAN, E. 1959. *The presentation of self in everyday life.* New York: Doubleday Anchor Books.

———— 1961. *Asylums.* Garden City, N.Y.: Doubleday.

———— 1961. *Encounters: two studies in the sociology of interaction.* Indianapolis: Bobbs-Merrill.

———— 1963. *Stigma: notes on the management of spoiled identity.* Englewood Cliffs, N.J.: Prentice-Hall.

GOLDBERG, C. 1976. Prediction and control as mediators of causal attribution. *Perceptual and Motor Skills* 42:183–195.

GOLDEN, R. K. 1976. Assembly-line violence: picture tube guns. *Cornell Journal of Social Relations* 11:39–45.

GOLDING, W. 1954. *Lord of the flies.* New York: Capricorn Books.

GOODE, W. J. 1960. A theory of role strain. *American Sociological Review* 25:483–496.

GOODMAN, M. E. 1964. *Race awareness in young children.* New York: Collier Books.

GORDON, C., and GERGEN, K. J. 1968. *The self in social interaction.* New York: John Wiley & Sons, Inc.

GORDON, R. L. 1952. Interaction between attitudes and the definition of the situation in the expression of opinion. *American Sociological Review* 17:50–58.

GOULDNER, A. W. 1960. The norm of reciprocity: a preliminary statement. *American Sociological Review* 25:161–179.

GRANOVETTER, M. 1978. Threshold models of collective behavior. *American Journal of Sociology* 83:1420–43.

GRAZIANO, W.; BROTHEN, T.; and BERSCHEID, E. 1978. Height and attraction: do men and women see eye-to-eye. *Journal of Personality* 46:128–145.

GREEN, D. 1974. Dissonance and self-perception analyses of forced compliance: when two theories make competing predictions. *Journal of Personality and Social Psychology* 29:819–828.

GREEN, R. B., and ROHWER, W. D. 1971. SES differences on learning and ability tests in black children. *American Educational Research Journal* 8:601–609.

GREENFIELD, M. 1978. The darker side. *Newsweek* 4 December: 132.

GREENFIELD, P. M., and SMITH, J. 1976. *The structure of communication in early language development.* New York: Academic Press.

GRIFFIN, J. H. 1961. *Black like me.* Boston: Houghton Mifflin.

GRIMSHAW, A., and HOLDEN, L. 1976. Postchildhood modifications of linguistic and social competence, *Items: Social Science Research Council,* 30:33–42.

GROSS, A. E. 1975. Generosity and legitimacy of a model as determinants of helping behavior. *Representative Research in Social Psychology* 6:45–50.

———; WALLSTON, B. S.; and PILIAVIN, I. M. 1975. Beneficiary attractiveness and cost as determinants of responses to routine requests for help. *Sociometry* 38:131–140.

GROSS, E., and STONE, G. P. 1964. Embarrassment and the analysis of role requirements. *American Journal of Sociology* 70:1–15.

GROSS, N.; MCEACHERN, A. W.; and MASON, W. S. 1966. Role conflict and its resolution. In *Role theory: concepts and research,* ed. B. J. Biddle and E. J. Thomas, pp. 287–96. New York: Wiley.

GUIOT, J. M. 1977. Attribution and identity construction: some comments. *American Sociological Review* 42:692–704.

GURR, T. R. 1970. *Why men rebel.* Princeton, N.J.: Princeton University Press.

GUTEN, S. and ALLEN, V. L. 1972. Likelihood of escape, likelihood of danger, and panic behavior. *Journal of Social Psychology* 87:29–36.

GUTTMAN, D. 1975. Parenthood: a key to the comparative study of the life cycle. In *Lifespan developmental psychology,* ed. N. Datan and L. H. Ginsberg, pp. 167–184. New York: Academic Press.

GUZMAN, J. P. 1969. Lynching. In *Racial violence in the United States,* ed. A. D. Grimshaw, pp. 56–59. Chicago: Aldine.

HADAMARD, J. 1949. *Psychology of invention in the mathematical field.* Princeton, New Jersey: Princeton University Press.

HALL, C. S. 1954. *A primer of freudian psychology,* New York: New American Library, Mentor Book.

HALL, E. T. 1959. *The silent language.* Garden City, New York: Doubleday.

HAMBLIN, R. L.; BRIDGER, D.; DAY, R. C.; and YANCEY, W. L. 1963. The interference-aggression law? *Sociometry* 26:190–216.

HAMBLIN, R. L.; BUCKHOLDT, D.; FERRITOR, D.; KOZLOFF, M.; and BLACKWELL, L. 1971. *The humanization process.* New York: Wiley-Intersciences.

HAMBURG, D. A. 1966. Effects of progesterone on behavior. In *Endocrines and the central nervous system,* vol. 43, ed. R. Levine, pp. 251–65. Baltimore, Md.: Williams & Williams.

HANER, C. F., and BROWN, P. A. 1955. Clarification of the instigation to action concept in the frustration–aggression hypothesis. *Journal of Abnormal and Social Psychology* 51:204–206.

HANNAN, M. T.; TUMA, N. B.; and GROENEVELD, L. P. 1977. Income and marital events: evidence from an income–maintenance program. *American Journal of Sociology* 82:1186–1211.

——— 1978. Income and independence effects on marital dissolution: results from the Seattle and Denver income–maintenance experiments. *American Journal of Sociology* 84:611–633.

HANRATTY, M. A.; LIEBERT, R. M.; MORRIS, L. W.; and FERNANDEZ, L. E. 1969. Imitation of film–mediated aggression against live and inanimate victims. In

Proceedings of the 77th annual convention of the American Psychological Association, pp. 457–458.

HARRIS, M. B., and BAUDIN, H. 1972. Models and vegetable eating: the power of Popeye. *Psychological Reports* 31:570.

HARRISON, J. 1978. Warning: the male sex role may be dangerous to your health. *Journal of Social Issues* 3:65–86.

HARRISON, M. I. 1977. Dimensions of involvement in social movements. *Sociological Focus* 10:353–366.

HARROW, M.; FOX, D. A.; MARKHUS, K. I.; STILLMAN, R.; and HALLOWELL, C. B. 1968. Changes in adolescents' self concepts and their parents' perceptions during psychiatric hospitalization. *Journal of Nervous and Mental Disease* 147:252–259.

HARTMAN, H.; KRIS, E.; and LOWENSTEIN, R. M. 1949. Notes on the theory of aggression. *The Psychoanalytic Study of the Child* 3–4:9–36.

HARTMAN, P. 1978. A perspective on the study of social attitudes. *European Journal of Social Psychology* 7:85–96.

HARTUP, W. W., and MOORE, S. G. 1963. Avoidance of inappropriate sex–typing by young children. *Journal of Consulting Psychology* 26:467–473.

HARVEY, J. H.; ARKIN, R. M.; GLEASON, J. M.: and JOHNSTON, S. 1974. Effects of expected and observed outcome of an action on the differential causal attributes of actor and observer. *Journal of Personality,* 42:62–77.

HASTORF, A. H.; SCHNEIDER, D. J.; and POLEFKA, J. 1970. *Person perception.* Reading, Mass: Addison-Wesley.

HAYAKAWA, S. I. 1950. Recognizing stereotypes as substitutes for thoughts. *Etc: Reviews of General Semantics* 7:208–210.

HAYES, C. 1951. *The ape in our house.* New York: Harper and Row.

HEIDER, F. 1944. Social perception and phenomenal causality. *Psychological Review* 51:358–374.

———— 1946. Attitudes and cognitive organization. *Journal of Psychology* 21:107–112.

———— 1958. *The psychology of interpersonal relations.* New York: Wiley.

HELFER, R. E., and KEMPE, C. H. 1976. *Child abuse and neglect: the family and the community.* Cambridge: Ballinger.

HELSON, H. 1948. Adaption–level as a basis for a quantitative theory of frames of reference. *Psychological Review* 55:297–313.

———— 1959. Adaptation–level theory. In *Psychology: A study of a science,* vol. 1, ed. S. Koch, pp. 565–621. New York: McGraw-Hill.

HENDRICK, C., and COSTANTINI, A. F. 1970. The effects of varying trait inconsistency and the response requirements on the primacy effect in impression formation. *Journal of Personality and Social Psychology* 15:158–164.

HENRY, J. 1973. *On sham, vulnerability and other forms of self–destruction.* New York: Vintage Books.

HENSLIN, J. 1967. Craps and magic. *American Journal of Sociology* 73:316–330.

HESHKA, J., and NELSON, Y. 1972. Interpersonal speaking distance as a function of age, sex, and relationship. *Sociometry* 35:491–498.

HETHERINGTON, E. M.; COX, M.; and COX, R. 1978. Family interaction and the social, emotional, and cognitive development of children following divorce. Paper read at the Symposium on the Family: Setting Priorities, sponsored by the Institute for Pediatrics Services, Johnson & Johnson Baby Co., May, Washington, D.C.

HINCKLEY, E. D. 1932. The influence of individual opinion on construction of an attitude scale. *Journal of Social Psychology* 3:283–296.

HODGKINS, B. J., and STAKENAS, R. G. 1969. A study of self–concepts of negro and white youths in segregated environments. *Journal of Negro Education* 38:370–377.

HOFFMAN, M. L. 1960. Power assertion by the parent and its impact on the child. *Child Development* 31:129–143.

_____, and SALTZSTEIN, H. D. 1967. Parent discipline and the child's moral development. *Journal of Personality and Social Psychology* 5:45–57.

HOLLANDER, E. P. 1964. *Leaders, groups, and influence.* New York: Oxford University Press.

_____ 1975. Independence, conformity, and civil liberties: some inplications from social psychological research. *Journal of Social Issues* 31:55–67.

HOMANS, G. C. 1958. Social behavior as exchange. *American Journal of Sociology* 63:-597–606.

_____ 1974. *Social behavior: its elementary forms.* New York: Harcourt Brace Jovanovich.

HORNIK, J. A. 1970. *Two approaches to individual differences in cooperative behavior in an expanded prisoner's dilemma game.* Unpublished master's level paper. Urbana; University of Illinois.

HOROWITZ, R. E. 1939. Racial aspects of self-identification in nursery school children. *Journal of Psychology* 7:91–99.

HOVLAND, C. I.; JANIS, I. L.; and KELLEY, H. H. 1953. *Communication and persuasion.* New Haven: Yale University Press.

HOVLAND, C. I.; LUMSDAINE, A.; and SHEFFIELD, F. 1949. *Experiments on mass communication.* Princeton, N.J.: Princeton University Press.

HOVLAND, C. I.; MENDAL, W.; CAMPBLL, E.; BROCK, T.; LUCHINS, A.; COHEN, A.; McGUIRE, W.; JANIS, E.; FEIERABEND, R.; and ANDERSON, N., eds. 1957. *The order of presentation in persuasion.* New Haven: Yale University Press.

HOVLAND, C. I., and SEARS, R. 1940. Mini studies of aggression: correlation of lynching with economic indices. *Journal of Psychology* 9:301–310.

HOVLAND, C. I., and SHERIF, M. 1952. Judgmental phenomena and scales of attitude measurement: item displacement in Thurstone scales. *Journal of Abnormal and Social Psychology* 47:822–832.

HOVLAND, C. I., and WEISS, W. 1951. The influence of source credibility on communication effectiveness. *Public Opinion Quarterly* 15:635–650.

HOWARD, W., and CRANO, W. D. 1974. Effects of sex, conversation, location, and size of observer group on bystander intervention in a high risk situation. *Sociometry* 37:491–507.

HULL, C. L. 1943. *Principles of behavior.* New York: Appleton-Century Crofts.

HUMPHREYS, L. 1970. *Tearoom trade: impersonal sex in public places.* Chicago: Aldine.

HURLOCK, E. B. 1968. *Developmental psychology,* 3rd ed. New York: McGraw Hill.

HUSTON, T. L.; GEIS, G.; and WRIGHT, R. 1976. The angry samaritans. *Psychology Today* 10:61–64.

HUSTON-STEIN, A. 1976. Issues in child development: new directions in understanding sex roles. *Newsletter: Society for Research in Child Development,* Summer.

HUTCHINSON, R. R.; ULRICH, R. E.; and AZRIN, N. H. 1965. Effects of age and related factors on the pain-aggression reaction. *Journal of Comparative Physiological Psychology* 59:365–369.

HUXLEY, A. 1932, 1960. *Brave new world.* New York: Harper & Row.

HYMAN, H. 1944. Do they tell the truth? *Public Opinion Quarterly* 8:557–559.

INKELES, A. 1969. Social structure and socialization. In *Handbook of socialization theory and research,* ed. D. A. Goslin, pp. 615–630. Chicago: Rand McNally.

JAKOBSON, R. 1968. *Child language aphasia and phonological universals.* The Hague: Mouton.

JAMES, W. 1968. *Psychology: the briefer course.* New York: Henry Holt & Co.

JANIS, I. L. 1967. Effects of fear arousal on attitude change: recent developments in theory and experimental research. In *Advances in experimental social psychology,* vol. 3, ed. L. Berkowitz, pp. 167–224. New York: Academic Press.

_____ 1972. *Victims of groupthink.* Boston: Houghton-Mifflin.

_____, and FESHBACK, S. 1953. Effects of fear–arousing communications. *Journal of Abnormal and Social Psychology* 48:78–92.

JANSYN, R., JR. 1966. Solidarity and delinquency in a street corner group. *American Sociological Review* 31:600–614.

JENNESS, A. 1932. The role of discussion in changing opinions regarding a matter of fact. *Journal of Abnormal and Social Psychology* 27:279–296.

JESPERSON, O. 1921. *Language: its nature, development, and origin.* New York: Macmillan.

JOHNSON, N. 1972. *Aggression in man and animals.* Philadelphia: W. B. Saunders Company.

JOHNSON, N. R. 1974. Collective behavior as group–induced shift. *Sociological Inquiry* 44:105–110.

_____; STEMLER, J. G.; and HUNTER, D. 1977. Crowd behavior as risky shift: a laboratory experiment. *Sociometry* 40:183–187.

JONES, E. E., and DAVIS, E. 1965. From acts to dispositions: the attribution process in person perception. In *Advances in experimental social psychology,* vol. 2, ed. L. Berkowitz, pp. 219–265. New York: Academic Press.

_____; and GERGEN, K. J. 1961. Role playing variations and their information value for person perception. *Journal of Abnormal and Social Psychology* 63:302–310.

JONES, E. E., and HARRIS, V. A. 1967. The attribution of attitudes. *Journal of Experimental Social Psychology* 3:1–24.

JONES, E. E., and NISBETT, R. E. 1971. The actor and the observer: divergent perceptions of the causes of behavior. Morristown, N.J.: General Learning Press.

JONES, E. E.; ROCK, I.; SHAVER, K. G.; GOETHALS, G. R.; and WARD, L. M. 1968. Patterns of performance and ability attribution: an unexpected primary effect. *Journal of Personality and Social Psychology* 10:317–340.

JONES, R. A.; LINDEN, D. E.; KIESLER, C. A.; ZANNA, M.; and BREHM, J. M. 1968. Internal states or external stimuli: observer's attitude judgments and the dissonance theory—self–persuasion controversy. *Journal of Experimental Social Psychology* 4:247–269.

JONES, W. H.; HANSSON, R. O.; and PHILLIPS, A. L. 1978. Physical attractiveness and judgments of psychopathology. *The Journal of Social Psychology* 105:79–84.

JOURARD, S. M. 1968. *Disclosing man to himself.* Princeton, New Jersey: Van Nostrand.

KAPLAN, H. B. 1975. *Self–attitudes and deviant behavior.* Pacific Palisades, Calif.: Goodyear Publishing Company, Inc.

_____, and MEYEROWITZ, J. H. 1970. Social and psychological correlates of drug abuse: a comparison of addict and non-addict populations from the perspective of self theory. *Social Science and Medicine* 4:203–25.

KAPLAN, R. M. 1978. Is beauty talent? Sex interaction in the attractiveness halo effect. *Sex Roles* 4:195–203.

KARLINS, M.; COFFMAN, T.; and WALTERS, G. 1964. On the fading of social stereotypes: studies in three generations of college students. *Journal of Personality and Social Psychology* 13:1–6.

KATZ, D. 1960. The functional approach to the study of attitude change. *Public Opinion Quarterly* 24:163–204.

KATZ, E., and LAZARSFELD, P. F. 1955. *Personal influence.* New York: Free Press.

KATZ, J. J. 1976. A hypothesis about the uniqueness of natural language. *Annals of the New York Academy of Sciences* 280:33–41.

KELLEY, H. H. 1950. The warm–cold variable in first impressions of persons. *Journal of Personality* 18:431–439.

_____ 1967. Attribution theory in social psychology. In *Nebraska symposium on motivation,* vol. 15, ed. D. Levine, pp. 192–240. Lincoln: University of Nebraska Press.

_____ 1971a. Attribution in social interaction. Morristown, N.J.: General Learning Press.

_____ 1971b. Causal schemata and the attribution process. Morristown, N.J.: General Learning Press.

————; CONDRY, J. C., JR.; DAHLKE, A. E.; and HILL, A. H. 1965. Collective behavior in a simulated panic situation. *Journal of experimental and social psychology* 1: 20–54.

KELLEY, H. H., and VOLKART, E. H. 1952. The resistance to change of group-anchored attitudes. *American Sociological Review* 17:453–465.

KELLOGG, W. N., and KELLOGG, L. A. 1933. *The ape and the child.* New York: McGraw-Hill.

KELLY, J. A., and WORELL, J. 1976. New formulations of sex roles and androgyny: a critical review. *Journal of Consulting and Clinical Psychology* 45:1101–1115.

KELMAN, H. C. 1961. Processes of opinion change. *Public Opinion Quarterly* 25:57–78.

———— 1974. Attitudes are alive and well and gainfully employed in the sphere of action. *American Psychologist* 29:310–324.

KEMPE, R. S., and KEMPE, C. H. 1978. *Child abuse.* Cambridge, Mass.: Harvard University Press.

KENDALL, P. L., and WOLFE, K. M. 1949. The analysis of deviant cases in communications research. In *Communications research,* ed. P. Lazarsfeld and F. Stanton, pp. 152–179. New York: Harper and Brothers.

KENT, J. 1972. *Eight months in the hospital.* Paper read at the 80th annual convention of the American Psychological Association, September 1–8. Honolulu, Hawaii.

KERCKHOFF, A. C., and BACK, K. W. 1968. *The June bug: a study of hysterical contagion.* New York: Appleton-Century-Crofts.

KERSHAW, D. N. 1972. A negative income-tax experiment. *Scientific American* 277: 19–25.

KETCHAM, H. 1975. *Play it again, Dennis.* Greenwich, Conn.: Fawcett Publications.

KIESLER, C. A.; COLLINS, B. E.; and MILLER, N. 1969. *Attitude change: a critical analysis of theoretical approaches.* New York: Wiley.

KILLIAN, L. M. 1964. Social movements. In *Handbook of modern sociology,* ed. R. E. L. FARIS, pp. 426–455: Chicago: Rand McNally.

KIMBALL, R. K., and HOLLANDER, E. P. 1974. Independence in the presence of an experienced but deviate group member. *Journal of Social Psychology* 93:281–292.

KIMBRELL, D., and BLAKE, R. 1958. Motivational factors in the violation of a prohibition. *Journal of Abnormal and Social Psychology* 56:132–137.

KING, C. W. 1965. *Social movements in the United States.* New York: Random House.

KIPARSKY, P. 1976. Historical linguistics and the origin of language. *Annals of the New York Academy of Sciences* 280:97–103.

KLAUS, M. H., and KENNELL, J. H. 1976. Parent to infant attachment. In *The family —can it be saved?,* ed. V. C. Vaughan, III, and T. B. Brazelton, pp. 115–122. Chicago: Year Book Medical Publishers.

KLUVER, H., and BUCY, P. C. 1937. Psychic blindness and other symptoms following bilateral lobotomy in rhesus monkeys. *American Journal of Physiology* 119:352–353.

KOHLBERG, L. 1966. A cognitive-developmental analysis of children's sex-role concepts and attitudes. In *The development of sex differences,* ed. E. E. Maccoby, pp. 82–173. Stanford, Calif.: Stanford University Press.

———— 1973. Stage and sequence: the cognitive-developmental approach. In *Handbook of socialization theory and research,* ed. D. A. Goslin, pp. 347–400. Chicago: Rand McNally.

KOHN M. L., and SCHOOLER, C. 1973. Occupational experience and psychological functioning: an assessment of reciprocal effects. *American Sociological Review* 68:471–480.

KORTE, C., and KERR, N. 1975. Response to altruistic opportunities in urban and nonurban settings. *Journal of Social Psychology* 95:183–184.

KORTE, C.; YPMA, I.; and TOPPEN, A. 1975. Helpfulness in Dutch society as a function of urbanization and environmental input level. *Journal of Personality and Social Psychology* 32:996–1003.

KRECH, D., and CRUTCHFIELD, R. S. 1948. *Theory and problems in social psychology.* New York: McGraw-Hill.

———— and BALLACHEY, E. L. 1962. *Individual in society.* New York: McGraw-Hill.

KUHN, M. H., and McPARTLAND, T. S. 1954. An empirical investigation of self attitudes. *American Sociological Review* 19:68–76.

KUTNER, B.; WILKINS, C.; and YARROW, P. 1952. Verbal attitudes and overt behavior involving racial predjudice. *Journal of Abnormal and Social Psychology* 47:649–652.

LANDERS, ANN. 1971. *Salt Lake Tribune,* Tuesday, July 22, Page 1, Section C.

LANTZ, D., and STEFFLRE, V. 1964. Language and cognition revisited. *Journal of Abnormal and Social Psychology* 69:472–481.

LaPIERE, R. 1934. Attitudes vs. action. *Social Forces* 13:230–237.

LATANE, B., and DARLEY, J. M. 1968. Group inhibition of bystander intervention in emergencies. *Journal of Personality and Social Psychology* 10:215–221.

———— 1969. Bystander apathy. *American Scientist* 57:244–268.

———— 1976. *Help in a crisis: bystander response to an emergency.* Morristown, N.J.: General Learning Press.

LATANE, B., and RODIN, J. 1969. A lady in distress: inhibiting effects of friends and strangers on bystander intervention. *Journal of Experimental Social Psychology* 5:189–202.

LAUER, R. H., and HANDEL, W. H. 1977. *Social psychology: the theory and application of symbolic interactionism.* Boston: Houghton Mifflin.

LAZARSFELD, P. F.; BERELSON, B. R.; and GAUDET, H. 1948. *The people's choice,* New York: Columbia University Press.

LAZARYS, A. A. 1971. *Behavior therapy and beyond.* New York: McGRAW HILL.

LEAVITT, H. J. 1951. Some effects of certain communication patterns on group performance. *Journal of Abnormal and Social Psychology* 46:38–50.

LeBON, G. 1896. *The crowd: a study of the popular mind.* London: Ernest Benn.

LEE, A. M. 1970. On context and relevance. In *The participant observer,* ed. G. Jacobs, pp. 3–18. New York: George Braziller.

LEFKOWITZ, M. M.; ERON, L. D.; WALDER, L. O.; and HUESMANN, L. R. 1971. Television violence and child aggression: a follow up study. In *Television and social behavior,* vol. 3, Surgeon General's Scientific Advisory Committee on Television and Social Behavior. Washington, D. C.: U.S. Government Printing Office.

LE MAIRE, L. 1956. Danish experiences regarding the castration of sexual offenders. *Journal of Criminal Law and Criminology* 47:294–310.

LEMERT, E. 1951 *Social pathology: a systematic approach to the theory of socio-pathic behavior.* New York: McGraw-Hill.

LENNEBERG, E. H. 1964. A biological perspective of language. In *New directions in the study of language,* ed. E. H. Lenneberg, pp. 65–88. Cambridge, Mass.: MIT Press.

———— 1967. *Biological foundations of language.* New York: Wiley.

————, and ROBERTS, J. M. 1956. *The language of experience.* Bloomington Ind.: Indiana University Press.

LERNER, M. J. 1965. Evaluation of performance as a function of performer's rewards and attractiveness. *Journal of Personality and Social Psychology* 3:355–360.

———— 1966. The unjust consequences of the need to believe in a just world. Paper read at the meeting of the American Psychological Association, September, New York.

———— 1970. The desire for justice and reactions to victims. In *Altruism and helping behavior: social psychological studies of some antecedents and consequences,* ed. J. Macaulay and L. Berkowitz, pp. 205–229. New York: Academic Press.

LESK, S., and ZIPPEL, B. 1975. Dependency, threat, and helping in a large city. *Journal of Social Psychology* 95:185–186.

LEVANTHAL, H. 1970. Findings and theory in the study of fear communications. In *Advances in experimental social psychology,* vol. 5, ed. L. Berkowitz, pp. 119–186. New York: Academic Press.

———, and NILES, P. 1965. Persistence of influence for varying durations of exposure to threat stimuli. *Psychological Reports* 16:223–233.

LEVANTHAL, H., and SINGER, R. 1966. Affect arousal and positioning of recommendations in persuasive communications. *Journal of Personality and Social Psychology* 4:137–146.

LEVY, L. 1969. Studies in conformity behavior: a methodological note. *Journal of Psychology* 50:39–41.

LEWIS, J. M. 1972. A study of the Kent State incident using Smelser's theory of collective behavior. *Sociological Inquiry* 42:87–96.

LIEBERMAN, P. 1974. On the evolution of language: a unified view. *Cognition* 2:59–94.

———; CRELIN, E.; and KLATT, D. 1972. Phonetic ability and related anatomy of the newborn and adult human, neanderthal man, and the chimpanzee. *American Anthropologist* 74:287–307.

LIEBERMAN, S. 1956. The effects of changes in roles on the attitudes of role occupants. *Human Relations* 9:385–403.

LIEBOW, E. 1967. *Talley's corner.* Boston: Little, Brown.

LIKERT, R. 1932. A technique for the measurement of attitudes. *Archives of Psychology,* No. 140.

LINDESMITH, A. R.; STRAUSS, A. L.; and DENZIN, N. K. 1977. *Social psychology,* 5th ed., Hinsdale, Ill.: Dryden.

LINN, L. 1965. Verbal attitudes and overt behavior: a study of racial discrimination. *Social Forces* 43:353–364.

LINTON, R. 1936. *The study of man.* New York: Appleton-Century.

——— 1947. *The cultural background of personality.* London: Kegan, Paul, Trech, Trubner.

LIPPMAN, W. 1922. *Public opinion.* New York: Harcourt Brace Jovanovich.

LISKA, A. E. 1974. Emergent issues in the attitude-behavior consistency controversy. *American Sociological Review* 39:261–272.

——— 1975. *The consistency controversy.* Cambridge, Mass: Schenkman.

LOHMAN, J. D., and REITZES, D. C. 1954. Deliberately organized groups and racial behavior. *American Sociological Review* 19:342–348.

LONG, B. H., and HENDERSON, E. H. 1968. Self-social concepts of disadvantaged school beginners. *Journal of Genetic Psychology* 113:41–51.

LORENZ, K. Z. 1958. The evolution of behavior. *Scientific American* 199:67–76, 78.

——— 1966. *On aggression,* translated by M. K. Wilson. New York: Harcourt Brace Jovanovich.

LOUIS, A. M. 1978. Should you buy biorhythms. *Psychology Today* 11:93–96.

LOYE, D. 1978. TV's impact on adults: it's not all bad news. *Psychology Today* 11: 86–94.

LUCHINS, A. S. 1957a. Experimental attempts to minimize the impact of first impressions. In *The order of presentation in persuasion,* ed. C. Hovland, et al., pp. 62–75. New Haven: Yale University Press.

——— 1957b. Primacy-recency in impression formation. In *The order of presentation in persuasion,* ed. C. Hovland, et al., pp. 33–61. New Haven: Yale University Press.

——— 1958. Definitiveness of impression and primacy-recency in communication. *Journal of Social Psychology* 48:275–290.

LYNN, D. B. 1966. The process of learning parental and sex-role identification. *Journal of Marriage and the Family* 28:788–805.

MACCOBY, E. E., 1968. The development of moral values and behavior in childhood. In *Socialization and society,* ed. J. A. Clausen, pp. 227–69. Boston: Little, Brown.

———— and JACKLIN, C. N., 1974. *The psychology of sex differences.* Stanford, Calif.: Stanford University Press.

MACKIE, M., 1973. Arriving at "truth" by definition: the case of stereotype inaccuracy. *Social Problems* 20:431–44.

MACNAMARA, J., 1972. Cognitive basis of language learning in infants. *Psychological Review* 79:1–14.

MANKOFF, M. L., and FLACKS, R. 1971. The changing social base of the American student movement. *Annals of the American Academy of Political and Social Science* 395:54–67.

MANIS, M. 1978. Cognitive social psychology and attitude change. *American Behavorial Scientist* 21:675–690.

MANN, L.; NAGEL, T.; and DOWLING, P. 1976. A study of economic panic: the "run" on the Hindmarsh Building Society. *Sociometry* 39:223–35.

MARINI, M. M. 1978. Sex differences in determination of adolescent aspirations: a review of research. *Sex Roles* 4:723–753.

MARK, V. H. and ERVIN, F. R. 1970. *Violence and the brain.* New York: Harper and Row.

MARTINDALE, D. 1960. *The nature and types of sociological theory.* Boston: Houghton Mifflin.

MARX, G. T. 1974. Thoughts on a neglected category of social movement participants: the agent provocateur and the informant. *American Journal of Sociology* 80:402–42.

MARX, G. T., and WOOD, J. L. 1975. Strands of theory and research in collective behavior. In *Annual review of sociology,* vol. 1, ed. A. Inkeles, J. Coleman, and N. Smelser, pp. 363–428. Palo Alto, Calif.: Annual Reviews.

MASLOW, A. H. 1943. A theory of human motivation. *Psychological Review* 50:370–396.

MASON, D. O.; CZAJKE, J. L.; and ARBER, S. 1976. Change in U.S. women's sex-role attitudes, 1964–1974. *American Sociological Review* 41:573–96.

MAUSNER, B., 1954. The effect of prior reinforcement on the interaction of observer pairs. *Journal of Abnormal and Social Psychology* 49:65–68.

MAUSS, A. L. 1971. On being strangled by the stars and stripes. *Journal of Social Issues* 27:183–202.

MCARTHUR, L. A. 1972. The how and the what of why: some determinants and consequences of causal attribution. *Journal of Personality and Social Psychology* 22:171–93.

MCCALL, G. J., and SIMMONS, J. L. 1966. *Identities and interaction.* New York: Free Press.

MCCARTHY, J. D., and ZALD, M. N. 1973. *The trend of social movements in America: professionalization and resource mobilization.* Morristown, N. J.: General Learning Press.

———— 1977. Resource mobilization and social movements: a partial theory. *American Journal of Sociology* 82:1212–41.

MCDANIEL, E. L. 1967. *Relationships between self-concept and specific variables in a low income culturally deficient population.* Final report on head start-evaluation and research: 1966–67, Institute for Educational Development, Section VIII. Aug. 31 ERIC: 019 124.

MCDOUGALL, W. 1908. *Introduction to social psychology.* London: Methuen.

———— 1923. *Outline of psychology.* New York: Scribner's.

MCGUIRE, W. J. 1964. Inducing resistance to persuasion: some contemporary approaches. In *Advances in experimental social psychology,* ed. L. Berkowitz, pp. 191–229. New York: Academic Press.

———— 1966. Attitudes and opinions. *Annual Review of Psychology* 17:475–514.

———— 1966. The current status of cognitive consistency theories. In *Cognitive consistency; motivational antecedents and behavioral consequents,* ed. S. Feldman, pp. 1–46. New York: Academic Press.

_____ 1967. Personality and susceptibility to social influence. In *Handbook of personality theory and research,* ed. E. F. Borgatta and W. W. Lambert, pp. 1130–1188 Chicago: Rand-McNally.

McKENNA, R. J. 1976. Good samaritanism in rural and urban settings: a nonreactive comparison of helping behavior of clergy and control subjects. *Representative Research in Social Psychology* 7:58–65.

McMAHAN, I. D. 1973. Relationship between causal attributions and expectancy of success. *Journal of Personality and Social Psychology* 28:108–14.

McNEIL, E. B. (ed.). 1965. *The nature of human conflict.* Englewood Cliffs, New Jersey: Prentice-Hall.

McNEILL, D., 1966a. The creation of language. *Discovery* 27:34–38.

_____ 1966b Developmental psycholinguistics. In *The genesis of language: a psycholinguistic approach.* ed. F. L. Smith and G. A. Miller, pp. 15–84. Cambridge, Mass.: MIT Press.

_____ 1970a. *The acquisition of language: the study of developmental psycholinguistics.* New York: Harper and Row.

_____ 1970b. The development of language. In *Carmichael's manual of child psychology,* vol. 1, ed. P. H. Mussen, pp. 1061–1161. New York: Wiley.

McPHAIL, C., and MILLER, D. 1973. The assembling process: a theoretical and empirical examination. *American Sociological Review* 38:721–35.

McWHIRTER, W. 1975. Is this what America has left? *Time* 7 April,:33–34

MEAD, G. H. 1934. *Mind, self and society.* Chicago: University of Chicago Press.

_____ 1938. *The philosophy of the act.* Chicago: University of Chicago Press.

_____ 1968. The genesis of the self and social control. *International Journal of Ethics* 35:251–73.

MEAD, M. 1935. *Sex and temperament in three primitive societies.* New York: Morro.

MEHRABIAN, A. 1968a. Inference of attitudes from the posture, orientation and distance of a communicator. *Journal of Consulting and Clinical Psychology* 32:-296–309.

_____ 1968b. Relationship of attitude to seated posture, orientation and distance. *Journal of Personality and Social Psychology* 10:26–30.

_____ 1972. *Nonverbal communication.* Chicago: Aldine.

MENZEL, E. W. 1971a. Communication about the environment in a group of young chimpanzees. *Polia Primatol* (Basel) 15:220–230.

_____ 1971b. Group behavior in young chimpanzees: responsiveness to cumulative novel changes in a large outdoor enclosure. *Journal of Comparative Physiological Psychology* 74:46–51.

_____ 1973. Leadership and communication in young chimpanzees. *Precultural Primate Behavior,* ed. E. W. Menzel, vol. 1, pp. 192–225. Basel, Switzerland: Karger.

_____ 1974. A group of young chimpanzees in a one-acre field. In *Behavior of nonhuman primates,* ed. A. M. Schrier and F. Stollintz, vol. 5, pp. 83–153. New York: Academic Press.

MENZEL, H. 1957. Public and private conformity under different conditions of acceptance in the group. *Journal of Abnormal and Social Psychology* 55:398–401.

MERTON, R. K. 1957a. *Social theory and social structure.* New York: Free Press.

_____ 1957b. The role-set: problems in sociological theory. *British Journal of Sociology* 8:106–20.

MICHENER, J. 1971. *Kent State: what happened and why.* New York: Random House.

MILES, L. W. 1976. Discussion paper: the communicative competence of child and chimpanzee, *Annals of the New York Academy of Sciences* 280:592–597.

MILGRAM, S. 1963. Behavioral study of obedience. *Journal of Abnormal and Social Psychology* 67:371–78.

_____ 1964. Group pressure and action against a person. *Journal of Abnormal and Social Psychology* 69:137–43.

————. 1965. Some conditions of obedience and disobedience to authority. *Human Relations* 18:57–76.

————. 1974. *Obedience to authority.* New York: Harper and Row.

————; BICKMAN, L.; and BERKOWITZ, L. 1969. Note on the drawing power of crowds of different size. *Journal of Personality and Social Psychology* 13:79–82.

MILGRAM, S. and SHOTLAND, R. 1973. *Television and antisocial behavior: field experiments.* New York: Academic Press.

MILGRAM, S., and TOCH, H. 1969. Collective behavior: crowds and social movements. In *Handbook of social psychology,* vol. 4, 2nd ed., ed. G. Lindzey and E. Aronson, pp. 507–610. Reading, Mass.: Addison Wesley.

MILLER, A. G. 1970. Role of physical attractiveness in impression formation. *Psychonomic Science* 19:241–43.

MILLER, D. L.; MIETUS, K. J.; and MATHERS, R. A. 1978. A critical examination of the social contagion image of collective behavior: the case of the Enfield Monster. *Sociological Quarterly* 19:129–40.

MILLER, D. R. 1969. Psychoanalytic theory development: a re-evaluation. In *Handbook of socialization theory and research,* ed. D. A. Goslin, pp. 481–502. Chicago: Rand McNally.

MILLER, G.; MAYERSON, N.; POGUE, M.; and WHITEHOUSE, D. 1977. Perceivers' explanations of their attributions of attitude. *Personality and Social Psychology Bulletin* 3:111–14.

MILLER, N. and CAMPBELL, D. 1959. Recency and primacy in persuasion as a function of the timing of speeches and measurements. *Journal of Abnormal and Social Psychology* 59:1–9.

MILLER, N. E., and DOLLARD, J. 1941. *Learning and imitation.* New Haven: Yale University Press.

MILLER, W. B. 1966. Violent crimes in city gangs. *Annals of American Academy of Political and Social Science* 364:96–112.

MILLS, C. W. 1968. *The power elite.* Boston: Beacon.

MILLS, J., and ARONSON, E. 1965. Opinion change as a function of communicator's attractiveness and desire to influence. *Journal of Personality and Social Psychology* 1:173–77.

MINARD, R. 1952. Race relationships in the Pocahontas coal field. *Journal of Social Issues* 8:29–44.

MINNIGERODE, F., and LEE, J. A. 1978. Young adults' perceptions of sex roles across the lifespan. *Sex Roles* 4:563–569.

MINTZ, A. 1951. Non-adaptive group behavior. *Journal of Abnormal and Social Psychology* 46:150–59.

MISCHEL, W. 1966. A social learning view of sex differences in behavior. In *The development of sex differences,* ed. E. E. Maccoby, pp. 56–81. Stanford, Calif.: Stanford University Press.

MODIGLIANI, A. 1971. Embarrassment, face-work, and eye-contact: testing a theory of embarrassment. *Journal of Personality and Social Psychology* 17:15–24.

MOEDE, W. 1920. *Experimentelle massenpsychologie.* Leipzig, Germany: S. Hirzel.

MOELLER, G., and APPLEZWEIG, M. H. 1957. A motivational factor in conformity. *Journal of Abnormal and Social Psychology* 55:114–20.

MONSON, T. C., and SNYDER, M. 1977. Actors, observers, and the attribution process: toward a reconceptualization. *Journal of Experimental Social Psychology* 13:89–111.

MONTAGUE, A. 1976. *The Nature of Human Aggression.* New York: Oxford University Press.

MOORE, W. E. 1969. Occupational socialization. In *Handbook of socialization theory and research,* ed. D. A. Goslin, pp. 861–84. Chicago: Rand McNally.

MORRIS, D. 1967. *The naked ape.* New York: McGraw-Hill.

———— 1969. *The human zoo.* New York: McGraw-Hill.

MORTON, J. H.; ADDISON, H.; ADDISON, R. G.; HUNT, L.; and SULLIVAN, J. J. 1953. A clinical study of premenstrual tension. *American Journal of Obstetrics and Gynecology* 65:1182–1191.

MOWRER, O. H. 1960a. *Learning theory and behavior.* New York: Wiley.

———— 1960b. *Learning theory and the symbolic processes.* New York: Wiley.

MUELLER, R. J. 1963. The role of the Wisconsin employment board arbitrator. *Wisconsin Law Review* 47–56.

MUNROE, R. L. 1955. *Schools of psychoanalytic thought.* New York: Holt.

MUNSTERBERG, H. 1914. *Psychology, general and applied.* New York: Appleton.

MURDOCK, G. P. 1937. Comparative data on the division of labor by sex. *Social Forces* 19:551–553.

MURPHY, J. M. 1972. Statement before the subcommittee on communication committee on commerce. *Hearings on the surgeon general's report by the scientific committee on television and social behavior,* March 21, p. 10. Washington, D. C.: U. S. Government Printing Office.

MYRDAL, G. 1944. *An American dilemma,* vol. 1. New York: Harper and Row.

NADLER, A.; FISHER, J. D.; and STREUFERT, S. 1976. When helping hurts: effects of donor-recipient similarity and recipient self-esteem on reactions to aid. *Journal of Personality* 44:392–409.

NAKAZIMA, S. 1962. A comparative study of the speech developments of Japanese and American English in childhood. I: A comparison of the developments of voices at the prelinguistic period. *Studia Phonologica* 2:27–46.

National advisory commission on civil disorders, 1968. *Report of the national advisory commission on civil disorders.* New York: Bantam Books, Inc.

National commission on the causes and prevention of violence. 1969. *To establish justice, to ensure domestic tranquility.* Washington, D. C.: U.S. Government Printing Office.

NELSON, L. D., and DYNES, R. R. 1976. The impact of devotionalism and attendance on ordinary and emergency helping behavior. *Journal for the Scientific Study of Religion* 15:47–59.

NESBITT, P. 1972. The effectiveness of student canvassers. *Journal of Applied Social Psychology* 2:252–58.

NEWCOMB, T. M. 1953. An approach to the study of communicative acts. *Psychological Review* 60:393–404.

———— 1958. Attitude development as a function of reference groups: the Bennington study. In *Readings in social psychology,* ed. E. Maccoby, T. M. Newcomb, and E. L. Hartley, pp. 265–73. New York: Holt, Rinehart and Winston.

———— 1961. *The acquaintance process.* New York: Holt, Rinehart, and Winston.

————; KOENIG, K.; FLACKS, R.; and WARWICK, D. 1967. *Persistence and change: Bennington College and its students after 25 years.* New York: Wiley.

Newsweek. 1975. Education section. (21 April):97.

———— 1976. Life with Father Moon. (14 June):60–66.

———— 1977. Is deprogramming legal? (21 February):44.

———— 1977. Newsmakers. (12 September):73.

———— 1978. The cult of death: special report. (4 December):38–81.

NIBLEY, H. W. 1978. Genesis of the written word. In *Nibley on the timely and the timeless,* ed. H. W. Nibley, pp. 101–127. Salt Lake City, Utah: Publishers Press.

NISBETT, R. E.; CAPUTO, G. C.; LEGANT, P.; and MARACEK, J. 1973. Behavior as seen by the actor and as seen by the observer. *Journal of Personality and Social Psychology* 27:154–64.

NKPA, N. K. U. 1977. Rumors of mass poisoning in Biafra. *Public Opinion Quarterly* 41:332–46.

NYE, F. I., and GECAS, V. 1976. The role concept: review and delineation. In *Role structure and analysis of the family,* ed. F. I. Nye, pp. 3–14. Beverly Hills, Calif.: Sage.

OBERSCHALL, A. 1973. *Social conflict and social movements.* Englewood Cliffs, N.J.: Prentice-Hall.

OPPENHEIM, A. N. 1966. *Questionnaire design and attitude measurement.* New York: Basic Books.

ORWELL, G. 1946. *Animal farm.* New York: Harcourt Brace Jovanovich.

OSGOOD, C. E.; SUCI, G. J.; and TANNENBAUM, P. H. 1957. *Measurement of meaning.* Urbana: University of Illinois Press.

OSGOOD, C. E., and TANNENBAUM, P. H. 1955. The principle of congruity in the prediction of attitude change. *Psychological Review* 62:42–55.

PARK, R. E., and BURGESS, E. W. 1921. *Introduction to the science of sociology.* Chicago: University of Chicago Press.

PATTERSON, F., and COHN, R. H. 1978. Conversations with a gorilla. *National Geographic* (October):438–465.

PAVLOV, I. P. 1927. *Conditioned reflexes,* trans. G. V. Anrep. London: Oxford University Press.

PEI, M. 1968. *What's in a word?* New York: Award Books.

PHILLIPS, T. R. 1973. Syntax and vocabulary of mother's speech to young children: age and sex comparisons. *Child Development* 44:182–85.

PIAGET, J. 1926. *The language and the thought of the child.* New York: Harcourt Brace Jovanovich.

——— 1954. *The construction of reality in the child.* New York: Basic Books.

PICKERING, M. O. 1887. *The life of John Pickering.* Boston, Mass.

PILIAVIN, I.; RODIN, J.; and PILIAVIN, J. 1969. Good samaritanism: an underground phenomenon? *Journal of Personality and Social Psychology* 13:289–299.

PINARD, M. 1971. *The rise of a third party: a study in crisis politics.* Englewood Cliffs, N. J.: Prentice-Hall.

PINTNER, R., and FORLANO, G. 1937. The influence of attitude upon scaling of attitude items. *Journal of Social Psychology* 8:39–45.

PITCHER, E., and PRELINGER, E. 1963. *Children tell stories.* New York: International University Press.

POMAZAL, R. J., and CLORE, G. L. 1973. Helping on the highways: the effects of dependency and sex. *Journal of Applied Social Psychology* 3:150–164.

POMAZAL, R. J., and JACCARD, J. J. 1976. An informational approach to altruistic behavior. *Journal of Personality and Social Psychology* 33:317–326.

PONTING, J. R. 1973. Rumor control centers: their emergence and operations. *American Behavioral Scientist* 16:391–401.

PREMACK, D. 1970a. A functional analysis of language. *Journal of the Experimental Analysis of Behavior* 14:107–25.

——— 1970b. The education of Sarah. *Psychology Today* 4:54–58.

——— 1971. Language in chimpanzee? *Science* 172:808–822.

President's commission on campus unrest. 1970. *Report of the president's commission on campus unrest.* Washington, D. C.: U.S. Government Printing Office.

PRUITT, DEAN G. 1971. Choice shifts in group discussion: an introductory review. *Journal of Personality and Social Psychology* 20:339–60.

RADBILL, S. X. 1968. A history of child abuse and infanticide. In *The battered child,* ed. R. E. Helfer and C. H. Kempe, pp. 3–21. Chicago: University of Chicago Press.

RADKE, MARIAN J., and TRAGER, H. G. 1950. Children's perceptions of the social roles of negroes and whites. *The Journal of Psychology* 29:3–33.

RAIFFA, H. 1970. *Decision analysis.* Reading, Mass.: Addison-Wesley.

RANSFORD, H. E. 1968. Isolation, powerlessness and violence. A study of attitudes and participation in the Watts riot. *American Journal of Sociology* 73:581–591.

RAPAPORT, D. 1959. The structure of psychoanalytic theory. In *Psychology: A Study of Science,* vol. 3, ed. S. Koch, pp. 55–183. New York: McGraw-Hill.

RAPER, A. 1933. *The tragedy of lynching.* Chapel Hill, N. C.: University of North Carolina Press.

RAVEN, B., and FRENCH, J. 1958. Legitimate power, coercive power, and observability in social influence. *Sociometry* 21:83–97.

REISS, I. L. 1967. *The social context of premarital sexual permissiveness.* New York: Holt, Rinehart and Winston.

REST, J. R.; TURIEL, E.; and KOHLBERG L. 1969. Level of moral development as a determinant of preference and comprehension of moral judgments made by others. *Journal of Personality* 37:225–52.

RHEINGOLD, H. L. 1969. The social and socializing infant. In *Handbook of socialization theory and research,* ed. D. A. Goslin, pp. 779–790. Chicago: Rand McNally.

RICCIUTI, H. N. 1965. Object grouping and selective ordering behavior in infants 12 to 24 months old. *Merrill-Palmer Quarterly* 11:129–148.

RIESMAN, D.; GLAZER, N.; and DENNEY, R. 1950. *The lonely crowd.* New Haven: Yale University Press.

RISKEY, D. R., and BIRNBAUM, M. H. 1974. Compensatory effects in moral judgments: two rights don't make up for a wrong? *Journal of Experimental Psychology* 103:171–73.

ROBINSON, J. P., and SHAVER, P. R. 1969. *Measures of social psychological attitudes.* Ann Arbor: Institute for Social Research, University of Michigan.

ROETHLISBERGER, F. J., and DICKSON, W. J. 1939. *Management and the worker.* Cambridge, Mass.: Harvard University Press.

ROGERS, C. M.; SMITH, M. D.; and COLEMAN, J. M. 1978. Social comparison in the classroom: the relationship between academic achievement and self-concept. *Journal of Educational Psychology,* 70:50–57.

ROGERS, C. R., and DYMOND, R. F. (eds.). 1954. *Psychotherapy and personality change.* Chicago: University of Chicago Press.

ROHNER, R. P. 1975. *They love me, they love me not.* New Haven: HRAF Press.

ROKEACH, M. 1967. Attitude change and behavior change. *Public Opinion Quarterly* 30:529–50.

———— 1970. Faith, hope, bigotry. *Psychology Today* 3:33–37.

ROLL, S., and VERINIS, J. 1971. Stereotypes of scalp and facial hair as measured by the semantic differential. *Psychological Reports* 28:975–80.

ROLLINS, B. C., and THOMAS, D. L. 1975. A theory of parental power and child compliance. In *Power in families,* ed. R. E. Cromwell and D. H. Olson. pp. 38–60 New York: Halsted Press.

———— 1979. Parental support, power and control techniques in the socialization of children. In *Contemporary theories about the family,* vol. 1, eds. W. R. Burr, R. Hill, I. L. Reiss, and F. I. Nye, pp. 317–64. New York: Free Press.

ROSCH, E. 1973. On the internal structure of perceptual and semantic categories. *Cognitive development and the acquisition of language.* New York: Academic Press.

ROSE, A. M. 1962. A systematic summary of symbolic interaction theory. In *Human behavior and social processes,* ed. A. M. Rose, pp. 3–19. Boston: Houghton Mifflin.

ROSENBAUM, M., and BLAKE, R. 1955. Volunteering as a function of field structure. *Journal of Abnormal and Social Psychology* 50:193–96.

ROSENBERG, F. R., and SIMMONS, R. G. 1975. Sex differences in the self-concept in adolescence. *Sex Roles* 1:147–59.

ROSENBERG, M. J. 1965a. An evaluation of models of attitude change, paper presented at the meeting of the American Psychological Association. Philadelphia, September.

———— 1965b. When dissonance fails: on eliminating evaluation apprehension from attitude measurement. *Journal of Personality and Social Psychology* 1:28–42.

———— and ABELSON, R. P. 1960. An analysis of cognitive balancing. In *Attitude organization and change,* ed., C. I. Hovland and I. K. Janis, pp. 112–63. New Haven: Yale University Press.

ROSENBERG, M. and SIMMONS, R. G. 1971. *Black and white self-esteem: the urban school child.* Washington, D.C.: American Sociological Association.

ROSENBERG, S.; NELSON, C.; and VIVEKANANTHAN, P. S. 1968. A multidimensional approach to the structure of personality impressions. *Journal of Personality and Social Psychology* 9:283–94.

ROSENTHAL, A. M. 1964. Study of the sickness called apathy. *New York Times Magazine,* 3 May: 24, 66, 69–70, 72.

ROSENTHAL, R. 1964. The effect of the experimenter on the results of psychological research. In *Progress in experimental personality research,* vol. 1, ed. B. A. Meher, pp. 79–114. New York: Academic Press.

———— 1966. *Experimenter effects in behavioral research.* New York: Appleton-Century-Crofts.

———— 1969. Interpersonal expectations: effects of the experimenter's hypothesis. In *Artifact in Behavioral Research,* ed. R. Rosenthal and R. L. Rosnow. pp. 182–277. New York: Academic Press.

———— 1973. The pygmalion effect lives. *Psychology Today* 7:56–63.

———— and JACOBSON, L. 1968. *Pygmalion in the classroom: teacher expectation and pupils' intellectual development.* New York: Holt, Rinehart and Winston.

ROSNOW, R. L., and FINE, G. A. 1976. *Rumor and gossip: the social psychology of hearsay.* New York: Elsevier.

ROSOW, I. 1965. Forms and function of adult socialization. *Social Forces* 44:35–45.

ROSS, E. A. 1908. *Social psychology.* New York: Macmillian.

ROSS, M., and SHALMAN, R. F. 1973. Increasing the salience of initial attitudes: dissonance versus self-perception theory. *Journal of Personality and Social Psychology* 28:138–44.

RUBIN, Z. 1970. Measurement of romantic love. *Journal of Personality and Social Psychology* 16:265–73.

RUDWICK E., and MEIER, A. 1972. The Kent State affair: social control of a putative value-oriented movement. *Sociological Inquiry* 42:81–86.

RUMBAUGH, D. M., and GILL, T. V. 1976. The mastery of language-type skills by the chimpanzee (Pan). *Annals of the New York Academy of Sciences* 280:562–77.

RYAN, V. L.; KRALL, C. A.; and HODGES, W. F. 1976. Self concept change in behavior modification. *Journal of Consulting and Clinical Psychology* 44:638–45.

SAILOR, W. 1971. Reinforcement and generalization of productive plural allomorphs in two retarded children. *Journal of Applied Behavior Analysis* 4:305–10.

Salt Lake Tribune. 1976. Girl slashes self with razor as Hartford crowd cheers. 22 August, p. A5.

SAMUEL, W. 1975. *Contemporary social psychology: an introduction.* Englewood Cliffs, N. J.: Prentice-Hall.

SARBIN, T. R., and ALLEN, V. L. 1968. Role Theory. In *Handbook of social psychology,* vol. 1, 2nd ed., ed. G. Lindzey and E. Aronson, pp. 488–567. Reading, Mass.: Addison-Wesley.

SCHACHTER, S. 1951. Deviation, rejection, and communication. *Journal of Abnormal and Social Psychology* 46:190–207.

————, and BURDICK, H. 1955. A field experiment on rumor transmission and distortion. *Journal of Abnormal and Social Psychology* 50:363–71.

SCHACHTER, S. and LATANÉ, B. 1964. Crime, cognition, and the autonomic nervous system. In *Nebraska symposium on motivation,* ed. D. Levine, pp. 221–73. Lincoln: University of Nebraska Press.

SCHAEFER, E. S. 1965a. A configurational analysis of children's reports of parent behavior. *Journal of Consulting and Clinical Psychology* 29:552–57.

———— 1965b. Childrens' reports of parental behavior: an inventory. *Child Development* 36:413–24.

SCHAFFER, R. 1977. *Mothering.* Cambridge, Mass.: Harvard University Press.

SCHANK, R. L. 1932. A study of a community and its groups and institutions conceived of as behaviors of individuals. *Psychological Monographs* 43:1–133.

SCHEFF, T. J. 1975. The labelling theory of mental illness. In *Labelling madness,* ed. T. J. Scheff. pp. 21–34. Englewood Cliffs, N.J.: Prentice-Hall.

SCHEFLEN, A. E. 1965. Quasi-courting behavior in psychotherapy. *Psychiatry* 28: 245–57.

SCHEIN, E. H.; SCHNEIER, I.; and BARKER, C. H. 1961. *Coercive persuasion.* New York: Norton.

SCHEIN, V. E. 1978. Sex role stereotyping ability and performance: prior research and new directions. *Personnel Psychology* 31:259–67.

SCHELLING, T. C. 1963. *The strategy of conflict.* New York: Oxford Press.

SCHNEIDER, D. J. 1973. Implicit personality theory: a review. *Psychological Bulletin* 79:294–309.

SCHREIBER, F. R. 1973. *Sybil.* New York: Warner Books.

SCHWARTZ, S. H. 1968a. Awareness of consequences and the influence of moral norms on interpersonal behavior. *Sociometry* 31:355–69.

———, 1968b. Words, deeds, and the perception of consequences and responsibility in action situations. *Journal of Personality and Social Psychology* 10:232–42.

——— 1970. Elicitation of moral obligation and self-sacrificing behavior: an experimental study of volunteering to be a bone marrow donor. *Journal of Personality and Social Psychology* 15:283–93.

——— 1977. Normative influences on altruism. In *Advances in experimental social psychology,* vol. 10, ed. L. Berkowitz, pp. 221–279. New York: Academic Press.

SCOTT, L. J. 1969. *An analysis of the self-concept of seventh grade students in segregated-desegregated schools of Oklahoma City.* Unpublished dissertation. Norman University of Oklahoma.

SCOTT, W. A. 1957. Attitude change through reward of verbal behavior. *Journal of Abnormal and Social Psychology* 55:72–75.

SEARS, R. R.; MACCOBY, E. E.; and LEVIN, H. 1957. *Patterns of child-rearing.* Evanston, Ill.: Row, Peterson.

SECORD, P. F., and BACKMAN, C. W. 1964. *Social psychology.* New York: McGraw-Hill.

SEIBER, S. D. 1974. Toward a theory of role accumulation. *American Sociological Review* 39:567–78.

SHAFFER, J. W.; SCHMIDT, C. W. Jr.; ZLOTOWITZ, H. I.; and FISHER, R. S. 1978. Biorhythms and highway crashes. *Archives of General Psychiatry* 35:41–46.

SHAH, S. A. 1970. *Report on the XYY chromosomal abnormality.* National Institutes of Mental Health Conference Report. Washington, D.C.: U.S. Government Printing Office.

SHAVER, K. G. 1975. *An introduction to attribution processes.* Englewood Cliffs, N.J.: Prentice-Hall.

SHAW, M. E. 1954a. Some effects of problem complexity upon problem solution efficiency in different communication networks. *Journal of Experimental Psychology* 48:211–17.

——— 1954b. Some effects of unequal distribution of information upon group performance in various communication nets. *Journal of Abnormal and Social Psychology* 49:547–53.

———, and WRIGHT, J. M. 1967. *Scales for the measurement of attitudes.* New York: McGraw-Hill.

SHAW, M. E., and COSTANZO, P. R. 1970. *Theories of social psychology.* New York: McGraw-Hill.

SHEEHAN, B. W. 1973. *Seeds of extinction: Jeffersonian philanthropy and the American indian.* Chapel Hill, N. C.: University of North Carolina.

SHERIF, M. 1935. A study of some social factors in perception. *Archiva Psychologia* 27, No. 187:1–60.

——— 1936. *The psychology of norms.* New York: Harper.

———, and HOVLAND, C. I. 1953. Judgmental phenomena and scales of attitude measurement: placement of items with individual choice of number of categories. *Journal of Abnormal and Social Psychology* 48:135–41.

SHIBUTANI, T. 1966. *Improvised news: a sociological study of rumor.* Indianapolis: Bobbs-Merrill.

———— 1961. *Society and personality: an interactionist's approach to social psychology.* Englewood Cliffs, N. J.: Prentice-Hall.

SHORT, J. F., Jr., and STRODTBECK, F. L. 1956. *Group process and gang delinquency.* Chicago: University of Chicago Press.

SILVERMAN, I. 1971. On the resolution and tolerance of cognitive inconsistency in a natural occurring event. *Journal of Personality and Social Psychology* 17:171–78.

SILVERTHORNE, C. 1971. Information input and the group shift phenomenon in risk taking. *Journal of Personality and Social Psychology* 20:456–61.

SIMMONS, R. G.; BROWN, L.; BUSH, D. M.; and BLYTH, D. A. 1978. Self-esteem and achievement of black and white adolescents. *Social Problems,* 26:86–96.

SIMMONS, R. G., and ROSENBERG, F. R. 1975. Sex, sex roles and self-images. *Journal of Youth and Adolescence* 4:229–258.

————; and ROSENBERG, M. 1973. Disturbance in the self-image at adolescence. *American Sociological Review* 38:553–68.

SINCLAIR-DE-ZWART, H. 1967. *Acquisition de langage et dévélopement de la pensée.* Paris: Dunod.

SINGER, J. E. 1961. Verbal conditioning and generalization of prodemocratic responses. *Journal of Abnormal and Social Psychology* 63:43–46.

SINGH, J. A. L., and ZINGG, R. M. 1966. *Wolf-children and feral man.* Hamden, Conn.: Archon Books.

SKINNER, B. F. 1957. *Verbal behavior.* Englewood Cliffs, NJ: Prentice-Hall, Inc.

———— 1959. *Cumulative record.* Englewood Cliffs, NJ: Prentice-Hall, Inc.

———— 1969. *Contingencies of reinforcement.* Englewood Cliffs, NJ: Prentice-Hall, Inc.

———— 1971. *Beyond freedom and dignity.* New York: Alfred A. Knopf and Bantam Books.

SLOBIN, D. I. 1971. *Psycholinguistics.* Glenview, Ill.: Scott, Foresman.

SMELSER, N. J. 1963. *A theory of collective behavior.* New York: Free Press.

SMITH, D. E.; KING, M. B.; and HOEBEL, B. C. 1970. Lateral hypothalmic control of killing: evidence for a cholinoceptive mechanism. *Science* 167:900–901.

SMITH, M. B. 1974. *Humanizing social psychology.* San Francisco: Jossey Bass.

————; BRUNER, J. S.; and WHITE, R. W. 1956. *Opinions and personality.* New York: Wiley.

SPENCER, H. 1862. *First principles.* Reprinted from 5th London ed. New York: Burt.

STAATS, A. W. 1961. Verbal habit-families, concepts, and the operant conditioning of word classes. *Psychological Review* 68:190–204.

———— 1968. *Learning, language and cognition.* New York: Holt, Rinehart and Winston.

———— 1975. *Social behaviorism.* Homewood, Ill.: Dorsey.

————, and STAATS, C. K. 1958a. Attitudes established by classical conditioning. *Journal of Abnormal and Social Psychology* 57:37–40.

———— 1958b. *Complex human behavior.* New York: Holt, Rinehart, and Winston.

STAM, J. H. 1977. The sapir-whorf hypothesis in historical perspective. *Annals of the New York Academy of Sciences* 291:306–316.

STARK, R. and McEVOY, J., III. 1970. Middle class violence. *Psychology Today* 4:52–3, 110–12.

STEFFENHAGEN, R. A. 1978. An Adlerian approach toward a self-esteem theory of deviance: a drug abuse model. *Journal of Alcohol and Drug Education* 24:1–13.

STEINFELD, J. I. 1973. T. V. violence is harmful. *Reader's Digest* 102:37–40 and 45.

STEPHAN, F. F., and MISHLER, E. G. 1952. The distribution of participation in small groups: an exponential approximation. *American Sociological Review* 17:599–608.

STEWART, R. 1965. Effects of continuous responding on the order effect in personality impression formation. *Journal of Personality and Social Psychology* 1:161–65.

STORMS, M. D. 1973. Videotape and the attibutional process: reversing actor's and observer's points of views. *Journal of Personality and Social Psychology* 27:165–75.

STORR, A. 1968. *Human aggression.* New York: Antheneum.

—— 1972. *Human destructiveness.* New York: Basic Books.

STRAUS, M. A. 1964. Power and support structure of the family in relation to socialization. *Journal of Marriage and the Family* 26:318–26.

STRICKLAND, B., and CROWN, D. P. 1962. Conformity under conditions of simulated group pressure as a function of the need for social approval. *Journal of Social Psychology* 58:171–81.

STRYKER, S. 1964. The interactional and situational approaches. In *Handbook of marriage and the family,* ed. H. T. Christensen, pp. 127–70. Chicago: Rand McNally.

Subcommittee to investigate juvenile delinquency. 1954. *Juvenile delinquency, television program.* Hearings of subcommittee to investigate juvenile delinquency of the committee on the Judiciary, U.S. Senate. Washington D.C.: U.S. Government Printing Office.

Subcommittee to investigate juvenile delinquency. 1965. *Effects on young people of violence and crime portrayed on television.* Hearing before the subcommittee to investigate juvenile delinquency of the committee on the judiciary, U.S. Senate. Washington, D.C.: U.S. Government Printing Office.

SUCZEK, B. 1972. The curious case of the "death" of Paul McCartney. *Urban Life and Culture* 1:61–76.

SULLIVAN, H. S. 1953. *The interpersonal theory of psychiatry.* New York: Norton.

SUMNER, W. G. 1904. *Folkways.* Boston: Ginn & Company.

SUPPES, P. 1976. Discussion. *Annals of the New York Academy of Sciences* 280:92–95.

Surgeon general's scientific advisory committee on television and social behavior. 1971–1972. *Television and Social Behavior,* vols. 1–8. Washington, D.C.: U.S. Government Printing Office.

SWEET, W. H.; ERVIN, F. R.; and MARK, V. H. 1969. The relationship of violent behavior to focal cerebral disease. In *Aggressive behavior,* ed. S. Garattini and E. Sigg, pp. 336–352. New York: Wiley.

TANNER, N., and ZIHLMAN, A. 1976. Discussion paper: the evolution of human communication: what can primates tell us? *Annals of the New York Academy of Sciences* 280:467–80.

TARTER, D. E. 1969. Toward predication of attitude-action discrepancy. *Social Forces* 47:398–405.

—— 1970. Attitude the mental myth. *The American Sociologist* 5: 276–78.

TERRACE, H. S., and BEVER, T. G. 1976. What might be learned from studying language in the chimpanzee? The importance of symbolizing oneself. *Annals of the New York Academy of Sciences* 280:579–87.

THIBAUT, J. W., and KELLEY, H. H. 1959. *The social psychology of groups.* New York: Wiley.

THISTLETHWAITE, D.; deHAAN, H.; and KAMENETZKY, J. 1955. The effects of "directive" and "nondirective" communication procedures on attitudes. *Journal of Abnormal and Social Psychology* 51: 107–13.

THOMAS D. L.; FRANKS, D. D.; CALONICO, J. M. 1972. Role-taking and power in social psychology. *American Sociological Review* 37:605–14.

THOMAS D. L.; GECAS, V.; WEIGERT, A.; and ROONEY, E. 1974. *Family socialization and the adolescent.* Lexington, Mass.: Lexington Books.

THOMAS, W. I., and THOMAS, D. S. 1928. *The child in America.* New York: Knopf.

THOMAS, W. I., and ZNANIECKI, F. 1918. *The Polish peasant in Europe and America,* vol. 1. Boston: Badger.

THORPE, W. H. 1956. *Learning and instinct in animals.* Cambridge, Mass.: Harvard University Press.

THURSTONE, L. L. 1928. Attitudes can be measured. *American Journal of Sociology* 33:529–554.

TILLY, C. 1973. Does modernization breed revolution? *Comparative Politics* 5:425–47.

———— 1975. Revolution and collective violence. In *Handbook of Political Science*, Vol. 3, ed. F. Greenstein and N. Polsky, pp. 483–555. Reading, Mass.: Addison-Wesley.

Time. 1975 Crumbling before the Juggernaut. 7 April, pp. 28–33.

———— 1975. Is this what America has left? 7 April, pp. 33–34.

———— 1977. Night of Terror. 25 July, pp. 12–23. Why the lights went out. pp. 24–25.

———— 1977. Law. 10 October, p. 87–88.

———— 1977. The stereotype could be true. 13 September, p. 30.

TOCH, H. 1965. *The social psychology of social movements*. New York: Bobbs-Merrill.

TÖNNIES, F. 1887. *Community and society*, trans. and ed. C. A. Loomis. East Lansing, Mich.: Michigan State University Press, 1957.

TRILLING, L. 1955. *Freud and the crisis of our culture*. Boston: Beacon Press.

TRAUGOTT, M. 1978. Reconceiving social movements. *Social Problems* 26:38–49.

TROWBRIDGE, N. T. 1972. Self-concept and socio-economic status in elementary school children. *American Educational Research Journal* 9:525–37.

TURNER, R. H. 1962. Role-taking: process versus conformity. In *Human behavior and social processes*, ed. A. M. Rose, pp. 20–40. Boston: Houghton Mifflin.

———— 1964. Collective behavior. In *Handbook of modern sociology*, ed. R. E. L. Faris, pp. 382–425. Chicago: Rand McNally.

———— 1966. Role-taking, role standpoint, and reference group behavior. In *Role theory: concepts and research*, ed. B. J. Biddle and E. J. Thomas, pp. 151–159. New York: Wiley.

———— 1968. Is the concept of attitude obsolete? Paper presented at meetings of the Pacific Sociological Association. San Francisco, March.

———— 1978. The role and the person. *American Journal of Sociology* 84:1–23.

————., and KILLIAN, L. M. 1972. *Collective behavior*, 2nd ed. Englewood Cliffs, N. J.: Prentice-Hall.

U. S. riot commission report, 1968. *Report of the national advisory commission on civil disorders*. New York: Bantam Books.

VAUGHAN, V. C., III. 1976. Perspectives from ethology. In *The family—can it be saved?*, ed. V. C. Vaughan, III, and T. B. Brazelton, pp. 123–27. Chicago: Year Book Medical Publishers.

VERINIS, J. and ROLL, S. 1970. Primary and secondary male characteristics: the hairiness and large penis stereotype. *Psychological Reports* 26:123–26.

VETTER, H. J. 1969. *Language behavior and communication*. Itasca, Ill.: Peacock.

VON FRISCH, K. 1954. *The dancing bees*. New York: Harcourt Brace Jovanovich.

VON HENTIG, H. 1947. Redhead and the outlaw: a study in criminal anthropology. *Journal of Criminal Law and Criminology* 38:1–16.

VON HOFFMAN, N. 1970. Sociological snoopers. *Transaction* 7:4–6.

VYGOTSKY, L. 1962. *Thought and language*. Cambridge, Mass.: MIT Press.

WALSTER, E.; ARONSON, E.; and ABRAHAMS, D. 1966. On increasing the persuasiveness of a low prestige communicator. *Journal of Experimental Social Psychology* 2:325–42.

WALSTER, E.; BERSCHEID, E.; and WALSTER, G. W. 1970. The exploited: justice or justification? In *Altruism and helping behavior: social psychological studies of some antecedents and consequences*, ed. J. Macaulay and L. Berkowitz, pp. 179–204. New York: Academic Press.

WALSTER, E., and PILIAVIN, J. 1972. Equity and the innocent bystander. *Journal of Social Issues* 28:165–89.

———— J. 1977. Normative influences on altruism. In *Advances in experimental social psychology*, vol. 10, ed. L. Berkowitz, pp. 221–79. New York: Academic Press.

WALTERS, J., and STINNETT, N. 1971. Parent-child relationships: a decade review of research. *Journal of Marriage and the Family* 33:70–111.

WALTERS, R. H., and KARAL, P. 1960. Social deprivation and verbal behavior. *Journal of Personality* 28:89–107.

WARNER, L. G., and DeFLEUR, M. L. 1969. Attitude as an interactional concept: social constraint and social distance as intervening variables between attitudes and actions. *American Sociological Review* 34:153–69.

WATSON, J. B., and RAYNER, R. 1920. Conditioned emotional reactions. *Journal of Experimental Psychology* 3:1–14.

WEBB, E. J.; CAMPBELL, D. T.; SCHWARTZ, R. D.; and SECHREST, L. 1966. *Unobtrusive measures: nonreactive research in the social sciences.* Chicago: Rand McNally.

WEINER, B. 1972. *Theories of motivation.* Chicago: Markham.

WEISS, W. 1971. Mass communication. In *Annual Review of Psychology,* vol. 22, ed. P. H. Mussen and M. R. Rosenzweig, pp. 309–339. Palo Alto, Calif.: Annual Reviews, Inc.

WEISSBERG, N. 1965. Commentary on DeFleur and Westie's attitude as a scientific concept. *Social Forces* 43:422–425.

WELLER, J. M., and QUARANTELLI, E. L. 1973. Neglected characteristics of collective behavior. *American Journal of Sociology* 79:665–85.

WERTHEIMER, M. 1977. Discussion. *Annals of the New York Academy of Sciences* 291: 317–320.

WEST, S. G., and BROWN, T. J. 1975. Physical attractiveness, the severity of the emergency and helping: a field experiment and interpersonal simulation. *Journal of Experimental Social Psychology* 11:531–38.

WEST, S. G.; WHITNEY, G.; and SCHNEDLER, R. 1975. Helping a motorist in distress: the effects of sex, race, and neighborhood. *Journal of Personality and Social Psychology* 31:691–98.

WHITE, R. W. 1961. Ego and reality in psychoanalytic theory: a proposal for independent ego energies. *Psychological Issues* 3.

WHITING, J. W. M., and CHILD, I. L. 1953. *Child training and personality: a cross cultural study.* New Haven: Yale University Press.

WHORF, B. 1956. *Language, thought,* and *reality.* New York: Published jointly by the Technology Press of MIT and John Wiley and Sons, Inc.

WHYTE, W. F. 1943. *Street corner society.* Chicago: University of Chicago Press.

WICKER, A. W. 1969. Attitudes vs. actions: the relationship of verbal and overt behavior responses to attitude objects. *Journal of Social Issues* 25:41–78.

WILLIAMS, J. E.; BENNETT, S. M.; and BEST, D. L. 1975. Awareness and expression of sex stereotypes in young children. *Developmental Psychology* 11:635–42.

WILLIAMS, J. H. 1973. The relationship of self-concept and reading achievement in first grade children. *Journal of Educational Research* 66:378–80.

WILSON, A. B. 1967. Educational consequences of segregation in a California community. In *Racial isolation in the public schools: a report of the U.S. Commission on Civil Rights.* Washington, D.C.: U.S. Government Printing Office.

WILSON, E. O. 1975. *Sociobiology: the new synthesis.* Cambridge, Mass.: Harvard University Press.

WILSON, J. 1973. *Introduction to social movements.* New York: Basic Books.

WISHNER, J. 1960. Reanalysis of impression of personality. *Psychological Review* 67: 96–112.

WOLFGANG, M. E. 1958. *Patterns of criminal homicide.* Philadelphia: University of Pennsylvania Press.

———, and FERRACUTI, F. 1968. *The subculture of violence: towards an integrated theory in criminology.* London: Tavistock-Social Science Paperbacks.

WOLLOCK, J. 1977. William Thornton, an eighteenth century American psycholinguist: background and influence. *Annals of the New York Academy of Sciences* 291:264–76.

Wooley, P. V., and Evans, W. A. 1955. Significance of the skeletal lesions in infants resembling those of traumatic origin. *Journal of the American Medical Association* 158:539–43.

Wright, J. D., and Wright, S. R. 1976. Social class and parental values for children: a partial replication and extension of Kohn's thesis. *American Sociological Review* 41:527–37.

Wrightsman, L. S. 1974. The most important social psychological research in this generation? A review of Milgram's obedience to authority. *Contemporary Psychology* 19:803–05.

Wrong, D. H. 1961. The oversocialized conception of man in modern sociology. *American Sociological Review* 26:183–93.

Wurtzel, A. 1977. Television violence and aggressive behavior. *ETC.* 34:212–25.

Wylie, R. C. 1961. *The self-concept.* Lincoln: University of Nebraska Press.

———— 1963. Children's estimates of their schoolwork ability as a function of sex, race and socioeconomic level. *Journal of Personality* 31:203–24.

Yinger, J. M. 1971. Personality, character and the self. In *Current perspectives in social psychology,* ed. E. P. Hollander and R. G. Hunt, 3rd ed. pp. 152–58, New York: Oxford University Press.

———— 1965. *Toward a field theory of behavior.* New York: McGraw-Hill.

Youniss, J.; Furth, H.; and Ross, B. 1971. Logical symbol use in deaf and hearing children and adolescents. *Developmental Psychology* 5:511–17.

Zajonc, R. B. 1968. Cognitive theories in social psychology. In *The handbook of social psychology,* vol. 1, 2nd ed., ed. G. Lindzey and E. Aronson, pp. 320–411. Reading, Mass.: Addison-Wesley.

Zald, M. N., and Ash, R. 1966. Social movement organizations: growth, decay, and change. *Social Forces* 44:327–41.

Zanna, M. P., and Hamilton, D. L. 1972. Attribute dimensions and patterns of trait inferences. *Psychonomic Science* 27:353–54.

Zawadzki, B. 1948. Limitations of the scapegoat theory of prejudice. *Journal of Abnormal and Social Psychology* 43:127–41.

Zigler, E., and Child, I. L. 1973. *Socialization and personality development.* Reading, Mass.: Addison-Welsey.

Zigler, E., and Seitz, V. 1978. Changing trends in socialization theory and research. *American Behavioral Scientist* 21:731–56.

Zimbardo, P. G., 1969. The human choice: individuation, reason, and order versus deindividuation, impulse, and chaos. In *Nebraska symposium on motivation,* ed. W. J. Arnold and D. Levine, pp. 237–307. Lincoln: University of Nebraska Press.

———— 1971. The psychological power and pathology of imprisonment. A statement prepared for the U.S. House of Representatives Committee on the Judiciary. Unpublished paper. Stanford, Calif.: Stanford University.

Zirkel, P. A. 1971. Self-concept and the "disadvantage" of ethnic group membership and mixture. *Review of Educational Research* 41:211–25.

————, and Moses, E. G. 1971. Self-concept and ethnic group membership among public school children. *American Educational Research Journal* 8:253–65.

Zurcher, L. A., Jr.; Kirkpatrick, R. G.; Cushing, R. G.; and Bowman, C. L. 1971. The anti-pornography campaign: a symbolic crusade. *Social problems* 19:217–38.

Zygmunt, J. F. 1972. When prophecies fail: a theoretical perspective on the comparative evidence. *American Behavioral Scientist* 16:245–68.

index

a

Abelson, R. P., 226
Aberle, D. F., 382
Abrahams, D., 243
Academic achievement, and gender, 109, 111
Acceptance, latitude of, 236–37
Acock, A. C., 218
Adams, J., 292
Adaptation-level theory, 238–40
Additive model, in impression formation, 275
Adrenalin, 318
Adults, socialization of, 114–23
Adventures with the Missing Link (Dart), 315
Affect
   attitudes and, 194–95, 197
   psychological continuum, 198
African Genesis (Ardrey), 315
Agentic state, 127
Agent provocateurs, 360
Agents, 172
Aggression. *See also* Violence.
   brain-damage theories, 319–21, 344
   chromosome abnormality theory, 321
   control of, 343–45

defined, 313
ethological theories, 314–18
frustration and, 322–24, 344–45
gender and, 109, 182
hormone theories, 318–19, 344
instinct theories, 314
pain and, 321–22
psychoanalytic theory, 314
social-learning theory, 324–28, 344
subculture-of-violence theory, 328–30
Aggressor, identification with, 99
Ajzen, I., 219, 220
Albrecht, S. L., 146, 148, 201, 218, 220
Alcoholics Anonymous, 82, 250
Alcorn, D. S., 256–57
Alexander, C. N., 274
Ali, Mohammud, 119
Allen, V. L., 116, 136, 362–63
Allport, Gordon W., 5, 6, 7, 127, 150, 192–93, 194, 288, 355, 370
Alpert, J. L., 45
Altruism, 284–310
   contemporary examples, 287
   decision making and, 305–6
   defined, 284
   diffusion of responsibility and, 295–99
   effect on recipients, 307
   genetic theory, 289

X

Y

Z